UNDERSTANDING AND APPLYING BASIC STATISTICAL METHODS USING R

UNDERSTANDING AND APPLYING BASIC STATISTICAL METHODS USING R

RAND R. WILCOX

WILEY

Published by John Wiley & Sons, Inc., Hoboken, New Jersey
Published simultaneously in Canada

Library of Congress Cataloging-in-Publication Data:

Names: Wilcox, Rand R., author.
Title: Understanding and applying basic statistical methods using R / Rand R.
   Wilcox.
Description: Hoboken, New Jersey : John Wiley & Sons, 2016. | Includes
   bibliographical references and index.
Identifiers: LCCN 2015050582| ISBN 9781119061397 | ISBN 9781119061410 (epub)
   | ISBN 9781119061403 (Adobe PDF)
Subjects: LCSH: Statistics–Computer programs. | R (Computer program language)
Classification: LCC QA276.45.R3 W55 2016 | DDC 519.50285/5133–dc23 LC record available at
   http://lccn.loc.gov/2015050582

Typeset in 10/12pt TimesLTStd by SPi Global, Chennai, India

Printed in the United States of America

10 9 8 7 6 5 4 3 2 1

CONTENTS

LIST OF SYMBOLS

α: Type I error probability (alpha)

β: Type II error probability (beta)

β_0:   The intercept of a regression line

β_1:   The slope of a regression line

δ: A measure of effect size (delta)

θ: Population median or the odds ratio (theta)

μ: Population mean (mu)

μ_t: Population trimmed mean

ν: Degrees of freedom (nu)

ρ: Pearson's correlation (rho)

ρ_s: Spearman's correlation

σ: Population standard deviation (sigma)

σ^2:   Population variance

$\sum$:   Summation

τ: Kendall's tau

ϕ: Phi coefficient

Ω: Odds (omega)

M: Sample median

p: Probability of success. Also used to indicate a p-value as well as a measure of effect size associated with the Wilcoxon–Mann–Whitney method

r: Estimate of ρ, Pearson's correlation

r_w: Winsorized correlation

r_e: A measure of effect size based on a robust generalization of Pearson's correlation

$\overline{X}$:   Sample mean, which estimates the population mean μ

s^2:   Sample variance, which estimates the population variance σ^2

s: Sample standard deviation, which estimates the population standard deviation σ

s_w^2:   Winsorized variance

s_w: Winsorized standard deviation

PREFACE

The goal of this book is to introduce basic statistical principles, techniques, and concepts in a relatively simple and concise manner. The book is designed for a one-semester course aimed at nonstatisticians. Numerous illustrations are provided using data from a wide range of disciplines. Answers to the exercises are in Appendix A. More detailed answers to all of the exercises and data sets for the exercises can be downloaded from www.wiley.com/go/Wilcox/Statistical_Methods_R.

There are, of course, basic methods that are routinely taught in the typical introductory course, which are covered here. A primary motivation for the book is to include a description of modern insights and advances that are relevant to basic techniques in terms of dealing with nonnormality, outliers, heteroscedasticity (unequal variances), and curvature. There is a growing awareness of the practical importance of these advances, they are explained in more advanced books, but at the moment, they are not covered in the typical introductory text. Put simply, when comparing groups of individuals, or when studying the association among variables, modern advances provide the opportunity to get a much deeper and more accurate understanding of data. This is due in part to a better understanding of when routinely taught methods perform well and when they can be highly unsatisfactory. In addition, many new methods have been developed to deal with the shortcomings of standard techniques, some of which are described in this book. A broad goal is to provide a conceptual basis for understanding the relative merits of the basic methods that are now available.

Today, there are many ways of comparing groups and studying associations that did not exist 50 years ago, which are readily applied with the software R. The author is frequently asked which method is best. But there is a seemingly better question: How many methods does it take to get a good understanding of data? Addressing this question requires a good conceptual understanding of what various methods tell us and what they do not tell us. The book includes detailed illustrations demonstrating the practical importance of multiple perspectives.

The following helps illustrate the motivation for this book. Conventional wisdom has long held that with a sample size of 40 or larger, normality can be assumed. Many introductory books still make this claim, this view is consistent with studies done many years ago, and in fairness, there are conditions where adhering to this view is innocuous. But numerous journal articles make it clear that when working with means, under very general conditions, this view is incorrect. A practical consequence is that discoveries are often lost due to using some conventional method that does not perform well when dealing with nonnormal distributions. Where did this erroneous view come from and what can be done about correcting any practical problems? Simple explanations are provided as well as easily applied techniques aimed at dealing with this issue.

Another insight is that outliers can destroy the ability of standard methods to detect and accurately reflect true differences among groups and the association among two or more variables. Highly misleading summaries of data can occur when using means, least squares regression, or Pearson's correlation. A seemingly natural strategy is to simply remove any outliers and apply standard methods to the remaining data. This is valid if a convincing argument can be made that the outliers are erroneous. But otherwise (when removing outliers among the dependent variable), invalid results are obtained even with a large sample size. Technically sound methods for dealing with outliers are described in the book.

A popular method for dealing with nonnormal distributions is to transform the data. But by modern standards, this is a relatively ineffective strategy for reasons that are explained and illustrated. Better methods for dealing with nonnormal distributions are described.

Yet another example of modern advances has to do with a routinely made assumption when comparing means or when using least squares regression: homoscedasticity. This assumption is fine when there is no association among the variables under study or when the groups being compared have identical distributions. But otherwise, it can result in erroneous conclusions and possibly missing differences among groups or an association among variables that have practical importance. There are methods for testing the homoscedasticity assumption, but they are known to be unsatisfactory under fairly general conditions. Effective methods for dealing with the violation of the homoscedasticity assumption are readily applied using the software R, as will be demonstrated.

Currently, there is a tremendous gap between advances in the statistics literature relevant to basic techniques and the methods that are routinely taught and used. The hope is that this book will help close this gap so that future researchers can take advantage of what modern technology has to offer.

Rand Wilcox
Los Angeles, California

ABOUT THE COMPANION WEBSITE

This book is accompanied by a companion website:
www.wiley.com/go/Wilcox/Statistical_Methods_R

The website includes:

- Instructor's solutions manual
- Datasets

1

INTRODUCTION

Why are statistical methods important? One reason is that they play a fundamental role in a wide range of disciplines including physics, chemistry, astronomy, manufacturing, agriculture, communications, pharmaceuticals, medicine, biology, kinesiology, sports, sociology, political science, linguistics, business, economics, education, and psychology. Basic statistical techniques impact your life.

At its simplest level, statistics involves the description and summary of events. How many home runs did Babe Ruth hit? What is the average rainfall in Seattle? But from a scientific point of view, it has come to mean much more. Broadly defined, it is the science, technology, and art of extracting information from observational data, with an emphasis on solving real-world problems. As Stigler (1986, p. 1) has so eloquently put it:

> Modern statistics provides a quantitative technology for empirical science; it is a logic and methodology for the measurement of uncertainty and for examination of the consequences of that uncertainty in the planning and interpretation of experimentation and observation.

To help elucidate the types of problems addressed in this book, consider an experiment aimed at investigating the effects of ozone on weight gain in rats (Doksum and Sievers, 1976). The experimental group consisted of 22 seventy-day-old rats kept in an ozone environment for 7 days. A control group of 23 rats, of the same age, was kept in an ozone-free environment. The results of this experiment are shown in Table 1.1.

How should these two groups be compared? A natural reaction is to compute the average weight gain for both groups. The averages turn out to be 11 for the ozone group and 22.4 for the control group. The average is higher for the control group

Understanding and Applying Basic Statistical Methods Using R, First Edition. Rand R. Wilcox.
© 2017 John Wiley & Sons, Inc. Published 2017 by John Wiley & Sons, Inc.
www.wiley.com/go/Wilcox/Statistical_Methods_R

TABLE 1.1   Weight Gain of Rats in Ozone Experiment

Control	41.0	38.4	24.4	25.9	21.9	18.3	13.1	27.3	28.5	−16.9
Ozone	10.1	6.1	20.4	7.3	14.3	15.5	−9.9	6.8	28.2	17.9
Control	26.0	17.4	21.8	15.4	27.4	19.2	22.4	17.7	26.0	29.4
Ozone	−9.0	−12.9	14.0	6.6	12.1	15.7	39.9	−15.9	54.6	−14.7
Control	21.4	26.6	22.7							
Ozone	44.1	−9.0								

suggesting that for the typical rat, weight gain will be less in an ozone environment. However, serious concerns come to mind upon a moment's reflection. Only 22 rats were kept in the ozone environment, and only 23 rats were in the control group. Suppose 100 rats had been used, or 1,000, or even a million. Is it reasonable to conclude that the ozone group would still have a smaller average than the control group? What about using the average to reflect the weight gain for the typical rat? Are there other methods for summarizing data that might have practical value when characterizing the differences between the groups? A goal of this book is to introduce the basic tools for answering these questions.

Most of the basic statistical methods currently taught and used were developed prior to the year 1960 and are based on strategies developed about 200 years ago. Of particular importance was the work of Pierre-Simon Laplace (1749–1827) and Carl Friedrich Gauss (1777–1855). Approximately a century ago, major advances began to appear, which dominate how researchers analyze data today. Especially important was the work of Karl Pearson (1857–1936) Jerzy Neyman (1894–1981), Egon Pearson (1895–1980), and Sir Ronald Fisher (1890–1962). For various reasons summarized in subsequent chapters, it was once thought that these methods generally perform well in terms of extracting accurate information from data. But in recent years, it has become evident that this is not always the case. Indeed, three major insights have revealed conditions where methods routinely used today can be highly unsatisfactory.

The good news is that many new and improved methods have been developed that are aimed at dealing with known problems associated with the more commonly used techniques. In practical terms, modern technology offers the opportunity to get a deeper and more accurate understanding of data. So, a major goal of this book is to introduce basic methods in a manner that builds a conceptual foundation for understanding when commonly used techniques perform in a satisfactory manner and when this is not the case. Another goal is to provide some understanding of when and why more modern methods have practical value.

This book does *not* describe the mathematical underpinnings of routinely used statistical techniques, but rather the concepts and principles that are used. Generally, the essence of statistical reasoning can be understood with little training in mathematics beyond basic high school algebra. However, there are several key components underlying the basic strategies to be described, the result being that it is easy to lose track of where we are going when the individual components are being explained. Consequently, it might help to provide a brief overview of what is covered in this book.

1.1 SAMPLES VERSUS POPULATIONS

A key aspect of most statistical methods is the distinction between a sample of participants or objects and a population of participants or objects. A *population* of participants or objects consists of all those participants or objects that are relevant in a particular study. In the weight-gain experiment with rats, there are millions of rats that could be used if sufficient resources were available. To be concrete, suppose there are a billion rats and the goal is to determine the average weight gain if all 1 billion were kept in an ozone environment. Then, these 1 billion rats compose the population of rats we wish to study. The average gain for these rats is called the *population mean*. In a similar manner, there is an average weight gain for all 1 billion rats that might be raised in an ozone-free environment instead. This is the *population mean* for rats raised in an ozone-free environment. The obvious problem is that it is impractical to measure all 1 billion rats. In the experiment, only 22 rats were kept in an ozone environment. These 22 rats are an example of a *sample*.

Definition. A *sample* is any subset of the population of individuals or things under study.

Example

Imagine that a new method for treating depression is tried on 20 individuals. Further imagine that after treatment with the new method, depressive symptoms are measured and the average is found to be 16. So, we have information about the 20 individuals in the study, but of particular importance is knowing the average that would result if all individuals suffering from depression were treated with the new method. The population corresponds to all individuals suffering from depression. The sample consists of the 20 individuals who were treated with the new method. A basic issue is the uncertainty of how well the average based on the 20 individuals in the study reflects the average if all depressed individuals were to receive the new treatment.

Example

Shortly after the Norman Conquest, around the year 1100, there was already a need for methods that indicate how well a sample reflects a population of objects. The population of objects in this case consisted of coins produced on any given day. It was desired that the weight of each coin be close to some specified amount. As a check on the manufacturing process, a selection of each day's coins was reserved in a box ("the Pyx") for inspection. In modern terminology, the coins selected for inspection are an example of a sample, and the goal is to generalize to the population of coins, which in this case is all the coins produced on that day.

Three Fundamental Components of Statistics Statistical techniques consist of a wide range of goals, techniques, and strategies. Three fundamental components worth stressing are given as follows:

1. *Design.* Roughly, this refers to a procedure for planning experiments so that data yield valid and objective conclusions. Well-chosen experimental designs

maximize the amount of information that can be obtained for a given amount of experimental effort.

2. *Description*. This refers to numerical and graphical methods for summarizing data.

3. *Inference*. This refers to making predictions or generalizations about a population of individuals or things based on a sample of observations.

Design is a vast subject, and only the most basic issues are discussed here. The immediate goal is to describe some fundamental reasons why design is important. As a simple illustration, imagine you are interested in factors that affect health. In North America, where fat accounts for a third of the calories consumed, the death rate from heart disease is 20 times higher than in rural China where the typical diet is closer to 10% fat. What are we to make of this? Should we eliminate as much fat from our diet as possible? Are all fats bad? Could it be that some are beneficial? This purely descriptive study does not address these issues in an adequate manner. This is not to say that descriptive studies have no merit, only that resolving important issues can be difficult or impossible without good experimental design. For example, heart disease is relatively rare in Mediterranean countries where fat intake can approach 40% of calories. One distinguishing feature between the American diet and the Mediterranean diet is the type of fat consumed. So, one possibility is that the amount of fat in a diet, without regard to the type of fat, might be a poor gauge of nutritional quality. Note, however, that in the observational study just described, nothing has been done to control other factors that might influence heart disease. Sorting out what does and does not contribute to heart disease requires good experimental design.

The ozone experiment provides a simple example where design considerations are important. It is evident that the age of young rats is related to their weight. So, the experiment was designed to control for age by using rats that have the same age and then manipulate the *single* factor that is of interest, namely, the amount of ozone in the air.

Description refers to ways of summarizing data that provide useful information about the phenomenon under study. It includes methods for describing both the sample available to us and the entire population of participants if only they could be measured. The average is one of the most common ways of summarizing data. As previously noted, the average for all the participants in a population is called the *population mean*; it is typically represented by the Greek letter mu, μ. The average based on a sample of participants is called a *sample mean*. The hope is that the sample mean provides a good reflection of the population mean. Inferential methods described in subsequent chapters are designed to determine the extent this goal is achieved.

1.2 COMMENTS ON SOFTWARE

As is probably evident, a key component to getting the most accurate and useful information from data is software. There are now several popular software packages for analyzing data. Perhaps the most important thing to keep in mind is that the choice of software can be crucial, particularly when the goal is to apply new and improved methods developed during the last half century. Presumably, no software package is perfect, based on all of the criteria that might be used to judge them, but the following comments about some of the choices might help.

Best Software The software R is arguably the best software package for applying all of the methods covered in this book. Moreover, it is free and available at http:// cran.R-project.org. Many modern methods developed in recent years, as well as all classic techniques, can be applied. One feature that makes R highly valuable from a research perspective is that a group of statisticians does an excellent job of constantly adding and updating routines aimed at applying modern techniques. A wide range of modern methods can be applied using the basic package and many specialized methods are available, some of which are described in this book.

Very Good Software SAS is another software package that provides power and excellent flexibility. Many modern methods can be applied, but a large number of the most recently developed techniques are not yet available via SAS. SAS code could be written by anyone reasonably familiar with SAS, and the company is fairly diligent about upgrading the routines in their package, but this has not been done yet for some of the methods covered in this book.

Good Software Minitab is fairly simple to use and provides a reasonable degree of flexibility when analyzing data. All of the standard methods developed prior to the year 1960 are readily available. Many modern methods could be run in Minitab, but doing so is not straightforward. Similarly to SAS, special Minitab code is needed, and writing this code would take some effort. Moreover, certain modern methods that are readily applied with R cannot be easily applied when using Minitab even if an investigator is willing to write the appropriate code.

Unsatisfactory Software SPSS is certainly one of the more popular and frequently used software packages. But in terms of providing access to the many new and improved methods for comparing groups and studying associations, which have appeared during the last half century, it must be given a poor rating. An additional concern is its lack of flexibility compared to R. It is a relatively simple matter for statisticians to create specialized R code that provides non-statisticians with easy access to modern methods. Some modern methods can be applied with SPSS, but often this task is difficult or virtually impossible.

The software EXCEL is relatively easy to use, it provides some flexibility, but generally modern methods are not readily applied. McCullough and Wilson (2005) conclude that this software package is not maintained in an adequate manner. (For a more detailed description of some problems with this software, see Heiser, 2006.) Even if EXCEL functions were available for all modern methods that might be used, features noted by McCullough and Wilson suggest that EXCEL should not be used. Some improvements were made in Microsoft Excel 2010, but serious concerns remain (Mélard, 2014).

1.3 R BASICS

R is a vast and powerful software package. Even a book completely dedicated to R cannot cover all of the methods and features that are available. The immediate goal is to describe the basic features that are needed in this book. Many additional features are introduced in subsequent chapters when they are required. Another resource for learning the basics of R is Swirl, which can be installed as described at http://swirlstats .com/. There are many books on R as a Google Search will reveal. A free manual is available at http://cran.r-project.org/. On the left side of this web page near the bottom under documentation, you will see a manual. Click on this link to gain access to the manual. Another free manual is available at http://cran.r-project.org/doc/contrib/ Verzani-SimpleR.pdf. (Or, google Verzani's simpleR.)

R can be downloaded from http://cran.r-project.org/. At the top of the web page, you will see three links:

- Download R for Linux
- Download R for (Mac) OS X
- Download R for Windows

Simply click on the link matching the computer you are using to download R. Once you start R, you will see this prompt:

```
>.
```

This means that R is waiting for a command. (You do not type > The prompt is used to indicate where you type commands.) To quit R, use the command

```
> q().
```

That is, type q() and hit Enter.

1.3.1   Entering Data

To begin with the simplest case, imagine you want to store the value 5 in an R variable called blob. This can be done with the command

```
blob=5.
```

Typing blob and hitting Enter will produce the value 5 on the computer screen.

An important feature of R is that a collection of values can be stored in a single R variable. One way of doing this is with the R command c, which stands for combine. For example, the values 2, 4, 6, 8, 12 can be stored in the R variable blob with the command

```
blob=c(2,4,6,8,12).
```

The first value, 2, is stored in blob[1], the second value is stored in blob[2], and so on. To determine how many values are stored in an R variable, use the R command length. In the example

```
length(blob)
```

would return the value 5.

R has various ways of reading data stored in a file. The R commands scan and read.table are the two basic ways of accomplishing this goal. The simplest version of the scan command assumes that a string of values is to be read. By default, R assumes that values are separated by one or more spaces. Missing values are assumed to be recorded as NA for "not available."

For example, imagine that a file called *ice.dat* contains

6 3 12 8 9.

Then, the command

```
ice=scan(file="ice.dat")
```

will read these values from the file and store them in the R variable ice. However, this assumes that the data are stored in the directory where R expects to find the file. Just where R expects to find the file depends on the hardware and how R is being accessed. (It might assume that data are stored in the main directory or in Documents, but other possibilities exist.) A simple way of dealing with this issue is to use the R command file.choose in conjunction with the scan command. That is, use the command

```
ice=scan(file.choose()).
```

This will open a window that lists the files on your computer. Simply click on the appropriate file.

If the data are not separated by one or more spaces, but rather some particular character, the argument sep tells R how the values are separated. For example, suppose the file contains

6, 3, 12, 8, 9.

That is, the values in the file are separated by a comma rather than a space. Now use the command

```
ice=scan(file.choose(),sep=",")
```

In other words, the argument sep tells R the character used to separate the values. If the values were separated by &, use the command

```
ice=scan(file.choose(),sep="&").
```

When you quit R with the command q(), R will ask whether you want to save your results. If you answer yes, R variables containing data will remain in R until they are removed. So, in this last example, if you quit R and then restart R, typing ice will again return the values 6, 3, 12, 8, 9. To remove data, use the rm command. For example,

```
rm(ice)
```

would remove the R variable ice.

R variables are case-sensitive. So, for example, the command

```
Ice=5
```

would store the value 5 in Ice, but the R variable ice would still contain the values listed previously, unless of course they had been removed.

The R command `read.table` is another commonly used method for reading data into R. It is designed to read columns of data where each column contains the values of some variable. It has the general form

```
read.table(file, header = FALSE, sep = "",na.strings =
"NA",skip=0)
```

where the argument file indicates the name of the file where the data are stored and the other arguments are explained momentarily. Notice that the first argument, `file`, does not contain an equal sign. This means that a value for this argument must be specified. With an equal sign, the argument defaults to the value shown. So, for `read.table`, `header` is an optional argument that will be taken to be `header=FALSE` if it is not used.

Example

Suppose a file called quake.dat contains three measures related to earthquakes:

```
magnitude length  duration
7.8          360      130
7.7          400      110
7.5           75       27
7.3           70       24
7.0           40        7
6.9           50       15
6.7           16        8
6.7           14        7
6.6           23       15
6.5           25        6
6.4           30       13
6.4           15        5
6.1           15        5
5.9           20        4
5.9            6        3
5.8            5        2
```

Then, the R command

```
quake=read.table('quake.dat',skip=1)
```

will read the data into the R variable `quake`, where the argument `skip=1` indicates that the first line of the data file is to be ignored, which in this case contains the three labels: magnitude, length, and duration. As with the `scan` command, you can point to the file to be read using the `file.choose` command. That is, use the command

```
quake=read.table(file.choose(),skip=1).
```

Typing `quake` and hitting Enter produce

```
      V1     V2     V3
1  7.8    360    130
2  7.7    400    110
```

```
 3  7.5    75     27
 4  7.3    70     24
 5  7.0    40      7
 6  6.9    50     15
 7  6.7    16      8
 8  6.7    14      7
 9  6.6    23     15
10  6.5    25      6
11  6.4    30     13
12  6.4    15      5
13  6.1    15      5
14  5.9    20      4
15  5.9     6      3
16  5.8     5      2
```

So, the columns of the data are given the names V1, V2, and V3, as indicated. Typing the R command

```
quake$V1
```

and hitting Enter would return the first column of data, namely the magnitude of the earthquakes. The command

```
quake[,1]
```

would accomplish the same goal. In a similar manner, quake[,2] contains the data in the second column and quake[,3] contains the data in the third column. In contrast, quake[1,] contains the data in the first row. So, typing the command

```
quake[1,]
```

and hitting Enter would return

7.8 360 130.

The command quake[1,1] would return the value 7.8, the value stored in the first row and the first column, and quake[1,2] would return 360.

Now consider the command

```
quake=read.table("quake.dat",header=TRUE).
```

The argument header=TRUE tells R that the first line in the file contains labels for the columns of data, which for the earthquake data are magnitude, length, and duration. Now the command

```
quake$magnitude
```

would print the first column of data on the computer screen. The R command

```
labels
```

returns the labels associated with an R variable. For the situation at hand,

```
labels(quake)
```

would return magnitude, length, and duration. The command

```
head(dat)
```

returns the first six lines of the data stored in `dat` and

```
tail(dat)
```

returns the final six lines. The R command

```
str(dat)
```

returns information about the number of observations, the number of variables, and it lists some of the values stored in `dat`. (It also indicates the storage mode of `dat`; storage modes are explained in Section 1.3.3.)

As was the case with the `scan` command, `read.table` assumes that values stored in a data file are separated by one or more spaces. But suppose the values are separated by some symbol, say &. Again, this can be handled via the argument `sep`. Now the command would resemble this:

```
quake=read.table("quake.dat",sep="&",header=TRUE)
```

Another common issue is reading data into R that are stored in some other software package such as SPSS. The seemingly easiest way of dealing with this is to first store the data in a .csv file, where csv stands for Comma Separated Values. (SPSS, EXCEL, and other popular software have a command to accomplish this goal.) Once this is done, the data can be read into R using the `read.csv` command, which is used in the same way as the `read.table` command.

Now imagine that some of the values in the quake file are missing and that missing values are indicated by M rather than NA. The argument `na.strings` can be used to indicate that missing values are stored as M. That is, now the data would be read using the R command

```
quake=read.table(quake.dat.txt,na.strings="M",header=TRUE).
```

1.3.2   Arithmetic Operations

In the simplest case, arithmetic operations can be performed on numbers using the operators +, −, * (multiplication), / (division), and ^ (exponentiation). For example, to compute 1 plus 5 squared, use the command

```
1+5^2
```

which returns

```
[1] 26.
```

To store the answer in an R variable, say `ans`, use the command

```
ans=1+5^2.
```

If two or more values are stored in an R variable, arithmetic operations applied to the variable name will be performed on all the values. For example, if the values 2, 5, 8, 12, and 25 are stored in the R variable vdat, then the command

```
vinv=1/vdat
```

will compute 1/2, 1/5, 1/8, 1/12, and 1/25, and store the results in the R variable vinv. The R command

```
2*vdat
```

multiplies every value in vdat by 2. For the situation at hand, it returns 4, 10, 16, 24, and 50. The command

```
vdat-2
```

returns 0, 3, 6, 10, and 23. That is, 2 is subtracted from every element in vdat.

Most R commands consist of a name of some function followed by one or more arguments enclosed in parentheses. There are hundreds of functions that come with R. Some of the more basic functions are listed as follows:

Function	Description
abs	Absolute value
exp	Exponential
log	Natural logarithm
sqrt	Square root
cor	Correlation (explained in Chapter 8)
mean	Arithmetic mean (with a trimming option)
median	Median (explained in Chapter 2)
min	Smallest value
max	Largest value
range	Determines the minimum and maximum values
sd	Standard deviation (explained in Chapter 2)
sum	Arithmetic sum
var	Variance (explained in Chapter 2) and covariance (explained in Chapter 8)
length	Indicates how many values are stored in an R variable.

Example

If the values 2, 7, 9, and 14 are stored in the R variable x, the command

```
min(x)
```

returns 2, the smallest of the four values stored in x. The average of the numbers is computed with the command

```
mean(x),
```

which returns the value 8. The command `range (x)` returns the largest and smallest values stored in x, which are 2 and 14, respectively. The command

```
v=range(x)
```

would result in the smallest value being stored in `v[1]` and the the largest value stored in `v[2]`. The command

```
sum(x)
```

returns the value $2 + 7 + 9 + 14 = 32$. The command

```
sum(x)/length(x)
```

is another way to compute the average.

1.3.3 Storage Types and Modes

R has several ways of storing data. The four types that are important in this book are vectors, matrices, data frames, and list mode.

Vectors are the most basic way of storing data. A vector is just a collection of values stored in some R variable. When data are read into R using the `scan` command, the data are stored in a vector. The R command

```
blob=c(2,4,6,8,12),
```

previously described, creates a vector containing the values 2, 4, 6, 8, and 12.

A matrix is a rectangular array of values having n rows and J columns. Imagine, for example, that the performance of 10 athletes is measured on three different occasions. Then, a convenient way of storing the data is in a matrix with $n = 10$ rows and $J = 3$ columns. So, the first row contains the three measures for the first individual, the second row contains the three measures for the second individual, and so on.

As another example, imagine that for each of 20 individuals you measure blood glucose levels, anxiety, height, and weight. Then, a convenient way of storing the data is in a matrix with $n = 20$ rows and $J = 4$ columns, where the first column contains blood glucose levels, the second column contains a measure of anxiety, and so forth. A vector can be thought of as a matrix with a single column, but R makes a distinction between a vector and a matrix. If, for example, x is a matrix with 10 rows and 2 columns, the R command

```
is.vector(x)
```

returns FALSE, meaning that the R variable x is not a vector. But the R command

```
is.vector(x[,1])
```

returns TRUE, meaning that column 1 of the matrix x is a vector. More generally, any single column of a matrix is a vector. The same is true for any row of x. For example,

```
is.vector(x[2,])
```

would return TRUE, meaning that the second row of x is a vector. In contrast,

```
is.matrix(x)
```

returns TRUE and the command

```
is.matrix(x[,1])
```

returns FALSE.

There are several ways a matrix can be created in R. For example, imagine that you already have an R variable BPS containing measures of systolic blood pressure for 30 individuals and for the same 30 individuals, the R variable BPD contains their diastolic blood pressure. The command

```
BP=cbind(BPS,BPD)
```

would result in a matrix with 30 rows and 2 columns. The command cbind(BPS, BPD) says to bind together BPS and BPD as columns. The R command rbind binds together rows.

To determine how many rows a matrix has, use the R command nrow. The command ncol returns the number of columns and dim returns both the number of rows and columns. Here, ncol(BP) would return the value 2.

You can apply arithmetic operations to specific rows or columns of a matrix. For example, to compute the average of all values in column 1 of the matrix m, use the command

```
mean(m[,1]).
```

The command

```
mean(m[2,])
```

computes the average of all values in row 2. In contrast, the command

```
mean(m)
```

would average all of the values in m. If you have several columns of data and want to compute the average for each column, there is a quick way of doing this via the apply command. The command

```
apply(m,2,mean)
```

computes the average for each column. The command

```
apply(m,1,mean)
```

computes the average for each row.

Another way to create a matrix is with the R command `matrix`.

Example

The command

```
matrix(c(1,4,8,3,7,2),ncol=2)
```

returns

```
     [,1] [,2]
[1,]    1    3
[2,]    4    7
[3,]    8    2
```

The argument `ncol` tells R how many columns the matrix is to have. Note that the first three numbers are stored in the first column and the other three are in column 2. In contrast, the command

```
matrix(c(1,4,8,3,7,2),ncol=2,byrow=TRUE)
```

returns

```
     [,1] [,2]
[1,]    1    4
[2,]    8    3
[3,]    7    2
```

Now the first two numbers are stored in the first row, the next two are stored in the second row, and the final two are stored in the third row. That is, it fills in the numbers by rows rather than columns.

There are several storage modes used by R. The four important ones in this book are the following: logical, numeric, character, and factor. As the name implies, numeric refers to numbers in contrast to characters such as "A." (Logical variables are discussed in Section 1.3.4.) For present purposes, factor variables can be viewed as a storage mode that indicates the group to which an individual belongs. Imagine, for example, a study dealing with hypertension where some individuals receive an experimental drug and others receive a placebo. Further imagine that the data are stored in the file BP_study containing two columns. The first column contains blood pressure measures and the second contains the letters E and P, where E indicates that an individual received the experimental drug and P indicates a placebo. So, the first few rows in the file might resemble this:

```
120   E
145   P
132   E
121   E
139   P
```

As previously explained, the R command

```
BP=read.table(file="BP_study")
```

can be used to read the data and store it in the R variable BP. When this is done, BP will be stored in what R calls a *data frame*. Similar to a matrix, a data frame consists of *n* rows and *J* columns. The advantage of a data frame over a matrix is that different columns of a data frame can contain different types of data. In contrast, a matrix cannot have a mix of data types. For example, it cannot contain both numeric and character data: it must be all numeric, or it can be all characters. A data frame is more flexible in the sense that some columns can have numeric data that are to be analyzed and other columns can be something other than numeric data such as a factor variable. When the R command read.table encounters a column of data in a file that is not numeric, it stores it as a factor. In the example, the second column would be read as a factor variable with two possible values: E and P.

When data are stored in a data frame, with some column having the factor mode, situations are encountered where it will be necessary to separate the data into R variables based on the values of the factor variable. In the last example, it might be necessary to separate the participants receiving the experimental drug from those who received the placebo. There are several ways to do this, but the details are postponed until they are needed. (Chapter 9 illustrates this process; see the discussion of the R commands split and fac2list.)

List mode is yet another convenient way of storing data. It will play an important role in Chapters 9–11. Imagine that three groups of participants are to be compared: those with little or no signs of depression, those with mild depression, and those with severe depression. Further suppose that there are 20, 30, and 10 individuals belonging to these groups, respectively, and that the data are stored in the R variables G1, G2, and G3. For various purposes, it can be convenient to store the data for all three groups in a single R variable. A matrix is not convenient because the number of individuals differs among the three groups. A more convenient way to combine the data into a single R variable is to use list mode. In this book, the most common way of storing data in list mode is via the R function fac2list, or the R function split, which are described and illustrated in Chapter 9. In case it helps, here is another way this can be done:

```
DEP=list()
DEP[[1]]=G1
DEP[[2]]=G2
DEP[[3]]=G3
```

The average of the data in the second group, for example, can be computed with the R command

```
mean(DEP[[2]]).
```

If the goal is to compute the average for all three groups, there is an easier way to do this via the R command lapply. The command

```
lapply(DEP,mean)
```

accomplishes this goal.

One more way of storing data in list mode is as follows. First create a variable having list mode. If you want the variable to be called gdat, use the command

```
gdat=list()
```

Then, the data for group 1 can be stored via the command

```
gdat[[1]]=c(36, 24, 82, 12, 90, 33, 14, 19)
```

the group 2 data would be stored via the command

```
gdat[[2]]=c(9, 17, 8, 22, 15)
```

and the group 3 data would be stored by using the command

```
gdat[[3]]=c(43, 56, 23, 10)
```

Typing the command gdat and hitting Enter return

```
[[1]]:
[1] 36 24 82 12 90 33 14 19

[[2]]:
[1]  9 17  8 22 15

[[3]]:
[1] 43 56 23 10
```

That is, gdat contains three vectors of numbers corresponding to the three groups under study.

Another way to store data in list mode is with a variation of the scan command. Suppose the data are stored in a file called *mydata.dat* and are arranged as follows:

```
36   9   43
24   17  56
82   8   23
12   22  10
90   15  NA
33   NA  NA
14   NA  NA
19   NA  NA
```

Then, the command

```
gdat=scan("mydata.dat",list(g1=0,g2=0,g3=0))
```

will store the data in gdat in list mode. Typing gdat and hitting Enter return

```
$g1:
[1] 36 24 82 12 90 33 14 19
$g2:
[1] 9 17 8 22 15 NA NA NA
$g3:
[1] 43 56 23 10 NA NA NA NA
```

So, the data for group 1 are stored in gdat$g1; for group 2, they are in gdat$g2; and for group 3, they are in gdat$g3. An alternative way of accessing the data in group 1 is with gdat[[1]]. Note that when scan is used to store data in list mode, it assumes that the data for group 1 are stored in column 1, group 2 data are stored in column 2, and group 3 data are stored in column 3.

1.3.4   Identifying and Analyzing Special Cases

There are various ways R can be used to examine a subset of the data. The earth-quake data, described at the end of Section 1.3.1, provide a glimpse of why this can be important and useful. Still assuming the data are stored in the R variable quake, the R command mean(quake[,2]) indicates that the average of the length variable (the average of the data in column 2) is 72.75. Note that among the 16 observations, only 3 have a value greater than 72.75. Also notice that the two largest length values, 360 and 400, appear to be unusually large compared to the other values. Do these two values have an inordinate impact on the average? A way of answering this question is to elim-inate these two values and averaging the remaining data. Noting that the two largest values are stored in rows 1 and 2, this can be accomplished by averaging the data in rows 3–16 of data frame quake. An R command that accomplishes this goal is

```
mean(quake[3:16,2]).
```

Now the average is only 28.86, suggesting that the two most extreme values have an inordinate impact on the average. In quake[3:16,2], the command 3:16 indicates that rows 3–16 of quake are to be used. Another but more tedious way of averaging over rows 3–16 is as follows:

```
id=c(3,4,5,6,7,8,9,10,11,12,13,14,15,16)
mean(quake[id,2]).
```

In this particular case, it was a simple matter to identify and ignore the rows of data that seem to be having an inordinate impact on the average length. But often, some alternative method for selecting special rows of data is required and *logical variables* provide a convenient way of accomplishing this goal. Again using the quake data, the following R commands illustrate one way of doing this:

```
flag=quake[,2]<360
mean(quake[flag,2]).
```

The first command creates a logical variable that contains TRUE or FALSE, depending on whether the length values (the values in column 2) are less than 360. That is, the command flag=quake[,2]<360 returns TRUE for any value in column 2 that is less than 360. Typing the R command flag and hitting Enter return

FALSE FALSE TRUE TRUE TRUE TRUE TRUE TRUE TRUE TRUE

TRUE TRUE TRUE TRUE TRUE TRUE

That is, flag[1]=FALSE, flag[2]=FALSE, flag[3]=TRUE, and so forth. The command

```
mean(quake[flag,2])
```

tells R to compute the mean using only those rows of quake for which flag is TRUE. Another way to accomplish the same goal is to use the R command

```
flag=which(quake[,2]<360).
```

Now flag indicates the row numbers for which the length is less than 360. That is, the values in flag are 3, 4, 5, 6, 7, 8, 9, 10, 11, 12, 13, 14, 15, 16. Yet another way is to eliminate or ignore the first two rows in quake when computing the average of the values in column 2. This can be done with the R command

```
mean(quake[c(-1,-2),2])
```

which again returns the value 28.86. That is, row numbers that are negative are ignored.

As just indicated, the command quake[flag,2]) tells R to use only those rows of quake for which flag is TRUE. The command quake[!flag,2]) tells R to use only those rows for which flag is FALSE. That is, the command ! means "not."

Logical variables provide one way of dealing with missing values. The R function is.na determines which values are missing, which can be used to eliminate them.

Example

Consider the R command

```
z=c(45, 23, NA, 19 , 12)
```

So, the third value, stored in z[3], is missing. The R command

```
is.na(z)
```

returns FALSE FALSE TRUE FALSE FALSE, where FALSE means the corresponding value is not missing, and TRUE means that it is missing. Remembering that ! means not, the command

```
flag=!is.na(z)
```

indicates which values are not missing. So, for example, flag[1]=TRUE, flag[3]=FALSE, and z[flag] contains 45, 23, 19, and 12. An even simpler way of eliminating missing values stored in z is with the command

```
z=z[!is.na(z)].
```

TABLE 1.2   A Summary of Basic Commands for Accessing Data When Working with a Vector x

`x[4]`	Access the fourth element in x
`x[c(1,4,7)]`	Access the first, fourth, and seventh elements in x
`x[c(-1,-4,-7)]`	Access all elements in x excluding elements 1, 4, and 7
`x[x>5]`	Access all elements in x having a value greater than 5
`x[x>=5]`	Access all elements in x having a value greater than or equal to 5
`x[x>=5 | x<0]`	Access all elements in x having a value greater than 5 or less than 0
`x[abs(x)>12 & x<8]`	Access all elements in x that have an absolute value greater than 12 and a value less than 8.
`x[!is.na(x)]`	Access all elements in x that are not missing
`which(x==min(x))`	Indicates which elements of x contain the smallest value

Table 1.2 summarizes some basic commands for accessing data when working with a vector x. The last six methods in Table 1.2 make use of logical variables that can be very helpful when manipulating data.

Example

The following illustrates the last command in Table 1.2:

```
x=c(8,12,9,2,23,19)
which(x==min(x)).
```

The second command, `which(x==min(x))`, returns the value 4, meaning that x[4] contains the smallest value.

Example

For the situation in the last example,

```
z=min(x)
```

stores a single value in z, namely the smallest value in x, which is 2. In contrast, the command

```
z=x==min(x)
```

stores

FALSE FALSE FALSE TRUE FALSE FALSE

in the R variable z. The command

```
x[z]
```

returns only those values in x for which the corresponding value in z is TRUE, which in this case is the value 2.

Example

To illustrate the next to last command in Table 1.2, suppose the values 22, NA, 13, 6, 19, 23 are stored in the R variable x. Then, the R command `mean` attempts to compute the average, but it returns NA because the second observation is missing (not available). One way to remove any missing values and compute the average of the remaining data is with the command

```
mean(x[!is.na(x)]).
```

Another way is to use the command

```
mean(x,na.rm=TRUE).
```

1.4   R PACKAGES

R has many built-in functions for applying the methods that are routinely taught and used. We will see, however, that these classic techniques can miss important features of data that are revealed when using more modern methods. An extremely important feature of R is that more modern methods are readily applied via freely available R packages that have been written by numerous statisticians. Literally, hundreds of new and improved techniques can now be used to gain a deeper and more accurate understanding of data. A few of these more modern methods are described in this book and will be seen to have considerable practical importance.

R packages are available from two sources. The first is located on the web at r-forge .r-project.org. The other is CRANS, located at cran.r-project.org. R packages available from CRANS can be installed with the R command `install.packages`. For example, the R command

```
install.packages("akima")
```

will install the R package akima, which is used when creating three-dimensional plots.

There is a particular R package that plays a central role in this book, and there are two ways it can be installed. The first and simplest method is to download the file Rallfun, which is stored at

http://dornsife.usc.edu/labs/rwilcox/software/.

The current version is labeled Rallfun-v28. Once the file is downloaded, use the R command

```
source("Rallfun-v28")
```

to execute the R commands stored in Rallfun-v28. This assumes that Rallfun-v28 is stored where R expects to find data. If Rallfun-v28 is not stored where R expects to find data, use the `source` command in conjunction with the `file.choose` command. That is, use the R command

```
source(file.choose()).
```

A previously explained, `file.choose` provides a way of finding where the file Rallfun-v28 is stored. By clicking on this file, the functions written for this book will be incorporated into your version of R. This file contains over 1,100 R functions for applying modern statistical methods.

A second way of gaining access is via the R package WRS (maintained by Felix Schönbrodt). Go to

https://github.com.

At the top of the web page, you will see Search GitHub. Type WRS and hit return. You can either download the Rallfun file, or you can install the WRS package using the R commands indicated on this web page. These R commands can also be located at

https://github.com/nicebread/WRS

Copy and paste the R commands into R. Then, use the R command

```
library(WRS)
```

to gain access to the functions.

A subset of the R functions in Rallfun is available in the R package WRS2 (created by Patrick Mair), which is stored on CRANS. A possible appeal of this package is that it contains help files and it is easily installed by using the R command

```
install.packages("WRS2").
```

The R command

```
library(WRS2)
```

provides access to the functions, and it lists the functions that are available. Currently, a negative feature is that WRS2 does not contain all of the functions described and illustrated in this book.

Information about built-in R functions, as well as functions in R packages downloaded from CRANS, can be obtained by typing the R command ? followed by the name of the function. For example, to get a brief summary of the R function `mean`, use the R command

```
?mean.
```

A window will appear that summarizes what the function does. For the functions in Rallfun, a different approach is required: type the name of the function and hit Enter. For example, there is a function called `yuen`, which is described in Chapter 9. The R command

```
yuen
```

lists the R code on your computer screen. At the top of the code, you will see

```
#
#   Perform Yuen's test for trimmed means on the data in x and y.
#   The default amount of trimming is 20%
#   Missing values (values stored as NA) are automatically removed.
#
#   A confidence interval for the trimmed mean of x minus the
#   the trimmed mean of y is computed and returned in yuen$ci.
#   The $p$-value is returned in yuen$p. value
#
```

These first few lines provide a quick summary of what the function does and how it is used. To see a list of the arguments used by the function, use the `args` command. For example,

```
args(yuen)
```

returns

```
function (x, y, tr = 0.2, alpha = 0.05).
```

So, the function expects to find data stored in two variables, labeled here as x and y. There are two optional arguments. The first is `tr`, which defaults to 0.2, and the second, `alpha`, which defaults to 0.05, both of which are explained in subsequent chapters.

Many of the R functions written for this book are based in part on other R packages available at CRANS. They include the following packages:

- akima
- MASS
- mgcv
- plotrix
- quantreg
- robust
- rrcov
- scatterplot3d
- stats

All of these packages can be installed with the `install.packages` command (assuming that you are connected to the web).

1.5   ACCESS TO DATA USED IN THIS BOOK

R has many built-in data sets. To see a list of the data sets that are available, type the R command

```
data().
```

Additional data sets used to illustrate the methods in this book can be downloaded from

http://dornsife.usc.edu/labs/rwilcox/datasets/.

1.6 ACCESSING MORE DETAILED ANSWERS TO THE EXERCISES

For each chapter in this book, brief answers to most of the exercises are located in Appendix A. More detailed answers for all of the exercises are located at http://dornsife.usc.edu/labs/rwilcox/books/ and are stored in the file answers_wiley.pdf.

1.7 EXERCISES

1. Store the values $-20, -15, -5, 8, 12, 9, 2, 23, 19$ in the R variable x and use the R command sum to verify that the sum of the values is 33.
2. For the data in Exercise 1, verify that the average is 3.67 using the R command mean.
3. What R commands can be used to compute an average without using the R command mean?
4. In Exercise 1, use R to sum the positive values ignoring the negative values.
5. In Exercise 1, use the which command to get the average of the values ignoring the largest value.
6. If the data in Exercise 1 are stored in the R variable x, speculate about the values corresponding to x[abs(x)>=8 & x<8]. Verify your speculation using this R command.
7. You record your commute time to work for 10 days, in minutes, and get 23, 18, 29, 22, 24, 27, 28, 19, 28, 23. Use R to determine the average, the shortest time, and the longest time.
8. Verify that the R commands

   ```
   y=c(2,4,8)
   z=c(1,5,2)
   2*y
   ```

   return the values 4, 8, 16. Also, verify that the R command y+z returns 3, 9, 10 and that the command y-2 returns 0, 2, 6.
9. Let x = c(1, 8, 2, 6, 3, 8, 5, 5, 5, 5). Use R to compute the average using the sum and length commands. Next, use a single command to subtract the value 4 from each value stored in x. Finally, find the difference between the largest and smallest values stored in x. (This difference is called the range.) You can use the max and min functions or the range function.
10. For the data in Exercise 9, use R to subtract the average from each value, and then sum the results.

11. Imagine a matrix m having 100 rows and 2 columns. Further imagine that some of the values in the first column are NA, missing. Describe how the R function is.na can be used to eliminate the rows with missing values.

12. R has a built-in data set called ChickWeight. Verify that the R command

    ```
    mean(ChickWeight[,1])
    ```

    returns 121.8 but that the command

    ```
    mean(ChickWeight[,3])
    ```

    returns NA and a warning message even though the values in column 3 appear to be numeric. The reason for the warning message is that column 3 is stored as a factor variable. Arithmetic operations can only by performed on numeric or logical variables. Verify that

    ```
    mean(as.numeric(ChickWeight[,3]))
    ```

    returns 26.26.

13. Create a matrix with two rows and five columns with some of the entries stored as NA. Verify that the R function

    ```
    elimna(x)
    ```

    eliminates the rows with missing values. (This function is contained in the file Rallfun and can be installed as described in Section 1.4.)

14. R has a built-in data set called chickwts, which is stored in a data frame with two columns. (It differs from the built-in data set ChickWeight.) The first column contains the weight of chicks, and the second column indicates the type of feed they received, one of which is labeled horsebean. Use R to compute the average weight among chicks that were fed horsebean.

15. Let x = c(1, 8, 2, 6, 3, 8, 5, 5, 5, 5). Describe two different R commands for summing the values in x ignoring the value 2 stored in x[3] and the value 3 stored in x[5].

16. For the values used in the previous exercise, use two different R commands to sum all of the values not equal to 5.

17. For the data used in the previous two exercises, use a single R command to change all values equal to 8 to 7.

18. Create a matrix with four rows and two columns with the values 1, 2, 3, 4 and in the first column and 5, 6, 7, 8 in the second column.

19. Create a matrix with four columns and two rows with the values 1, 2, 3, 4 and in the first row and 11, 12, 13, 14 in the second row.

2

NUMERICAL SUMMARIES OF DATA

Chapter 1 made a distinction between a population and a sample and noted that a fundamental issue is understanding the extent to which inferences about a population can be made based on a sample. The focus in this chapter is on numerical methods for summarizing a sample. Chapters 4 and 5 describe the key components that will be needed to make inferences about the population.

To help motivate this chapter, imagine a study conducted on the effects of a drug designed to lower cholesterol levels. The study begins by measuring the cholesterol level of 171 participants and then measuring each participant's cholesterol level after 1 month on the drug. Table 2.1 shows the change between the two measurements. (The data are stored in the file ibtable2_1_dat.txt, which can be downloaded from the author's web page as described in Section 1.5.) The first entry is −23, indicating that the cholesterol level of this particular individual decreased by 23 units. Further imagine that a placebo is given to 176 participants, resulting in the changes in cholesterol as shown in Table 2.2. Although we have information on the effect of the drug, there is the practical problem of conveying this information in a useful manner. Simply looking at the values, it is difficult determining how the experimental drug compares to the placebo. In general, how might we summarize the data in a manner that helps us judge any differences that might exist?

This chapter describes numerical summaries of data called *descriptive measures* or *descriptive statistics* that are aimed at addressing the issue just raised. Many descriptive measures have been proposed, but only a few are described here. There are two types that play a particularly important role when trying to understand data: *measures of location* and measures of dispersion. Measures of location, also called *measures of central tendency*, are traditionally thought of as attempts to find a single numerical quantity that reflects the "typical" observed value. But this description can

Understanding and Applying Basic Statistical Methods Using R, First Edition. Rand R. Wilcox.
© 2017 John Wiley & Sons, Inc. Published 2017 by John Wiley & Sons, Inc.
www.wiley.com/go/Wilcox/Statistical_Methods_R

be misleading and is too narrow in a sense that will be made clear in Section 2.2. Roughly, measures of dispersion reflect how spread out the data happen to be. That is, they reflect the variability among the observed values.

2.1 SUMMATION NOTATION

Before continuing, some basic notation should be introduced. Arithmetic operations associated with statistical techniques can get quite involved, and so a mathematical shorthand is typically used to make sure that there is no ambiguity about how the computations are to be performed. Generally, some letter is used to represent whatever is being measured; the letter X is the most common choice. So, in Tables 2.1 and 2.2, X represents the change in cholesterol levels, but it could just as easily be used to represent how much weight is lost using a particular diet, how much money is earned using a particular investment strategy, or how often a particular surgical procedure is successful. The notation X_1 is used to indicate the first observation. In Table 2.1, the first observed value is -23, and this is written as $X_1 = -23$. The next observation is -11, which is written as $X_2 = -11$, and the last observation is $X_{171} = -4$. In a similar manner, in Table 2.2, $X_1 = 8$, $X_6 = 26$, and the last observation is $X_{177} = -19$. More generally, n is typically used to represent the total number of observations, and the

TABLE 2.1   Changes in Cholesterol Level after 1 Month on an Experimental Drug

```
−23 −11 −7 −13 4 −32 −20 −18 1 7 −32 −14 −18 6 10 −4 −15 −7
−21 −10 10 −20 −15 −10 −11 −10 −5 0 −13 −14 −6 9 −19 −10 −19 −11
5 −6 −17 −6 −15 6 −8 −17 −8 −16 2 −6 −14 −22 −11 −23 −6 −5
−12 −12 0 0 −3 −14 −34 −8 −19 −30 −17 −17 −1 −30 −31 −17 −16 −5
8 −23 −12 9 −33 4 −18 −34 −2 −28 −10 −8 −20 −8 19 −12 −11 0
−19 −12 −10 −20 −11 −2 −17 −24 −18 −18 −13 25 4 −13 −1 −7 −2
−22 −25 −19 −8 −17 −10 −27 −1 −6 −19 4 −16 −29 4 −8 −16
−16 1 −7 −31 −9 0 −4 −16 −5 −6 −14 −3 0 31 −10 −23
−14 −24 −11 −2 20 −5 −21 −1 −2 −3 −21 −5 −10 −12 0 −5
10 −26 −9 −10 16 −15 −26 1 −18 −19 −16 10 0 4 −9 −4
```

TABLE 2.2   Changes in Cholesterol Level after 1 Month of Taking a Placebo

```
8 7 2 5 11 26 2 0 −10 6 −28 3 −14 2 −27 1 12 0
17 68 14 −16 10 10 30 −27 −35 6 −1 22 2 1 0 −11 −5 −36
10 4 7 15 −6 10 −8 −4 6 −2 −2 −1 10 34 39 4 15 −4
−7 1 −8 −4 −7 −3 −12 0 −17 −1 −17 7 −16 −1 15 20 1 −9
1 −3 −14 0 2 1 7 2 −17 −25 −7 −16 3 −1 −2 9 11 0
13 8 −20 0 −3 10 −1 −4 −9 −7 9 −7 9 −43 10 −17 −10 −18
11 −11 −22 0 11 11 10 6 −5 8 71 −11 −9 −1 12 0 −6 −1
−21 11 5 −3 24 −11 −36 −1 4 18 −8 −8 1 −1 3 0 6 3
−5 8 0 −4 −7 11 0 16 −1 −3 −11 −16 −14 −12 6 −5 21 −16
−11 6 −10 3 13 −5 13 5 −1 −1 −8 5 −9 18 −19
```

observations themselves are represented by

$$X_1, X_2, \ldots, X_n.$$

So, in Table 2.1, $n = 171$ and in Table 2.2, $n = 177$.

Summation notation is a way of saying that a collection of numbers is to be added. In symbols, adding the numbers $X_1, X_2, \ldots, X_n$ is denoted by

$$\sum_{i=1}^{n} X_i = X_1 + X_2 + \ldots + X_n,$$

where $\sum$ is an uppercase Greek sigma. The subscript i is the *index of summation*, and the 1 and n that appear respectively below and above the symbol $\sum$ designate the range of the summation. So, if X represents the changes in cholesterol levels in Table 2.2,

$$\sum_{i=1}^{n} X_i = 8 + 7 + 2 \ldots = 22.$$

In most situations, the sum extends over all n observations, in which case it is customary to omit the index of summation. That is, simply use the notation

$$\sum_i X_i = X_1 + X_2 + \ldots + X_n.$$

Example

Imagine you work for a software company, and you want to know, when customers call for help, how long it takes them to reach the appropriate department. To keep the illustration simple, imagine that you have data on five individuals and that their times (in minutes) are as follows:

$$1.2, 2.2, 6.4, 3.8, 0.9.$$

Then,

$$\sum_{i=2}^{4} X_i = 2.2 + 6.4 + 3.8 = 12.4$$

and

$$\sum_i X_i = 1.2 + 2.2 + 6.4 + 3.8 + 0.9 = 14.5.$$

Another common arithmetic operation consists of squaring each observed value and summing the results. This is written as

$$\sum_i X_i^2 = X_1^2 + X_2^2 + \ldots + X_n^2.$$

Note that this is not necessarily the same as adding all the values and squaring the result. This latter operation is denoted by

$$\left(\sum X_i\right)^2.$$

Example

For the data in the last example,

$$\sum X_i^2 = 1.2^2 + 2.2^2 + 6.4^2 + 3.8^2 + 0.9^2 = 62.49$$

and

$$\left(\sum X_i\right)^2 = (1.2 + 2.2 + 6.4 + 3.8 + 0.9)^2 = 14.5^2 = 210.25.$$

Let c be any constant. In some situations, it helps to note that multiplying each value by c and adding the results is the same as first computing the sum and then multiplying by c. In symbols,

$$\sum cX_i = c \sum X_i.$$

Example

Consider again the data used in the last two examples, and suppose we convert the observed values into seconds by multiplying each value by 60. Then, the sum, using times in seconds, is

$$\sum 60X_i = 60 \sum X_i = 60 \times 14.5 = 870.$$

Another common operation is to subtract a constant from each observed value, square each difference, and add the results. In summation notation, this is written as

$$\sum (X_i - c)^2.$$

Example

For the data in the examples just described, suppose we want to subtract 2.9 from each value, square each of the results, and then sum these squared differences. So $c = 2.9$, and

$$\sum (X_i - c)^2 = (1.2 - 2.9)^2 + (2.2 - 2.9)^2 + \dots + (0.9 - 2.9)^2 = 20.44.$$

One more summation rule should be noted. If we sum a constant c n times, we get nc. This is written as

$$\sum c = c + \dots + c = nc.$$

2.2   MEASURES OF LOCATION

As previously noted, measures of location, frequently called *measures of central tendency*, are often described as attempts to find a single numerical quantity that reflects the typical observed value. Literally, hundreds of such measures have been proposed and studied. Two, called the sample mean and median, are easily computed and routinely used. But acquiring a good understanding of their relative merits will take some time.

2.2.1   The Sample Mean

The *sample mean* is just the average of the values and is generally labeled $\overline{X}$. The notation $\overline{X}$ is read as X bar. In summation notation,

$$\overline{X} = \frac{1}{n} \sum X_i.$$

Example

A commercial trout farm wants to advertise, and as part of their promotion plan, they want to tell customers how much their typical trout weighs. To keep things simple for the moment, suppose they catch five trout having weights 1.1, 2.3, 1.7, 0.9, and 3.1 pounds. The trout farm does not want to report all five weights to the public but rather one number that conveys the typical weight among the five trout caught. For these five trout, a measure of the typical weight is the sample mean,

$$\overline{X} = \frac{1}{5}(1.1 + 2.3 + 1.7 + 0.9 + 3.1) = 1.82.$$

Example

You sample 10 married couples and determine the number of children they have. The results are 0, 4, 3, 2, 2, 3, 2, 1, 0, 8. The sample mean is $\overline{X} = (0 + 4 + 3 + 2 + 2 + 3 + 2 + 1 + 0 + 8)/10 = 2.5$. Of course, nobody has 2.5 children. The intention is to provide a number that is centrally located among the 10 observations with the goal of conveying what is typical. The sample mean is frequently used for this purpose, in part because it greatly simplifies technical issues related to methods covered in subsequent chapters. In some cases, the sample mean suffices as a summary of data, but it is important to keep in mind that for various reasons, it can be highly unsatisfactory. One reason is that a few unusually large or small values can have an inordinately large impact on its value. That is, the sample mean can poorly reflect the typical value. We have already seen this in Chapter 1 in connection with the earthquake data.

Example

As another example, imagine that an investment firm is trying to recruit you. As a lure, they tell you that among the 11 individuals currently working at the company, the average salary, in thousands of dollars, is 88.7. However, on closer inspection, you find that the salaries are

$$30, 25, 32, 28, 35, 31, 30, 36, 29, 200, 500,$$

where the two largest salaries correspond to the vice president and president, respectively. The average is 88.7, as claimed, but an argument can be made that this is hardly typical because the salaries of the president and vice president distort the sample mean. Note that the sample mean is considerably larger than 9 of the 11 salaries.

Example

Pedersen et al. (2002) conducted a study, a portion of which dealt with the sexual attitudes of undergraduate students. Among other things, the students were asked how many sexual partners they desired over the next 30 years. The responses of 105 males are shown in Table 2.3. The sample mean is $\overline{X} = 64.9$. But this is hardly typical because 102 of the 105 males gave a response less than the sample mean.

Outliers are values that are unusually large or small. In the last example, one participant responded that he wanted 6,000 sexual partners over the next 30 years, which is clearly unusual, compared to the other 104 students. Also, two gave the response 150, which again is relatively unusual. An important point made by these last two examples is that the sample mean can be highly influenced by one or more outliers. That is, care must be exercised when using the sample mean because its value can be highly atypical and therefore potentially misleading. Also, outliers are not necessarily mistakes or inaccurate reflections of what was intended. For example, it might be argued that nobody would seriously want 6,000 sexual partners, but similar studies confirm that generally a small proportion of individuals will give a relatively extreme response.

2.2.2   The Median

Another important measure of location is called the sample median. The basic idea is easily described using the example based on the trout farm data. The observed weights were

$$1.1, 2.3, 1.7, 0.9, 3.1$$

TABLE 2.3   Responses by Males in the Sexual Attitude Study

6 1 1 3 1 1 1 1 1 1 6 1 1 1 4
5 3 9 1 1 1 5 12 10 4 2 1 1 4 45
8 5 0 1 150 13 19 2 1 18 3 1 3 1 11
1 2 1 1 1 12 1 1 2 6 1 1 1 1 4
1 150 6 40 4 30 10 1 1 0 3 4 1 4 7
1 10 0 19 1 9 1 1 1 1 5 0 1 1 15 4
1 4 1 1 11 1 1 1 30 12 6,000 1 0 1 1 15

Putting the values in ascending order yields

$$0.9, 1.1, \mathbf{1.7}, 2.3, 3.1.$$

Notice that the value 1.7 divides the observations in the middle in the sense that half of the remaining observations are less than 1.7 and half are larger. If, instead, the observations are

$$0.8, 4.5, 1.2, 1.3, 3.1, 2.7, 2.6, 2.7, 1.8,$$

we can again find a middle value by putting the observations in order yielding

$$0.8, 1.2, 1.3, 1.8, \mathbf{2.6}, 2.7, 2.7, 3.1, 4.5.$$

Then, 2.6 is a middle value in the sense that half of the observations are less than 2.6 and half are larger. This middle value is an example of what is called a *sample median*.

Notice that there are an odd number of observations in the last two illustrations; the last illustration has $n = 9$. If, instead, we have an even number of observations, there is no middle value, in which case the most common strategy is to average the two middle values to get the so-called sample median. For the last illustration, suppose we eliminate the value 1.2, so now $n = 8$ and the observations, written in ascending order, are

$$0.8, 1.3, 1.8, \mathbf{2.6}, \mathbf{2.7}, 2.7, 3.1, 4.5.$$

The sample median in this case is taken to be the average of 2.6 and 2.7, namely $(2.6 + 2.7)/2 = 2.65$. In general, with n odd, the median is a value in your sample, but with n, even this is not necessarily the case.

A more formal description of the sample median illustrates some commonly used notation. Recall that the notation $X_1, \ldots, X_n$ is typically used to represent the observations associated with n individuals or objects. Consider again the trout example where $n = 5$ and the observations are $X_1 = 1.1$, $X_2 = 2.3$, $X_3 = 1.7$, $X_4 = 0.9$, and $X_5 = 3.1$ pounds. That is, the first trout that is caught weighs 1.1 pounds, the second weighs 2.3 pounds, and so on. The notation $X_{(1)}$ is used to indicate the smallest observation. In the illustration, the smallest of the five observations is 0.9, so $X_{(1)} = 0.9$. The smallest of the remaining four observations is 1.1, and this is written as $X_{(2)} = 1.1$. The smallest of the remaining three observations is 1.7, so $X_{(3)} = 1.7$, the largest of the five values is 3.1, and this is written as $X_{(5)} = 3.1$. More generally,

$$X_{(1)} \leq X_{(2)} \leq X_{(3)} \leq \ldots \leq X_{(n)}$$

is the notation used to indicate that n values are to be put in ascending order.

The *sample median* is computed in one of two ways:

1. If the number of observations, n, is odd, compute $m = (n + 1)/2$. Then, the sample median is
$$M = X_{(m)},$$
the mth value after the observations are put in ascending order.

2. If the number of observations, n, is even, compute $m = n/2$. Then, the sample median is

$$M = \frac{(X_{(m)} + X_{(m+1)})}{2},$$

the average of the mth and $(m + 1)$th observations after putting the observed values in ascending order.

Example

Seven individuals are given a test that measures depression. The observed scores are

$$34, 29, 55, 45, 21, 32, 39.$$

Because the number of observations is $n = 7$, which is odd, $m = (7 + 1)/2 = 4$. Putting the observations in ascending order yields

$$21, 29, 32, \mathbf{34}, 39, 45, 55.$$

So, the sample median is $M = X_{(4)} = 34$.

Example

The last example is repeated, only with six test scores

$$29, 55, 45, 21, 32, 39.$$

Because the number of observations is $n = 6$, which is even, $m = 6/2 = 3$. Putting the observations in ascending order yields

$$21, 29, \mathbf{32}, \mathbf{39}, 45, 55.$$

So, $X_{(3)} = 32$ and $X_{(4)} = 39$, and the sample median is $M = (32 + 39)/2 = 35.5$.

Example

Consider again the data in the example dealing with salaries. We saw that the sample mean is 88.7. In contrast, the sample median is $M = 31$, providing a substantially different impression of the typical salary earned. This illustrates that the sample median is relatively insensitive to outliers for the simple reason that the smallest and largest values are trimmed when it is computed. For this reason, the median is called a *resistant measure of location*. The sample mean is an example of a measure of location that is not resistant to outliers.

Example

As previously noted, the sample mean for the sexual attitude data in Table 2.3 is $\overline{X} = 64.9$. But the median is $M = 1$, which provides a substantially different perspective on what is typical.

With the sample mean and median in hand, we can now be a bit more formal and precise about what is meant by a measure of location.

Definition. A summary of data, based on the observations $X_1, \ldots, X_n$, is called a *measure of location* if it satisfies three properties. First, its value must lie somewhere between the smallest and largest values observed. In symbols, a measure of location must have a value that is greater than or equal to $X_{(1)}$ and simultaneously less than or equal to $X_{(n)}$. Second, if all observations are multiplied by some constant c, then the measure of location is multiplied by c as well. Third, if c is added to every value, the measure of location is increased by the same amount.

Example

You measure the height, in feet, of 10 women, yielding the values 5.2, 5.9, 6.0, 5.11, 5.0, 5.5, 5.6, 5.7, 5.2, 5.8. The sample mean is $\overline{X} = 5.501$. Notice that the mean cannot be less than the smallest value and it cannot be greater than the largest value. More formally, $X_{(1)} \leq \overline{X} \leq X_{(n)}$, so the sample mean satisfies the first criterion for being a measure of location. We could get the mean in inches by multiplying each value by 12 and recomputing the average, but it is easier to simply multiply the mean by 12, yielding 66.012. Finally, if, for example, 3 is added to each value, it can be seen that the sample mean is now $5.501 + 3 = 8.501$. More generally, if c is added to very value, the sample mean, $\overline{X}$, is increased by c as well.

Similarly, the median is 5.55 feet, and in inches it is easily verified that the median is $12 \times 5.55 = 66.6$. More generally, if M is the median, and if each value is multiplied by some number c, the median becomes cM. If c is added to very value, now the median is $M + c$. This illustrates that both the mean and median satisfy the second and third conditions in the definition of a measure location.

The practical point being made here is that when a statistician refers to a measure of location, this does not necessarily imply that this measure reflects what is typical. We have already seen that the sample mean can be very atypical, yet it is generally referred to as a measure of location or a measure of central tendency.

2.2.3 Sample Mean versus Sample Median

How do we choose between the mean and median? It might seem that because the median is resistant to outliers and the mean is not, use the median. But this issue is not simple. Indeed, for various reasons outlined later in this book, both the mean and median can be unsatisfactory, but this is not to suggest that they never have practical value. What is needed is a good understanding of their relative merits, which includes issues covered in subsequent chapters. To complicate matters, even when the mean and median have identical values, it will be seen that for purposes beyond merely describing the data, the choice between these two measures of location can be crucial. It is also noted that although the median can better reflect what is typical, in some situations, its resistance to outliers can be undesirable.

Example

Imagine someone invests $200,000 and reports that the median amount earned per year, over a 10-year period, is $100,000. This sounds great, but now imagine that the earnings for each year are as follows: $100,000, $200,000, $200,000, $200,000, $200,000, $200,000, $200,000, $300,000, $300,000, −$2,000,000. So, at the end of 10 years this individual has earned nothing and in fact lost the $200,000 initial investment. (The sample mean is −$200,000.) Certainly, the long-term total amount earned is relevant in which case the sample mean provides a useful summary of the investment strategy that was followed.

2.2.4 Trimmed Mean

The mean and median are the two best-known measures of location, with the mean being used in a large proportion of applied investigations. There are circumstances where using a mean gives satisfactory results. Indeed, there are conditions where it is optimal, compared to any other measure of location that might be used. There are conditions where the median is an excellent choice, but situations are encountered where both the mean and median can be unsatisfactory. Many new methods have been developed for dealing with known problems, some of which are based in part on using measures of location other than the mean and median. One of the simpler alternatives is introduced here.

The sample median is an example of what is called a trimmed mean; it trims all but one or two values. Although there are circumstances where this extreme amount of trimming can be beneficial, for various reasons covered in subsequent chapters, this extreme amount of trimming can be detrimental. The sample mean represents the other extreme: zero trimming. We have already seen that this can result in a measure of location that is a rather poor reflection of what is a typical observation. But even when it provides a good indication of the typical value, many basic methods based on the mean suffer from other fundamental concerns yet to be described. One way of reducing these problems is to use a compromise amount of trimming. That is, trim some values, but not as many as done by the median. No specific amount of trimming is always best, but for various reasons, 20% trimming is often a good choice. This means that the smallest 20% and the largest 20% are trimmed and the average of the remaining data is computed. In symbols, first compute $0.2n$, round down to the nearest integer, call this result g, in which case the 20% trimmed mean is given by

$$\overline{X}_t = \frac{1}{n - 2g}(X_{(g+1)} + \cdots + X_{(n-g)}). \tag{2.1}$$

Example

Consider the values

$$46, 12, 33, 15, 29, 19, 4, 24, 11, 31, 38, 69, 10.$$

Putting these values in ascending order yields,

$$4, 10, 11, 12, 15, 19, 24, 29, 31, 33, 38, 46, 69.$$

The number of observations is $n = 13$, $0.2(n) = 0.2(13) = 2.6$, and rounding 2.6 down to the nearest integer yields $g = 2$. That is, when computing a 20% trimmed mean for the data at hand, trim the two smallest values, 4 and 10, trim the two largest values, 46 and 69, and average the numbers that remain yielding

$$\overline{X}_t = \frac{1}{9}(11 + 12 + 15 + 19 + 24 + 29 + 31 + 33 + 38) = 23.56.$$

Example

Imagine a figure skating contest that uses nine judges who rate a skater on a six-point scale. Suppose the nine ratings are

$$5.1, 5.3, 5.3, 5.5, 5.0, 5.1, 5.4, 4.2, 5.2.$$

A natural concern is that some raters might not be fair under certain circumstances, or they might provide a poor reflection of how most raters would judge the skater, which in turn might make a difference in a competition. From a statistical point of view, we do not want an unusual rating to overly influence our measure of the typical rating a skater would receive. For the data at hand, the sample mean is 5.1, but notice that the rating 4.2 is unusually small, compared to the remaining eight. To guard against unusually high or low ratings, it is common in skating competitions to throw out the highest and lowest scores and average those that remain. Here, $n = 9$, $0.2n = 1.8$, so $g = 1$. That is, a 20% trimmed mean corresponds to throwing out the lowest and highest scores and averaging the ratings that remain yielding $\overline{X}_t = 5.2$.

2.2.5 R function mean, tmean, and median

As noted in Chapter 1, the mean can be computed with the R function

```
mean(x,tr = 0, na.rm = FALSE).
```

The optional argument `tr` controls the amount of trimming and defaults to 0, no trimming. The argument `na.rm=FALSE` means that missing values will not be removed. Consequently, if there are missing values, `mean` will return NA. To remove missing values, set the argument `na.rm=TRUE`.

The R function

```
median(x, na.rm = FALSE)
```

computes the median.

A common choice for the amount of trimming is 20%, so for convenience, the R function

```
tmean(x, tr=0.2)
```

has been included in the file Rallfun and the R package WRS described in Section 1.4. Again, the amount of trimming is controlled by the argument `tr`. Unlike `mean`, `tmean` automatically removes missing values.

2.3 QUARTILES

As already explained and illustrated, the sample median divides the data into two parts: the lower half and the upper half after putting the observations in ascending order. *Quartiles* are measures of location aimed at dividing data into four parts. This is done with two additional measures of location called the lower and upper quartiles. The median is sometimes called the middle quartile. Roughly, the *lower quartile* is the median of the smaller half of the data and the *upper quartile* is the median of the upper half. So, it will be approximately the case that a fourth of the data are below the lower quartile, a fourth are between the lower quartile and the median, a fourth are between the median and the upper quartile, and a fourth are above the upper quartile.

There are, in fact, many suggestions about how the lower and upper quartiles should be computed. Again let $X_{(1)} \leq \ldots \leq X_{(n)}$ denote the observations written in ascending order. A simple approach is to take the lower quartile to be $X_{(j)}$, where $j = n/4$. If $n = 16$, for example, then $j = 4$ and a fourth of the values will be less than or equal to $X_{(4)}$, and using $X_{(4)}$ is consistent with how the lower quartile is defined. But when $n = 10$, this simple approach is unsatisfactory. Should we use $j = 10/4$ rounded down to the value 2, or should we use j rounded up to the value 3? Here we deal with this issue using a method that is relatively simple and that has been found to be well suited for another problem considered later in this chapter. The method is based on what are called the *ideal fourths*. To explain, let j be the integer portion of $(n/4) + (5/12)$, meaning that j is $(n/4) + (5/12)$ rounded down to the nearest integer, and let

$$h = \frac{n}{4} + \frac{5}{12} - j.$$

The lower quartile is taken to be

$$q_1 = (1 - h)X_{(j)} + hX_{(j+1)}. \tag{2.2}$$

Letting $k = n - j + 1$, the upper quartile is

$$q_2 = (1 - h)X_{(k)} + hX_{(k-1)}. \tag{2.3}$$

Example

Consider the values

$$-29.6, \ -20.9, \ -19.7, \ -15.4, \ -12.3, \ -8.0, \ -4.3, 0.8, 2.0, 6.2, 11.2, 25.0.$$

There are 12 values, so $n = 12$, and

$$\frac{n}{4} + \frac{5}{12} = 3.41667.$$

Rounding this last quantity down to the nearest integer gives $j = 3$. That is, j is just the number to the left of the decimal. Also, $h = 3.416667 - 3 = 0.41667$. That is, h

is the decimal portion of 3.41667. Because $X_{(3)} = -19.7$ and $X_{(4)} = -15.4$, the lower quartile is

$$q_1 = (1 - 0.41667)(-19.7) + 0.41667(-15.4) = -17.9.$$

In a similar manner, the upper quartile is

$$q_2 = (1 - 0.41667)(6.2) + 0.41667(2) = 4.45.$$

An important feature of the lower quartile is that it is insensitive to the smallest values. In modern terminology, it is resistant to outliers. In the last example, the smallest value is -29.6. If the value -29.6 is lowered to -100, or even $-1,000,000$, the lower quartile does not change. In a similar manner, the upper quartile is resistant to outliers as well. (This property will be exploited in Section 2.4.)

2.3.1   R function idealf and summary

The R function

```
idealf(x),
```

which is included in the Rallfun file described in Section 1.4, computes the ideal fourths. The built-in R function

```
summary(x,na.rm=FALSE),
```

computes what is generally called the *five number summary*: (1) the smallest observed value, (2) the lower quartile, (3) the median, (4) the upper quartile, and (5) the largest observed value. The lower and upper quartiles are computed using a method that differs slightly from the ideal fourths. The function `summary` also returns the mean.

2.4   MEASURES OF VARIATION

Often, measures of location are of particular interest. But measures of variation play a central role as well. Indeed, it is variation among responses that motivates many of the statistical methods covered in this book.

For example, imagine that a new diet for losing weight is under investigation. Of course, some individuals will lose more weight than others and some might gain weight. How might we take this variation into account when trying to assess the efficacy of this new diet? When a new drug is being researched, the drug might have no detrimental effect for some patients, but it might cause liver damage in others. What must be done to establish that the severity of liver damage is small? When asked whether they approve of how a political leader is performing, some will say they approve and others will give the opposite response. How can we take this variability into account when trying to assess the proportion of individuals who approve? The first step toward answering these questions is to introduce measures of variation, which play a central role when summarizing data. (The manner in which these measures are used to address the problems just described will be covered in subsequent chapters.)

2.4.1 The Range

The *range* is just the difference between the largest and smallest observations. In symbols, it is $X_{(n)} - X_{(1)}$. In Table 2.1, the largest value is 31, the smallest is -34, so the range is $31 - (-34) = 65$. The range provides information about the variability of the data, but relative to other measures that might be used, it plays a minor role.

2.4.2 R function Range

The R function

$$range(x, na.rm=FALSE),$$

does not compute the range as just defined. Rather, it determines the smallest and largest values stored in x.

Example

If the values 2, 7, 9, and 14 are stored in the R variable x, the commands

```
v=range(x)
v[2]-v[1]
```

would compute the range, which is equal to $14-2=12$. The commands

```
range(x)[2]-range(x)[1]
```

and

```
max(x)-min(x)
```

are two other ways of computing the range.

2.4.3 Deviation Scores, Variance, and Standard Deviation

Deviation scores are just the difference between each observation and the sample mean. For example, the deviation score for the first observation, X_1, is $X_1 - \overline{X}$. In a similar manner, the deviation score for the second observation is $X_2 - \overline{X}$.

Example

For various reasons, a diet with a reasonable amount of fiber is thought to promote good health. Among cereals regarded to have high fiber, is there much variation in the actual amount of fiber contained in one cup? For 11 such cereals, the amount of fiber (in grams), written in ascending order, is

$$7.5, 8.0, 8.0, 8.5, 9.0, 11.0, 19.5, 19.5, 28.5, 31.0, 36.0.$$

The sample mean is $\overline{X} = 17$, so the deviation scores are

$$-9.5, \ -9.0, \ -9.0, \ -8.5, \ -8.0, \ -6.0, 2.5, 2.5, 11.5, 14.0, 19.0.$$

Deviation scores reflect how far each observation is from the mean, but often it is convenient and desirable to find a single numerical quantity that summarizes the amount of variation. An initial suggestion might be to simply average the deviation scores. That is, use

$$\frac{1}{n} \sum (X_i - \overline{X}).$$

But using the rules for summation already described, it can be seen that this average difference is always zero, so this approach is unsatisfactory. Another possibility is to use the average of the absolute deviation scores:

$$\frac{1}{n} \sum |X_i - \overline{X}|.$$

This is reasonable, but it makes certain theoretical developments difficult. It turns out that using the squared differences instead greatly reduces certain technical issues related to methods covered in subsequent chapters. That is, use what is called the *sample variance*, which is

$$s^2 = \frac{1}{n-1} \sum (X_i - \overline{X})^2.$$

In other words, use the average squared difference from the mean. The sample *standard deviation* is the (positive) square root of the variance, s.

Notice that when computing the sample mean, we divide by n, the number of observations, but when computing the sample variance, s^2, we divide by $n - 1$. When first encountered, this usually seems strange, but it is too soon to explain why this is done.

Example

Imagine that for a sample of 10 adults ($n = 10$), each is asked to rate the performance of the president on a 10-point scale and the responses are as follows:

$$3, 9, 10, 4, 7, 8, 9, 5, 7, 8.$$

The sample mean is $\overline{X} = 7$, $\sum (X_i - \overline{X})^2 = 48$, so the sample variance is $s^2 = 48/9 = 5.33$ and the standard deviation is $s = \sqrt{5.33} = 2.31$. A more detailed summary of the calculations is as follows:

i	X_i	$X_i - \overline{X}$	$(X_i - \overline{X})^2$
1	3	−4	16
2	9	2	4
3	10	3	9
4	4	−3	9
5	7	0	0
6	8	1	1
7	9	2	4
8	5	−2	4
9	7	0	0
10	8	1	1
$\sum$		0	48

The sum of the observations in the last column is $\sum (X_i - \overline{X})^2 = 48$. So again, $s^2 = 48/9 = 5.33$.

The interpretation and practical utility of the sample variance, s^2, is unclear at this point. For now, the main message is that for some purposes, it is very useful, as will be seen. But simultaneously, there are various situations where it can be highly unsatisfactory. What is needed is a basic understanding of when it performs well, and when and why it can yield highly misleading results. One of the main reasons it can be unsatisfactory is its sensitivity to outliers.

Example

Consider the 10 values 50, 50, 50, 50, 50, 50, 50, 50, 50, 50. As is evident, the sample mean is $\overline{X} = 50$, and because all values are equal to the sample mean, $s^2 = 0$. Suppose we decrease the first value to 45 and increase the last to 55. Now $s^2 = 5.56$. If we decrease the first value to 20 and increase the last to 80, $s^2 = 200$. The point is that the sample variance can be highly influenced by unusually large or small values, even when the bulk of the values are tightly clustered together. Put another way, the sample variance can be small only when *all* of the values are tightly clustered together. If even a single value is unusually large or small, the sample variance will tend to be large regardless of how bunched together the other values might be. This property can wreak havoc on methods routinely used to analyze data, as will be seen. Fortunately, many new methods have been derived that deal effectively with this problem.

2.4.4   R Functions var and sd

The R function

```
var(x,na.rm=FALSE),
```

computes the sample variance and the R function

```
sd(x,na.rm=FALSE)
```

computes the standard deviation.

2.4.5 The Interquartile Range

For some purposes, it is important to measure the variability of the centrally located values. If, for example, we put the observations in ascending order, how much variability is there among the central half of the data? One approach is the *interquartile range*, which is just $q_2 - q_1$, the difference between the upper and lower quartiles.

Notice that the interquartile range is insensitive to the more extreme values. As previously noted, the upper and lower quartiles are resistant to outliers, which means that the most extreme values do not affect the values of q_1 and q_2. Consequently, the interquartile range is resistant to outliers as well.

Example

Consider again the 10 values 50, 50, 50, 50, 50, 50, 50, 50, 50, 50. The interquartile range is zero. If we decrease the first value to 20 and increase the last to 80, the interquartile range is still zero because it measures the variability of the central half of the data, while ignoring the upper and lower fourth of the observations. Indeed, no matter how small we make the first value, and no matter how much we increase the last value, the interquartile range remains zero.

2.4.6 MAD and the Winsorized Variance

In recent years, two other measures of variation have played a prominent role in the statistics literature: the median absolute deviation (MAD) and the Winsorized variance. MAD plays an important role when the goal is to detect outliers for reasons described in the next section. The Winsorized variance plays a fundamental role when analyzing data using a trimmed mean, as will be made evident in Chapters 5–7.

MAD is computed by subtracting the median from each observation, taking the absolute value of each difference, and then computing the median. In symbols, MAD is the median of

$$|X_1 - M|, \ \ldots \ , |X_n - M|.$$

Example

Consider the values

$$12, 45, 23, 79, 19, 92, 30, 58, 132.$$

The median is $M = 45$. Subtracting the median from each value and computing the absolute value yield

$$33, 0, 22, 34, 26, 47, 15, 13, 87.$$

Putting these values in ascending order yields

$$0, 13, 15, 22, \mathbf{26}, 33, 34, 47, 87.$$

MAD is the median of these nine values: 26.

Typically, MAD is divided by 0.6745 for reasons that are difficult to explain at the moment. For convenience, we set

$$\text{MADN} = \frac{\text{MAD}}{0.6745}. \tag{2.4}$$

When using a trimmed mean, certain types of analyses, to be covered, require a Winsorized variance. The process of Winsorizing data by 20% is related to 20% trimming. Recall that when computing a 20% trimmed mean, the g smallest and the g largest observations are removed, where $g = 0.2n$ rounded down to the nearest integer, in which case the 20% trimmed mean is the average of the remaining values. Winsorizing the data by 20% means that the g smallest values are not trimmed, but rather, they are set equal to the smallest value not trimmed. Similarly, the g largest values are set equal to the largest value not trimmed.

Example

Suppose the reaction times of individuals are measured, yielding

$$2, 3, 4, 5, 6, 7, 8, 9, 10, 50.$$

There are $n = 10$ values, $0.2(10) = 2$, so $g = 2$. Here, 20% Winsorizing of the data means that the two smallest values are set equal to 4, which is the smallest value not trimmed. Simultaneously, the two largest observations, 10 and 50, are set equal to 9, the largest value not trimmed. That is, 20% Winsorizing of the data yields

$$4, 4, 4, 5, 6, 7, 8, 9, 9, 9.$$

In symbols, the observations $X_1, \ldots, X_n$ are Winsorized by first putting the observations in ascending order, yielding $X_{(1)} \le X_{(2)} \le \ldots \le X_{(n)}$. Then, the g smallest observations are replaced by $X_{(g+1)}$, and the g largest observations are replaced by $X_{(n-g)}$.

Example

To Winsorize the values

$$10, 8, 22, 35, 42, 2, 9, 18, 27, 1, 16, 29$$

using 20% Winsorization, first note that there are $n = 12$ observations, $0.2 \times 12 = 2.4$, and rounding down gives $g = 2$. Putting the values in ascending order yields

$$1, 2, 8, 9, 10, 16, 18, 22, 27, 29, 35, 42.$$

Then, the two smallest values are replaced by $X_{(g+1)} = X_{(3)} = 8$, the two largest values are replaced by $X_{(n-g)} = X_{(10)} = 29$, and the resulting Winsorized values are

$$8, 8, 8, 9, 10, 16, 18, 22, 27, 29, 29, 29.$$

The sample mean of the Winsorized values, $\overline{W}$, is called the *Winsorized mean*. In symbols, if $W_1, \ldots, W_n$ are the Winsorized values,

$$\overline{W} = \frac{1}{n} \sum W_i.$$

The *Winsorized variance* is just the sample variance based on the Winsorized values and will be labeled s_w^2. In symbols,

$$s_w^2 = \frac{1}{n-1} \sum (W_i - \overline{W})^2. \tag{2.5}$$

The *Winsorized sample standard deviation* is the square root of the Winsorized sample variance, s_w.

Example

To compute the 20% Winsorized mean and variance for the observations

$$1, 2, 8, 9, 10, 16, 18, 22, 27, 29, 35, 42,$$

first Winsorize these values, yielding

$$8, 8, 8, 9, 10, 16, 18, 22, 27, 29, 29, 29.$$

The mean of these Winsorized values is the 20% Winsorized mean given by

$$\overline{W} = \frac{8 + 8 + 8 + 9 + 10 + 16 + 18 + 22 + 27 + 29 + 29 + 29}{12} = 17.75.$$

The 20% Winsorized sample variance is

$$s_w^2 = \frac{(8 - 17.75)^2 + (8 - 17.75)^2 + \ldots + (29 - 17.75)^2}{12 - 1} = 82.57.$$

The 20% Winsorized sample standard deviation is $s_w = \sqrt{82.57} = 9.1$.

For the observations in the last example, the sample mean is $\overline{X} = 18.25$ and the sample variance is $s^2 = 170.57$, which is about twice as large as the sample Winsorized variance, $s_w^2 = 82.57$. The 20% Winsorized variance is relatively insensitive to extreme observations roughly because extreme values do not impact its value. In contrast, the sample variance, s^2, is highly sensitive to extreme values. This difference between the sample variance and the 20% Winsorized sample variance will be seen to be important.

Example

For the data in the last example, suppose the largest value, 42, is increased to 60. Then, the sample mean increases from 18.25 to 19.75 and the sample variance, s^2, increases from 170.57 to 275.3. In contrast, the 20% Winsorized sample mean and variance do not increase at all, they are still equal to 17.75 and 82.57, respectively. Because there are $n = 12$ values, $g = 2$, so increasing the two largest values or decreasing the two smallest values does not alter the sample 20% Winsorized variance. That is, the Winsorized variance is resistant to outliers, which will turn out to have great practical value.

2.4.7   R Functions winvar, winsd, idealfIQR, and mad

The R function

$$\text{winvar}(x, tr=0.2)$$

computes the Winsorized variance and

$$\text{winsd}(x, tr=0.2)$$

computes the Winsorized standard deviation (assuming that the R package WRS has been installed or that the Rallfun file, described in Section 1.4, has been sourced). The argument tr controls the amount of Winsorizing and defaults to 0.2. The R function

$$\text{idealfIQR}(x)$$

computes the interquartile range based on the ideal fourths. (The built-in R function IQR uses a different method for computing the interquartile range.)

The built-in R function

$$\text{mad}(x).$$

computes MADN (not MAD).

2.5   DETECTING OUTLIERS

The detection of outliers will be seen to be important for a variety of reasons. A glimpse of one concern was provided in Chapter 1: A few outliers can have a major impact on the mean, as was indicated by the earthquake data. That is, the mean can poorly reflect the typical response. In this chapter, we have seen that outliers can have a major impact on the sample variance, which creates several practical concerns, one of which is described and illustrated in Section 2.5.1.

A rather mundane reason for using a good outlier detection method is that it can help identify erroneously recorded results. We have already seen that even a single outlier can grossly affect the sample mean and variance, and of course, we do not want a typing error to substantially alter our perceptions of the data. Such errors seem to be rampant in applied work, and the subsequent cost of such errors can be enormous (De Veaux and Hand, 2005). So, it can be prudent to check for outliers and, if any are found, make sure they are valid.

But even when data are recorded accurately, it cannot be stressed too strongly that modern outlier detection techniques suggest that outliers are more the rule rather than the exception. That is, unusually small or large values occur naturally in a wide range of situations. Interestingly, in 1960, the renowned statistician John Tukey (1915–2000) predicted that, in general, we should expect outliers. What is fascinating about his prediction is that it was made before good outlier detection techniques were available.

A fundamental requirement of any outlier detection technique is that it does not suffer from masking. An outlier detection technique is said to suffer from *masking* if the very presence of outliers causes them to be missed. The remainder of this section describes several methods for detecting outliers and their relative merits, in terms of masking, are discussed.

2.5.1   A Classic Outlier Detection Method

A classic outlier detection technique illustrates the problem of masking. This classic technique declares the value X an outlier if

$$\frac{|X - \overline{X}|}{s} > 2. \tag{2.6}$$

In words, declare X an outlier if it is more than two standard deviations from the mean. (The value 2 in this last equation is motivated by results covered in Chapter 4.) A commonly used variation of this rule is to declare a value an outlier if it is more than three standard deviations from the mean. In symbols, declare X an outlier if

$$\frac{|X - \overline{X}|}{s} > 3. \tag{2.7}$$

Example

Consider the values

$$2, 2, 2, 2, 2, 3, 3, 3, 3, 3, 4, 4, 4, 4, 4, 1, 000.$$

The sample mean is $\overline{X} = 65.3$, the sample standard deviation is $s = 249.1$,

$$\frac{|1, 000 - 65.3|}{249.25} = 3.75,$$

3.75 is greater than 2, so the value 1,000 is declared an outlier. In this particular case, the classic outlier detection method is performing in a reasonable manner; it identifies what is surely an usual value.

Example

Now consider the values

$$2, 2, 3, 3, 3, 4, 4, 4, 100, 000, 100, 000.$$

The sample mean is $\overline{X} = 20,002.5$, the sample standard deviation is $s = 42,162.38$,

$$\frac{|100,000 - 20,002.5|}{42,162.38} = 1.897,$$

and so the classic method would not declare the value 100,000 an outlier even though certainly it is highly unusual relative to the other eight values. The problem is that the sample mean and, particularly, the sample standard deviation are sensitive to outliers. Consequently, the classic method for detecting outliers suffers from masking. It is left as an exercise to show that even if the two values 100,000 in this example are increased to 10,000,000, the value 10,000,000 is not declared an outlier.

Example

Consider the sexual attitude data in Table 2.3. It is evident that the response 6,000 is unusually large and the classic rule declares it an outlier. But even the response 150 seems very unusual relative to the majority of values listed, yet the classic rule does not flag it as an outlier.

2.5.2   The Boxplot Rule

One of the earliest improvements on the classic outlier detection rule is called the boxplot rule. It is based on the fundamental strategy of avoiding masking by replacing the mean and standard deviation with measures of location and dispersion that are relatively insensitive to outliers. In particular, the *boxplot rule* declares the value X an outlier if

$$X < q_1 - 1.5(q_2 - q_1) \tag{2.8}$$

or

$$X > q_2 + 1.5(q_2 - q_1). \tag{2.9}$$

So, the rule is based on the lower and upper quartiles, as well as the interquartile range, which provide resistance to outliers.

Example

Consider the values

$$1, 2, 3, 4, 5, 6, 7, 8, 9, 10, 11, 12, 13, 14, 100, 500.$$

A little arithmetic shows that the lower quartile is $q_1 = 4.417$, the upper quartile is $q_2 = 12.583$, so $q_2 + 1.5(q_2 - q_1) = 12.583 + 1.5(12.583 - 4.417) = 24.83$. That is, any value greater than 24.83 is declared an outlier. In particular, the values 100 and 500 are labeled outliers. Using instead the two standard deviations rule given by Equation (2.6), only 500 is declared an outlier.

Example

For the sexual attitude data in Table 2.3, the classic outlier detection rule declares only one value to be an outlier: the largest response, 6,000. In contrast, the boxplot rule labels all values greater than 13.5 as outliers. So, of the 105 responses, the classic outlier detection rule finds only 1 outlier and the boxplot rule finds 12.

2.5.3   The MAD–Median Rule

In terms of avoiding masking, the boxplot rule often suffices because more than 25% of the values must be outliers before masking becomes an issue. But situations are encountered where the boxplot rule breaks down. An outlier detection rule that can deal with an even larger proportion of outliers without suffering from masking is the MAD–median rule: Declare X an outlier if

$$\frac{|X - M|}{\text{MADN}} > 2.24. \tag{2.10}$$

(The value 2.24 in this last equation stems from Rousseeuw and van Zomeren, 1990.)

Example

Consider again the sexual attitude data. As previously indicated, the boxplot rule finds that 12 of the 105 values are outliers. In contrast, the MAD–median rule flags 33 values as outliers, the only point being that the outlier detection method that is used can make a practical difference.

2.5.4   R Functions outms, outbox, and out

The R function

```
outms(x,crit=2)
```

checks for outliers using the mean and standard deviation. In practice, this method is not recommended. This R function is provided merely to help illustrate that the classic outlier detection rule can be unsatisfactory due to masking. By default, the function uses Equation (2.6). To use Equation (2.7), set the argument `crit=3`. The R function

```
outbox(x).
```

checks for outliers using the boxplot rule and the R function

```
outpro(x).
```

uses the MAD–median rule.

Example

The earthquake data in Chapter 1 are used to illustrate the output from these functions. Focusing on the length variable, again assuming the data are stored in the R matrix quake and that the length data are stored in column 2, the R command

```
outbox(quake[,2])
```

returns

```
$out.val
[1] 360 400

$out.id
[1] 1 2

$keep
 [1]  3  4  5  6  7  8  9 10 11 12 13 14 15 16

$n
[1] 16

$n.out
[1] 2

$cl
[1] $-$55

$cu
[1] 131.6667
```

So, the values flagged as outliers are 360 and 400 and $out.id indicates that they are the first and second values stored in quake [,2]. That is, the outliers are stored in quake [1,2] (the first row and second column of quake) and quake [2,2] (the second row and second column). The output $keep indicates where the values not declared outliers are stored. So, from Chapter 1, the R commands

```
flag=outbox(quake[,2])$keep

mean(quake[flag,2])
```

would compute the mean using only those values not declared outliers. Finally, $n is the sample size, $n.out is the number of values declared an outlier, $cl indicates how small a value must be to be declared an outlier, and $cu is how large a value must be to be declared an outlier.

2.6 SKIPPED MEASURES OF LOCATION

Skipped estimators of location are based on the strategy of removing outliers and computing the mean of the remaining data. The previous section illustrated this process using the boxplot rule. Removing outliers based on the MAD–median rule and averaging the remaining values is called a modified one-step M-estimator (MOM). The resulting average will be denoted by $\overline{X}_{mm}$. (One-step M-estimators have been studied extensively, they have excellent theoretical properties, but the details go beyond the scope of this book. See Wilcox, 2012b, for more information.)

At some level, skipped estimators might seem preferable to using a trimmed mean. A trimmed mean might trim values that are not outliers, and a natural reaction is that values that are not outliers should not be trimmed. But this issue is not simple. Subsequent chapters provide more details.

2.6.1 R Function MOM

The R function

$$\mathrm{mom}(x)$$

computes the modified one-step M-estimator.

2.7 SUMMARY

- Several measures of location were introduced. How and when should one measure of location be preferred over another? Sensitivity to outliers is one way of addressing this issue. But there are other issues that need to be taken into account that are based on concepts yet to be described.
- The sample mean can be highly sensitive to outliers. For some purposes, this is desirable, but in many situations, this creates practical problems, as will be further demonstrated in subsequent chapters.
- The median is highly insensitive to outliers. It plays an important role in some situations, but the median has some negative characteristics yet to be described.
- In terms of sensitivity to outliers, the 20% trimmed mean lies between two extremes: no trimming (the mean) and the maximum amount of trimming (the median). Similarly to the median, the modified one-step M-estimator is highly insensitive to outliers.
- The sample variance is highly sensitive to outliers. This property creates difficulties when it is used to check for outliers. More precisely, it results in masking, and some additional concerns will become evident later in this book.
- The interquartile range measures variability without being sensitive to the more extreme values. This property makes it well suited for detecting outliers.
- The 20% Winsorized variance also measures variation without being sensitive to the more extreme values. But it is too soon to explain why it has practical importance.

2.8   EXERCISES

Brief answers to the exercises are located in Appendix A. More detailed answers are
located at http://dornsife.usc.edu/labs/rwilcox/books/ in the file answers_wiley.pdf.

1. Suppose

$$X_1 = 1 \qquad\qquad X_2 = 3 \qquad\qquad X_3 = 0$$
$$X_4 = -2 \qquad\qquad X_5 = 4 \qquad\qquad X_6 = -1$$
$$X_7 = 5 \qquad\qquad X_8 = 2 \qquad\qquad X_9 = 10$$

   Use R to find
   (a) $\sum X_i$, (b) $\sum_{i=3}^{5} X_i$, (c) $\sum_{i=1}^{4} X_i^3$, (d) $(\sum X_i)^2$, (e) $\sum 3$, (f) $\sum (X_i - 7)$
   (g) $3\sum_{i=1}^{5} X_i - \sum_{i=6}^{9} X_i$, (h) $\sum 10X_i$, (i) $\sum_{i=2}^{6} iX_i$, (j) $\sum 6$

2. Express the following in summation notation. (a) $X_1 + \frac{X_2}{2} + \frac{X_3}{3} + \frac{X_4}{4}$, (b) $U_1 + U_2^2 + U_3^3 + U_4^4$, (c) $(Y_1 + Y_2 + Y_3)^4$

3. Show by numerical example that $\sum X_i^2$ is not necessarily equal to $(\sum X_i)^2$.

4. Find the mean and median of the following sets of numbers. (a) $-1, 0, 3, 0,$
   $2, -5$. (b) $2, 2, 3, 10, 100, 1,000$.

5. The final exam scores for 15 students are $73, 74, 92, 98, 100, 72, 74, 85, 76, 94,$
   $89, 73, 76, 99$. Compute the mean, 20% trimmed mean, and median using R.

6. The average of 23 numbers is 14.7. What is the sum of these numbers?

7. Consider the 10 values $3, 6, 8, 12, 23, 26, 37, 42, 49, 63$. The mean is $\overline{X} = 26.9$.
   (a) What is the value of the mean if the largest value, 63, is increased to 100?
   (b) What is the mean if 63 is increased to 1,000? (c) What is the mean if 63 is
   increased to 10,000? What do these results illustrate about the sample mean?

8. Repeat the previous exercise, only compute the median instead.

9. In general, how many values must be altered to make the sample mean arbitrarily large?

10. What is the minimum number of values that must be altered to make the 20%
    trimmed mean and sample median arbitrarily large?

11. For the values $0, 23, -1, 12, -10, -7, 1, -19, -6, 12, 1, -3$, compute the
    lower and upper quartiles using the ideal fourths.

12. For the values $-1, -10, 2, 2, -7, -2, 3, 3, -6, 12, -1, -12, -6, 8, 6$, compute
    the lower and upper quartiles (the ideal fourths).

13. Approximately how many values must be altered to make q_2, the estimate of
    the upper quartile based on the ideal fourths, arbitrarily large?

14. Argue that the smallest observed value, $X_{(1)}$, satisfies the definition of a mea-
    sure of location.

15. The height of 10 plants is measured in inches and found to be $12, 6, 15, 3, 12,$
    $6, 21, 15, 18,$ and 12. Verify that $\sum (X_i - \overline{X}) = 0$.

16. For the data in the previous exercise, compute the range, variance, and stan-
    dard deviation.

17. Use the rules of summation notation to show that it is always the case that
    $\sum (X_i - \overline{X}) = 0$.

18. Seven different thermometers were used to measure the temperature of a substance. The reading in degrees Celsius are $-4.10, -4.13, -5.09, -4.08, -4.10,$ $-4.09,$ and -4.12. Find the variance and standard deviation.

19. A weightlifter's maximum bench press (in pounds) in each of 6 successive weeks was 280, 295, 275, 305, 300, 290. Find the standard deviation.

20. For the values

$$20, 121, 132, 123, 145, 151, 119, 133, 134, 130, 200$$

use the classic outlier detection rule, via the R function outms, to determine whether any outliers exist.

21. Apply the boxplot rule and the MAD–median rule using the values in the preceding exercise. Note that the results differ, compared to using the classic rule. Explain why this happened.

22. Consider the values

$$0, 121, 132, 123, 145, 151, 119, 133, 134, 130, 250.$$

Are the values 0 and 250 declared outliers using the classic outlier detection rule?

23. Verify that for the data in the previous exercise, the boxplot rule declares the values 0 and 250 outliers.

24. Consider the values

$$20, 121, 132, 123, 145, 151, 119, 133, 134, 240, 250.$$

Verify that no outliers are found using the classic outlier detection rule.

25. Verify that for the data in the previous exercise, the boxplot rule declares the values 20, 240, and 250 outliers.

26. What do the last three exercises suggest about the boxplot rule versus the classic rule for detecting outliers?

27. What is the typical pulse rate (beats per minute) among adults? Imagine that you sample 21 adults, measure their pulse rate, and get

$$80, 85, 81, 75, 77, 79, 74, 86, 79, 55, 82, 89, 73, 79, 83, 82, 88, 79, 77, 81, 82.$$

Compute the 20% trimmed mean.

28. For the observations

$$21, 36, 42, 24, 25, 36, 35, 49, 32$$

verify that the sample mean, 20% trimmed mean, and median are $\overline{X} = 33.33$, $\overline{X}_t = 32.9$, and $M = 35$.

29. The largest observation in the last problem is 49. If 49 is replaced by the value 200, verify that the sample mean is now $\overline{X} = 50.1$ but the 20% trimmed mean and median are not changed.

30. For the data in Exercise 28, what is the minimum number of observations that must be altered so that the 20% trimmed mean is greater than 1,000?

31. Repeat the previous exercise, but use the median instead. What does this illustrate about the resistance of the mean, median, and 20% trimmed mean?

32. For the observations

$$6, 3, 2, 7, 6, 5, 8, 9, 8, 11$$

use R to verify that the sample mean, 20% trimmed mean, and median are $\overline{X} = 6.5$, $\overline{X}_t = 6.7$, and $M = 6.5$, respectively.

33. In general, when you have n observations, what is the minimum number of values that must be altered to make the 20% trimmed mean as large as you want.

34. A class of fourth graders was asked to bring a pumpkin to school. Each of the 29 students counted the number of seeds in their pumpkin, and the results were

$$250, 220, 281, 247, 230, 209, 240, 160, 370, 274, 210, 204, 243, 251, 190,$$

$$200, 130, 150, 177, 475, 221, 350, 224, 163, 272, 236, 200, 171, 98.$$

Using R, compute the sample mean, 20% trimmed mean, median, and MOM.

35. Compute the 20% Winsorized values for the observations

$$21, 36, 42, 24, 25, 36, 35, 49, 32.$$

36. For the observations in the previous problem, use R to verify that the 20% Winsorized variance is 51.36.

37. In the previous problem, would you expect the sample variance to be larger or smaller than 51.36? Verify your answer.

38. In general, will the Winsorized sample variance, s_w^2, be less than the sample variance, s^2?

39. For the observations

$$6, 3, 2, 7, 6, 5, 8, 9, 8, 11$$

verify that the sample variance and 20% Winsorized variance are 7.4 and 1.8, respectively.

40. Consider again the number of pumpkin seeds given in Exercise 34. Compute the 20% Winsorized variance.

41. Snedecor and Cochran (1967) report results from an experiment dealing with weight gain in rats as a function of source and amount of protein. One of the groups was fed beef with a low amount of protein. The weight gains were

$$90, 76, 90, 64, 86, 51, 72, 90, 95, 78.$$

Compute the 20% trimmed mean and the 20% Winsorized variance.

3

PLOTS PLUS MORE BASICS ON SUMMARIZING DATA

This chapter covers some of the more basic methods for graphically summarizing data, and it expands on the numerical methods for characterizing data that were described in Chapter 2. (Many additional methods for plotting data are available with the R package ggplot2. See, e.g., Chang, 2013; Field et al., 2012; Wickham, 2009.) Included in this chapter are some modern insights regarding when basic graphical methods perform well and when and why they might be unsatisfactory for certain purposes. Generally, plots can reveal important features of data that are easily missed or underappreciated when relying solely on numerical summaries of data. This is particularly true when comparing two groups of individuals, as we will see in Chapter 9, and when studying the association between two variables as will be illustrated in Chapter 8.

3.1 PLOTTING RELATIVE FREQUENCIES

We begin with the situation where the variable of interest can take on a relatively small number of values. For example, individuals might be asked to rate the amount of pain they have after surgery on a scale from 0 to 5, or they might be asked whether they agree, disagree, or have no opinion about some political issue.

The notation f_x is used to denote the *frequency* or number of times the value x occurs. To be concrete, imagine that 100 individuals are asked to rate a recently released movie using a 10-point scale, where a 1 means the movie received a poor rating and a 10 indicates an excellent film. Suppose the results are as shown in Table 3.1, which for convenience are written in ascending order. In Table 3.1, the value 2 occurs five times, which is written as $f_2 = 5$, the number 3 occurs 18 times, so $f_3 = 18$. In a

Understanding and Applying Basic Statistical Methods Using R, First Edition. Rand R. Wilcox.
© 2017 John Wiley & Sons, Inc. Published 2017 by John Wiley & Sons, Inc.
www.wiley.com/go/Wilcox/Statistical_Methods_R

TABLE 3.1   One Hundred Ratings of a Film

2 2 2 2 2 3 3 3 3 3 3 3 3 3 3 3 3 3 3 3 3 3 3 3 4 4 4 4 4 4 4 4 4 4 4 4 4 4
4 4 4 4 4 4 4 4 4 4 5 5 5 5 5 5 5 5 5 5 5 5 5 5 5 5 5 5 5 5 5 5 5 5 5 5 6 6
6 6 6 6 6 6 6 6 6 6 6 6 7 7 7 7 7 7 7 7 7 8 8 8 8

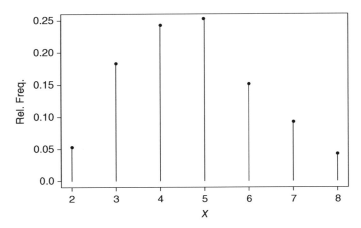

Figure 3.1   Relative frequencies for the data in Table 3.1

similar manner, $f_4 = 24, f_5 = 25, f_6 = 15, f_7 = 9$, and $f_9 = 4$. The *relative frequency* is the frequency divided by the sample size. That is, the relative frequency associated with the value x is f_x/n, the proportion of times the value x occurs among the n observations. The value having the largest frequency is called the *mode*. The plot used to indicate the relative frequencies consists of the possible x values along the x-axis with the height of spikes used to indicate the relative frequencies. The relative frequencies, taken as whole, are called an *empirical distribution*. Figure 3.1 shows a plot of the relative frequencies (the empirical distribution) for the data in Table 3.1. The mode is 5.

Note that for every possible value x, a certain proportion of the observed values will be less than or equal to x, which will be denoted by $F(x)$. These proportions, taken as a whole, are called the *empirical cumulative distribution function*. In Table 3.1, for example, the value 2 occurred five times, there are no values smaller than 2, so the proportion of values less than or equal to 2 is 5/100. In symbols, $f_2 = 5$, $n = 100$, and $F(2) = 5/100$. The next largest value that was observed is 3, 23 of the 100 values are less than or equal to 3, so $F(3) = 23/100$.

3.1.1   R Functions table, plot, splot, barplot, and cumsum

The R function

$$\texttt{table(x)}$$

provides a convenient way of computing the frequencies associated with the values stored in some R variable. One way of plotting the frequencies or relative frequencies is to use the R function `plot` in conjunction with `table`. For example, to plot the frequencies, use the R command

```
plot(table(x)).
```

Alternatively, use the R function

```
splot(x,op = TRUE, VL = FALSE, xlab= 'X',ylab= 'Rel.Freq.',
                    frame.plot = TRUE),
```

which is included in the file Rallfun mentioned in Section 1.4. By default, when using the R function `splot`, the relative frequencies are plotted and are connected by a line. Setting the argument `op=FALSE`, no lines are plotted. Setting `VL=TRUE`, vertical lines are plotted; the heights of the vertical lines indicate the relative frequencies. The arguments `xlab` and `ylab` can be used to label the x-axis and y-axis, respectively.

To compute the cumulative relative frequencies, use the command

```
cumsum(splot(x)$frequencies)/length(x).
```

Example
If the data in Table 3.1 are stored in the R variable `film`, the R command

```
table(film)
```

returns

```
film
 2   3   4   5   6   7   8
 5  18  24  25  15   9   4
```

The first row indicates the values that were found in `film` and the second line indicates the corresponding frequencies. For example, the value 2 occurred five times. To plot the relative frequencies, use the command

```
plot(table(film)/length(film)).
```

Alternatively, use the R command

```
splot(film,VL=TRUE),
```

which was used to create Figure 3.1.

It is noted that *bar plots* are sometimes used to summarize relative frequencies rather than vertical lines as done in Figure 3.1. This just means that the height of a rectangle is used to indicate the relative frequency rather than a vertical line. The R command

```
barplot(table(film)/length(film))
```

creates a bar plot for the film data.

3.1.2 Computing the Mean and Variance Based on the Relative Frequencies

This section indicates how the sample mean can be computed using relative frequencies. Observe that the sum of the frequencies yields the sample size, n. That is,

$$n = \sum f_x,$$

where now the summation is over all possible values of x. For the data in Table 3.1,

$$\sum f_x = f_1 + f_2 + f_3 + f_4 + f_5 + f_6 + f_7 + f_8 + f_9 + f_{10}$$
$$= 0 + 5 + 18 + 24 + 25 + 15 + 9 + 40 + 0 + 0$$
$$= 100.$$

The sample mean is

$$\overline{X} = \frac{1}{n} \sum x f_x = \sum x \frac{f_x}{n}. \tag{3.1}$$

So, if we know the relative frequencies, f_x/n, it is a simple matter to compute the mean even when the number of observations, n, is large. (And writing the sample mean in terms of relative frequencies helps elucidate a basic principle covered in Chapter 4.) The sample variance is

$$s^2 = \frac{n}{n-1} \sum (x - \overline{X})^2 \frac{f_x}{n}. \tag{3.2}$$

Example

One million couples are asked how many children they have. For illustrative purposes, suppose that the maximum number of possible children is 5 and that the relative frequencies are $f_0/n = 0.10, f_1/n = 0.20, f_2/n = 0.25, f_3/n = 0.29, f_4/n = 0.12$, and $f_5/n = 0.04$. Then, the sample mean is

$$\overline{X} = 0(0.10) + 1(0.20) + 2(0.25) + 3(0.29) + 4(0.12) + 5(0.04) = 2.25.$$

To compute the sample variance, first compute

$$(0 - 2.25)^2 0.10 + (1 - 2.25)^2 0.20 + \cdots + (5 - 2.25)^2 0.04 = 1.6675.$$

Because $n/(n - 1) = 1,000,000/999,999 = 1.000001$, the sample variance is $1.000001(1.6675) = 1.667502$.

3.1.3 Some Features of the Mean and Variance

Plots of relative frequencies help add perspective on the sample variance, mean, and median introduced in Chapter 2. Look at Figure 3.2. Figure 3.2a shows five relative frequencies where the middle spike is the highest and the other spikes are symmetric about this middle value. When this happens, the middle value corresponds to the mode, median, mean, and 20% trimmed mean. So, in Figure 3.2, all of these measures of location are equal to 3. Figure 3.2b shows another plot of relative frequencies symmetric about the value 3 (again the mean), but now the relative frequencies associated with the values 1 and 5 are much smaller, and the relative frequencies associated with the values 2 and 4 are larger. This indicates that the sample variance is smaller in Figure 3.2b, compared to Figure 3.2a, roughly because in Figure 3.2a, values are more likely to be relatively far from the mean. In Figure 3.2a, the data used to create the plot has a sample variance of 1.21, and in Figure 3.2b, it is 0.63.

3.2 HISTOGRAMS AND KERNEL DENSITY ESTIMATORS

An important feature of the data previously used to illustrate plots of relative frequencies is that only a few values occur many times. In Figure 3.2, for example, the responses are limited to five values. But when there are many values, with most values occurring a small number of times, plots of relatively frequencies can be rather uninteresting. If each value occurs only once, a plot of the relative frequencies would consist of n spikes, each having height $1/n$. A histogram is one way of trying to deal

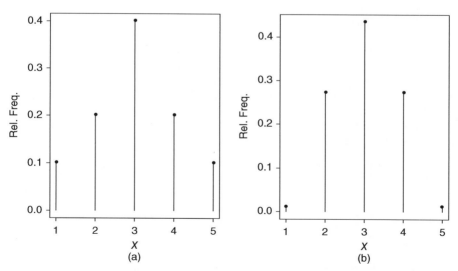

Figure 3.2 Relative frequencies that are symmetric about a central value. For this special case, the mean and median have identical values, the middle value, which here is 3. The relative frequencies in (a) are higher for the more extreme values, compared to (b), indicating that the variance associated with (a) is higher

with this problem. It is similar to bar plots of relative frequencies, the main difference being that values are binned together to get a more useful plot. That is, a histogram simply groups the data into categories and plots the corresponding frequencies using the height of a rectangle.

3.2.1   R Function hist

The R function

$$hist(x)$$

creates a histogram. This function has many optional arguments that are not particularly relevant for present purposes. (For information about these optional arguments, use the R command ?hist.) As usual, the label on the x-axis can be specified via the argument xlab.

Example

A histogram is illustrated with data from a heart transplant study conducted at Stanford University between October 1, 1967 and April 1, 1974. (The data are stored in the file mismatch, which can be downloaded from the author's web page as described in Section 1.5.) Of primary concern is whether a transplanted heart will be rejected by the recipient. With the goal of trying to address this issue, a so-called T5 mismatch score was developed by Dr C. Bieber. It measures the degree of dissimilarity between the donor and the recipient tissue with respect to HL-A antigens. Scores less than 1 represent a good match and scores greater than 1 a poor match. The T5 scores, written in ascending order, are shown in Table 3.2 and are taken from Miller (1976). Suppose the T5 values are grouped into seven categories: values between 0.0 and 0.5, values greater than 0.5 but less than or equal to 1, values greater than 1 but less than or equal to 1.5, and so on. The beginning and end of each interval are called *boundaries* or *class intervals* and the point midway between any two boundaries is called the *class mark* or *midpoint*. So here, the first interval has boundaries 0.0 and 0.5, and the corresponding class mark or midpoint is $(0 + 0.5)/2 = 0.25$. Similarly, the second interval has boundaries 0.5 and 1, so the class mark is $(0.5 + 1)/2 = 0.75$. Note that all of the categories have the same length, which is a feature routinely used. The frequency and relative frequency associated with each of these intervals are shown in Table 3.3. For example, there are 9 T5 mismatch scores in the interval extending from 0.0 to 0.5 and the proportion of all scores belonging to this interval is 0.138. Assuming that the data

TABLE 3.2   T5 Mismatch Scores from a Heart Transplant Study

0.00 0.12 0.16 0.19 0.33 0.36 0.38 0.46 0.47 0.60 0.61 0.61 0.66 0.67 0.68
0.69 0.75 0.77 0.81 0.81 0.82 0.87 0.87 0.87 0.91 0.96 0.97 0.98 0.98 1.02
1.06 1.08 1.08 1.11 1.12 1.12 1.13 1.20 1.20 1.32 1.33 1.35 1.38 1.38 1.41
1.44 1.46 1.51 1.58 1.62 1.66 1.68 1.68 1.70 1.78 1.82 1.89 1.93 1.94 2.05
2.09 2.16 2.25 2.76 3.05

TABLE 3.3 **Frequencies and Relative Frequencies for Grouped T5 Scores, $n = 65$**

Test Score (x)	Frequency	Relative Frequency
0.0–0.5	9	$9/65 = 0.138$
0.5–1.0	20	$20/65 = 0.308$
1.0–1.5	18	$18/65 = 0.277$
1.5–2.0	12	$12/65 = 0.138$
2.0–2.5	4	$4/65 = 0.062$
2.5–3.0	1	$1/65 = 0.015$
3.0–3.5	1	$1/65 = 0.015$

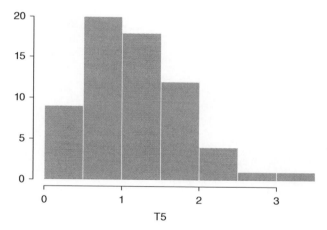

Figure 3.3 A histogram of the heart transplant data in Table 3.2

are stored in the R variable TS, Figure 3.3 shows the resulting histogram based on the R command

```
hist(TS,xlab='T5').
```

How many bins should be used when constructing a histogram and how should the length of the bins be chosen? The general goal is to choose the number of bins so as to get an informative plot of the data. If we have one bin only, this tells us little about the data, and too many bins suffer from the same problem. There are simple rules for choosing the number of bins. (R uses Sturges' rule, but the details are not important for present purposes.)

3.2.2 What Do Histograms Tell Us?

Similarly to so many graphical summaries of data, histograms attempt, among other things, to tell us something about the shape of the data. One issue of some concern is

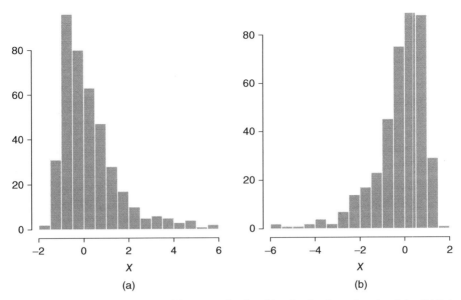

Figure 3.4 (a) An example of a histogram that is said to be the skewed to the right. (b) It is skewed to the left

whether data are reasonably symmetric about some central value. In Figure 3.2, we see exact symmetry, but often data are highly skewed, and this can be a serious practical problem when dealing with inferential techniques yet to be described. Figure 3.4a shows data that are not symmetric, but rather *skewed to the right*. Figure 3.4b shows data that are *skewed to the left*. In recent years, skewness, roughly referring to a lack of symmetry, has been found to be a much more serious problem than once thought for reasons that are best postponed for now. But one important point that should be stressed is that when distributions are skewed, generally the mean, median, and 20% trimmed mean will differ. In some cases, they differ by very little, but these measures of location can differ substantially, as was illustrated in Chapter 2. Moreover, even when these measures of location are virtually identical, subsequent chapters will demonstrate that often the choice for a measure of location can make a practical difference when addressing common problems yet to be described.

Example

A study (by M. Earleywine) was performed that generally dealt with the effects of consuming alcohol. A portion of the study was concerned with measuring hangover symptoms after consuming a specific amount of alcohol in a laboratory setting. The resulting measures, written in ascending order, were

0 0 0 0 0 0 0 0 0 0 0 0 0 0 0 0 0 0 0 0 0 0 0 0 0 1 2 2 2 3 3 3 6 8 9 11 11 11 12 18

32 32 41.

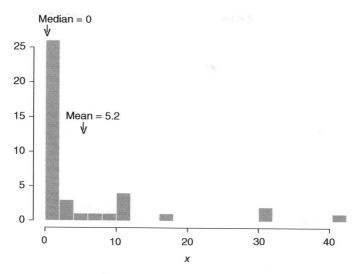

Figure 3.5   A histogram based on a measure of hangover symptoms

Figure 3.5 shows a histogram based on these data. As is evident, the histogram is skewed to the right with a fairly large difference between the median and mean. Note that the right-most portion indicates three bins that are separated from the rest of the plot. This might suggest that any value greater than 16 should be flagged an outlier, but the boxplot rule indicates that only values greater than or equal to 32 are outliers. Although a histogram can provide a useful summary of data, as an outlier detection method, it is not very satisfactory. One fundamental problem is that, when using a histogram, there is no precise rule for deciding whether a value should be declared an outlier. Without a precise rule, there can be no agreement on the extent to which masking (described in Chapter 2) is avoided. Also, examples will be seen where extremely unlikely values occur, yet a histogram does not suggest that they are unusual. As a general rule, histograms might suggest that certain values are outliers, but when making a decision about which values are outliers, it is better to use methods specifically designed for this task, such as the boxplot rule.

3.2.3   Populations, Samples, and Potential Concerns about Histograms

Histograms are routinely taught in an introductory statistics course, and in some cases, they provide useful information about data. But, similar to so many methods covered in this book, it is important to understand not only when histograms perform well but also when, and in what sense, they might be highly misleading. Without a basic understanding of the relative merits of a method, there is the potential of drawing erroneous conclusions as well as missing interesting results. The immediate goal is to illustrate a fundamental concern with histograms.

As mentioned in Chapter 1, there is an important distinction between samples of individuals or things in contrast to a population of individuals or things. Samples represent a subset of the population under study. Consider, for example, the last example dealing with hangover symptoms. There were 40 participants who represent only a small proportion of the individuals who might have taken part in this study. Ideally, the available participants will provide a reasonably accurate reflection of the histogram we would obtain if all participants could be measured. In some cases, a histogram satisfies this goal. But an important practical issue is whether it can be highly unsatisfactory. And if it can be unsatisfactory, is there some strategy that might give substantially better results? It turns out that a histogram can indeed be unsatisfactory and fundamental improvements are now available (e.g., Silverman, 1986). The goal here is to illustrate what might go wrong and provide some information about better techniques.

First, we consider a situation where the histogram tends to perform tolerably well. Imagine that the population consists of 1 million individuals and that if we could measure everyone, the resulting histogram would appear as in Figure 3.6. (Here, the y-axis indicates the relative frequencies.) Now imagine that 100 individuals are selected from the 1 million individuals in the population, with every individual having the same probability of being chosen. An issue of fundamental importance is the extent to which a histogram based on a sample of only 100 individuals will reflect the histogram we would get if all individuals could be measured. Mimicking this process on a computer resulted in the histogram shown in Figure 3.7. So, in this particular case, the histogram provides a reasonable reflection of the population histogram, roughly capturing its bell shape. A criticism of this illustration is that maybe we just got lucky. That is, in general, perhaps with only 100 individuals, the histogram will not accurately reflect the population. This might indeed happen, but generally it gives a reasonable sense of the shape of the population histogram.

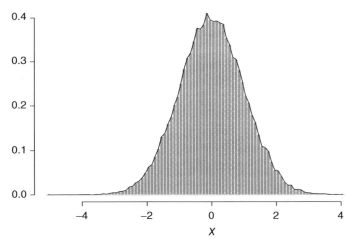

Figure 3.6   A histogram of an entire population that is symmetric about 0 with relatively light tails, meaning outliers tend to be rare

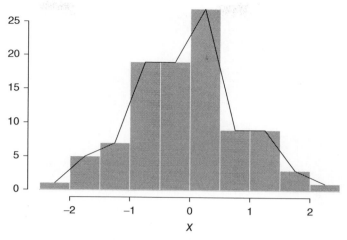

Figure 3.7 A histogram based on a sample of 100 observations generated from the histogram in Figure 3.6

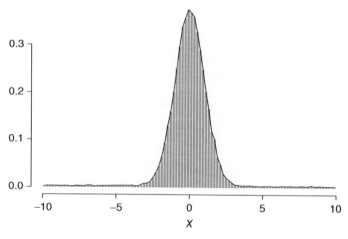

Figure 3.8 A histogram of an entire population that is symmetric about 0 with relatively heavy tails, meaning outliers tend to be common

Now consider the population histogram in Figure 3.8. This histogram has the same bell shape as in Figure 3.6, but the tails extend out a bit farther. This reflects the fact that for this particular population, there are more outliers or extreme values. Now look at Figure 3.9, which is based on 100 individuals sampled from the population histogram in Figure 3.8. As is evident, it provides a poor indication of what the population histogram resembles. Figure 3.9 also provides another illustration that the histogram can perform rather poorly as an outlier detection rule. It suggests that values greater than 10 are highly unusual, which turns out to be true based on how the

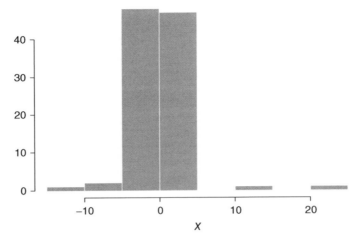

Figure 3.9 A histogram based on a sample of 100 observations generated from the histogram in Figure 3.8

data were generated. But values less than −5 are also highly unusual, which is less evident here. The fact that the histogram can miss outliers limits its ability to deal with problems yet to be described.

A rough characterization of the examples just given is that when the population histogram is symmetric and bell-shaped, and outliers tend to be rare, it performs tolerably well with 100 observations in terms of indicating the shape of the population histogram. But when outliers are relatively common, the reverse is true.

3.2.4 Kernel Density Estimators

We have seen that in terms of providing information about the shape of the population histogram, a histogram based on 100 observations can be relatively ineffective in certain situations. There is a vast literature on how this problem might be addressed using what are called *kernel density estimators*. (The term density estimator will be made clearer in Chapter 4.) There are in fact many variations, some of which appear to perform very well over a fairly broad range of situations. None of the involved computations are provided here, but some R functions for using kernel density estimators are described and illustrated.

3.2.5 R Functions Density and Akerd

The built-in R function

```
density(x)
```

is one way of possibly improving on a histogram. To create a plot of the data, use the command

```
plot(density(x)).
```

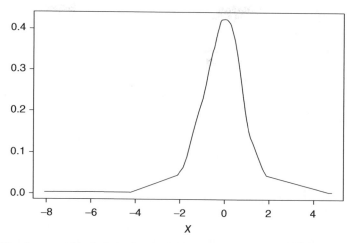

Figure 3.10 An example of a kernel density plot based on the same 100 observations generated from Figure 3.8 and used in Figure 3.9. Note how the kernel density plot does a better job of capturing the shape of the population histogram in Figure 3.8

As usual, when using the function `plot`, the argument `xlab` can be used to label the x-axis. A possible way of getting an even better plot is via the R function

```
akerd(x,xlab='', ylab ='').
```

The arguments `xlab` and `ylab` can be used to label the x-axis and y-axis, respectively. The function applies what is called an *adaptive kernel density estimator* (cf. Harpole et al., 2014).

Example

Consider again the data used to create the histogram shown in Figure 3.9. Recall that the 100 observations were sampled from a population having the symmetric histogram shown in Figure 3.8, yet the histogram in Figure 3.9 suggests a certain amount of asymmetry. In particular, the right tail differs from the left; values in the right tail appear to be outliers and the values in the left tail seem to have a low relatively frequency, but otherwise, there is no sense that they are unusually far from the central values. Figure 3.10 shows a plot of the data in Figure 3.9 using the R function `akerd`. The plot does not capture the exact symmetry of the population histogram, but typically it does a better job of indicating its shape, compared to the histogram.

3.3 BOXPLOTS AND STEM-AND-LEAF DISPLAYS

A stem-and-leaf display is another method designed to provide some overall sense of what data are like. The method is illustrated with measures taken from a study

TABLE 3.4   Word Identification Scores

58 58 58 58 58 64 64 68 72 72 72 75 75 77 77 79 80 82 82 82 82
82 84 84 85 85 90 91 91 92 93 93 93 95 95 95 95 95 95 95 95 98
98 99 101 101 101 102 102 102 102 102 103 104 104 104 104 104
105 105 105 105 105 107 108 108 110 111 112 114 119 122 122 125
125 125 127 129 129 132 134

aimed at understanding how children acquire reading skills. A portion of the study was based on a measure that reflects the ability of children to identify words. (The data were supplied by L. Doi.) Table 3.4 lists the observed scores in ascending order.

The construction of a stem-and-leaf display begins by separating each value into two components. The first is the *leaf*, which in this example is the number in the ones position (the single digit just to the left of the decimal place). For example, the leaf corresponding to the value 58 is 8. The leaf for the value 64 is 4, and the leaf for 125 is 5. The digits to the left of the leaf are called the *stem*. Here the stem of 58 is 5, the number to the left of 8. Similarly, 64 has a stem of 6 and 125 has a stem of 12. We can display the results for all 81 children as follows:

Stems	Leaves
5	88888
6	448
7	22255779
8	0222224455
9	011233355555555889
10	1112222234444455555788
11	01249
12	22555799
13	24

There are five children who have the score 58, so there are five scores with a leaf of 8, and this is reflected by the five 8s displayed to the right of the stem 5 and under the column headed by Leaves. Two children got the score 64, and one child got the score 68. That is, for the stem 6, there are two leaves equal to 4 and one equal to 8, as indicated by the list of leaves in the display. Now look at the third row of numbers where the stem is 7. The leaves listed are 2, 2, 2, 5, 5, 7, 7, and 9. This indicates that the value 72 occurred three times, the value 75 occurred two times, as did the value 77, and the value 79 occurred once. Notice that the display of the leaves gives us some indication of the values that occur most frequently and which are relatively rare. Similarly to the histogram, the stem-and-leaf display gives us an overall sense of what the values are like.

The leaf always consists of the numbers corresponding to a specified digit. For example, the leaf might correspond to the tenths digit, meaning that the leaf is the first number to the right of the decimal, in which case the stem consists of all the numbers to the left of the leaf. So, for the number 158.234, the leaf would be 2 and the stem would be 158. If we specify the leaf to be the hundredths digit, the leaf would now be 3 and the stem would be 158.2. The choice of which digit is to be used as the leaf depends in part on which digit provides a useful graphical summary of the data. But details about how to address this problem are not covered here. Suffice it to say that algorithms have been proposed for deciding which digit should be used as the leaf and determining how many lines a stem-and-leaf display should have (e.g., Emerson and Hoaglin, 1983).

3.3.1   R Function stem

The R function

$$stem(x)$$

creates a stem-and-leaf plot.

Example

The output from stem, based on the T5 mismatch data, resembles this:

```
The decimal point is at the |

  0 | 0122344
  0 | 556667777888889999
  1 | 00000111111223344444
  1 | 5566777788999
  2 | 1123
  2 | 8
  3 | 1
```

So, this plot suggests that the data are somewhat skewed to the right. Also, there are no values visibly separated from the overall plot suggesting that there are no outliers. But the boxplot rule and the MAD–median rule are better techniques for detecting outliers.

3.3.2   Boxplot

Proposed by Tukey (1977), a boxplot is a commonly used graphical summary of data, an example of which is shown in Figure 3.11 As indicated, the ends of the rectangular box mark the lower and upper quartiles. That is, the box indicates where the middle half of the data lie. The horizontal line inside the box indicates the position of the median. The lines extending out from the box are called *whiskers*. Figure 3.12 shows a boxplot with two outliers. The ends of the whiskers are called *adjacent values*. They are the smallest and largest values not declared outliers.

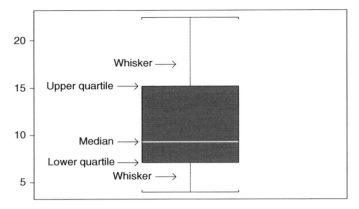

Figure 3.11   An example of a boxplot with no outliers

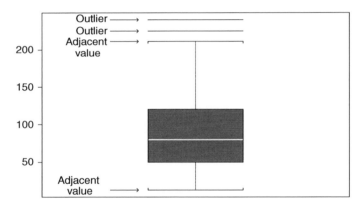

Figure 3.12   An example of a boxplot with outliers

3.3.3   R Function boxplot

The R function

```
boxplot(x)
```

creates a boxplot. It should be noted that this function does not use the ideal fourths when computing the lower and upper quartiles; it uses an estimator that can result in slightly different values.

3.4   SUMMARY

- No single graphical summary of data is always best. Different methods provide different and potentially interesting perspectives. That is, more than one method might be needed to get a good sense of the overall nature of the data.

- The histogram is a classic, routinely taught method, but it is suggested that kernel density estimators be given serious consideration. Perhaps the most important point to keep in mind is that the histogram performs rather poorly as an outlier detection technique.

- The boxplot is one of the more useful graphical tools for summarizing data. It conveys certain important features that were described and illustrated, but kernel density estimators can help add perspective.

- The stem-and-leaf display can be useful when trying to understand the overall pattern of the data. But with large sample sizes, it can be highly unsatisfactory.

3.5 EXERCISES

1. Based on a sample of 100 individuals, the values 1, 2, 3, 4, 5 are observed with relative frequencies 0.2, 0.3, 0.1, 0.25, 0.15, respectively. Compute the mean, variance, and standard deviation.

2. Fifty individuals are rated on how open-minded they are. The ratings have the values 1, 2, 3, 4, and the corresponding relative frequencies are 0.2, 0.24, 0.4, 0.16, respectively. Compute the mean, variance, and standard deviation.

3. For the values 0, 1, 2, 3, 4, 5, 6, the corresponding relative frequencies based on a sample of 10,000 observations are 0.015625, 0.093750, 0.234375, 0.312500, 0.234375, 0.093750, 0.015625, respectively. Determine the mean, variance, and standard deviation.

4. For a local charity, the donations in dollars received during the last month were 5, 10, 15, 20, 25, 50, having the frequencies 20, 30, 10, 40, 50, 5, respectively. Compute the mean, variance, and standard deviation.

5. The values 1, 5, 10, 20 have the frequencies 10, 20, 40, 30. Compute the mean, variance, and standard deviation.

6. For the data in Table 2.1, dealing with changes in cholesterol levels, create a histogram with the R function hist. (The data are stored in the file ibtable2_1_dat.txt, which can be downloaded as described in Section 1.5.) Based on the histogram, guess about whether there are any outliers and then note that the R function outbox finds two outliers and the R function outpro finds four.

7. For the data in Table 2.2, create a histogram using the R function hist and speculate about whether values less than zero are outliers. (The data are stored in the file ibtable2_2_dat.txt, which can be downloaded as described in Section 1.5.) Then, compare your answer to the result obtained using the R function outbox.

8. The heights of 30 male Egyptian skulls from 4000 BC are reported by Thomson and Randall-Maciver (1905) to be

121 124 129 129 130 130 131 131 132 132 132 133 133 134 134 134

134 135 135 136 136 136 136 137 137 138 138 138 140 143

TABLE 3.5   Examination Scores

83	69	82	72	63	88	92	81	54
57	79	84	99	74	86	71	94	71
80	51	68	81	84	92	63	99	91

Create a histogram with the R function hist. (The data are stored in the file skull_height_dat.txt, which can be downloaded as described in Section 1.5.) Note that there is no indication of any outliers. Verify that the R function outbox flags one value as an outlier and that the MAD–median rule, applied via the R function outpro, finds three outliers.

9. For the data in the previous exercise, verify that the classic outlier detection rule, given by Equation (2.6), finds three outliers, which match the values flagged as outliers by the MAD–median rule. Despite this result, what are the concerns with the classic outlier detection rule?

10. What do Exercises 6 and 7 suggest about using a histogram to detect outliers?

11. Table 3.5 shows the exam scores for 27 students. Create a stem-and-leaf display using R.

12. If the leaf is the hundredths digit, what is the stem for the number 34.679?

13. Consider the values 5.134, 5.532, 5.869, 5.809, 5.268, 5.495, 5.142, 5.483, 5.329, 5.149, 5.240, 5.823. If the leaf is taken to be the tenths digit, why would this make an uninteresting stem-and-leaf display?

14. For the boxplot in Figure 3.11, determine, approximately, the quartiles, the interquartile range, and the median. Approximately how large is the largest value not declared an outlier.

15. In Figure 3.11, about how large must a value be to be declared an outlier? How small must it be?

16. Use R to create both a boxplot and a plot of the relative frequencies using the film data in Table 3.1.

17. Use R to create a boxplot and a kernel density estimate using the data in Table 3.2.

18. Describe a situation where the sample histogram is likely to give a good indication of the population histogram based on 100 observations.

19. Comment generally on how large of a sample size is needed to ensure that the sample histogram will likely provide a good indication of the population histogram?

20. When trying to detect outliers, discuss the relative merits of using a histogram versus a boxplot.

21. A sample histogram indicates that the data are highly skewed to the right. Is this a reliable indication that if all individuals of interest could be measured, the resulting histogram would also be highly skewed?

4

PROBABILITY AND RELATED CONCEPTS

As indicated in Chapter 1, a fundamental goal is making inferences about a population of individuals or things based on a sample or subset of the population that is available. Basic probability plays a key role when addressing this issue. This chapter covers the fundamentals of probability and some related concepts and results that will be needed. Section 4.7 is particularly important in terms of understanding one of the reasons that many of the statistical methods developed during the last 50 years have practical value.

4.1 THE MEANING OF PROBABILITY

Coming up with an acceptable definition of the term probability turns out to be a nontrivial task. For example, imagine a bowl with 100 marbles, of which 50 are blue and the other 50 are green. When someone picks a marble from the bowl, without looking, what is the probability that the marble will be blue? A seemingly natural response is 0.5 because half the marbles are blue. But suppose all of the green marbles are on the bottom of the bowl and the person picking a marble has a penchant for picking marbles from those on top. Then, the probability of a blue marble is virtually 1; it will happen with near certainty unless this individual decides to reach deeply into the bowl. Of course, we can mix the marbles in the bowl so that not all of the blue marbles are at the top. But when is the bowl of marbles sufficiently mixed so that the probability of a blue marble is 0.5? A response might be that all marbles must have the same probability of being chosen. But we cannot use the term probability as if we know what it means in our attempt to define probability.

Understanding and Applying Basic Statistical Methods Using R, First Edition. Rand R. Wilcox.
© 2017 John Wiley & Sons, Inc. Published 2017 by John Wiley & Sons, Inc.
www.wiley.com/go/Wilcox/Statistical_Methods_R

Another seemingly natural way of defining probability is in terms of a long series of events. For example, if you flip a coin, what is the probability of a head? You might flip the coin a 100 times, a 1,000 times, and we can conceive of flipping the coin billions of times with the idea that the proportion of times we observe a head is equal to the probability of a head on any one flip. There is a famous result (called the law of large numbers) telling us the conditions under which the proportion of heads will indeed converge to the true probability of a head. This result says that if the probability of a head is the same on every flip, as we increase the number of flips, the proportion of times we observe a head will converge to the true probability. But again, we used the term probability as if we already know what it means.

4.2 PROBABILITY FUNCTIONS

The typical way of dealing with probability, at least for the problems covered in this book, is to view probability in terms of what are called probability functions, which must obey certain rules that are about to be described. This approach does not define probability, but rather makes precise the rules of probability that are needed for analyzing data. But first, some new terms and notation are needed.

A *random variable* refers to a measurement or observation that cannot be known in advance. If someone with heart disease is put on a new medication, will they have a heart attack during the next 12 months? How much weight will someone lose if they follow Aunt Sally's weight reduction method for 4 weeks? Consistent with previous chapters, usually some uppercase Roman letter is used to represent a random variable, the most common letter being X. That is, X is a generic symbol representing whatever we want to measure. A lowercase x is used to represent an observed value corresponding to the random variable X. So, the notation $X = x$ means that the observed value of X is x. For instance, we might let a 1 indicate that someone has a heart attack and no heart attack is indicated by a 0. So, $X = 1$ indicates that a heart attack occurred and $X = 0$ means that it did not occur. This is an example of what is called a *discrete random variable*, meaning that there are gaps between any value and the next possible value. Here, there are only two possible values, the next possible value after 0 is 1, no value between 0 and 1 is possible, so X is discrete. In terms of Aunt Sally's weight reduction method, X represents how much weight was lost and $X = 12$ refers to the event that someone lost 12 pounds. In principle, this is a *continuous random variable*, meaning that for any two outcomes, any value between these two values is possible. For example, someone might lose 12 pounds, 13 pounds, or any amount between 12 and 13 pounds.

The set of all possible outcomes or values of X we might observe is called the *sample space*. For the heart disease example, the sample space consists of two outcomes: heart attack or no heart attack, or in numerical terms, 1 and 0. For the weight loss example, the sample space consists of all possible results we might observe in terms of how much weight was lost or gained. Unless stated otherwise, the elements of the sample space are assumed to be *mutually exclusive*. That is, one and only one element of the sample space can occur. In the heart disease example, $X = 0$ and $X = 1$ are two mutually exclusive events simply because if an individual did not have a heart attack

($X = 0$), this eliminates the possibility that a heart attack occurred ($X = 1$). In a similar manner, in the weight loss example, all possible outcomes are mutually exclusive.

Example

An investment strategy for buying stocks has been recommended to you. You plan to try out the new strategy by buying 10 stocks and observing how many stocks gain value after 6 months. Here, X represents the number of stocks that gain value and the sample space is 0, 1, 2, 3, 4, 5, 6, 7, 8, 9, and 10. This is an example of a discrete random variable.

Next, the notion of a probability function is introduced, which for convenience is described in terms of a discrete random variable, still assuming that the elements of the sample space are mutually exclusive.

Definition. A *probability function* is a rule, denoted by $P(x)$, that assigns numbers to elements of the sample space with the following properties:

1. $P(x) \geq 0$.
2. For any two distinct elements in the sample space, say x and y, $P(x$ or $y) = P(x) + P(y)$. In words, the probability of observing the value x or y is equal to the sum of the individual probabilities (assuming that these two events are mutually exclusive).
3. The sum of the probabilities associated with all of the elements in the sample space is 1. That is, $\sum P(x) = 1$.

The definition of a probability function is somewhat abstract, but it is easy to understand if we think of probabilities in terms of proportions. To be concrete, imagine that 100 students are asked to rate their college experience on a five-point scale: 1, 2, 3, 4, 5. Further imagine that among the 100 students, 10 respond 1, 20 respond 2, 35 respond 3, 30 respond 4, and 5 respond 5. So, the proportions corresponding to 1, 2, 3, 4, 5 are 0.1, 0.2, 0.35, 0.3, and 0.05, respectively. Now think of these proportions as probabilities. It is evident that all proportions are greater than or equal to 0. Consider any two responses, say 2 and 4. The number of students responding 2 or 4 is $20 + 30 = 50$, so the proportion responding 2 or 4 is 0.5. In symbols, letting $P(2$ or $4)$ be the probability of a 2 or 4, $P(2$ or $4) = P(2) + P(4) = 0.2 + 0.3 = 0.5$. That is, condition 2 in the definition of a probability function is satisfied for these two values and for any other two values we might choose. Condition 3 is satisfied because the proportions sum to 1.

Example

Imagine that the sample space consists of the values

$$x : 0, 1, 2, 3, 4$$

and consider

$$P(x) : 0.1, 0.2, 0.25, 0.3, 0.25, 0.2.$$

That is, $P(0) = 0.1, P(1) = 0.2$, and so on. Then, $P(x)$ does not qualify as a probability function because the sum of all five $P(x)$ values is greater than 1.

4.3   EXPECTED VALUES, POPULATION MEAN AND VARIANCE

The notion of expected values is important for two general reasons. First, it provides a precise definition of quantities associated with populations that play a fundamental role in the methods to be described. Second, it provides a link between samples and populations in a sense explained in Chapter 5.

Consider any random variable X with probability function $P(x)$. The *expected value* of X is

$$E(X) = \sum xP(x). \tag{4.1}$$

In words, multiply every value in the sample space by its probability and sum the results. The expected value of a random variable plays fundamental role, and it has been given a special name - the population mean, which is typically written as μ (a lowercase Greek mu). That is, $\mu = E(X)$.

The notion of an expected value might be made clearer by noting that it is similar to how the sample mean was defined in Chapter 3. Recall that if f_x/n is the relative frequency associated with the value x, the sample mean is

$$\overline{X} = \sum x\frac{f_x}{n}.$$

Now imagine that an entire population consists of N individuals and that the relative frequencies are f_x/N. Further assume that we view these relative frequencies as probabilities. That is, $P(x)$ is taken to be f_x/N. Then, the average value for the population of individuals is

$$\mu = E(X) = \sum x\frac{f_x}{N}.$$

That is, the population mean is just the average of all the individuals in the population, if only they could be measured.

Example
For

$$x : 1, 5, 10$$

and

$$P(x) : 0.2, 0.5, 0.3$$

the population mean is

$$\mu = 1(0.2) + 5(0.5) + 10(0.3) = 5.7.$$

Example

A carnival game costs 2 dollars to play, and for each play, a contestant can win 1, 2, or 3 dollars. Imagine that the probabilities associated with these three outcomes are 0.25, 0.40, and 0.35, respectively. That is, $P(1) = 0.25$, $P(2) = 0.4$, and $P(3) = 0.35$. Then, the expected winnings is

$$\sum xP(x) = 1(0.25) + 2(0.40) + 3(0.35) = 2.10.$$

This says that on average, a contestant would win $2.10 and, because it costs $2.00 to play, on average, the carnival would lose 10 cents.

Example

Imagine that when buying a car, you are offered an extended warranty for $200. To keep the example simple, further imagine that four outcomes are possible: no repairs are needed, or one of three repairs can occur costing $50, $150, and $250. If the probabilities corresponding to these four outcomes are 0.7, 0.15, 0.10, and 0.05, respectively, the expected cost of a repair is

$$0(0.7) + 50(0.15) + 150(0.10) + 200(0.05) = 30.$$

This says that on average, the cost to customers who buy this warranty is $200−$30=$170.

Example

Consider a population of 1 million individuals who have played a particular video game. Further assume that if asked to rate the game on a five-point scale, the proportion who would give a rating of 1, 2, 3, 4, and 5 would be 0.1, 0.15, 0.35, 0.30, and 0.1, respectively. If we view these proportions as probabilities, the mean or expected rating is

$$\mu = 1(0.1) + 2(0.15) + 3(0.35) + 4(0.30) + 5(0.1) = 3.15.$$

A population mean is an example of what is called a *population parameter*, which is a quantity that is generally unknown because it is impossible to measure everyone in the population. The sample mean is an example of an *estimator*, a value computed based on data available to us and based on a sample taken from the population. As is probably evident, the sample mean $\overline{X}$ is intended as an estimate of the population mean, μ. A fundamental issue is how well the sample mean $\overline{X}$ estimates the population mean, μ, an issue we will begin to address in Chapters 5 and 6.

4.3.1   Population Variance

We have seen that there are two types of means: a population mean, which is the average, μ, we would get if all individuals or things could be measured, and there is a sample mean, $\overline{X}$, which is just the average based on a sample from the population. In a similar manner, there is both a sample variance, s^2, introduced in Chapter 2, and a population variance, which is the average squared difference between the population mean and the measures associated with all individuals or things in the population under study. More formally, the *population variance* is

$$\sigma^2 = \sum (x - \mu)^2 P(x), \tag{4.2}$$

where σ is a lowercase Greek sigma. The (positive) square root of the population variance, σ, is called the *population standard deviation*.

Example

Consider the following probability function.

x:	0	1	2	3
$P(x)$:	0.1	0.3	0.4	0.2

The population mean is $\mu = 1.7$. So, for the value 0, its squared distance from the population mean is $(0 - 1.7)^2 = 2.89$ and reflects how far away the value 0 is from the population mean. Moreover, the probability associated with this squared difference is 0.1, the probability of observing the value 0. In a similar manner, the squared difference between 1 and the population mean is 0.49, and the probability associated with this squared difference is 0.3, the same probability associated with the value 1. Continuing in this manner, the population variance is

$$\sigma^2 = (0 - 1.7)^2(0.1) + (1 - 1.7)^2(0.3) + (2 - 1.7)^2(0.4) + (3 - 1.7)^2(0.2) = 0.81.$$

Example

For a five-point scale measuring anxiety, the probability function for all adults living in New York City is

x:	1	2	3	4	5
$P(x)$:	0.05	0.1	0.7	0.1	0.05

The population mean is

$$\mu = 1(0.05) + 2(0.1) + 3(0.7) + 4(0.1) + 5(0.05) = 3,$$

so the population variance is

$$\sigma^2 = (1-3)^2(0.05) + (2-3)^2(0.1) + (3-3)^2(0.7)$$
$$+ (4-3)^2(0.1) + (5-3)^2(0.05) = 0.6,$$

and the population standard deviation is $\sigma = \sqrt{0.6} = 0.775$.

4.4 CONDITIONAL PROBABILITY AND INDEPENDENCE

Conditional probability refers to the probability of some event given that some other event has occurred. For example, what is the probability of developing heart disease given that someone's cholesterol level is 250? What is the probability of developing stomach cancer given that someone drinks two glasses of wine every day?

A convenient way of illustrating how conditional probabilities are computed is in terms of what are called *contingency tables*, an example of which is shown in Table 4.1. In the contingency table are the probabilities associated with four mutually exclusive groups: individuals who (1) receive a flu shot and get the flu, (2) do not receive a flu shot and get the flu, (3) receive a flu shot and do not get the flu, and (4) do not receive a flu shot and do not get the flu. The last column shows what are called the *marginal probabilities*. For example, the probability of getting a flu shot is $0.25 + 0.20 = 0.45$. Put another way, it is the sum of the probabilities associated with two mutually exclusive events. The first event is getting the flu and simultaneously getting a flu shot, which has probability 0.25. The second event is not getting the flu and simultaneously getting a flu shot, which has probability 0.2. The last line in Table 4.1 shows the marginal probabilities associated with getting or not getting the flu. For example, the probability of getting the flu is $0.25 + 0.28 = 0.53$.

Now consider the probability of someone getting the flu given that they receive a flu shot, and for convenience, view probabilities as proportions. According to Table 4.1, the proportion of people who got a flu shot is 0.45. Among the people who got a flu shot, the proportion who got the flu is $0.25/0.45 = 0.56$. That is, the probability of getting the flu, given that an individual received a flu shot, is 0.56.

Notice that a conditional probability is determined by altering the sample space. In the illustration, the proportion of all people who got a flu shot is 0.45. But restricting

TABLE 4.1 Hypothetical Probabilities for Getting a Flu Shot and Getting the Flu

Get a Shot	Get the Flu		
	Yes	No	
Yes	0.25	0.20	0.45
No	0.28	0.27	0.55
	0.53	0.47	1.00

attention to individuals who got a flu shot means that the sample space has been altered. More precisely, the contingency table reflects four possible outcomes, but by focusing exclusively on individuals who got a flu shot, the sample space is reduced to two outcomes.

In a more general notation, if A and B are any two events, and if we let $P(A)$ represent the probability of event A and $P(A$ and $B)$ represent the probability that events A and B occur simultaneously, then the conditional probability of A, given that B has occurred, is

$$P(A|B) = \frac{P(A \text{ and } B)}{P(B)}. \tag{4.3}$$

In the illustration, A is the event of getting the flu and B is the event of getting a flu shot. So, according to Table 4.1, $P(A$ and $B) = 0.25$, $P(B) = 0.45$, so $P(A|B) = 0.25/0.45$, as previously indicated.

Example

Based on Table 4.1, the probability that someone does not get the flu, given that they get a flu shot, is

$$\frac{0.20}{0.45} = 0.44.$$

4.4.1 Independence and Dependence

Roughly, two events are *independent* if the probability associated with the first event is not altered when the second event is known. If the probability is altered, the events are *dependent*.

Example

According to Table 4.1, the probability of getting the flu is 0.53. Getting the flu is independent of getting a flu shot if among the individuals getting a shot, the probability of getting the flu remains 0.53. We have seen, however, that the probability of getting the flu, given that the person gets a shot, is 0.56, so these two events are dependent.

Consider any two variables, say X and Y, and let x and y be any two possible values corresponding to these variables. The variables X and Y are independent if for any x and y,

$$P(Y = y|X = x) = P(Y = y). \tag{4.4}$$

Otherwise, they are dependent.

Example

Imagine that married couples are asked to rate the extent to which marital strife is reduced by following the advice in a book on having a happy marriage. Assume that both husbands and wives rate the effectiveness of the book with the values 1, 2, and 3, where the values stand for fair, good, and excellent, respectively. Further assume that

TABLE 4.2 Hypothetical Probabilities for Rating a Book

Wife (Y)	Husband (X) 1	2	3	
1	0.02	0.10	0.08	0.2
2	0.07	0.35	0.28	0.7
3	0.01	0.05	0.04	0.1
	0.1	0.5	0.4	

the probabilities associated with the possible outcomes are as shown in Table 4.2. We see that the probability a wife (Y) gives a rating of 1 is 0.2. In symbols, $P(Y = 1) = 0.2$. Furthermore, $P(Y = 1|X = 1) = 0.02/0.1 = 0.2$, where $X = 1$ indicates that the wife's husband gave a rating of 1. So, the event $Y = 1$ is independent of the event $X = 1$. If the probability had changed, we could stop and say that X and Y are dependent. But to say that they are independent requires that we check all possible outcomes. For example, another possible outcome is $Y = 1$ and $X = 2$. We see that $P(Y = 1|X = 2) = 0.1/0.5 = 0.2$, which again is equal to $P(Y = 1)$. Continuing in this manner, it can be seen that for any possible values for Y and X, the corresponding events are independent, so X and Y are independent.

Now the notion of *dependence* is described in a slightly more general context that contains contingency tables as a special case. A common and fundamental question in applied research is whether information about one variable influences the probabilities associated with another variable. For example, in a study dealing with diabetes in children, one issue of interest was the association between a child's age and the level of serum C-peptide at diagnosis. For convenience, let X represent age and Y represent C-peptide concentration. For any child we might observe, there is some probability that her C-peptide concentration is less than 3, or less than 4, or less than c, where c is any constant we might pick. The issue at hand is whether information about X (a child's age) alters the probabilities associated with Y (a child's C-peptide level). That is, does the conditional probability of Y, given X, differ from the probabilities associated with Y when X is not known or ignored. If knowing X does not alter the probabilities associated with Y, X and Y are independent. Equation (4.4) is one way of providing a formal definition of independence. An alternative way is to say that X and Y are independent if

$$P(Y \leq y|X = x) = P(Y \leq y) \tag{4.5}$$

for all possible x and y values. Equation (4.4) implies Equation (4.5). Yet another way of describing independence is that for all possible x and y values,

$$\frac{P(Y = y \text{ and } X = x)}{P(X = x)} = P(Y = y), \tag{4.6}$$

which follows from Equation (4.4). From this last equation, it can be seen that if X and Y are independent, then

$$P(X = x \text{ and } Y = y) = P(X = x)P(Y = y). \tag{4.7}$$

Equation (4.7) is called the *product rule* and says that if two events are independent, the probability that they occur simultaneously is equal to the product of their individual probabilities.

Example

In Table 4.1, if getting a flu shot is independent of getting the flu, then the probability of both getting a flu shot and getting the flu is $0.45 \times 0.53 = 0.2385$. But according to Table 4.1, the probability of getting a flu shot and getting the flu is 0.25. So, these two events are dependent.

Example

Consider again the diabetes in children study where one of the variables of interest was C-peptide concentrations at diagnosis. Suppose that for all children we might measure, the probability of having a C-peptide concentration less than or equal to 3 is $P(Y \leq 3) = 0.4$. Now consider only children who are 7 years old, and imagine that for this subpopulation of children, the probability of having a C-peptide concentration less than 3 is 0.2. In symbols, $P(Y \leq 3 | X = 7) = 0.2$. Then, C-peptide concentrations and age are dependent because knowing that the child's age is 7 alters the probability that the child's C-peptide concentration is less than or equal to 3. If, instead, $P(Y \leq 3 | X = 7) = 0.4$, the events $Y \leq 3$ and $X = 7$ are independent. More generally, if for any x and y, $P(Y \leq y | X = x) = P(Y \leq y)$, then C-peptide concentrations and age are independent.

4.5   THE BINOMIAL PROBABILITY FUNCTION

A discrete distribution of particular importance is the binomial distribution. It arises in situations where each observation among n observations is binary. For example, each of n individuals might respond yes or no, or agree or disagree. Or, the outcome for each of n trials might be labeled a success or failure. Typically, the number 1 is used to represent a success and a failure is represented by 0. A common convention is to let p represent the probability of success and to let $q = 1 - p$ be the probability of a failure.

Let the random variable X represent the total number of successes among n observations. The immediate goal is to describe how to compute the probability of x successes among n trials or observations. In symbols, we want to evaluate $P(X = x)$. For example, imagine that five people undergo a new type of surgery and you observe whether the disorder is successfully treated. If the probability of a success is $p = 0.6$, what is the probability that exactly three of the five surgeries will be a success?

Assuming that the outcomes are independent and that the probability of success is the same every time the surgery is performed, there is a convenient formula for solving this problem based on the *binomial probability function*. It says that among n observations, the probability of exactly x successes is given by

$$P(x) = \binom{n}{x} p^x q^{n-x}. \tag{4.8}$$

Here, $n = 5$, $x = 3$, and the goal is to determine $P(3)$. The first term on the right side of this equation, called the binomial coefficient, is defined to be

$$\binom{n}{x} = \frac{n!}{x!(n-x)!},$$

where $n!$ represents n factorial. That is,

$$n! = 1 \times 2 \times 3 \times \cdots \times (n-1) \times n.$$

For example, $1! = 1, 2! = 2$, and $3! = 6$. By convention, $0! = 1$.

Example

For the situation just described regarding whether a surgical procedure is a success, the probability of exactly three successes can be determined as follows.

$$n! = 1 \times 2 \times 3 \times 4 \times 5 = 120,$$

$$x! = 1 \times 2 \times 3 = 6,$$

$$(n-x)! = 2! = 2,$$

in which case

$$P(3) = \frac{120}{6 \times 2}(0.6^3)(0.4^2) = 0.3456.$$

Example

Imagine 10 couples who recently got married. What is the probability that 4 of the 10 couples will report that they are happily married at the end of 1 year? Assuming that responses by couples are independent and that the probability of success is $p = 0.3$, the probability that exactly $x = 4$ couples will report that they are happily married is

$$P(4) = \frac{10!}{4! \times 6!}(0.3^4)(0.7^6) = 0.2001.$$

Often, attention is focused on the probability of *at least* x successes in n trials or *at most* x successes, rather than the probability of getting *exactly* x successes. In the last illustration, you might want to know the probability that four couples or fewer are happily married as opposed to exactly 4. The former probability consists of five mutually exclusive events, namely, $x = 0, x = 1, x = 2, x = 3$, and $x = 4$. Thus, the probability that four couples or fewer are happily married is

$$P(X \leq 4) = P(0) + P(1) + P(2) + P(3) + P(4).$$

In summation notation,

$$P(X \leq 4) = \sum_{k=0}^{4} P(k).$$

More generally, the probability of x successes or less in n trials is

$$P(X \leq x) = \sum_{k=0}^{x} P(k)$$

$$= \sum_{k=0}^{x} \binom{n}{k} p^k q^{n-k}.$$

For any x between 0 and n, Table B.2 in Appendix B gives the value of $P(X \leq x)$ for various values of n and p. Returning to the illustration where $p = 0.3$ and $n = 10$, Table B.2 reports that the probability of 4 successes or less is 0.85. Notice that the probability of 5 successes or more is just the complement of getting 4 successes or less, so

$$P(X \geq 5) = 1 - P(X \leq 4)$$

$$= 1 - 0.85$$

$$= 0.15.$$

In general,

$$P(X \geq x) = 1 - P(X \leq x - 1),$$

so $P(X \geq x)$ is easily evaluated with Table B.2.

Expressions such as

$$P(2 \leq X \leq 8),$$

meaning you want to know the probability that the number of successes is between 2 and 8, inclusive, can be evaluated with Table B.2 by noting that

$$P(2 \leq X \leq 8) = P(X \leq 8) - P(X \leq 1).$$

In words, the event of 8 successes or less can be broken down into the sum of two mutually exclusive events: the event that the number of successes is less than or equal to 1 and the event that the number of successes is between 2 and 8, inclusive. Rearranging terms yields the last equation. The point is that $P(2 \leq X \leq 8)$ can be written in terms of two expressions that are easily evaluated with Table B.2 in Appendix B.

Example

Assume $n = 10$ and $p = 0.5$. From Table B.2 in Appendix B, $P(X \leq 1) = 0.011$ and $P(X \leq 8) = 0.989$, so

$$P(2 \leq X \leq 8) = 0.989 - 0.011 = 0.978.$$

A related problem is determining the probability of 1 success or less or 9 successes or more. The first part is simply read from Table B.2 and can be seen to be 0.011. The probability of 9 successes or more is the complement of 8 successes or less, so

$$P(X \geq 9) = 1 - P(X \leq 8) = 1 - 0.989 = 0.011,$$

again assuming that $n = 10$ and $p = 0.5$. Thus, the probability of 1 success or less or 9 successes or more is $0.011 + 0.011 = 0.022$. In symbols,

$$P(X \leq 1 \text{ or } X \geq 9) = 0.022.$$

There are times when you will need to compute the mean and variance of a binomial probability function once you are given n and p. It can be shown that the (population) mean and variance are given by

$$\mu = E(X)$$
$$= np,$$

and

$$\sigma^2 = npq$$

respectively.

Example

If $n = 16$ and $p = 0.5$, the mean of the binomial probability function is $\mu = np = 16(0.5) = 8$. That is, on average, 8 of the 16 observations will be a success. The variance is $\sigma^2 = npq = 16(0.5)(0.5) = 4$, so the standard deviation is $\sigma = \sqrt{4} = 2$. If, instead, $p = 0.3$, then $\mu = 16(0.3) = 4.8$. That is, the average number of successes is 4.8.

In most situations, p, the probability of a success, is not known and must be estimated based on x, the observed number of successes. The estimate typically used is x/n, the proportion of observed successes. Often, this estimator is written as

$$\hat{p} = \frac{x}{n},$$

where $\hat{p}$ is read as p hat. It can be shown that

$$E(\hat{p}) = p.$$

That is, if an experiment were repeated millions of times (and, in theory, infinitely many times), each time sampling n observations, the average of the resulting $\hat{p}$ values would be p. It can be shown that the variance of $\hat{p}$ is

$$\sigma_{\hat{p}}^2 = \frac{pq}{n}.$$

Example

Assuming independence, a sample size of 25 and that the probability of success is 0.4, the variance of $\hat{p}$ is

$$\sigma_{\hat{p}}^2 = \frac{0.4 \times 0.6}{25} = 0.098.$$

The characteristics and properties of the binomial probability function can be summarized as follows:

- The experiment consists of exactly n independent trials.
- Only two possible outcomes are possible on each trial, usually called *success* and *failure*.
- Each trial has the same probability of success, p.
- $q = 1 - p$ is the probability of a failure.
- There are x successes among the n trials.
- $P(x) = \binom{n}{x} p^x q^{n-x}$.
- $\binom{n}{x} = \frac{n!}{x!(n-x)!}$.
- The usual estimate of p is $\hat{p} = \frac{x}{n}$.
- $E(\hat{p}) = p$.
- The variance of $\hat{p}$ is $\sigma_{\hat{p}}^2 = \frac{pq}{n}$.
- The average or expected number of successes in n trials is $\mu = E(X) = np$.
- The variance associated with X, the total number of successes, is $\sigma^2 = npq$.

Example

Two basketball teams are contending for the title of national champion. The first team to win four games is declared champion. If we assume that the probability of a win is the same each time they play and that the outcomes for any two games are independent, can we use the binomial probability function to determine the probability of four wins? The answer is no. The problem here is that the number of games to be played, n, is not fixed. If the two teams played exactly seven games, then the binomial probability function would apply. But the total number of games to be played is 4, 5, 6, or 7.

4.5.1   R Functions dbinom and pbinom

The R function

$$\text{dbinom}(\text{x, size, prob})$$

computes the probability of exactly x successes, where the argument `size` indicates the number of trials, n, and `prob` indicates the probability of success, p. The R function

$$\text{pbinom}(\text{q, size, prob})$$

computes the probability of q successes or less where again the argument `size` indicates the number of trials, n, and `prob` indicates the probability of success, p.

Example

For $n = 12$ trials and a probability of success $p = 0.6$, the probability of exactly 5 successes can be determined with the R command

```
dbinom(5,12,0.6).
```

The answer is 0.1009. The R command

```
pbinom(5,12,0.6).
```

returns 0.15821, meaning that the probability of 5 successes or less is 0.15821.

4.6   THE NORMAL DISTRIBUTION

In contrast to discrete variables, probabilities associated with continuous variables are given by the area under a curve. The equation for this curve is called a *probability density function*, which is typically labeled $f(x)$. (Kernel density estimators, introduced in Section 3.2.4, are designed to estimate $f(x)$.)

This section focuses on a particular choice for the probability density function, called a normal distribution, which plays a central role in a wide range of statistical techniques as will become evident. Moreover, many published papers make it clear that for a wide range of situations, a normal distribution provides a very convenient and highly accurate method for analyzing data. But there is also a wide range of situations where it performs poorly. So, in terms of building a good foundation for understanding data, a crucial component is understanding when the normal distribution serves us well and when it can be misleading and highly unsatisfactory.

An example of a normal distribution is shown in Figure 4.1. Note the vertical line at -1. It can be shown that the area under this normal curve and to the left of -1 is 0.158655. This means that if a random variable X has the normal distribution shown in Figure 4.1, the probability that X is less than or equal to -1 is 0.158655. In symbols, $P(X \leq -1) = 0.158655$.

Normal distributions have the following important properties:

1. The total area under the curve is 1. (This is a requirement of any probability density function.)
2. All normal distributions are bell-shaped and symmetric about their mean, μ.
3. Although not indicated in Figure 4.1, all normal curves extend from $-\infty$ to ∞ along the x-axis.
4. If the variable X has a normal distribution, the probability that X has a value within one standard deviation of the mean is 0.68 as indicated in Figure 4.2. In symbols, if X has a normal distribution, $P(\mu - \sigma \leq X \leq \mu + \sigma) = 0.68$ regardless of what the population mean and variance happen to be. The probability

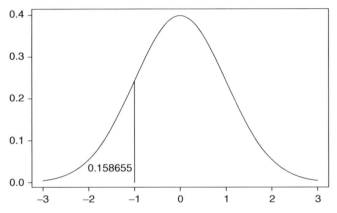

Figure 4.1   A normal distribution having mean $\mu = 0$. The area under the curve and to the left of -1 is 0.158655, which is the probability that an observation is less than or equal to -1

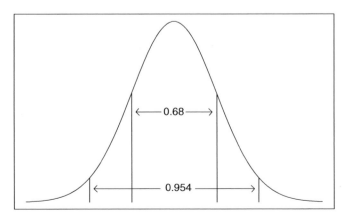

Figure 4.2   For all normal distributions, the probability that an observation is within one standard deviation of the mean is 0.68. The probability of being within two standard deviations is 0.954

of being within two standard deviations is approximately 0.954. In symbols, $P(\mu - 2\sigma \leq X \leq \mu + 2\sigma) = 0.954$. The probability of being within three standard deviations is $P(\mu - 3\sigma \leq X \leq \mu + 3\sigma) = 0.9975$.

5. The probability density function of a normal distribution is

$$f(x) = \frac{1}{\sigma\sqrt{2\pi}} \exp\left[-\frac{(x-\mu)^2}{2\sigma^2}\right], \tag{4.9}$$

where as usual, μ and σ^2 are the mean and variance. (The notation $\exp(x)$ refers to the exponential function, which means that e is raised to the power x, where e, the base of the natural logarithm, is approximately 2.71828. E.g., $\exp(2) = 2.71828^2 = 7.389$.) This equation does not play a direct role in this book and is reported simply for informational purposes. The main point is that for any distribution to qualify as a normal distribution, its probability density function must be given by this last equation. It turns out that many distributions are symmetric and bell-shaped, yet they do not qualify as a normal distribution. That is, the equation for these distributions does not conform to the equation for a normal curve. Another important point is that the probability density function is determined by the mean and variance. If, for example, we want to determine the probability that a variable is less than 25, this probability is completely determined by the mean and variance *if* we assume normality.

Figure 4.3 shows three normal distributions, two of which have means equal to 0 but standard deviations $\sigma = 1$ and $\sigma = 1.5$. The other distribution again has a standard deviation $\sigma = 1$, but now the mean is $\mu = 2$. There are two things to notice. First, if two normal distributions have equal variances but unequal means, the two probability curves are centered around different values, but otherwise they are identical. Second, for *normal* distributions, there is a distinct and rather noticeable difference between the two curves when the standard deviation increases from 1 to 1.5.

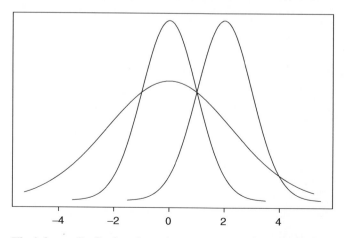

Figure 4.3 The left two distributions have the same mean but different standard deviations, namely, 1 and 1.5. The right distribution has a mean of 2 and standard deviation 1

4.6.1   Some Remarks about the Normal Distribution

Some brief comments about the history of the normal distribution will help put its relative merits in perspective. Consider a binomial probability function with $n = 1,000$ and $p = 0.5$. To be concrete, imagine we flip a coin 1,000 times and that unknown to us, the probability of a head is 0.5. Note that if we get 450 heads, we would estimate the probability of a head to be 0.45. In a similar manner, if we get 550 heads, we would estimate the probability of a head to be 0.55. Abraham de Moivre (1667–1754) derived a method for addressing the following question: what is the probability of getting between 450 and 550 heads? That is, what is the probability that the estimate of p will be between 0.45 and 0.55 when in fact $p = 0.5$. Put another way, what is the probability that the estimated probability of a success will be close to its true value?

The problem, of course, is that, without a computer, the calculations needed to answer this question are prohibitive. Even calculating the probability of exactly 450 heads is a tremendously difficult task, and the problem requires that one also compute the probability of exactly 451 heads, 452 heads, and so on, until we get to 550 heads, and then these 101 values would need to be summed. So, de Moivre set out to find a reasonably accurate approximation for solving this problem. Over 12 years later, he had a solution based on the normal distribution, which he announced in 1733.

Many years later, Laplace was searching for a family of distributions that might be used to solve some of the basic problems covered in this book. But his best attempt led to an approach that proved to be highly impractical in terms of both theoretical and computational details. In 1809, with the goal of rationalizing the use of the sample mean, Gauss derived the normal distribution, which in essence is a slight modification of a family of distributions derived by Laplace. (In 1809, the mathematician R. Adrain also derived the normal distribution.) Gauss's work was so influential, the normal curve is sometimes called the Gaussian distribution. Although the normal curve proved to be extremely convenient from a mathematical point of view, both Laplace and Gauss were concerned about how to justify the use of the normal distribution when addressing practical problems. In 1809, Gauss described his first attempt at solving this problem, which proved to be highly unsatisfactory. In 1810, Laplace announced an alternative approach, what is called the central limit theorem, the details of which are covered in Chapter 5. Laplace's result forms the basis for assuming normality for an extremely wide range of problems. We will see that in some instances, this justification for assuming normality is very successful, but in others, it is not.

Another issue should be discussed: If we could measure all the individuals (or things) who constitute a population of interest, will a plot of the observations follow a normal distribution? The answer is rarely, and some would argue never. The first study to determine whether data have a normal distribution was conducted by Wilhelm Bessel (1784–1846) in the year 1818. His astronomical data appeared to be reasonably bell-shaped, consistent with a normal curve, but Bessel made an important observation: The distribution of his data had thicker or heavier tails than what would be expected for a normal curve. Bessel appears to have made an extremely important observation. The reason is that heavy-tailed distributions tend to generate outliers, which turn out to create practical problems to be illustrated. But it would be about another 1.5 centuries before the practical importance of Bessel's observation would be fully appreciated.

During the nineteenth century, various researchers came to the conclusion that data follow a normal curve, a view that stems from results covered in Chapter 5. Indeed, the term normal distribution stems from the first paper ever published by Karl Pearson. He was so convinced that the bell-shaped distribution used by Laplace and Gauss reflected reality, he named it the normal distribution, meaning the distribution we should expect. But to his credit, Pearson examined data from actual studies to see whether his belief could be confirmed, and eventually, he concluded that his initial speculation was incorrect. He attempted to deal with this problem by introducing a larger family of distributions for describing data, but his approach does not play a role today when analyzing data. More modern investigations confirm Pearson's conclusion that data generally do not follow a normal curve (e.g., Micceri, 1989), but this does not mean that the normal curve has no practical value. What is important is whether it provides an adequate approximation, and as already mentioned, in some cases it does, and in others it does not.

4.6.2 The Standard Normal Distribution

For the moment, we ignore any practical limitations associated with the normal curve and focus on some basic issues when the normal distribution is used. We begin with the issue of how to compute probabilities. To be concrete, assume that human infants have birth weights that are normally distributed with a mean of 3,700 g and a standard deviation of 200 g. What is the probability that a baby's birth weight will be less than or equal to 3,000 g? As previously explained, this probability is given by the area under the normal curve, but simple methods for computing this area are required. Today, the answer is easily obtained on a computer. But for pedagogical reasons, a more traditional method is covered here. We begin by considering the special case where the mean is 0 and the standard deviation is 1 ($\mu = 0$, $\sigma = 1$), after which we illustrate how to compute probabilities for any mean and standard deviation.

The *standard normal distribution* is a normal distribution with mean $\mu = 0$ and standard deviation $\sigma = 1$; it plays a central role in many areas of statistics. As is typically done, Z is used to represent a variable that has a standard normal distribution. The immediate goal is to describe how to determine the probability that an observation randomly sampled from a standard normal distribution is less than or equal to any constant c we might choose.

These probabilities are easily determined using Table B.1 in Appendix B, which reports the probability that a standard normal random variable has probability less than or equal to c for $c = -3.00, -2.99, -2.98, \ldots, -0.01, 0, 0.01, \ldots, 3.00$. The first entry in the first column shows -3. The column next to it gives the corresponding probability, 0.0013. That is, the probability that a standard normal random variables is less than or equal to -3 is $P(Z \leq -3) = 0.0013$. Going down the first column, we see the entry -2.08, and the column next to it indicates that the probability of a standard

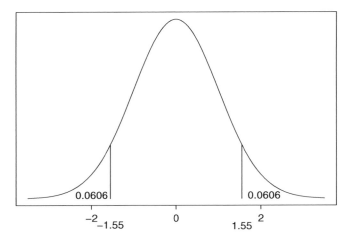

Figure 4.4   The left tail indicates that for a standard normal distribution, the probability of a value less than or equal to -1.55 is 0.0606, and the probability of a value greater than or equal to 1.55 is 0.0606 as well

normal variable being less than or equal to -2.08 is 0.0188. Looking at the last entry in the third column, we see -1.55, the entry just to the right, in the fourth column, is 0.0606, so $P(Z \leq -1.55) = 0.0606$. This probability corresponds to the area in the left portion of Figure 4.4. Because the standard normal curve is symmetric about zero, the probability that X is greater than 1.55 is also 0.0606, which is shown in the right portion of Figure 4.4. Again, looking at the first column of Table B.1 in Appendix B, we see the value $c = 1.53$, and next to it is the value 0.9370 meaning that $P(Z \leq 1.53) = 0.9370$.

In applied work, there are three types of probabilities that need to be determined:

1. $P(Z \leq c)$, the probability that a standard normal random variable is less than or equal to c,
2. $P(Z \geq c)$, the probability that a standard normal random variable is greater than or equal to c, and
3. $P(a \leq Z \leq b)$, the probability that a standard normal random variable is between the values a and b.

The first of these is determined from Table B.1 in Appendix B, as already indicated. Because the area under the curve is 1, the second is given by

$$P(Z \geq c) = 1 - P(Z \leq c).$$

The third is given by

$$P(a \leq Z \leq b) = P(Z \leq b) - P(Z \leq a).$$

Example

Determine $P(Z \geq 1.5)$, the probability that a standard normal random variable is greater than or equal to 1.5. From Table B.1 in Appendix B, $P(Z \leq 1.5) = 0.9332$. Therefore, $P(Z \geq 1.5) = 1 - 0.9332 = 0.0668$.

Example

Determine $P(-1.96 \leq Z \leq 1.96)$, the probability that a standard normal random variable is between -1.96 and 1.96. From Table B.1 in Appendix B, $P(Z \leq 1.96) = 0.975$. Also, $P(Z \leq -1.96) = 0.025$, so $P(-1.96 \leq Z \leq 1.96) = 0.975 - 0.025 = 0.95$.

In some situations, it is necessary to use Table B.1 (in Appendix B) backward. That is, we are given a probability and the goal is to determine c. For example, if we are told that $P(Z \leq c) = 0.99$, what is c? We simply find 0.99 in Table B.1 under the columns headed by $P(Z \leq c)$ and then read the number to the left, under the column headed by c. The answer is 2.33.

Before continuing, this is a convenient moment to illustrate the notion of a *quantile*. If for any variable X, $P(X \leq c) = 0.5$, then c is said to be the 0.5 quantile. The 0.5 quantile corresponds to the *population median*, which is estimated with the sample median described in Chapter 2. If $P(X \leq c) = 0.2$, c is the 0.2 quantile, and if $P(X \leq c) = 0.75$, c is the 0.75 quantile. *Percentiles* are quantiles multiplied by 100. If $P(X \leq c) = 0.75$, c is the 75th percentile.

Example

We have seen that for a standard normal distribution, $P(Z \leq 2.33) = 0.99$. This says that 2.33 is the 0.99 quantile (or the 99th percentile). From Table B.1 in Appendix B, $P(Z \leq -1.96) = 0.025$. Said another way, -1.96 is the 0.025 quantile of a standard normal distribution. To determine the 0.4013 quantile of a standard normal distribution, go to Table B.1 in Appendix B and find the value c such that $P(Z \leq c) = 0.4013$. The answer is -0.25.

When using Table B.1 in Appendix B, two related problems also arise. The first is determining c given the value of

$$P(Z \geq c).$$

A solution is obtained by noting that the area under the curve is 1, so $P(Z \geq c) = 1 - P(Z \leq c)$, which involves a quantity that can be determined from Table B.1. That is, compute $d = 1 - P(Z \geq c)$ and then determine c such that

$$P(Z \leq c) = d.$$

Example

To determine c if $P(Z \geq c) = 0.9$, first compute $d = 1 - P(Z \leq c) = 1 - 0.9 = 0.1$. Then, c is given by $P(Z \leq c) = 0.1$. Referring to Table B.1 in Appendix B, $c = -1.28$.

The other type of problem is determining c given

$$P(-c \leq Z \leq c).$$

Letting $d = P(-c \leq Z \leq c)$, the answer is given by

$$P(Z \leq c) = \frac{1+d}{2}.$$

Example

To determine c if $P(-c \leq Z \leq c) = 0.9$, let $d = P(-c \leq Z \leq c) = 0.9$ and compute $(1+d)/2 = (1+0.9)/2 = 0.95$. Then, c is given by $P(Z \leq c) = 0.95$. Referring to Table B.1 in Appendix B, $c = 1.645$.

4.6.3   Computing Probabilities for Any Normal Distribution

Now consider any normal random variable having mean μ and standard deviation σ. The next goal is to describe how to determine the probability of an observation being less than or equal to c, where as usual, c is any constant that might be of interest. The solution is based on *standardizing* a normal random variable, which means that we subtract the population mean μ and divide by the standard deviation, σ. In symbols, we standardize a normal random variable X by transforming it to

$$Z = \frac{X - \mu}{\sigma}. \tag{4.10}$$

The quantity Z is often called a Z score; it reflects how far the value X is from the mean in terms of the standard deviation.

Example

If $Z = 0.5$, then X is a half standard deviation away from the mean. That is, $X - \mu = 0.5\sigma$. If $Z = 2$, then X is two standard deviations away from the mean.

It can be shown that if X has a normal distribution, then the distribution of Z is standard normal. In particular, the probability that a normal random variable X is less than or equal to c is

$$P(X \leq c) = P\left(Z \leq \frac{c - \mu}{\sigma}\right). \tag{4.11}$$

Example

Someone claims that the cholesterol levels in adults have a normal distribution with mean $\mu = 230$ and standard deviation $\sigma = 20$. If this is true, what is the probability that an adult will have a cholesterol level less than or equal to 200? Referring to Equation (4.11), the answer is

$$P(X \leq 200) = P\left(Z \leq \frac{200 - 230}{20}\right) = P(Z < -1.5) = 0.0668,$$

where 0.0668 is read from Table B.1 in Appendix B.

In a similar manner, we can determine the probability that an observation is greater than or equal to 240 or between 210 and 250. More generally, for any constant c that is of interest, we can determine the probability that an observation is greater than or equal to c with the equation

$$P(X \geq c) = 1 - P(X \leq c),$$

the point being that the right side of this equation can be determined with Equation (4.11). In a similar manner, for any two constants a and b,

$$P(a \leq X \leq b) = P(X \leq b) - P(X \leq a).$$

Example

Continuing the last example, determine the probability of observing an adult with a cholesterol level greater than or equal to 240. We have that

$$P(X \geq 240) = 1 - P(X \leq 240).$$

Referring to Equation (4.11),

$$P(X \leq 240) = P\left(Z \leq \frac{240 - 230}{20}\right) = P(Z \leq 0.5) = 0.6915,$$

so

$$P(X \geq 240) = 1 - 0.6915 = 0.3085.$$

In words, the probability of an adult having a cholesterol level greater than or equal to 240 is 0.3085.

Example

Continuing the cholesterol example, we determine

$$P(210 \leq X \leq 250).$$

We have that

$$P(210 \leq X \leq 250) = P(X \leq 250) - P(X \leq 210).$$

Now

$$P(X \leq 250) = P\left(Z \leq \frac{250 - 230}{20}\right) = P(Z \leq 1) = 0.8413$$

and

$$P(X \leq 210) = P\left(Z \leq \frac{210 - 230}{20}\right) = P(Z \leq -1) = 0.1587,$$

so
$$P(210 \leq X \leq 250) = 0.8413 - 0.1587 = 0.6826,$$

meaning that the probability of observing a cholesterol level between 210 and 250 is 0.6826.

4.6.4   R Functions pnorm and qnorm

The R function
```
pnorm(c, mean = 0, sd = 1)
```

computes the probability that a normal random variable is less than or equal to c. By default, a standard normal distribution is used but the mean and standard deviation can be altered via the arguments mean and sd, respectively. For example, pnorm(2, mean = 1, sd = 3) would compute $P(X \leq 2)$, where X has a normal distribution with mean $\mu = 1$ and standard deviation $\sigma = 3$.
     The R function

```
qnorm(p, mean = 0, sd = 1)
```

computes the pth quantile of a normal distribution, For example, qnorm(0.975) returns 1.96, meaning that 1.96 is the 0.975 quantile of a standard normal distribution.

4.7   NONNORMALITY AND THE POPULATION VARIANCE

There are many methods for making inferences about a population of individuals based on a sample of individuals. They include classic methods that assume sampling is from a normal distribution as well as more modern methods aimed at dealing with nonnormal distributions, both of which will be described in subsequent chapters. Of fundamental importance is building a conceptual basis for understanding the relative merits of these techniques. There are several aspects of this issue, one of which has to do with the sensitivity of the population variance to the tails of a distribution. It can be formally shown that a very small change in a distribution can have a relatively large impact on the value of the population variance, σ^2, which will be seen to have important practical implications about how best to analyze data. In particular, even a small departure from normality can inflate σ^2, which can alter how results based on σ^2 should be interpreted. The immediate goal is to illustrate one aspect of this issue. Subsequent chapters will elaborate on the practical implications.
     The so-called contaminated or mixed normal distribution is a classic way of illustrating that a small departure from normality can have a large impact on the population variance, σ^2. The mixed normal arises as follows. Consider two populations of individuals or things. Assume each population has a normal distribution, but they differ in terms of their means, or variances, or both. When we mix the two populations together, we get what is called a *mixed normal* distribution. Generally, mixed normals

fall outside the class of normal distributions. That is, for a distribution to qualify as normal, the equation for its curve must have the form given by Equation (4.9), and a mixed normal distribution does not satisfy this requirement. When the two normals mixed together have a common mean, but unequal variances, the resulting probability curve is again symmetric about the mean, but even now the mixed normal is not a normal distribution.

Henceforth, the focus will be on a particular mixed normal distribution, sometimes called a contaminated normal distribution, which is often used to illustrate the impact of slight departures from a normal distribution. To provide a concrete description, let X represent the amount of weight that was gained or lost during the last year among all adults. Imagine that we divide the population of adults into two groups: those who have tried some form of dieting to lose weight and those that have not. For illustrative purposes, assume that for adults who have not tried to lose weight, the distribution of their weight loss is standard normal (so $\mu = 0$ and $\sigma = 1$). As for adults who have dieted to lose weight, assume that their weight loss is normally distributed again with mean $\mu = 0$ but with standard deviation $\sigma = 10$. Finally, suppose that 10% of all adults went on a diet last year to lose weight. That is, there is a 10% chance of selecting an observation from a normal distribution having standard deviation 10, so there is a 90% chance of selecting an observation from a normal curve having a standard deviation of 1.

Now, if we mix these two populations of adults together, the exact distribution can be derived and is shown in Figure 4.5. Also shown is the standard normal distribution, and as is evident, there is little separating the two curves. Note that in Figure 4.5, the tails of the mixed normal lie above the tails of the normal distribution. For this reason, this mixed normal distribution is often described as being *heavy-tailed*. Because the area under the extreme portions of a heavy-tailed distribution is larger than the area under a normal curve, extreme values or outliers are more likely when sampling from the mixed normal.

Here is the point: Very small departures from normality can greatly influence the value of the population variance. For the standard normal, the variance is 1, but for the mixed normal, it is 10.9. A related implication is that slight changes in any distribution, not just normal distributions, can have a big impact on the population variance. The full implications of this result are impossible to appreciate at this point, but they will become clear in subsequent chapters. But two implications can be illustrated here.

We have seen that for any normal distribution, the probability of being within one standard deviation of the mean is 0.68, as illustrated in Figure 4.2. In symbols, if X has a normal distribution,

$$P(\mu - \sigma \leq X \leq \mu + \sigma) = 0.68.$$

More generally, if a distribution is symmetric and bell-shaped, but not a normal distribution, is it approximately true that the probability of being within one standard deviation of the mean is 0.68? The answer is no, not necessarily. For the mixed normal considered here, this probability exceeds 0.925.

A criticism of this last example is that perhaps we never encounter a mixed normal distribution in practice, but this misses the point. The mixed normal distribution illustrates a basic principle: The value of the population variance is highly sensitive to the tails of a distribution. Even slight changes in the tails in any distribution can inflate the population variance, which in turn means that certain interpretations of the standard deviation that are reasonable under normality can be highly inaccurate. And we will see that other uses of the standard deviation can result in serious practical problems yet to be described.

Here is another implication worth mentioning. As previously pointed out, normal curves are completely determined by their mean and variance, and Figure 4.3 illustrated that under normality, increasing the variance from 1 to 1.5 results in a very noticeable difference in the graphs of the probability curves. If we assume that distributions are at least approximately normal, this might suggest that in general, if two distributions have equal means and variances, they will be very similar in shape. But this is not necessarily true even when the two curves are symmetric about the population mean and are bell-shaped. Figure 4.6 illustrates that two curves can have equal means and variances yet differ substantially. Figure 4.6 was created by plotting the mixed normal distribution in Figure 4.5 and then plotting a normal distribution that has the same mean and variance.

The illustration just given is not intended to suggest that the variance be abandoned when trying to understand data. Rather, the main message is that when learning basic statistical techniques, it is important to be aware of when the variance provides accurate and useful information and when and why it might be unsatisfactory. That is, basic training should include concepts and results that help avoid reading more into data than is warranted.

A feature of heavy-tailed distributions is that they tend to result in more outliers, compared to samples drawn from a normal distribution.

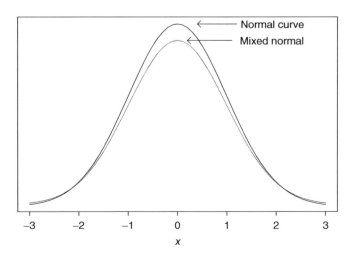

Figure 4.5   Shown is the standard normal and the mixed normal described in the text

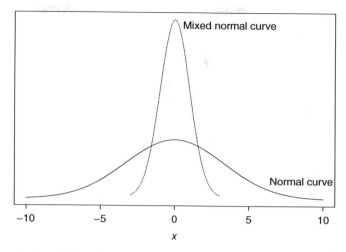

Figure 4.6 Two distributions with equal means and variances

Example

Forty observations were generated from a normal distribution using the R command `rnorm(40)` and the number of outliers, based on the boxplot rule, was noted. This process was repeated 1,000 times, and the average number of outliers was 0.44. The median number of outliers was 0. The same was done again; only now values were generated from a mixed normal via the R command `cnorm(40)`. Now the mean number of outliers was 3.3 and the median number was 3. One implication is that the sample variance, s^2, will tend to be larger when observations are sampled from a mixed normal, compared to situations where observations are sampled from a normal distribution. The reason is that outliers tend to inflate the sample variance as noted in Chapter 2. This has important implications about methods based on means described in subsequent chapters.

4.7.1 Skewed Distributions

Heavy-tailed distributions are one source of concern when using means. Another is skewed distributions, which generally refer to distributions that are not exactly symmetric. It is too soon to discuss all of the practical problems associated with skewed distributions, but one of the more fundamental issues can be described here.

Consider the issue of choosing a single number to represent the typical individual or thing under study. A seemingly natural approach is to use the population mean. If a distribution is symmetric about its mean, as is the case when a distribution is normal, there is general agreement that the population mean is indeed a reasonable reflection of what is typical. But when distributions are skewed, at some point, doubt begins to arise as to whether the mean is a good choice. Consider, for example, the distribution shown in Figure 4.7, which is skewed to the right. In this particular case, the population mean is located in the extreme right portion of the curve. In fact, the

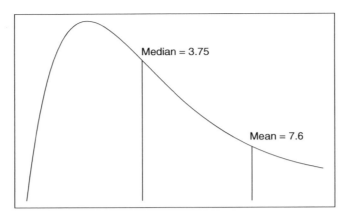

Figure 4.7   For skewed distributions, the population mean and median can differ tremendously

probability that an observation is less than the population mean is 0.74. So, from a probabilistic point of view, the population mean is rather atypical. In contrast, the median is located near the more likely outcomes and would seem to better reflect what is typical.

4.7.2   Comments on Transforming Data

A common suggestion regarding how to deal with skewed distributions is to transform the data. Two standard strategies are to use the square root of the original data or to use logarithms. In some cases, this creates a more symmetric looking plot of the data, but even when using more complex transformations, a plot of the data can remain skewed. Another important point is that this is a relatively ineffective way of dealing with outliers. Although simple transformations might reduce outliers, often the number of outliers remains the same, and in some instances, the number of outliers actually increases. There are more effective methods for dealing with skewed distributions, some of which are covered later in this book.

Example

Figure 4.8a shows a plot of 100 observations generated on a computer. Using the boxplot rule, five of the values are declared outliers. Figure 4.8b shows a plot of the same data after taking the logarithm of each value. The plot appears to be more symmetric, but an important point is that the same five values are again declared outliers.

Example

Figure 4.9a shows a plot of another 100 observations generated on a computer, only this time the data were generated from a distribution a bit more skewed than the

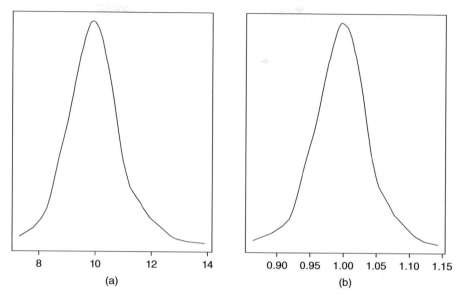

Figure 4.8 Taking logarithms sometimes results in a plot of the data being more symmetric, as illustrated here, but outliers can remain

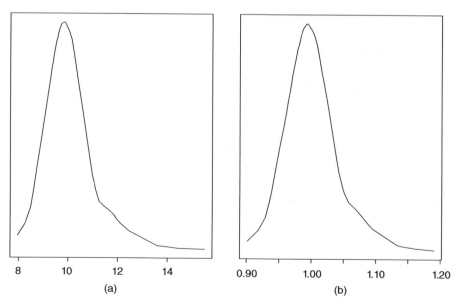

Figure 4.9 Taking logarithms sometimes reduces skewness but does not eliminate it, as illustrated here

distribution used in Figure 4.8. Using the boxplot rule, six of the values are declared outliers. Figure 4.9b shows a plot of the same data after taking the logarithm of each value. Note that the plot is again noticeably skewed. The number of outliers is reduced to four, this is better than six, but the more salient point is that the presence of outliers is not eliminated.

This next example illustrates yet one more important point. Consider the following values:

$$1, 2, 3, 4, 5, 6, 7, 8, 9, 10, 200, 500$$

The sample mean is 62.9 and the median is 6.5. If we take logarithms (to the base 10), the values are now

0.0000000, 0.3010300, 0.4771213, 0.6020600, 0.6989700, 0.7781513,

0.8450980, 0.9030900, 0.9542425, 1.0000000, 2.3010300, 2.6989700.

The mean of these values is 0.8116246. Does this somehow provide an estimate of the mean before we transformed the data? In general, transforming data makes it difficult to estimate the mean of the original values. If we simply transform back by raising 10 to the power 0.8116246, we get $10^{0.8116246} = 6.48$, a value close to the median of the original values, but quite different from the mean. This illustrates a common situation: Using the mean of values after taking logarithms often results in using a measure of location that is close to the median of the original values, rather than the mean. This does not necessarily mean that transformations are bad. But it is important to be aware of this property.

4.8 SUMMARY

- Expected values provide a formal definition of parameters that characterize a distribution such as the population mean and variance. (In Chapter 5, expected values provide an important link between the sample mean and the population mean.)
- Basic properties of the binomial distribution were summarized, which will play an important role in subsequent chapters.
- Normal distributions were introduced and some of their properties were described. One important property has to do with the fact that the standard deviation determines the probability that an observation is close to the mean. For example, the probability that an observation is within one standard deviation of the mean is 0.68, as was illustrated.
- In various situations, normal distributions have considerable practical value, but this is not always the case. An important goal in this chapter was to provide a foundation for understanding one reason why it can be unsatisfactory. This was done with the mixed normal distribution, which illustrates that even when a distribution is bell-shaped, certain properties of normal distributions cannot be

assumed to be true. For example, the probability that an observation is within one standard deviation of the mean can exceed 0.925 when dealing with the mixed normal distribution. Also, outliers are more common when dealing with heavy-tailed distributions, compared to sampling from a normal distribution. The practical implications associated with these results will become clear in the next three chapters.

- The population variance σ^2 is not robust in the sense that a very small change in a distribution can have a large impact on its value (e.g., Staudte and Sheather, 1990; Wilcox, 2012b). The mixed normal distribution illustrates this point.
- Even when an entire population of individuals is measured, the mean, median, and 20% trimmed mean can differ substantially.
- Transforming data might reduce skewness, but a fair amount of skewness can remain. Also, transforming data represents an unsatisfactory approach when dealing with outliers.

4.9   EXERCISES

1. If the possible values for x are 0, 1, 2, 3, 4, 5, and the corresponding values for $P(x)$ are 0.2, 0.2, 0.15, 0.3, 0.35, 0.2, 0.1, respectively, does $P(x)$ qualify as a probability function?

2. If the possible values for x are 2, 3, 4, and the corresponding values for $P(x)$ are 0.2, −0.1, 0.9, respectively, does $P(x)$ qualify as a probability function?

3. If the possible values for x are 1, 2, 3, 4, and the corresponding values for $P(x)$ are 0.1, 0.15, 0.5, 0.25, respectively, does $P(x)$ qualify as a probability function?

4. If the possible values for x are 2, 3, 4, 5, and the corresponding values for $P(x)$ are 0.2, 0.3, 0.4, 0.1, respectively, what is the probability of observing a value less than or equal to 3.4?

5. In Exercise 4, what is the probability of observing a value less than or equal to 1?

6. In Exercise 4, what is the probability of observing a value greater than 3?

7. In Exercise 4, what is the probability of observing a value greater than or equal to 3?

8. If the probability of observing a value less than or equal to 6 is 0.3, what is the probability of observing a value greater than 6?

9. For the probability function

$$x : 0, 1$$

$$P(x) : 0.7, 0.3$$

verify that the mean and variance are 0.3 and 0.21, respectively. What is the probability of getting a value less than the mean?

10. Imagine that an auto manufacturer wants to evaluate how potential customers will rate handling for a new car being considered for production. Also, suppose that if all potential customers were to rate handling on a four-point scale, 1 being poor and 4 being excellent, the corresponding probabilities associated with these ratings would be $P(1) = 0.2$, $P(2) = 0.4$, $P(3) = 0.3$, and $P(4) = 0.1$. Determine the population mean, variance, and standard deviation.

11. If the possible values for x are 1, 2, 3, 4, 5 with probabilities 0.2, 0.1, 0.1, 0.5, 0.1, respectively, what are the population mean, variance, and standard deviation?

12. In Exercise 11, determine the probability of getting a value within one standard deviation of the mean. That is, determine the probability of getting a value between $\mu - \sigma$ and $\mu + \sigma$.

13. If the possible values for x are 1, 2, 3 with probabilities 0.2, 0.6, and 0.2, respectively, what is the mean and standard deviation?

14. In Exercise 13, suppose the possible values for x are now 0, 2, 4 with the same probabilities as before. Will the standard deviation increase, decrease, or stay the same?

15. For the probability function

$$x : 1, 2, 3, 4, 5$$

$$P(x) : 0.15, 0.2, 0.3, 0.2, 0.15$$

determine the mean, the variance, and the probability that a value is less than the mean.

16. For the probability function

$$x : 1, 2, 3, 4, 5$$

$$P(x) : 0.1, 0.25, 0.3, 0.25, 0.1$$

would you expect the variance to be larger or smaller than the variance associated with the probability function used in the previous exercise? Verify your answer by computing the variance for the probability function given here.

17. For the probability function

$$x : 1, 2, 3, 4, 5$$

$$P(x) : 0.2, 0.2, 0.2, 0.2, 0.2$$

would you expect the variance to be larger or smaller than the variance associated with the probability function used in the previous exercise. Verify your answer by computing the variance.

18. For the following probabilities

		Income	
Age	High	Medium	Low
< 30	0.030	0.180	0.090
30–50	0.052	0.312	0.156
> 50	0.018	0.108	0.054

   determine (a) the probability that someone is under 30, (b) the probability that someone has a high income given that they are under 30, (3) the probability of someone having a low income given that they are under 30, and (4) the probability of a medium income given that they are over 50.

19. For the previous exercise, are income and age independent?

20. Coleman (1964) interviewed 3,398 schoolboys and asked them about their self-perceived membership in the "leading crowd." Their response was either yes, they were a member, or no they were not. The same boys were also asked about their attitude concerning the leading crowd. In particular, they were asked whether membership meant that it does not require going against one's principles sometimes or whether they think it does. Here, the first response will be indicated by a 1, while the second will be indicated by a 0. The results were as follows:

	Attitude	
Member	1	0
Yes	757	496
No	1,071	1,074

   So, for example, the relative frequency of the event (yes, 1) is 757/3,398. Treat the relative frequencies as probabilities and determine (a) the probability that an arbitrarily chosen boy responds yes, (b) $P(\text{yes}|1)$, (c) $P(1|\text{yes})$, (d) whether the response yes is independent of the attitude 0, (e) the probability of a (yes and 1) or a (no and 0) response, (f) the probability of not responding (yes and 1), (g) the probability of responding yes or 1.

21. Let Y be the cost of a home and let X be a measure of the crime rate. If the variance of the cost of a home changes with X, does this mean that the cost of a home and the crime rate are dependent?

22. If the probability of $Y < 6$ is 0.4 given that $X = 2$, and if the probability of $Y < 6$ is 0.3 given that $X = 4$, does this mean that X and Y are dependent?

23. If the range of possible Y values varies with X, does this mean that X and Y are dependent?

24. For a binomial with $n = 10$ and $p = 0.4$, use Table B.2 in Appendix B to determine (a) $P(0)$, the probability of exactly 0 successes, (b) $P(X \leq 3)$, (c) $P(X < 3)$, (d) $P(X > 4)$, (e) $P(2 \leq X \leq 5)$.

25. For a binomial with $n = 15$ and $p = 0.3$, use Table B.2 in Appendix B to determine (a) $P(0)$, the probability of exactly 0 successes, (b) $P(X \leq 3)$, (c) $P(X < 3)$, (d) $P(X > 4)$, (e) $P(2 \leq X \leq 5)$.

26. For a binomial with $n = 15$ and $p = 0.6$, use Table B.2 to determine the probability of exactly 10 successes.

27. For a binomial with $n = 7$ and $p = 0.35$, what is the probability of exactly 2 successes.

28. For a binomial with $n = 18$ and $p = 0.6$, determine the mean and variance of X, the total number of successes.

29. For a binomial with $n = 22$ and $p = 0.2$, determine the mean and variance of X, the total number of successes.

30. For a binomial with $n = 20$ and $p = 0.7$, determine the mean and variance of $\hat{p}$, the proportion of observed successes.

31. For a binomial with $n = 30$ and $p = 0.3$, determine the mean and variance of $\hat{p}$.

32. For a binomial with $n = 10$ and $p = 0.8$, determine (a) the probability that $\hat{p}$ is less than or equal to 0.7, (b) the probability that $\hat{p}$ is greater than or equal to 0.8, (c) the probability that $\hat{p}$ is exactly equal to 0.8.

33. A coin is rigged so that when it is flipped, the probability of a head is 0.7. If the coin is flipped three times, which is the more likely outcome, exactly three heads, or two heads and a tail?

34. Imagine that the probability of head when flipping a coin is given by the binomial probability function with $p = 0.5$. (So, the outcomes are independent.) If you flip the coin nine times and get nine heads, what is the probability of a head on the 10th flip?

35. The Department of Agriculture of the United States reports that 75% of all people who invest in the futures market lose money. Based on the binomial probability function, with $n = 5$, determine

    (a) the probability that all five lose money.

    (b) the probability that all five make money.

    (c) the probability that at least two lose money.

36. If for a binomial distribution $p = 0.4$ and $n = 25$, determine (a) $P(X < 11)$, (b) $P(X \leq 11)$, (c) $P(X > 9)$, and (d) $P(X \geq 9)$.

37. In the previous problem, determine the mean of X, the variance of X, the mean of $\hat{p}$, and the variance of $\hat{p}$.

38. Given that Z has a standard normal distribution, use Table B.1 in Appendix B to determine (a) $P(Z \geq 1.5)$, (b) $P(Z \leq -2.5)$, (c) $P(Z < -2.5)$, (d) $P(-1 \leq Z \leq 1)$.

39. If Z has a standard normal distribution, determine (a) $P(Z \leq 0.5)$, (b) $P(Z > -1.25)$, (c) $P(-1.2 < Z < 1.2)$, (d) $P(-1.8 \leq Z < 1.8)$.

40. If Z has a standard normal distribution, determine (a) $P(Z < -0.5)$, (b) $P(Z < 1.2)$, (c) $P(Z > 2.1)$, (d) $P(-0.28 < Z < 0.28)$.

41. If Z has a standard normal distribution, find c such that (a) $P(Z \le c) = 0.0099$, (b) $P(Z < c) = 0.9732$, (c) $P(Z > c) = 0.5691$, (d) $P(-c \le Z \le c) = 0.2358$.

42. If Z has a standard normal distribution, use R to find c such that (a) $P(Z > c) = 0.0764$, (b) $P(Z > c) = 0.5040$, (c) $P(-c \le Z < c) = 0.9108$, (d) $P(-c \le Z \le c) = 0.8$.

43. If X has a normal distribution with mean $\mu = 50$ and standard deviation $\sigma = 9$, use Table B.1 in Appendix B to determine (a) $P(X \le 40)$, (b) $P(X < 55)$, (c) $P(X > 60)$, (d) $P(40 \le X \le 60)$.

44. If X has a normal distribution with mean $\mu = 20$ and standard deviation $\sigma = 9$, use R to determine (a) $P(X < 22)$, (b) $P(X > 17)$, (c) $P(X > 15)$, (d) $P(2 < X < 38)$.

45. If X has a normal distribution with mean $\mu = 0.75$ and standard deviation $\sigma = 0.5$, use R to determine (a) $P(0.5 < X < 1)$, (b) $P(0.25 < X < 1.25)$.

46. If X has a normal distribution, determine c such that

$$P(\mu - c\sigma < X < \mu + c\sigma) = 0.95.$$

Hint: Convert the given expression so that the middle term has a standard normal distribution.

47. If X has a normal distribution, determine c such that

$$P(\mu - c\sigma < X < \mu + c\sigma) = 0.8.$$

48. Assuming that the scores on a math achievement test are normally distributed with mean $\mu = 68$ and standard deviation $\sigma = 10$, what is the probability of getting a score greater than 78?

49. In the previous problem, how high must someone score to be in the top 5%? That is, determine c such that $P(X > c) = 0.05$.

50. A manufacturer of car batteries claims that the life of their batteries is normally distributed with mean $\mu = 58$ months and standard deviation $\sigma = 3$. Determine the probability that a randomly selected battery will last at least 62 months.

51. Assume that the income of pediatricians is normally distributed with mean $\mu = \$100,000$ and standard deviation $\sigma = 10,000$. Determine the probability of observing an income between \$85,000 and \$115,000.

52. Suppose the winnings of gamblers at Las Vegas are normally distributed with mean $\mu = -300$ (the typical person loses \$300), and standard deviation $\sigma = 100$. Determine the probability that a gambler does not lose any money.

53. A large computer company claims that their salaries are normally distributed with mean \$50,000 and standard deviation 10,000. What is the probability of observing an income between \$40,000 and \$60,000?

54. Suppose the daily amount of solar radiation in Los Angeles is normally distribution with mean 450 calories and standard deviation 50. Determine the probability that for a randomly chosen day, the amount of solar radiation is between 350 and 550.

55. If the cholesterol levels of adults are normally distributed with mean 230 and standard deviation 25, what is the probability that a randomly sampled adult has a cholesterol level greater than 260?

56. If after 1 year, the annual mileage of privately owned cars is normally distributed with mean 14,000 miles and standard deviation 3,500, what is the probability that a car has mileage greater than 20,000 miles?

57. Can small changes in the tails of a distribution result in large changes in the population mean, μ, relative to changes in the median?

58. Explain in what sense the population variance is sensitive to small changes in a distribution.

59. For normal random variables, the probability of being within one standard deviation of the mean is 0.68. That is, $P(\mu - \sigma \le X \le \mu + \sigma) = 0.68$ if X has a normal distribution. For nonnormal distributions, is it safe to assume that this probability is again 0.68? Explain your answer.

60. If a distribution appears to be bell-shaped and symmetric about its mean, can we assume that the probability of being within one standard deviation of the mean is 0.68?

61. Can two distributions differ by a large amount yet have equal means and variances?

62. If a distribution is skewed, is it possible that the mean exceeds the 0.85 quantile?

5

SAMPLING DISTRIBUTIONS

This chapter deals with the notion of a sampling distribution, which plays a fundamental role when trying to generalize from a sample to a population of individuals or things. Sampling distributions also provide perspective on the relative merits of the location estimators introduced in Chapter 2.

As previously explained, the population mean μ represents the average of all individuals or things that are of interest in a particular study. But typically not all individuals of interest can be measured, in which case the sample mean, $\overline{X}$, is used to estimate the population mean μ. The sample mean is the average based on a subset of the population of interest, and so it will generally be the case that the sample mean is not equal to the population mean. That is, generally $\overline{X} \neq \mu$. Consequently, an issue of fundamental importance is how well the sample mean estimates the population mean. If the sample mean is $\overline{X} = 23$, we estimate that the population mean is 23, but can we be reasonably certain that the population mean is less than 42? Can we be reasonably certain that the population mean is greater than 16? In a similar manner, when we compute the sample median, M, how well does it estimate the population median? Given some data, is there some method that allows us to conclude, for example, the population median is between 8 and 10? When working with the binomial distribution, if we observe 67 successes among 100 observations, we estimate the probability of success to be 0.67. But how might we assess the accuracy of this estimate? A key component when trying to address these problems is the notion of a sampling distribution.

Notice that if a study is replicated, chances are that the sample means will differ. Imagine a study that yields $\overline{X} = 23$. If the study is replicated with a new sample of individuals, this might yield $\overline{X} = 19$. In a third study, we might get $\overline{X} = 34$. In

Understanding and Applying Basic Statistical Methods Using R, First Edition. Rand R. Wilcox.
© 2017 John Wiley & Sons, Inc. Published 2017 by John Wiley & Sons, Inc.
www.wiley.com/go/Wilcox/Statistical_Methods_R

general, many replications of a study will yield a collection of sample means, which can be depicted as follows:

Study: 1   2   3   4 $\cdots$
Means: $\overline{X}_1$ $\overline{X}_2$ $\overline{X}_3$ $\overline{X}_4$ $\cdots$

Now, over many studies, a certain proportion of the sample means will be less than or equal to 10. Thinking of probabilities in terms of proportions, if 20% of all studies yield a sample mean less than or equal to 10, this is taken to mean that the probability of a sample mean less than or equal to 10 is 0.2. In symbols, $P(\overline{X} \leq 10) = 0.2$. In a similar manner, $P(\overline{X} \leq 20) = 0.8$ indicates that 80% of all sample means are less than or equal to 20. The difficulty is that replicating a study many times is not practical. What is needed is some way of determining these probabilities without actually replicating a study. The collection of probabilities associated with all possible values of $\overline{X}$ is called the *sampling distribution* of $\overline{X}$. Sections 5.1–5.4 describe basic strategies for determining these probabilities and subsequent chapters illustrate their practical importance.

5.1   SAMPLING DISTRIBUTION OF $\hat{P}$, THE PROPORTION OF SUCCESSES

Elaborating on the notion of a sampling distribution is perhaps easiest when dealing with a binomial distribution where the probability of success is estimated with the proportion of successes, $\hat{p}$. Similar to the sample mean, $\hat{p}$ also has a distribution over many studies. The first study might yield $\hat{p} = 0.2$, the next study might yield $\hat{p} = 0.5$, and so on. But before continuing, it helps to first describe the binomial distribution in a slightly different manner than was done in Chapter 4, and the notion of random sampling needs to be made more precise.

As was done in Chapter 2, consider n observations, which are labeled $X_1, \ldots, X_n$. To be concrete, suppose we want to determine the proportion of adults over the age of 40 who suffer from arthritis. For the first person in our study, set $X_1 = 1$ if this individual has arthritis, otherwise set $X_1 = 0$. Similarly, for the second person, set $X_2 = 1$ if this individual has arthritis, otherwise set $X_2 = 0$. We repeat this process n times, so each of the variables $X_1, \ldots, X_n$ has the value 0 or 1. These n values are said to be a *random sample* if two conditions are met:

- Any two observations are independent.
- Each observation has the same probability function.

For the situation at hand where the outcome is either 0 or 1, the second condition merely means that for every observation made, the probability of getting a 1 is the same, which we label p. In symbols, for the n observations available,

$$P(X_1 = 1) = P(X_2 = 1) = \cdots = P(X_n = 1) = p.$$

The sample mean of these n values is typically denoted by $\hat{p}$. That is,

$$\hat{p} = \frac{1}{n} \sum X_i,$$

which is just the proportion of 1's among the n observations.

Example

Imagine you want to know what percentage of marriages end in divorce among couples living in Iceland. You do not have the resources to check all records, so you want to estimate this percentage based on available data. To keep the illustration simple, suppose you have data on 10 couples:

$$X_1 = 1, X_2 = 0, X_3 = 0, X_4 = 0, X_5 = 1,$$
$$X_6 = 0, X_7 = 0, X_8 = 0, X_9 = 0, X_{10} = 1.$$

That is, the first couple got a divorce, the next three couples did not get a divorce, the fifth couple got a divorce, and so on. The number of divorces among these 10 couples is

$$\sum X_i = 1 + 0 + 0 + 0 + 1 + 0 + 0 + 0 + 0 + 1 = 3,$$

so the estimated probability of a divorce is

$$\hat{p} = \frac{3}{10} = 0.3.$$

Notice that if we knew the true probability of a divorce, p, we could compute the probability of getting $\hat{p} = 0.3$ based on a sample of size 10. When $n = 10$, it is just the probability of observing three divorces. From Section 4.5, this probability is

$$P(3) = \binom{10}{3} p^3 q^7,$$

where $q = 1 - p$. Moreover, if we are told that the probability of a divorce is $p = 0.4$, for example, then the probability of exactly three divorces can be determined using the R function dbinom, as indicated in Chapter 4. In particular, dbinom(3,10,.4) returns 0.215. That is, the probability of getting $\hat{p} = 0.3$ is 0.215. The probability that the number of divorces is less than or equal to 3 can be determined with the R function pbinom, or Table B.2 in Appendix B could be used. Using pbinom(3,10,.4), this probability is found to be 0.382.

Generalizing, consider any binomial distribution where $X = x$ represents the number of successes in n trials, in which case the estimate of p is $\hat{p} = x/n$. The event of getting x successes in n trials occurs with probability $P(x)$, where $P(x)$ is the binomial probability function given by Equation (4.8) in Section 4.5. For instance, if $X = 3$ successes are observed, the estimated probability of success is $3/n$, which occurs with probability $P(3)$.

Example

Consider a binomial distribution with $p = 0.4$ and $n = 10$ trials. Then, as previously explained, the probability of getting three successes or less is

$$P(X \leq 3) = P(0) + P(1) + P(2) + P(3)$$
$$= 0.382.$$

Noting that 0, 1, 2, and 3 successes correspond to the $\hat{p}$ values 0/10, 1/10, 2/10, and 3/10, it follows that

$$P(\hat{p} \leq 0.3) = 0.382.$$

Here is how $P(\hat{p} \leq c)$ can be computed for any value c between 0 and 1 when we are told the number of trials n and the probability of success p:

- Compute $m = [nc]$, where the notation $[nc]$ means that nc is rounded down to the nearest integer. For example, $[67 \times 0.4] = [26.8] = 26$.
- Then, $P(\hat{p} \leq c) = P(X \leq m)$, where X is a binomial random variable having probability of success p.
- The value of $P(X \leq m)$ can be determined using Table B.2 in Appendix B, as already explained in Chapter 4, or the R function pbinom can be used.

Example

Various research teams plan to conduct a study aimed at estimating the occurrence of tooth decay among adults living in a particular geographic region. Assume random sampling, that each team plans to base their estimate on five individuals, and that unknown to them, the proportion of people with tooth decay is 30%. So, $n = 5$ and $p = 0.3$. Then for each research team that might investigate this issue, the possible values for $\hat{p}$ are 0/5, 1/5, 2/5, 3/5, 4/5, 5/5, and the corresponding probabilities are 0.16807, 0.36015, 0.30870, 0.13230, 0.02835, and 0.00243, respectively, which correspond to the probability of a 0, 1, 2, 3, 4, and 5 "successes" based on the binomial probability function. So, from Chapter 4, the average value of $\hat{p}$, among the many research teams, is $p = 0.3$, and the variance of the $\hat{p}$ values is $p(1 - p)/n = 0.3(0.7)/5 = 0.042$. To determine the probability of getting $\hat{p} \leq 0.3$, compute 0.3×5 and round down yielding $m = 1$. The R command pbinom(1,5,0.3) yields 0.52822. That is, $P(\hat{p} \leq 0.3) = 0.52822$.

Example

A college president claims that the proportion of students at her institution with an IQ greater than 120 is 0.4. If someone plans to sample 20 students, what is the probability that the proportion having an IQ greater than 120 will be less than or equal to 4/20 if the claim is correct? An estimate less than or equal to 4/20 corresponds to getting 0 or 1 or 2 or 3 or 4 students with an IQ greater than 120. Or, in the notation just introduced, $c = 4/20$, $m = 4$, and so $P(\hat{p} \leq c) = P(X \leq 4)$. If the claim $p = 0.4$ is correct, then from Table B.2 in Appendix B (with $n = 20$), or using the R function pbinom, the probability of getting four or fewer students with an IQ greater than 120 is 0.051. That is, if the president's claim is correct, it would be rather unusual to get $\hat{p} \leq 4/20$, suggesting that perhaps the claim is wrong.

5.2 SAMPLING DISTRIBUTION OF THE MEAN UNDER NORMALITY

The goal in this section is to extend the notion of a sampling distribution to situations where data have a normal distribution. Again, we have n observations $X_1, \ldots, X_n$, but rather than having a value of 0 or 1, as was the case when working with the binomial distribution, these variables are continuous with mean μ and standard deviation σ. And if all individuals could be measured, a plot of the data would have the normal distribution described in Chapter 4.

As with the binomial distribution, we imagine that many research teams plan to conduct the same study or that the same research team plans to repeat their study many times. To be concrete, imagine that the goal is to estimate how many additional hours of sleep an individual gets after taking a particular drug. Further suppose that the drug is tried on 20 individuals yielding a sample mean of $\overline{X} = 0.8$ hours. But if the study were repeated with another 20 participants, chances are we would get a different result as previously discussed. The goal is to be able to determine the probability that the sample mean is less than or equal to 0.5, less than or equal to 1, less than equal to 1.3, and more generally, less than or equal c, where c is any constant we might choose. In symbols, we want to be able to determine $P(\overline{X} \leq c)$ for any constant c. Three key results provide a solution based on a single study:

- Under random sampling, the average value of the sample mean, over (infinitely) many studies, can be shown to be equal to μ, the population mean. In symbols, $E(\overline{X}) = \mu$. Said another way, in any given study, chances are that the sample mean will not be equal to the population mean. But on average (over many studies), the sample mean provides a correct estimate of the population mean.

- Under random sampling, the variance of the sample mean, generally known as the *squared standard error* of the sample mean, can be shown to be σ^2/n. That is, the average squared difference between the sample mean and the population mean is σ^2/n. In symbols, the variance (or squared standard error) of the sample mean is

$$E[(\overline{X} - \mu)^2] = \frac{\sigma^2}{n}.$$

The (positive) square root, $\sigma/\sqrt{n}$, is called the *standard error* of the sample mean, which will be seen to play a central role when analyzing data.

- When observations are randomly sampled from a normal distribution, the sample mean also has a normal distribution. Said more succinctly, when n observations are randomly sampled from a normal distribution with mean μ and variance σ^2, the sample mean has a normal distribution with mean μ and variance σ^2/n. The practical implication is that the probability of getting a value for $\overline{X}$ less than or equal to 1, 3, or c, for any c we might choose, can be determined under normality when the mean, variance, and sample size are known, as will be illustrated.

It is noted that the first two results require the assumption of random sampling only—normality is not required. The third result assumes normality. As previously remarked, normality is rarely if ever true, so there is the issue of how to deal with the more realistic situation where data do not follow a normal curve. For the moment this issue is ignored, but it will be discussed in detail at various points.

As just noted, the variance of the sample mean is called the *squared standard error* of the sample mean. Often, this variance is written as $\text{VAR}(\overline{X})$ or $\sigma^2_{\overline{X}}$ and as previously indicated

$$\sigma^2_{\overline{X}} = \frac{\sigma^2}{n}.$$

In words, the variance of the sample mean is equal to the variance of the distribution from which the observations were sampled, divided by the sample size, assuming random sampling only. In practice, typically σ^2 is unknown, but as previously indicated, it can be estimated with the sample variance, s^2. Consequently, the squared standard error can be estimated as well and is simply s^2/n, and an estimate of the standard error is $s/\sqrt{n}$.

Example

Depressive symptoms are measured for 10 randomly sampled individuals and found to be

$$55, 69, 77, 53, 63, 71, 58, 62, 80, 61.$$

The sample variance is $s^2 = 82.54$, so an estimate of σ^2/n, the squared standard error of the sample mean, is $82.54/10 = 8.254$ and an estimate of the standard error is $\sqrt{8.254} = 2.87$.

Example

Sixteen observations are randomly sampled from a normal distribution having a population mean equal to 10 and standard deviation equal to 1. That is, $n = 16$, $\mu = 10$, and $\sigma = 1$. By chance, we might get $\overline{X} = 9.92$. If we repeat this study, again with $n = 16$, now we might get $\overline{X} = 10.76$. If we continue to repeat this study (infinitely) many times, the average of the sample means will be 10. If we were to compute the variance of these sample means, we would get $\sigma^2/n = 1^2/16 = 0.0625$, and the standard error of the sample mean is $\sigma/\sqrt{n} = 1/4 = 0.25$.

Figure 5.1 shows the normal distribution used in the last example, which is indicated by $n = 1$. Recall that σ^2 reflects how closely a *single* observation tends to be to the population mean. Also shown is the sampling distribution of the sample mean, $\overline{X}$, which is the distribution indicated by $n = 16$. For example, the area under this curve and to left of the value 1 corresponds to the probability that a sample mean, based

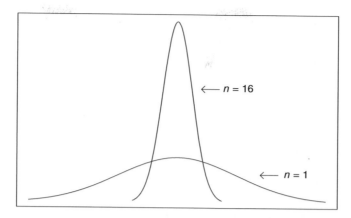

Figure 5.1   An illustration of how the sampling distribution of the sample mean, $\overline{X}$, changes with the sample size when sampling from a normal distribution

on 16 observations, will have a value less than or equal to 1, assuming normality. Because its variance is σ^2/n, which is smaller than the variance based on a single observation, the sample mean tends to be closer to the population mean, on average. Indeed, as we increase the sample size, σ^2/n decreases. Intuition suggests that the larger the sample size, the more accurate will be the sample mean in terms of estimating the population mean. The result just given helps quantify just how much more accurate it will be.

> *Definition* An *estimator* is some expression, based on the observations made, intended to estimate some feature of the population under study. The sample mean, $\overline{X}$, is an estimator of the population mean, and its observed value is called an *estimate*. The sample variance, s^2, is an estimator, and its observed value is said to be an estimate of the population variance.

> *Definition* An estimator is *unbiased* if its expected value, roughly meaning its average value over (infinitely) many studies, is equal to the quantity it is trying to estimate. The sample mean is an unbiased estimator of the population mean because its expected value can be shown to be $E(\overline{X}) = \mu$. For the binomial distribution, $E(\hat{p}) = p$, so $\hat{p}$ is an unbiased estimator of the true probability of success, p. It can be shown that on average, the sample variance, s^2, is equal to σ^2. That is, s^2 is an unbiased estimator of the population variance. In symbols, $E(s^2) = \sigma^2$.

5.2.1   Determining Probabilities Associated with the Sample Mean

The results just described make it possible to address the following type of problem. If we are told that data are randomly sampled from a normal distribution with a specified sample size, population mean, and population variance, what is the probability that the sample mean is less than or equal to 10, less than or equal to 20, or less than or equal to c for any constant c we might pick? In symbols, we want to know $P(\overline{X} \leq c)$.

Recall from Chapter 4 that if X has a normal distribution, we can determine $P(X \leq c)$ by standardizing X. That is, if we subtract the population mean and divide by the population standard deviation, X is transformed to a standard normal random variable. In symbols, we used the fact that

$$P(X \leq c) = P\left(Z \leq \frac{c - \mu}{\sigma}\right),$$

where Z has a standard normal distribution. Here, the same strategy is used when working with the sample mean, the main difference being that the sample mean has standard deviation $\sigma/\sqrt{n}$ rather than σ. In symbols, under random sampling from a normal distribution,

$$Z = \frac{\overline{X} - \mu}{\sigma/\sqrt{n}}$$

has a standard normal distribution. This means that

$$P(\overline{X} \leq c) = P\left(Z \leq \frac{c - \mu}{\sigma/\sqrt{n}}\right), \tag{5.1}$$

which can be determined by referring to Table B.1 in Appendix B. In addition, the probability that the sample mean is greater than or equal to c is

$$P(\overline{X} \geq c) = 1 - P\left(Z \leq \frac{c - \mu}{\sigma/\sqrt{n}}\right), \tag{5.2}$$

and the probability that the sample mean is between the constants a and b is

$$P(a \leq \overline{X} \leq b) = P\left(Z \leq \frac{b - \mu}{\sigma/\sqrt{n}}\right) - P\left(Z \leq \frac{a - \mu}{\sigma/\sqrt{n}}\right). \tag{5.3}$$

Chapter 4 also pointed out that probabilities associated with a normal distribution can be determined with the R function pnorm. From a computational point of view, this is much easier than standardizing and then using Table B.1 in Appendix B. However, standardizing the sample mean, as done here, reflects a basic strategy for analyzing data. Some awareness of this strategy and its relative merits can be important from a practical point of view, as will be indicated in subsequent chapters.

Example

If 25 observations are randomly sampled from a normal distribution with mean 50 and standard deviation 10, what is the probability that the sample mean will be less than or equal to 45? We have that $n = 25$, $\mu = 50$, $\sigma = 10$, and $c = 45$, so

$$P(\overline{X} \leq 45) = P\left(Z \leq \frac{45 - 50}{10/\sqrt{25}}\right)$$

$$= P(Z \leq -2.5)$$

$$= 0.0062.$$

Example

A company claims that after years of experience, the average SAT score among students who take their training program is 30 points higher than the average for students who do not take their course. They further claim that the increase in the scores has a normal distribution with a standard deviation of 12. As a check on their claim, you randomly sample 16 students and find that the average score is 21 points higher than the score among students who do not take the course. The company argues that this does not refute their claim because getting a sample mean of 21 or less is not that unlikely. To determine whether their claim has merit, you compute

$$P(\overline{X} \le 21) = P\left(Z \le \frac{21 - 30}{12/\sqrt{16}}\right)$$
$$= P(Z \le -3)$$
$$= 0.0013,$$

which indicates that getting a sample mean as small or smaller than 21 is a relatively unlikely event. That is, there is empirical evidence that the claim made by the company is probably incorrect.

Example

A researcher claims that for college students taking a particular test of spatial ability, the scores have a normal distribution with mean 27 and variance 49. If this claim is correct, and you randomly sample 36 students, what is the probability that the sample mean will be greater than or equal to 28? First compute

$$\frac{c - \mu}{\sigma/\sqrt{n}} = \frac{28 - 27}{\sqrt{49/36}} = 0.857.$$

Because $P(Z \le 0.857) = 0.80$, Equation (5.2) says that $P(\overline{X} \ge 28) = 1 - P(Z \le 0.857) = 1 - 0.80 = 0.20$. This says that if we randomly sample $n = 25$ students, and the claims made by the researcher are true, the probability of getting a sample mean greater than or equal to 28 is 0.2.

Example

Thirty-six observations are randomly sampled from a normal distribution with $\mu = 5$ and $\sigma = 3$. What is the probability that the sample mean will be between 4 and 6? In the notation used here, $a = 4$ and $b = 6$. To find out, first determine $P(\overline{X} \le 6)$ by computing

$$\frac{b - \mu}{\sigma/\sqrt{n}} = \frac{6 - 5}{3/\sqrt{36}} = 2.$$

Referring to Table B.1 in Appendix B, $P(\overline{X} \le 6) = P(Z \le 2) = 0.9772$. Similarly,

$$\frac{a - \mu}{\sigma/\sqrt{n}} = \frac{4 - 5}{3/\sqrt{36}} = -2,$$

and $P(Z \leq -2) = 0.0228$. So, according to Equation (5.3),

$$P(2 \leq \overline{X} \leq 6) = 0.9772 - 0.0228 = 0.9544.$$

5.2.2 But Typically σ Is Not Known. Now What?

In the examples just given, we are told the value of σ, the population standard deviation. But in practice, it is rarely known. So, how can we compute probabilities associated with the sample mean?

Recall that the sample standard deviation s estimates the population standard deviation σ. So, a seemingly natural strategy is to replace Equation (5.1), for example, with

$$P(\overline{X} \leq c) = P\left(Z \leq \frac{c - \mu}{s/\sqrt{n}}\right), \tag{5.4}$$

Said another way, the standard error of the sample mean is not known, so we estimate it with $s/\sqrt{n}$. When dealing with normal distributions, this is reasonable (assuming random sampling) provided the sample size is sufficiently large, say greater than or equal to 120. But when dealing with small sample sizes, an alternative method is typically used, which is introduced in Chapter 6.

5.3 NONNORMALITY AND THE SAMPLING DISTRIBUTION OF THE SAMPLE MEAN

During the early years of the nineteenth century, it was realized that assuming data have a normal distribution is highly convenient from both a theoretical and computational point of view. But this left open an issue of fundamental importance: How might one justify the use of the normal distribution beyond mere mathematical convenience? In particular, when approximating the sampling distribution of the sample mean, under what circumstances is it reasonable to assume that the normal distribution can be used as described and illustrated in the previous section? Gauss worked on this problem over a number of years, but it is a result derived by Laplace that is routinely used today. Announced in the year 1810, Laplace called his result the central limit theorem, where the word central is intended to mean fundamental.

Roughly, the *central limit theorem* says that under random sampling, as the sample size gets large, the sampling distribution of the sample mean approaches a normal distribution with mean μ and variance σ^2/n. Put another way, if a random sample is sufficiently large, we can assume that the sample mean has a normal distribution. This means that with a *sufficiently large* sample size, it can be assumed that

$$Z = \frac{\overline{X} - \mu}{\sigma/\sqrt{n}}$$

has a standard normal distribution.

An important aspect of the central limit theorem, particularly in light of some modern insights, is the phrase sufficiently large. This is rather vague. Just how large must the sample size be in order to justify the assumption that the sample mean has a normal distribution? For reasons to be described, a common claim is that $n = 40$ generally suffices. But in subsequent chapters, it will become evident that two key components of this issue were overlooked. In particular, general situations will be described where a much larger sample size is required when attention is restricted to the mean. There are many recently derived methods that provide improved strategies for dealing with small sample sizes, and a glimpse of some of these techniques will be provided.

5.3.1 Approximating the Binomial Distribution

We have seen that when dealing with a binomial distribution, the probability of success is estimated with $\hat{p}$, which is just a sample mean based on n variables having the value 0 or 1. Consequently, under random sampling, the central limit theorem says that if the sample size is sufficiently large, $\hat{p}$ will have, approximately, a normal distribution with mean p (the true probability of success) and variance $p(1 - p)/n$. This means that if $\hat{p}$ is standardized by subtracting its mean and dividing by its standard error, the result will be a variable having, approximately, a standard normal distribution. In symbols,

$$Z = \frac{\hat{p} - p}{\sqrt{p(1 - p)/n}}$$

will have, approximately, a standard normal distribution. This implies that for any constant c, if n is sufficiently large, it will be approximately true that

$$P(\hat{p} \leq c) = P\left(Z \leq \frac{c - p}{\sqrt{p(1 - p)/n}} \right), \tag{5.5}$$

where Z is a standard normal random variable. That is, this probability can be determined with Table B.1 in Appendix B. For any constants a and b,

$$P(a \leq \hat{p} \leq b) = P\left(Z \leq \frac{b - p}{\sqrt{p(1 - p)/n}} \right) - P\left(Z \leq \frac{a - p}{\sqrt{p(1 - p)/n}} \right). \tag{5.6}$$

The accuracy of these approximations depends on both n and p. The approximation performs best when $p = 0.5$. When p is close to 0 or 1, much larger sample sizes are needed to get a good approximation. A commonly used rule is that if both np and $n(1 - p)$ are greater than 15, the normal approximation will perform reasonably well. Figure 5.2a shows a plot of the probability function for $\hat{p}$ when $n = 10$ and $p = 0.5$, and Figure 5.2b is when $n = 100$, again with $p = 0.5$. Based on these plots, it does not seem too surprising that the normal distribution provides a good approximation of the sampling distribution of $\hat{p}$ when the sample size is not too small.

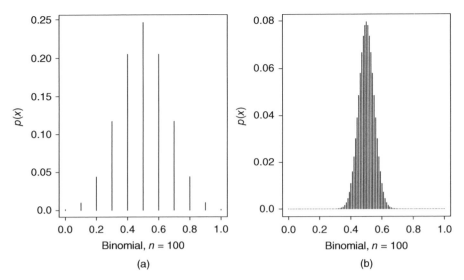

Figure 5.2   The sampling distribution of $\hat{p}$, the proportion of successes, when randomly sampling from a binomial distribution having probability of success $p = 0.5$

Example

Consider a binomial distribution with $p = 0.5$ and $n = 10$, and imagine that we want to determine the probability that $\hat{p}$ will have a value less than or equal to 7/10. That is, the goal is to determine $P(\hat{p} \leq 0.7)$. Using methods already described, the exact probability is 0.945. Using the approximation given by Equation (5.5),

$$P(\hat{p} \leq 0.7) = P\left(Z \leq \frac{0.7 - 0.5}{\sqrt{0.5(1 - 0.5)/10}} \right) = P(Z \leq 1.264911).$$

Referring to Table B.1 in Appendix B, $P(Z \leq 1.264911) = 0.897$, which differs from the exact value by $0.945 - 0.897 = 0.048$.

Example

We repeat the previous example, only now we approximate $P(0.3 \leq \hat{p} \leq 0.7)$. So, referring to Equation (5.6), $b = 0.7$,

$$\frac{b - p}{\sqrt{p(1 - p)/n}} = \frac{0.7 - 0.5}{\sqrt{0.5(1 - 0.5)/10}} = 1.264911$$

$$\frac{a - p}{\sqrt{p(1 - p)/n}} = \frac{0.3 - 0.5}{\sqrt{0.5(1 - 0.5)/10}} = -1.264911,$$

so the approximation of $P(0.3 \leq \hat{p} \leq 0.7)$ is

$$P(Z \leq 1.264911) - P(Z \leq -1.264911) = 0.8970484 - 0.1029516 = 0.7940968.$$

The exact value is 0.890625. (There are many ways of improving the approximation when n is small, some of which are mentioned in later chapters.)

Example

Consider a binomial distribution with $p = 0.5$ and $n = 100$, and imagine that we want to determine the probability that $\hat{p}$ will have a value less than or equal to 0.55. The exact value is 0.8643735. The approximation based on the central limit theorem is

$$P(\hat{p} \leq 0.55) = P(Z \leq 1) = 0.8413447.$$

So, compared to the examples based on $n = 10$, we see that we get a better approximation here. This is to be expected based on the central limit theorem, which says that the approximation will improve as the sample size gets large.

Example

We repeat the last example, only now we compute the probability that $\hat{p}$ will have a value between 0.45 and 0.55. Referring to Equation (5.6), the approximate value of this probability is

$$P(Z \leq 1) - P(Z \leq -1) = 0.6826895.$$

The exact value is 0.6802727. So, again, we see that the approximation is performing better compared to the situation where $n = 10$.

Example

Again, consider the case $n = 100$, only now $p = 0.05$, and we want to determine the probability that $\hat{p}$ will be less than or equal to 0.03. So, now

$$\frac{c - p}{\sqrt{p(1-p)/n}} = \frac{0.03 - 0.05}{\sqrt{0.05(1 - 0.05)/100}} = -0.917663,$$

and based on the central limit theorem, $P(\hat{p} \leq 0.03)$ is approximately equal to $P(Z \leq -0.9176629) = 0.1794$. The exact value is 0.2578387. In contrast, with $n = 10$, the approximate value is 0.386 and the exact value 0.599, again illustrating that the approximation improves as the sample size gets large and that the approximation is less accurate than when p is close to 0 or 1.

5.3.2   Approximating the Sampling Distribution of the Sample Mean: The General Case

This section deals with approximating the distribution of the sample mean, via the central limit theorem, for the more general case where X is virtually any variable having some unknown nonnormal distribution. Of particular importance is gaining some sense of when reliance on the central limit theorem provides a reasonably accurate approximation and when it can be unsatisfactory. This issue can be addressed using a *simulation study*. That is, observations are generated from some specified distribution, the sample mean is computed, and this process is repeated many times. If, for example, 5,000 sample means are generated in this manner, a fairly good approximation of the sampling distribution of the sample mean is obtained. Moreover, a plot of the resulting sample means provides an indication of the extent to which the sample mean has a normal distribution.

The immediate goal is to consider what happens when observations are sampled from a symmetric distribution where outliers tend to be common. In particular, consider the situation where 10 observations are randomly sampling from the mixed normal distribution in Figure 4.5, the sample mean is computed and this process is repeated 5,000 times yielding 5,000 sample means. (R code illustrating how to perform this type of simulation is described in Section 5.5. Values from a mixed normal distribution can be generated with the R function `cnorm`.). A plot of the resulting sample means is shown in Figure 5.3a. Also shown is the approximation of the distribution stemming from the central limit theorem. Figure 5.3b shows the distribution of the sample means when the sample size is increased to $n = 40$ and the approximation based on the central limit theorem. The approximation is fairly good with $n = 10$, and for $n = 40$, it is quite accurate.

Next, consider the sampling distribution of the sample mean when sampling from the skewed distributions shown in Figure 5.4 The distribution shown in Figure 5.4a is relatively light-tailed, roughly meaning that a random sample tends to contain a

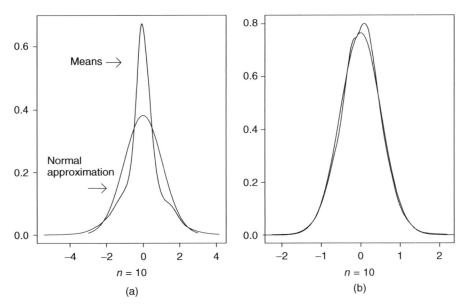

Figure 5.3   As the sample size gets large, the sampling distribution of the sample mean will approach a normal distribution under random sampling. Here, observations were sampled from a symmetric distribution where outliers tend to occur

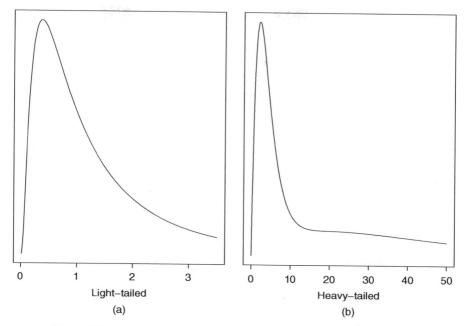

0   1   2   3   0   10   20   30   40   50

Light–tailed   Heavy–tailed

(a)   (b)

Figure 5.4   Examples of skewed distributions having light and heavy tails

relatively small proportion of outliers. The distribution in Figure 5.4b is heavier tailed, meaning that outliers are more common.

The top left panel of Figure 5.5 shows a plot of 5,000 sample means when sampling from the light-tailed distribution with $n = 10$, and the top right panel is the sampling distribution when $n = 40$. The bottom two panels show plots of the sample means when sampling from the heavy-tailed distribution instead, again with $n = 10$ and 40. When $n = 10$, the approximation based on the central limit theorem is not very satisfactory, especially when dealing with a heavy-tailed distribution. When $n = 40$, the approximation is better as expected based on the central limit theorem, but note that again the approximation is noticeably worse when sampling is from the skewed, heavy-tailed distribution, particularly in the left tail.

Important Comment Figures 5.3 and 5.5 illustrate why it is commonly assumed that with a sample size of 40 or more, normality can be assumed when using the sample mean. Historically, the classic illustrations of the central limit theorem were based on two specific distributions. One is called a uniform distribution for which outliers are very rare. (The uniform distribution is a symmetric distribution with no tails.) The other is called an exponential distribution, which is skewed and light-tailed, again meaning that few outliers are typically encountered. Both of these distributions look nothing like a normal distribution, and again we find that with $n = 40$, the sampling distribution of the sample mean is well approximated by a normal distribution. These findings have had a tremendous influence regarding views about how large the sample size must be to justify normality when using the sample mean. But despite the

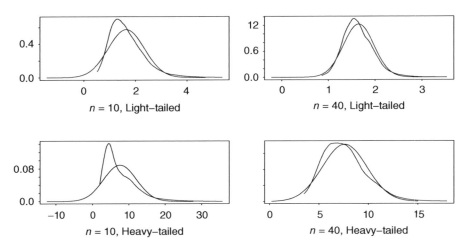

Figure 5.5   The distributions of 5,000 sample means when sampling from the skewed distributions in Figure 5.4. The symmetric distributions are the distributions of the sample mean based on the central limit theorem. With skewed, light-tailed distributions, smaller sample sizes are needed to assume that the sample mean has a normal distribution compared to situations where sampling is from a heavy-tailed distribution

illustrations of the central limit theorem provided here, nonnormality can be a very serious concern when using the mean for reasons that will made evident in subsequent chapters.

Although an argument can be made that in general, the sampling distribution of the mean is approximately normal with $n = 40$, it should be noted that there are circumstances where this rule breaks down. One such situation is the binomial distribution where the probability of success, p, is close to 0 or 1. Another situation is where extreme outliers occur.

Example

Forty values were sampled, with replacement, from the sexual attitude data in Table 2.3. If the data are stored in the R variable sexm, this can be done with the R command

```
sample(sexm,40,replace=TRUE).
```

This process was repeated 5,000 times, each time computing the sample mean. A plot of the means is shown in Figure 5.6a. As is evident, now the sampling distribution of the mean looks nothing like a normal distribution. The problem here is that sampling is from a highly skewed distribution with an extreme outlier. If the extreme outlier is removed, the resulting plot of the means is shown in Figure 5.6b. Even now, the plot of the means differs from a normal distribution in an obvious way.

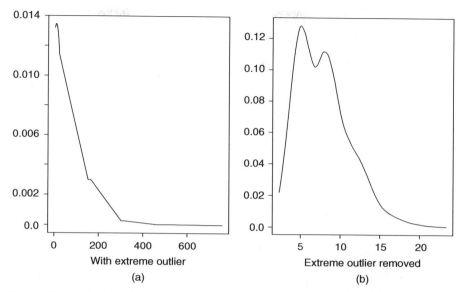

Figure 5.6   Although it is often the case that with a sample size of 40, the sampling distribution of the sample mean will be approximately normal, exceptions arise as illustrated here using the sexual attitude data

5.4   SAMPLING DISTRIBUTION OF THE MEDIAN AND 20% TRIMMED MEAN

All estimators, such as the median, 20% trimmed mean, the sample variance, and the interquartile range, have sampling distributions. The focus here is on the sampling distribution of the median and 20% trimmed mean. The median is of interest in its own right, and it helps provide perspective when trying to understand the relative merits of the mean.

An issue that has considerable practical importance is whether a version of the central limit theorem applies. That is, when can it be assumed that the median and 20% trimmed mean have, approximately, a normal distribution? The answer to this question plays a vital role in subsequent chapters.

The term *tied values* refers to a situation where duplicate values occur. For example, among the values 2, 4, 8, 12, 23, 34, 56, there are no tied values, each value occurs only once. Among the values 2, 3, 3, 4, 8, 12, 12, 12, 19, 33, 45, there are tied values: 3 occurs twice and 12 occurs three times. First, consider a situation where tied values never occur. Then, a version of the central limit theorem indicates that the sampling distribution of both the sample median and 20% trimmed mean will be approximately normal provided the sample size is not too small. But when tied values can occur, the distribution of the median does not necessarily converge to a normal distribution as the sample size increases.

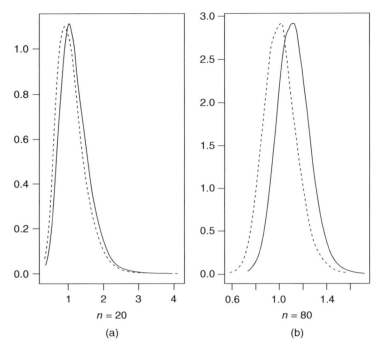

Figure 5.7   Plots of 5,000 trimmed means (solid line) and medians (dashed line). (a) Plots based on a sample size of $n = 20$. (b) The sample size is 80. As the sample size increases, the sample medians converge to a normal distribution centered around the population median, which here is 1. The 20% trimmed means converge to a normal distribution centered around the population 20% trimmed means, which here is 1.65

Example

First, consider the situation where observations are randomly sampled from a (continuous) distribution where tied values are virtually impossible. The focus here is on the skewed distribution in Figure 5.4a. Twenty values were generated (using the R function `rlnorm`), the 20% trimmed mean and median were computed, and this process was repeated 5,000 times. Figure 5.7a shows a plot of the resulting distributions. The solid line is the plot of the 20% trimmed means and the dashed line is the plot of the medians. Figure 5.7b shows the results when the sample size is $n = 80$. The population median is 1. As the sample size gets large, the medians approach a normal distribution centered around the population median. The population 20% trimmed mean is 1.11 and the sample trimmed means converge to a normal distribution centered around the population 20% trimmed mean.

Example

The last example is repeated, only observations are generated from a discrete distribution with a sample space consisting of the integers $0, 1, \ldots, 10$. Two sample sizes are considered: $n = 20$ and $n = 80$. So, tied values will occur. (The probabilities

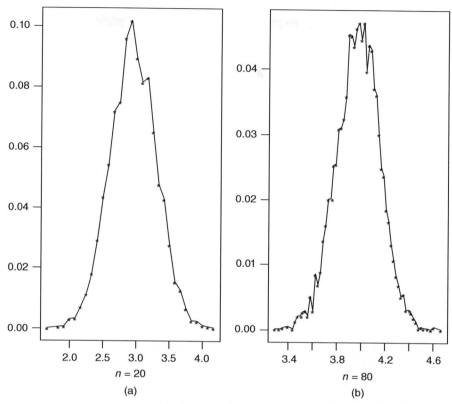

Figure 5.8   Plots of 20% trimmed means when data are generated from a discrete distribution where tied values will occur and repeated 5,000 times. (a) Plots based on a sample size of $n = 20$ and shows the relative frequencies among the observed 20% trimmed means. (b) The sample size is 80, which illustrates that the distribution of the 20% sample trimmed mean approaches a normal distribution as the sample size increases

associated with this sample space correspond to the number of success associated with a binomial distribution where the probability of success is $p = 0.4$. Data were generated with the R function rbinom.) Figure 5.8 shows the relative frequencies associated with the observed 20% trimmed means. Again, as the sample size gets large, the distribution of the 20% trimmed mean approaches a normal distribution.

But now look at the results based on the median, which are shown in Figure 5.9. In contrast to the mean and 20% trimmed mean, the distribution of the median does not converge to a normal distribution. This has important implications about how to analyze data based on the median, as will become evident in subsequent chapters. Perhaps when tied values rarely occur, the distribution of the median will converge to a normal distribution, but it is unclear when this is the case. The best strategy at the moment is that if tied values occur, do not assume that the sampling distribution of the median converges to a normal distribution.

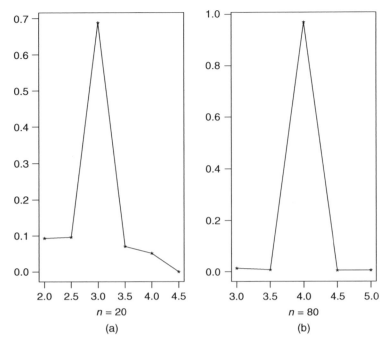

Figure 5.9 Plots of 5,000 medians when data are generated from the same discrete distribution used in Figure 5.8. (a) Plots based on a sample size of $n = 20$ and shows the relative frequencies among the observed medians. Notice that only seven values for the median were observed. (b) The sample size is 80. Now there are only five observed values for the median. In this particular case, the median does not converge to a normal distribution

5.4.1   Estimating the Standard Error of the Median

Estimating the standard error of the sample mean is straightforward: use $s/\sqrt{n}$. But when dealing with the median, no single estimator is routinely recommended. Here, a simple estimator is used that has practical value in situations to be described *provided that tied values are virtually impossible*. For a discrete distribution where tied values will occur, there is no known way of estimating the standard error of the median in a reasonably accurate manner. This is a practical concern because subsequent chapters will make it clear that standard errors play a fundamental role among many routinely used techniques. Because the standard error of the median can be estimated poorly when there are tied values, alternative methods that do not rely on the standard error will be needed.

The estimate of the standard error used here, assuming that tied values are virtually impossible, was derived by McKean and Schrader (1984). To apply it, first put the observations in ascending order, which is denoted by $X_{(1)} \le X_{(2)} \le \cdots \le X_{(n)}$. Next, compute

$$\frac{n+1}{2} - 2.5758\sqrt{\frac{n}{4}},$$

round this value to the nearest integer, and call it k. The McKean–Schrader estimate of the squared standard error of the median is

$$s_M^2 = \left(\frac{X_{(n-k+1)} - X_{(k)}}{5.1517} \right)^2$$

and the estimate of the standard error is s_M.

5.4.2   R Function msmedse

The R function

```
msmedse(x)
```

computes the McKean–Schrader estimate of the standard error of the median.

Example

The values

$$2.2, -11.0, -7.6, 7.3, -12.5, 7.5, -3.2, -14.9, -15.0, 1.1$$

are used to illustrate how to estimate the standard error of the median. Putting these values in ascending order yields

$$-15.0, -14.9, -12.5, -11.0, -7.6, -3.2, 1.1, 2.2, 7.3, 7.5.$$

So $X_{(1)} = -15$, $X_{(2)} = -14.9$, and $X_{(10)} = 7.5$. The sample size is $n = 10$ and

$$\frac{10+1}{2} - 2.5758\sqrt{\frac{10}{4}} = 1.4.$$

Rounding 1.4 to the nearest integer yields $k = 1$. Because $n - k + 1 = 10 - 1 + 1 = 10$, the squared standard error of the sample median is estimated to be

$$\left(\frac{X_{(10)} - X_{(1)}}{5.1517} \right)^2 = \left(\frac{7.5 - (-15)}{5.1517} \right)^2 = 19.075.$$

Consequently, the standard error is estimated to be $\sqrt{19.075} = 4.4$. Here are the steps using R:

```
x=c(-15.0, -14.9, -12.5, -11.0, -7.6, -3.2, 1.1, 2.2, 7.3, 7.5)

msmedse(x)
```

which returns 4.3675.

Example

There are realistic situations where the estimated standard error of the median can be substantially smaller than the estimated standard error of the mean. For example,

Harrison and Rubinfeld (1978) conducted a study dealing with the cost of homes in regions near Boston, MA. One of the variables of interest dealt with crime rates. Based on a sample size of 504, the estimated standard error of the median was 0.035 compared to 0.382 for the mean, which is more than 10 times as large as the standard error of the median. This is a substantial difference for reasons described in Chapters 6 and 7.

Example

Imagine that a training program for investing in stocks is rated on a scale between 0 and 10. So, only 11 possible outcomes are possible. Further assume that for the population of individuals who have taken the training program, the probability function corresponds to a binomial distribution with 10 trials and probability of success 0.4. If 100 observations are sampled from this distribution, it can be shown that the standard error of the median is approximately 0.098. But over 75% of the time, the McKean–Schrader estimate exceeds 0.19. That is, typically, the estimate is about twice as large as it should be, which will be seen to be a source of practical concern. Roughly, the problem here is that because the only possible values are the integers from 0 to 10, tied values will occur.

5.4.3 Approximating the Sampling Distribution of the Sample Median

Section 5.2.1 described how to compute $P(\overline{X} \leq c)$, the probability that the sample mean is less than or equal to some number c that is of interest, assuming that sampling is from a normal distribution and the population variance is known. Section 5.3 explained that for nonnormal distributions, normality can be assumed if the sample size is sufficiently large. That is, again $P(\overline{X} \leq c)$ can be computed. When duplicate values are virtually impossible, probabilities associated with the sample median can be determined as well. Letting θ (a lowercase Greek theta) represent the population median, this means that if we are given the value of the standard error of the median, say σ_M, then

$$Z = \frac{M - \theta}{\sigma_M}$$

will have, approximately, a standard normal distribution. Consequently, for any constant c, it will be approximately true that

$$P(M \leq c) = P\left(Z \leq \frac{c - \theta}{\sigma_M}\right).$$

In words, this probability can be determined by computing $(c - \theta)/\sigma_M$ and using Table B.1 in Appendix B. In practice, σ_M is not known, but it can be estimated with s_M, suggesting the approximation

$$P(M \leq c) = P\left(Z \leq \frac{c - \theta}{s_M}\right), \tag{5.7}$$

and it turns out that this approximation can be very useful.

Example

For a continuous distribution where the standard error of the median is 0.5, someone claims that the population median is 10. In symbols, the claim is that $\theta = 10$. If you collect data and find that the median is $M = 9$, and if the claim is correct, is it unusual to get a sample median this small or smaller? To find out, we determine $P(M \leq 9)$. We see that $(c - \theta)/\sigma_M = (9 - 10)/0.5 = -2$, and from Table B.1 in Appendix B, $P(Z \leq -2) = 0.023$, suggesting that the claim might be incorrect.

Example

Based on 40 values sampled from a distribution for which tied values never occur, a researcher computes the McKean–Schrader estimate of the standard error of the sample median, M, and gets $s_M = 2$. Of interest is the probability of getting a sample median less than or equal to 24 if the population median is 26. To approximate this probability, compute $(c - \theta)/S_m = (24 - 26)/2 = -1$. So, the approximate probability is $P(Z \leq -1) = 0.1587$.

Example

A study is conducted yielding the following values: 1, 3, 4, 3, 4, 2, 3, 1, 2, 3, 4, 1, 2, 1, 2. In this case, it would not be advisable to assume that the sampling distribution of the median is normal because tied (duplicated) values are common. In particular, the McKean–Schrader estimate of the standard error might perform poorly in this case.

5.4.4 Estimating the Standard Error of a Trimmed Mean

There is a simple method for estimating the squared standard error of a 20% trimmed mean:

$$\frac{s_w^2}{0.6^2 n},$$ (5.8)

where s_w^2 is the 20% Winsorized sample variance introduced in Chapter 2. The 0.6 in the denominator is related to the amount of trimming, which is assumed to be 20%. If 10% trimming is used instead, the 0.6 is replaced by 0.8. That is, double the proportion that is trimmed and subtract it from 1. The standard error of the 20% trimmed mean is estimated with the (positive) square root of this last equation:

$$\frac{s_w}{0.6\sqrt{n}}.$$ (5.9)

In practice, situations are encountered where the standard error of the mean is about as small or slightly smaller than the standard error of the 20% trimmed mean. But as will be illustrated, the standard error of the 20% trimmed mean can be substantially smaller than the standard error of the mean, which has important implications when analyzing data using methods to be described.

5.4.5   R Function trimse

The R function

```
trimse(x,tr=0.2)
```

computes an estimate of the standard error of a trimmed mean. By default, a 20% trimmed mean is used, as indicated by the argument `tr`. Setting `tr=0.1`, the function returns the standard error based on the 10% trimmed mean. Setting `tr=0`, the function returns the standard error of the sample mean, $s/\sqrt{n}$.

Example

Suppose rats are subjected to a drug that might affect aggression and that the measures of aggression are

$$5, 12, 23, 24, 18, 9, 18, 11, 36, 15.$$

The 20% Winsorized standard deviation can be computed as described in Chapter 4 and is equal to 27.1667, so the Winsorized standard deviation is 5.21. Because $n = 10$, the squared standard error of the 20% trimmed mean is estimated to be

$$\frac{27.1667}{0.36(10)} = 7.546$$

and the estimate of the standard error is $\sqrt{7.546} = 2.747$. Using the R function `trimse` instead,

```
x=c(5, 12, 23, 24, 18, 9, 18, 11, 36, 15)
trimse(x)
```

returns the value 2.747.

5.4.6   Estimating the Standard Error When Outliers Are Discarded: A Technically Unsound Approach

In recent years, there has been an increasing awareness that outliers are a serious practical concern when analyzing data using means. A seemingly natural strategy is to check for outliers, remove any that are found, and compute the mean with the remaining data. There are situations where this approach has practical value, but there are serious technical issues that are not immediately evident. One fundamental concern is estimating the standard error when outliers are removed.

To elaborate, imagine that for a random sample of n observations, we check for outliers, remove them, and now m values remain. If the sample mean is computed based on the remaining m values, how should the squared standard error be estimated? It might seem that the problem is trivial: compute the sample variance using the remaining m values and divide the result by m. This would be valid if $n - m$ values were randomly removed. But this was not done: only extreme values were removed. It can be shown that this strategy can result in a highly inaccurate estimate of the standard error regardless of how large the sample size might be (e.g., Staudte and Sheather, 1990; Wilcox, 2012a), but the technical details go beyond the scope of this book. However, we can illustrate the seriousness of this issue using methods covered in this chapter.

A 20% trimmed mean reduces the negative consequences of outliers simply because it eliminates extreme values. Notice that when using the 20% trimmed mean, the sample variance of the values left after trimming was not used when estimating the squared standard error. Rather, the 20% Winsorized variance was used, and this value was divided by $0.36n$, not m. The next example illustrates that the two methods can give substantially different results. That is, using a technically sound method can make a practical difference. Generally, a correct estimate of the standard error depends in part on how outliers are identified and removed. If, for example, outliers are identified via a boxplot, and then removed, special methods for estimating the standard error are required that are covered in more advanced books.

Example

For the data in Table 2.3, the estimated standard error of the 20% trimmed mean is 0.532 using the technically correct estimate of the standard error based on the Winsorized variance and given by Equation (5.9). There are 63 values left after trimming. Imagine that instead of using Equation (5.9), we simply use the method for the sample mean using these 63 values only. That is, compute s using these 63 values and then compute $s/\sqrt{63}$. This yields 0.28, which is about half of the value based on the Equation (5.9). Subsequent chapters will reveal that the discrepancy between these two values is substantial.

5.5 THE MEAN VERSUS THE MEDIAN AND 20% TRIMMED MEAN

One reason sampling distributions are important is that they play a fundamental role in terms of understanding the relative merits of various methods that might be used to analyze data. Consider, for example, the issue of choosing between the sample mean, a 20% trimmed mean, or the median. When and why should one be preferred over the others? A detailed answer is difficult in an introductory course: advanced training and experience are needed. However, it is important to provide at least a glimpse of some of the issues.

Momentarily consider the situation where the population of individuals under study has a standard normal distribution, in which case the mean is $\mu = 0$ and the standard deviation is $\sigma = 1$. Because the distribution is symmetric, the sample mean, 20% trimmed mean, and median are just different ways of estimating the population mean μ. Over many studies, which one performs best?

One way of addressing this issue is in terms of which one tends to be closest to the population mean over many studies. Although we cannot replicate a study numerous times, we can mimic this process on a computer, which can provide a fairly accurate answer to the question just raised. This section describes this strategy using R, which helps illustrate the notion of a sampling distribution.

Suppose we want to simulate a situation where a study is replicated 10,000 times and for each study the sample mean is computed based on $n = 20$ observations sampled from a standard normal distribution. Here are the steps that can be used with R:

```
mean.vals=NULL
for(study in 1:10000){
x=rnorm(20)
mean.vals[study]=mean(x)
}
```

The first command initializes an R variable called `mean.vals` where sample means will be stored. The command

```
for(study in 1:10000)
```

creates a loop, which in this case means that the commands within the braces will be performed 10,000 times. The first loop consists of setting the R variable `study` equal to 1 and then performing the command

```
x=rnorm(20)
```

followed by the command

```
mean.vals[study]=mean(x).
```

The command `rnorm(20)` generates data from a standard normal distribution. As indicated in Chapter 2, the R function `mean` computes the sample mean. The result is that a sample mean is stored in `mean.vals[1]`. Next, R sets `study=2`, generates a new set of 20 values, computes the mean, and stores the result in `mean.vals[2]`, and it continues in this manner 10,000 times. So, we now have 10,000 sample means stored in the R variable `mean.vals`. Notice that the process is easily replicated using the median by replacing the R command `mean.vals[study]=mean(x)` with `mean.vals[study]=median(x)`. For the 20% trimmed mean, replace `mean(x)` with the R command `mean(x,0.2)`.

Figure 5.10 shows boxplots of the resulting means, medians, and 20% trimmed means that were obtained using the R commands just described. Notice that the 10,000 means are more tightly centered around the population mean compared to the 20% trimmed means and medians. Roughly, this indicates that over many studies, the sample mean $\overline{X}$ will tend to be closer to the population mean μ.

But what happens when values are sampled from a nonnormal distribution? In some situations, the sample mean will again have less variation than median and 20% trimmed mean, but there are situations where the reverse is true, sometimes strikingly so. As an illustration, the simulation study is repeated, only now values

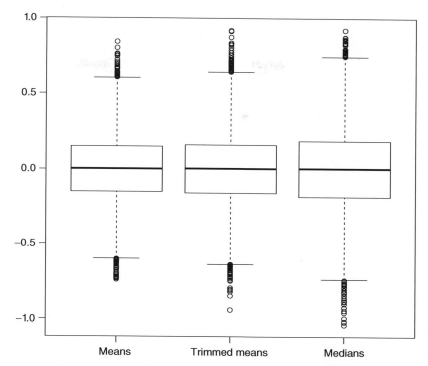

Figure 5.10 Boxplots of 10,000 means, 20% trimmed means, and medians using data sampled from a normal distribution

are generated from the mixed normal shown in Figure 4.5. (This can be done using R by replacing the R function `rnorm(20)` with `cnorm(20)`, assuming that the R functions written for this book have been installed as described in Section 1.4.) Figure 5.11 shows the resulting boxplots. Now there is substantially more variation among the means.

We repeat the simulation study, only this time observations are sampled from a skewed distribution for which the proportion of values flagged as an outlier tends to be relatively small. A plot of the distribution from which observations are sampled is shown in Figure 5.4a. Now data are generated with the R command `rlnorm(20)`. The resulting boxplots are shown in Figure 5.12. As is evident, there is substantially more variation among the means compared to the 20% trimmed means and medians. Notice that the means tend to be larger than the 20% trimmed means and medians simply because for a skewed distribution, the mean, 20% trimmed mean, and median are estimating different values. That is, the population mean, 20% trimmed mean, and median generally differ when dealing with a skewed distribution.

The main point for now is that in some situations, the sample mean has less variation compared to the 20% trimmed mean and median, but in other situations, the reverse is true, sometimes substantially so. Gaining a deep and accurate understanding of data requires in part some awareness of this fact and how it might be addressed. Subsequent chapters elaborate on this issue.

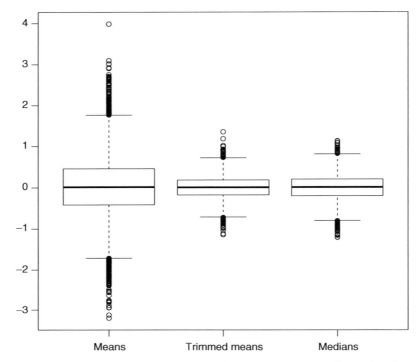

Figure 5.11 Boxplots of 10,000 means, 20% trimmed means, and medians using data sampled from a mixed normal distribution

Example

We have seen situations where there is less variability among the trimmed means and medians over many studies compared to the variability among the means. A practical issue is whether the standard errors of the trimmed mean and median are ever substantially smaller than the standard error of the mean when dealing with data from actual studies. Consider data from a study on self-awareness. A portion of the study dealt with how long a participant could keep a portion of an apparatus in contact with a specified target. Here are the results:

$$77, 87, 88, 114, 151, 210, 219, 246, 253, 262, 296, 299, 306, 376, 428, 515,$$

$$666, 1310, 2611.$$

The trimmed mean is $\overline{X}_t = 283$ and its estimated standard error is 56.1. In contrast, the standard error of the sample mean is $s/\sqrt{n} = 136$, a value approximately 2.4 times larger than the sample standard error of the trimmed mean. So, the trimmed mean has a much smaller standard error than the mean. The sample median has an estimated standard error of 77.8.

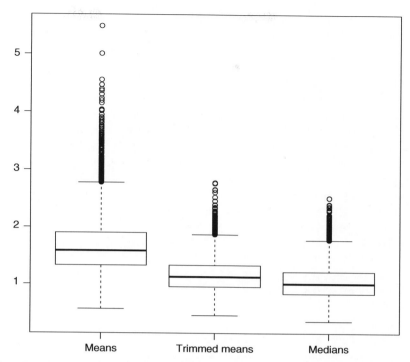

Figure 5.12 Boxplots of 10,000 means, 20% trimmed means, and medians using data sampled from the skewed distribution in Figure 5.4a for which the proportion of values declared an outlier is typically small

5.6 SUMMARY

- The sampling distribution of the sample mean reflects the likelihood of getting particular values for $\overline{X}$. In particular, it provides information about the likelihood that $\overline{X}$ will be close to the population mean, μ, when a study is repeated many times. That is, the sampling distribution of the sample mean provides some sense of how well $\overline{X}$ estimates the population mean μ. The accuracy of $\overline{X}$, in terms of estimating the population mean, is reflected by its standard error, $\sigma/\sqrt{n}$.

- All estimators, such as the sample median, the 20% trimmed mean, and the sample variance have a sampling distribution. If a study could be repeated millions of times, each time yielding a sample variance, s^2, we would know, for example, the sampling distribution of s^2 to a high degree of accuracy. That is, we could determine $P(s^2 \leq c)$ for any constant c.

- Under normality and random sampling, the sampling distribution of $\overline{X}$ is also normal with mean μ and variance σ^2/n.

- The standard errors corresponding to the mean, the 20% trimmed mean, and the median can differ substantially. For the special case where sampling is from a perfectly symmetric distribution, this means that there are conditions where the median and 20% trimmed mean can provide a much more accurate estimate of the population mean relative to the sample mean, $\overline{X}$.

- Estimating the standard error of the mean and 20% trimmed mean is relatively simple. The same is true when using the median provided tied values never occur. But with tied values, obtaining a reasonably accurate estimate of the standard error of the median can be difficult even with very large sample sizes.

- The central limit theorem indicates that with a sufficiently large sample size, the sample mean will have, approximately, a normal distribution. It appears that usually, but not always, normality can be assumed with a sample size of $n \geq 40$. This result is sometimes taken to mean that normality can be assumed when using basic methods based on the mean, which are covered in subsequent chapters. But it is stressed that this is not always the case, even when outliers are relatively rare, for reasons that will be described in Section 6.5.1.

- A version of the central limit theorem also indicates that the sampling distribution of the 20% trimmed mean will be approximately normal provided the sample size is not too small. Currently, it seems that tied values have little or no impact on this result. But when dealing with the median, assuming normality can be highly unsatisfactory when tied values can occur.

5.7   EXERCISES

1. For a binomial with $n = 25$ and $p = 0.5$, determine (a) $P(\hat{p} \leq 15/25)$, (b) $P(\hat{p} > 15/25)$, (c) $P(10/25 \leq \hat{p} \leq 15/25)$.

2. Many research teams intend to conduct a study regarding the proportion of people who have colon cancer. If a random sample of 10 individuals could be obtained, and if the probability of having colon cancer is 0.05, what is the probability that a research team will get $\hat{p} = 0.1$?

3. In the previous problem, what is the probability of $\hat{p} = 0.05$?

4. Someone claims that the probability of losing money, when using an investment strategy for buying and selling commodities, is 0.1. If this claim is correct, what is the probability of getting $\hat{p} \leq 0.05$ based on a random sample of 25 investors?

5. You interview a married couple and ask the wife whether she supports the current leader of their country. Her husband is asked the same question. Describe why it might be unreasonable to view these two responses as a random sample.

6. Imagine that 1,000 research teams draw a random sample from a binomial distribution with $p = 0.4$, with each study based on a sample size of 30. So, this would result in 1,000 $\hat{p}$ values. If these 1,000 values were averaged, what, approximately, would be the result?

7. In the previous problem, if you computed the sample variance of the $\hat{p}$ values, what, approximately, would be the result?

8. Suppose $n = 16$, $\sigma = 2$, and $\mu = 30$. Assume normality and determine (a) $P(\overline{X} \le 29)$, (b) $P(\overline{X} \ge 30.5)$, (c) $P(29 \le \overline{X} \le 31)$.

9. Suppose $n = 25$, $\sigma = 5$, and $\mu = 5$. Assume normality and determine (a) $P(\overline{X} \le 4)$, (b) $P(\overline{X} \ge 7)$, (c) $P(3 \le \overline{X} \le 7)$.

10. Someone claims that within a certain neighborhood, the average cost of a house is $\mu = \$100,000$ with a standard deviation of $\sigma = \$10,000$. Suppose that based on $n = 16$ homes, you find that the average cost of a house is $\overline{X} = \$95,000$. Assuming normality, what is the probability of getting a sample mean this low or lower if the claims about the mean and standard deviation are true?

11. In the previous problem, what is the probability of getting a sample mean between $\$97,500$ and $\$102,500$?

12. A company claims that the premiums paid by its clients for auto insurance has a normal distribution with mean $\mu = \$750$ dollars and standard deviation $\sigma = 100$. Assuming normality, what is the probability that for $n = 9$ randomly sampled clients, the sample mean will have a value between $\$700$ and $\$800$?

13. Imagine you are a health professional interested in the effects of medication on the diastolic blood pressure of adult women. For a particular drug being investigated, you find that for $n = 9$ women, the sample mean is $\overline{X} = 85$ and the sample variance is $s^2 = 160.78$. Estimate the standard error of the sample mean, assuming random sampling.

14. You randomly sample 16 observations from a discrete distribution with mean $\mu = 36$ and variance $\sigma^2 = 25$. Use the central limit theorem to determine (a) $P(\overline{X} \le 34)$, (b) $P(\overline{X} \le 37)$, (c) $P(\overline{X} \ge 33)$, (d) $P(34 \le \overline{X} \le 37)$.

15. You sample 25 observations from a nonnormal distribution with mean $\mu = 25$ and variance $\sigma^2 = 9$. Use the central limit theorem to determine (a) $P(\overline{X} \le 24)$, (b) $P(\overline{X} \le 26)$, (c) $P(\overline{X} \ge 24)$, (d) $P(24 \le \overline{X} \le 26)$.

16. Describe a situation where reliance on the central limit theorem to determine $P(\overline{X} \le 24)$ might be unsatisfactory.

17. Describe situations where a normal distribution provides a good approximation of the sampling distribution of the mean.

18. For the values 4, 8, 23, 43, 12, 11, 32, 15, 6, 29, verify that the McKean–Schrader estimate of the standard error of the median is 7.57.

19. In the previous exercise, how would you argue that the method used to estimate the standard error of the median is a reasonable approach?

20. For the values 5, 7, 2, 3, 4, 5, 2, 6, 7, 3, 4, 6, 1, 7, 4, verify that the McKean–Schrader estimate of the standard error of the median is 0.97.

21. In the previous exercise, how would you argue that the method used to estimate the standard error of the median might be highly inaccurate?

22. In Exercise 20, would it be advisable to approximate $P(M \le 4)$, the probability that the sample median is less than or equal to 4, using Equation (5.7)?

23. For the values 2, 3, 5, 6, 8, 12, 14, 18, 19, 22, 201, why would you suspect that the McKean–Schrader estimate of the standard error of the median will be smaller than the standard error of the mean? (Hint: Consider features of data that can have

a large impact on s, the sample standard deviation, and recall that the standard error of the mean is $s/\sqrt{n}$.) Verify that this speculation is correct.

24. Summarize when it would and would not be reasonable to assume that the sampling distribution of M, the sample median, is normal.

25. For the values

$$59, 106, 174, 207, 219, 237, 313, 365, 458, 497, 515,$$

$$529, 557, 615, 625, 645, 973, 1065, 3215,$$

estimate the standard error of the 20% trimmed mean.

26. For the data in Exercise 25, why would you suspect that the standard error of the sample mean will be larger than the standard error of the 20% trimmed mean? Verify that this speculation is correct.

27. The ideal estimator of location would have a smaller standard error than any other estimator we might use. Explain why such an estimator does not exist.

28. Under normality, the sample mean has a smaller standard error than the 20% trimmed mean or median. If observations are sampled from a distribution that appears to be normal, does this suggest that the mean should be preferred over the trimmed mean and median?

29. If the sample mean and 20% trimmed mean are nearly identical, it might be thought that for future studies, it will make little difference which measure of location is used. Comment on why this is not necessarily the case.

30. Observations can be generated from the distribution in Figure 5.4a using the R command rlnorm. For example, rlnorm(25) would generate 25 observations. Indicate the R commands for determining the sampling distribution of the sample median, M. In particular, how would you determine the probability that M will have a value less than 1.5?

6

CONFIDENCE INTERVALS

As pointed out in the previous chapters, the sample mean, $\overline{X}$, estimates the population mean μ, but typically the estimate will not be exactly correct. That is, it is generally the case that $\overline{X} \neq \mu$. Consequently, a fundamental goal is determining what values for the population mean are reasonable based on the available data. In a similar manner, $\hat{p}$, the proportion of successes among n observations, estimates the true probability of success p associated with a binomial distribution, but generally $\hat{p} \neq p$. Based on data, how might we determine a range of values that is likely to contain the true value of p? For example, imagine that based on 100 observations $\hat{p} = 0.8$. Is it reasonable to conclude that p, the true probability of success, is at least 0.5?

A classic strategy for addressing these problems, one that is routinely used today, was derived by Laplace about two centuries ago. The basic idea is to take advantage of results related to sampling distributions covered in Chapter 5. There are conditions where this classic strategy performs very well, but today it is realized that there are general conditions where some of the better-known techniques can fail miserably as will be illustrated. So, an important goal is understanding when routinely used methods are satisfactory as well as when and why they can be unsatisfactory. Another important goal is to provide a glimpse of modern robust methods that are designed to deal with the shortcomings with techniques typically covered in an introductory course.

6.1 CONFIDENCE INTERVAL FOR THE MEAN

A *confidence interval* for the population mean μ is an interval, based on the observed data, that contains μ with some specified probability. Generally, confidence intervals

Understanding and Applying Basic Statistical Methods Using R, First Edition. Rand R. Wilcox.
© 2017 John Wiley & Sons, Inc. Published 2017 by John Wiley & Sons, Inc.
www.wiley.com/go/Wilcox/Statistical_Methods_R

will vary over studies. For instance, one study might suggest that the interval $(2, 14)$ contains μ, and another study might suggest that the interval $(5, 10)$ contains μ. If, for example, 95% of the confidence intervals over (infinitely) many studies contain μ, then the resulting confidence interval is said to be a 0.95 confidence interval for μ. That is, consistent with Chapter 5, probabilities are viewed as proportions over many studies.

To describe how a confidence interval is computed, a distinction is made between two situations. The first is that σ^2 is known (i.e., you are given the value of σ^2 in a problem). The second is that σ^2 is not known, but the sample variance s^2 is available, which provides an estimate of σ^2.

6.1.1 Computing a Confidence Interval Given σ^2

We begin with the simplest case where sampling is from a normal distribution and the population variance, σ^2, is known. In reality, σ^2 is rarely known, but momentarily assuming that σ^2 is known simplifies the reasoning and helps make clear the principles underlying the method. Once the basic principle is described, more realistic situations are covered where σ^2 is unknown, in which case it is estimated with the sample variance s^2. Strategies for handling nonnormal distributions will be covered as well.

The key to computing a confidence interval when σ is known is being able to determine the quantiles of

$$Z = \frac{\overline{X} - \mu}{\sigma / \sqrt{n}}. \tag{6.1}$$

As explained in Chapter 5, this can be done when sampling from a normal distribution because Z has a standard normal distribution. For example, from Chapter 5, when normality is assumed,

$$P(-1.96 \leq Z \leq 1.96) = 0.95.$$

Because Z is given by Equation (6.1), this last equation becomes

$$P\left(-1.96 \leq \frac{\overline{X} - \mu}{\sigma / \sqrt{n}} \leq 1.96\right) = 0.95.$$

Here is the point: Rearranging terms in this last equation, we see that

$$P\left(\overline{X} - 1.96 \frac{\sigma}{\sqrt{n}} \leq \mu \leq \overline{X} + 1.96 \frac{\sigma}{\sqrt{n}}\right) = 0.95.$$

That is, the population mean μ is not known, but with probability 0.95, the population mean is between $\overline{X} - 1.96\sigma/\sqrt{n}$ and $\overline{X} + 1.96\sigma/\sqrt{n}$. The interval

$$\left(\overline{X} - 1.96 \frac{\sigma}{\sqrt{n}}, \overline{X} + 1.96 \frac{\sigma}{\sqrt{n}}\right)$$

is a 0.95 confidence interval for the population mean.

TABLE 6.1 Additional Hours Sleep Gained by Using an Experimental Drug

Patient	Increase
1	1.2
2	2.4
3	1.3
4	1.3
5	0.0
6	1.0
7	1.8
8	0.8
9	4.6
10	1.4

Example

Ten patients were given a drug to increase the number of hours they sleep. Table 6.1 shows some hypothetical data for which the sample mean is $\overline{X} = 1.58$. Momentarily assume that among all patients who might have been measured, the increase in the amount of sleep has a normal distribution with variance $\sigma^2 = 1.664$. So, the standard error of the sample mean is $\sigma/\sqrt{n} = \sqrt{1.1664/10} = 0.408$ and

$$P\left(-1.96 \leq \frac{\overline{X} - \mu}{0.408} \leq 1.96\right) = 0.95.$$

Rearranging terms in this last equation and noting that $1.96 \times 0.408 = 0.8$, we see that

$$P(\overline{X} - 0.8 \leq \mu \leq \overline{X} + 0.8) = 0.95. \tag{6.2}$$

In words, there is a 95% chance that the interval $(\overline{X} - 0.8, \overline{X} + 0.8)$ contains the unknown population mean, μ. For the data at hand, $\overline{X} = 1.58$, so

$$(\overline{X} - 0.8, \overline{X} + 0.8) = (0.78, 2.38) \tag{6.3}$$

is a 0.95 confidence interval for the mean. That is, different studies will result in different sample means, but the confidence interval was constructed so that with probability 0.95, it will contain the unknown population mean.

Rather than compute a 0.95 confidence interval, it might be desired to compute a 0.99 or 0.90 confidence interval instead. From Table B.1 in Appendix B, or as pointed out in Chapter 4, it can be seen that the probability of a standard normal random variable having a value between -2.58 and 2.58 is 0.99. That is,

$$P(-2.58 \leq Z \leq 2.58) = 0.99.$$

Proceeding as was done in the last paragraph, this implies that

$$\left(\overline{X} - 2.58\frac{\sigma}{\sqrt{n}}, \overline{X} + 2.58\frac{\sigma}{\sqrt{n}} \right)$$

is a 0.99 confidence interval for μ. In the last example, $\sigma/\sqrt{10} = 0.408$, so now the confidence interval for μ is $(0.53, 2.63)$.

> *Notation.* A common notation for the probability that a confidence interval does *not* contain the population mean μ is α, where α is a lowercase Greek alpha. When computing a 0.95 confidence interval, $\alpha = 1 - 0.95 = 0.05$. For a 0.99 confidence interval, $\alpha = 0.01$, meaning that there is a 0.01 probability that the resulting confidence interval does not contain the population mean.

Constructing a confidence interval for the mean can be described in a slightly more general context as follows, still assuming that sampling is from a normal distribution. Imagine that the goal is to compute a $1 - \alpha$ confidence interval. The first step is to determine c such that the probability of a standard normal random variable being between $-c$ and c is $1 - \alpha$. In symbols, determine c such that

$$P(-c \leq Z \leq c) = 1 - \alpha.$$

From Chapter 4, this means that

$$P(Z \leq c) = \frac{1 + (1 - \alpha)}{2}$$
$$= 1 - \frac{\alpha}{2}.$$

Put another way, c is the $1 - \alpha/2$ quantile of a standard normal distribution. For example, if the goal is to compute a $1 - \alpha = 0.95$ confidence interval, then

$$\frac{1 + (1 - \alpha)}{2} = \frac{1 + 0.95}{2} = 0.975,$$

and from Table B.1 in Appendix B,

$$P(Z \leq 1.96) = 0.975,$$

so $c = 1.96$. For convenience, Table 6.2 lists the value of c for three common choices for $1 - \alpha$.

Once c is determined, a $1 - \alpha$ confidence interval for μ is

$$\left(\overline{X} - c\frac{\sigma}{\sqrt{n}}, \overline{X} + c\frac{\sigma}{\sqrt{n}} \right). \tag{6.4}$$

As indicated in Chapter 5, probabilities are being viewed in terms of proportions over many studies. For example, a 0.95 confidence interval for μ means that over (infinitely) many studies, 95% of the intervals will contain μ.

TABLE 6.2 Common Choices for $1 - \alpha$ and c

$1 - \alpha$	c
0.90	1.645
0.95	1.96
0.99	2.58

Definition. The *probability coverage* of a confidence interval is the probability that the interval contains the unknown parameter being estimated. The desired probability coverage is typically represented by $1 - \alpha$, with $1 - \alpha = 0.95$ or 0.99 being common choices. For the situation at hand, $1 - \alpha$ refers to the probability that Equation (6.4) will contain the population mean μ. The value $1 - \alpha$ is called the *confidence level* or *confidence coefficient* associated with a confidence interval.

Example

Imagine that a training program for improving SAT scores has been used for years and that among the thousands of students who have enrolled in the program, the average increase in their scores is 48. For illustrative purposes, imagine that the number of students is so large that for all practical purposes, it is known that the population mean is $\mu = 48$. Now imagine that a study is performed aimed at estimating the effectiveness of a new training method and that based on $n = 25$ students, the resulting sample mean is $\overline{X} = 54$. That is, the average effectiveness of the new method is estimated to be greater than the average increase using the standard method, suggesting that the new method is better for the typical student. But the sample mean is probably not equal to the population mean, so there is uncertainty about whether the experimental method would be better, on average, than the standard method if all students were to attend the new training program. For illustrative purposes, assume that the population standard deviation is known and equal to 9. That is, $\sigma = 9$. Then a 0.95 confidence interval for the unknown mean associated with the experimental method is

$$\left(54 - 1.96\frac{9}{\sqrt{25}}, 54 + 1.96\frac{9}{\sqrt{25}}\right) = (50.5, 57.5).$$

So based on the 25 students that are available, their SAT scores indicate that μ is somewhere between 50.5 and 57.5, and by design, the probability coverage (or confidence level) is 0.95, assuming normality. This interval does not contain the value 48, suggesting that the experimental method is better, on average, than the standard training technique.

Example

The last example is repeated, only this time a 0.99 confidence interval is computed instead. From Table 6.2 $c = 2.58$, so the 0.99 confidence interval for μ is

$$\left(54 - 2.58\frac{9}{\sqrt{25}}, 54 + 2.58\frac{9}{\sqrt{25}}\right) = (49.4, 58.6).$$

Note that this interval does not contain 48, again suggesting that the experimental method is better on average.

Example

Suppose that for $n = 16$ observations randomly sampled from a normal distribution, $\overline{X} = 32$, for the entire population $\sigma = 4$, and the goal is to compute a 0.9 confidence interval. So, $1 - \alpha = 0.9$ and referring to Table 6.2, $c = 1.645$. Without Table 6.2, proceed by first noting that $(1 + 0.9)/2 = 0.95$. Referring to Table B.1 in Appendix B, $P(Z \le 1.645) = 0.95$, so again $c = 1.645$. Therefore, a 0.9 confidence interval for μ is

$$\left(32 - 1.645\frac{4}{\sqrt{16}}, 32 + 1.645\frac{4}{\sqrt{16}} \right) = (30.355, 33.645).$$

Although $\overline{X}$ is not, in general, equal to μ, note that the length of the confidence interval provides some sense of how well $\overline{X}$ estimates the population mean. Here the length is $33.645 - 30.355 = 3.29$.

Example

A college president claims that IQ scores at her institution are normally distributed with a mean of $\mu = 123$ and a standard deviation of $\sigma = 12$. Suppose you randomly sample $n = 20$ students and find that $\overline{X} = 110$. Does the $1 - \alpha = 0.95$ confidence interval for the mean support the claim that the average of all IQ scores at the college is $\mu = 123$? Because $1 - \alpha = 0.95$, $c = 1.96$ and the 0.95 confidence interval for the population mean is

$$\left(110 - 1.96\frac{14}{\sqrt{20}}, 110 + 1.96\frac{14}{\sqrt{20}} \right) = (103.9, 116.1).$$

The interval $(103.9, 116.1)$ does not contain the value 123, suggesting that the president's claim might be false. But there is a 0.05 probability that the confidence interval will not contain the true population mean, so there is some possibility that the president's claim is correct.

Important Conceptual Point

In the last example, suppose that the 0.95 confidence interval is $(119, 125)$. Would it be reasonable to conclude that the president's claim (that $\mu = 123$) is correct? The answer is no. It could be that the population mean μ is 120 or 124 for example; these values would not be ruled out based on the confidence interval. Confidence intervals can provide empirical evidence that certain values for the parameter being estimated (in this case, the population mean) can probably be ruled out. But proving that the population mean is exactly 123 is virtually impossible without measuring the entire population of students under study. We can, however, improve the precision of the estimate by increasing the sample size, n. Looking at Equation (6.4), we see that the length of a confidence interval is

$$\left(\overline{X} + c\frac{\sigma}{\sqrt{n}}\right) - \left(\overline{X} - c\frac{\sigma}{\sqrt{n}}\right) = 2c\frac{\sigma}{\sqrt{n}}.$$

So, by increasing the sample size n, the length of the confidence interval decreases and reflects the extent to which the sample mean gives an improved estimate of the population mean.

Use Caution When Interpreting Confidence Intervals

Care must be taken to not read more into a confidence interval than is warranted. For the situation at hand, the probability coverage of a confidence interval reflects the likelihood, over many studies, that the confidence interval will contain the unknown population mean, μ. But there are several ways in which a confidence interval can be interpreted incorrectly, which are illustrated with the last example where 0.95 confidence interval for the average IQ score at some university was found to be (103.9, 116.1):

- 95% of all students have an IQ between 103.9 and 116.1. The error here is interpreting the ends of the confidence intervals as quantiles. That is, if among all students, the 0.025 quantile is 100.5 and the 0.975 quantile is 120.2, this means that 95% of all students have an IQ between 100.5 and 120.2. But confidence intervals for the population mean tell us nothing about the quantiles associated with all students at this university.

- There is a 0.95 probability that a randomly sampled student will have an IQ between 100.5 and 120.2. This erroneous interpretation is similar to the one just described. Again, confidence intervals do not indicate the likelihood of observing a particular IQ, but rather indicate a range of values that are likely to include μ.

- All sample means among future studies will have a value between 103.9 and 116.1 with probability 0.95. This statement is incorrect because it is about the sample mean, not the population mean. (For more details about this particular misinterpretation, see Cumming and Maillardet, 2006.)

6.2 CONFIDENCE INTERVALS FOR THE MEAN USING S (σ NOT KNOWN)

As explained in the previous section, the key to computing a confidence interval when σ is known is being able to determine the quantiles of

$$Z = \frac{\overline{X} - \mu}{\sigma/\sqrt{n}}.$$

When the standard deviation σ is not known, we estimate σ with the sample standard deviation s in which case Z becomes

$$T = \frac{\overline{X} - \mu}{s/\sqrt{n}}. \tag{6.5}$$

So now, the key to computing a confidence interval is determining the quantiles of T. A simple strategy is to assume that T has a standard normal distribution and proceed as was done in the previous section. Assuming random sampling from a normal distribution, this approach is reasonable provided the sample size is reasonably large. With a sample size of $n \geq 120$, fairly accurate confidence intervals will result when sampling from a normal distribution.

But there are two practical concerns with this approach. The first is how to deal with relatively small sample sizes. The other is that distributions are rarely if ever exactly normal. Assuming normality is convenient from a technical point of view, but to what extent does it provide a reasonably accurate approximation? If, for example, someone claims that a 0.95 confidence interval for the population mean has been computed, is it possible that the probability coverage is only 0.9 or even 0.8? Under what conditions is the actual probability coverage reasonably close to 0.95? Here, we first focus on how to proceed when the standard deviation σ is not known, still assuming normality. Then we will discuss the effects of nonnormality and how they might be addressed.

Assuming normality, William Sealy Gosset (1876–1937) derived a method for determining the quantiles of T that is routinely used today. Gosset worked for Arthur Guinness and Son, a Dublin brewery. His applied work dealt with quality control issues relevant to making beer, typically he was forced to make inferences based on small sample sizes, and so he set out to find a method that takes into account the fact that s might be a rather unsatisfactory estimate of σ. He published his results in a now famous 1908 paper, "The Probable Error of a Mean."

But initially Guinness did not allow Gosset to publish his results. Eventually, however, he was allowed to publish provided that he use a pseudonym chosen by the managing director of Guinness, C. D. La Touche. The pseudonym chosen by La Touche was "Student." For this reason, the distribution of T is called *Student's T Distribution*. The main point is that under normality, we can determine the probability that T is less than 1, less than 2, or less than t for any constant t we might choose. It turns out that the distribution of T depends on the sample size, n. By convention, the quantiles of the distribution are reported in terms of *degrees of freedom*: $\nu = n - 1$, where ν is a lower-case Greek nu. Figure 6.1 shows Student's T distribution with $\nu = 4$ degrees of freedom. Observe that the distribution is similar to a standard normal distribution. In particular, it is symmetric and bell-shaped about zero with thicker or heavier tails. With infinite degrees of freedom, Student's T and the standard normal are identical. But otherwise, Student's T distribution does not belong to the class of normal distributions, even though it has a symmetric, bell shape. That is, a distribution is called normal if the equation for the curve has the form indicated by Equation (4.6). Generally, the equation for Student's T does not have this form. Put another way, all normal distributions are symmetric and bell-shaped, but there are infinitely many symmetric and bell-shaped distributions that are not normal.

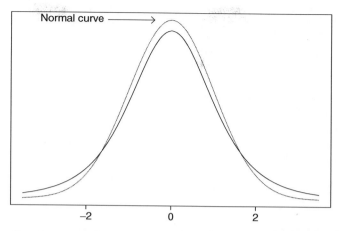

Figure 6.1   Shown is a standard normal curve and a Student's T distribution with four degrees of freedom. Student's T distributions are symmetric about zero, but they have thicker tails than a normal distribution

Table B.4 in Appendix B reports some quantiles of Student's T distribution. The first column gives the degrees of freedom. The next column, headed by $t_{0.9}$, reports the 0.9 quantiles. For example, with $v = 1$, we see 3.078 under the column headed by $t_{0.9}$. This means that $P(T \leq 3.078) = 0.9$. That is, if we randomly sample two observations from a normal distribution, in which case $v = n - 1 = 1$, there is a 0.9 probability that the resulting value for T is less than or equal to 3.078. Similarly, if $v = 24$, $P(T \leq 1.318) = 0.9$. The column headed by $t_{0.99}$ lists the 0.99 quantiles. For example, if $v = 3$, we see 4.541 under the column headed by $t_{0.99}$, so the probability that T is less than or equal to 4.541 is 0.99. If $v = 40$, Table B.2 indicates that $P(T \leq 2.423) = 0.99$. Similar to the situation when working with normal distributions,

$$P(T \geq t) = 1 - P(T \leq t), \tag{6.6}$$

where t is any constant that might be of interest. For example, with $v = 4$, $P(T \leq 2.132) = 0.95$, as previously indicated, so $P(T \geq 2.132) = 1 - P(T \leq 2.132) = 0.05$.

Computing a Confidence Interval for the Mean Using Student's T

Confidence intervals are readily computed using R. But it is instructive to be aware of the underlying strategy and how it is applied. Here are the steps for computing a $1 - \alpha$ confidence interval when working with the sample standard deviation s:

- Compute the degrees of freedom: $v = n - 1$.
- Determine the $1 - \alpha/2$ quantile, $t_{1-\alpha/2}$, using Table B.4 in Appendix B.
- The $1 - \alpha$ confidence interval for the mean is

$$\left(\overline{X} - t_{1-\alpha/2}\frac{s}{\sqrt{n}}, \overline{X} + t_{1-\alpha/2}\frac{s}{\sqrt{n}} \right). \tag{6.7}$$

Note that the confidence interval given by Equation (6.7) is similar to the confidence interval given by Equation (6.4), but with c and σ in Equation (6.4) replaced by $t_{1-\alpha/2}$ and s, respectively.

Example

Imagine that you are a health professional interested in the effects of medication on the diastolic blood pressure of adult women. For nine women taking a particular drug, their diastolic blood pressure is measured, the sample mean is $\overline{X} = 85$, and the sample variance is $s^2 = 160.78$. So, although we do not know the population variance σ^2, we have an estimate of it, namely $s^2 = 160.78$. Because $n = 9$, $s/\sqrt{n} = 4.2$. The degrees of freedom are $v = 9 - 1 = 8$, and from Table B.4 in Appendix B, the corresponding 0.975 quantile of T is $t_{0.975} = 2.306$. So, a 0.95 confidence interval for the population mean μ is
$$(85 - 2.306(4.2), 85 + 2.306(4.2)) = (75.3, 94.7).$$

Example

Doksum and Sievers (1976) report data on weight gain among rats. One group was the control and the other was exposed to an ozone environment. For illustrative purposes, attention is focused on the control group and the goal is to determine a range of possible values for the population mean that are reasonable based on the available data. Here, we compute a 0.95 confidence interval. Because there are $n = 22$ rats, the degrees of freedom are $n - 1 = 22 - 1 = 21$. Because $1 - \alpha = 0.95$, $\alpha = 0.05$, so $\alpha/2 = 0.025$, and $1 - \alpha/2 = 0.975$. Referring to Table B.4 in Appendix B, we see that the 0.975 quantile of Student's T distribution with 21 degrees of freedom is approximately $t_{0.975} = 2.08$. Because $\overline{X} = 11$ and $s = 19$, a 0.95 confidence interval is
$$11 \pm 2.08\frac{19}{\sqrt{22}} = (2.6, 19.4).$$

6.2.1   R Function t.test

The R function

```
t.test(x,conf.level=0.95)
```

computes a confidence interval for the mean using Student's T. (There are additional arguments associated with this R function that are explained in subsequent chapters.) The probability coverage is controlled via the argument conf.level, which defaults to 0.95. Setting conf.level=0.99, for example, would result in a 0.99 confidence interval.

Example

Imagine that you are interested in the reading abilities of fourth graders. A new method for enhancing reading is being considered, you try the new method on 11 students and then administer a reading test yielding the scores

12, 20, 34, 45, 34, 36, 37, 50, 11, 32, 29.

For illustrative purposes, suppose that after years of using a standard method for teaching reading, the average scores on the reading test has been found to be $\mu = 25$. Someone claims that if the new teaching method is used, the population mean will remain 25. The goal here is to determine whether this claim is consistent with the 0.99 confidence interval for μ. That is, does the 0.99 confidence interval contain the value 25? The following R commands address this issue:

```
grades=c(12, 20, 34, 45, 34, 36, 37, 50, 11, 32, 29)
t.test(gades,conf.level=0.99)
```

A portion of the output looks like this:

```
99 percent confidence interval:
       19.11674 42.70144
       sample estimates:
          mean of x
          30.90909
```

We see that the 0.99 confidence interval is (19.11674, 42.70144), the interval contains the value 25, so the results do not provide evidence that $\mu = 25$ is unreasonable. The sample mean is greater than 25, suggesting that on average the new method is better, but based on the 0.99 confidence interval, there is some possibility that on average it is actually worse than the standard method. With only 11 participants, the confidence interval is too long to resolve whether this might be the case.

6.3 A CONFIDENCE INTERVAL FOR THE POPULATION TRIMMED MEAN

As was the case when working with the population mean, we want to know how well the sample trimmed mean, $\overline{X}_t$, estimates the population trimmed mean, μ_t. What is needed is a method for computing a $1 - \alpha$ confidence interval for μ_t and here the method derived by Tukey and McLaughlin (1963) is used. Let h be the number of observations left after trimming. Similar to Student's T, let $t_{1-\alpha/2}$ be the $1 - \alpha/2$ quantile of Student's T distribution with $h - 1$ degrees of freedom and let s_w be the Winsorized sample standard deviation. The Tukey–McLaughlin confidence interval for a 20% trimmed mean is

$$\left(\overline{X}_t - t_{1-\alpha/2} \frac{s_w}{0.6\sqrt{n}}, \overline{X}_t + t_{1-\alpha/2} \frac{s_w}{0.6\sqrt{n}} \right). \tag{6.8}$$

As in Chapter 5, the 0.6 in this last equation is related to the amount of trimming, which is assumed to be 20%. If 10% trimming is used instead, the 0.6 is replaced by 0.8. That is, double the proportion that is trimmed and subtract it from 1. In terms of probability coverage, we get reasonably accurate confidence intervals for a much broader range of nonnormal distributions compared to confidence intervals for μ based on Student's T. But if the goal is to get a confidence interval for the mean, the Tukey–McLaughlin method is inappropriate when dealing with a skewed distribution because it provides a confidence interval for the population trimmed mean, which generally differs from the population mean.

6.3.1   R Function trimci

The R function

```
trimci(x,tr=0.2,alpha=0.05,null.value=0)
```

computes a $1 - \alpha$ confidence interval for μ_t, the population trimmed mean. The amount of trimming, indicated by the argument tr, defaults to 20%. If the argument alpha is unspecified, $\alpha = 0.05$ is used. (The argument null.value=0 is explained in Chapter 7.)

Example

In a sexual attitude study, different from the one described in Chapter 2, 2,282 women were asked how many sexual partners they wanted during the next 30 years. (The data are stored in the file miller_dat.txt, which can be downloaded from the author's web page as described in Section 1.5.) Storing the data in the R variable sexf, the command

```
trimci(sexf)
```

returns a 0.95 confidence interval for the 20% trimmed mean: (1.082, 1.197). The command

```
trimci(sexf,tr=0)
```

returns a 0.95 confidence interval for the mean: (0.773, 6.174). Notice that the confidence interval for the mean is substantially longer than the confidence interval for the 20% trimmed mean despite the relatively large sample size. This is because there are outliers that inflate the standard error of the mean; the standard error of the 20% trimmed mean is not affected as much by outliers because it is based in part on the Winsorized variance.

Example

The data in Table 6.3 are from a study on self-awareness and reflect how long a participant could keep a portion of an apparatus in contact with a specified target. The 20% trimmed mean is $\overline{X}_t = 283$ and its estimated standard error is $s_w/(0.6\sqrt{n}) = 146.804/(0.6\sqrt{19}) = 56.1$. In contrast, the standard error of the sample mean is $s/\sqrt{n} = 136$, a value approximately 2.4 times larger than the estimated standard error of the 20% trimmed mean. The number of observations

TABLE 6.3   Self-Awareness Data

77	87	88	114	151	210	219	246	253	262
296	299	306	376	428	515	666	1,310	2,611	

trimmed is 6, so the number of observations left after trimming is $h = 19 - 6 = 13$ and the degrees of freedom are $v = h - 1 = 12$. When computing a 0.95 confidence interval, $1 - \alpha/2 = 0.975$, and referring to Table B.4 in Appendix B, $t = 2.18$. So, the 0.95 confidence interval for the population trimmed mean is

$$283 \pm 2.18(56.1) = (160.7, 405.3).$$

The data in Table 6.3 are stored in the file dana_dat.txt, which can be downloaded as described in Section 1.5. The file contains two columns of numbers, each column corresponding to a different group. The data in Table 6.3 are stored in the first column. Here is how the analysis can be done using R:

```
aware=read.table(file='dana_dat.txt')
trimci(aware[,1])
```

As explained in Chapter 1, the first R command reads the data and stores it in the R variable `aware`. Or the command

```
aware=read.table(file.choose())
```

can be used. The R variable `aware` will have two columns with the data used here stored in aware[,1], the first column. The 0.95 confidence interval returned by `trimci` is (160.4, 405.0). It differs slightly from the numeric illustration because the calculations performed by R are accurate to more decimal places.

6.4   CONFIDENCE INTERVALS FOR THE POPULATION MEDIAN

This section describes and illustrates two methods for computing a confidence interval for the population median, θ. (Again, θ is a lowercase Greek theta.) The first method is included partly to illustrate a basic strategy used by many conventional methods for computing confidence intervals. But the other has certain practical advantages to be described.

Recall from Chapter 5 that similar to the sample mean, the sample median has a sampling distribution. Momentarily, it is assumed that there are no tied values. As noted in Chapter 5, one way of estimating the squared standard error of the sample median is with the McKean–Schrader estimator, S_M^2. The (positive) square root of this last value, S_M, estimates the standard error.

A version of the central limit theorem says that under random sampling,

$$Z_M = \frac{M - \theta}{S_M}$$

will have, approximately, a standard normal distribution if the sample size is sufficiently large. Note the similarity between this last equation and the methods for computing confidence intervals for the population mean. In practical terms, a confidence interval for the population median can be computed by assuming that Z_M has a standard normal distribution. So, an approximate 0.95 confidence interval for the population median is

$$(M - 1.96S_M, M + 1.96S_M). \tag{6.9}$$

More generally, if c is the $1 - \alpha/2$ quantile of a standard normal distribution,

$$(M - cS_M, M + cS_M) \tag{6.10}$$

is an approximate $1 - \alpha$ confidence interval for the population median.

6.4.1 R Function msmedci

The R function

```
msmedci(x,alpha=0.05,null.value=0)
```

computes a $1 - \alpha$ confidence interval for θ, the population median, using the McKean–Schrader estimate of the standard error. (The argument null.value=0 is explained in Chapter 7.) The function checks for tied values and prints a warning message if any are found.

6.4.2 Underscoring a Basic Strategy

The methods for computing a confidence interval for the mean, 20% trimmed mean, and median illustrate a general strategy for computing confidence intervals that currently dominates applied research. It is important to be aware of this strategy and to develop some sense about its relative merits compared to more modern techniques.

Consider any unknown parameter of interest, such as the population median, mean, or trimmed mean. When computing a confidence interval, the most basic strategy stems from Laplace and consists of standardizing the estimator being used. That is, subtract the parameter being estimated, divide by the standard error of the estimator, and then assume that this standardized variable has, approximately, a standard normal distribution when the sample size is reasonably large. When working with means, $\overline{X}$ estimates μ, an estimate of the standard error of $\overline{X}$ is $s/\sqrt{n}$, so this standardization takes the form

$$T = \frac{\overline{X} - \mu}{s/\sqrt{n}},$$

and an improvement on Laplace's approach was to approximate the distribution of T with Student's T distribution. When the goal is to make inferences about the population median, the sample median M estimates the population median θ, S_M estimates the standard error of M, so this same strategy suggests assuming that

$$Z_M = \frac{M - \theta}{S_M}$$

has a standard normal distribution, which in turn means that a confidence interval for the median can be computed.

It is stressed that the confidence interval for the median given by Equation (6.10) might perform poorly when duplicate or *tied* values tend to occur. As a reminder, if we observe the values 4, 7, 8, 19, 34, 1, all values occur only once, so it is said that there are no tied values. But if we observe 23, 11, 9, 8, 23, 6, 7, 1, 11, 19, 11, there are tied values because the value 11 occurred three times and the value 23 occurred twice. In Chapter 5, it was pointed out that when tied values tend to occur, S_M can be a highly unsatisfactory estimate of the standard error of the median. Consequently, any confidence interval based on S_M can be inaccurate as well.

6.4.3   A Distribution-Free Confidence Interval for the Median Even When There Are Tied Values

There are methods for computing a confidence interval for the median that perform well even when there are tied values. One such method is described here, which is *distribution free*. This means that the exact probability coverage can be determined assuming random sampling only. That is, normality is not required, even when dealing with a small sample size. The main reason for including the method based on the McKean–Schrader estimator is that it can be extended to situations where the goal is to compare two or more groups of participants. The distribution-free method described here is limited to making inferences about the population median associated with a single variable. For various situations considered in subsequent chapters, there is no extension of the method in this section that can be used.

Let Y be a binomial random variable with probability of success $p = 0.5$. Given the sample size n, consider any integer k greater than 0 but less than or equal to $n/2$. Let $A = P(Y < k)$ and recall from Chapter 4 that A can be determined from Table B.2 in Appendix B by noting that $P(Y < k) = P(Y \leq k - 1)$. Put the observations $X_1, \ldots, X_n$ in ascending order yielding $X_{(1)} \leq \cdots \leq X_{(n)}$. Then

$$(X_{(k)}, X_{(n-k+1)})$$

is a confidence interval for the population median having probability coverage $1 - 2A$, assuming random sampling only.

Example

To illustrate the method, imagine a study yielding the values

4, 12, 14, 19, 23, 26, 28, 32, 39, 43.

Note that the values are written in ascending order, so in the notation used here, $X_{(1)} = 4$, $X_{(2)} = 12$, and $X_{(10)} = 43$. Also note that the sample size is $n = 10$. The method uses confidence intervals having the form

$$(X_{(k)}, X_{(n-k+1)}),$$

where k is some integer between 1 and $n/2$. The problem is, given some choice for k, what is the probability coverage? For illustrative purposes, first consider $k = 1$ in which case $n - k + 1 = 10$. Then $P(Y < 1) = P(Y \leq 0) = 0.001$, where Y is a binomial random variable with probability of success $p = 0.5$ and $n = 10$. This means that $(X_{(1)}, X_{(10)}) = (4, 43)$ is a $1 - 2(0.001) = 0.998$ confidence interval for the population median. For $k = 2$, the confidence interval becomes $(12, 39)$. Because $P(Y < 1) = 0.010742$ (using the R function pbinom), the method used to compute a confidence interval has probability $1 - 2(0.010742) = 0.9785$ of containing the population median.

Example

To illustrate the method again, suppose $n = 15$ and consider $k = 5$. Then $P(Y < k) = P(Y \leq 4) = 0.059$ and $n - k + 1 = 11$. So $(X_{(5)}, X_{(11)})$ is a confidence interval for the population median having probability coverage $1 - 2(0.059) = 0.882$.

A limitation of the method is that if, for example, the goal is to compute a 0.95 confidence interval for the median, this cannot be done exactly because there is no choice for k such that $P(Y < k) = 0.025$ is exactly true. There is a refinement of the method aimed at dealing with this issue, but the computational details are not important for the present purposes. Rather, the R function in Section 6.4.4 is provided, which performs the calculations.

6.4.4   R Function sint

The R function

```
sint(x,alpha=0.05)
```

computes a $1 - \alpha$ confidence interval for the median using a refinement of the method in the previous section.

Example

Consider the sleep data in Table 6.1. R can be used to compute an approximate 0.95 confidence interval for the median using the following two commands:

```
x=c(1.2,2.4,1.3,1.3,0,1,1.8,.8,4.6,1.4)
sint(x)
```

The function `sint` returns two numbers: 0.93 and 2.01. That is, (0.93, 2.01) is, to a close approximation, a 0.95 confidence interval for the median. To compute a 0.99 confidence interval, use the command

```
sint(x,alpha=0.01)
```

The confidence interval returned by this command is (0.691, 2.701).

Example

Consider again the sleep data in Table 6.1 and note that there are tied values. In this case, the McKean–Schrader estimate of the standard error should not be used. To provide some perspective on why tied values are a practical concern, first note that the sample median is $M = 1.3$, the McKean–Schrader estimate of the standard error is $S_M = 0.8929$, and the 0.95 confidence interval for the population median is

$$1.3 \pm 1.96(0.8929) = (-0.45, 3.05).$$

Notice that the length of the confidence interval is 3.5. Using `sint` instead, the length of the confidence interval is much shorter: $2.01 - 0.93 = 1.08$.

6.5 THE IMPACT OF NONNORMALITY ON CONFIDENCE INTERVALS

An issue of fundamental importance is understanding when a method for computing a confidence interval continues to give reasonably accurate results when dealing with a nonnormal distribution. Said another way, how might we characterize the situations where they perform in an unsatisfactory manner? What are the relative merits of using Student's T compared to using a 20% trimmed mean or median? This section deals with these issues.

6.5.1 Student's T and Nonnormality

As previously explained, confidence intervals based on Student's T hinge on being able to determine the quantiles of

$$T = \frac{\overline{X} - \mu}{s/\sqrt{n}},$$

and when dealing with a normal distribution this is easily done. To gain a deeper understanding of how well Student's T performs when computing a confidence interval, we focus on four types of distributions:

1. Symmetric distributions that have relatively light tails, roughly meaning that the proportion of points declared outliers tends to be relatively small. This includes normal distributions as a special case.
2. Symmetric, heavy-tailed distribution: Outliers tend to be more common compared to the normal distribution.

3. Skewed, light-tailed distribution.

4. Skewed, heavy-tailed distribution.

For symmetric, light-tailed distributions, confidence intervals based on Student's T perform well. For normal distributions, the probability coverage is exact and the length of the confidence will be shorter than a confidence interval based on the 20% trimmed mean or median.

A positive feature of Student's T when dealing with a symmetric, heavy-tailed distribution is that when computing a $1 - \alpha$ confidence interval, the actual probability coverage will be at least $1 - \alpha$ and typically larger. But a concern is that the length of the confidence interval can be relatively high compared to methods based on the median or 20% trimmed mean even when a distribution appears to be approximately normal. Roughly, the reason is that the standard error of the median or 20% trimmed mean can be substantially smaller than the standard error of the mean.

Example

To illustrate the point just made, 30 observations were sampled from a mixed normal distribution using the R function cnorm. The 0.95 confidence interval based on Student's T was $(-3.62, 1.71)$, compared to $(-0.49, 0.34)$ using the median. Both confidence intervals contain zero (the true value of the population mean and median), as they should, but the confidence interval based on the median gives us a much more precise indication of the value of the population mean and median.

Next, consider a skewed, light-tailed distribution. Recall that in Chapter 5, we saw how R can be used to approximate the distribution of the sample mean via a simulation. The same strategy is used here to determine the distribution of T when dealing with nonnormal distributions. (This also helps provide a foundation for some modern inferential methods, called bootstrap techniques, to be covered.)

To outline the strategy, momentarily imagine that we know the population mean μ, we sample 21 observations, and then compute the sample mean $\overline{X}$ and the standard deviation, s. Then, of course, we can compute

$$T = \frac{\overline{X} - \mu}{s/\sqrt{n}}.$$

Further imagine that we repeat this process thousands of times. Then a plot of the resulting T values would provide a very accurate approximation of the actual distribution of T. If, for example, the proportion of T values less than or equal to 2.086 is 0.975, and if the proportion of T values less than -2.086 is 0.025, then we would know how to compute a 0.95 confidence interval for the population mean: use $t_{0.975} = 2.086$ in Equation (6.7).

Example

Consider the situation where $n = 25$ observations are generated from the distribution in Figure 6.2. The issue is whether a confidence interval based on Student's T, which assumes normality, continues to perform reasonably well when dealing with the

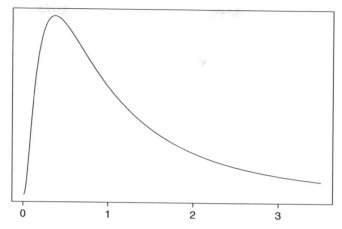

Figure 6.2   A skewed, light-tailed distribution used to illustrate the effects of nonnormality
when using Student's T

skewed, light-tailed distribution being considered here. This issue can be addressed
using a simulation study. (See Exercise 41 for details about how this can be done
using R for the situation at hand.) Briefly, generate data from the distribution in
Figure 6.2, compute T, and repeat this many times to get an approximation of the
distribution of T.

Figure 6.3 shows a plot of 5,000 T values that were generated in the manner just
described. Also shown is Student's T distribution with 24 degrees of freedom (the
distribution of T when sampling from a normal distribution). As is evident, the actual

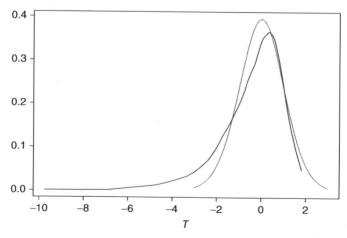

Figure 6.3   Shown is the distribution of T (solid line) when sampling from the skewed,
light-tailed distribution in Figure 6.2 and the distribution of T when sampling from a normal
distribution (dotted line)

distribution of T is poorly approximated by a Student's T distribution with 24 degrees of freedom. One obvious concern is that the actual distribution of T is not even symmetric. Suppose the goal is to compute a 0.95 confidence interval. When sampling from a normal distribution, we would use $t_{0.975} = 2.086$. That is, it is being assumed that $P(T \leq -2.086) = 0.025$ and $P(T \geq 2.086) = 0.975$. But when sampling from the skewed distribution used here, $P(T \leq -2.086)$ is approximately 0.12. The probability that T is greater than 2.086 is approximately 0.02. When computing a 0.95 confidence interval, the actual probability coverage is only 0.88, not 0.95 as intended.

It is stressed that even when the sample mean has, approximately, a normal distribution, this does not necessarily mean that Student's T will provide an accurate confidence interval. For the skewed, light-tailed distribution considered here, the distribution of the sample mean is approximately normal as was illustrated in the upper right panel of Figure 5.5. But despite this, the confidence interval for the mean is fairly inaccurate based on Student's T, as was just illustrated.

Example

Consider yet another skewed, light-tailed distribution, which is shown in Figure 6.4a. If the sample mean is based on 40 observations, its distribution is approximately normal as indicated in Figure 6.4b. The dotted curve is the normal curve used to approximate the plot of the sample means via the central limit theorem. Now look at Figure 6.5. The solid line is a plot of 5,000 T values when data are sampled from the distribution in Figure 6.4a and the dashed line is the distribution of T assuming

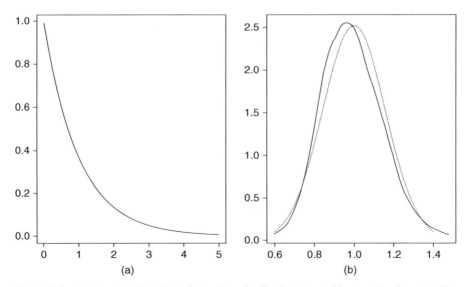

Figure 6.4 When sampling data from the distribution (a), with $n = 40$, the sampling distribution of the sample mean is approximately normal (b). But compare this to the sampling distribution of T shown in Figure 6.5

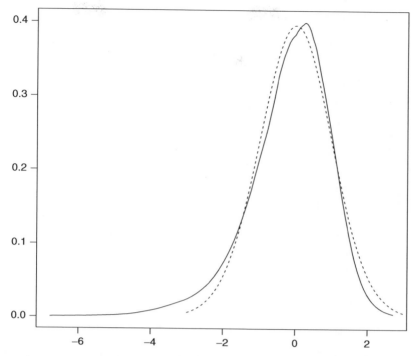

Figure 6.5 When sampling data from the distribution in Figure 6.4a, with $n = 40$, the sampling distribution of T, indicated by the solid line, differs substantially from a Student's T distribution, indicated by the dotted line, even though the sampling distribution of the sample mean is approximately normal

normality. Assuming normality, the 0.025 and 0.975 quantiles of T are -2.02 and 2.02, respectively. But the correct values when sampling from the distribution in Figure 6.4a are approximately -2.98 and 1.66, respectively, which are not reasonably close to the values under normality.

Next, consider skewed, heavy-tailed distributions. It was mentioned in Chapter 5 that roughly, when dealing with skewed distributions, as the likelihood of observing outliers increases, the larger the sample size we might need when trying to approximate the sampling distribution of the sample mean with a normal curve. When dealing with Student's T, this remains true. That is, large sample sizes might be needed so that the actual distribution of the T values will be approximately the same as the distribution under normality. Suppose that a confidence interval is considered to be reasonably accurate if the actual probability coverage is between 0.925 and 0.975. Then a sample size of 300 or more can be required.

Example

Table 2.3 reports the responses of 105 undergraduate males regarding how many sexual partners they desired over the next 30 years. Here the extreme outlier is

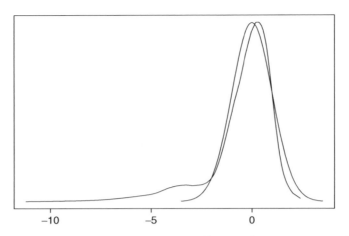

Figure 6.6   When dealing with data from actual studies, situations are encountered where the actual distribution of T differs even more from the distribution of T under normality than is indicated in Figures 6.3 and 6.5. Shown is the distribution of T when sampling from the data in Table 2.3, with the extreme outlier removed. The sample size is $n = 104$. With the extreme outlier included, the distribution of T becomes even more skewed to the left

removed, leaving 104 observations. Imagine that we resample, with replacement, 104 observations from these values. (Sampling with replacement means that when an observation is sampled, it is put back, so it has the possibility of being chosen again.) In effect, we are sampling from a distribution with a known mean, which is the sample mean of our observed data. Consequently, we can compute T. Repeating this process 1,000 times yields an approximation of the distribution of T, which is shown in Figure 6.6. (In essence, this is a bootstrap-t technique, which is discussed later in this chapter.) The smooth symmetric curve is the distribution of T assuming normality. As is evident, the two curves differ substantially.

The performance of Student's T can be summarized as follows:

- When sampling from a symmetric distribution where outliers tend to be rare, such as any normal distribution, Student's T performs well in terms of both probability coverage and the length of the resulting confidence interval relative to other methods that might be used.
- When sampling from an asymmetric distribution where outliers tend to be rare, a sample size of 200 or more might be needed to get a reasonably accurate confidence interval. A positive feature is that the length of the confidence interval continues to compete well with other methods. Also, even when the distribution of the sample mean is approximately normal, it is possible that Student's T is providing inaccurate confidence intervals unless the sample size is fairly large.
- When sampling from a symmetric distribution where outliers tend to be common, the probability coverage of a confidence interval based on Student's

T will generally be greater than or equal to the intended level. But the confidence interval based on Student's T might be substantially wider relative to other methods that might be used.

- When sampling from an asymmetric distribution where outliers tend to be common, a sample size of 300 or more might be needed to get accurate probability coverage, and the length of the confidence interval will tend to be large compared to alternative techniques.

6.5.2 Nonnormality and the 20% Trimmed Mean

The Tukey–McLaughlin method for computing a confidence interval for a 20% trimmed mean assumes that

$$T_t = \frac{0.6(\overline{X}_t - \mu_t)}{s_w/\sqrt{n}} \tag{6.11}$$

has a Student's T distribution with $h - 1$ degrees of freedom, where h is the number of observations left after trimming. This assumption is reasonable when sampling from a normal distribution. To get some idea about how it performs when sampling from a nonnormal distribution, consider again the distribution in Figure 6.2. We repeat the simulation study done using Student's T, only now we use the Tukey–McLaughlin method based on a 20% trimmed mean. Again the sample size is taken to be 25. Figure 6.7 shows a plot of the distribution of T_t as well as a plot of Student's T distribution with 14 degrees of freedom. Comparing Figure 6.7 to Figure 6.3, we see that there is now a closer match with a Student's T distribution when using a 20%

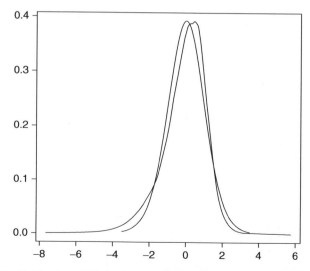

Figure 6.7 The distribution of T_t based on $n = 25\%$ and 20% trimming when sampling observations from the distribution in Figure 6.2. The distribution of T_t when sampling from a normal distribution is indicated by the dashed line. Compare this to Figure 6.3

trimmed mean. The left tail again extends out farther than is assumed when using a 20% trimmed mean, but the accuracy of the confidence interval is better using a 20% trimmed mean rather than the mean. For the mean, the actual probability coverage is only 0.88 when attempting to compute a 0.95 confidence interval, as previously indicated. For the 20% trimmed mean, the actual probability coverage is 0.936.

6.5.3   Nonnormality and the Median

The confidence interval for the population median, based on the McKean–Schrader estimate of the standard error, assumes that

$$Z_M = \frac{M - \theta}{S_M}$$

has a standard normal distribution. Again, an important issue is the extent to which this assumption is reasonable when sampling from a nonnormal distribution. To provide some perspective, again, observations are sampled from the distribution shown in Figure 6.2. Figure 6.8 shows the distribution of Z_M as well as a standard normal distribution. Now, when attempting to compute a 0.95 confidence interval, the actual probability coverage is 0.975. Notice that as the amount of trimming increases, sampling from the skewed distribution considered here has less of an impact on the accuracy of the confidence interval. Also, in this particular case, there is little difference between the 20% trimmed mean and median in terms of achieving accurate probability coverage. But we will see that the choice between these two estimators can make a practical difference.

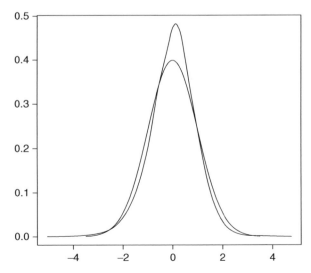

Figure 6.8   The distribution of Z_M based on $n = 25$ and when sampling observations from the distribution in Figure 6.2. The distribution of Z_M when sampling from a normal distribution is indicated by the dashed line. Compare this to Figures 6.3 and 6.7

When tied values are virtually impossible, Z_M can be assumed to have a standard normal distribution under fairly general conditions. With a few tied values, it might be that Z_M again has, approximately, a standard normal distribution. But at some point, this is no longer the case. To be safe, the method in Section 6.4.3 should be used when computing a confidence interval for the population median.

6.6   SOME BASIC BOOTSTRAP METHODS

This section introduces two basic bootstrap methods for computing a confidence interval: a percentile bootstrap method and a bootstrap-t method. Bootstrap methods are not a panacea for analyzing data. But for certain goals that have considerable practical importance, bootstrap methods are the only known techniques that perform reasonably well, as will be made clear in subsequent chapters. For the goal of computing confidence intervals for the population mean, bootstrap methods can reduce some practical concerns, as will be illustrated here, but concerns remain. When using a median or 20% trimmed mean, bootstrap methods perform very well even with a relatively small sample size. (For a theoretical justification of the methods described in this section, see Liu et al., 1999.)

6.6.1   The Percentile Bootstrap Method

Before describing how a percentile bootstrap method is applied, a rough indication of the strategy behind the method is provided. Again, imagine that a study is repeated thousands of times and that the sample median is computed each time. Further imagine that among these thousands of sample medians, 95% of them are between 3 and 10. Said more formally, numerous studies indicate that 3 and 10 are the 0.025 and 0.975 quantiles of the distribution of the sample median M. This suggests that a reasonable 0.95 confidence interval for the population median is (3, 10). This is the approach used by a percentile bootstrap method, only rather than repeat a study thousands of times, simulations are performed using the data from a single study with the goal of estimating the sampling distribution of the median.

Imagine that we have n observations, say $X_1, \ldots, X_n$. A *bootstrap sample* of size n is obtained by randomly sampling, with replacement, n observations from $X_1, \ldots, X_n$ yielding, say, $X_1^*, \ldots, X_n^*$.

Example

Suppose we observe the 10 values

1, 4, 2, 19, 4, 12, 29, 4, 9, 16.

If we randomly sample a single observation from among these 10 values, we might get the value 2. If we randomly sample another observation, we might again get the value 2, or we might get the value 9 or any of the other values listed. If we perform this process 10 times, we might get the values

2, 9, 16, 2, 4, 12, 4, 29, 16, 19.

This is an example of a bootstrap sample of size 10. If we were to get another bootstrap sample of size 10, this time we might get

29, 16, 29, 19, 2, 16, 2, 9, 4, 29.

Now suppose we create many bootstrap samples in the manner just described and for each bootstrap sample we compute the median. For illustrative purposes, imagine that we repeat this process 1,000 times, yielding 1,000 (bootstrap) sample medians, which can be done very quickly on modern computers. If we put these 1,000 sample medians in ascending order, then the middle 95% form an approximate 0.95 confidence interval for the population median. In terms of achieving accurate probability coverage, this method performs very well when using a median or 20% trimmed mean, but it does not perform well when using the mean; a bootstrap-t method (described in Section 6.6.3) is preferable. When sample sizes are sufficiently large, the percentile bootstrap is not necessary when working with a 20% trimmed mean, but for small sample sizes, it is preferable and in fact works very well, even in situations where all methods based on means perform poorly. The percentile bootstrap method is not necessary when computing a confidence interval for the population median. But when using the median in various situations described in subsequent chapters, it is the only method that continues to perform well when there are tied values.

6.6.2   R Functions trimpb

The R function

```
trimpb(x,tr=0.2,alpha=0.05,nboot=2000)
```

computes a percentile bootstrap confidence interval for a trimmed mean. The argument tr indicates the amount of trimming and defaults to 0.2 (a 20% trimmed mean) if not specified. Again, the argument alpha is α and defaults to 0.05, meaning that by default, a 0.95 confidence interval is computed. To get a 0.99 confidence interval, for example, set alpha=0.01. The argument nboot controls how many bootstrap samples are generated. The default is nboot=2000, meaning that 2,000 (bootstrap) trimmed means will be generated.

6.6.3   Bootstrap-t

As previously explained, a confidence interval for the population mean can be computed if the distribution of T can be determined. Assuming normality, we are able to determine, for example, t such that $P(-t \leq T \leq t) = 0.95$, which leads to the 0.95 confidence interval given by

$$\overline{X} \pm t \frac{s}{\sqrt{n}}. \tag{6.12}$$

Rather than assume normality, the bootstrap-t method approximates the distribution of T by performing a simulation on the observed data. The simulation yields a value for t such that $P(-t \leq T \leq t) = 1 - \alpha$ is approximately true in which case an approximate $1 - \alpha$ confidence interval for the population mean μ is given by Equation (6.12). An R function is supplied, which performs the calculations. The resulting confidence interval is said to be a *symmetric* confidence interval. To illustrate what this means, suppose $\overline{X} = 32$ and that $t\frac{s}{\sqrt{n}} = 3$. Then the confidence interval is $(32 - 3, 32 + 3) = (29, 35)$. That is, the confidence interval is symmetric about 32 because the same amount is both added to 32 and subtracted from 32.

For a normal distribution, T has a symmetric distribution about zero, but when sampling from a skewed distribution, the distribution of T is also skewed as was previously illustrated. Another approach to computing a confidence interval is to use simulations to determine values a and b such that $P(T \leq a) = \alpha/2$ and $P(T \geq b) = \alpha/2$. Now the $1 - \alpha$ confidence interval for the mean is

$$\left(\overline{X} - b\frac{s}{\sqrt{n}}, \overline{X} - a\frac{s}{\sqrt{n}} \right). \tag{6.13}$$

This is called an *equal-tailed* confidence interval because $P(T \leq a) = P(T \geq b)$. Note that b is used to compute the lower end of the confidence, not the upper end. Also, the upper end, $\overline{X} - a\frac{s}{\sqrt{n}}$, might appear to be a typo. But a is always a negative number, so in effect $-a\frac{s}{\sqrt{n}}$ is a positive number that is being added to the sample mean. Again, a more detailed description of the calculations is not provided; an R function is supplied instead that applies the method. (For readers interested in more details, see the answer to Exercise 42 located at http://dornsife.usc.edu/labs/rwilcox/ books/ and stored in the file answers_wiley.pdf.) The only goal here is to provide a rough indication of the strategy underlying the bootstrap-t method.

Table 6.4 shows the actual probability coverage, estimated via a simulation study, when computing a 0.95 confidence interval for the mean and observations are sampled from four types of distributions: normal, symmetric and heavy-tailed

TABLE 6.4 Actual Probability Coverage for Three Methods Designed to Compute a 0.95 Confidence Interval for the Population Mean

		Method	
Distribution	BT	SB	T
	$n = 20$		
N	0.946	0.949	0.950
SL	0.922	0.907	0.860
MN	0.900	0.986	0.978
SH	0.802	0.829	0.798
	$n = 100$		
N	0.952	0.962	0.950
SL	0.942	0.942	0.917
MN	0.908	0.982	0.959
SH	0.832	0.827	0.810

N=normal; SL=skewed, light-tailed; MN=mixed normal; SH=skewed, heavy-tailed; BT=equal-tailed, bootstrap-t; SB=symmetric bootstrap-t; T=Student's T

TABLE 6.5 Actual Probability Coverage When Computing a 0.95 Confidence Interval for the Population 20% Trimmed Mean

Distribution	Method			
	BT	SB	P	TM
		$n = 20$		
N	0.933	0.948	0.937	0.958
SL	0.951	0.950	0.934	0.932
MN	0.978	0.981	0.947	0.985
SH	0.986	0.982	0.934	0.980

N=normal, SL=skewed, light-tailed; MN=mixed normal; SH=skewed, heavy-tailed; BT=equal-tailed, bootstrap-t; SB=symmetric bootstrap-t; P=Percentile bootstrap; TM=Tukey–McLaughlin.

(outliers are common), skewed and light-tailed (outliers are relatively rare), and skewed and heavy-tailed. If, for example, a method is judged to be reasonably satisfactory when the actual probability coverage is between 0.925 and 0.975, all three methods are unsatisfactory with a sample size of $n = 20$ except when dealing with a normal distribution. Increasing the sample size to $n = 100$, the bootstrap methods perform reasonably well for light-tailed distributions (outliers are relatively rare), but they remain unsatisfactory when dealing with heavy-tailed distributions.

Table 6.5 shows the actual probability coverage when the goal is to compute a 0.95 confidence interval for the 20% population trimmed mean. Even with a sample size of 20, all four methods have an actual probability coverage greater than 0.925. The main difficulty is that, except for the percentile bootstrap method, the actual probability coverage can exceed 0.975. That is, the confidence interval is wider than necessary, given the goal of computing a 0.95 confidence interval. Note that generally, the actual probability coverage is closer to the nominal 0.95 level when using a 20% trimmed mean rather than the mean. It should be mentioned, however, that as the amount of trimming increases, at some point, only the percentile bootstrap method performs well. The other methods are unsatisfactory when the amount of trimming is relatively high roughly because the estimate of the standard error, based in part on the Winsorized variance, breaks down. This is not an issue when using the percentile bootstrap method because it does not use an estimate of the standard error. But as previously noted, if the amount of trimming is close to zero, a bootstrap-t method performs better than the percentile bootstrap method.

6.6.4 R Function trimcibt

The R function

```
trimcibt(x, tr = 0.2, alpha = 0.05, nboot = 599, side =
TRUE)
```

computes a bootstrap-t confidence interval for a trimmed mean. To compute a confidence interval for the population mean, set the argument `tr=0`. The argument side indicates whether an equal-tailed or a symmetric confidence interval is to be computed. The default is `side=TRUE`, resulting in a symmetric confidence interval. Using `side=FALSE` means that an equal-tailed confidence interval will be computed.

Example

Table 3.2 reports data on the desired number of sexual partners among 105 college males. As previously indicated, these data are highly skewed with a relatively large number of outliers, and this can have a deleterious effect on many methods for computing a confidence interval. If we compute the Tukey–McLaughlin 0.95 confidence interval for the 20% trimmed, we get $(1.62, 3.75)$. Using the R function `trimcibt` with `side=FALSE` returns an equal-tailed 0.95 confidence interval: $(1.79, 4.11)$. With `side=TRUE` the 0.95 confidence interval is $(1.49, 3.88)$. Using the percentile bootstrap method, the R function `trimpb` returns $(1.86, 3.89)$. So in this particular case, the lengths of the confidence intervals do not vary that much among the methods used, but the intervals are centered around different values, which might affect any conclusions made. If `trimcibt` is used to compute a 0.95 confidence interval for the mean (by setting the argument tr=0), the result is $(-2.46, 4704.59)$ with the argument `side=FALSE`, which differs substantially from the confidence intervals for a 20% trimmed mean. With `side=TRUE`, the 0.95 confidence interval for the mean is $(-2249.14, 2378.99)$.

6.7 CONFIDENCE INTERVAL FOR THE PROBABILITY OF SUCCESS

A common goal is making inferences about the unknown probability of success, p, associated with a binomial distribution. Briefly reviewing details given in Chapters 4 and 5, we observe $X_1, \cdots, X_n$, where $X_1 = 1$ or 0, $X_2 = 1$ or 0, and so on. The sample mean of these n values corresponds to the proportion of successes among the n observations. But rather than label the average of these values $\overline{X}$, the more common notation is to use $\hat{p}$. That is,

$$\hat{p} = \frac{1}{n} \sum X_i \tag{6.14}$$

is the observed proportion of successes and estimates the unknown probability of success, p. In fact, $\hat{p}$ can be shown to be an unbiased estimate of p (meaning that $E(\hat{p}) = p$) and its squared standard error (its variance over many studies) is

$$VAR(\hat{p}) = \frac{p(1-p)}{n}.$$

So its standard error is

$$SE(\hat{p}) = \sqrt{\frac{p(1-p)}{n}}.$$

As noted in Chapter 5, the central limit theorem applies and says that if the sample size is sufficiently large,

$$\frac{\hat{p} - p}{\sqrt{p(1-p)/n}}$$

will have, approximately, a standard normal distribution. In the present context, this means that Laplace's method is readily applied when computing a confidence interval for p. It is given by

$$\hat{p} \pm c\sqrt{\frac{p(1-p)}{n}},$$

where c is the $1 - \alpha/2$ quantile of a standard normal distribution. We do not know the value of the quantity under the radical, but it can be estimated with $\hat{p}$, in which case a simple $1 - \alpha$ confidence interval for p is

$$\hat{p} \pm c\sqrt{\frac{\hat{p}(1-\hat{p})}{n}}. \tag{6.15}$$

Example

Among all registered voters, let p be the proportion who approve of how the president of the United States is handling his job. Suppose 10 randomly sampled individuals are asked whether they approve of the president's performance. Further imagine that the responses are

1, 1, 1, 0, 0, 1, 0, 1, 1, 0

and the goal is to compute a 0.95 confidence interval for p. So $c = 1.96$, which is read from Table B.1 in Appendix B and corresponds to the 0.975 quantile of a standard normal distribution. In terms of the aforementioned notation, $X_1 = 1$ (the first individual responded that she approves), $X_2 = 1$ and $X_4 = 0$, and the proportion who approve is $\hat{p} = 6/10$. So the estimated standard error associated with $\hat{p}$ is $\sqrt{0.6(1-0.6)/10} = 0.155$ and a 0.95 confidence interval is

$$0.6 \pm 1.96(0.155) = (0.296, 0.904).$$

In words, the true value of p is unknown, but based on the available information, if we assume random sampling and that $\hat{p}$ has a normal distribution, we can be reasonably certain that p has a value between 0.296 and 0.904.

Example

Among a random sample of 100 voters, 64 favored a bond issue. To assess the proportion of all voters who favor the bond issue, we compute a 0.95 confidence interval for p, the proportion of all voters who favor the bond issue. So $n = 100$, $\hat{p} = 0.64$, $c = 1.96$,

$$\sqrt{\frac{\hat{p}(1-\hat{p})}{n}} = \sqrt{\frac{0.64 \times 0.36}{100}} = 0.048,$$

$1.96 \times 0.048 = 0.094$ and the 0.95 confidence interval is

$$(0.64 - 0.094, 0.64 + 0.094) = (0.546, 0.734).$$

6.7.1   Agresti–Coull Method

The confidence interval given by Equation (6.15) illustrates basic principles. But the accuracy of this confidence interval depends on both the sample size n and the unknown probability of success, p. Generally, the closer p happens to be to 0 or 1, the larger the sample size must be to get an accurate confidence interval. But p is not known, which has raised practical concerns when computing a confidence interval using Equation (6.15). Brown et al. (2002) compared several methods aimed at improving on Equation (6.15) and found that a simple generalization of a method derived by Agresti and Coull (1998) performs relatively well.

The Agresti–Coull method is applied as follows. Let x represent the observed number of successes among n observations, in which case

$$\hat{p} = \frac{x}{n}$$

is the proportion of successes among the n observations. As before, let c be the $1 - \alpha/2$ quantile of a standard normal distribution. Compute

$$\tilde{n} = n + c^2,$$

$$\tilde{x} = x + \frac{c^2}{2},$$

and

$$\tilde{p} = \frac{\tilde{x}}{\tilde{n}}.$$

Then the $1 - \alpha$ confidence interval for p is

$$\tilde{p} \pm c\sqrt{\frac{\tilde{p}(1 - \tilde{p})}{\tilde{n}}}.$$

6.7.2   Blyth's Method

For the special cases where the number of successes is $X = 0, 1, n - 1$, and n, Blyth (1986) suggests computing a $1 - \alpha$ confidence interval for p as follows:

- If $x = 0$, use

$$(0, 1 - \alpha^{1/n}).$$

- If $x = 1$, use

$$\left(1 - \left(1 - \frac{\alpha}{2}\right)^{1/n}, 1 - \left(\frac{\alpha}{2}\right)^{1/n}\right).$$

- If $x = n - 1$, use

$$\left(\left(\frac{\alpha}{2} \right)^{1/n}, \left(1 - \frac{\alpha}{2} \right)^{1/n} \right).$$

- If $x = n$, use

$$(\alpha^{1/n}, 1).$$

6.7.3 Schilling–Doi Method

The Agresti–Coull method provides an approximate confidence interval that is simple and relatively effective among the many methods that have been derived. Approximate means that when computing a 0.95 confidence interval, for example, the actual probability coverage might be less than 0.95. More recently, Schilling and Doi (2014) derived a more complex method that guarantees that the actual probability coverage is greater than or equal to the specified level. For example, if the goal is to compute a 0.95 confidence interval, the actual probability that the confidence interval contains the true probability of success, p, is at least 0.95. In addition, the Schilling–Doi method is designed to provide the optimal confidence interval. This means that when computing a $1 - \alpha$ confidence interval, the shortest possible confidence interval is computed that guarantees that the probability coverage is at least $1 - \alpha$. The involved calculations are not described here, but an R function for applying the method is supplied.

6.7.4 R Functions acbinomci and binomLCO

The R function

```
acbinomci(x = sum(y), nn = length(y), y = NULL, alpha = 0.05)
```

computes a $1 - \alpha$ confidence interval for the probability of success using the Agresti–Coull method. If the number of successes is 0, 1, $n - 1$, or n, Blyth's method is used. The argument x indicates the number of successes and the argument nn corresponds to the sample size. If the data are stored as a collection of 0's and 1's, use the argument y. For example, if the data are stored in the R variable bindat, acbinomci(y=bindat) would be used. If the argument y is not specified, the function assumes that the number of successes is indicated by the argument x and the sample size is specified by the argument nn. The function returns an estimate of p, which is labeled $phat, and a confidence interval indicated by $ci.

The R function

```
binomLCO(x = sum(y), nn = length(y), y = NULL, alpha = 0.05)
```

applies the Schilling–Doi method and is used in the same manner as the R function acbinomci. A possible concern is that with a large sample size, execution time using the Schilling–Doi method can be prohibitive.

Example

If the number of successes is 23 based on a sample size of $n = 34$, `acbinomci(23,34)` returns an approximate 0.95 confidence interval.

Example

For zero successes among $n = 15$ trials, the 0.95 confidence interval returned by `binomci` is $(0, 0.181)$. The 0.95 confidence interval returned by `binomLCO` is $(0, 0.222)$.

Example

Data were generated from a binomial distribution (using the R function rbinom) with the probability of success set at 0.3. The results were: 0, 0, 1, 0, 0, 1, 0, 1, 0, 0, 1, 1, 0, 0, 1, 0, 0, 0, 0, 0, 0, 0, 0. Here is how to use `acbinomci` to get a confidence interval:

```
bdat=c(0,0,1,0,0,1,0,1,0,0,1,1,0,0,1,0,0,0,0,0,0,0,0)
acbinomci(y=bdat).
```

The estimate of p is $\hat{p} = 0.23$. The approximate 0.95 confidence interval returned by `acbinomci` is $(0.123, 0.468)$, which in this particular case contains the true probability of success, 0.3. The confidence interval returned by `binomLCO` is $(0.120, 0.478)$.

Example

Some years ago, a television news program covered a story about a problem that sometimes arose among people undergoing surgery. Some patients would wake up, become aware of what was happening to them, and they would have nightmares later about their experience. Some surgeons decided to monitor brain function in order to be alerted if someone was regaining consciousness. In the event this happened, they would give the patient more medication to keep them under. Among 200,000 surgeries, zero patients woke up under this experimental method. But hospital administrators, worried about the added cost of monitoring brain function, argued that with only 200,000 surgeries, it is impossible to be very certain about the actual probability of someone waking up. Note, however, that we can compute a 0.95 confidence interval using Blyth's method. The number of times a patient woke up is $x = 0$, the number of observations is $n = 200,000$, so an approximate 0.95 confidence interval for the probability of waking up is

$$(0, 1 - 0.05^{1/200000}) = (0, 0.000015).$$

Example

Consider again the first example in this section dealing with the approval rating of the president, only now we compute the Agresti–Coull 0.95 confidence interval. As before, $x = 6$, $n = 10$, and $c = 1.96$. So, $\tilde{n} = 10 + 1.96^2 = 13.84$, $\tilde{x} = 6 + 1.96^2/2 = 7.92$, and $\tilde{p} = 7.92/13.84 = 0.5723$. The 0.95 confidence interval is

$$0.5723 \pm 1.96\sqrt{\frac{0.5723(1 - 0.5723)}{13.84}} = (0.31, 0.83).$$

Using the R command `acbinomci(6,10)` returns the same result. In contrast, using Equation (6.15), the 0.95 confidence interval is $(0.296, 0.904)$. Notice that the upper end of this confidence interval, 0.904, differs substantially from the Agresti–Coull upper end, 0.83. The 0.95 confidence interval based on the Schilling–Doi method is $(0.291, 0.850)$.

6.8   SUMMARY

- Confidence intervals provide a fundamental way of determining which values for a population measure of location are reasonable based on the available data. Probability coverage of a confidence interval refers to the probability, over many studies, that the resulting confidence intervals will contain the population parameter being estimated.

- The classic and routinely used method for computing a confidence interval for μ, the population mean, is based on Student's T. For symmetric, light-tailed distributions, its actual probability coverage tends to be reasonably close to the nominal level. For symmetric, heavy-tailed distributions, the actual probability coverage tends to be higher than the stated level. But for skewed distributions, the probability coverage can be substantially less than intended, particularly when outliers are common. An accurate confidence can require a sample size of $n = 300$ or more.

- In terms of achieving accurate probability coverage and relatively short confidence intervals, Student's T is the best method when dealing with a normal distribution. But methods based on a 20% trimmed mean perform better than methods based on means for a wide range of situations. For symmetric, heavy-tailed distributions for which outliers are common, using a 20% trimmed mean or a median can result in a substantially shorter confidence interval for the population mean compared to methods based on the sample mean. For skewed distributions, methods based on a 20% trimmed mean or median do not provide a satisfactory confidence interval for μ, but they do provide a satisfactory confidence interval for the population trimmed mean and population median that might better reflect what is typical.

- When computing a confidence interval for the population median, the method in Section 6.4.3 has appeal because it is based on a relatively weak assumption: random sampling only. But the other methods covered in this chapter are important because they can be extended to comparing two or more groups of participants, unlike the method in Section 6.4.3. (An exception occurs when comparing two dependent groups, as will be seen in Chapter 11.) A point worth stressing is that the method based on Equation (6.10), which uses the McKean–Schrader estimate of the standard error, is appropriate when tied values never occur. At some point, as the number of tied values increases, it performs poorly. So if any tied values occur, it is safer to use something other than the method based on the McKean–Schrader estimator. Two possibilities are the method in Section 6.4.3 or a percentile bootstrap method. With tied values, a percentile bootstrap will be seen to be important when comparing the medians of two or more groups.

- Equation (6.15) is the basic method for computing a confidence interval for p, the probability of success associated with a binomial distribution, which is typically covered in an introductory course. But the Agresti–Coull method is generally preferable in practice. For the special cases where the number of successes is 0, 1, $n - 1$, or n, use Blyth's method. To guarantee that the probability coverage is at least as large as intended, use the Schilling–Doi method.

- Regarding bootstrap methods, there are conditions where they provide little improvement, but there are situations where they have considerable practical value. When working with the mean, a bootstrap-t method is better than a percentile bootstrap method. But as the amount of trimming increases, at some point the percentile bootstrap method performs better than a bootstrap-t method. The relative merits of these methods will be discussed in more detail in subsequent chapters.

6.9   EXERCISES

1. Explain the meaning of a 0.95 confidence interval.

2. If the goal is to compute a 0.80, or 0.92, or a 0.98 confidence interval for μ when σ is known, and sampling is from a normal distribution, what values for c should be used in Equation (6.4)?

3. Assuming random sampling is from a normal distribution with standard deviation $\sigma = 5$, if the sample mean is $\overline{X} = 45$ based on $n = 25$ participants, what is the 0.95 confidence interval for μ?

4. Repeat the previous example, only compute a 0.99 confidence interval instead.

5. A manufacturer claims that their light bulbs have an average life span that follows a normal distribution with $\mu = 1,200$ hours and a standard deviation of $\sigma = 25$. If you randomly test 36 light bulbs and find that their average life span is $\overline{X} = 1,150$, does a 0.95 confidence interval for μ suggest that the claim $\mu = 1,200$ is reasonable?

6. Compute a 0.95 confidence interval for the mean, assuming normality, for the following situations: (a) $n = 12$, $\sigma = 22$, $\overline{X} = 65$, (b) $n = 22$, $\sigma = 10$, $\overline{X} = 185$, (c) $n = 50$, $\sigma = 30$, $\overline{X} = 19$.

7. What happens to the length of a confidence interval for the mean of a normal distribution when the sample size is doubled? In particular, what is the ratio of the lengths? What is the ratio of the lengths if the sample size is quadrupled?

8. The length of a bolt made by a machine parts company has a normal distribution with standard deviation σ equal to 0.01 mm. The lengths of four randomly selected bolts are as follows: 20.01, 19.88, 20.00, 19.99. (a) Compute a 0.95 confidence interval for the mean. (b) Specifications require a mean length μ of 20.00 mm for the population of bolts. Do the data indicate that this specification is being met? (c) Given that the 0.95 confidence interval contains the value 20, why might it be inappropriate to conclude that the specification is being met?

9. The weight of trout sold at a trout farm has a standard deviation of 0.25. Based on a sample of 10 trout, the average weight is 2.10 lb. Use R to compute a 0.99 confidence interval for the population mean, assuming normality. Note: the quantiles of a standard normal distribution can be computed with the R command qnorm. For example, qnorm(0.975) returns the 0.975 quantile, which is 1.96.

10. The average bounce of 45 randomly selected tennis balls is found to be $\overline{X} = 1.70$. Assuming that the standard deviation of the bounce is 0.30, compute a 0.90 confidence interval for the average bounce assuming normality?

11. Assuming that the degrees of freedom are 20, find the value t for which
    (a) $P(T \leq t) = 0.995$,
    (b) $P(T \geq t) = 0.025$,
    (c) $P(-t \leq T \leq t) = 0.90$.

12. Compute a 0.95 confidence interval if
    (a) $n = 10, \overline{X} = 26, s = 9$,
    (b) $n = 18, \overline{X} = 132, s = 20$,
    (c) $n = 25, \overline{X} = 52, s = 12$.

13. Repeat the previous exercise, but compute a 0.99 confidence interval instead.

14. For a study on self-awareness, the observed values for one of the groups were

$$77, 87, 88, 114, 151, 210, 219, 246, 253, 262, 296, 299, 306, 376, 428,$$

$$515, 666, 1, 310, 2, 611.$$

Using R, compute 0.95 confidence interval for the mean assuming normality. Compare the result to the bootstrap-t confidence interval obtained via the R function trimcibt. Comment on why the two confidence intervals differ substantially.

15. Rats are subjected to a drug that might affect aggression. Suppose that for a random sample of rats, measures of aggression are found to be

$$5, 12, 23, 24, 18, 9, 18, 11, 36, 15.$$

Compute a 0.95 confidence interval for the mean assuming that the scores are from a normal distribution.

16. Suppose $M = 34$ and the McKean–Schrader estimate of the standard error of M is $S_M = 3$. Compute a 0.95 confidence interval for the population median.

17. For the data in Exercise 14, the McKean–Schrader estimate of the standard error of M is $S_M = 77.8$ and the sample median is 262. Compute a 0.99 confidence interval for the population median.

18. If $n = 10$ and a confidence interval for the median is computed using $(X_{(k)}, X_{(n-k)})$, as described in Section 6.4.3, what is the probability that this interval contains the population median if $k = 2$?

19. Repeat the previous exercise, only use R to determine the probability coverage when $n = 15$ and $k = 4$.

20. For the data in Exercise 14, if you use (88, 515) as a confidence interval for the median, what is the probability this interval contains the population median?

21. You observe the following successes and failures: 1, 1, 1, 1, 1, 0, 0, 0, 0, 0, 0, 0, 0, 0, 0. Compute a 0.95 confidence interval for p using Equation (6.15) as well as the Agresti–Coull method.

22. Given the following results for a sample from a binomial distribution, compute the squared standard error of $\hat{p}$. (a) $n = 25$, $X = 5$. (b) $n = 48$, $X = 12$. (c) $n = 100$, $X = 80$. (d) $n = 300$, $X = 160$.

23. Among 100 randomly sampled adults, 10 were found to be unemployed. Compute a 0.95 confidence interval for the percentage of adults unemployed using Equation (6.15). Compare this result to the Agresti–Coull confidence interval.

24. A sample of 1,000 fishes was obtained from a lake. It was found that 290 were members of the bass family. Compute a 0.95 confidence interval for the percentage of bass in the lake using Equation (6.15).

25. Among a random sample of 1,000 adults, 60 reported never having any legal problems. Use Equation (6.15) to compute a 0.95 confidence interval for the percentage of adults who have never had legal problems.

26. Among a sample of 600 items, only one was found to be defective. Explain why using Equation (6.15) might be unsatisfactory when computing a confidence interval for the probability that an item is defective.

27. In the previous exercise, compute a 0.90 confidence interval for the probability that an item is defective.

28. One-fourth of 300 persons in a large city stated that they are opposed to a certain political issue favored by the mayor. Using Equation (6.15), calculate a 0.99 confidence interval for the fraction of individuals opposed to this issue.

29. Consider a method for detecting a type of cancer that is highly accurate but very expensive and invasive, resulting in a great deal of discomfort for the patient. An alternative test to detect this type of cancer has been developed, and it is of interest to know the probability of a false-negative indication, meaning that the test fails to detect cancer when it is present. The test is conducted on 250 patients known to have cancer, and 5 tests fail to show its presence. Use Equation (6.15) to determine a 0.95 confidence interval for the probability of a false-negative indication.

30. In the previous exercise, imagine that 0 false-negative indications were found. Determine a 0.99 confidence interval for the probability of a false-negative indication.

31. A cosmetic company found that 180 of 1,000 randomly selected women in New York city have seen the company's latest television ad. Use Equation (6.15) to compute a 0.95 confidence interval for the percentage of women in New York city who have seen the ad.

32. Describe in general terms how nonnormality can affect Student's T distribution.

33. Chapter 5 illustrated that when randomly sampling observations from a skewed distribution where outliers are rare, it is generally reasonable to assume that plots of sample means over many studies have, approximately, a normal distribution. This means that reasonably accurate confidence intervals for the mean can be computed when the standard deviation, σ, is known. Based on the information summarized in this chapter, how does this contrast with the situation where the variance is not known and confidence intervals are computed using Student's T distribution?

34. Listed here are the average LSAT scores for the 1973 entering classes of 15 American law schools.

545	555	558	572	575	576	578	580
594	605	635	651	653	661	666	

(LSAT is a national test for prospective lawyers.) The 0.95 confidence interval for the population mean μ is $(577.1, 623.4)$. Use a boxplot to verify that there are no outliers and that the data appear have a skewed distribution. Argue that as a result, the confidence interval for the mean, based on Student's T, might be inaccurate.

35. Compute a 0.95 confidence interval for the 20% trimmed mean if (a) $n = 24$, $s_w^2 = 12$, $\overline{X}_t = 52$, (b) $n = 36$, $s_w^2 = 30$, $\overline{X}_t = 10$, (c) $n = 12$, $s_w^2 = 9$, $\overline{X}_t = 16$.

36. Repeat the previous exercise, but compute a 0.99 confidence interval instead.

37. The last example at the end of Section 6.3.1 used data from a study of self-awareness. In another portion of the study, a group of participants had the following values.

$$59, 106, 174, 207, 219, 237, 313, 365, 458, 497, 515,$$

$$529, 557, 615, 625, 645, 973, 1,065, 3,215.$$

Compute a 0.95 confidence interval for both the population mean and 20% trimmed mean. Also compute a 0.95 confidence interval using the R function trimci in Section 6.3.1. (If again the data are read into the variable aware, as described in Section 6.3.1, the data will be stored in the second column, namely, aware[,2].)

38. The ideal method for computing a confidence interval for the mean would have a shorter length than any other method that might be used. Explain why such a method does not exist even when sampling from a perfectly symmetric distribution.

39. For the values
$$5, 60, 43, 56, 32, 43, 47, 79, 39, 41$$

compute a 0.95 confidence interval for the 20% trimmed mean and compare the results to the 0.95 confidence interval for the mean.

40. In the previous exercise, the confidence interval for the 20% trimmed mean is shorter than the confidence interval for the mean. Explain why this is not surprising.

41. Here is R code for estimating the distribution of Student's T when data are sampled from a skewed, light-tailed distribution that has a population mean $\mu = 1.649$:

```
t.vals=NULL
for(study in 1:1000){
x=rlnorm(25)
t.vals[study]=trimci(x,tr=0,null.value=1.649)$test.stat
}
```

The first command initializes an R variable where the T values will be stored. The argument `null.value=1.649`, used by `trimci`, indicates that the mean of the distribution being used is 1.649 and the argument `tr=0` indicates no trimming, meaning that a confidence interval for the population mean is computed. These commands result in 1,000 T values being stored in the R variable `t.vals`. If the goal is to compute a 0.95 confidence interval for the mean, describe how to do this based on the simulation results.

42. How would you modify the code in the last exercise to use data from an actual study to compute a confidence interval for the mean? In essence, how would you create R code to apply a bootstrap-t method using the data stored in the R variable x? Hint: the R command `sample(x,n,replace=TRUE)` samples with replacement n values from the data stored in x, where the argument n is the number of observations stored in x.

7

HYPOTHESIS TESTING

The previous chapter described confidence intervals, which provide a fundamental strategy for making inferences about population measures of location such as the population mean μ and the population median. About a century after Laplace's groundbreaking work on sampling distributions, new techniques were developed for making inferences about parameters that add perspective and are routinely used. One of the main architects of this new perspective was Jerzy Neyman. Forced to leave Poland due to the war between Poland and Russia, Neyman eventually moved to London in 1924 where he met Egon Pearson (son of Karl Pearson, whom we met in Chapter 1). Their joint efforts led to the Neyman–Pearson framework for testing hypotheses, which is the subject of this chapter.

7.1 TESTING HYPOTHESES ABOUT THE MEAN, σ KNOWN

The essence of hypothesis testing methods is quite simple. A researcher formulates some speculation about the population under study. Typically, the speculation has to do with the value of some unknown population parameter, such as the population mean. Then, data are analyzed with the goal of determining whether the stated speculation is unreasonable. That is, is there empirical evidence indicating that the speculation is probably incorrect? The speculation about the value of a parameter is called a *null hypothesis*.

Example

A manufacturer of a high-definition television claims that the average life of the bulb used in their rear projection model lasts an average of at least 48 months. Imagine that

Understanding and Applying Basic Statistical Methods Using R, First Edition. Rand R. Wilcox.
© 2017 John Wiley & Sons, Inc. Published 2017 by John Wiley & Sons, Inc.
www.wiley.com/go/Wilcox/Statistical_Methods_R

you want to collect data with the goal of determining whether this claim is correct. Then, the null hypothesis is that the population mean for all televisions is at least 48. This is written as

$$H_0 : \mu \geq 48, \tag{7.1}$$

where the notation H_0 is read H naught. The alternative to the null hypothesis is written as

$$H_a : \mu < 48. \tag{7.2}$$

Suppose that for 10 televisions, you determine how long the bulb lasts and find that the average life is $\overline{X} = 50$ months. That is, you estimate that μ is equal to 50, which supports the claim that the population mean is at least 48. So, in particular, you would not reject the stated hypothesis. But suppose you get a sample mean of $\overline{X} = 46$. Now the estimate is that the population mean is less than 48, but the manufacturer might claim that if the population mean is 48, a sample mean of 46 is not all that unusual. The issue is how low does the sample mean have to be in order to argue that the null hypothesis is unlikely to be true?

For the moment, three fundamental assumptions are made:

- Random sampling
- Normality
- σ is known.

As noted in Chapter 6, assuming that σ is known is generally unrealistic, it is rarely known exactly, but it provides a convenient framework for describing the basic principles and concepts underlying hypothesis testing methods. For convenience, we denote some hypothesized value for μ by μ_0. In the last example, $\mu_0 = 48$.

7.1.1 Details for Three Types of Hypotheses

There are three types of null hypotheses:

1. $H_0: \mu \geq \mu_0$.
2. $H_0: \mu \leq \mu_0$.
3. $H_0: \mu = \mu_0$.

Consider the first hypothesis. The basic strategy is to momentarily assume that $\mu = \mu_0$ and to consider the probabilistic implications associated with the observed value of the sample mean. So, in the example dealing with how long a bulb lasts, we give the manufacturer the benefit of the doubt and momentarily assume that $\mu = 48$. The idea is that if we find empirical evidence strongly suggesting that the mean is less than 48, then we would conclude that the hypothesis $H_0: \mu \geq 48$ should be rejected.

If $\mu = \mu_0$ and the three assumptions are true, then from Chapter 6,

$$Z = \frac{\overline{X} - \mu_0}{\sigma / \sqrt{n}} \tag{7.3}$$

has a standard normal distribution. Consider the rule: reject the null hypothesis if $Z \leq c$, where c is the 0.05 quantile of a standard normal distribution. That is, $P(Z \leq c) = 0.05$ and from Table 7.1 in Appendix B, $c = -1.645$. This means that the probability of erroneously rejecting, when in fact $\mu = \mu_0$, is 0.05.

It might help to note that the rule just given is tantamount to rejecting if the sample mean is sufficiently smaller than the hypothesized value. More precisely, rejecting if $Z \leq c$ is the same as rejecting if

$$\overline{X} \leq \mu_0 + c\frac{\sigma}{\sqrt{n}}.$$

In the previous paragraph, $c = -1.645$, so the rule would be to reject if $\overline{X} \leq \mu_0 - 1.645\sigma/\sqrt{n}$. But for convenience, the rule is usually stated in terms of Z.

> *Definition* 7.1. Rejecting a null hypothesis, when in fact it is true, is called a *Type I error*. For the situation just described, assuming that the underlying assumptions are true, the probability of a Type I error is 0.05 when $\mu = \mu_0$.

We can summarize a decision rule for H_0: $\mu \geq \mu_0$ in more general terms as follows. Let c be the α quantile of a standard normal distribution, and suppose this null hypothesis is rejected if $Z \leq c$. Then, if the three underlying assumptions are true, the probability of a Type I error is α.

Example

A researcher claims that on a test of open-mindedness, the population mean for adult men is at least 50 with a standard deviation of $\sigma = 12$. So, in the notation used in this chapter, $\mu_0 = 50$ and the null hypothesis is H_0: $\mu \geq 50$. Based on 10 adult males, would the researcher's claim be rejected if the sample mean is $\overline{X} = 48$ and the Type I error probability is to be 0.025? To find out, first note that from Table B.1 in Appendix B, the 0.025 quantile of a standard normal distribution is $c = -1.96$. Because $n = 10$, we have that

$$Z = \frac{\overline{X} - \mu_0}{\sigma/\sqrt{n}} = \frac{48 - 50}{12/\sqrt{10}} = -0.53.$$

Because -0.53 is greater than -1.96, the null hypothesis is not rejected.

Example

We repeat the last example, only now suppose the sample mean is $\overline{X} = 40$. Then, $Z = -2.635$, this is less than -1.96, so reject the null hypothesis. That is, there is empirical evidence that the claim is unlikely to be true.

Now consider the second type of null hypothesis, H_0: $\mu \leq \mu_0$. For this case, we would not reject if the sample mean is less than the hypothesized value μ_0 for the simple reason that if the null hypothesis is true, this is the type of result we would expect. Rather, we would reject if the sample mean is sufficiently larger than the null value, which means that we would reject if Z is sufficiently large. More formally, if we want the probability of a Type I error to be α when in fact $\mu = \mu_0$, let c be the $1 - \alpha$ quantile of a standard normal distribution and reject null hypothesis if $Z \geq c$.

Example

Imagine that the goal is to test H_0: $\mu \leq 15$ assuming normality, $\sigma = 4$, and that the Type I error probability is to be 0.01. Then, $1 - \alpha = 0.99$ and from Table B.1 in Appendix B, $c = 2.33$. If based on a sample of size 25, the sample mean is $\overline{X} = 18$, then

$$Z = \frac{18 - 15}{4/\sqrt{25}} = 3.75.$$

Because 3.75 is greater than 2.33, reject the null hypothesis.

Finally, consider the third type of null hypothesis, H_0: $\mu = \mu_0$. Now the null hypothesis would be rejected if the sample mean is sufficiently smaller or larger than the hypothesized value, μ_0. In symbols, if the goal is to have the probability of a Type I error equal to α, reject if Z is less than or equal to the $\alpha/2$ quantile of a standard normal distribution or if Z is greater than or equal to the $1 - \alpha/2$ quantile. Said another way, reject if $|Z| \geq c$, where now c is the $1 - \alpha/2$ quantile of a standard normal distribution.

Example

Imagine you want to test H_0: $\mu = \mu_0$ with $\alpha = 0.05$. Then, $\alpha/2 = 0.025$, so $1 - \alpha/2 = 0.975$, meaning that the hypothesis is rejected if $|Z| \geq 1.96$, the 0.975 quantile of a standard normal distribution. The shaded region in Figure 7.1 indicates the *critical*

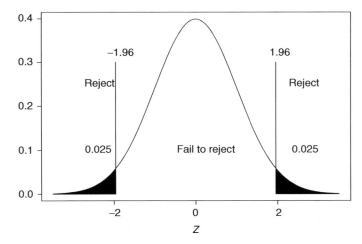

Figure 7.1 A graphical depiction of the rejection rule when using Z and $\alpha = 0.05$. The shaded portions indicate the rejection regions

region, meaning the collection of Z values for which the null hypothesis would be rejected. Here, the critical region consists of all values less than or equal to -1.96 as well as all values greater than or equal to 1.96. The constant c is called a *critical value*.

Example

Suppose the goal is to test H_0: $\mu = 15$, assuming normality, $\sigma = 4$, $n = 25$, $\overline{X} = 18$, and the Type I error probability is to be 0.01. So, $\alpha/2 = 0.005$, $1 - \alpha/2 = 0.995$, and from Table B.1 in Appendix B, $c = 2.58$. Because $|Z| = 3.75 > 2.58$, reject the null hypothesis.

Summary

The details of the three hypothesis testing methods are summarized here for convenience, assuming that the probability of a Type I error is to be α. Once the sample mean has been determined, compute

$$Z = \frac{\overline{X} - \mu_0}{\sigma/\sqrt{n}}.$$

Case 1. H_0: $\mu \geq \mu_0$. Reject H_0 if $Z \leq c$, the α quantile of a standard normal distribution.

Case 2. H_0: $\mu \leq \mu_0$. Reject H_0 if $Z \geq c$, the $1 - \alpha$ quantile of a standard normal distribution.

Case 3. H_0: $\mu = \mu_0$. Reject H_0 if $Z \geq c$ or if $Z \leq -c$, where now c is the $1 - \frac{\alpha}{2}$ quantile of a standard normal distribution. Equivalently, reject if $|Z| \geq c$.

The hypotheses $H_0 : \mu \geq \mu_0$ and $H_0 : \mu \leq \mu_0$ are called *one-sided hypotheses*. In contrast, $H_0 : \mu = \mu_0$ is called a *two-sided hypothesis*. The constant c is called a *critical value*.

7.1.2 Testing for Exact Equality and Tukey's Three-Decision Rule

There are some issues regarding the goal of testing for exact equality that should be discussed. Some authorities criticize this commonly sought goal on the grounds that exact equality is rarely if ever true. The argument is that if we test H_0: $\mu = 89$, for example, we can be reasonably certain that the actual value of the population mean differs at some decimal place from 89. For example, it might be 89.00012. In more general terms, it can be argued that without any data, one can make the argument that the hypothesis of exact equality is false. A related criticism is that as a consequence, we should never accept the null hypothesis as being true, so why test this hypothesis?

Momentarily, imagine that we accept the argument that the population mean is never exactly equal to the hypothesized value. There is a way of salvaging hypothesis testing by interpreting it in terms of what is called *Tukey's three-decision rule*. (For more details, see Jones and Tukey, 2000.) This means that when assessing the meaning of the test statistic Z, one of three conclusions is reached regarding how the population mean compares to the hypothesized value. The three possible conclusions are as follows:

- If $H_0 : \mu = \mu_0$ is rejected and $\overline{X} < \mu_0$, conclude that $\mu < \mu_0$.
- If $H_0 : \mu = \mu_0$ is rejected and $\overline{X} > \mu_0$, conclude that $\mu > \mu_0$.
- Otherwise, make no decision about whether μ is greater than or less than the hypothesized value.

So, the goal is not to test for exactly equality, but rather to make a decision about whether the population mean is less than or greater than the hypothesized value.

Note that the first two conclusions are subject to a possible error. You might erroneously conclude, for example, that the population mean is greater than the hypothesized value. Or, you might erroneously conclude that the population mean is less than the hypothesized value. But, assuming normality, if we test at the α level, the probability associated with each of these mistakes is at most $\alpha/2$. If, for example, $\alpha = 0.05$, the probability of erroneously concluding that the population mean is greater than the hypothesized value is at most 0.025. And similarly, the probability of erroneously concluding that the population mean is less than the hypothesized value is at most 0.025.

Example

Consider an expensive prescription medication for which its average effectiveness is found to be 48 based on some relevant measure. A company wants to market an alternative drug that is less expensive, but there is the issue of how its effectiveness compares to the medication currently being used. One possibility is to test the hypothesis that the effectiveness of a new medication is equal to 48 and conclude that it is more effective if $H_0 : \mu = 48$ is rejected and the sample mean, $\overline{X}$, is greater than 48. If $H_0 : \mu = 48$ is rejected and the sample mean is less than 48, conclude that the new medication is less effective on average. If the null hypothesis is not rejected, make no decision about the effectiveness of the new medication.

7.1.3 p-Values

Notice that if you are told that the null hypothesis is rejected with $\alpha = 0.05$, and nothing else, it is unknown whether you would also reject with $\alpha = 0.025$, $\alpha = 0.01$, or $\alpha = 0.001$. Generally, what is the smallest α value that would result in rejecting the null hypothesis? This smallest α value is called a *p-value* and can be determined by using the observed value of Z as a critical value. Generally, p-values have values between 0 and 1. The closer the p-value is to zero, the stronger the evidence that the null hypothesis should be rejected. When testing for exact equality, a p-value reflects the strength of the empirical evidence that a decision can be made about whether the population mean is greater or less than the hypothesized value.

Example

Imagine that the goal is to test $H_0: \mu \geq 6$ and that the value of the test statistic is $Z = -1.8$. If the probability of a Type I error is chosen to be $\alpha = 0.05$, then the critical value would be $c = -1.645$. Because the value of Z is less than the critical value, the null hypothesis would be rejected. But suppose you had used a critical value equal to the observed value of Z, namely -1.8. Then, the corresponding probability of a Type I error is called the p-value and is equal to $P(Z \leq -1.8)$. From Table B.1 in Appendix B, the p-value is equal to 0.036. So, in particular, you would reject if the desired Type I error probability were 0.05, 0.04, or even 0.036, but not for $\alpha = 0.03$.

For the three types of hypotheses that arise, here is a more detailed description of how to compute the p-value given $\overline{X}$, μ_0, n, and σ, which will help make clear a certain conceptual issue to be described.

Case 1. $H_0: \mu \geq \mu_0$. The p-value is

$$p = P\left(Z \leq \frac{\overline{X} - \mu_0}{\sigma/\sqrt{n}}\right), \qquad (7.4)$$

which can be determined using Table B.1 in Appendix B.

Case 2. $H_0: \mu \leq \mu_0$. The p-value is

$$p = P\left(Z \geq \frac{\overline{X} - \mu_0}{\sigma/\sqrt{n}}\right). \qquad (7.5)$$

Case 3. $H_0: \mu = \mu_0$. The p-value is

$$p = 2\left(1 - P\left(Z \leq \frac{|\overline{X} - \mu_0|}{\sigma/\sqrt{n}}\right)\right). \qquad (7.6)$$

Example

Imagine that $n = 36$, $\sigma = 5$, $\overline{X} = 44$, and you test $H_0: \mu \geq 45$, which corresponds to case 1. Then, $Z = -1.5$, and the p-value is the probability that a standard normal random variable has a value less than or equal to -1.5, which is $P(Z \leq -1.5) = 0.0668$. Because the p-value is greater than 0.05, you would not reject if you wanted the Type I error to be 0.05. If the p-value were 0.015, then, in particular, you would reject if the largest Type I error probability you wanted to allow were $\alpha = 0.05$ or 0.025, but not if $\alpha = 0.01$.

Example

We repeat the previous example, only with $\overline{X} = 46$. Then, $Z = 1.5$ and the p-value is $P(Z \leq 1.5) = 0.933$. So, this is not even close to rejecting, which is not surprising because the hypothesis is that μ is greater than or equal to 45, and the sample mean is consistent with this speculation.

Example

A company claims that on average, their beef hotdogs have 150 calories. Assume normality and that $\sigma = 10$. Imagine that the average calories for 12 hotdogs is $\overline{X} = 145$ and the goal is to check the company's claim. In formal terms, the goal is to test H_0: $\mu = 150$, which corresponds to case 3. The test statistic is $Z = -1.73$. The corresponding p-value is

$$p = 2(1 - P(Z \leq |-1.73|)) = 2(1 - 0.958) = 0.084.$$

So, the null hypothesis would not be rejected if the desired Type I error probability were 0.05. In terms of Tukey's three-decision rule, the sample mean indicates that the population mean is less than 150, but no decision about whether this is the case would be made with $\alpha = 0.05$.

7.1.4 Interpreting p-Values

From the point of view of Tukey's three-decision rule, p-values reflect the strength of the empirical evidence that a decision can be made about whether the population mean is less than or greater than some specified value. But care must be taken not to read more into a p-value than is warranted. Notice that the expressions for computing a p-value make it clear that it is influenced by three factors:

1. The difference between the sample mean and the hypothesized value, $\overline{X} - \mu_0$
2. the magnitude of the standard deviation, σ
3. the sample size, n.

Said another way, a p-value is determined by the difference between the sample mean and the hypothesized population mean, $\overline{X} - \mu_0$, as well as the standard error of the sample mean, $\sigma/\sqrt{n}$. The point is that if a p-value is close to zero, and we are told nothing else, it is not necessarily the case that the estimate of the population mean, $\overline{X}$, differs substantially from the hypothesized value. The reason could be that the standard deviation is small relative to the sample size. In particular, a small p-value does *not* necessarily mean that the difference between the null value of the mean and its actual value, namely $\mu - \mu_0$, is large.

Here is another perspective that is helpful. It can be shown that on average, if $\mu = \mu_0$, and sampling is from a normal distribution, the p-value will be 0.5. That is, the p-value will differ from one study to the next, but over many studies, its average value is 0.5 if the population mean is equal to the hypothesized value, μ_0. This is related to the fact that when $\mu = \mu_0$, Z has a standard normal distribution, meaning that with probability 0.5, its value will be greater than 0. But when dealing with a nonnormal distribution, we will see that skewness and outliers affect the magnitude of the p-value.

Another important point is that p-values do not indicate the likelihood of replicating a decision about the null hypothesis. For example, if the p-value is 0.001, what is the probability of rejecting at the 0.05 level if the study is conducted again? This is a power issue, a topic that is introduced in Section 7.2.

A common convention is to describe a test of some hypothesis as *significant* if the p-value is small, say less than or equal to 0.05. But the term significant is a statistical term meaning that there is strong evidence that the null hypothesis should be rejected. It does not necessarily mean that there is an important or large difference between the hypothesized value of the population mean and its actual value. One way to assess the magnitude of $\mu - \mu_0$ is to compute a confidence interval for μ using the methods in Chapter 6.

7.1.5 Confidence Intervals versus Hypothesis Testing

There is a simple connection between confidence intervals covered in Chapter 6 and tests of hypotheses. As an illustration, imagine that the goal is to test H_0: $\mu = 64$ with a Type I error probability of $\alpha = 0.05$. Rather than proceed as was done here, simply compute a 0.95 confidence interval for the population mean and reject if this interval does not contain the hypothesized value, 64. Assuming normality and random sampling, the probability of a Type I error will be $1 - 0.95 = 0.05$. More generally, if a $1 - \alpha$ confidence interval is computed, and the null hypothesis is rejected if this interval does not contain the hypothesized value, the probability of a Type I error will be α. Both approaches have their own advantages. Confidence intervals not only tell us whether we should reject some hypothesis of interest, they also provide information about the accuracy of our estimate of μ as well as which values for μ appear to be reasonable and which do not. If we are told only that the null hypothesis is rejected, this tells us nothing about the magnitude of $\mu - \mu_0$, the difference between actual population mean and its hypothesized value. This difference is an example of what is called an *effect size*, which is a general term for measures aimed at quantifying the extent to which the null hypothesis is false. The issue of measuring effect size is discussed in some detail in Sections 9.7 and 11.2.2. In contrast to confidence intervals, from the point of view of Tukey's three-decision rule, p-values reflect the strength of the empirical evidence that a decision can be made about whether the population mean is less than or greater than some specified value. It is stressed, however, that a p-value does not indicate the probability that a correct decision has been made.

A fundamental issue is whether the sample size is sufficiently large. One way of addressing this issue is in terms of the length of the confidence interval as noted in Section 6.1.1. Hypothesis testing provides an alternative perspective on whether the sample size is sufficiently large. This perspective is based on the notion of power, which is described in the next section.

7.2 POWER AND TYPE II ERRORS

There are two fundamental types of errors when testing hypotheses. The first is a Type I error, which has already been discussed. The second is called a *Type II* error, meaning that the null hypothesis is false but was not rejected. The probability of a Type II error is usually labeled β, a lowercase Greek beta. The probability of rejecting, when the null hypothesis is false, is called *power* and is labeled $1 - \beta$. That is, power is the probability of making a correct decision about the null hypothesis when the hypothesis is false. Or, in terms of Tukey's three-decision rule, power is the probability of being able to make a decision about whether the measure of location is greater than or less than the hypothesized value. Table 7.1 summarizes

TABLE 7.1   Four Possible Outcomes When Testing Hypotheses

Decision	Reality	
	H_0 True	H_0 False
H_0 true	Correct decision	Type II error (probability β)
H_0 false	Type I error (probability α)	Correct decision (power)

the four possible outcomes when testing hypotheses. Power is of critical importance for reasons illustrated by the next example.

Example

Imagine that a new drug for treating hypertension is being studied, but there is an issue about whether the drug causes liver damage. For illustrative purposes, suppose that based on some appropriate measure, liver damage is of little concern if $\mu \leq 14$. If a pharmaceutical firm reports that they tested H_0: $\mu \leq 14$ and failed to reject, is it reasonable to assume that the drug is safe? Based only on the information given, the answer is not known. Imagine, for example, that if $\mu = 16$, severe liver damage could result. The concern is that if in reality $\mu = 16$, by chance we might fail to reject. For example, if the pharmaceutical firm reveals that a sample size of only 10 was used, intuitively one would be suspicious about any conclusions regarding the entire population of individuals who might take this drug. In statistical terms, the issue is how much power is afforded with a sample size of only 10. If power is only $1 - \beta = 0.2$, there are serious concerns because this means that there is only a 20% chance of discovering a practical problem with this drug.

For the situation at hand where sampling is from a normal distribution and σ is known, power depends on four quantities: σ, α, n, and the value of $\mu - \mu_0$, which is the difference between the true value and the hypothesized value of the population mean. Here is how power is computed for the three types of hypotheses previously described.

Case 1. H_0: $\mu \leq \mu_0$. Determine the critical value c as previously described. (The critical value is the $1 - \alpha$ quantile of a standard normal distribution.) Then, power, the probability of rejecting the null hypothesis, is

$$1 - \beta = P\left(Z \geq c - \frac{\sqrt{n}(\mu - \mu_0)}{\sigma} \right).$$

In words, power is equal to the probability that a standard normal random variable is greater than or equal to

$$c - \frac{\sqrt{n}(\mu - \mu_0)}{\sigma}.$$

Case 2. $H_0: \mu \geq \mu_0$. Determine the critical value c, which is now the α quantile of a standard normal distribution. Then, power is

$$1 - \beta = P\left(Z \leq c - \frac{\sqrt{n}(\mu - \mu_0)}{\sigma} \right).$$

Case 3. $H_0: \mu = \mu_0$. Now c is the $1 - \frac{\alpha}{2}$ quantile of a standard normal distribution. Power is

$$1 - \beta = P\left(Z \leq -c - \frac{\sqrt{n}(\mu - \mu_0)}{\sigma} \right) + P\left(Z \geq c - \frac{\sqrt{n}(\mu - \mu_0)}{\sigma} \right).$$

Example

After years of production, a manufacturer of batteries for automobiles finds that, on average, their batteries last 42.3 months with a standard deviation of $\sigma = 4$. A new manufacturing process is being contemplated, and one goal is to determine whether the batteries have a longer life on average based on 10 batteries produced by the new method. For illustrative purposes, assume that the standard deviation is again $\sigma = 4$ and that the manufacturer decides to test $H_0: \mu \leq 42.3$ with the idea that if they reject, there is evidence that the new manufacturing process is better on average. Moreover, if in reality $\mu = 44$, and the Type I error probability is set at $\alpha = 0.05$, the manufacturer wants a high probability of rejecting the null hypothesis and adopting the new method. So, a practical issue is how much power there is when $\mu = 44$. With $\alpha = 0.05$, the critical value is $c = 1.645$. So, power is

$$1 - \beta = P\left(Z \geq c - \frac{\sqrt{n}(\mu - \mu_0)}{\sigma} \right)$$

$$= P\left(Z \geq 1.645 - \frac{\sqrt{10}(44 - 42.3)}{4} \right)$$

$$= P(Z \geq 0.30)$$

$$= 0.38.$$

Example

We repeat the last example, only now we determine power when the sample size is increased to 20. Now, power is

$$1 - \beta = P\left(Z \geq c - \frac{\sqrt{n}(\mu - \mu_0)}{\sigma} \right)$$

$$= P\left(Z \geq 1.645 - \frac{\sqrt{20}(44 - 42.3)}{4} \right)$$

$$= P(Z \geq -0.256)$$
$$= 0.60.$$

Increasing n to 30, it can be seen that power is now $1 - \beta = 0.75$, meaning that the probability of correctly identifying an improved manufacturing process, when $\mu = 44$, is 0.75. A rough explanation of why this occurs is as follows. Recall that the accuracy of the sample mean, as an estimate of the population mean, is reflected by its squared standard error, σ^2/n. So, as n gets large, its squared standard error decreases, meaning that it is more likely that the sample mean will be close to the true population mean, 44, as opposed to the hypothesized value, 42.3.

We have just illustrated that increasing the sample size can increase power, roughly because this lowers the standard error. Now, it is illustrated that the larger σ happens to be, the lower the power will be, given α, n, and a value for $\mu - \mu_0$. This is because increasing σ increases the standard error.

Example

For the battery example, again consider $\alpha = 0.05$, $\mu - \mu_0 = 44 - 42.3 = 1.7$, and $n = 30$ with $\sigma = 4$. Then, power is 0.75 as previously indicated. But if $\sigma = 8$, power is now 0.31. If $\sigma = 12$, power is only 0.19.

Finally, the smaller α happens to be, the lower will be the power, given values for n, σ, and $\mu - \mu_0$. This is because, as we lower α, the critical value increases, meaning that the value for Z needed to reject increases as well.

Example

For the battery example with $n = 30$, consider three choices for α: 0.05, 0.025, and 0.01. For $\alpha = 0.05$, we have already seen that power is 0.75 when testing $H_0 : \mu < 42.3$ and $\mu = 44$. For $\alpha = 0.025$, the critical value is now $c = 1.96$, so power is

$$1 - \beta = P\left(Z \geq c - \frac{\sqrt{n}(\mu - \mu_0)}{\sigma} \right)$$

$$= P\left(Z \geq 1.96 - \frac{\sqrt{20}(44 - 42.3)}{4} \right)$$

$$= P(Z \geq 0.059)$$

$$= 0.47.$$

If, instead, $\alpha = 0.01$ is used, the critical value is now $c = 2.33$ and power can be seen to be 0.33. This illustrates that if we adjust the critical value so that the probability of a Type I error goes down, power goes down as well. Put another way, the more careful we are to not commit a Type I error by choosing α close to zero, the more likely we are to commit a Type II error if the null hypothesis happens to be false.

The results just described on how n, α, and σ are related to power can be summarized as follows:

- As the sample size, n, gets large, power goes up, so the probability of a Type II error goes down.
- As α goes down, in which case the probability of a Type I error goes down, power goes down and the probability of a Type II error goes up.
- As the standard deviation, σ, goes up, with n, α, and $\mu - \mu_0$ fixed, power goes down.

7.2.1 Power and p-Values

As previously noted, p-values do not indicate the probability of rejecting again if a study is replicated. If unknown to us, power is 0.2 when testing with $\alpha = 0.05$, then the probability of rejecting again, if the study is replicated, is 0.2 regardless of what the p-value happens to be. If, for example, the null hypothesis happens to be true, and by chance the p-value is 0.001, the probability of rejecting again is 0.05 or whatever α value we happen to use.

7.3 TESTING HYPOTHESES ABOUT THE MEAN, σ NOT KNOWN

When the variance is not known, one simply estimates it with the sample variance, in which case the test statistic

$$Z = \frac{\overline{X} - \mu_0}{\sigma/\sqrt{n}}$$

becomes

$$T = \frac{\overline{X} - \mu_0}{s/\sqrt{n}}. \tag{7.7}$$

When the null hypothesis is true, T has a Student's T distribution with $v = n - 1$ degrees of freedom when sampling from a normal distribution. This means that the critical value is read from Table B.4 in Appendix B. The details can be summarized as follows.

Assumptions:

- Random sampling
- normality

Decision Rules:

- For $H_0 : \mu \geq \mu_0$, reject if $T \leq t_\alpha$, where t_α is the α quantile of Student's T distribution with $v = n - 1$ degrees of freedom and T is given by Equation (7.7).

- For $H_0 : \mu \le \mu_0$, reject if $T \ge t_{1-\alpha}$, where now $t_{1-\alpha}$ is the $1 - \alpha$ quantile of Student's T distribution with $v = n - 1$ degrees of freedom.
- For $H_0 : \mu = \mu_0$, reject if $T \ge t_{1-\alpha/2}$ or $T \le t_{\alpha/2}$, where $t_{1-\alpha/2}$ and $t_{\alpha/2}$ are the $1 - \frac{\alpha}{2}$ and the $\alpha/2$ quantiles, respectively, of a Student's T distribution with $v = n - 1$ degrees of freedom. Equivalently, (because $-t_{\alpha/2} = t_{1-\alpha/2}$), reject if $|T| \ge t_{1-\alpha/2}$.

Example

Imagine that for a general measure of anxiety, a researcher claims that the population of college students has a population mean equal to 50. As a check on this claim, suppose that 10 college students are randomly sampled with the goal of testing H_0: $\mu = 50$ with $\alpha = 0.10$. Or, in the context of Tukey's three-decision rule, is it reasonable to make a decision about whether the population mean is less than or greater than 50? Further imagine that the sample standard deviation is $s = 11.4$, and the sample mean is $\overline{X} = 44.5$. Because $n = 10$, the degrees of freedom are $v = n - 1 = 9$ and

$$T = \frac{\overline{X} - \mu_0}{s/\sqrt{n}} = \frac{44.5 - 50}{11.4/\sqrt{10}} = -1.5.$$

Referring to Table B.4 in Appendix B, $P(T \le 1.83) = 0.95$. This means that if we reject when T is less than or equal to -1.83, or greater than or equal to 1.83, the probability of a Type I error will be 0.10, assuming normality. Because the observed value of T is -1.5, which is between the two critical values, fail to reject. In other words, the sample mean is not sufficiently smaller than 50 to be reasonably certain that the population mean μ is less than 50. Note that the steps used to test hypotheses, when σ is not known, mirror the steps used to test hypotheses when σ is known.

Example

Suppose you observe the values

$$12, 20, 34, 45, 34, 36, 37, 50, 11, 32, 29$$

and the goal is to test $H_0 : \mu = 25$ such that the probability of a Type I error is $\alpha = 0.05$. Here, $n = 11$, $\mu_0 = 25$, and it can be seen that $\overline{X} = 33.24$, $s/\sqrt{11} = 3.7$, so

$$T = \frac{\overline{X} - \mu_0}{s/\sqrt{n}} = \frac{33.24 - 25}{3.7} = 2.23.$$

The null hypothesis is that the population mean is exactly equal to 25. So, the critical value is the $1 - \frac{\alpha}{2} = 0.975$ quantile of Student's T distribution with degrees of freedom $v = 11 - 1 = 10$. Table B.4 in Appendix B indicates that

$$P(T \le 2.28) = 0.975,$$

so the decision rule is to reject H_0 if the value of T is greater than or equal to 2.28, or less than or equal to -2.28. Because the absolute value of T is less than 2.28, fail to reject.

7.3.1 R Function t.test

The R function

```
t.test(x,alternative = c('two.sided', 'less', 'greater'), mu =
                0, conf.level = 0.95),
```

which was introduced in Section 6.2.1, can be used to test hypotheses based on Student's T. The argument mu indicates the hypothesized value, μ_0, and defaults to zero. The argument conf.level indicates the value of $1 - \alpha$, in which case the probability of a Type I error is α. By default, $\alpha = 0.05$. If, for example, the goal is to have a Type I error rate equal to 0.01, set the argument conf.level=0.99 and reject if the resulting confidence interval does not contain the hypothesized value. By default, the function tests for equality. If the goal is to test $H_0 : \mu \leq \mu_0$, set the argument alternative="greater," meaning that the goal is to reject if the population mean is greater than the hypothesized value. For $H_0 : \mu \geq \mu_0$, use alternative="less." The function also returns a *p*-value.

Example

The R command

```
t.test(x,alternative="less,"mu=30,conf.level=0.9)
```

tests the hypothesis $H_0 : \mu \geq 30$ with the Type I error probability set to $\alpha = 0.1$.

7.4 STUDENT'S *T* AND NONNORMALITY

An issue of fundamental importance is how well Student's T performs under nonnormality. There are situations where it performs well compared to alternative methods that might be used. But based on properties of Student's T described in Chapter 6, a natural guess is that practical problems might arise, and this speculation turns out to be correct.

As done in Chapter 6, four types of distributions are used to illustrate the impact of nonnormality on Student's T. The first is a symmetric, light-tailed distribution where outliers tend to be rare, which includes normal distributions as a special case. For this case, Student's T performs well in terms of both Type I errors and power compared to alternative methods that might be used. For example, the mean and median are estimating the same unknown value, but the mean offers a power advantage compared to the median. The median offers no power advantage for the situation at hand, roughly because its standard error tends to be larger than the standard error of the mean due to trimming nearly all of the data. For normal distributions, Student's T is optimal, in terms of power, compared to any other estimator that might be used.

When sampling from a symmetric, heavy-tailed distribution, generally the actual probability of a Type I error, when using Student's T, is less than the nominal level. A crude explanation is that outliers tend to inflate the sample variance, a large sample variance lowers the value of T, which in turn makes it less likely to reject. For example, if you test the hypothesis of a zero mean when sampling from the mixed normal shown in Figure 4.5, with $n = 20$ and $\alpha = 0.05$, the actual probability of a Type I error is approximately 0.025. But in terms of power, Student's T performs poorly compared to other methods that might be used. The essential reason is that the standard error of the mean can be relatively large. As an example, imagine that the goal is to test the hypothesis of a zero mean and that observations are sampled from a distribution such as the mixed normal distribution in Figure 4.5, only the population mean is 0.5, in which case power is approximately 0.11 when $n = 20$. But if we test the hypothesis of a zero median instead, using Equation (7.8), power is approximately 0.35.

Next, consider skewed, light-tailed distributions. We saw in Chapter 6 that the distribution of T can be asymmetric, rather than symmetric. When sampling from any symmetric distribution, T also has a symmetric distribution, but, otherwise, its distribution is generally asymmetric. In addition, the actual quantiles can differ substantially from the quantiles of Student's T under normality, resulting in poor control over the probability of a Type I error. Imagine, for example, that observations are randomly sampled from the distribution shown in Figure 6.2 with the goal of having a Type I error probability of 0.05. For sample sizes 40, 80, and 160, the actual probability of a Type I error is 0.149, 0.124, and 0.109, respectively. So, control over the probability of a Type I error improves as the sample size increases, in accordance with a generalization of the central limit theorem, but if we want the probability of a Type I error to be under 0.075, a sample size of about 200 is needed.

As for skewed, heavy-tailed distributions, control over the probability of a Type I error deteriorates. Now, a sample size of more than 300 might be needed to get adequate control over the probability of a Type I error. An added concern is that when outliers are likely to occur, the standard error of the sample mean is relatively large, which could mean relatively poor power. Note that by implication, skewness and outliers affect p-values, which complicates their interpretation. Despite this, we will see situations in later chapters where p-values have practical value.

Here is a brief summary of how Student's T performs under nonnormality:

- For symmetric, light-tailed distributions, Student's T performs relatively well in terms of both Type I errors and power.
- For symmetric, heavy-tailed distributions, the actual probability of a Type I error will not exceed the nominal level, but power can be relatively poor.
- For asymmetric, light-tailed distributions, good control over the probability of a Type I error might require a sample size of 200 or more. Poor power can be an issue.

- For asymmetric, heavy-tailed distributions, serious concerns about Type I errors and power arise, and a sample size of 300 or more might be needed to correct any practical problems.

7.4.1 Bootstrap-t

The bootstrap-t method, introduced in Section 6.6.3, can help improve control over the Type I error probability when testing hypotheses about the population mean, but it does not eliminate all practical concerns. In terms of low power due to a relatively large standard error, the bootstrap-t method offers little or no advantage. In the present context, the strategy behind the bootstrap-t method is to perform a simulation on the observed data, as described in Chapter 6, with the goal of determining an appropriate critical value. That is, rather than assume normality to determine a critical value, use the observed data to determine a critical value. Chapter 6 also noted that there are two variations of the bootstrap-t: equal-tailed and symmetric, both of which can be applied with the R function `trimcibt` in Section 7.6.1. Table 7.2 compares these methods in terms of their ability to control the Type I error probability.

Example

Section 3.2.2 described a study dealing with hangover symptoms when drinking alcohol. Another portion of the study resulted in the following hangover symptoms:

1, 0, 3, 0, 3, 0, 15, 0, 6, 10, 1, 1, 0, 2, 24, 42, 0, 0, 0, 2.

TABLE 7.2 Actual Type I Error Probabilities When Testing Some Hypothesis about the Mean at the $\alpha = 0.05$ Level

Dist.	Method		
	BT	SB	*T*
		n = 20	
N	0.054	0.051	0.050
SL	0.078	0.093	0.140
MN	0.100	0.014	0.022
SH	0.198	0.171	0.202
		n = 100	
N	0.048	0.038	0.050
SL	0.058	0.058	0.083
MN	0.092	0.018	0.041
SH	0.168	0.173	0.190

N, normal; SL, skewed, light-tailed; MN, mixed normal; SH, skewed, heavy-tailed; BT, equal-tailed, bootstrap-t; SB, symmetric bootstrap-t; *T*, Student's *T*.

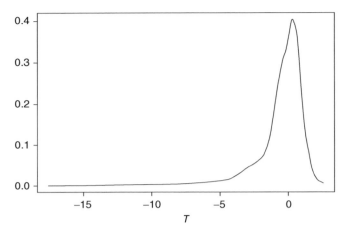

Figure 7.2   The distribution of T based on the bootstrap-t method and the data stemming from a study on hangover symptoms

A bootstrap-t method generates a bootstrap sample as described in Section 6.6.1. It then computes T based on this bootstrap sample, and this process is repeated many times. For the data at hand, 1,000 bootstrap samples were generated, resulting in 1,000 T values. A plot of the resulting T values is shown in Figure 7.2. Under the assumption of normality and with $\alpha = 0.05$, the hypothesis H_0: $\mu = 5.5$ would be rejected if $T \leq -2.09$ or if $T \geq 2.09$. But based on equal-tailed bootstrap-t method, the null hypothesis would be rejected if $T \leq -5.9$ or if $T \geq 1.4$.

7.4.2   Transforming Data

Another strategy for trying to improve the control over the Type I error probability when using Student's T is to transform the data. For example, take the square root of every value and then test some hypothesis. Using logarithms is another common strategy. There are conditions where this approach does indeed improve the control over the Type I error probability. But by modern standards, this technique is relatively ineffective because typically the data remain skewed and transformations generally do not deal with outliers in an effective manner.

7.5   TESTING HYPOTHESES ABOUT MEDIANS

One way of testing hypotheses about the median is to use a strategy similar to Student's T. That is, subtract the hypothesized value from the sample median and divide by an estimate of the standard error. In symbols, if θ_0 represents some hypothesized value for the population median, the test statistic is

$$Z = \frac{M - \theta_0}{S_M}, \tag{7.8}$$

where S_M is the McKean–Schrader estimate of the standard error described in Section 5.4.1. As pointed out in Chapter 6, if tied (duplicated) values are virtually impossible, Z has, approximately, a standard normal distribution, assuming that the null hypothesis is true. This means that hypotheses are tested in essentially the same manner as in Section 7.1. For instance, when testing H_0: $\theta = \theta_0$, reject if $|Z| \geq c$, the $1 - \alpha/2$ quantile of a standard normal distribution. But as previously noted, tied values might result in a poor estimate of the standard error, in which case the confidence interval described in Section 6.4.3 can be used. That is, reject the null hypothesis if the confidence interval does not contain the hypothesized value.

7.5.1   R Function msmedci and sintv2

The R function

```
msmedci(x,alpha=0.05,null.value=0),
```

introduced in Section 6.4.1, can be used to test hypotheses about the population median using the McKean–Schrader estimate of the standard error. The argument `alpha` is the desired Type I error probability, which defaults to 0.05, and `null.value` is the hypothesized value. When dealing with tied values, a slight extension of the method in Section 6.4.3 can be used to compute a p-value. The computations are done via a generalization of the R function `sint` in Section 6.4.4, namely

```
sintv2(x,alpha=0.05,null.value=0).
```

Example

A researcher claims that in 4000 B.C., the median height of adult male skulls was 132 mm. As a check on this claim, consider the following values for 30 skulls:

121, 124, 129, 129, 130, 130, 131, 131, 132, 132, 132, 133, 133, 134, 134,

134, 134, 135, 135, 136, 136, 136, 136, 137, 137, 138, 138, 138, 140, 143.

To test H_0: $\theta = 132$ with a Type I error probability of 0.05, compute the sample median, yielding $M = 134$. The value of S_M can be seen to be 0.97056, so the test statistic is $Z = (134 - 132)/0.97056 = 2.06$. The critical value is the 0.975 quantile of a standard normal distribution, which is read from Table B.1 in Appendix B and found to be 1.96. Because $|Z| \geq 1.96$, reject and conclude that the population median is greater than 132. The p-value is

$$2(1 - P(Z \leq 2.06)) = 0.039.$$

Because there are tied values, the analysis just described might be unsatisfactory in terms of controlling the Type I error probability. Having tied values does not necessarily mean disaster, but the reality is that serious practical problems can occur. For the skull data, using instead the R function `sintv2`, the p-value is 0.043. So, in this particular case, the choice of method made little difference, but the only reliable way of determining whether this is the case is to try both methods.

7.6   TESTING HYPOTHESES BASED ON A TRIMMED MEAN

The methods for computing a confidence interval for a trimmed mean, described in Chapter 6, are readily adapted to testing hypotheses. For example, to test $H_0: \mu_t = \mu_0$ based on a 20% trimmed mean, the test statistic based on the Tukey–McLaughlin method is

$$T_t = \frac{0.6(\overline{X}_t - \mu_0)}{s_w/\sqrt{n}},$$

where s_w is the 20% Winsorized standard deviation.

Decision Rule: The hypothesis $H_0: \mu_t = \mu_0$ is rejected if $T_t \leq t_{\alpha/2}$ or $T_t \geq t_{1-\alpha/2}$, where now $t_{\alpha/2}$ and $t_{1-\alpha/2}$ are the $\alpha/2$ and $1 - \alpha/2$ quantiles of a Student's T distribution with $h - 1$ degrees of freedom, where h is the number of observations left after trimming.

In the context of hypothesis testing, the Tukey–McLaughlin method has several advantages. It performs much better than Student's T in terms of controlling the probability of a Type I error, meaning that it performs well over a much broader range of situations. But even the Tukey–McLaughlin method can be unsatisfactory in terms of Type I errors when the sample size is small and the departure from normality is sufficiently severe: When dealing with distributions where outliers are common, the actual Type I error can be substantially smaller than intended, which might negatively impact power. Another advantage is that under normality, its power is nearly comparable to Student's T and it has higher power than methods based on the median. Compared to Student's T, it has higher power when sampling from symmetric distributions where outliers are common. But if the number of outliers is sufficiently high, using the median can result in even higher power. Also, when dealing with skewed distributions, it is prudent to keep in mind that the population mean, 20% trimmed mean, and median differ, sometimes by a substantial amount. That is, hypotheses about means are not the same as hypotheses about medians.

Chapter 6 described how to compute a confidence interval using a bootstrap-t or percentile bootstrap method. Both can be used to test hypotheses: reject if the resulting confidence interval does not contain the hypothesized value. When using the percentile bootstrap method, here is how a p-value is computed when testing H_0: $\mu_t = \mu_0$. Imagine that B bootstrap samples are taken, resulting in B trimmed means. Let A be the number of bootstrap trimmed means that are less than the hypothesized value, μ_0, and let $p^* = A/B$. Then, the p-value, when testing for exact equality, is $2p^*$ or $2(1 - p^*)$, whichever is smaller. Or, in terms of Tukey's three-decision rule, p^* reflects the strength of the empirical evidence that a decision can be made about whether μ_t is greater than or less than μ_0.

7.6.1   R Functions trimci, trimcipb, and trimcibt

The R functions introduced in Chapter 6 for computing a confidence interval for a trimmed mean can be used to test hypotheses. The R function

```
trimci(x,tr=.2,alpha=0.05,null.value=0)
```

tests H_0: $\mu_t = \mu_0$, where the argument `null.value` indicates the null value, μ_0. The amount of trimming, indicated by the argument `tr`, defaults to 20% and the Type I error probability is indicated by the argument `alpha`. To test H_0: $\mu_t > 0$, for example, with the Type I error probability equal to $\alpha = 0.05$, say, use the command `trimci(x,tr=.2,alpha=0.10)` and reject if the upper end of the confidence interval is negative. That is, simply double the value of the argument `alpha`. If, for example, the 0.90 confidence interval is $(-6, -1)$, reject H_0: $\mu_t > 0$ when testing at the 0.05 level. If the confidence interval is $(-3, 2)$, fail to reject.

The R function

```
trimcibt(x, tr = 0.2, alpha = 0.05, nboot = 599, side = TRUE)
```

uses a bootstrap-t method, where again `side=TRUE` results in a symmetric confidence interval and `side=FALSE` means that an equal-tailed confidence interval will be computed. (The null hypothesis is rejected if the confidence interval does not contain the hypothesized value.) The R function

```
trimpb(x,tr=0.2,alpha=0.05,nboot=2000)
```

uses a percentile bootstrap method.

Table 7.3 compares these methods in terms of controlling the Type I error probability with a sample size of $n = 20$ and when the desired Type I error probability is set at 0.05. If the goal is to guarantee that the Type I error probability does not exceed 0.05, the symmetric bootstrap-t performs relatively well. But the actual Type I error probability can be well below 0.05, raising the concern that power might be relatively low. The same concern applies when using the equal-tailed, bootstrap-t and the Tukey–McLaughlin method. From the point of view of getting a Type I error probability reasonably close to the nominal 0.05 level among the four situations considered, the percentile bootstrap seems to have an advantage.

TABLE 7.3 **Actual Probability of a Type I Error When Using a 20% Trimmed Mean, $\alpha = 0.05$**

Dist.	\multicolumn{4}{c}{Method}			
	BT	SB	P	TM
\multicolumn{5}{c}{$n = 20$}				
N	0.067	0.052	0.063	0.042
SL	0.049	0.050	0.066	0.068
MN	0.022	0.019	0.053	0.015
SH	0.014	0.018	0.066	0.020

N, normal; SL, skewed, light-tailed; MN, mixed normal; SH, skewed, heavy-tailed; BT, equal-tailed, bootstrap-t; SB, symmetric bootstrap-t; P, Percentile bootstrap; TM, Tukey–McLaughlin.

Example

Doksum and Sievers (1976) report data on weight gain among rats. One group was the control and the other was exposed to an ozone environment. For illustrative purposes, attention is focused on the control group and we consider the claim that the typical weight gain is 26.4, as measured by the 20% trimmed mean. The sample size is $n = 23$, the 20% trimmed mean is $\overline{X}_t = 23.3$, $s_w = 3.9$, and for $H_0 : \mu_t = 26.4$, we see that

$$T_t = \frac{0.6(\overline{X}_t - \mu_0)}{s_w/\sqrt{n}} = \frac{0.6(23.3 - 26.4)}{3.9/\sqrt{23}} = -2.3.$$

Because there are 23 rats and 8 values are trimmed, the degrees of freedom are $\nu = 23 - 8 - 1 = 14$, and the critical value (read from Table B.4 in Appendix B) is $t = 2.14$. The p-value is 0.037. Because $|T| = |-2.3| = 2.3$ is greater than the critical value, and because the sample trimmed mean is less than the hypothesized value, reject the null hypothesis and conclude that the population trimmed mean is less than 26.4.

7.7 SKIPPED ESTIMATORS

Chapter 2 mentioned a skipped estimator where values flagged as outliers by the MAD–median rule are removed and the average of the remaining data is computed. This is the modified one-step M-estimator (MOM). The only known way of computing a reasonably accurate confidence interval is via the percentile bootstrap method. When testing hypotheses, reject if the confidence interval does not contain the hypothesized value.

A point that cannot be stressed enough is that different methods can provide different perspectives that can paint a decidedly different picture about the nature of the data. Consequently, understanding data can require, among other things, a good understanding of the features of data that can impact a particular hypothesis testing method. One reason different methods can give different results is that when distributions are skewed, generally the population mean, MOM, median, and 20% trimmed mean differ. So, for example, if the goal is to test the hypothesis that the population mean is 20, this hypothesis could be true even when the population median has some other value. In practical terms, if there is interest in making inferences about the mean when a distribution is skewed, methods based on a 20% trimmed mean, MOM, or median can be highly unsatisfactory. Another reason different methods can give different results is that the standard errors of the mean, 20% trimmed mean, and median can differ substantially, which in turn can impact power.

7.7.1 R Function momci

The R function

```
momci(x,alpha=0.05,nboot=2000,null.value=0)
```

tests hypotheses based on the skipped estimator MOM. As usual, the argument `null.value` is the hypothesized value, which defaults to zero. The function returns a p-value as well as a confidence interval.

Example

Consider again the sexual attitude data in Table 2.3, and suppose someone claims the typical male desires one sexual partner during the next 30 years. Testing the hypothesis H_0: $\mu = 1$ with Student's T, the p-value is $p = 0.266$. Using the Tukey–McLaughlin method with a 20% trimmed mean, $p = 0.002$. Using a percentile bootstrap method, again with a 20% trimmed mean, $p < 0.001$. Using the median via the R function `sintv2`, $p = 0.99$. Using the R function `momci`, which is based on the MOM estimator, $p = 0.232$. These strikingly different results stem from the fact that the methods used are sensitive to different features of the data and that the data at hand are highly skewed with outliers, as noted in Chapter 2.

One final comment might help. Based on the many negative features associated with Student's T, the utility of methods based on means might seem rather bleak in the sense that there is concern about the possibility of making a Type I error or having relatively low power, unless perhaps the sample size is quite large. Despite known problems covered here, plus some additional concerns covered in subsequent chapters, methods based on means can be argued to have practical value, provided the results are interpreted in a manner that takes into account modern insights, some of which are yet to be described.

7.8 SUMMARY

- When using Student's T test, the actual probability of a Type I error will be fairly close to the nominal level when sampling from symmetric distributions where outliers are rare. If sampling is from a symmetric distribution where outliers are common, the actual probability of a Type I error can drop well below the intended level.

- When using Student's T test, control over the probability of a Type I error can exceed the intended level when sampling from skewed distributions, particularly when dealing with situations where outliers are common. In some situations, even with a sample size of $n = 300$, Student's T test performs poorly.

- Skewness and outliers can adversely affect the power of Student's T.

- From the perspective of hypothesis testing, p-values and confidence intervals complement one another. That is, they provide different information. If a confidence interval does not contain the hypothesized value, the null hypothesis is rejected and the confidence interval provides information about the range of values that are likely to contain the true value of the measure of location—assuming that an accurate confidence can be computed. A p-value supplements a confidence interval, from the point of view of Tukey's three-decision rule, by quantifying the extent it is reasonable to make a decision about whether a measure of location is greater than or less than the hypothesized value.

- When using Equation (7.8) to test hypotheses about the median, control over the probability of a Type I error is reasonably good when tied values never occur. But when tied values can occur, it should be used with caution if at all. Use, instead, the method in Section 6.4.3. A p-value can be computed via the R function sintv2, which was described in Section 7.5.1.
- In terms of controlling the probability of a Type I error, the Tukey–McLaughlin method based on Equation (7.9) with a 20% trimmed mean performs reasonably well over a broader range of situations compared to methods based on the mean. But for skewed distributions, it is inappropriate in terms of testing hypotheses about the population mean.
- Generally, some type of bootstrap method has practical value in terms of controlling the probability of a Type I error. In some situations, it is the only reasonable option, such as when using the skipped estimator MOM.

7.9 EXERCISES

1. Given that $\overline{X} = 78$, $\sigma^2 = 25$, $n = 10$, and $\alpha = 0.05$, test $H_0 : \mu \geq 80$, assuming that observations are randomly sampled from a normal distribution.
2. Repeat the previous exercise but test $H_0 : \mu = 80$.
3. For the data in Exercise 1, compute a 0.95 confidence interval and verify that this interval is consistent with your decision about whether to reject the null hypothesis $H_0 : \mu = 80$.
4. For Exercise 1, determine the p-value.
5. For Exercise 2, determine the p-value.
6. Given that $\overline{X} = 120$, $\sigma = 5$, $n = 49$, and $\alpha = 0.05$, test $H_0 : \mu \geq 130$, assuming that observations are randomly sampled from a normal distribution.
7. Repeat the previous exercise but test $H_0 : \mu = 130$.
8. For the previous exercise, compute a 0.95 confidence interval and compare the result with your decision about whether to reject H_0.
9. If $\overline{X} = 23$ and $\alpha = 0.025$, can you make a decision about whether to reject $H_0 : \mu \leq 25$ without knowing σ?
10. An electronics firm mass-produces a component for which there is a standard measure of quality. Based on testing vast numbers of these components, the company has found that the average quality is $\mu = 232$ with $\sigma = 4$. However, in recent years, the quality has not been checked, so management asks you to check their claim with the goal of being reasonably certain that an average quality of less than 232 can be ruled out. That is, assume that the quality is poor and in fact less than 232 with the goal of empirically establishing that this assumption is unlikely. You get $\overline{X} = 240$ based on a sample $n = 25$ components, and you want the probability of a Type I error to be 0.01. State the null hypothesis and perform the appropriate test, assuming normality.

11. An antipollution device for cars is claimed to have an average effectiveness of exactly 546. Based on a test of 20 such devices, you find that $\overline{X} = 565$. Assuming normality and that $\sigma = 40$, would you rule out the claim with a Type I error probability of 0.05?

12. Comment on the relative merits of using a 0.95 confidence interval for addressing the effectiveness of the antipollution device in the previous exercise rather than testing the hypothesis $H_0: \mu = 232$.

13. For $n = 25$, $\alpha = 0.01$, $\sigma = 5$, and $H_0 : \mu \geq 60$, verify that power is 0.95 when $\mu = 56$.

14. For $n = 36$, $\alpha = 0.025$, $\sigma = 8$, and $H_0 : \mu \leq 100$, verify that power is 0.61 when $\mu = 103$.

15. For $n = 49$, $\alpha = 0.05$, $\sigma = 10$, and $H_0 : \mu = 50$, verify that power is approximately 0.56 when $\mu = 47$.

16. A manufacturer of medication for migraine headaches knows that their product can damage the stomach if taken too often. Imagine that by a standard measuring process, the average damage is $\mu = 48$. A modification of their product is being contemplated, and based on 10 trials, it is found that $\overline{X} = 46$. Assuming $\sigma = 5$, they test $H_0: \mu \geq 48$, the idea being that if they reject, there is convincing evidence that the average amount of damage is less than 48. Then,

$$Z = \frac{46 - 48}{5/\sqrt{10}} = -1.3.$$

With $\alpha = 0.05$, the critical value is -1.645, so they do not reject because Z is not less than the critical value. What might be wrong with accepting H_0 and concluding that the modification results in an average amount of damage greater than or equal to 48?

17. For the previous exercise, verify that power is 0.35 if $\mu = 46$.

18. The previous exercise indicates that power is relatively low with only $n = 10$ observations. Imagine that you want power to be at least 0.8. One way of getting more power is to increase the sample size, n. Verify that for sample sizes of 20, 30, and 40, power is 0.56, 0.71, and 0.81, respectively.

19. For the previous exercise, rather than increase the sample size, what else might you do to increase power? What is a negative consequence of using this strategy?

20. Given the following values for $\overline{X}$ and s: (a) $\overline{X} = 44$, $s = 10$, (b) $\overline{X} = 43$, $s = 10$, (c) $\overline{X} = 43$, $s = 2$, test the hypothesis $H_0: \mu = 42$ with $\alpha = 0.05$ and $n = 25$.

21. For part b of the last exercise, you fail to reject but you reject for the situation in part c. What does this illustrate about power?

22. Test the hypothesis $H_0 : \mu \leq 42$ with $\alpha = 0.05$ and $n = 16$ for the following values for $\overline{X}$ and s: (a) $\overline{X} = 44$, $s = 10$, (b) $\overline{X} = 43$, $s = 10$, (c) $\overline{X} = 43$, $s = 2$.

23. Repeat the previous exercise and only test $H_0 : \mu \geq 42$.

24. A company claims that on average, when their toothpaste is used, 45% of all bacteria related to gingivitis is killed. For 10 individuals, it is found that the

percentages of bacteria killed are 38, 44, 62, 72, 43, 40, 43, 42, 39, 41. The mean and standard deviation of these values are $\overline{X} = 46.4$ and $s = 11.27$, respectively. Assuming normality, test the hypothesis that the average percentage is 45 with $\alpha = 0.05$.

25. A portion of a study by Wechsler (1958) reports that for 100 males taking the Wechsler Adult Intelligent Scale (WAIS), the sample mean and variance on picture completion are $\overline{X} = 9.79$ and $s = 2.72$, respectively. Test the hypothesis $H_0 : \mu \geq 10.5$ with $\alpha = 0.025$.

26. Given that $n = 16$, $\overline{X} = 40$, and $s = 4$, test $H_0: \mu \leq 38$ with $\alpha = 0.01$.

27. Given that $n = 9$, $\overline{X} = 33$, and $s = 4$, test $H_0: \mu = 32$ with $\alpha = 0.05$.

28. An engineer believes it takes an average of 150 man-hours to assemble a portion of an automobile. As a check, the time to assemble 10 such parts was ascertained, yielding $\overline{X} = 146$ and $s = 2.5$. Test the engineer's belief with $\alpha = 0.05$.

29. In a study of court administration, the following times to disposition were determined for 20 cases and found to be

$$42, 90, 84, 87, 116, 95, 86, 99, 93, 92$$

$$121, 71, 66, 98, 79, 102, 60, 112, 105, 98.$$

Use R to test the hypothesis that the average time to disposition is less than or equal to 80. Use $\alpha = 0.01$.

30. Assuming 20% trimming, test the hypothesis $H_0 : \mu_t = 42$ with $\alpha = 0.05$ and $n = 20$ given the following values for $\overline{X}_t$ and s_w: (a) $\overline{X}_t = 44, s_w = 9$, (b) $\overline{X}_t = 43$, $s_w = 9$, (c) $\overline{X}_t = 43, s_w = 3$.

31. Repeat the previous exercise, only test the hypothesis $H_0 : \mu_t \leq 42$ with $\alpha = 0.05$ and $n = 16$.

32. For the data in Exercise 24, the 20% trimmed mean is $\overline{X}_t = 42.17$ with a Winsorized standard deviation of $s_w = 1.73$. Test the hypothesis that the population trimmed mean is 45 with $\alpha = 0.05$.

33. A standard measure of aggression in 7-year-old children has been found to have a 20% trimmed mean of 4.8 based on years of experience. A psychologist wants to know whether the trimmed mean for children with divorced parents is greater than or less than 4.8. Suppose $\overline{X}_t = 5.1$ with $s_w = 7$ based on $n = 25$. Test the hypothesis that the population trimmed mean is exactly 4.8 with $\alpha = 0.01$ and state whether a decision can be made.

34. Summarize the relative merits of using a percentile bootstrap method.

35. For the data in the R variable x, imagine that you want to compute Z with the goal of testing the hypothesis that $\mu = 6$. Assuming that the R variable null.value contains the hypothesized value and that sigma contains the standard deviation, indicate the R commands for computing Z.

36. R has a built-in data set called ToothGrowth. Information about the data can be obtained with the R command ?ToothGrowth. The first column contains measures of tooth growth in guinea pigs and the third column indicates the dose

levels of vitamin C that were used in the experiment. Consider the claim that the typical growth is 8 when the vitamin C level is 0.5 mg. Using R, verify that with Student's T and $\alpha = 0.05$, it would be decided that the population mean is larger than 8. Verify that no decision would be made based on the Tukey–McLauglin method with a 20% trimmed mean. Plot the data and comment on why the two methods give different results.

37. Based on the results for the previous exercise, speculate about whether you would reject using a median or MOM. Use R to check your speculation.

8

CORRELATION AND REGRESSION

A common goal is determining whether two variables are dependent and, if they are dependent, trying to understand the nature of the association. Is there an association between breast cancer rates and exposure to solar radiation? If yes, how might it be described in an effective manner? What is the association between weight gain in infants and the amount of ozone in the air? How strong is the association? This chapter describes some of the more basic techniques aimed at answering these questions.

8.1 REGRESSION BASICS

A fundamental issue in a regression analysis can be described in general terms as follows. Consider any two variables, say X (e.g., marital aggression in the home) and Y (e.g., cognitive functioning of children living in the home). How might we estimate the typical value of Y if we are told the value of X? If marital aggression in the home is relatively low, is the typical level of cognitive functioning of children living in the home higher compared to homes where marital aggression is relatively high? The most common strategy for answering this type of question is to assume that the typical value of Y can be modeled with a straight line. In symbols, it is assumed that the typical value of Y is given by

$$Y = \beta_0 + \beta_1 X, \tag{8.1}$$

where β_0 and β_1 are the unknown intercept and slope, respectively, which are estimated based on observations to be made. The variable X has been given several

Understanding and Applying Basic Statistical Methods Using R, First Edition. Rand R. Wilcox.
© 2017 John Wiley & Sons, Inc. Published 2017 by John Wiley & Sons, Inc.
www.wiley.com/go/Wilcox/Statistical_Methods_R

names: predictor, regressor, the explanatory variable, and the independent variable. The variable Y is called the dependent variable.

Example

Consider the population of children living in a home for which marital aggression is $X = 6$. Assuming that the model given by Equation (8.1) is true, and if $\beta_1 = 0.5$ and $\beta_0 = 10$, then the typical level of cognitive functioning among all of these children is $10 + 0.5 \times 6 = 13$.

Assuming that the typical value of Y, given X, can be modeled with a straight line given by Equation (8.1), there is the problem of estimating β_1, the slope, and β_0, the intercept, based on the available data. There are many methods aimed at addressing this problem. Today, the most popular method is based on what is called the *least squares* principle, and, therefore, understanding its relative merits is essential. It has various advantages over competing methods, but it also has serious deficiencies, as we shall see. To provide some sense of when it performs well and when it performs poorly, and why the method remains popular today, it helps to describe some of the reasons the method rose to prominence.

A simple example of some historical interest will help set the stage. Newton, in his *Principia*, argued that the earth bulges at the equator due to its rotation. In contrast, based on empirical measures, the astronomer Cassini suspected that the earth bulges at the poles, but because of possible measurement errors, there was uncertainty about whether Cassini's data could be used to make valid inferences. In an attempt to resolve the issue, the French government funded expeditions to measure the linear length of a degree of latitude at several places on the earth. Newton's arguments suggested that there would be an approximately linear association between a certain transformation of the latitude and measures of arc length. For convenience, let X represent the transformed latitude and let Y represent the arc length. According to Newton, it should be the case that $\beta_1/3\beta_0$ is approximately $1/230$.

During the second half of the eighteenth century, Roger Boscovich attempted to resolve the shape of the earth using the data in Table 8.1. Recall that any two distinct points determine a line. If we denote the two points by (X_1, Y_1) and (X_2, Y_2), then the slope is given by

$$b_1 = \frac{Y_2 - Y_1}{X_2 - X_1},$$

the difference between the Y values divided by the difference between the X values. The intercept is given by

$$b_0 = \overline{Y} - b_1\overline{X}.$$

So, for the first and last points in Table 8.1, the slope is

$$b_1 = \frac{57,422 - 56,751}{0.8386 - 0} = 800.14,$$

TABLE 8.1   Boscovich's Data on Meridian Arcs

Place	Transformed Latitude	Arc Length
Quito	0.0000	56,751
Cape of Good Hope	0.2987	57,037
Rome	0.4648	56,979
Paris	0.5762	57,074
Lapland	0.8386	57,422

and the intercept is given by

$$b_0 = 57,086.5 - 800.14(0.4193) = 56,751.$$

But Boscovich has a problem: he has five points and each pair of points gives a different value for the slope and intercept. Differences were to be expected because the measurements of arc length and latitude cannot be done precisely. That is, there is measurement error due to the instruments being used and variations due to the individuals taking the measurements. So, an issue is whether the different slopes can be combined in some manner to produce a reasonable estimate of the true slope and intercept (β_1 and β_0) if no measurement errors were made.

For the data at hand, there are 10 pairs of points that could be used to estimate the slope and intercept. The corresponding estimates of the slopes, written in ascending order, are

$$-349.19, 133.33, 490.53, 560.57, 713.09, 800.14, 852.79, 957.48, 1185.13, 1326.22.$$

One possibility is to simply average these 10 values yielding a single estimate of the unknown slope, an idea that dates back to at least the year 1750. This yields 667. Although averaging the slopes is reasonable, from a practical point of view, it has two serious difficulties. The first is that in general, as the number of points increases, the number of pairs of points that must be averaged quickly becomes impractical without a computer. For example, if Boscovich had 50 points rather than only 5, he would need to average 1,225 slopes. With a 100 points, he would need to average 4,950 slopes. The second problem is that it is not immediately clear how to assess the precision of the estimate. That is, how might we compute a confidence interval for the true slope? It might seem that we could somehow extend the methods in Chapters 5 and 6 to get a solution, but there are technical problems that are very difficult to address in a reasonably simple fashion.

8.1.1   Residuals and a Method for Estimating the Median of Y Given X

Two major advances have played a fundamental role when trying to address the two practical problems just described. The first stems from Boscovich who suggested that the fit of a regression line be judged based on what are called residuals. The basic idea is to judge a choice for the slope and intercept based on the overall discrepancy between the observed Y values and those predicted by some regression equation under consideration. If we denote candidate choices for the slope and intercept by b_1 and b_0, then the typical value of Y, given a value for X, is taken to be

$$\hat{Y} = b_0 + b_1 X,$$

where the notation $\hat{Y}$ is traditionally used to make a distinction between the observed Y value and the value predicted by the regression equation. Boscovich's suggestion was to judge how well the choice for the slope and intercept performs in terms of the discrepancy between the observed Y value and the predicted value, $\hat{Y}$.

In more formal terms, imagine we have n points: $(X_1, Y_1), \ldots, (X_n, Y_n)$. Further imagine that consideration is being given to predicting Y with X using the equation $\hat{Y} = b_0 + b_1 X$. Then, the *residuals* corresponding to these n points are

$$r_1 = Y_1 - \hat{Y}_1, r_2 = Y_2 - \hat{Y}_2, \ldots, r_n = Y_n - \hat{Y}_n,$$

which reflect the discrepancies between the observed Y values and the predicted values, $\hat{Y}$.

Example

Consider again Boscovich's data, and suppose the goal is to judge how well some choice for the intercept and slope performs. To be concrete, imagine that consideration is being given to the possibility that the slope is $b_1 = 800.14$ and the intercept is $b_0 = 56,751$. So for Boscovich's data, we are considering the regression equation $\hat{Y} = 56,751 + 800.14X$, and the goal is to get some overall sense of how well this equation performs. The resulting values for $\hat{Y}$ and the residuals are as follows:

i	Y_i	$\hat{Y}_i$	r_i (Residuals)
1	56,751	56,737.43	13.57
2	57,037	56,953.52	83.48
3	56,979	57,073.68	−94.68
4	57,074	57,154.27	−80.27
5	57,422	57,344.10	77.90

But there are infinitely many choices for the slope and intercept. How might the slope and intercept be chosen so that they are optimal in some sense? Boscovich went on to suggest that the overall effectiveness of a regression line be judged by the sum of the absolute values of the residuals. In particular, his suggestion was to choose the slope and intercept to be the values b_1 and b_0 that minimize

$$\sum |r_i|.$$

That is, determine the values for b_1 and b_0 that minimize

$$\sum |Y_i - b_1 X_i - b_0|. \tag{8.2}$$

Today, this called is *least absolute value regression*. Boscovich devised a numerical method for determining the slope and intercept, it reflected an important advance over simply averaging the slopes of all pairs of points, but major practical problems remained. It was still relatively difficult to perform the calculations with many pairs of points, and without a computer, computing confidence intervals cannot be done in a practical manner.

There is a feature of Boscovich's method that should be stressed. It can be shown that his method for determining the slope and intercept is tantamount to estimating the median of Y given X with $\hat{Y} = b_0 + b_1 X$. For Boscovich's data, the values for the slope and intercept that minimize Equation (8.2) are $b_1 = 800.14$ and $b_0 = 56,751$, respectively. This means, for example, that the median arc length among all measures that might be taken, given that the latitude is 0.5, is estimated to be $Y = 56,751 + 800.14(0.5) = 57,151.07$.

8.1.2   R function qreg and Qreg

Assuming that the R package quant as well as the functions in the file Rallfun have been installed (as described in Section 1.4), the R function

```
qreg(x,y,qval=0.5,q=NULL,xout=FALSE,outfun=outpro,
        plotit=FALSE,xlab='X',ylab='Y')
```

computes the least absolute value regression estimates of the slope and intercept. The argument qval indicates the quantile to be used, which defaults to 0.5, the median. That is, the regression line is designed to estimate the median of Y given X. If the goal is to estimate the upper quartile of Y given X, setting the argument qval=0.75 accomplishes this goal using a generalization of the least absolute value regression estimator derived by Koenker and Bassett (1978). The argument q can be used instead of the argument qval to alter the quantile to be used. The argument xout indicates whether data are to be removed if the value of the independent variable is flagged as an outlier. (Section 8.3 elaborates on this issue.) The argument outfun indicates the method used to detect outliers, which defaults to the MAD–median rule when there is only one independent variable. Setting the argument plotit=TRUE results in a scatterplot of the data that includes the estimated regression line. The arguments xlab and ylab can be used to label the *x*-axis and *y*-axis, respectively.

Suppose the values for the dependent variable are 6, 2, 12, 17, 6, 21, 19. Note that there are tied (duplicated) values; the value 6 occurs twice. In seemingly rare instances, qreg might not function properly when there are tied values among the dependent variable, in which case the R function

```
Qreg(x,y,q=0.5,xout=FALSE,outfun=outpro,
        plotit=FALSE,xlab='X',ylab='Y')
```

can be used. The R function qreg has a lower execution time than Qreg, which might be an issue when using a bootstrap technique. Often, these two functions give identical values, but the estimates can differ somewhat due to using different numerical algorithms to estimate the slope and intercept.

8.2   LEAST SQUARES REGRESSION

In the year 1809, about 50 years after Boscovich's suggestion to use least absolute value regression to determine the slope and intercept, Legendre published a paper describing a slight variation of Boscovich's method that would prove to be a major breakthrough. Indeed, Legendre's modification continues to be the most commonly used technique today. His idea was to use the sum of the squared residuals when judging how well a regression line performs as opposed to the sum of the absolute values. So, Legendre's suggestion is to choose values for the slope (b_1) and intercept (b_0) that minimize

$$\sum r_i^2. \tag{8.3}$$

That is, determine the values for b_1 and b_0 that minimize

$$\sum (Y_i - b_1 X_i - b_0)^2. \tag{8.4}$$

This is an example of what is called the *least squares principle*. Initially, it might seem that this modification makes little practical difference, but it greatly simplifies the calculations and provides a convenient framework for developing a method for computing confidence intervals and testing hypotheses. For convenience, let

$$A = \sum (X_i - \overline{X})(Y_i - \overline{Y})$$

and

$$C = \sum (X_i - \overline{X})^2.$$

Then, based on the least squares principle, it can be shown that the slope is given by

$$b_1 = \frac{A}{C} \tag{8.5}$$

and the intercept is given by

$$b_0 = \overline{Y} - b_1 \overline{X}. \tag{8.6}$$

Example
Table 8.2 summarizes the computational details using Boscovich's data in Table 8.1. As indicated, $A = 283.24$, $C = 0.3915$, so the slope is estimated to be $b_1 = 283.24/0.3915 = 723.5$. Because $\overline{Y} = 57,052.6$ and $\overline{X} = 0.43566$, the intercept is $b_0 = 57,052.6 - 723.5(0.43566) = 56,737.4$.

As previously noted, least absolute value regression results in an estimate of the median of Y given X. In contrast, least squares regression attempts to estimate the mean of Y given X.

TABLE 8.2   Computing the Least Squares Slope Using Boscovich's Data

i	$X_i - \overline{X}$	$Y_i - \overline{Y}$	$(X_i - \overline{X})^2$	$(X_i - \overline{X})(Y_i - \overline{Y})$
1	−0.43566	−301.6	0.18980	131.395
2	−0.13696	−15.6	0.01876	2.137
3	0.02914	−73.6	0.00085	−2.145
4	0.14054	21.4	0.01975	3.008
5	0.40294	369.4	0.16236	148.846
Sum			0.3915	283.24

To illustrate what this means, consider a study conducted by E. Sockett and colleagues that deals with children diagnosed with diabetes. (The data are given in Exercise 14, and they are stored in the file diabetes_sockett_dat.txt, which can be downloaded from the author's web page as described in Section 1.5.) One of the goals was to understand how a child's age is related to their C-peptide concentrations. Consider all children of age 7. For various reasons, C-peptide concentrations among these children will vary. One issue of possible interest is determining the average C-peptide concentration among 7-year-old children. Similarly, one might want to know the average C-peptide concentration among all children of age 8 or 7.5, and so on. If we fit a least squares line to the data, it is assumed that the mean C-peptide concentration, given a child's age, is equal to $\beta_0 + \beta_1(\text{Age})$ for some unknown slope (β_1) and intercept (β_0) that are to be estimated based on observations to be made. In the notation of Chapter 4, another way to write this is

$$E(Y|X) = \beta_0 + \beta_1 X,$$

which says that the conditional mean of Y (C-peptide concentration in the example), given X (age in the example) is given by $\beta_0 + \beta_1 X$.

Example

Imagine you want to buy a house in a particular suburb of Los Angeles. Table 8.3 shows the selling price of homes during the month of May 1998, plus the size of the home in square feet. Given that you are interested in buying a home with 2,000 square feet, what would you expect to pay? What would you expect to pay if the house has 1,500 square feet instead? It can be seen that the least squares regression line for predicting the selling price, given the size of the house, is $\hat{Y} = 0.215(X) + 38.192$. So, an estimate of the average cost of a home having 1,500 square feet is $360,692.

Example

We saw that for Boscovich's data in Table 8.1, the least squares regression estimate of β_1 is $b_1 = 723.44$ and the estimate of β_0 is 56,737.43. This says, for example, that the estimated mean arc length, corresponding to a transformed latitude of 0.4, is $\hat{Y} = 723.44(0.4) + 56,737.43 = 57,026.81$. Using least absolute value regression yields

TABLE 8.3 Sale Price of Homes (Divided by 1,000) and Size in Square Feet

Home i	Size (X_i)	Sales Price (Y_i)	Home i	Size (X_i)	Sales Price (Y_i)
1	2,359	510	15	3,883	859
2	3,397	690	16	1,937	435
3	1,232	365	17	2,565	555
4	2,608	592	18	2,722	525
5	4,870	1,125	19	4,231	805
6	4,225	850	20	1,488	369
7	1,390	363	21	4,261	930
8	2,028	559	22	1,613	375
9	3,700	860	23	2,746	670
10	2,949	695	24	1,550	290
11	688	182	25	3,000	715
12	3,147	860	26	1,743	365
13	4,000	1,050	27	2,388	610
14	4,180	675	28	4,522	1,290

$b_1 = 755.62$ and $b_0 = 56,686.32$. So, the estimated median arc length, corresponding to a transformed latitude of 0.4, is $\hat{Y} = 755.62(0.4) + 56,686.32 = 56,988.57$. In this particular case, there is little difference between the estimated mean of Y, $\hat{Y} = 57,026.81$, compared to the estimated median of Y, $\hat{Y} = 56,988.57$. But as pointed out in Chapter 2, the mean and median can differ substantially because the mean is sensitive to even a single outlier in contrast to the median, which is highly insensitive to outliers. In a similar manner, least squares and least absolute value regression can result in substantially different estimates for the slope and intercept as illustrated in Section 8.3.

8.2.1   R Functions lsfit, lm, ols, plot, and abline

The built-in R function

```
lsfit(x, y)
```

computes the least squares estimate of the slope and intercept. The built-in R function

```
lm(y ~ x)
```

also computes the least squares estimate of the slope and intercept. The R command y~x is an example of what R calls a *formula*. Roughly, it indicates that the goal is to determine the typical value of Y, given some value for X.

The R function

```
ols(x,y,xout=FALSE,outfun=outpro,plotit=FALSE,
        xlab='X',ylab='Y',zlab='Z'),
```

written for this book, also computes the least squares estimate of the slope and intercept. (OLS is a commonly used acronym for ordinary least squares.) It is generally prudent to check on the impact of outliers among the independent variable. This can be done by setting the argument xout=TRUE, which indicates that data are to be removed if the value of the independent variable is flagged as an outlier. The argument outfun indicates the outlier detection method to be used, which defaults to the MAD–median rule when there is only one independent variable. Setting the argument plotit=TRUE, the function creates a scatterplot of the data and plots the regression line as well. Labels for the x-axis and y-axis can be supplied via the arguments xlab and ylab. (If there are two independent variables, a regression plane is plotted and the argument zlab can be used to label the z-axis.) Plotting the data can be invaluable as will be illustrated.

Another way to plot the least squares regression line is to first create a scatterplot of the data with the R function

$$plot(x,y)$$

and then add the regression line to the plot with the R command

$$abline(lsfit(x,y)\$coef).$$

(When using the R function plot, again xlab and ylab can be used to label the x-axis and y-axis, respectively.)

8.3   DEALING WITH OUTLIERS

Outliers can have a major impact on the estimate of the slope and intercept of a regression line. Outliers among both the independent and dependent variables are a concern and are generally treated in a different manner.

8.3.1   Outliers among the Independent Variable

First, focus on outliers among the independent variable X, which are called *leverage points*. When using least squares regression, even a single outlier has the potential of resulting in a regression line that poorly fits the bulk of the points. Indeed, a properly placed outlier can make the estimate of the slope arbitrarily large or small. Even when using robust regression estimators, we will see that it is generally a good idea to check on the impact of leverage points. There is a simple strategy for doing this: remove any data for which the independent variable is flagged an outlier and compare the estimates of the slope and intercept to the estimates obtained when using all of the data. As indicated in Sections 8.1.2 and 8.2.1, this is easily done when using the R functions ols, qreg, and Qreg by setting the argument xout=TRUE. The same can be done when using other robust estimators via R functions to be described.

Example

Figure 8.1, which shows a scatterplot of the surface temperature of 47 stars and their light intensity, illustrates that removing outliers among the independent variable can have a major impact on the least squares regression estimate of the slope and intercept. Assuming the data are stored in the R variable star, a matrix with surface temperatures in column 1 and light intensity in column 2, Figure 8.1 was created with two commands:

```
ols(star[,1],star[,2],plotit=TRUE,xlab='Surface Tempera-
ture',

ylab='Light Intensity')
abline(ols(star[,1],star[,2],xout=TRUE)$coef,lty=2).
```

The first command creates the scatterplot and the least squares regression line using all of the data. This is the solid line with the negative slope in Figure 8.1. The second command adds the regression line when the observations associated with leverage points are removed. The R argument lty=2 tells R to plot a dashed line rather than a solid line.

Notice that the four points in the upper-left portion of the plot appear to be outliers and the MAD–Median rule confirms that among the values of the independent variable (surface temperature) this is indeed the case. Restricting the range of the independent variable to values greater than 3.6 effectively removes these four outliers; the resulting estimate of the slope is now $b_1 = 2.05$. But the MAD–median rule indicates that there is one more leverage point where the surface temperature is 3.84. Removing all of the data associated with leverage points, the estimated slope of the regression line is now $b_1 = 2.98$, which corresponds to the dotted line in Figure 8.1.

Although the least absolute value regression estimator is aimed at estimating the median of Y, given X, even a single leverage point can have a tremendous impact on the estimate of the slope and intercept. For the star data in Figure 8.1, the R function qreg estimates the slope and intercept to be $b_1 = -0.69$ and $b_0 = 8.15$. Removing observations associated with leverage points by setting the argument xout=TRUE, the estimates are $b_1 = 3.28$ and $b_0 = -9.54$.

8.3.2   Dealing with Outliers among the Dependent Variable

Many regression estimators have been proposed for dealing with outliers among the dependent variable Y (e.g., Wilcox, 2012b), but no single estimator is always best. This section describes one of these estimators that has been studied extensively and found to perform relatively well.

As pointed out in Section 8.1, an early strategy for estimating the slope, β_1, was to compute the slope for all pairs of points and average them. The Theil (1950) and Sen (1968) estimator is simply the median of the slopes rather than their average, which is labeled b_{1ts}. The intercept is estimated to be

$$b_{0ts} = M_y - b_{1ts}M_x,$$

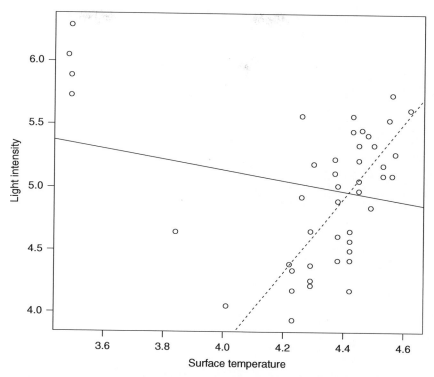

Figure 8.1 A few outliers among the independent variable can drastically alter the least squares regression line. Here, the outliers in the upper-left corner result in a regression line having a slightly negative slope. The MAD–median rule indicates that the five smallest surface temperature values are outliers. These are the four points in the upper-left corner, as well as the surface temperature value 3.84. If these outliers are removed, the slope is positive and better reflects the association among the bulk of the points

where M_x and M_y are the medians of the X and Y values, respectively. For Boscovich's data in Table 8.1, the Theil–Sen estimate of the slope is

$$b_{1ts} = 756.6.$$

It can be seen that $M_x = 0.4648$, $M_y = 57,037$, so the estimate of the intercept is

$$b_{0ts} = 57,037 - 756.6(0.4648) = 56,685.3.$$

A technical concern with both the least squares estimator and the least absolute value estimator is that the estimates of the slope and intercept can be made arbitrarily large, or arbitrarily small, by a single outlier. The least absolute value estimator mitigates the impact of outliers among the dependent variable, but it does not deal effectively with leverage points (outliers among the independent variable). The Theil–Sen estimator deals with both leverage points and outliers among the values of the dependent variable: about 30% of the points must be altered to make the estimates of the slope and intercept arbitrarily large. That is, there is a sense in which the Theil–Sen estimator is less sensitive to outliers. Nevertheless, leverage points can have a substantial impact on the Theil–Sen estimator as will be illustrated. (The same is true for many other robust estimators that have been derived. See Wilcox, 2012b, for details.) In practical terms, it is prudent to always check on the impact of removing leverage points, which is easily done using the R functions written for this book via the argument xout.

When there are tied values among the dependent variable, there is a modification of the Theil–Sen estimator that might provide more power when testing hypotheses (Wilcox and Clark, 2013). Details about the modification are not important for present purposes but an R function that computes the modification is provided.

8.3.3   R Functions tsreg and tshdreg

The R function

```
tsreg(x,y,xout=FALSE,outfun=out,plotit=FALSE,
    xlab='X',ylab='Y',...)
```

computes the Theil–Sen regression estimator. The R function

```
tshdreg(x,y,xout=FALSE,outfun=out,plotit=FALSE,
    xlab='X',ylab='Y',...)
```

computes the modification of the Theil–Sen regression estimator that is designed for tied values among the dependent variable.

Example

The Theil–Sen estimator can mitigate the impact of leverage points. But leverage points can impact the Theil–Sen estimator to the point that removing leverage points can have a substantial impact on the estimate of the slope and intercept. As an illustration, consider again the star data in Figure 8.1. The estimate of the slope using all of the data is 1.73. This is in contrast to using the least squares estimator as well as the least absolute value estimator, both of which estimate the slope to be negative. However, removing leverage points, now the Theil–Sen estimate of slope is 3.22. So in this case, the Theil–Sen estimator provides improved protection from the deleterious impact of leverage points, but when all leverage points are removed, the estimate of the slope nearly doubles.

Example

To illustrate that outliers among the dependent variable can make a practical difference when using the least squares estimator rather than the Theil–Sen estimator, even when there are no leverage points, consider again the star data, only now the goal is to predict the surface temperature of stars given its light intensity. The least squares estimate of the slope is −0.107, suggesting a negative association. But the Theil–Sen estimate is positive: 0.123.

8.3.4 Extrapolation Can Be Dangerous

Care must be taken when making predictions about Y when using some value for X that lies outside the range of values used to obtain the slope and intercept. When making a prediction about Y using some value for X that is less than any value used to compute the least squares slope and intercept, or when using any other estimator covered in this chapter, highly inaccurate results might be obtained. In a similar manner, making predictions using some value for X that is larger than any value used to compute b_1 and b_0, again highly inaccurate results might result.

Example

Consider again the data in Table 8.3 dealing with the cost of a home based on how many square feet it has. The sizes of the homes range between 688 and 4,870 square feet. What would you estimate the cost of a lot to be with no home on it? The least squares regression line is $\hat{Y} = 215(X) + 38,192$. An empty lot corresponds to $X = 0$ square feet. The temptation, based on the least squares regression line, might be to estimate the cost of the lot to be $\hat{Y} = 215(0) + 38,192 = 38,192$. This is an absurd result, however, because at the time, for this particular suburb, it was impossible to find any lot this inexpensive.

8.4 HYPOTHESIS TESTING

In the previous chapters, we saw how we might make inferences about some measure of location such as the population mean μ. In particular, methods for computing confidence intervals and testing hypotheses were described. The goal of this section is to extend these methods so as to be able to test hypotheses and compute confidence intervals when dealing with the slope and intercept of a regression line. For example, based on available observations, is it reasonable to rule out the possibility that the true (population) slope, β_1, is equal to zero? Is it reasonable to conclude that it is at least 1.2?

Of particular interest is testing

$$H_0 : \beta_1 = 0, \tag{8.7}$$

the hypothesis that the slope is zero. If this hypothesis is rejected, and the slope is positive, this suggests that as the independent variable increases, the typical value of the dependent variable increases as well. In a similar manner, evidence of a negative slope is typically taken to mean that as the independent variable increases, the typical value of the dependent variable decreases. However, this interpretation must be used with caution because as previously illustrated, outliers can have a major impact on the estimate of both the slope and intercept. Section 8.9 describes and illustrates some additional reasons this interpretation can be misleading.

8.4.1   Inferences about the Least Squares Slope and Intercept

The most commonly used approach to testing the hypothesis of a zero slope is based on the least squares regression estimator. The derivation of the least squares regression estimator makes no assumption about the distribution of the dependent variable or the independent variable. But the classic method for testing Equation (8.7) makes three assumptions. The first is random sampling.

The second assumption is that for any given value of the independent variable, the corresponding values of the dependent variable have a normal distribution. To provide a concrete example, consider again the diabetes study where the goal is to estimate C-peptide levels based on a child's age at diagnosis. Consider all children who are 7 years old. Among all of these children, there will be some variation among their C-peptide levels, some will have a higher level than others. The assumption is that their C-peptide levels have a normal distribution. Similarly, among children 8 years old, their C-peptide levels are assumed to have a normal distribution.

The third assumption is called homoscedasticity. *Homoscedasticity*, in the context of regression, refers to a situation where the variance of the dependent variable does not depend on the value of the independent variable. In the diabetes study, for example, it is assumed that the variance of the C-peptide levels at age 7 is the same as it is at age 8, or 9, or any age we might pick. If somehow we could measure millions of children at different ages, a plot of the data might resemble Figure 8.2 for children who are age 7, 8, or 9. Notice that the variation among the Y values is the same regardless of which age we consider. This is in contrast to *heteroscedasticity*, where the variation differs at two or more age levels as illustrated in Figure 8.3.

In a more general and more formal manner, homoscedasticity can be described as follows. Consider any two variables X and Y, and let $VAR(Y|X)$ be the conditional variance of Y, given X. In the diabetes example, Y is C-peptide levels and X is age, so $VAR(Y|8)$, for example, represents the variance of C-peptide levels among all 8-year-old children. Homoscedasticity means that variance of the Y values does not depend on the value for X. Usually, this common (unknown) variance is represented by σ^2. So, homoscedasticity means that regardless of what the value of X might be, $VAR(Y|X) = \sigma^2$.

If homoscedasticity is assumed, how do we estimate the common variance σ^2? When using least squares regression, the estimate typically used is

$$s_{Y.X}^2 = \frac{1}{n-2} \sum r_i^2. \tag{8.8}$$

That is, estimate the assumed common variance by summing the squared residuals and dividing by $n-2$.

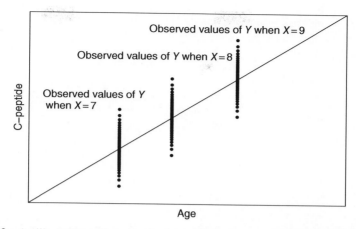

Figure 8.2 An illustration of homoscedasticity: The variation associated with the dependent variable Y (C-peptide) does not depend on the value of the independent variable X (the age of the participant)

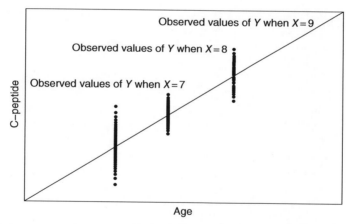

Figure 8.3 An illustration of heteroscedasticity: The variation associated with the dependent variable Y (C-peptide) depends on the value of the independent variable X (the age of the participant)

Example

For Boscovich's data in Table 8.1, the residuals based on the least squares estimate of the slope and intercept are as follows:

$$13.57393, 83.48236, -94.68105, -80.27228, 77.89704.$$

Squaring each of these values and adding the results yield $\sum r_i^2 = 28,629.64$. There are five points ($n = 5$), so the estimate of the assumed common variance is $s_{Y.X}^2 = 28,629.64/3 = 9,543.21$.

Estimating the Standard Errors

Based on the homoscedasticity assumption, it can be shown that when estimating the slope with the least squares estimator b_1 given by Equation (8.5), the squared standard error of b_1 is

$$\frac{\sigma^2}{\sum (X_i - \overline{X})^2}. \tag{8.9}$$

That is, b_1 has a sampling distribution, just as the sample mean has a sampling distribution as described in Chapter 5, and if we were to repeat an experiment (infinitely) many times, the variance of the resulting estimates of the slope would be given by Equation (8.9). In practice, we do not know σ^2, but we can estimate σ^2 with $s_{Y.X}^2$ given by Equation (8.8), in which case the squared standard error of b_1 is estimated with

$$\frac{s_{Y.X}^2}{\sum (X_i - \overline{X})^2}. \tag{8.10}$$

The squared standard error of b_0 is estimated with

$$\frac{s_{Y.X}^2 \sum X_i^2}{n \sum (X_i - \overline{X})}. \tag{8.11}$$

Computing a Confidence Interval for the Slope and Intercept

When there is homoscedasticity, random sampling, and when for any X, the corresponding Y values have a normal distribution, exact confidence intervals for the slope (β_1) and intercept (β_0) can be computed using Student's T distribution introduced in Chapter 5. Now the degrees of freedom are $v = n - 2$. The confidence interval for the slope is

$$b_1 \pm t \sqrt{\frac{s_{Y.X}^2}{\sum (X_i - \overline{X})^2}}, \tag{8.12}$$

where t is the $1 - \alpha/2$ quantile of Student's T distribution with $v = n - 2$ degrees of freedom. (The value of t is read from Table B.4 in Appendix B.) The confidence interval for the intercept is

$$b_0 \pm t \sqrt{\frac{s_{Y.X}^2 \sum X_i^2}{n \sum (X_i - \overline{X})^2}}. \tag{8.13}$$

One way of testing

$$H_0 : \beta_1 = 0, \tag{8.14}$$

the hypothesis that the slope is zero is to compute a confidence interval for β_1 and reject if this interval does not contain the hypothesized value, 0. Alternatively, compute

$$T = b_1 \sqrt{\frac{\sum (X_i - \overline{X})^2}{s_{Y.X}^2}} \tag{8.15}$$

and reject if

$$|T| \geq t,$$

where again t is the $1 - \alpha/2$ quantile of Student's T distribution with $v = n - 2$ degrees of freedom.

8.4.2 R Functions lm, summary, and ols

The built-in R function

$$\text{lm}(y \sim x)$$

introduced in Section 8.2.1 can be used in conjunction with the R command summary to test hypotheses about the slope and intercept. To test the hypothesis that the slope and the intercept are equal to zero, use the R command

$$\text{summary}(\text{lm}(y \sim x))$$

It returns a p-value but no confidence interval.

The R function

```
ols(x,y,xout=FALSE,outfun=outpro,plotit=FALSE,

    xlab='X',ylab='Y',zlab='Z'),
```

introduced in Section 8.2.1, also tests the hypotheses that the slope and intercept are equal to zero with the advantage of providing a simple way of checking on the impact of removing leverage points via the argument xout.

Example

A general goal of a study conducted by G. Margolin and A. Medina was to examine how children's information processing is related to a history of exposure to marital aggression. Results for two of the measures are shown in Table 8.4. (The data are stored in the file marital_agg_dat.txt, which can be downloaded from the author's web page as described in Section 1.5.) The first, labeled X, is a measure of marital aggression that reflects physical, verbal, and emotional aggression during the last year, and Y is a child's score on a recall test. If aggression in the home (X) has a relatively low value, what would we expect a child to score on the recall test (Y)? If the measure of aggression is high, now what would we expect the recall test score to be? As aggression increases, do test scores tend to decrease? Can we be reasonably

TABLE 8.4   Measures of Marital Aggression and Recall Test Scores

Family i	Aggression X_i	Test Score Y_i	Family i	Aggression X_i	Test Score Y_i
1	3	0	25	34	2
2	104	5	26	14	0
3	50	0	27	9	4
4	9	0	28	28	0
5	68	0	29	7	4
6	29	6	30	11	6
7	74	0	31	21	4
8	11	1	32	30	4
9	18	1	33	26	1
10	39	2	34	2	6
11	0	17	35	11	6
12	56	0	36	12	13
13	54	3	37	6	3
14	77	6	38	3	1
15	14	4	39	3	0
16	32	2	40	47	3
17	34	4	41	19	1
18	13	2	42	2	6
19	96	0	43	25	1
20	84	0	44	37	0
21	5	13	57	11	2
22	4	9	46	14	11
23	18	1	47	0	3
24	76	4			

certain that there is some association between marital aggression and scores on the recall test?

If there is no association between aggression measures and recall test scores, then the slope of the least squares regression line is zero. That is, the hypothesis H_0: $\beta_1 = 0$ is true. Suppose the goal is to test this hypothesis so that the probability of a Type I error is $\alpha = 0.05$. Then, $1 - \alpha/2 = 0.975$. There are $n = 47$ participants, so the degrees of freedom are $v = 47 - 2 = 45$, and the critical value (read from Table B.4) is $t = 2.01$. The least squares estimate of the slope is $b_1 = -0.0405$. It can be seen that $\sum(X_i - \overline{X})^2 = 34,659.74$ and that the estimate of the assumed common variance is $s_{Y.X}^2 = 14.15$, so the test statistic is

$$T = -0.0405\sqrt{\frac{34,659.74}{14.5}} = -1.98.$$

Because $|T| = 1.98 < 2.01$, fail to reject. The p-value returned by the R function ols is 0.052. Removing data associated with leverage points by setting the argument xout=TRUE in the R function ols, now the p-value is 0.023. Because the slope is estimated to be negative, this analysis suggests that as aggression in the home increases, the typical recall test score decreases. (But methods described in the next two sections as well as in Section 9.5.1 suggest that this interpretation is misleading.)

8.4.3   Heteroscedcasticity: Some Practical Concerns and How to Address Them

The homoscedasticity assumption made in Section 8.4.1, when testing hypotheses about the slope and intercept based on the least squares regression estimator, has been routinely adopted for about two centuries. There is a very simple reason for this: It was unclear how to deal with heteroscedasticity. Even today, homoscedasticity is typically assumed. But to what extent does the homoscedasticity assumption provide reasonably good control over the the Type I error probability and reasonably accurate confidence intervals?

If two variables are independent, this implies homoscedasticity. That is, the homoscedasticity assumption is reasonable. If there is an association, in theory, homoscedasticity is possible, but there is no reason to assume that this is the case and an argument can be made that surely there is some degree of heteroscedasticity. A concern is that if there is heteroscedasticity, the test statistic given by Equation (8.15) and the confidence interval given by Equation (8.13) are using the wrong standard error (e.g., Cribari-Neto, 2004; Godfrey, 2006; Long and Ervin, 2000), which can result in inaccurate confidence intervals. Moreover, the probability of rejecting the hypothesis that the slope is zero, using Equation (8.15), depends on the value of the population slope β_1, as well as the degree to which there is heteroscedasticity. Even when the hypothesis of a zero slope is true, if there is heteroscedasticity, there can be a high probability of rejecting, particularly when the sample size is large (e.g., Wilcox, 2012a).

A strategy for justifying the homoscedasticity assumption is to test the hypothesis that the homoscedasticity assumption is true and assume homoscedasticity if such a test fails to reject. However, published results do not support this approach (Ng and Wilcox, 2011). Imagine that unknown to us, we are dealing with a situation where heteroscedasticity is a practical concern when making inferences about the slope and intercept. The issue, then, is whether the test of the homoscedasticity assumption has enough power to detect the fact that we are dealing with a situation where heteroscedasticity results in poor control over the Type I error probability and inaccurate confidence intervals. Presumably, with a sufficiently large sample size, methods for testing the homoscedasticity assumption would have sufficient power to detect heteroscedasticity when it is a practical concern. But it is unknown how to determine when this is the case. In practical terms, when testing the hypothesis of a zero slope with Student's T via Equation (8.15), it is reasonable to conclude that there is an association when Student's T rejects. But the accuracy of the confidence interval given by Equation (8.12) is in doubt.

Today, there are several technically sound methods for estimating the standard error of b_1 and b_0 when using least squares regression and there is heteroscedasticity. The computational details are not described but an R function is provided that uses the so-called HC4 estimate of the standard error. (For details about the HC4 estimator, see Godfrey, 2006, or Wilcox, 2012b.)

8.4.4   R Function olshc4

The R function

```
olshc4(x,y,xout=FALSE,outfun=outpro,plotit=FALSE,
       xlab='X',ylab='Y',zlab='Z')
```

tests the hypothesis of a zero slope using least squares regression in conjunction with a method that allows heteroscedasticity. (The function olsci performs the same computations as olshc4.)

Example

Consider again the illustration in Section 8.4.2 dealing with marital aggression in the home, only now the HC4 estimator is used to deal with heteroscedasticity. Testing the hypothesis of a zero slope with the R function olshc4, the p-value is 0.092. This is in contrast to the homoscedastic method used in Section 8.4.2 where the p-value is 0.051. The estimate of the slope is -0.041, so the homoscedastic method suggests that there is an association and because the slope is negative, the natural conclusion is that the average recall test score decreases as marital aggression scores increase. But to what extent is the true nature of association understood? To address this issue, it helps to plot the data and the regression line.

Assuming the data have been read into the R variable agg, a matrix with marital aggression scores in column 2 and recall test scores in column 3, the R command

```
olshc4(agg[,2],agg[,3],plotit=TRUE,xlab='Aggression',
ylab='Recall Test Scores')
```

creates the scatterplot in Figure 8.3, and it plots the least squares regression line as well. Why does Student's T have a lower p-value than the method based on the HC4 estimator? A possible explanation is that there is heteroscedasticity, and Figure 8.3 suggests that this is indeed the case: there appears to be more variation among the recall test scores when aggression is relatively low. (Results in Section 9.5.1 lend support to this speculation.) Notice the five points in the upper-left corner. They are flagged as outliers based on the MAD–median rule applied to the recall test scores. If they are eliminated, the regression line is nearly horizontal. (It is left as an exercise to verify that this is the case.)

Now consider the data from a slightly different perspective. The plot suggests that among homes with low marital aggression scores, relatively high recall test scores occur, but as marital aggression scores increase, at some point this is less likely to be the case. Indeed, for marital aggression scores greater than 20, no association is found and a plot indicates that the regression line is nearly horizontal. That is, there is the possibility that there is an association between these two variables, but one that is not modeled well by a straight least squares regression line based on all of the data.

8.4.5 Outliers among the Dependent Variable: A Cautionary Note

In the last example, a technically invalid strategy is to eliminate the outliers among the dependent variable (the recall test scores) and test the hypothesis that the slope is zero using the method in Section 8.4.1 or the heteroscedastic method in Section 8.4.3. The reason is that the derivation of the standard error is no longer valid. Recall from Chapters 6 and 7, when using Student's T or Welch's method, discarding outliers and applying these techniques to the remaining data result in inaccurate confidence intervals and poor control over the Type I error probability. Special techniques, such as the Tukey–McLaughlin method, are needed for handling outliers in a technically sound manner. The same is true when working with regression estimators: special methods are needed to deal with outliers among the dependent variable. In contrast, outliers among the independent variable can be discarded.

8.4.6 Inferences Based on the Theil–Sen Estimator

When testing hypotheses, a way of dealing with outliers among the dependent variable in a technically sound manner, and simultaneously dealing with heteroscedasticity, is to use the Theil–Sen estimator in conjunction with a percentile bootstrap method. (A percentile bootstrap method continues to perform well when using other robust regression estimators not covered in this book.) In the present context, a bootstrap sample refers to resampling with replacement n points from among the available data. In symbols, the data consists of the n points $(X_1, Y_1), \ldots, (X_n, Y_n)$. A bootstrap sample is obtained by resampling with replacement n points, yielding say $(X_1^*, Y_1^*), \ldots, (X_n^*, Y_n^*)$. Based on this bootstrap sample, let b_0^* and b_1^* be the estimate of the intercept and slope, respectively, using the Theil–Sen estimator. Repeat this process many times, and put the resulting b_1^* values in ascending order. The middle 95% provides a 0.95 confidence interval for the slope. A p-value can be computed in essentially the same manner as in Chapter 7. Let A be the number of bootstrap estimates of the slope that are less than zero, let B be the number of bootstrap samples, and let $p^* = A/B$. Then, the p-value is $2p^*$ or $2(1 - p^*)$, whichever is smaller. A confidence interval and p-value for the intercept are computed in a similar manner.

To provide a bit more detail regarding how to compute a $1 - \alpha$ confidence interval for the slope, denote the B bootstrap estimates of the slope by $b_1^*, \ldots, b_B^*$. Put these B values in ascending order, yielding $b_{(1)}^* \leq \cdots \leq b_{(B)}^*$. Let $L = \alpha B/2$ rounded to the nearest integer, and let $U = B - L$. Then, a $1 - \alpha$ confidence interval for the slope is

$$(b_{(L+1)}^*, b_{(U)}^*).$$

8.4.7 R Functions regci and regplot

The R function

```
regci(x,y,regfun=tsreg,nboot=599,alpha=0.05,
      xout=FALSE,outfun=outpro)
```

tests the hypothesis of a zero slope using a percentile bootstrap method that allows heteroscedasticity. The argument `regfun` indicates the regression estimator to be used and defaults to `tsreg`, the Theil–Sen estimator. The argument `alpha=0.05` indicates that a $1 - \alpha = 0.95$ confidence interval will be computed. (For a summary of additional estimators that are available, see Wilcox, 2012b.) The other arguments have their usual meaning.

The R function `regci` does not contain an option for creating a scatterplot and plotting the regression line. But this can be done with the R function

```
regplot(x,y,regfun=tsreg, xlab='X',ylab='Y',

        xout=FALSE,outfun=out,...)
```

Example

Consider again the marital aggression data in Figure 8.4. The *p*-value for the slope returned by the R function `regci` is 0.235. However, the function also prints a message that tied values were detected among the dependent variable and that using `regfun=tshdreg` might provide more power. This refers to the modification of the Theil–Sen estimator mentioned at the end of Section 8.3.2. Setting the argument `regfun=tshdreg`, now the *p*-value is 0.087, the only point being that using the modified Theil–Sen estimator can make a substantial difference. Again, the hypothesis of a zero slope is not rejected at the 0.05 level, but this was somewhat expected

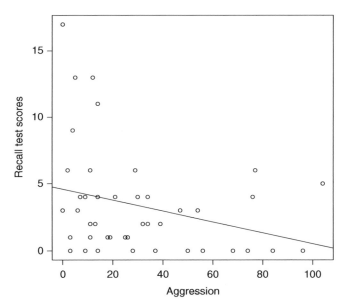

Figure 8.4 A scatterplot of the marital aggression data. Also shown is the least squares regression line. Notice the apparent outliers in the upper-left corner. Removing these five points, now the regression line is nearly horizontal

because the Theil–Sen estimator and its modification are relatively insensitive to the outliers in the upper-left corner of Figure 8.4.

8.5 CORRELATION

Rejecting the hypothesis that a regression line has a zero slope establishes that there is an association. But how strong is the association? For example, age might be associated with blood glucose levels. If we knew the average blood glucose levels among all adults, this average could be used to predict the blood glucose level of a randomly sampled individual. If we are told that the age of the randomly sampled person is 50, to what extent does this help predict her blood glucose level? How might the strength of any association be characterized?

8.5.1 Pearson's Correlation

The classic and most frequently used method for answering the question just posed is called *Pearson's correlation* or the *product moment correlation coefficient*. The computation of Pearson's correlation is described first followed by a description of what it tells us and, just as important, what it does not tell us.

Pearson's correlation is

$$r = b_1 \frac{s_x}{s_y}, \tag{8.16}$$

where b_1 is the least squares estimate of the regression slope, and s_x and s_y are the sample standard deviations associated with the independent variable X and the dependent variable Y, respectively. An alternative way of computing r is

$$r = \frac{A}{\sqrt{CD}}, \tag{8.17}$$

where

$$A = \sum (X_i - \overline{X})(Y_i - \overline{Y}),$$

$$C = \sum (X_i - \overline{X})^2$$

and

$$D = \sum (Y_i - \overline{Y})^2.$$

It can be shown that Pearson's correlation always has a value between -1 and 1. More succinctly,

$$-1 \leq r \leq 1.$$

Pearson's correlation dates back to at least the year 1846 when it was studied by A. Bravais. During the late nineteenth century, Galton made a considerable effort at applying the correlation coefficient. About this time, Pearson solved some technical problems and provided a mathematical account that helped sway many natural scientists and mathematicians that it has value in the analysis of biological observations, which led to the common practice of calling this measure of association Pearson's correlation.

There is another way of relating Pearson's correlation to least squares regression that provides a useful perspective on how it can be interpreted. Note that if the value of the independent variable X is not known, a natural guess about the value of the dependent variable Y is the average of the Y values, $\overline{Y}$. In the diabetes data, for example, if we were given no information about a child's age or C-peptide level, and we want to guess what the child's C-peptide level happens to be, a reasonable guess would be $\overline{Y}$, the average of all the C-peptide levels available to us. One way of measuring the accuracy of this estimate is with $\sum (Y_i - \overline{Y})^2$, the sum of squared differences between the observed Y values and the mean, $\overline{Y}$. Recall that this sum is the numerator of the sample variance of the Y values. In a similar manner, $\sum (Y_i - \hat{Y}_i)^2$ reflects how well we can predict Y using the least squares regression line and X. The improvement in estimating Y with $\hat{Y}$ over $\overline{Y}$ is the difference between these two sums:

$$\sum (Y_i - \overline{Y})^2 - \sum (Y_i - \hat{Y}_i)^2.$$

The reduction in error using $\hat{Y}$, relative to using $\overline{Y}$, is

$$r^2 = \frac{\sum (Y_i - \overline{Y})^2 - \sum (Y_i - \hat{Y}_i)^2}{\sum (Y_i - \overline{Y})^2}, \tag{8.18}$$

the squared value of Pearson's correlation. The quantity r^2 is called the *coefficient of determination*, which reflects *the proportion of variance accounted for using a least squares regression line and X* to predict Y. In the diabetes study, for example, $r^2 = 0.151$, meaning that when using a least squares regression line to predict C-peptide levels, given a child's age, 15% of the variation among C-peptide levels is accounted for based on a child's age. Because r has a value between -1 and 1, the coefficient of determination has a value between 0 and 1.

Here is another way of describing the coefficient of determination. The variance of the C-peptide levels is 0.519. The variance of the residuals is 0.441. So, the fraction of the variance *not* accounted for is $0.441/0.519 = 0.850$, or 85%. The fraction that is accounted for is $100\%-85\%=15\%$, which is the value of r^2.

Yet another way of describing the coefficient of determination is that it reflects the variation in the predicted Y values (the $\hat{Y}$ values), based on the least squares regression line, relative to the variation in the Y values. In the diabetes example, it can be seen that the variance of the predicted C-peptide levels values is 0.0783. The variance of the observed C-peptide levels is 0.5192, so the proportion of variance accounted for is $0.0783/0.5192 = 0.15$, which is again equal to r^2. In symbols,

$$r^2 = \frac{VAR(\hat{Y})}{VAR(Y)}.$$

A fundamental property of the correlation coefficient is that if all participants could be measured and if X and Y are independent, then Pearson's correlation is zero. This fact can be used to establish dependence using methods described in Section 8.5.2.

Interpreting r

A good understanding of r requires an understanding not only of what it tells us about an association, but also what it does not tell us. That is, care must be taken to not read more into the value of r than is warranted. Interpreting r is complicated by the fact that various features of the data under study affect its magnitude. Five such features are described here.

Assuming that the regression line between and X and Y is straight, the first feature is the magnitude of the residuals. Generally, large residuals tend to result in low values for r.

Figure 8.5a shows a scatterplot of points with $r = 0.92$. Figure 8.5b shows another scatterplot of points that are centered around the same line as in (a), only they are farther from the line. Now $r = 0.42$.

A second feature that affects the magnitude of r is the magnitude of the slope around which the points are centered (e.g., Barrett, 1974; Loh, 1987). The closer the slope happens to be to zero, the lower will be the value of r.

A third feature of data that affects r is outliers. For the star data in Figure 8.1, $r = -0.21$, which is consistent with the negative slope associated with the least squares regression line. But we have already seen that for the bulk of the points, there is a positive association. Generally, a single unusual value can have a tremendous impact on the value of r resulting in a poor reflection of the association among the

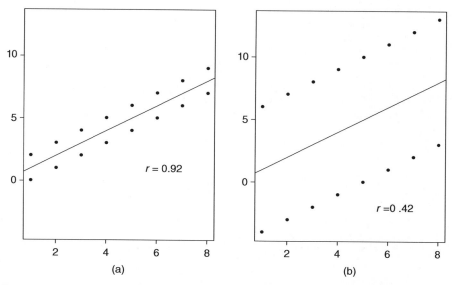

Figure 8.5 An illustration that the magnitude of Pearson's correlation is influenced by the magnitude of the residuals

majority of points. In fact, regardless of how many observations we might have, slight departures from normality can substantially alter r.

A fourth feature is restricting the range of the X or Y values. For the star data in Figure 8.1, $r = -0.21$. If we restrict the range of the X values by considering only X values greater than 3.6, which eliminates the obvious outliers, now $r = 0.61$. Restricting the range of X or Y can lower r as well.

A fifth feature is curvature. Suppose that unknown to us, the mean of Y given X is X^2, but it is erroneously assumed that the mean of Y given X is X. That is, the mean of Y given X is assumed to be given by a straight line $\beta_0 + \beta_1 X$, but in reality, it has the form $\beta_0 + \beta_1 X^2$. There is a positive correlation between Y and X^2, but the correlation between Y and X is zero. In general, assuming that the regression line is straight, when in fact this is not the case, can impact the correlation.

In summary, the following features of data influence the magnitude of Pearson's correlation:

- The slope of the line around which points are clustered
- The magnitude of the residuals
- Outliers
- Restricting the range of the X values, which can cause r to go up or down
- Curvature.

8.5.2   Inferences about the Population Correlation, ρ

There is a population analog of r, typically written as ρ, where ρ is a lowercase Greek rho. Roughly, ρ is the value of r if all individuals of interest could be measured. Usually, not all individuals can be measured, so we estimate ρ with r (in much the same way we estimate the population mean μ with the sample mean $\overline{X}$). It can be shown that

$$-1 \leq \rho \leq 1.$$

That is, the population analog of Pearson's correlation has a value between -1 and 1. Moreover, if two variables are independent, then $\rho = 0$. So, if there is strong empirical evidence that $\rho \neq 0$, this indicates that there is an association between the two variables of interest.

The classic method for testing

$$H_0 : \rho = 0, \tag{8.19}$$

the hypothesis that the population value of Pearson's correlation is zero is based on the assumption that X and Y are independent and that X or Y has a normal distribution. The test statistic is

$$T = r\sqrt{\frac{n-2}{1-r^2}}. \tag{8.20}$$

If the null hypothesis is true and the assumptions are met, then T has a Student's T distribution with $n - 2$ degrees of freedom.

Decision Rule: If the goal is to have the probability of a Type I error equal to α, reject if $|T| \geq t$, where t is the $1 - \alpha/2$ quantile of Student's T distribution, which is read from Table B.4 in Appendix B with $v = n - 2$ degrees of freedom.

Example

For the aggression data in Table 8.3, $n = 47$, $r = -0.286$, so $v = 45$ and

$$T = -0.286\sqrt{\frac{45}{1 - (-0.286)^2}} = -2.$$

With $\alpha = 0.05$, $1 - \alpha/2 = 0.975$, and from Table B.4 in Appendix B, the critical value is $t = 2.01$, and because $|-2| < 2.01$, fail to reject. That is, we are unable to conclude that the aggression scores and recall test scores are dependent with $\alpha = 0.05$.

The intelligent use and interpretation of the hypothesis testing method just described require a closer look at the underlying assumptions. It can be shown that if two variables are independent, then there is homoscedasticity. Moreover, the assumption of homoscedasticity plays a crucial role in the mathematical derivation of the test statistic T. If there is heteroscedasticity, then the test statistic T is using the wrong standard error, which can have practical implications when interpreting data. For example, it is possible to have $\rho = 0$, yet the probability of rejecting increases as the sample size gets large. That is, regardless of how large the sample size might be, the probability of a Type I error is not controlled when using T to test the hypothesis that $\rho = 0$. However, if X and Y are independent, a correct estimate of the standard error is being used, and now the probability of a Type I error can be controlled reasonably well. So, in a very real sense, the test statistic T is best described as a test of the hypothesis that X and Y are independent, rather than a test of the hypothesis that $\rho = 0$. Another concern is that using the wrong standard error can affect power, the probability of detecting dependence when it exists. A simple way of dealing with heteroscedasticity is to use the HC4 estimate of the standard error.

Use Caution When Rejecting the Hypothesis that Pearson's Correlation is Equal to Zero

If the hypothesis that $\rho = 0$ is rejected, a common interpretation is that if r is greater than 0, than generally, as X increases, Y increases as well. Similarly, if $r < 0$, a natural speculation is that as X increases, Y decreases. This interpretation is consistent with the least squares regression line because the slope is given by

$$b_1 = r\frac{s_y}{s_x}.$$

So if $r > 0$, the least squares regression line has a positive slope, and if $r < 0$, the reverse is true. *Perhaps this interpretation is usually correct, but this should not be taken for granted.* In Figure 8.1, for example, r is negative, but generally, as X increases, Y increases too. Many methods have been derived to get a more exact understanding of how X and Y are related. One simple recommendation is to always plot the data, as well as the least squares regression line, as opposed to relying completely on the value of r to interpret how two variables are related. At a minimum, the least squares regression line should look reasonable when viewed within a plot of the data. But even if it gives a reasonable summary of the data, there can be a considerable practical advantage to using an alternative regression estimator.

A Summary of How to Use r

To summarize, Pearson's correlation, r, has two useful functions. First, it can be used to establish dependence between two variables by testing and rejecting the hypothesis that ρ is equal to zero. Second, r^2 (the coefficient of determination), reflects the extent to which the least squares regression estimate of Y, namely $\hat{Y}$, improves upon the sample mean, $\overline{Y}$, in terms of predicting Y.

However, even if r^2 is close to 1, this does not necessarily mean that the least squares estimate of Y is performing well. It might be, for example, that both $\hat{Y}$ and $\overline{Y}$ perform poorly. Even when Pearson's correlation is very close to 1, this does not necessarily mean that the least squares regression line provides a highly accurate estimate of Y, given X. Finally, compared to more modern methods, Pearson's correlation can be relatively ineffective in terms of describing and detecting dependence. This is not always the case, but it is imprudent to assume that it always provides an adequate method for detecting and describing an association. Put another way, rejecting the hypothesis that $\rho = 0$ provides empirical evidence that there is dependence, but failing to reject is not a compelling reason to conclude that two variables are independent. More modern methods can be sensitive to types of dependence that are difficult to discover when using Pearson's correlation only.

Example

Mednick conducted a study aimed at understanding the association among some variables related to schizophrenia. With two of the variables, he got a Pearson correlation very close to 1. Momentarily, he thought he had a major breakthrough. Fortunately, he checked a scatterplot of his data and found an obvious outlier. This one outlier resulted in r being close to 1, but with the outlier removed, no association was found.

8.5.3   R Functions pcor and pcorhc4

The R function

```
pcor(x,y)
```

tests the hypothesis of a zero correlation using Equation (8.20), which assumes homoscedasticity and that at least one of the variables has a normal distribution. The R function

```
pcorhc4(x,y)
```

also tests the hypothesis that Pearson's correlation is zero, still assuming normality, but it allows heteroscedasticity.

8.6   DETECTING OUTLIERS WHEN DEALING WITH TWO OR MORE VARIABLES

Before continuing, it helps to discuss briefly the issue of detecting outliers when dealing with bivariate data. Look at the scatterplot in Figure 8.6a. What method should be used to check for outliers? A seemingly natural guess is to simply check for outliers among the first variable, ignoring the second variable, and then check for outliers among the second variable, ignoring the first. But this can result in missing unusual data points as illustrated in Figure 8.6. The point indicated by the arrow in the lower-right corner is very unusual based on how the data were generated. That is, it is an outlier. But when checking for outliers based on the data for the first variable, ignoring the second variable, no outliers are detected, as indicated by the first boxplot in Figure 8.6b. Similarly, when checking for outliers based on data for the second variable, ignoring the first variable, no outliers are detected. What is needed is a method for detecting outliers that takes into account the overall structure of the data. To provide a more concrete example of what this means, it is not unusual for

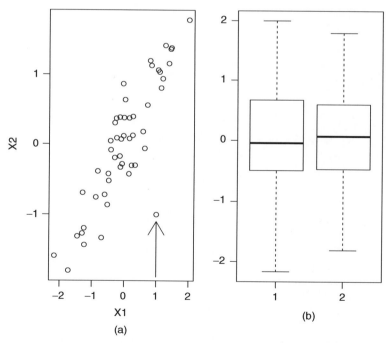

Figure 8.6   When checking for outliers among bivariate data, simply applying the boxplot rule for each of the variables can miss outliers, as illustrated here. The first boxplot in (b) is based on the data stored in the variable x1, ignoring the data stored in x2. The other boxplot is based on the data stored in x2, ignoring x1. No outliers are detected by the boxplots, but the point indicated by the arrow in (a) is an outlier. What is needed is an outlier detection method that takes into account the overall structure of the data

someone to be young, it is not unusual for someone to have heart disease, but it is unusual for someone to be both young and have heart disease.

Several methods have been proposed for detecting outliers in a manner that takes into account the overall structure of the data when dealing with two or more variables. But no single method is always best. A so-called projection method performs relatively well and is the default method used by many of the R functions written for this book. Another well-known method in the statistics literature is based on what is called the minimum volume ellipsoid (MVE) estimator. For a detailed description of the strategy behind these methods, as well as some alternative methods that deserve serious consideration, see Rousseeuw and Leroy (1987), Rousseeuw and van Zomeren (1990), and Wilcox (2012b). Both the projection method and the MVE estimator perform well in terms of avoiding masking. Both methods can handle situations where the goal is to detect outliers among more than two variables. A possible criticism of the MVE method is that it might flag too many points as outliers. (This is called swamping.) A positive feature of the MVE method is that execution time on a computer can be much lower, compared to the projection method, when dealing with a very large sample size.

8.6.1   R Functions out and outpro

The R functions

$$\text{out}(x)$$

and

$$\text{outpro}(x)$$

are designed to check for outliers in a manner that takes into account the overall structure of the data when dealing with two or more variables. The first function checks for outliers using the MVE method, and the second function uses the projection method. The argument x can be a matrix or a data frame. When the argument x is a single variable, both out and outpro use the MAD–median rule.

8.7   MEASURES OF ASSOCIATION: DEALING WITH OUTLIERS

Similar to least squares regression, Pearson's correlation is highly sensitive to outliers: even a single outlier can suggest a strong association when in fact there is little or no association among the bulk of the points, and a strong association can be missed as well. There are several ways this concern might be addressed, some of which are described in this section.

8.7.1   Kendall's Tau

Kendall's tau is based on the following idea. Consider two pairs of observations, which are labeled (X_1, Y_1) and (X_2, Y_2). These two pairs of numbers are said to be concordant if Y increases as X increases, or if Y decreases as X decreases. So if $X_1 <$ X_2 and simultaneously $Y_1 < Y_2$, these two points are concordant. Put another way, if the slope between these two points is positive, they are concordant. If two pairs of observations are not concordant, meaning that the slope is negative, they are said to be discordant.

Roughly, Kendall's tau reflects the extent to which X and Y have a monotonic association. A monotonic relationship is one that consistently increases or decreases, but the increase (or decrease) does not necessarily follow a straight line. If in general, as one variable increases, the other tends to increase as well, then Kendall's tau will be positive. In a similar manner, if in general, as one variable increases, the other tends to decrease, then Kendall's tau will be negative.

Based on all pairs of points, Kendall's tau is the difference between the number of positive slopes and the number of negative slopes divided by the total number of slopes. Consequently, its value is between -1 and 1. Said another way, among all pairs of points, Kendall's tau is just the average number that are concordant minus the average number that are discordant. If two variables are independent, then this difference should be approximately equal to zero. If all pairs of points are concordant, meaning that as the first variable increases, the second always increases as well, Kendall's tau is equal to 1. If all pairs of points are discordant, Kendall's tau is equal to -1.

Example

The points $(X_1, Y_1) = (12, 32)$ and $(X_2, Y_2) = (14, 42)$ are concordant because X increases from 12 to 14 and the corresponding Y values increase as well. That is, the slope between these two points is positive. The pairs of points $(X_1, Y_1) = (10, 28)$ and $(X_2, Y_2) = (14, 24)$ have a negative slope and are discordant: X increases from 10 to 14 and Y decreases from 28 to 24.

To describe how to compute tau in a more formal manner, let $K_{ij} = 1$ if the ith and jth points are concordant, otherwise $K_{ij} = -1$. Next, sum all of the K_{ij} for which $i < j$, which is denoted by

$$\sum_{i<j} K_{ij}.$$

Then, Kendall's tau is given by

$$\hat{\tau} = \frac{2\sum_{i<j} K_{ij}}{n(n-1)}, \tag{8.21}$$

where τ is a lowercase Greek tau. In words, Kendall's tau is just the average of the K_{ij} values. (In the notation used here, the number of K_{ij} values is $n(n-1)/2$.) As previously indicated, $\hat{\tau}$ has a value between -1 and 1. If $\hat{\tau}$ is positive, there is a tendency for Y to increase with X and if $\hat{\tau}$ is negative, the reverse is true.

Example

Consider the values

$$(X_1, Y_1) = (2, 1)$$
$$(X_2, Y_2) = (6, 5)$$
$$(X_3, Y_3) = (8, 7)$$
$$(X_4, Y_4) = (3, 12).$$

We see that for the first two points ($i = 1$ and $j = 2$), X increases from 2 to 6, Y increases from 1 to 5, so they are concordant. That is, $K_{12} = 1$. More generally, we see that

i	j	K_{ij}
1	2	1
1	3	1
1	4	1
2	3	1
2	4	-1
3	4	-1

Then, Kendall's tau is $\hat{\tau} = 0.333$, the average of these six K_{ij} values. To illustrate the notation, $\sum_{i<j} K_{ij} = 2$, $n = 4$, so again

$$\hat{\tau} = \frac{2(2)}{4(3)} = 0.333.$$

The population analog of $\hat{\tau}$ is labeled τ and can be shown to be zero when X and Y are independent. That is, τ is the value of Kendall's tau if all individuals could be measured, and if there is no association, $\tau = 0$. So if there is empirical evidence that $\tau \neq 0$, this indicates that X and Y are dependent. *If X and Y are independent, and if tied values never occur*, it can be shown that the variance of $\hat{\tau}$ over many studies, which is the squared standard error of $\hat{\tau}$, is given by

$$\sigma_\tau^2 = \frac{2(2n + 5)}{9n(n - 1)}.$$

To test

$$H_0 : \tau = 0,$$

compute

$$Z = \frac{\hat{\tau}}{\sigma_\tau}.$$

Decision Rule: Reject if

$$|Z| \geq c,$$

where c is the $1 - \alpha/2$ quantile of a standard normal distribution, which can be read from Table B.1 in Appendix B.

This hypothesis testing method is routinely taught and used. However, a criticism of this method is that it is affected by heteroscedasticity. That is, when it rejects, it is reasonable to conclude that the variables are dependent, but there is a sense in which it is not a satisfactory test of the hypothesis that Kendall's tau is zero. A way of dealing with heteroscedasticity is to use instead a percentile bootstrap method, which can be applied with the R function `tauci` described in the next section.

Example

Continuing the last example, there are four points $(n = 4)$, $2(2n + 5) = 26$, $9n(n - 1) = 108$, so $\sigma_\tau^2 = 26/108 = 0.2407$, and $Z = 0.333/\sqrt{0.2407} = 0.68$. With $\alpha = 0.05$, $c = 1.96$, so fail to reject.

Kendall's tau provides protection against outliers among the X values, ignoring Y, as well as outliers among the Y values, ignoring X. Imagine that $\hat{\tau} = 0.4$ and that the largest X value is 40. If this largest X value is increased to 1 million, $\hat{\tau}$ is not altered, it remains equal to 0.4. Nevertheless, a few unusual points, properly placed, can have a tremendous influence on the value of Kendall's tau.

Example

Look at Figure 8.7. The points indicated by an o were generated where the slope is 0.6 and the common standard deviation is $\sigma = 0.67$. Then, two outliers were added, which are indicated by an * in the lower-right corner of Figure 8.7. Ignoring these two outliers, Kendall's tau is $\hat{\tau} = 0.49$, and the hypothesis that $\tau = 0$ is rejected with the Type I error set at $\alpha = 0.05$. (The p-value is 0.003 using the test statistic Z, and it is 0.002 using a percentile bootstrap method.) But if we include these two outliers, Kendall's tau drops to $\hat{\tau} = 0.31$ and the p-value increases to 0.055 using Z and 0.086 using a percentile bootstrap method. So in particular, we no longer reject at the 0.05 level even though all but two of the values were generated in a manner where X and Y are dependent.

8.7.2   R Functions tau and tauci

The R function

```
tau(x,y=NULL)
```

computes Kendall's tau, and it returns a p-value when testing the hypothesis that Kendall's tau is zero using the method in the previous section, which assumes homoscedasticity. The argument x can be a matrix or data frame with two columns, in which case Kendall's tau is computed based on these two columns of data. Or, x can be a single variable, in which case data are assumed to be stored in y, and Kendall's tau is computed using the data in x and y.

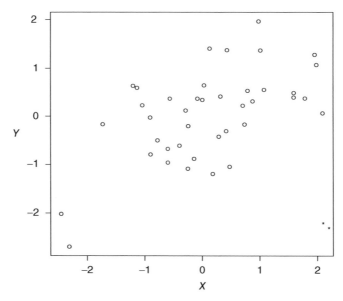

Figure 8.7 This scatterplot illustrates that outliers, properly placed, can have a large influence on both Kendall's tau and Spearman's rho. The two points in the lower-right corner are outliers based on how the data were generated. Kendall's tau, using all of the data, is 0.31, but ignoring the two outliers it is 0.49. Spearman's rho is 0.29 using all of the data and 0.48 when the two outliers are ignored

The R function

```
tauci(x,y, nboot=1000, alpha=0.05)
```

tests the hypothesis that Kendall's tau is zero using a percentile bootstrap method that allows heteroscedasticity. The argument nboot controls the number of bootstrap samples and defaults to 1,000. The function returns a *p*-value as well as a confidence interval; the probability coverage is determined by the argument alpha. By default, alpha is 0.05, meaning that a 0.95 confidence interval will be computed.

8.7.3 Spearman's Rho

Spearman's rho, labeled r_s, is just Pearson's correlation based on what are called the ranks associated with X and the ranks associated with Y. To explain what this means, consider the values 33, 7, 12, 18, 9, 23, and 6. The smallest value is said to have a rank of 1, the next smallest a rank of 2, and so on. So, converting these seven values to ranks yields

$$7, 2, 4, 5, 3, 6, 1.$$

Spearman's rho begins by converting the X values to ranks, the same is done for the Y values, and then Pearson's correlation is computed based on the ranks.

Under independence, the population analog of r_s, ρ_s, is zero. Also, similar to Kendall's tau, Spearman's rho is exactly equal to 1 if there is a monotonic increasing relationship between X and Y. That is, Y always increases as X gets large. And $\rho_s = -1$ if the association is monotonic decreasing instead. Similar to Kendall's tau, there is no assumption that the regression line is straight.

The usual approach to testing

$$H_0 : \rho_s = 0$$

is based on

$$T = r_s \frac{\sqrt{n-2}}{\sqrt{1 - r_s^2}}.$$

Decision Rule: When there is independence, T has, approximately, a Student's T distribution with $v = n - 2$ degrees of freedom. So, reject and conclude that there is an association if $|T| \geq t$, where t is the $1 - \alpha/2$ quantile of a Student's T distribution with $n - 2$ degrees of freedom.

Similar to the test based on Kendall's tau, a criticism of this method is that it is affected by heteroscedasticity. That is, a more accurate description of the method is that it tests the hypothesis of independence rather than the hypothesis that Spearman's rho is zero. A way of testing the hypothesis that Spearman's rho is zero, in a manner that allows heteroscedasticity, is to use instead a percentile bootstrap method.

Similar to Kendall's tau, Spearman's rho provides protection against outliers among the X values, ignoring Y, as well as outliers among the Y values, ignoring X, yet unusual points can have a big impact on its value.

Example

Figure 8.7 illustrated that Kendall's tau can be influenced by a few unusual values. The same is true when using Spearman's rho. Ignoring the two outliers in the lower-right corner of Figure 8.7, Spearman's rho is $r_s = 0.48$ and the hypothesis of independence is rejected with $\alpha = 0.05$. (The p-value is 0.002 using the test statistic T.) But when the two outliers are included, $r_s = 0.29$ and the p-value is 0.06. So now, no association is detected when testing at the 0.05 level.

8.7.4   R Functions spear and spearci

The R function

```
spear(x,y=NULL)
```

computes Spearman's rho. The function also returns a p-value based on Student's T, which was described in the previous section. The argument x can be a matrix or data frame with two columns, in which case Spearman's rho is computed based on these two columns of data. Or, x can be a single variable, in which case data are assumed to be stored in y and Spearman's rho is computed using the data in x and y.

The R function

$$\texttt{spearci(x,y,nboot=1000,alpha=0.05)}$$

tests the hypothesis that Spearman's rho is zero using a percentile bootstrap method, which allows heteroscedasticity. The argument nboot indicates how many bootstrap samples will be used and defaults to 1,000. The function returns a p-value as well as a confidence interval. By default, alpha is 0.05, meaning that a 0.95 confidence interval will be computed. Using alpha=0.01, for example, would result in a 0.99 confidence interval.

8.7.5 Winsorized and Skipped Correlations

There are many robust correlation coefficients beyond Spearman's rho and Kendall's tau (e.g., Wilcox, 2012b, Chapter 9). This section provides a brief description of two of them: a Winsorized correlation and a skipped correlation.

Rather than replace the observed X and Y values with their ranks, as done by Spearman's correlation, the Winsorized correlation Winsorizes the values as described in Section 2.4.6. The Winsorized correlation is Pearson's correlation based on the Winsorized values. Unlike Spearman's rho and Kendall's tau, the Winsorized correlation reflects the strength of the association based on a regression line having the form $Y = \beta_0 + \beta_1 X$. That is, the regression line is assumed to be straight. The population Winsorized correlation is denoted by ρ_w. When two variables are independent, $\rho_w = 0$.

Figure 8.7 illustrated that Spearman's rho and Kendall's tau can be influenced by outliers. The same is true of the Winsorized correlation despite the fact that it guards against outliers among the X values ignoring Y, as well as outliers among the Y values, ignoring X.

A test of the hypothesis

$$H_0 : \rho_w = 0$$

that allows heteroscedasticity can be performed using a percentile bootstrap method. A method that assumes homoscedasticity is based on

$$T = r_w \sqrt{\frac{n-2}{1-r_w^2}}.$$

When there is independence, T has, approximately, a Student's T distribution with $v = n - 2g - 2$ degrees of freedom, where $2g$ indicates the total number of observations that were Winsorized. For a 20% Winsorized correlation, $g = 0.2n$ rounded down to the nearest integer. For example, if $n = 10$, then $g = 2$, meaning that the two smallest values and the two largest values are Winsorized.

Decision Rule: Reject and conclude that there is an association if $|T| \geq t$, where t is the $1 - \alpha/2$ quantile of a Student's T distribution with $n - 2g - 2$ degrees of freedom. So, t can be read from Table B.4 in Appendix B.

A skipped correlation means that a method for detecting outliers is applied that takes into account the overall structure of the data as discussed in Section 8.6. Here the R function outpro, described in Section 8.6.1, is used to detect outliers. Then, any points flagged as an outlier are removed and Pearson's correlation is applied to the remaining data. (Other possibilities are to apply Spearman's rho or Kendall's tau after outliers are removed.) So, a skipped correlation is designed to be insensitive to the outliers in Figure 8.7. A method for testing the hypothesis that two variable are independent can be performed via the R function scor described in the next section. The R function scorci tests the hypothesis that the skipped correlation is zero using a percentile bootstrap method that allows heteroscedasticity.

8.7.6 R Functions scor, scorci, scorciMC, wincor, and wincorci

The R function

$$\text{wincor}(x,y,tr=0.2)$$

computes the Winsorized correlation coefficient and tests the hypothesis

$$H_0 : \rho_w = 0$$

using the test statistic T given in the previous section. The argument tr indicates the amount of Winsorizing. When tr=0, Pearson's correlation is computed. Homoscedasticity is assumed. So to be precise, this function is actually testing the hypothesis that two variables are independent. To test the hypothesis that the Winsorized correlation is zero in a manner that allows heteroscedasticity, use the R function

$$\text{wincorci}(x,y,nboot=1000,alpha=0.05,tr=0.2).$$

The argument alpha=0.05 indicates that a 0.95 confidence interval will be computed. As usual, the argument nboot indicates the number of bootstrap samples that will be used and tr indicates the amount of Winsorizing, which defaults to 20%. The function returns an estimate of the Winsorized correlation and a p-value.

The R function

$$\text{scor}(x,y,MC=FALSE)$$

computes the skipped correlation coefficient described in the previous section. The function reports a test statistic and a critical value for testing the hypothesis of independence with a Type I error probability $\alpha = 0.05$. Reject the hypothesis that the two variables are independent if the test statistic is greater than or equal to the critical value. Setting the argument MC=TRUE, the function will take advantage of a multicore processor if one is available, which can reduce execution time.

A criticism of the R function scor is that the Type I error probability is 0.05 and cannot be altered. Also, no p-value is reported and the method is not designed to handle heteroscedasticity. The R function

$$\text{scorci}(x,y,nboot=1000,plotit=TRUE)$$

uses a percentile bootstrap method to deal with these concerns at the expense of higher execution time. The argument `plotit=TRUE` means that a scatterplot of the data will be created with an indication of which points are outliers. The R function

```
scorciMC(x,y,nboot=1000,plotit=TRUE)
```

is exactly similar to the function `scorci`, only it takes advantage of a multicore processor if one is available, which might reduce execution time considerably.

Example

As previously noted, when using all of the data in Figure 8.7, both Kendall's tau and Spearman's rho fail to reject at the 0.05 level. In contrast, the p-value when testing the hypothesis of a zero correlation using the R function `scorci` is 0.032. In effect, the skipped correlation is insensitive to the two outliers in the lower-right corner.

Example

This example provides another illustration that the choice of method can make a practical difference. Doi conducted a study aimed at finding good predictors of reading ability in children. A portion of her study considered predicting a measure of the ability to identify words (Y) with a measure of speeded naming for digits (X). The values are shown in Table 8.5. The data for all of the variables in this study are stored the file reading.txt on the author's web page and can be downloaded as described in Section 1.5. The data used here are in columns 4 and 8. Pearson's correlation is $r = -0.035$ and the p-value is 0.76 based on Student's T test in Section 8.5.2. Kendall's tau is -0.197 and the p-value is 0.011 using the R function `tau`, and it is 0.022 using the R function `tauci`. The 20% Winsorized correlation is -0.27 and the p-value returned by `wincorci` is 0.022. The skipped correlation is -0.386. Assuming that the data have been read into the R variable `read`, the command

```
scorci(read[,4],read[,8])
```

returns a 0.95 confidence interval, namely $(-0.666, -0.135)$. Homoscedasticity was not assumed. The p-value is 0.006. Pearson's correlation is routinely used, but these

TABLE 8.5   Reading Data

X:	34 49 49 44 66 48 49 39 54 57 39 65 43 43 44 42 71 40 41
	38 42 77 40 38 43 42 36 55 57 57 41 66 69 38 49 51 45 141
	133 76 44 40 56 50 75 44 181 45 61 15 23 42 61 146 144 89 71
	83 49 43 68 57 60 56 63 136 49 57 64 43 71 38 74 84 75 64 48
Y:	129 107 91 110 104 101 105 125 82 92 104 134 105 95 101 104 105 122 98
	104 95 93 105 132 98 112 95 102 72 103 102 102 80 125 93 105 79 125
	102 91 58 104 58 129 58 90 108 95 85 84 77 85 82 82 111 58 99
	77 102 82 95 95 82 72 93 114 108 95 72 95 68 119 84 75 75 122 127

results demonstrate once again that alternative methods can make a substantial difference.

8.8 MULTIPLE REGRESSION

The focus has been on situations where there is a single predictor, but often there is interest in taking into account two or more predictors. For example, how is the average fuel consumption of a car related to its weight and horsepower? In this case, there are two predictors (weight and horsepower), which again are called *explanatory variables* or *independent variables*, as opposed to the quantity to be predicted (average fuel consumption), which is called the *dependent variable* or *outcome variable*. What happens to this association if, in addition to weight and horsepower, the speed of the car is considered as well? How are grades in law school related to undergraduate grade-point averages and scores on the LSAT (a law school admission test)? What is the association among the heights of college students and the height of both parents?

In general terms, a fundamental goal is to find some way to predict the typical value of Y, given values for p independent variables $X_1, \ldots, X_p$. The most basic approach is to assume that the typical value of Y is given by

$$Y = \beta_0 + \beta_1 X_1 + \cdots + \beta_p X_p. \tag{8.22}$$

In the law school example, this means that the typical grade-point average in law school is given by

$$\beta_0 + \beta_1(\text{GPA}) + \beta_2(\text{LSAT}),$$

where GPA is a student's undergraduate grade-point average, and the goal is to use data to determine values for the intercept (β_0) and the two slopes (β_1 and β_2). All of the regression estimators previously described can be applied when there are two or more independent variables. The next section elaborates slightly on how the slopes and the intercept are estimated when using least squares regression. The computational details associated with the least absolute value regression method, as well as the Theil–Sen estimator, go beyond the scope of this book. But these methods are readily applied using the R functions in Sections 8.1.2 and 8.3.3.

8.8.1 Least Squares Regression

The least squares principle can be extended to the situation at hand in a straightforward manner. Imagine that for each of n individuals, we have the following information:

$$(X_{11}, \ldots, X_{1p}, Y_1), (X_{21}, \ldots, X_{2p}, Y_2), \ldots, (X_{n1}, \ldots, X_{np}, Y_n).$$

The unknown values of $\beta_0, \beta_1, \ldots, \beta_p$ are estimated with the values $b_0, b_1, \ldots, b_p$ that minimize

$$\sum_{i=1}^{n} (Y_i - b_0 - b_1 X_{i1} - \cdots - b_p X_{ip})^2. \tag{8.23}$$

The computations are performed by the R functions previously described in Section 8.4.2. Similar to the case of a single predictor, it is assumed that the mean of Y, given $X_1, \ldots, X_p$, is

$$\beta_0 + \beta_1 X_1 + \beta_2 X_2 + \cdots + \beta_p X_p.$$

Said a bit more formally, when using least squares regression, it is assumed that

$$E(Y|X_1, \ldots, X_p) = \beta_0 + \beta_1 X_1 + \beta_2 X_2 + \cdots + \beta_p X_p. \tag{8.24}$$

Again, even a single outlier can have an inordinate impact on the least squares estimate of the slopes and intercept. Two ways of dealing with outliers among the dependent variable are to use the least absolute value regression estimator or the Theil–Sen estimator. Regardless of which estimator is used, again it is prudent to check on the impact of removing outliers among the independent variables.

8.8.2 Hypothesis Testing

A common goal is to test the hypothesis that all of the slope parameters are zero. In symbols, the goal is to test

$$H_0 : \beta_1 = \cdots = \beta_p = 0. \tag{8.25}$$

The classic strategy for accomplishing this goal is based on the least squares regression estimator and assumptions similar to the single predictor case ($p = 1$). In particular, given values for the predictor variables, $X_1, \ldots, X_p$, the corresponding Y values are assumed to have a normal distribution. In more formal terms, the conditional distribution of Y, given $X_1, \ldots, X_p$, is normal. An additional assumption is homoscedasticity. That is, the variance of the Y values does not depend on the values of the independent variables.

Let

$$\hat{Y} = b_0 + b_1 X_1 + \cdots + b_p X_p$$

be the least squares estimate of Y given $X_1, \ldots, X_p$. That is, the values $b_0, b_1, \ldots, b_p$ minimize $\sum (Y_i - \hat{Y}_i)^2$, the sum of the squared residuals. The *squared multiple correlation coefficient* is

$$R^2 = 1 - \frac{\sum (Y_i - \hat{Y}_i)^2}{\sum (Y_i - \overline{Y})^2}. \tag{8.26}$$

The classic method for testing the hypothesis given by Equation (8.25) is based on the test statistic

$$F = \left(\frac{n - p - 1}{p} \right) \left(\frac{R^2}{1 - R^2} \right). \tag{8.27}$$

Under normality and homoscedasticity, F has what is called an F distribution with $\nu_1 = p$ and $\nu_2 = n - p - 1$ degrees of freedom.

Decision Rule: Reject the null hypothesis if $F \geq f_{1-\alpha}$, the $1 - \alpha$ quantile of an F distribution with v_1 and v_2 degrees of freedom. If the Type I error is to be 0.1, 0.05, 0.025, or 0.01, the value of $f_{1-\alpha}$ can be read from Tables B.5, B.6, B.7, and B.8, respectively, in Appendix B. For example, with $\alpha = 0.05$, $v_1 = 3$ and $v_2 = 40$, Table B.6 indicates that the 0.95 quantile is $f_{0.95} = 2.84$. That is, there is a 0.05 probability of getting an F value greater than or equal to 2.84 when the null hypothesis is true and the underlying assumptions are true as well. For $\alpha = 0.01$, Table B.8 says that the 0.99 quantile is 4.31. This means that if the null hypothesis is rejected when $F \geq 4.31$, the probability of a Type I error will be 0.01, assuming random sampling, normality, and homoscedasticity.

Example

Imagine a study aimed at predicting depression in young adults based on three independent variables and a random sample of 63 participants. Suppose $R^2 = 0.3$ and that it is desired to test the hypothesis that all of the slope parameters are zero with the Type I error probability set equal to $\alpha = 0.05$. Then, $n = 63, p = 3$,

$$F = \left(\frac{63 - 3 - 1}{3} \right) \left(\frac{0.3}{1 - 0.3} \right) = 8.4,$$

the degrees of freedom are $v_1 = 3$, $v_2 = 60$, and from Table B.8 in Appendix B, $f_{0.95} = 2.76$. Because $8.4 > 2.76$, reject and conclude that not all of the slopes are equal to zero, assuming normality and homoscedasticity.

There is a connection between the squared multiple correlation coefficient, R^2, given by Equation (8.26), and Pearson's correlation. R^2 can be seen to be the squared Pearson correlation between the observed Y values (the Y_i values) and the predicted Y values (the $\hat{Y}_i$ values) based on the least squares regression line.

There are methods for dealing with heteroscedasticity when testing Equation (8.25), the hypothesis that all of the slope parameters are equal to zero. Currently, the most effective method appears to be one based on a *wild bootstrap* method (Ng and Wilcox, 2009), which differs from the percentile and bootstrap-t methods described in the previous chapters. The method can be applied with the R function `olstest` described in the next section.

A point worth stressing is that the magnitude of the slope for the first independent variable, X_1, can depend substantially on which additional independent variables are included. In particular, the estimated slope associated with X_1, b_1, can be positive and differ significantly from zero when ignoring all other independent variables, yet when some additional independent variable is added to the model, now b_1 does not differ significantly from zero and can be relatively small.

Example

The following R commands illustrate the point just made.

```
x=rmul(50,rho=0.6)

y=rnorm(50,mean=x[,1])
```

```
olshc4 (x[,2],y)

olshc4 (x,y)
```

The first command generates a matrix of data with 50 rows and 2 columns. (For readers who want to duplicate the results, use the R command set.seed(1) before generating the data.) Each column of the data is generated from a standard normal distribution and Pearson's correlation between these two variables is $\rho = 0.6$. The command rnorm(50,mean=x[,1]) generates 50 values from a normal distribution having means equal to the values in x[,1] and variance 1. For example, x[1,1] is equal to -0.468, so y[1] contains a value generated from a normal distribution with mean -0.468 and variance 1. In a similar manner, x[2,1] is equal to -0.019, so y[2] contains a value generated from a normal distribution with mean -0.019. More formally, the command generates data for which the mean of Y is $\beta_1 X_1 + \beta_2 X_2$, where $\beta_1 = 1$ and $\beta_2 = 0$. The command olshc4(x[,2],y) tests $H_0: \beta_2 = 0$, the hypothesis that the second independent variable has a zero slope using the data in x[,2], ignoring the data in x[,1]. The estimate of the slope is $b_2 = 0.52$ and the p-value is 0.003. Roughly, even though the values for the dependent variable were generated in a manner that ignores the second independent variable, an association is found due to the correlation between the second independent variable and the first independent variable. The final command includes both independent variables when testing for a zero slope. Now the estimate of β_2 is -0.006, very close to the true value, and the p-value is 0.976. As for the slope associated with the first independent variable, the estimate is $b_1 = 1.03$, very close to the true value, and the p-value is less than 0.001. This is not to suggest that if two independent variables are correlated, ignoring one of the independent variables will necessarily have a strong impact on the estimate of the regression coefficient associated with other independent variable. The only point is that such a result is possible.

8.8.3 R Function olstest

When using least squares regression, the R function

```
olstest (x,y,nboot=500,xout=FALSE,outfun=outpro)
```

tests the hypothesis that all of the slope parameters are equal to zero in a manner that allows heteroscedasticity. When there is more than one independent variable, the argument x is assumed to be a matrix or data frame having n rows and p columns. (Any row in x with missing values is automatically deleted.) To test the hypothesis of a zero slope for each of the p slopes, the R function olshc4 in Section 8.4.4 can be used, which allows heteroscedasticity. The function ols in Section 8.4.2 tests the hypothesis that all of the slope parameters are equal to zero, and it also performs a test for each of the individual slopes, assuming homoscedasticity.

8.8.4 Inferences Based on a Robust Estimator

It is briefly noted that when using a robust regression estimator, such as the Theil–Sen estimator, the hypothesis that all of the slope parameters are equal to zero can be tested via a bootstrap method (e.g., Wilcox, 2012b). Heteroscedasticity is allowed. The method is based on a generalization of the percentile bootstrap and can be applied with the R function in the next section. The computational details are somewhat involved and are not provided.

8.8.5   R Function regtest

The R function

```
regtest(x,y,regfun=tsreg, nboot=600, alpha=0.05,
        plotit=TRUE, xout=FALSE,outfun=outpro)
```

can be used to test the hypothesis that all of the slope parameters are equal to zero when the slope parameters are estimated via some robust regression estimator. By default, the Theil–Sen estimator is used but other robust estimators can be used via the argument `regfun`. For example, `regfun=tshdreg` would use the modification of the Theil–Sen estimator that is designed to handle tied values among the dependent variable. If the goal is to test the hypothesis of a zero slope for each of the individual independent variables, rather than the global hypothesis that all of the slopes are zero, use the R function `regci` in Section 8.4.7.

8.9   DEALING WITH CURVATURE

Caution must be exercised when assuming that a regression line is straight. Close examination of data often reveals that over some intervals of the independent variable, a straight line provides a reasonable description of the association. But over larger ranges, often a straight line becomes unsatisfactory. The next example illustrates this point and provides another example of why extrapolation can be dangerous.

Example

Vitamin A is necessary for good health. Imagine a study relating the intake of vitamin A to some measure of good health. For illustrative purposes, suppose the largest intake of vitamin A used in the study is 2,000 international units and that a straight regression line is found to provide a reasonably accurate prediction of good health based on the amount of vitamin A intake. Is it reasonable to assume that 8,000 international units of vitamin A would have positive health benefits? The answer is no. Indeed, if we keep increasing the amount of vitamin A, eventually poor health would result. In fact, a sufficiently high dose of vitamin A can cause death. There are two issues here. One is extrapolation because the study is limited to situations where the amount of vitamin A intake is less than or equal to 2,000 international units. There are no data regarding the impact of 8,000 international units of vitamin A on health. The second issue is that over short intervals, using a straight regression line is reasonable. But over a sufficiently wide range of vitamin A intake, using a straight regression line is no longer satisfactory.

In general, how should the issue of curvature be addressed? A seemingly natural suggestion is to include a quadratic term in the regression model. That is, for a single independent variable, assume that the typical value of Y, given X, is given by

$$Y = \beta_0 + \beta_1 X + \beta_2 X^2.$$

Or, some variation might be used such as the square root of X. But often, a more flexible approach to curvature is required that does not specify a particular equation for the typical value of Y given X. Many such methods have been derived and are generally known as *smoothers* or *nonparametric regression* estimators.

To provide a very rough description of the strategy behind smoothers, consider again the goal of predicting a child's C-peptide concentrations based on the child's age at the time diabetes is diagnosed. There were 43 children in the study, one of whom was 8.1 years old. Momentarily, focus on the age of this particular child and consider the goal of predicting the child's C-peptide level. A smoother focuses on all children who are close to being 8.1 years old and ignores those children who are substantially younger or older. Among the available data, more attention or weight is given to participants who are approximately 8.1 years old. Then, one strategy is to fit a straight regression using this subset of the data (using a generalization of the least squares estimator), which yields a predicted C-peptide level given that the child is 8.1 years old. This process is performed for each of the 43 values of the independent variable (age) that are available, resulting in 43 predicted values for the dependent variable. In symbols, we now have

$$(X_1, \hat{Y}_1), \; \ldots \; , (X_n, \hat{Y}_n),$$

where $\hat{Y}_i$ is the predicted value of Y_i corresponding to X_i $(i = 1, \ldots , n)$. The values of the independent variable and the corresponding predicted values are then plotted in order to get some visual indication of the nature of the association. The regression line resulting from this process, meaning the line connecting the points $(X_1, \hat{Y}_1), \; \ldots \; , (X_n, \hat{Y}_n)$, is called a *smooth*. This is a very crude description of the strategy behind the smoother derived by Cleveland (1979), generally known as LOESS.

Again focusing on the child who is 8.1 years old, another strategy is to apply a trimmed mean (or some other robust estimator) to the C-peptide values for which the corresponding ages are close to 8.1. In contrast to LOESS, a regression estimator plays no role. This process can be repeated for each age that is available, and the results can again be plotted to get a visual sense about the nature of the association. This is a very crude description of the running interval smoother. (Details for both methods can be found in Wilcox, 2012b.) The goal here is to describe R functions for applying these two particular smoothers and to illustrate why they have practical value.

8.9.1   R Function lplot and rplot

The R function

```
lplot(x, y, pyhat=FALSE, xout=FALSE, outfun=outpro,
plotit=TRUE, xlab='X', ylab='Y', zlab='Z',theta=50,
phi=25,out=FALSE,ticktype='simple', outfun=outpro)
```

plots Cleveland's smooth (LOESS) using the data in the arguments x and y. As usual, setting the argument xout=TRUE removes data associated with leverage points. If the argument pyhat=TRUE, the function returns the predicted values of the dependent variable. (The function contains several other optional arguments that are explained in Wilcox, 2012b.) The function is designed to estimate the mean of the dependent variable given some value for the independent variable, but it provides some protection against outliers among the dependent variable.

Smoothers can be used when there are two or more independent variables. If there are two independent variables, the argument zlab can be used to label the z-axis when plotting the regression surface, the argument theta can be used to rotate the plot and phi can be used to tilt the plot. The argument tick-type='simple' means that values along the axes are not included in the plot. Setting ticktype='detail', values are included.

The R function

```
rplot(x, y, est=tmean, scat =TRUE, plotit=TRUE,
pyhat = FALSE, theta = 50, phi = 25, outfun=outpro,
xout=FALSE,out=FALSE, eout=FALSE, xlab ='X', ylab='Y',
zlab=' ', ticktype='simple')
```

applies the running interval smoother. It defaults to estimating the 20% trimmed mean of the dependent variable given some value for the independent variable, but virtually any measure of location can be used via the argument est. For example, est=median would use the median rather than the 20% trimmed mean. A scatter-plot is created unless the argument scat=FALSE, in which case only the regression line is plotted. Similar to lplot, rplot can be used when there are two independent variables.

Example

The Well Elderly 2 study by Clark et al. (2012) was generally aimed at assessing the impact of an intervention program designed to enhance the physical and emotional well-being of older adults. A portion of the study dealt with the association between the cortisol awakening response (CAR) and a measure of depressive symptoms, which is labeled CESD. Cortisol is a hormone produced by the adrenal cortex. The

CAR refers to the change in cortisol upon awakening and measured again 30–60 minutes later. Here the focus is on measures taken after 6 months of intervention. The sample size is $n = 328$. Using least squares regression, which is the most commonly used method for detecting an association, no association is found. The p-value is 0.218. Using least squares regression in conjunction with a method that allows heteroscedasticity (via the R function olshc4), the p-value is 0.168. Using the Theil–Sen estimator (via the R function regci), the p-value is 0.531. Eliminating leverage points and again using the Theil–Sen estimator, the p-value is 0.242. Given the reasonably large sample size, these results might suggest that there is little or no association. However, look at Figure 8.8, which shows a plot of the regression line using the running interval smoother. (The data are stored on the author's web page in the file A3B3C.txt, which can be downloaded as described in Section 1.5.) Assuming the data have been read into the R variable A3B3C, here are the R commands that were used:

```
dif=A3B3C$cort1-A3B3C$cort2

rplot(dif,A3B3C$CESD,xout=TRUE,xlab='CAR',ylab='CESD').
```

The R variable A3B3C$cort1 contains the cortisol measures upon awakening and A3B3C$cort2 contains the cortisol measures 30–60 minutes after awakening. So, the first R command stores the CAR values in the R variable dif. The argument

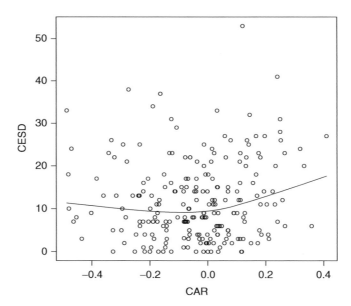

Figure 8.8 Shown is the smooth created by the R function rplot. The solid line reflects an estimate of the typical CESD measure (depressive symptoms) given a value for the CAR (the cortisol awakening response). Notice that there appears to be a distinct bend close to where the CAR is zero

xout=TRUE indicates that observations associated with leverage points were removed. Notice that when the CAR is negative (cortisol increases after awakening), the regression line appears to be nearly horizontal. But when the CAR is positive, there appears to be a positive association with CESD (depressive symptoms).

Rather than fit a straight regression line using all of the data, suppose only the data for which the CAR is positive are used. Then, the the p-value associated with the slope, based on the Theil–Sen estimator, is 0.038. Fitting a straight regression line using only data for which the CAR is negative, no association is found; the p-value is 0.631.

It should be stressed that these results, coupled with the smooth in Figure 8.8, suggest that there is curvature, but it can be argued that more compelling evidence is needed to establish that there is indeed curvature. For the situation at hand, one way of doing this is to test the hypothesis that slope based on the data when the CAR is negative is equal to the slope based on the data when the CAR is positive. If a straight regression line is appropriate using all of the data, these two slopes should be equal. Section 9.12.4 describes how to compare these two slopes. As will be seen, the results indicate that the slope based on the positive CAR values is larger than the slope when using only the negative the CAR values. This suggests that the nature of the association between the CAR and depressive symptoms depends on whether the CAR is positive or negative.

Example

Consider again the diabetes study where the goal is to predict a child's C-peptide levels based on the child's age at the time diabetes is diagnosed. Using least squares to test the hypothesis of zero slope, the p-value (based on olshc4) is 0.039. The slope is positive, so a conventional analysis suggests that the typical C-peptide level increases with age. Using the Theil–Sen estimator, the p-value is 0.150, indicating that no decision about the slope should be made with a Type I error probability equal to 0.05. But Figure 8.9, based on the R function lplot, suggests that there is a positive association up to about the age of 7 and that beyond the age of 7, there seems to be little or no association. Focusing on only the data for which age is less than or equal to 7, now both least squares and the Theil–Sen estimator reject at the 0.05 level. The p-values are 0.026 and 0.023, respectively. But for children older than 7, both methods fail to find an association.

Example

Consider again the Well Elderly study, only now the goal is to predict a measure of meaningful activities, labeled MAPA, using two independent variables: the CAR and CESD (a measure of depressive symptoms). Using least squares regression, the slope associated with the CAR is not significant using the R function olshc4; the p-value is 0.787 (with leverage points removed). So when taking CESD into account, the usual regression model does not indicate any association between the CAR and MAPA. Also, a smooth indicates a fairly straight, horizontal regression line between MAPA and the CAR (ignoring CESD), and no association is found using least squares

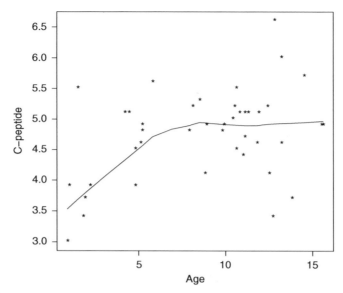

Figure 8.9   Shown is the smooth created by the R function lplot using the diabetes data. The smooth suggests that there is a positive association up to about the age of 7, but for older children, there seems to be little or no association

or the Theil–Sen estimator when ignoring CESD. Moreover, no association between MAPA and the CAR is found when focusing on only the CAR values greater than zero. That is, unlike depressive symptoms, no association is found between the CAR and MAPA when cortisol decreases shortly after awakening. (The same is true when CAR is negative.) In summary, all of the analyses just described find no association between MAPA and the CAR.

However, look at Figure 8.10, which shows the regression surface for predicting MAPA, given a value for CAR and CESD. Notice the distinct bend close to where CESD is 16. The nature of the association appears to depend crucially on whether depressive symptoms are high or low. Applying least squares regression again, but now using only the data for which the CAR is less than 16, both slopes for predicting MAPA are significant when testing at the 0.05 level. For the slope associated with CAR, the p-value is 0.022, and for the slope associated with CESD, the p-value is less than 0.001. Here are the R commands that were used to compute these p-values, again assuming that the data have been read into the R variable A3B3C:

```
dif=A3B3C$cort1-A3B3C$cort2

flag2=A3B3C$CESD<16

olshc4(cbind(dif[flag2],A3B3C$CESD[flag2]),A3B3C$MAPAGLOB
[flag2], xout=T).
```

It is noted, though, that if CESD is ignored, again no association between the CAR and MAPA is found when testing at the 0.05 level; the p-value is 0.09. So this example

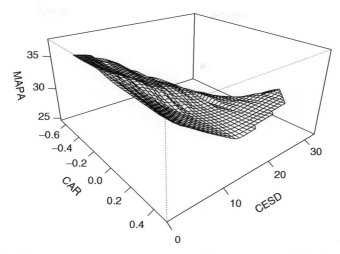

Figure 8.10 Shown is the smooth created by the R function `lplot` using the CAR and CESD to predict the typical MAPA score. Notice the distinct bend close to where CESD is equal to 16. Focusing on only those participants who have a CESD score less than 16, an association is found between CAR and MAPA, in contrast to an analysis where any possibility of curvature is ignored

touches on two points: curvature can mask an association when it is assumed that a regression surface is a plane and detecting whether an independent variable is associated with a dependent variable can depend on the other independent variables included in the model.

A common assumption is that with two independent variables, the regression surface is a plane, and it seems that often this is a reasonable approximation. But experience with smoothers indicates that taking this for granted is unwise as was just illustrated. The next example is intended to underscore this point.

Example

One goal in a study conducted by Tom and Schwartz was to understand the association between a Totagg score and two predictors: grade point average (GPA) and a measure of academic engagement. The Totagg score was a sum of peer nomination items that were based on an inventory that included descriptors focusing on adolescents' behaviors and social standing. (The peer nomination items were obtained by giving children a roster sheet and asking them to nominate a certain amount of peers who fit particular behavioral descriptors.) The sample size is $n = 336$. Figure 8.11 shows the smooth created by the R function `rplot`. Notice that there appears to be curvature and that the nature of the association between Totagg and the two independent variables appears to depend on the values of the independent variables in a rather complex manner. If the apparent curvature is ignored and least squares regression is used, the p-value for the slope associated with GPA is 0.005, and for the variable engage, it is 0.304. But if only the data for which engage is less than or equal to 3

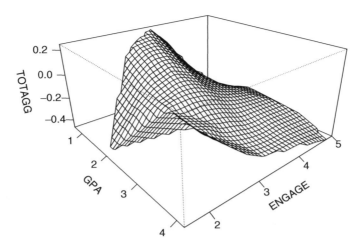

Figure 8.11 Shown is the smooth created by the R function `rplot` where the goal is to predict the typical Totagg score, given values for engage and GPA. This illustrates again that curvature can mask an association and that assuming that a regression surface is a plane can yield misleading results

are used, now the *p*-value for the slope associated with GPA is 0.773, and for the variable engage, it is 0.037. So, a conventional regression model does not detect an association between Totagg and engage when taking GPA into account, but a smooth suggests that the nature of the association depends on whether engage is relatively high or low. More broadly, associations are typically modeled using Equation (8.22). This example illustrates that using Equation (8.22) might perform poorly in terms of modeling the association.

8.10 SUMMARY

- A good regression analysis requires taking into account several issues that include outliers among the independent variable, outliers among the the dependent variable, heteroscedasticity, and curvature. Consequently, more than one method might be needed to get a good understanding of the association between an dependent variable and one or more independent variables.
- Least squares regression and Pearson's correlation are the most commonly used methods for studying associations. Currently, they are typically used in conjunction with inferential methods that assume homoscedasticity and normality. A positive feature of these methods is that when they reject, it is reasonable to conclude that there is an association. But more needs to be done to ensure that the nature of the association is well understood. In some cases, these classic hypothesis testing techniques continue to perform well when violating the normality and homoscedasticity assumptions. But at some point, they break down and become highly unsatisfactory.

- Pearson's correlation is useful for establishing dependence. It provides an indication of whether the least squares regression line has a positive or negative slope, but in terms of measuring the strength of an association, it has the potential of being highly misleading. It is even possible for Pearson's correlation to be positive when for the bulk of the data there is a negative association. Spearman's correlation, Kendall's tau, and the Winsorized and skipped correlations provide ways of dealing with outliers.

- Failure to detect an association with Pearson's correlation or least squares regression is not convincing evidence that no association exists, even with large sample sizes. True associations can be masked due to outliers and curvature. Heteroscedasticity also can mask an association if a hypothesis testing method is used that assumes homoscedasticity.

- Methods for testing hypotheses that allow heteroscedasticity were described and are readily applied using R. They help provide more accurate confidence intervals for the slope and intercept.

- It is prudent to always check on the impact of removing data associated with outliers among the independent variables. This is readily accomplished using the R functions in this chapter by setting the argument xout=TRUE.

- Robust regression estimators, which include the Theil–Sen estimator as a special case, are designed to deal with outliers among the dependent variable. Many other robust regression estimators have the potential of substantially improving upon the least squares estimator. But a brief yet informative summary of the relative merits of these alternative robust estimators is difficult.

- Smoothers provide a flexible approach to dealing with curvature that can be invaluable, as was illustrated.

The purpose of this chapter was to introduce basic concepts and to describe standard hypothesis testing methods associated with least squares regression. Another goal was to provide some indication of what might go wrong with standard methods and to briefly outline how some of these problems can be corrected. Generally, it is suggested that the students seek advanced training before attempting any regression analysis. Also, improved techniques continue to emerge. For more about regression, see Li (1985), Montgomery and Peck (1992), Staudte and Sheather (1990), Hampel et al. (1986), Huber and Ronchetti (2009), Rousseeuw and Leroy (1987), Belsley et al. (1980), Cook and Weisberg (1992), Carroll and Ruppert (1988), Hettmansperger (1984), Hettmansperger and McKean (1977) and Wilcox (2012a, b).

8.11 EXERCISES

1. For the following data, use R to verify that the least squares regression line is $\hat{Y} = 1.8X - 8.5$.

$$X : 5, 8, 9, 7, 14$$

$$Y : 3, 1, 6, 7, 19.$$

Also verify that using the Theil–Sen estimator, the slope is estimated to be 1.746 and the intercept is estimated to be −7.968.

2. Using the R function `lsfit`, compute the residuals using the data in Exercise 1. Verify that if you square and sum the residuals, you get 46.584. (Hint: `lsfit(x,y)$residuals` returns the residuals.)

3. Verify that for the data in Exercise 1, if you use $\hat{Y} = 2X - 9$, the sum of the squared residuals is greater than 46.584. Why would you expect a value greater than 46.584?

4. Suppose that based on $n = 25$ values, $s_x^2 = 12$ and $\sum(X_i - \overline{X})(Y_i - \overline{Y}) = 144$. What is the slope of the least squares regression?

5. The following table reports breast cancer rates plus levels of solar radiation (in calories per day) for various cities in the United States. The data are stored in the file cancer_rate_dat.txt on the author's web page. (Section 1.5 indicates how to access the data.) Note that the values in this file are separated by & and the first line in the file contains labels for the variables. Use R to fit a least squares regression line to the data with the goal of predicting cancer rates and comment on what this line suggests.

City	Rate	Daily Calories	City	Rate	Daily calories
New York	32.75	300	Chicago	30.75	275
Pittsburgh	28.00	280	Seattle	27.25	270
Boston	30.75	305	Cleveland	31.00	335
Columbus	29.00	340	Indianapolis	26.50	342
New Orleans	27.00	348	Nashville	23.50	354
Washington, DC	31.20	357	Salt Lake City	22.70	394
Omaha	27.00	380	San Diego	25.80	383
Atlanta	27.00	397	Los Angeles	27.80	450
Miami	23.50	453	Fort Worth	21.50	446
Tampa	21.00	456	Albuquerque	22.50	513
Las Vegas	21.50	510	Honolulu	20.60	520
El Paso	22.80	535	Phoenix	21.00	520

6. For the following data, use R to compute the least squares regression line for predicting GPA given SAT.

SAT	500	530	590	660	610	700	570	640
GPA	2.3	3.1	2.6	3.0	2.4	3.3	2.6	3.5

7. Compute the residuals for the data used in the previous problem and verify that they sum to zero.

8. For the following data, use R to compute the least squares regression line for predicting Y from X.

X	40	41	42	43	44	45	46
Y	1.62	1.63	1.90	2.64	2.05	2.13	1.94

9. In Exercise 5, what would be the least squares estimate of the cancer rate given a solar radiation of 600? Indicate why this estimate might be unreasonable.

10. Maximal oxygen uptake (MOU) is a measure of an individual's physical fitness. You want to know how MOU is related to how fast someone can run a mile. Suppose you randomly sample six athletes and get

    MOU (ml/kg) 63.3 60.1 53.6 58.8 67.5 62.5

    Time (seconds) 241.5 249.8 246.1 232.4 237.2 238.4

    Compute the least squares regression line and comment on what the results suggest.

11. Verify that for the following pairs of points, the least squares regression line has a slope of zero. Plot the points and comment on the assumption that the regression line is straight.

    X 1 2 3 4 5 6

    Y 1 4 7 7 4 1

12. Repeat the last exercise, only for the points

    X 1 2 3 4 5 6

    Y 4 5 6 7 8 2

13. Vitamin A is required for good health. However, one bite of polar bear liver results in death because it contains a high concentration of vitamin A. Comment on this fact in terms of extrapolation.

14. Sockett et al. (1987) report data related to patterns of residual insulin secretion in children. A portion of the study was concerned with whether age can be used to predict the logarithm of C-peptide concentrations at diagnosis. The observed values are

    Age (X) 5.2 8.8 10.5 10.6 10.4 1.8 12.7 15.6 5.8 1.9 2.2 4.8 7.9 5.2 0.9 11.8 7.9 1.5 10.6 8.5 11.1 12.8 11.3 1.0 14.5 11.9 8.1 13.8 15.5 9.8 11.0 12.4 11.1 5.1 4.8 4.2 6.9 13.2 9.9 12.5 13.2 8.9 10.8

    C-peptide (Y) 4.8 4.1 5.2 5.5 5.0 3.4 3.4 4.9 5.6 3.7 3.9 4.5 4.8 4.9 3.0 4.6 4.8 5.5 4.5 5.3 4.7 6.6 5.1 3.9 5.7 5.1 5.2 3.7 4.9 4.8 4.4 5.2 5.1 4.6 3.9 5.1 5.1 6.0 4.9 4.1 4.6 4.9 5.1

Duplicate the smooth in Figure 8.8. (The data are stored on the author's web page in the file diabetes_sockett_dat.txt and can be downloaded as described in Section 1.5.)

15. For the data in the last exercise, use R to verify that a least squares regression line using only X values (age) less than or equal to 7 yields a p-value equal to 0.026 when using the R function olsch4. Also verify that the p-value, when using the Theil–Sen estimator, is 0.0233.

16. For the reading data in Table 8.5, verify that the R function spearci returns a p-value equal to 0.014 and that scorci returns a p-value equal to 0.002. Based on the plot returned by scorci, why is it not surprising that these two functions give similar results?

17. Given that $b_1 = -1.5$, $n = 10$, $s_{Y.X}^2 = 35$, and $\sum (X_i - \overline{X})^2 = 140$, assume normality and homoscedasticity and compute a 0.95 confidence interval for slope, β_1.

18. Repeat the previous problem, only compute a 0.98 confidence interval.

19. Based on results covered in the previous chapters, speculate about why the confidence intervals computed in the last two problems might be inaccurate.

20. Assume normality and homoscedasticity and suppose $n = 30$, $\sum X_i = 15$, $\sum Y_i = 30$, $\sum (X_i - \overline{X})(Y_i - \overline{Y}) = 30$, and $\sum (X_i - \overline{X})^2 = 10$. Determine the least squares estimates of the slope and intercept.

21. Assume normality and homoscedasticity and suppose $n = 38$, $\overline{Y} = 20$, $\sum X_i^2 = 1,922$, $\overline{X} = 7$, $\sum (X_1 - \overline{X})(Y_i - \overline{Y}) = 180$, $\sum (X_i - \overline{X})^2 = 60$, and $s_{Y.X}^2 = 121$.
    (a) Determine the least squares estimates of the slope and intercept.
    (b) Test the hypothesis H_0: $\beta_0 = 0$ with $\alpha = 0.02$.
    (c) Compute a 0.9 confidence interval for β_1.

22. Assume normality and homoscedasticity and suppose $n = 41$, $\overline{Y} = 10$, $\overline{X} = 12$, $\sum (X_1 - \overline{X})(Y_i - \overline{Y}) = 100$, $\sum (X_i - \overline{X})^2 = 400$, and $s_{Y.X}^2 = 144$. (a) Determine the least squares estimate of the slope and intercept. (b) Compute a 0.9 confidence interval for β_1.

23. Assume normality and homoscedasticity and suppose $n = 18$, $b_1 = 3.1$, $\sum (X_i - \overline{X})^2 = 144$ and $s_{Y.X}^2 = 36$. Compute a 0.95 confidence interval for β_1. Would you conclude that $\beta_1 > 2$?

24. Assume normality and homoscedasticity and suppose $n = 20$, $b_0 = 6$, $\sum X_i^2 = 169$, $s_{Y.X}^2 = 25$ and $\sum (X_i - \overline{X})^2 = 90$. Compute a 0.95 confidence interval for β_0.

25. Given the following quantities, find the sample correlation coefficient, r, and test $H_0 : \rho = 0$ at the indicated value for α.
    (a) $n = 27$, $\sum (Y_i - \overline{Y})^2 = 100$, $\sum (X_i - \overline{X})^2 = 625$, $\sum (X_i - \overline{X})(Y_i - \overline{Y}) = 200$, $\alpha = 0.01$.
    (b) $n = 5$, $\sum (Y_i - \overline{Y})^2 = 16$, $\sum (X_i - \overline{X})^2 = 25$, $\sum (X_i - \overline{X})(Y_i - \overline{Y}) = 10$, $\alpha = 0.05$.

26. The high school grade-point average (X) and college grade-point (Y) for 29 randomly sampled college freshman yielded the following results: $\sum(Y_i - \overline{Y})^2 = 64$, $\sum(X_i - \overline{X})^2 = 100$, $\sum(X_i - \overline{X})(Y_i - \overline{Y}) = 40$. Test H_0 : $\rho = 0$ with $\alpha = 0.1$ and interpret the results.

27. For the previous exercise, answer the following questions:

    (a) Is it reasonable to conclude that the least squares regression line has a positive slope?

    (b) Is it possible that despite the value for r, as high school grade-point averages increase, college grade-point averages decrease? Explain your answer.

    (c) What might you do, beyond considering r, to decide whether it is reasonable to conclude that as high school grade-point averages increase, college grade-point averages increase as well?

28. Using R, determine what happens to Pearson's correlation between X and Y if the Y values are multiplied by 3. Argue that if Y is multiplied by any constant $c \neq 0$, Pearson's correlation does not change.

29. Repeat the previous problem, only determine what happens to the slope of the least squares regression line.

30. Consider a least squares regression line $Y = 0.5X + 2$, assume homoscedasticity and consider the situation where the common variance is $\sigma^2 = 1$. What happens to the correlation between X and Y if instead $\sigma^2 = 2$? Hint: What happens to the residuals?

31. The numerator of the coefficient of determination is $\sum(Y_i - \overline{Y})^2 - \sum(Y_i - \hat{Y}_i)^2$. Based on the least squares principle, why is this value always greater than or equal to zero?

32. Imagine a study where the correlation between some amount of an experimental drug and liver damage yields a value for r close to zero and the hypothesis $H_0: \rho = 0$ is not rejected. Why might it be unreasonable to conclude that the two variables are independent?

33. Suppose $r^2 = 0.95$. Explain why this does not provide convincing evidence that the least squares line provides a good fit to a scatterplot of the points.

34. Imagine a situation where points are removed for which the X values are judged to be outliers. Note that this restricts the range of X values. Without looking at the data, can someone predict whether Pearson's correlation will increase or decrease after these points are removed?

35. If the normality assumption is violated, what effect might this have when computing confidence intervals for the slope and intercept as described in Section 8.4.1?

36. If the homoscedasticity assumption is violated, what effect might this have when computing confidence intervals as described in Section 8.4.1?

9

COMPARING TWO INDEPENDENT GROUPS

Chapters 6 and 7 described how to make inferences about the population mean, and other measures of location, associated with a single population of individuals or things. This chapter extends these methods to situations where the goal is to compare two independent groups. For example, Table 2.1 reports data from a study on changes in cholesterol levels when participants take an experimental drug. Of fundamental interest is how the changes compare to individuals who receive a placebo instead. Section 6.2 described an experiment on the effect of ozone on weight gain among rats. The two groups in this study consisted of rats living in an ozone environment and ones that lived in an ozone-free environment. Do weight gains differ for these groups, and if they do, how might this difference be described? Two training programs are available for learning how to invest in stocks. To what extent, if any, do these training programs differ? How does the reading ability of children who watch 30 hours or more of television per week compare to children who watch 10 hours or less? How does the birth weight of newborns among mothers who smoke compare to the birth weight among mothers who do not smoke? In general terms, if we have two independent variables, how might we compare them?

A basic goal in this chapter is to describe and illustrate methods that can be used to compare groups, and to discuss their relative merits regarding their ability to control the Type I error probability and provide relatively high power. But there is a broader goal, which is to make it clear that different methods provide different perspectives and that more than one perspective might be needed to get a deep and accurate understanding of how groups compare. Sometimes, a simple model for comparing groups is satisfactory: assume both groups have normal distributions and that comparing means suffices in terms of understanding whether and how the groups differ. But we

Understanding and Applying Basic Statistical Methods Using R, First Edition. Rand R. Wilcox.
© 2017 John Wiley & Sons, Inc. Published 2017 by John Wiley & Sons, Inc.
www.wiley.com/go/Wilcox/Statistical_Methods_R

will see that a more nuanced approach to comparing groups can be important and that multiple methods can be needed in order to get a reasonably accurate sense of how groups compare.

9.1   COMPARING MEANS

When trying to detect and describe differences between groups, by far the most common strategy is to use means. We begin with a classic method designed for two independent groups. By independent groups is meant that the observations in the first group are independent of the observations in the second. In particular, the sample means for the two groups, say $\overline{X}_1$ and $\overline{X}_2$, are independent. So in the example dealing with weight gain among rats, it is assumed that one group of rats is exposed to an ozone environment, and a separate group of rats, not associated with the first group, is exposed to an ozone-free environment. This is in contrast to using, for example, the same rats under both conditions, or using rats from the same litter, in which case the sample means might be dependent.

9.1.1   The Two-Sample Student's T Test

The classic and best-known method for comparing the means of two independent groups is called the *two-sample Student's T test*. Here, we let μ_1 and μ_2 represent the two population means, and the corresponding standard deviations are denoted by σ_1 and σ_2. The goal is to test

$$H_0 : \mu_1 = \mu_2, \tag{9.1}$$

the hypothesis that the population means are equal. Exact control over the probability of a Type I error can be achieved if the following three assumptions are true:

- Random sampling
- Normality
- Equal variances. That is, $\sigma_1 = \sigma_2$, which is called the *homoscedasticity* assumption.

Before describing how to test the hypothesis of equal means, first consider how we might estimate the assumed common variance. For convenience, let σ_p^2 represent the common variance and let s_1^2 and s_2^2 be the sample variances corresponding to the two groups. Also, let n_1 and n_2 represent the corresponding sample sizes. The typical estimate of σ_p^2 is

$$s_p^2 = \frac{(n_1 - 1)s_1^2 + (n_2 - 1)s_2^2}{n_1 + n_2 - 2}. \tag{9.2}$$

For the special case where the sample sizes are equal, meaning that $n_1 = n_2$, s_p^2 is just the average of the two sample variances. That is,

$$s_p^2 = \frac{s_1^2 + s_2^2}{2}.$$

Under the assumptions already stated, and when the hypothesis of equal means is true,

$$T = \frac{\overline{X}_1 - \overline{X}_2}{\sqrt{s_p^2 \left(\frac{1}{n_1} + \frac{1}{n_2} \right)}} \qquad (9.3)$$

has a Student's T distribution with $v = n_1 + n_2 - 2$ degrees of freedom. So if the assumptions of normality and equal variances are true, exact control over the Type I error probability can be achieved.

Decision Rule: As usual, let α denote the desired Type I error probability. Then, reject the hypothesis of equal means if

$$|T| \geq t, \qquad (9.4)$$

where the critical value t is the $1 - \alpha/2$ quantile of Student's T distribution with $v = n_1 + n_2 - 2$ degrees of freedom, which is read from Table B.4 in Appendix B. An exact $1 - \alpha$ confidence interval for the difference between the population means, still assuming normality and homoscedasticity, is

$$(\overline{X}_1 - \overline{X}_2) \pm t \sqrt{s_p^2 \left(\frac{1}{n_1} + \frac{1}{n_2} \right)}. \qquad (9.5)$$

Example

Salk (1973) conducted a study where the general goal was to examine the soothing effects of a mother's heartbeat on her newborn infant. Infants were placed in a nursery immediately after birth, and they remained there for 4 days except when being fed by their mothers. The infants were divided into two groups. The first group was continuously exposed to the sound of an adult's heartbeat; the other group was not. Salk measured, among other things, the weight change of the babies from birth to the fourth day. Table 9.1 reports the weight change for the babies weighing at least 3,510 g at birth. As indicated, the sample standard deviations are $s_1 = 60.1$ and $s_2 = 88.4$. The estimate of the assumed common variance is

$$s_p^2 = \frac{(20 - 1)(60.1^2) + (36 - 1)(88.4^2)}{20 + 36 - 2} = 6,335.9.$$

So

$$T = \frac{18 - (-52.1)}{\sqrt{6,335.9 \left(\frac{1}{20} + \frac{1}{36} \right)}} = \frac{70.1}{22.2} = 3.2.$$

The sample sizes are $n_1 = 20$ and $n_2 = 36$, so the degrees of freedom are $v = 20 + 36 - 2 = 54$. If we want the Type I error probability to be $\alpha = 0.05$, then $1 - \alpha/2 = 0.975$, and from Table B.4 in Appendix B, the critical value is $t = 2.01$. Because $|T| = 3.2$, which is greater than 2.01, reject the hypothesis of equal population means.

TABLE 9.1　Weight Gain, in Grams, for Large Babies

	Group 1 (Heartbeat)		
Subject	Gain	Subject	Gain
1	190	11	10
2	80	12	10
3	80	13	0
4	75	14	0
5	50	15	−10
6	40	16	−25
7	30	17	−30
8	20	18	−45
9	20	19	−60
10	10	20	−85

			Group 2 (No Heartbeat)				
Subject	Gain	Subject	Gain	Subject	Gain	Subject	Gain
1	140	11	−25	21	−50	31	−130
2	100	12	−25	22	−50	32	−155
3	100	13	−25	23	−60	33	−155
4	70	14	−30	24	−75	34	−180
5	25	15	−30	25	−75	35	−240
6	20	16	−30	26	−85	36	−290
7	10	17	−45	27	−85		
8	0	18	−45	28	−100		
9	−10	19	−45	29	−110		
10	−10	20	−50	30	−130		

$n_1 = 20, \overline{X}_1 = 18.0, s_1 = 60.1, s_1/\sqrt{n_1} = 13.$
$n_2 = 36, \overline{X}_2 = -52.1, s_2 = 88.4, s_2/\sqrt{n_2} = 15.$

Because the sample mean for the infants exposed to the sound of a heartbeat is greater than the sample mean for the control group, the results indicate that for the population of all newborns, the average weight gain would be higher among babies exposed to the sound of a heartbeat. The 0.95 confidence interval for $\mu_1 - \mu_2$, the difference between the population means, is

$$[18 - (-52.1)] \pm 2.01 \sqrt{6,335.9 \left(\frac{1}{20} + \frac{1}{36} \right)} = (25.5, 114.7).$$

This interval does not contain zero, so again reject the hypothesis of equal means.

9.1.2　Violating Assumptions When Using Student's *T*

There are two conditions where the assumption of normality, or equal variances, can be violated and yet, Student's *T* appears to continue to perform well in terms of Type I errors and accurate confidence intervals. The homoscedasticity assumption can be violated if both distributions are normal and the sample sizes are equal and not overly small, say less than 8 (Ramsey, 1980). As for nonnormality, Student's T appears to perform well in terms of Type I error probabilities provided the two distributions are identical. That is, not only do they have the same means, they have the same variances, the same amount of skewness, the tails of the distribution are identical, and so on. So if we were to plot the distributions, the plots would be exactly the same. If, for example, the desired probability of a Type I error is 0.05, generally, the actual Type I error probability will be less than or equal to 0.05.

If the goal is to test the hypothesis of equal means, without being sensitive to other ways the groups might differ, Student's T can be unsatisfactory in terms of Type I errors. A related concern is that it can yield inaccurate confidence intervals when sampling from normal distributions with unequal sample sizes and unequal variances. Problems due to unequal variances are exacerbated when sampling from nonnormal distributions, and now concerns arise even with equal sample sizes (e.g., Algina et al., 1994; Wilcox, 1990). When dealing with groups that differ in skewness, again problems with controlling the probability of a Type I error occur, and the combination of unequal variances and different amounts of skewness makes matters worse. Some degree of unequal variances, as well as mild differences in skewness, can be tolerated. But the extent to which this is true, based on the data under study, is difficult to determine in an accurate manner.

Example

Recall from Chapter 6 that one of way of determining the distribution of T under normality when dealing with a single populations is to use simulations. That is, generate data from a normal distribution, compute T, and repeat this process many times. With the aid of a computer, we can extend this method when sampling from two distributions that have equal means but which have unequal variances and differ in terms of skewness as well. Imagine, for example, that Student's T is computed based on 40 observations randomly sampled from a standard normal distribution and 60 observations randomly sampled from the distribution shown in Figure 9.1, which has a population mean of zero. Repeating this process 5,000 times provides an estimate of the distribution of T when the null hypothesis of equal means is true. Figure 9.2 shows a plot of the results plus the distribution of T assuming normality. Under normality, and with a Type I error probability of $\alpha = 0.05$, Student's T rejects the hypothesis of equal means if $T \leq -2.002$ or if $T \geq 2.002$. But the 5,000 T values indicate that we should reject if $T \leq -2.41$ or if $T \geq 1.45$, values that differ substantially from what would be used under normality. If, instead, 60 observations are randomly sampled from a standard normal distribution and 40 observations from the distribution shown in Figure 9.1, Student's T performs even more poorly. Now we should reject if $T \leq -2.89$ or if $T \geq 1.82$. If Student's T is applied assuming normality, the actual Type I error probability is approximately 0.10 rather than 0.05 as intended.

Some authorities might criticize this last example on the grounds that if groups differ in terms of the variances and the amount of skewness, surely the means differ as well. That is, they would argue that Type I errors are not an issue in this case. But

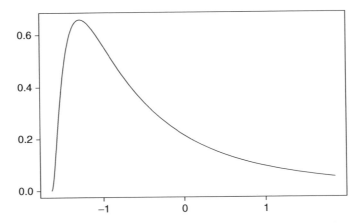

Figure 9.1   A skewed distribution with a mean of zero

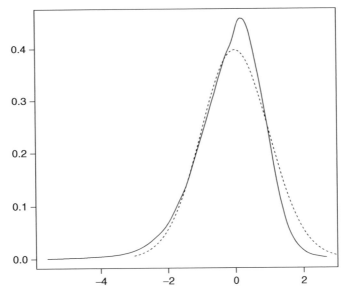

Figure 9.2   The distribution of T (the solid line) when sampling 40 values from a standard normal distribution and 60 values from the distribution in Figure 9.1. Also shown is the distribution of T when both groups have normal distributions. This illustrates that differences in skewness can have an important impact on T

even if we accept this point of view, this last illustration can be seen to create concerns about power, and it indicates that confidence intervals based on Student's T can be relatively inaccurate.

Usually, a basic requirement of any method is that with sufficiently large sample sizes, good control over the Type I error probability and accurate confidence intervals will be obtained. There are theoretical results indicating that under general conditions, when the goal is to compare the means without being sensitive to other features of the distribution (such as unequal variances), Student's T can be unsatisfactory regardless of how large the sample sizes might be (Cressie and Whitford, 1986). An exception is when the sample sizes are equal and when both groups have identical distributions. This means that Student's T provides a valid test of the hypothesis that the distributions are identical, but it can be unsatisfactory when computing confidence intervals for the difference between the means or when testing the hypothesis that groups have equal means.

Finally, in terms of Type II errors and power, Student's T can perform very poorly, compared to alternative techniques, when outliers tend to occur. Even a small departure from normality can be a source for concern. The presence of outliers does not necessarily mean relatively low power, but the reality is that power might be increased substantially when comparing groups with something other than the means, as will be illustrated. (Some additional concerns about Student's T are summarized in Wilcox, 2012a, b.)

The classic illustration that small departures from normality can result in poor power is shown in Figure 9.3. Figure 9.3a shows two normal distributions, both have variance 1, the first has a mean of 0, and the other has a mean of 1. With sample sizes $n_1 = n_2 = 25$, and when testing at the $\alpha = 0.05$ level, the probability of rejecting with Student's T (power) is 0.96. The distributions in Figure 9.3b are mixed normals that have variance 10.9. Now, power is only 0.28 despite the obvious similarity with the distributions in Figure 9.3a. This illustrates that the power of any method based on means is highly sensitive to small changes in the tails of the distributions and that situations where outliers tend to occur have the potential of masking an important difference among the bulk of the participants.

9.1.3 Why Testing Assumptions Can Be Unsatisfactory

Some commercial software now contains a test of the assumption that two groups have equal variances. The idea is that if the hypothesis of equal variances is not rejected, one would then use Student's T. But a *basic principle* is that failing to reject a null hypothesis is not, by itself, compelling evidence that the null hypothesis should be accepted or that the null hypothesis is approximately true. Accepting the null hypothesis is only reasonable if the probability of rejecting (power) is sufficiently high to ensure that differences that have practical importance will be detected. If there is a low probability of detecting a difference that is deemed important, concluding that no difference exists is difficult to defend. In the case of Student's T, would a test of the assumption of equal variances have enough power to detect a situation where unequal variances cause a problem? All indications are that the answer is no (e.g., Markowski and Markowski, 1990; Moser et al., 1989; Wilcox et al., 1986; Zimmerman, 2004; Hayes and Cai, 2007). Presumably, exceptions occur if the sample sizes are sufficiently large, but it is unclear when this is the case. Part of the problem is that the extent to which the variances can differ, without having a major impact on the Type I error probability, is a complicated function of the sample sizes, the extent

to which groups differ in terms of skewness, and the likelihood of observing outliers. Testing the hypothesis that data have a normal distribution is another strategy
that might be followed. But when do such tests have enough power to detect departures from normality that are a concern? The answer is not remotely clear, so this
approach cannot be recommended. A better strategy is to use more modern methods
that perform reasonably well under normality, but which continue to perform well
under nonnormality and when groups have unequal variances.

There are many alternatives to Student's T. Because testing assumptions seems
dubious, how can we tell whether some alternative technique might give a substantially different sense about whether and how the groups differ? Currently, the only
known strategy that answers this question in an adequate manner is to simply try
alternative methods, some of which are outlined later in this chapter. However, a criticism of applying many methods is that control over the probability of one or more
Type I errors can become an issue. Methods for dealing with this issue are described
and illustrated in Chapter 12.

9.1.4   Interpreting Student's T When It Rejects

Despite its many practical problems, Student's T does have a positive feature. If its
p-value is close to zero, this is a good indication that the distributions differ in some
manner. This is because when the distributions do not differ, it controls the probability of a Type I error fairly well. But even though the method is designed to compare
means, in reality it is also sensitive to differences in variances and skewness. As previously noted, some would argue that if the distributions differ, surely the means differ.
However, when Student's T rejects, it is unclear whether the main reason is due to
differences between the means. The main reason could be differences between the

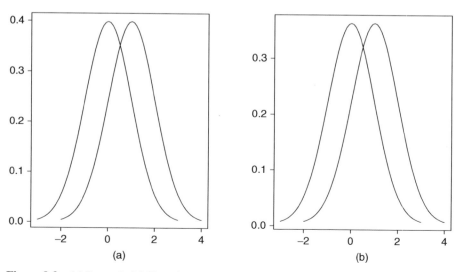

Figure 9.3   (a) Power is 0.96 based on Student's T, $\alpha = 0.05$ and sample sizes $n_1 = n_2 = 25$.
(b) The distributions are not normal, but rather mixed normals, and now, power is only 0.28

variances or differences in skewness. Moreover, rejecting with Student's T raises concerns about whether the confidence interval, given by Equation (9.5), is reasonably accurate. In summary, when rejecting with Student's T, it is reasonable to conclude that the groups differ in some manner. But there are concerns that the nature of the difference is not being revealed in a reasonably accurate manner. When Student's T fails to reject, this alone is not compelling evidence that the groups do not differ in any important way.

9.1.5 Dealing with Unequal Variances: Welch's Test

Many methods have been proposed for comparing means when the population variances (σ_1^2 and σ_2^2) differ. None are completely satisfactory. Here, we describe one such method that seems to perform relatively well compared to other techniques that have been proposed. Popular commercial software now contains this method, which stems from Welch (1938).

Recall from Chapter 5 that the sampling distribution of the sample mean has variance σ^2/n, which is called the squared standard error of the sample mean. For the situation at hand, the difference between the sample means, $\overline{X}_1 - \overline{X}_2$, also has a sampling distribution. Moreover, the population mean of this sampling distribution is $\mu_1 - \mu_2$, the difference between the population means. Roughly, if a study is repeated millions of times, and the differences between the sample means resulting from each study were averaged, the result would be $\mu_1 \mu_2$, the difference between the population means. Said another way, on average, over many studies, $\overline{X}_1 - \overline{X}_2$ estimates $\mu_1 - \mu_2$. Moreover, the variance (or squared standard error) of the difference between the sample means can be shown to be

$$VAR(\overline{X}_1 - \overline{X}_2) = \frac{\sigma_1^2}{n_1} + \frac{\sigma_2^2}{n_2}.$$

Also recall from Chapter 6 that under normality, if we standardize a variable by subtracting its (population) mean, and then dividing by its standard error, we get a standard normal distribution. That is, if a variable has a normal distribution, then in general,

$$\frac{\text{variable} - \text{population mean of the variable}}{\text{standard error of the variable}}, \tag{9.6}$$

will have a standard normal distribution. Here, the variable of interest is $\overline{X}_1 - \overline{X}_2$, the difference between the sample means, which has a population mean of $\mu_1 - \mu_2$. Consequently, based on the equation for the squared standard error, $VAR(\overline{X}_1 - \overline{X}_2)$, it follows that

$$\frac{\overline{X}_1 - \overline{X}_2 - (\mu_1 - \mu_2)}{\sqrt{\frac{\sigma_1^2}{n_1} + \frac{\sigma_2^2}{n_2}}}$$

has a standard normal distribution. *If* the hypothesis of equal means is true, then $\mu_1 - \mu_2 = 0$, in which case this last equation becomes

$$\frac{\overline{X}_1 - \overline{X}_2}{\sqrt{\frac{\sigma_1^2}{n_1} + \frac{\sigma_2^2}{n_2}}},$$

which again has a standard normal distribution. As usual, the population variances are rarely known, but they can be estimated with the sample variances, in which case this last equation becomes

$$W = \frac{(\overline{X}_1 - \overline{X}_2)}{\sqrt{\frac{s_1^2}{n_1} + \frac{s_2^2}{n_2}}}, \tag{9.7}$$

where as before, s_1^2 and s_2^2 are the sample variances corresponding to the two groups being compared. This is the test statistic used by Welch's test.

When the hypothesis of equal means is true, W will have, approximately, a standard normal distribution if the sample sizes are sufficiently large, thanks to a generalization of the central limit theorem. That is, we can determine how large W must be to reject the hypothesis of equal means using values in Table B.1. But in general, W will not have a normal distribution, so some other approximation of an appropriate critical value is required. Welch's approach to this problem is implemented in the following manner. For convenience, let

$$q_1 = \frac{s_1^2}{n_1} \text{ and } q_2 = \frac{s_2^2}{n_2}. \tag{9.8}$$

As was done with Student's T, Table B.4 in Appendix B is used to determine a critical value, t, but now the degrees of freedom are

$$\nu = \frac{(q_1 + q_2)^2}{\frac{q_1^2}{n_1 - 1} + \frac{q_2^2}{n_2 - 1}}. \tag{9.9}$$

Decision Rule: Under normality, W has, approximately, a Student's T distribution with degrees of freedom given by Equation (9.9). That is, reject the hypothesis of equal means if $|W| \geq t$, where t is the $1 - \alpha/2$ quantile of a Student's T distribution with degrees of freedom given by Equation (9.9). The $1 - \alpha$ confidence interval for the difference between the means, $\mu_1 - \mu_2$, is

$$(\overline{X}_1 - \overline{X}_2) \pm t\sqrt{\frac{s_1^2}{n_1} + \frac{s_2^2}{n_2}}. \tag{9.10}$$

A concern with Welch's test is that when distributions differ in skewness, control over the Type I error probability can be unsatisfactory. A way of possibly reducing this concern is to use a bootstrap-t method to determine a critical value rather than the method just described. That is, use simulations performed on the available data to determine an appropriate critical value. This can be accomplished with the R function yuenbt in Section 9.3.1.

9.1.6 R Function t.test

The built-in R function

```
t.test(x, y = NULL,var.equal=FALSE,conf.level=0.95)
```

performs Welch's test by default. It performs the two-sample Student's T test when the argument var.equal=TRUE. (If the second argument, y, is omitted, the one-sample Student's T test in Chapter 5 is performed.) The function also returns a p-value and a confidence interval, which by default has a probability coverage 0.95. To get a 0.99 confidence interval, for example, set the argument conf.level=0.99.

Example

Imagine that the data in Table 9.1 are stored in the R variables salk1 and salk2. Then, the command

```
t.test(salk1,salk2,var.equal=T,conf.level=0.9)
```

applies Student's T, assuming equal variances, and results in the following output:

```
          Standard Two-Sample t-Test

data:   salk1 and salk2
t = 3.1564, df = 54, p-value = 0.0026
alternative hypothesis: true difference in means is not equal to 0
90 percent confidence interval:
  32.92384 107.24282
sample estimates:
 mean of x mean of y
        18 -52.08333
```

Example

Tables 2.1 and 2.2 report data on the effectiveness of a drug to lower cholesterol levels. For the data in Table 2.1, corresponding to the group that received the experimental drug, the sample size is $n_1 = 171$, the sample variance is $s_1^2 = 133.51$, and the sample mean is $\overline{X}_1 = -9.854$. For the group that received the placebo, $n_2 = 177$, $s_2^2 = 213.97$, and $\overline{X}_2 = 0.124$. To apply Welch's test, compute $q_1 = 133.51/171 = 0.78076$ and $q_2 = 213.97/177 = 1.20887$, in which case the degrees of freedom are

$$v = \frac{(0.78076 + 1.20887)^2}{\frac{0.78076^2}{171-1} + \frac{1.2088^2}{177-1}} = 332.99.$$

The test statistic is $W = 7.07$, the $\alpha = 0.05$ critical value is 1.967, and because $|7.07| \geq 1.967$, reject the null hypothesis.

Data are often stored in a file where some column corresponds to some variable of interest and another column indicates whether it belongs to the first or second group. For example, the file mitch_dat.txt, stored on the author's web page, contains data from a study dealing with the effects of consuming alcohol. Hangover symptoms were measured after consuming a specific amount of alcohol in a laboratory setting. The first four rows of the data resemble this:

2	0	2	1
1	0	4	0
1	32	15	25
2	0	0	0

The first column indicates whether a participant is the son of an alcoholic or belongs to the control group. The value 1 indicates the control group and 2 indicates that the participant is the son of an alcoholic. Hangover symptoms were measured on three different occasions, which correspond to columns 2, 3, and 4. So, the first row indicates that this particular person was the son of an alcoholic and that the hangover symptoms at times 1, 2, and 3 were 0, 2, and 1, respectively. Focus on the second column and suppose the goal is to compare the mean hangover symptoms of sons of alcoholics to the mean for the control group. Assuming that the data have been read into the R variable hang (using the read.table command), here is an R command that accomplishes that goal:

```
t.test(hang[,2]~hang[,1]).
```

The command hang[,2]~hang[,1] is another example of an R command called a *formula*, which was introduced in Section 8.2.1 in connection with least squares regression. Basically, in the present context, it separates the data in the second column, hang[,2], into groups based on the corresponding values in the first column, hang[,1].

9.1.7   Student's *T* versus Welch's Test

Some brief comments about the relative merits of Student's *T* compared to Welch's test should be made. When comparing groups that do not differ in any manner, there is little reason to prefer Student's *T* over Welch's test. But if the distributions differ in some way, such as having unequal variances, the choice of method can make a practical difference. Welch's test reduces problems with unequal variances, given the goal of comparing means, but it does not eliminate them. Differences in skewness remain a concern, and as is the case with all methods based on means, outliers can destroy power. So when rejecting with Welch's test, similarly to Student's *T* test, it is reasonable to conclude that the distributions differ in some manner, but there is uncertainty about whether the main reason has to do with differences between the population means; the primary reason could be unequal variances or differences in skewness. When Welch's test fails to reject, this could be because the population means differ by very little, but another possibility is that power is low due to sample sizes that are too small, differences in skewness, or outliers.

In fairness, there are situations where Student's T correctly concludes that groups differ in some manner when Welch's test does not. This can happen because Student's T can be more sensitive to certain types of differences, such as unequal variances.

A positive feature of Welch's method is that with sufficiently large sample sizes, it will control the probability of a Type I error given the goal of comparing means, and it provides accurate confidence intervals as well, assuming random sampling only. This is in contrast to Student's T, which does not satisfy this goal when the sample sizes are unequal and the groups differ in skewness. A rough explanation is that under random sampling, regardless of whether the groups differ, Welch's test uses a correct estimate of the standard error associated with the difference between the means, $\overline{X}_1 - \overline{X}_2$, but there are conditions where this is not the case when using Student's T (Cressie and Whitford, 1986). As previously noted, an exception is when groups have identical distributions. So again, an argument for considering Student's T is that if it rejects, a good argument can be made that the groups differ in some manner.

9.1.8 The Impact of Outliers When Comparing Means

We have seen that any method for comparing groups based on means runs the risk of relatively low power. As noted in the previous chapters, outliers can inflate the sample variance, which in turn can result in low power, and there is some possibility that the mean will poorly reflect what is typical. The next example provides a different perspective on the impact of outliers.

Example

Imagine that an experimental drug is under investigation and that there is concern that it might damage the stomach. For illustrative purposes, suppose the drug is given to a sample of rats, a placebo is given to a control group, and the results are follows.

$$\text{Experimental drug: } 4, 5, 6, 7, 8, 9, 10, 11, 12, 13$$

$$\text{Placebo: } 1, 2, 3, 4, 5, 6, 7, 8, 9, 10$$

The goal is to determine whether the average amount of stomach damage differs for these two groups. The corresponding sample means are $\overline{X}_1 = 8.5$ and $\overline{X}_2 = 5.5$ and $T = 2.22$. With $\alpha = 0.05$, the critical value is $t = 2.1$, so Student's T rejects the hypothesis of equal means, and it would be decided that the first group has a larger population mean than the second group (because the first group has the larger sample mean). Now, if the largest observation in the first group is increased from 13 to 23, the sample mean increases to $\overline{X}_1 = 9.5$. So, the difference between $\overline{X}_1$ and $\overline{X}_2$ has increased from 3 to 4, and this would seem to suggest that there is stronger evidence that the population means differ and in fact the first group has the larger population mean. However, increasing the largest observation in the first group also inflates the corresponding sample variance, s_1^2. In particular, s_1^2 increases from 9.17 to 29.17. The result is that T *decreases* to $T = 2.04$ and it no longer rejects. That is, increasing the largest observation has more of an effect on the sample variance than the sample mean in the sense that now we are no longer able to conclude that the population means differ. Increasing the largest observation in the first group to 33, the sample mean increases to 10.5, the difference between the two sample means increases to 5, and now $T = 1.79$. So again, the hypothesis of equal means is not rejected and in fact the test statistic is getting smaller. It is left as an exercise to show that a similar result is obtained when using Welch's test.

9.2 COMPARING MEDIANS

Outliers can destroy the power of any method based on means, and there is a concern that the mean might reflect a highly atypical response. One strategy for dealing with this problem is to compare medians instead, roughly because the median is highly insensitive to outliers. Many methods have been proposed for comparing the population medians of two independent groups, most of which are rather unsatisfactory in terms of controlling the Type I error probability or computing a reasonably accurate confidence interval. This section describes two methods for comparing medians that perform fairly well. The first is based on the McKean–Schrader estimate of the standard errors and can be used when tied values are virtually impossible. The second uses a percentile bootstrap method that generally performs well even when tied values are likely to occur.

Two methods that are sometimes suggested for comparing medians, but which are unsatisfactory, should be mentioned. The first is called a *permutation method* that should not be used for reasons described in Romano (1990). The second is the Wilcoxon–Mann–Whitney test, described in Section 9.6.

9.2.1 A Method Based on the McKean–Schrader Estimator

Let M_1 and M_2 be the sample medians for the two groups, and let S_1^2 and S_2^2 be the corresponding McKean–Schrader estimates of the squared standard errors. Then, an approximate $1 - \alpha$ confidence interval for the difference between the population medians is

$$(M_1 - M_2) \pm c\sqrt{S_1^2 + S_2^2},$$

where c is the $1 - \alpha/2$ quantile of a standard normal distribution. The hypothesis of equal population medians is rejected if this interval does not contain zero. Alternatively, reject the hypothesis of equal population medians if

$$\frac{|M_1 - M_2|}{\sqrt{S_1^2 + S_2^2}} \geq c.$$

Example

Imagine a study aimed at measuring the extent men and women are addicted to nicotine. Based on a measure of dependence on nicotine, 30 men are found to have a median value of 4 and 20 women have a median value of 2. If the McKean–Schrader estimates of the corresponding squared standard errors are 0.8 and 0.6, then

$$\frac{|M_1 - M_2|}{\sqrt{S_1^2 + S_2^2}} = \frac{|4 - 2|}{\sqrt{0.8 + 0.6}} = 1.69.$$

With $\alpha = 0.05$, $1 - \alpha/2 = 0.975$, and from Table B.1 in Appendix B, the 0.975 quantile for a standard normal distribution is $c = 1.96$. Because 1.69 is less than the critical value, fail to reject.

9.2.2 A Percentile Bootstrap Method

The percentile bootstrap method, which was outlined in Chapters 6 and 7, is readily extended to comparing the medians of two independent groups. Among the various methods that might be used to compare medians, it performs relatively well. Currently, it is the only method for comparing medians that has been found to provide reasonably accurate control over the probability of a Type I error when tied (duplicated) values are likely to occur.

The method begins by generating a bootstrap sample from the first group. That is, randomly sample, with replacement, n_1 observations from the first group. The median, based on this bootstrap sample, is labeled M_1^*. Proceed in the same manner for the second group yielding M_2^*. Then, one of three outcomes will occur: $M_1^* < M_2^*$, $M_1^* = M_2^*$ or $M_1^* > M_2^*$. Next, this process is repeated B times, and for the sake of illustration, $B = 1,000$ is used. Let A be the number of times $M_1^* < M_2^*$, and let C be the number of times $M_1^* = M_2^*$. Proceeding in a manner similar to what was done in Chapter 7, let $Q = (A + 0.5C)/B$ and set P equal to Q or $1 - Q$, whichever is smaller. Then, a p-value for testing H_0: $\theta_1 = \theta_2$, the hypothesis that the population medians are equal, is $2P$.

A confidence interval for the difference between the population medians can be computed as well. Let $U^* = M_1^* - M_2^*$. That is, based on a bootstrap sample from each group, U^* is the difference between the resulting medians. Repeating this process 1,000 times yields 1,000 U^* values, which are labeled $U_1^*, \dots, U_{1,000}^*$. If we put these 1,000 values in ascending order, the middle 95% provide a 0.95 confidence interval for the difference between the population medians.

Example

Using a computer, it is found that among 1,000 bootstrap samples from each of two independent groups, there were 900 instances where $M_1^* < M_2^*$ and there were 26 instances where $M_1^* = M_2^*$. That is, $B = 1,000$, $A = 900$, and $C = 26$. Consequently,

$Q = (A + 0.5C)/B = (900 + 0.5(26))/1,000 = 0.913$. Because $Q > 0.5$, set $P = 1 - 0.913 = 0.087$ in which case the p-value is $2P = 2 \times 0.087 = 0.174$.

9.2.3   R Functions msmed, medpb2, split, and fac2list

The R function

$$msmed(x,y,alpha=0.05)$$

compares medians using the McKean–Schrader estimate of the standard error. (If tied values are detected, this function prints a warning message.) The arguments x and y are assumed to contain the data for the first and second group, respectively. As usual, the argument alpha indicates the desired Type I error probability and defaults to 0.05.
    The R function

$$medpb2(x, \ y, \ alpha=0.05, \ nboot=2000)$$

uses a percentile bootstrap method to compare medians. The argument nboot corresponds to B, the number of bootstrap samples that will be used, which defaults to 2,000.

Example

The weight gain data in Table 9.1 are stored in the file salk_dat.txt, which can be downloaded from the author's web page as described in Section 1.5. Imagine that the data have been stored in the R variable salk using the read.table command (as described in Section 1.3.1). So the data will be stored in a data frame having two columns corresponding to the two groups being compared. Then, the command

```
msmed(salk[,1],salk[,2])
```

compares the medians using the McKean–Schrader estimate of the standard errors. The function indicates that a 0.95 confidence interval for the difference between the (population) medians is (18.46, 91.54). However, the function prints a warning message that tied values were detected and that the estimates of the standard errors might be inaccurate. The command

```
medpb2(salk[,1],salk[,2])
```

uses a percentile bootstrap method instead, which allows tied values, and it indicates that a 0.95 confidence interval for the difference between the (population) medians is (30, 90). So the upper ends of the two confidence intervals do not differ very much, but the lower ends differ considerably. That is, using a method that allows tied values can make a practical difference.

    Section 9.1.6 described how to compare means using R when working with a data file where one of the columns indicates whether a participant belongs to group 1 or 2. It was noted that this can be done with a formula, and an illustration was provided based on the hangover data. The R functions in this section do not accept a formula for indicating group membership, so another method must be used to sort the data into groups. The R function

$$fac2list(x,g)$$

is one way of doing this. It sorts the data stored in the argument x into groups based on the corresponding values stored in the argument g. The function returns the data in an R variable having list mode. (List mode was described in Section 1.3.3.) Another way of doing this is with the R function

$$split(x,g).$$

(Also see the R function unstack.)

Example

As was done in Section 9.1.6, assume that the hangover data have been read into the R variable hang, where the first column indicates whether a participant is the son of an alcoholic and column 2 contains a measure of the hangover symptoms on the first occasion measures were taken. The R commands for comparing medians using the percentile bootstrap method are as follows:

```
z=fac2list(hang[,2],hang[,1])
medpb2(z[[1]],z[[2]]).
```

When using fac2list, it indicates how many groups were found as well as the values that were found in the second argument g. In the last example, the command

```
z=fac2list(hang[,2],hang[,1])
```

returns

```
"Group Levels:"
[1] 1 2
```

That is, for the first column of data, two unique values were found: 1 and 2. So there are two groups simply because only two unique values were found. The R function split does not explicitly indicate the values found in g, but it does add labels based on these values. For example, if the command z=split(hang[,2],hang[,1]) is used, z$'1' contains the data for first group in the hangover data.

9.2.4 An Important Issue: The Choice of Method can Matter

It cannot be emphasized too strongly that when comparing groups, the choice of method can matter not only in terms of detecting differences, but in terms of assessing the magnitude of the difference as well. Also, a *basic principle* is that failing to reject when comparing groups does not necessarily mean that any difference between the groups is relatively small or that no difference exists. Different methods provide different perspectives on how groups differ and by how much. This suggests using several methods for comparing groups. But a criticism of this strategy is that performing multiple tests increases the likelihood of a Type I error when the groups do not differ. Chapter 12 elaborates on this issue and how it might be addressed.

Example

Dana (1990) conducted a study aimed at investigating issues related to self-awareness and self-evaluation. (This study was previously mentioned in Section 6.5. Plots of the data are shown in Figure 9.5 in Section 9.8.) In one portion of the study, he recorded the times individuals could keep an apparatus in contact with a specified target. The results, in hundredths of second, are shown in Table 9.2. Comparing the groups with Student's T, the p-value is 0.4752, and for Welch's test, it is 0.4753. So, both methods give very similar results and provide no indication that the groups differ. However, comparing medians with the R function msmed, the p-value is 0.0417, indicating that, in particular, the hypothesis of equal medians is rejected with the Type I error probability set at $\alpha = 0.05$. (There are no tied values, suggesting that this method for comparing medians provides reasonably good control over the probability of a Type I error.)

Why is it that means and medians can yield substantially different p-values? There are at least two fundamental reasons why this can happen. For skewed distributions, means and medians can differ substantially. For the two groups in the last example, the means are 448 and 598, with a difference of $448 - 598 = -150$. The medians are 262 and 497, with a difference of -235, which is larger in absolute value than the difference between the means. Also, the estimated standard errors of the means are 136.4 and 157.9 compared to 77.8 and 85.02 for the medians. As a result, it was concluded that the population medians differ, but there is no evidence that the means differ as well. In fairness, however, situations are encountered where the difference between the means is larger than the difference between the medians, in which case comparing means might result in more power.

9.3 COMPARING TRIMMED MEANS

Yet another approach to comparing groups is to use a compromised amount of trimming and as previously noted, 20% trimming is often a good choice. One method

TABLE 9.2 Self-Awareness Data

Group 1:	77 87 88 114 151 210 219 246 253
	262 296 299 306 376 428 515 666 1,310 2,611
Group 2:	59 106 174 207 219 237 313 365 458 497 515
	529 557 615 625 645 973 1,065 3,215

for comparing 20% trimmed means was derived by Yuen (1974), which reduces to Welch's test when there is no trimming. The computational details, assuming 20% trimming, are as follows.

Let h_1 and h_2 be the number of observations left after trimming when computing the 20% trimmed mean for the first and second groups, respectively. Let $\overline{X}_{t1}$ and $\overline{X}_{t2}$ be the 20% trimmed means and let s_{w1}^2 and s_{w2}^2 be the corresponding 20% Winsorized variances. Let

$$d_1 = \frac{(n_1 - 1)s_{w1}^2}{h_1(h_1 - 1)}$$

and

$$d_2 = \frac{(n_2 - 1)s_{w2}^2}{h_2(h_2 - 1)}.$$

Yuen's test statistic is

$$T_y = \frac{\overline{X}_{t1} - \overline{X}_{t2}}{\sqrt{d_1 + d_2}} \tag{9.11}$$

and the degrees of freedom are

$$\nu_y = \frac{(d_1 + d_2)^2}{\frac{d_1^2}{h_1 - 1} + \frac{d_2^2}{h_2 - 1}}.$$

Decision Rule: The hypothesis of equal trimmed means,

$$H_0 : \mu_{t1} = \mu_{t2},$$

is rejected if

$$|T_y| \geq t,$$

where t is the $1 - \alpha/2$ quantile of Student's T distribution with ν_y degrees of freedom. The $1 - \alpha$ confidence interval for $\mu_{t1} - \mu_{t2}$, the difference between the population trimmed means, is

$$(\overline{X}_{t1} - \overline{X}_{t2}) \pm t\sqrt{d_1 + d_2}. \tag{9.12}$$

It is noted that a percentile bootstrap method is another option for comparing trimmed means. Simply proceed as described in Section 9.2.2, only use a trimmed mean rather than the median. This approach performs relatively well with a 20% trimmed mean, but it performs poorly when comparing means. When the amount of trimming is close to zero, a bootstrap-t method is preferable, again meaning that simulations based on the observed data are used to determine a critical value.

In terms of Type I errors and power, Yuen's method can have a substantial advantage over Welch's test. However, when dealing with distributions that are skewed, differences between means can be larger than differences between trimmed means or medians, which might mean more power when comparing means. Also, methods based on means can be sensitive to differences between groups, such as differences in skewness, which are missed when comparing 20% trimmed means. Generally, however, means usually offer little advantage in terms of power, and trimmed means often provide a substantial advantage. Wu (2002) compared the power of a variety of methods for comparing two independent groups using data from 24 dissertations. No single method was always best, and in some cases, methods based on means performed well. But in general, methods based on means had the poorest power and typically the best power was achieved with methods based on 20% trimmed means.

Example

Consider again the self-awareness data in Section 9.2.4. We saw that the hypothesis of equal medians was rejected with the Type I error probability set at $\alpha = 0.05$; the p-value was 0.047. In contrast, comparisons based on the means did not come close to rejecting. Applying Yuen's test, it can be seen that $\overline{X}_{t1} = 282.7, \overline{X}_{t2} = 444.8$, $v = 23$, $T_y = 2.044$, and with $\alpha = 0.05$, $t = 2.069$, so Yuen's method does not quite reject. (The p-value is 0.052.) In this particular case, methods for comparing 20% trimmed means and medians give similar results (their p-values differ by very little). But compared to using Student's T and Welch's method, both of these methods differ considerably in terms of whether a decision can be made about which group has the larger measure of location.

A basic principle underlying this last example is that when groups do not differ in any manner, meaning that they have identical distributions, the choice of method for comparing the groups makes little difference. But if the groups differ, situations are encountered where the choice of method can make a considerable difference.

9.3.1   R Functions yuen, yuenbt, and trimpb2

The R function

```
yuen(x,y,tr=0.2,alpha=0.05)
```

performs Yuen's test. As usual, the argument `tr` indicates the amount of trimming and defaults to 20%.

The R function

```
yuenbt(x,y,tr=0.2,alpha=0.05,nboot=599,side=TRUE,nullval=0)
```

compares trimmed means using a bootstrap-t method. As was the case in Chapter 6, the argument `side=FALSE` means that an equal-tailed confidence interval will be used. Setting `side=TRUE`, a symmetric confidence interval is computed instead. The function returns a p-value only when `side=TRUE`.

The R function

```
trimpb2(x,y,tr=0.2,alpha=0.05,nboot=2000)
```

compares trimmed means using a percentile bootstrap method. This function performs well when comparing 20% trimmed means. But when the amount of trimming is small, the function `yuenbt` is better in terms of providing an accurate confidence interval.

Example

The hangover data mentioned in Section 9.1.6 are used to illustrate that the choice between the bootstrap-t and the percentile bootstrap method can matter when comparing 20% trimmed means. Using the bootstrap-t method via the R function `yuenbt` with `side=TRUE`, the p-value is 0.102. Using the percentile bootstrap method, the p-value is 0.048.

9.3.2 Skipped Measures of Location and Deleting Outliers

A point worth stressing is that simply deleting valid observations that happen to be outliers, and then comparing the groups using Welch's test, is technically unsound and generally results in poor control over the Type I error probability as well as inaccurate confidence intervals (e.g., Bakker and Wicherts, 2014). As noted in Section 5.4.6, this approach uses an invalid estimate of the standard error regardless of how large the sample sizes might be. Technically sound techniques must take into account how outliers are treated. When using a trimmed mean, for example, this was done by using an estimate of the standard error that is based in part on the Winsorized variance. Section 2.6 mentioned skipped measures of location where the mean is computed after deleting outliers. When comparing groups using these measures of location, a percentile bootstrap method can be used. Briefly, proceed as described in Section 9.2.2, only compute skipped estimators of location rather than medians.

9.3.3 R Function pb2gen

The R function

```
pb2gen(x,y,alpha = 0.05, nboot = 2000,est=onestep)
```

can be used to compare two independent groups via skipped measures of location in conjunction with a percentile bootstrap method. By default, it uses a one-step M-estimator, which is not covered in this book. (It is closely related to the modified one-step M estimator, MOM, in Section 2.6.) To compare groups using the modified one-step M estimator, set the argument `est=mom`.

9.4 TUKEY'S THREE-DECISION RULE

Recall from Chapter 7 that testing for exact equality has been criticized on the grounds that surely the measure of location being used differs from the hypothesized value at some decimal place. A similar criticism applies when testing the hypothesis that two groups have equal measures of location such as equal means or medians. A way of dealing with this issue is to again use Tukey's three-decision rule. When comparing medians, for example, make one of three decisions:

- If the hypothesis of equal medians is rejected, and the first group has the larger sample median, decide that the first group has the larger population median.
- If the hypothesis is rejected, and the first group has the smaller sample median, decide that the first group has the smaller population median.
- If the hypothesis is not rejected, make no decision.

So the goal is not to test for exactly equality; the goal is to determine whether a decision can be made about which group has the larger measure of location. From this perspective, a p-value reflects the extent to which it is reasonable to make a decision. The smaller the p-value, the more reasonable it is to make a decision. It is stressed, however, that a p-value *does not* indicate the probability that a correct decision has been made.

9.5   COMPARING VARIANCES

Although the most common approach to comparing two independent groups is to use some measure of location such as the mean or median, situations arise where there is interest in comparing variances or some other measure of dispersion. For example, in agriculture, one goal when comparing two crop varieties might be to assess their relative stability. One approach is to declare the variety with the smaller variance as being more stable (e.g., Piepho, 1997). As another example, consider two methods for training raters of some human characteristic. For instance, raters might judge athletic ability or they might be asked to rate aggression among children in a classroom. Then, one issue is whether the variances of the ratings differ depending on how the raters were trained. Also, in some situations, two groups might differ primarily in terms of the variances rather than their means or some other measure of location.

There is a vast literature on comparing variances. The method typically mentioned in an introductory course assumes normality and is based on the ratio of the sample variances, s_1^2/s_2^2. But this approach has long been known to be highly unsatisfactory when distributions are nonnormal (e.g., Box, 1953), so it is not described.

Currently, the one method that appears to perform well is based on a modified percentile bootstrap method (Wilcox, 2002). Roughly, for large sample sizes, a percentile bootstrap method is used. For small sample sizes, the confidence interval is adjusted (it is lengthened) so that the probability coverage is more accurate. The computational details are not important for present purposes; an R function for applying the method is supplied instead. A limitation of the method is that it can only be applied when the Type I error is set at $\alpha = 0.05$. The method can be used to compute a confidence interval but not a p-value.

Two other well-known methods for comparing variances should be mentioned. The first is Levene's (1960) test and the other is a method derived by Brown and Forsythe (1974). But in terms of controlling the probability of a Type I error, these methods can be unsatisfactory when dealing with nonnormal distributions, so further details are omitted.

9.5.1   R Function comvar2

The R function

$$\texttt{comvar2(x,y,nboot=1000)}$$

compares the variances of two independent groups using the modified percentile bootstrap method just described.

Example

Consider again the marital aggression study in Section 8.4.4 and look again at Figure 8.4. The goal was to predict recall test scores based on marital aggression in the home. It was noted that assuming homoscedasticity, the p-value is 0.051 when testing the hypothesis of a zero slope using Student's T and the least squares regression line. But using a method that allows heteroscedasticity, the p-value is 0.092. One possible explanation for this result is that there is more variation among the recall test scores when marital aggression is less than or equal to 20, as suggested in Figure 8.4. That is, there appears to be heteroscedasticity. As a check on this possibility, we can compare the variance of the recall test scores when marital aggression is less than or equal to 20 to the variance when marital aggression is greater than 20. Here are the R commands that can be used, again assuming that the data are stored in the R variable `agg` with column 2 containing measures of marital aggression and column 3 containing recall test scores:

```
flag=agg[,2]<=20
comvar2(agg[flag,3],agg[!flag,3]).
```

The resulting 0.95 confidence interval for the difference between the variances is $(1.80, 34.38)$, this interval does not contain zero, so reject the hypothesis of equal variances. That is, there is evidence that there is more variability among homes with a relatively low measure of marital aggression.

9.6   RANK-BASED (NONPARAMETRIC) METHODS

This section describes some techniques for comparing two independent groups that generally fall under the rubric of rank-based or nonparametric methods. At a minimum, these methods provide a perspective that differs from any method based on comparing measures of location. Generally, the methods in this section guard against low power due to outliers. In some situations, they provide more power than other methods that might be used, but the reverse is also true.

9.6.1   Wilcoxon–Mann–Whitney Test

Let p be the probability that a randomly sampled observation from the first group is less than a randomly sampled observation from the second group. (Momentarily, it is assumed that tied values never occur.) If the groups do not differ, then $p = 0.5$ and a basic issue is whether the null hypothesis

$$H_0 : p = 0.5 \tag{9.13}$$

can be rejected. Or, in the context of Tukey's three-decision rule, can a decision be made about whether p is less than or greater than 0.5 based on the available data? The quantity p has been called a *probabilistic measure of effect size*, the *probability of concordance*, the measure of *stochastic superiority*, and the *common language measure of effect size*. This section describes a classic technique for comparing two independent groups, called the Wilcoxon–Mann–Whitney (WMW) test, which is based on a direct estimate of p. The method was originally derived by Wilcoxon (1945), and later it was realized that Wilcoxon's method is the same as a procedure derived by Mann and Whitney (1947). Section 9.6.3 describes a substantially better method for testing (9.13). But the Wilcoxon–Mann–Whitney method is widely known and used, so it is important to know what it tells us and what it does not tell us.

First, consider the problem of estimating p, and for illustrative purposes, suppose we observe

Group 1: 30, 60, 28, 38, 42, 54

Group 2: 19, 21, 27, 73, 71, 25, 59, 61.

Now, focus on the first value in the first group, 30, and notice that it is less than four of the eight observations in the second group. So, a reasonable estimate of p, the probability that an observation from the first group is less than an observation from the second, is $4/8$. In a similar manner, the second observation in the first group is 60. It is less than three of the values in the second group, so a reasonable estimate of p is $3/8$. These two estimates of p differ, and a natural way of combining them into a single estimate of p is to average them. More generally, if we have n_1 observations in group 1 and n_2 observations in group 2, focus on the ith observation in the first group and suppose that this value is less than V_i of the observation in group 2. So, based on the ith observation in group 1, an estimate of p is V_i/n_2, and we have n_1 estimates of p: $V_1/n_2, \cdots, V_{n_1}/n_2$. To combine these n_1 estimates of p into a single estimate, average them, yielding

$$\hat{p} = \frac{1}{n_1 n_2} \sum V_i. \tag{9.14}$$

Typically, the WMW method is described in terms of

$$U = n_1 n_2 \hat{p} \tag{9.15}$$

rather than $\hat{p}$. So when using software that reports U, an estimate p is

$$\hat{p} = \frac{U}{n_1 n_2}.$$

In other words, to estimate the probability that an observation from group 1 is less than an observation from group 2, divide U by $n_1 n_2$, the product of the sample sizes, which on average will be equal to be true probability p. The quantity U is called the Mann–Whitney U statistic.

Next, consider the problem of estimating VAR(U), the squared standard error of U. If we assume that there are no tied values and both groups have identical distributions, the classic estimate of the standard error can be derived. (Again, by no tied values, it is meant that each observed value occurs only once. So if we observe the value 6, e.g., it never occurs again among the remaining observations.) When the two groups have identical distributions, in which case the null hypothesis H_0: $p = 0.5$ is true, it can be seen that VAR(U) is

$$\sigma_u^2 = \frac{n_1 n_2 (n_1 + n_2 + 1)}{12}.$$

Also, when the null hypothesis is true, Equation (9.15) indicates that the expected value of U is $n_1 n_2 / 2$. This means that the null hypothesis can be tested with

$$Z = \frac{U - \frac{n_1 n_2}{2}}{\sigma_u}, \tag{9.16}$$

which has, approximately, a standard normal distribution when the groups have identical distributions. In particular, reject if

$$|Z| \geq c,$$

where c is the $1 - \alpha/2$ quantile of a standard normal distribution.

Example

For the data described at the beginning of this section, it can be seen that $\hat{p} = 0.479$, $n_1 = 6$, $n_2 = 8$, so $U = 23$ and

$$Z = \frac{23 - 24}{7.75} = -0.129.$$

With $\alpha = 0.05$, the critical value is $c = 1.96$, $|Z|$ is less than 1.96, so fail to reject.

An alternative method for estimating p is described that explains why the Wilcoxon–Mann–Whitney method is called a *rank-based* technique. The method begins by combining the observations into a single group, writing them ascending order, and then assigning ranks. This means that the smallest value among all of the observations gets a rank of 1, the next smallest gets a rank of 2, and the largest observation gets a rank of $n_1 + n_2$. Next, compute S, the sum of the ranks associated with the first group. Then,

$$U = n_1 n_2 + \frac{n_1(n_1 + 1)}{2} - S.$$

Example

Consider again the data described at the beginning of this section. Pooling the observations into a single group, writing them in ascending order, and assigning ranks yield

Pooled Data: **19 21 25 27** 28 30 38 42 54 **59** 60 **61 71 73**
Ranks: **1 2 3 4** 5 6 7 8 9 **10** 11 **12 13 14**.

For convenience, the values corresponding to the second group and their corresponding ranks are written in boldface. The sum of the ranks associated with the first group is

$$S = 5 + 6 + 7 + 8 + 9 + 11 = 46,$$

so

$$U = 6(8) + \frac{6(7)}{2} - 46 = 23,$$

and

$$\hat{p} = \frac{23}{6(8)} = 0.479.$$

There is the issue of how to compute ranks when there are tied values. The usual strategy is to use what are called midranks. Consider the values 45, 12, 13, 64, 13, and 25. Putting these values in ascending order yields

$$12, 13, 13, 25, 45, 64.$$

So, the value 12 gets a rank of 1, but there are two identical values having a rank of 2 and 3. The *midrank* is simply the average of the ranks among the tied values. Here, this means that the rank assigned to the two values equal to 13 would be $(2 + 3)/2 = 2.5$, the average of their corresponding ranks. So, the ranks for all six values would be 1, 2.5, 2.5, 4, 5, 6.

Generalizing, consider

$$7, 7.5, 7.5, 8, 8, 8.5, 9, 11, 11, 11.$$

There are 10 values, so if there were no tied values, their ranks would be 1, 2, 3, 4, 5, 6, 7, 8, 9, and 10. But because there are two values equal to 7.5, their ranks are averaged, yielding a rank of 2.5 for each. There are two values equal to 8, their original ranks were 4 and 5, so their final ranks (their midranks) are both 4.5. There are three values equal to 11, their original ranks were 8, 9, and 10, the average of these ranks is 9, so their midranks are all equal to 9. In summary, the ranks for the 10 observations are

$$1, 2.5, 2.5, 4.5, 4.5, 6, 7, 9, 9, 9.$$

Sometimes, the Wilcoxon–Mann–Whitney test is described as a method for comparing medians. However, it is unsatisfactory for this purpose, as are other rank-based methods, unless certain highly restrictive assumptions are met (e.g., Fung, 1980). A crude explanation is that the Wilcoxon–Mann–Whitney test is not based on an estimate of the population medians. One practical concern is that there are situations where power decreases as the difference between the population medians increases. Moreover, there are general conditions under which an accurate confidence interval for the difference between the medians cannot be computed based on the Wilcoxon–Mann–Whitney test (Kendall and Stuart, 1973; Hettmansperger, 1984).

In a very real sense, a more accurate description of the Wilcoxon–Mann–Whitney test is that it provides a test of the hypothesis that two distributions are identical. The situation is similar to Student's T test. When the two distributions are identical, a correct estimate of the squared standard error, σ_u^2, is being used. But otherwise, under general conditions, an incorrect estimate is being used, which results in practical concerns in terms of both Type I errors and power when using Equation (9.16) to test $H_0 : p = 0.5$.

9.6.2   R Function wmw

The R function

$$\text{wmw}(x, y)$$

performs the Wilcoxon–Mann–Whitney test. The function returns a p-value and an estimate of p, which is labeled p.hat.

9.6.3   Handling Heteroscedasticity

As previously noted, a serious limitation associated with the Wilcoxon–Mann–Whitney test is that if groups differ, then under general conditions the wrong standard error is being used, which can result in relatively poor power and an unsatisfactory confidence interval for p, the probability that a randomly sampled observation from the first group is less than a randomly sampled observation from the second group. Numerous methods have been proposed for improving on the Wilcoxon–Mann–Whitney test. Currently, a method derived by Cliff (1996) appears to perform relatively well, particularly when the sample sizes are small (Neuhäuser et al., 2007). Eight other methods were compared by Newcombe (2006). Twelve methods were compared by Ruscio and Mullen (2012), who found that if the total sample size, $n_1 + n_2$, is greater than or equal to 60, a bootstrap method not covered here tends to provide a more accurate confidence interval than Cliff's method.

Consider a situation where tied values can occur and note that if we randomly sample a single observation from both groups, there are three possible outcomes: the observation from the first group is greater than the observation from the second, the observations have identical values, or the observation from the first group is less than the observation from the second. The probabilities associated with these three mutually exclusive outcomes are labeled p_1, p_2, and p_3. In symbols, if X is some value randomly sampled from the first group and Y is some value randomly sampled from the second group,

$$p_1 = P(X > Y),$$
$$p_2 = P(X = Y),$$

and

$$p_3 = P(X < Y).$$

Let $P = p_3 + 0.5p_2$. The goal is to test

$$H_0 : P = 0.5. \tag{9.17}$$

When tied values are impossible, $p_2 = 0$, so $P = p_3 = P(X < Y)$. Cliff's method yields a confidence interval for P, but the rather lengthy calculations are not described. (The computational details can be found in Cliff, 1996, or Wilcox, 2012a.) If the confidence interval for P does not contain 0.5, reject H_0: $P = 0.5$. A p-value can be computed as well.

Let $D = X - Y$ be the difference between a randomly sampled observation from the first group and a randomly sampled observation from the second group. For convenience, momentarily assume that tied values are impossible. Notice that $P(X < Y)$, the probability that a randomly sampled observation from the first group is less than randomly sampled observation from the second, is the same as the probability that D is negative. That is, the hypothesis $H_0 : p_3 = 0.5$ is just another way of writing $H_0 : P(D < 0) = 0.5$. But by definition, if $P(D < 0) = 0.5$, the median of D is zero. So, Cliff's method is not based on estimates of the medians associated with the two groups (the population medians associated with X and Y). But it does have a connection with the (population) median of D; it tests the hypothesis that the median of D is zero.

9.6.4   R Functions cid and cidv2

The R function

```
cid(x,y,alpha=0.05,plotit=FALSE),
```

computes a confidence interval for $P = p_3 + 0.5p_2$ using Cliff's method, which is labeled ci.p. The estimate of P is labeled p.hat. To get a p-value, use the function

```
cidv2(x,y,alpha=0.05,plotit=FALSE).
```

When the argument plotit=TRUE, these functions plot the distribution of D, where D is the difference between a randomly sampled observation from the first group and a randomly sampled observation from the second group. D will have a symmetric distribution around zero when the distributions of the groups being compared are identical. The plot provides perspective on the extent to which this is the case.

Example

For the hangover data in Section 9.1.6, a portion of the output from the R function cidv2 looks like this:

```
$p. value
[1] 0.049

$p.hat
[1] 0.33125

$p.ci
[1] 0.1977060 0.4989051
```

So, the p-value based Cliff's method is 0.049, the estimate of P is 0.331, and the 0.95 confidence interval for P is (0.198, 0.499). In contrast, the p-value based on the Wilcoxon–Mann–Whitney method is 0.068.

9.7   MEASURING EFFECT SIZE

As noted in Chapter 7, when dealing with hypotheses about a single mean (or any other measure of location), p-values provide an indication of whether some hypothesis should be rejected. From the point of view of Tukey's three-decision rule, a p-value reflects the strength of the empirical evidence that a decision can be made about whether the mean is greater or less than some specified value. However, it is unsatisfactory in terms of understanding the extent to which the mean differs from the hypothesized value. A similar result applies when comparing the means of two independent groups. If, for example, the hypothesis of equal means is rejected at the 0.001 level and the first group has a larger sample mean than the second group, use Tukey's three-decision rule and conclude that the first group has the larger population mean. But generally, this tells us nothing about the magnitude of the difference.

Example

An article in *Nutrition Today* (1984, *19*, 22–29) illustrates the importance of this issue. A study was conducted on whether a particular drug lowers the risk of heart attacks. Those in favor of using the drug pointed out that the number of heart attacks in the group receiving the drug was significantly lower than the group receiving a placebo. As noted in Section 7.1.4, when a researcher reports that a significant difference was found, typically the word significant is being used to signify that a small p-value was obtained. In the study, the hypothesis of equal means was rejected at the $\alpha = 0.001$ level, and often, such a result is described as *highly significant*. However, critics of the drug argued that the difference between the number of heart attacks was trivially small. They concluded that because of the expense and side effects of using the drug, there is no compelling evidence that patients with high cholesterol levels should be put on this medication. A closer examination of the data revealed that the standard errors corresponding to the two groups were very small, so it was possible to get a statistically significant result that was clinically unimportant.

Acquiring a good understanding of how groups differ can be a nontrivial problem that might require several perspectives. One possibility is to simply use the difference between the sample means. In some situations, this simple approach will suffice. But if we limit our choice to the means, there is a practical concern: different measures of location can provide a different sense about how much the groups differ. As already illustrated, if we switch to medians, this can alter our sense about whether there is a large difference between the groups. Although we have already seen serious negative features associated with the mean, this is not to suggest that this approach should be abandoned. Rather, the issue is, if we limit ourselves to means, are there important details that are being missed? Often, the answer is yes.

9.7.1 Cohen's d

Currently, there is a method for measuring effect size, based, in part, on the means, which is used by many researchers and therefore important to know. The method was derived assuming that both groups have normal distributions with a common variance (homoscedasticity), which we again label σ_p^2. That is, $\sigma_1^2 = \sigma_2^2 = \sigma_p^2$ is assumed. Then, the so-called standardized difference between the groups is

$$\delta = \frac{\mu_1 - \mu_2}{\sigma_p}, \tag{9.18}$$

where δ is a lower-case Greek delta. Assuming normality, δ can be interpreted in a simple manner. For example, if $\delta = 2$, then the difference between the means is two standard deviations, and for normal distributions, we have some probabilistic sense of what this means. A common practice is to interpret δ values of 0.2, 0.5, and 0.8 as small, medium, and large effect sizes, respectively. It is known, however, that under general conditions, this oversimplifies the issue of measuring effect size for reasons indicated in the next section. The usual estimate of δ is

$$d = \frac{\overline{X}_1 - \overline{X}_2}{s_p},$$

where s_p^2 is given by Equation (9.2), and is often called *Cohen's d*.

The original motivation for Cohen's d stemmed from a criticism of p-values. The argument was that p-values provide no information about the magnitude of the difference between the means. Interestingly, when the normality and homoscedasticity assumptions are true, a p-value, coupled with the sample sizes, can be used to compute Cohen's d (Browne, 2010). But the details are not provided because there are several concerns with Cohen's d that are described in the next section.

9.7.2   Concerns about Cohen's d and How They Might Be Addressed

There are at least three major concerns with Cohen's d. The first is that even small departures from normality can result in missing an important difference among the bulk of the participants. Put another way, when dealing with distributions where outliers are likely to occur, Cohen's d can be highly misleading. Recall from Chapter 2 that even a few outliers can have a major impact on the sample variance. That is, outliers can inflate the denominator of Cohen's d, s_p, which in turn can make d relatively small even when for the bulk of the participants there is an important difference. This is a concern even with large sample sizes. To illustrate this point, look at Figure 9.3. In Figure 9.3a $\delta = 1$, which is traditionally viewed as a large effect size. But in Figure 9.3b, $\delta = 0.3$, which is typically viewed as being relatively small, despite the apparent similarity with Figure 9.3a.

The second concern is that Cohen's d assumes equal variances (homoscedasticity). If groups differ, there is no reason to assume that the variances are equal. Indeed, some authorities would argue that surely they must be unequal. We could test the hypothesis of equal variances, but how much power is needed to justify the conclusion that the variances are reasonably equal if we fail to reject? Another strategy is to replace σ_p with the standard deviation from one of the groups. That is, use

$$\delta_1 = \frac{\mu_1 - \mu_2}{\sigma_1}$$

or

$$\delta_2 = \frac{\mu_1 - \mu_2}{\sigma_2}$$

which are estimated with

$$d_1 = \frac{\overline{X}_1 - \overline{X}_2}{s_1}$$

and

$$d_2 = \frac{\overline{X}_1 - \overline{X}_2}{s_2},$$

respectively. A concern, however, is that there is the potential of getting two seemingly conflicting conclusions: δ_1, for example, might suggest a large effect size, while δ_2 indicates a small effect size.

A third concern with Cohen's d is that it is based on the means, so d might poorly reflect the typical difference, or it might miss a difference that is clinically important.

Many new methods have been derived with the goal of better understanding how groups differ. Some of these methods are described here and the plots in Section 9.8 help add perspective.

Algina et al., (2005) proposed a generalization of Cohen's d that is based on trimmed means and the Winsorized variances, assuming that the groups have equal (population) Winsorized variances. When using 20% trimming, their measure of effect size is

$$d_t = 0.642\frac{\overline{X}_{t1} - \overline{X}_{t2}}{S_w},$$

where

$$S_w^2 = \frac{(n_1 - 1)s_{w1}^2 + (n_2 - 1)s_{w2}^2}{n_1 + n_2 - 2}$$

is the pooled Winsorized variance. Under normality, and when the variances are equal ($\sigma_1^2 = \sigma_2^2$), both d and d_t are estimating the same measure of effect size, namely δ. An advantage of d_t is that it deals with the negative impact of outliers on Cohen's d, but a concern is the assumption that the (population) Winsorized variances are the same for both groups.

Another approach that deals with both outliers and unequal variances is to use a measure that reflects a robust generalization of Pearson's correlation (e.g., Wilcox, 2012a, p. 381). Recall from Section 8.5.1 that the estimate of Pearson's correlation can be written as

$$r^2 = \frac{VAR(\hat{Y})}{VAR(Y)},$$

where $VAR(\hat{Y})$ is the variation among the predicted values of the dependent variable based on some regression model, and $VAR(Y)$ is the variation associated with the dependent variable. In the present context, imagine that if we are told that a participant belongs to group 1, we predict that their observed value is equal to the trimmed mean associated with group 1. Similarly, if we are told that a participant belongs to group 2, predict that their observed value is equal to the trimmed mean associated with group 2. Roughly, the strength of the association based on this prediction rule is the variation among the trimmed means relative to the Winsorized variance of the pooled distributions, which will be labeled r_e^2. The square root of r_e^2, r_e, is called an *explanatory measure of effect size* because it reflects the strength of the association when the response of a participant is predicted to be $\overline{X}_{t1}$ or $\overline{X}_{t2}$ based on whether the participant was sampled from the first or second group. There is an extension of this method when dealing with medians, no details are supplied, but an R function for applying it is provided.

As noted in Chapter 8, a common convention is to regard the values 0.1, 0.3, and 0.5 for Pearson's correlation as being relatively small, medium, and large, respectively. To the extent this seems reasonable, the same would be done when using r_e to characterize the extent two groups differ.

One more approach is to use the probability that a randomly sampled observation from the first group is less than a randomly sampled observation from the second group, which can be estimated as described in Section 9.6.

The main point, which cannot be stressed too strongly, is that a single numerical quantity, aimed at assessing how groups differ and by how much, can be unsatisfactory and too simplistic. This is not always the case, but assuming that a single measure of effect size is adequate is a strategy that cannot be recommended. The general issue of assessing effect size in a satisfactory manner is a complex problem that might require multiple perspectives.

9.7.3 R Functions akp.effect, yuenv2, and med.effect

The R function

```
akp.effect(x,y,EQVAR=TRUE,tr=0.2)
```

computes the measure of effect size d_t, which defaults to using a 20% trimmed mean. If the argument EQVAR=FALSE, the function returns estimates of both δ_1 and δ_2. Setting tr=0, akp.effect returns Cohen's d when EQVAR=TRUE.

The R function

```
yuenv2(x,y,tr=0.2)
```

is exactly similar to the R function yuen, only it also reports r_e, the explanatory measure of effect size.

For the special case where groups are compared based on the medians, yuenv2 should not be used. Use, instead, the R function

```
med.effect(x,y,HD=TRUE).
```

The argument HD=TRUE means that the population median is estimated using an alternative to the usual sample median, the details of which go beyond the scope of this book. To use the usual sample median M, use HD=FALSE.

Example

Table 2.3 reports data on how many sexual partners undergraduate males want during the next 30 years. In the same study, 156 undergraduate females were asked the same question and researchers have tried to understand the extent to which males and females differ in their responses. Imagine that the data are stored in the R files sexm and sexf. Then, the R command

```
akp.effect(sexm,sext,tr=0)
```

indicates that Cohen's d is 0.16, which would typically be interpreted as being a small effect size. But with only 1% trimming (setting the argument tr=0.01), the measure of effect size is 0.314, nearly twice as large as Cohen's d, which would traditionally be characterized as being between a small and a medium effect size. The explanatory measure of effect size, based on a 20% trimmed mean, is $r_e = 0.35$, which would typically be interpreted as a medium effect size. With no trimming, $r_e = 0.106$, which would typically be considered to be relatively small. For both groups, the sample medians are 1, so now the effect size is zero, the point being that assessing effect size must be done with care because different methods provide different perspectives.

Another perspective is the probability that a randomly sampled male gives a response that is greater than the response given by a randomly sampled female. The R function `cidv2` estimates this probability to be 0.429. The probability of equal responses is estimated to be 0.316, and the probability that a randomly sampled female gives a greater response, compared to a randomly sample male, is 0.255. The p-value returned by `cidv2` is 0.014. So, the data indicate that males are more likely to give a greater response than females.

9.8 PLOTTING DATA

Various graphical methods can help provide perspective on how groups differ and by how much. That is, they can help assess effect size. Among some researchers, one popular graphical tool is called an *error bar*, which is just a plot of the means for the two groups under study plus an interval around each mean based on the standard error. An example is shown in Figure 9.4 using the self-awareness data in Table 9.2. The circles indicate the means. The ends of the lines extending above the circles indicate the value of the sample mean plus two standard errors. Similarly, the lines extending below the circles indicate the value of the sample mean minus two standard errors. In symbols, the top and bottom ends of the lines indicate the value of $\overline{X} + 2s/\sqrt{n}$ and $\overline{X} - 2s/\sqrt{n}$, respectively. For the first group, the sample mean is $\overline{X} = 448.1$ and the estimated standard error is $s/\sqrt{n} = 136.425$. Consequently, the bottom end of the first vertical line marks the value of $\overline{X} - 2s/\sqrt{n} = 175.25$ and the top end indicates the value $\overline{X} + 2s/\sqrt{n} = 720.95$. That is, the ends of the lines indicate a confidence interval for the population mean.

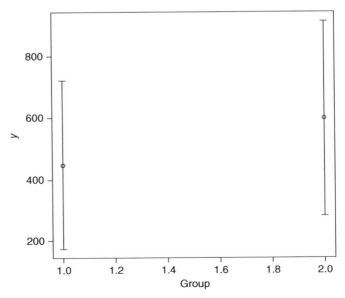

Figure 9.4 Examples of error bars using the self-awareness data in Section 9.1

Two alternative strategies are to use boxplots or plots of the two distributions. Boxplots for two or more groups can be included in a single figure as indicated in the next section. Distributions can be plotted using a kernel density estimator via the R function g2plot in Section 9.8.1.

Example

Figure 9.5a shows plots of the distributions based on the self-awareness data, which was created with the R function g2plot described in the next section. Figure 9.5b shows boxplots based on the same data. Notice that Figure 9.5 suggests that there is a fairly striking difference between the two groups in contrast to the error bars in Figure 9.4. As previously illustrated, comparing means is not significant; Welch's test returns a p-value equal to 0.48. However, comparing medians using the R function msmed, the p-value is 0.042.

Although error bars provide useful information, they can be relatively uninformative compared to the other plots that might be used as illustrated in Figures 9.4 and 9.5. That is, errors bars can fail to convey information that can be useful when

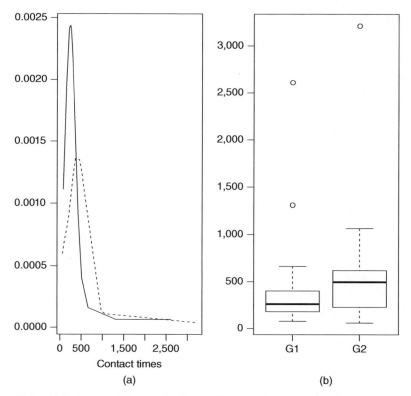

(a)   (b)

Figure 9.5   (a) Estimates of the two distributions in the self-awareness study. (b) The boxplots are based on the same data

trying to understand the nature of the difference between groups. Yet one more concern about error bars should be noted. Imagine that the error bars are constructed so as to indicate a 0.95 confidence interval for each mean. If the intervals do not overlap, this might suggest that the hypothesis of equal means should be rejected. If they overlap, as is the case in Figure 9.4, this might suggest that the hypothesis of equal means should not be rejected. It can be seen, however, that even if both intervals have exactly a 0.95 probability of containing the population mean, this approach does not control the probability of a Type I error when testing the hypothesis of equal means, even with large sample sizes (e.g., Schenker and Gentleman, 2001; Wilcox, 2012a, Section 8.9).

9.8.1   R Functions ebarplot, ebarplot.med, g2plot, and boxplot

The R function

```
ebarplot(x,y=NULL,nse=2,xlab='Groups',ylab=NULL,tr=0)
```

creates error bars using the data stored in the variables x and y, assuming that the R library plotrix has been installed using the R command install.packages as described in Section 1.4. If the argument y is not supplied, the function assumes that x is a matrix (with columns corresponding to groups) or that x has list mode. If, for example, x is a matrix with five columns, five plots will be created for each of the five groups. The argument nse defaults to 2, indicating that two standard errors are used when creating the plots. Setting nse=3 would use three standard errors. The arguments xlab and ylab can be used to generate labels for the *x*-axis and *y*-axis, respectively. Error bars based on trimmed means can be created using the argument tr. For example, tr=0.2 will use 20% trimmed means and the appropriate standard error.

To plot error bars using medians, use the R function

```
ebarplot.med(x,y = NULL, nse=2,xlab='Groups',ylab=NULL).
```

To plot two distributions, as was done in Figure 9.5, use the R function

```
g2plot(x1,x2,xlab='X', ylab=' ').
```

Boxplots for two or more groups can be created via the R command boxplot introduced in Section 3.3.3. If data are stored in a matrix or a data frame, say x having two or more columns, boxplot(x) will create a boxplot for each column of data. If the argument x has list mode, again a boxplot is created for each group. The argument names can be used to label the boxplots. For example, the R command used to create Figure 9.5b was

```
boxplot(dana,names=c('G1','G2')),
```

where dana is a data frame with two columns.

9.9   COMPARING QUANTILES

When comparing groups, a natural approach is to use a measure of location that reflects the typical value such as the median or 20% trimmed mean. But in some situations, there is interest in comparing the tails of a distribution. Said more formally, it can be informative to compare the lower or upper quantiles.

Example

One goal in the study by Clark et al., (2012) was to assess the effectiveness of an intervention program in terms of its ability to reduce depressive symptoms in older adults. Figure 9.6 shows a plot of the distributions (based on the R function g2plot) where the solid line is the distribution for a control group. Notice that there appears to be little difference between the central portions of the distributions, but the right tails appear to differ. Most of the participants did not score very high on a measure of depression prior to intervention, so it did not seem surprising that for the typical participant, depressive symptoms did not decrease much for the typical individual

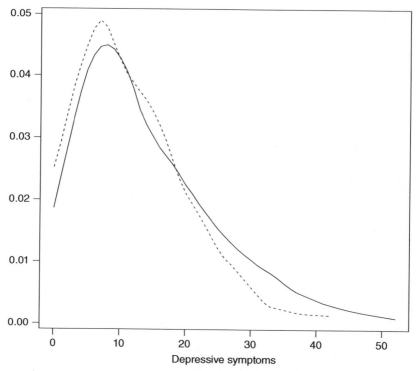

Figure 9.6   The distribution of depressive symptoms for a control group (solid line) and an experimental group (dotted line). The plot suggests that relatively high measures of depressive symptoms are more likely for the control group compared to the group that received intervention

after intervention. An issue was whether among participants with higher measures of depressive symptoms, does the control group differ from the experimental group? A way of dealing with this issue is to compare the upper quantiles. For example, do the upper quartiles differ? Do the 0.8 or 0.9 quantiles differ? In the study, the 0.8 quantile for the control group was estimated to be 23.3. That is, it was estimated that 80% of the participants in the control population have a measure of depression less than or equal to 23.3. For the experimental group, the estimate was 19.4. That is, for the population of individuals receiving intervention, it is estimated that 80% have a measure of depression less than or equal to 19.4. This suggests that for the experimental group, scores greater than or equal to 23.3 are less likely compared to the control group. But there is the issue of whether the observed difference is significant. That is, can a decision be made about which group has the larger 0.8 quantile?

A method that performs well when comparing quantiles, even when there are tied values, is based in part on a percentile bootstrap method coupled with a particular technique for estimating quantiles (Wilcox et al., 2013). The details of the method go beyond the scope of this book. But an R function for applying the method is provided.

9.9.1 R Function qcomhd

The R function

```
qcomhd(x,y,q=c(0.01,0.25,0.5,0.75,0.9),nboot
            =2000,plotit=TRUE,
SEED=TRUE,xlab='Group 1',ylab='Est.1-Est.2',
            alpha=0.05)
```

compares the quantiles of two independent groups. By default, it compares the 0.1, 0.25 (lower quartiles), 0.5 (medians), 0.75 (upper quartiles), and the 0.9 quantiles, but other quantiles can be compared via the argument q. For example, q=0.4 would compare the 0.4 quantiles. When comparing the quartiles and the Type I error probability is taken to be 0.05, the method has been found to control the actual Type I error probability fairly well when the smallest sample size is at least 20. When comparing the 0.9 quantiles, the smallest sample size should be at least 30.

Example

For the intervention study aimed at reducing depressive symptoms, which was described in the previous section, comparing medians and 20% trimmed means fail to reject. But comparing the 0.85 quantiles, $p = 0.006$. That is, there are indications that intervention is effective among the participants having higher levels of depression. But, perhaps, a more important point is that different methods are sensitive to different features of the data. Understanding whether groups differ and how groups differ might require multiple techniques.

9.10   COMPARING TWO BINOMIAL DISTRIBUTIONS

In many situations, comparing groups involves comparing two binomial distributions. For example, if the probability of surviving an operation using method 1 is p_1, and if the probability of surviving using method 2 is p_2, do p_1 and p_2 differ, and if they do differ, by how much? As another example, how does the proportion of women who believe the president of France is an effective leader compare to the corresponding proportion for men.

An appropriate test statistic can be derived using the same strategy used by Welch's method. From Chapters 4 and 5, if $\hat{p}$ indicates the proportion of successes, the corresponding squared standard error is $p(1-p)/n$. For two independent proportions, $\hat{p}_1$ and $\hat{p}_2$, the variance or squared standard error of their difference can be shown to be

$$VAR(\hat{p}_1 - \hat{p}_2) = \frac{p_1(1-p_1)}{n_1} + \frac{p_2(1-p_2)}{n_2},$$

and an estimate of this squared standard error is simply

$$\frac{\hat{p}_1(1-\hat{p}_1)}{n_1} + \frac{\hat{p}_2(1-\hat{p}_2)}{n_2}.$$

So, when the hypothesis

$$H_0 : p_1 = p_2 \tag{9.19}$$

is true

$$Z = \frac{\hat{p}_1 - \hat{p}_2}{\sqrt{\frac{\hat{p}_1(1-\hat{p}_1)}{n_1} + \frac{\hat{p}_2(1-\hat{p}_2)}{n_2}}}, \tag{9.20}$$

will have, approximately, a standard normal distribution.

Decision Rule: Reject the null hypothesis given by Equation (9.19) if

$$|Z| \geq c,$$

where c is the $1 - \alpha/2$ quantile of a standard normal distribution, which is read from Table B.1 in Appendix B. A $1 - \alpha$ confidence interval for the difference between the two probabilities is

$$(\hat{p}_1 - \hat{p}_2) \pm c\sqrt{\frac{\hat{p}_1(1-\hat{p}_1)}{n_1} + \frac{\hat{p}_2(1-\hat{p}_2)}{n_2}}. \tag{9.21}$$

9.10.1   Improved Methods

The method for comparing binomial distributions, just described, illustrates basic principles and so is particularly appropriate for an introductory course. A positive feature is that it performs reasonably well when the probability of success for the two groups is not too close to 0 or 1. But otherwise it can be unsatisfactory in terms of controlling the Type I error probability. Many improved methods have been proposed, comparisons of which are reported by Storer and Kim (1990) and Beal (1987). For more recent suggestions, see Berger (1996) and Coe and Tamhane (1993). The basic idea behind the Storer–Kim method is to estimate the probability of getting an estimated difference, $|\hat{p}_1 - \hat{p}_2|$, as large or larger than what was observed. This probability can be determined if p_1 and p_2 are known. They are not known, but they can be estimated based on the available data, which can be used to compute a p-value. A criticism of the Storer–Kim method is that it does not provide a confidence interval, only a p-value. But it can have more power than Beal's method.

The somewhat involved computational details of the Storer–Kim method and Beal's method are not important for present purposes, so they are not provided. Instead, R functions are supplied for applying them. (Computational details for both methods are summarized in Wilcox, 2012a.)

9.10.2   R Functions twobinom and twobicipv

The R function

```
twobinom(r1=sum(x),n1=length(x),r2=sum(y),

         n2=length(y),  x=NA,y=NA)
```

tests H_0: $p_1 = p_2$ using the Storer–Kim method; the function returns a p-value. The function can be used either by specifying the number of successes in each group (arguments r1 and r2) and the sample sizes (arguments n1 and n2), or the data can be passed to the function in R variables containing a collection of 1's and 0's, in which case the arguments x and y are used.

Beal's method can be applied with the R function

```
twobicipv(r1=sum(x),n1=length(x),r2=sum(y),

          n2=length(y),  x=NA,y=NA,alpha=0.05).
```

The function returns a p-value and a confidence interval for $p_1 - p_2$, the difference between the probabilities.

Example

Imagine that a new treatment for alcoholism is under investigation and that a method has been agreed upon for assessing whether the treatment is deemed effective after 12 months. An issue is whether the probability of success differs for men compared to women. For illustrative purposes, suppose that for 7 out 12 males, the treatment is a success, so $\hat{p}_1 = 7/12 = 0.58$, and that for 25 women, there are 22 successes, in which case $\hat{p}_2 = 22/25 = 0.88$. Then, simple calculations, based on Equation (9.20), show that $Z = -1.896$. If we want the probability of a Type I error to be 0.05, the critical value is $c = 1.96$, and because $|-1.896| < 1.96$, fail to reject. That is, the probability of success among women is estimated to be higher than it is for men, but some would argue that the strength of the empirical evidence that this is the case is not completely convincing because the null hypothesis of equal probabilities was not rejected.

Using, instead, the R function twobinom (the Storer–Kim method), the command

```
twobinom(7,12,22,25)
```

returns a p-value equal to 0.045. Now, the empirical evidence is stronger that women have a higher probability of success. Using, instead, twobicipv, the p-value is 0.114, the point being that the choice of method can make a practical difference in terms of whether the hypothesis is rejected.

Example

Consider again the data on how many sexual partners undergraduate males want during the next 30 years. Among the 105 males, 49 said that they want one partner. So, the estimated probability of answering 1 is $\hat{p}_1 = 49/105 = 0.47$. In the same study, 101 of 156 females also responded that they want one sexual partner during the next 30 years, so $\hat{p}_2 = 101/156 = 0.65$. For the entire population of undergraduates, and assuming random sampling, do the corresponding population probabilities, p_1 and p_2, differ? If the answer is yes, what can be said about the magnitude of the difference? Using Equation (9.22), it can be seen that $Z = -2.92$, and the null hypothesis would be rejected with a Type I error of $\alpha = 0.01$. So, the conclusion would be that females are more likely to respond 1 compared to the males. The estimated difference between the two probabilities is -0.181 and the 0.99 confidence interval is $(-0.340, -0.021)$. Roughly, we can be reasonably certain that the difference is between -0.021 and -0.34.

9.11   A METHOD FOR DISCRETE OR CATEGORICAL DATA

The binomial distribution deals with a situation where only two outcomes are possible. When there are more than two possible outcomes, there is an extension of the Storer–Kim method that can be used to compare two independent groups. (For computational details, see Wilcox et al., 2013.) Here, it is assumed that there are K possible responses where $K \geq 2$ but relatively small. For example, participants might be asked whether they agree, disagree, or have no opinion about some political issue. So, $K = 3$ and there are three probabilities of interest: the probability that someone responds agree, or disagree, or no opinion. A goal might be to compare males to females based on these probabilities. Or, based on a scale ranging from 1 to 5, participants might be asked to rate their satisfaction when getting their car serviced, where a 1 indicates very poor service and 5 indicates excellent service. So, $K = 5$ and a goal might be to compare the probabilities associated with the ratings for Toyota dealers to the probabilities for Nissan dealers. R functions for comparing these probabilities are described and illustrated in the next section.

9.11.1   R Functions disc2com, binband, and splotg2

The R function

$$\text{disc2com}(x,y,\text{alpha}=0.05)$$

tests the hypothesis that the probabilities associated with K possible responses are the same for two independent groups. When it rejects, this indicates that one or more of the probabilities differ, but it does not indicate which ones. To get more detail about how the K probabilities compare, use the R function

$$\text{binband}(x,y,\text{alpha}=0.05,\text{KMS}=\text{FALSE}).$$

It returns the estimated probability for each possible response, and it tests the hypothesis that the corresponding probabilities do not differ using the Storer–Kim Method. Setting the argument KMS=TRUE, the method derived by Kulinskaya et al., (2010) is used to compare the probabilities, which has the advantage of providing confidence intervals but possibly less power.

The R function

$$\text{splotg2}(x,y,\text{xlab} = `X', \ \text{ylab} = `\text{Rel. Freq.'})$$

plots the relative frequencies associated with the two groups being compared.

Example

A study was conducted aimed at comparing two methods for reducing shoulder pain after surgery. For the first method, the shoulder pain measures were as follows:

2, 4, 4, 2, 2, 2, 4, 3, 2, 4, 2, 3, 2, 4, 3, 2, 2, 3, 5, 5, 2, 2

and for the second method they were

5, 1, 4, 4, 2, 3, 3, 1, 1, 1, 1, 2, 2, 1, 1, 5, 3, 5.

Assuming that the data are stored in the R variables g1 and g2, disc2com(g1, g2) returns a p-value equal to 0.011. In contrast, for both Student's T and Welch's method, the p-value is 0.25. This illustrates that even when there are no outliers, using something other than the mean to compare groups can make a substantial difference. The R function binband returns:

Value	p1.est	p2.est	p1−p2	p.value
1	0.00000000	0.3888889	−0.38888889	0.00183865
2	0.50000000	0.1666667	0.33333333	0.02827202
3	0.18181818	0.1666667	0.01515152	0.94561448
4	0.22727273	0.1111111	0.11616162	0.36498427
5	0.09090909	0.1666667	−0.07575758	0.49846008

For the response 1, the p-value is 0.001839, indicating that it is reasonable to conclude that the second group is more likely to respond 1 compared to the first group. In contrast, for the probability of a response 5, the p-value is 0.56. So, the data indicate that the second group is more likely to respond 5, but based on Tukey's three-decision rule, no decision is made about which group is more likely to rate the pain as being 5. (The function `binband` also returns a column headed by `p.crit`, which is based on Hochberg's method as described in Section 12.8.3.)

Example

Erceg-Hurn and Steed (2011) investigated the degree to which smokers experience negative emotional responses (such as anger and irritation) upon being exposed to antismoking warnings on cigarette packets. Smokers were randomly allocated to view warnings that contained only text, such as "Smoking Kills," or warnings that contained text and graphics, such as pictures of rotting teeth and gangrene. Negative emotional reactions to the warnings were measured on a scale that produced a score between 0 and 16 for each smoker, where larger scores indicate greater levels of negative emotions. (The data are stored on the author's web page in the file smoke.csv and can be read into R using the `read.csv` command.) The means and medians differ significantly. But to get a deeper understanding of how the groups differ, look at Figure 9.7, which shows plots of the relative frequencies based on the R function `splotg2`. Note that the plot suggests that the main difference between the groups has to do with the response zero: the proportion of participants in the text-only group responding zero is 0.512 compared to 0.192 for the graphics group. Testing the hypothesis that the corresponding probabilities are equal, based on the R function `binband`, the p-value is less than 0.0001. The probabilities associated with the other possible responses do not differ significantly at the 0.05 level except for the response 16; the p-value is 0.0031. For the graphics group, the probability of responding 16 is 0.096 compared to 0.008 for the text-only group. So, a closer look at the data, beyond comparing means and medians, suggests that the main difference between the groups has to do with the likelihood of giving the most extreme responses possible, particularly the response zero.

9.12 COMPARING REGRESSION LINES

This section briefly describes some classic methods for comparing the regression lines of two independent groups as well as some modern improvements. We begin with a classic method known as the analysis of covariance or ANCOVA. The Well Elderly 2 study by Clark et al., (2012), previously described in Section 9.9, provides a concrete example. A particular goal was to assess the impact of intervention on a measure of meaningful activities. One strategy would be to compare a control group to a group that received intervention using one of the methods already covered in this chapter. However, numerous studies indicate an association between measures of stress and what is known as the cortisol awakening response (CAR). Cortisol is a

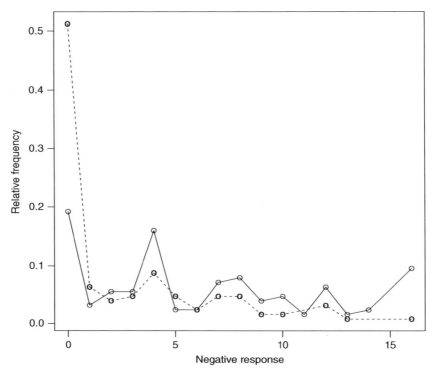

Figure 9.7 Pots of the relative frequencies for the graphics group (solid line) and the text-only group (dashed line)

hormone produced by the adrenal cortex. The CAR refers to the change in cortisol upon awakening and measured again 30–60 minutes later. Because CAR was found to be associated with the measure of meaningful activities (MAPA), a possibility is that the effectiveness of intervention on increasing meaningful activities might depend on the CAR. For example, a possibility is that MAPA scores are higher after intervention when cortisol increases after awakening, and perhaps, the opposite is true when cortisol decreases. Is it the case that the more cortisol increases after awakening, intervention is more effective?

As another example, consider a study aimed at comparing males and females based on their plasma retinol levels. Retinol levels have been found to be associated with age. So, a possibility is that the extent to which females differ from males in terms of their retinol levels depends on the age of the participants.

In the present context, what was called the independent variable in Chapter 8 is known as a *covariate*. In the meaningful activities example, the CAR is the covariate and the goal is to take this covariate into account when comparing the control group to the experimental group in terms of a measure of meaningful activities. In the plasma retinol example, age is the covariate.

9.12.1 Classic ANCOVA

The classic and best-known ANCOVA method makes the following assumptions:

- Random sampling.
- The typical value of the dependent variable Y, given some value for the independent variable X, is $Y_1 = \beta_{01} + \beta_{11}X_1$ for the first group and $Y_2 = \beta_{02} + \beta_{12}X_2$ for the second group. That is, the regression lines are assumed to be straight.
- As in Chapter 8, for any given value for the independent variable X, the dependent variable Y has a normal distribution. Said a bit more formally, the conditional distribution of Y, given X, is a normal distribution.
- The variance of Y does not depend on the value of the independent variable X. In symbols, it is assumed that for the first group $\text{VAR}(Y_1|X_1) = \sigma_1^2$ and for the second group $\text{VAR}(Y_2|X_2) = \sigma_2^2$. This is called the within group homoscedasticity assumption.
- $\sigma_1^2 = \sigma_2^2$, which is called the between group homoscedasticity assumption.
- $\beta_{11} = \beta_{12}$. That is, the regression lines are assumed to be parallel; they have the same slope.
- Least squares regression provides a satisfactory estimate of the slope and intercept.

Based on the aforementioned assumptions, the goal is to test

$$H_0 : \beta_{01} = \beta_{02}, \tag{9.22}$$

the hypothesis that the intercepts are the same.

For reasons already covered, these assumptions are highly restrictive. If these assumptions are true, exact control over the Type I error probability can be obtained when testing (9.22). But violating any one of these assumptions is a serious concern and violating two or more simultaneously only makes matters worse. A fairly common suggestion is to first test the hypothesis that the regression lines are parallel and if this hypothesis is not rejected, test (9.22). But testing the assumption that the regression lines are parallel raises a fundamental issue: when is power sufficiently high enough to detect situations where violating this assumption is a practical concern? A satisfactory method for answering this question has not been derived. Similarly to Student's T test in Chapter 8, when the classic ANCOVA method in this section rejects, it is reasonable to conclude that the groups differ in some manner. But understanding the nature of the difference requires using other methods described in this section.

9.12.2 R Function CLASSanc

The R function

```
CLASSanc(x1,y1,x2,y2,xout=FALSE, outfun=out)
```

performs the classic ANCOVA method described in the previous section. From a robustness point of view, this function provides the opportunity to remove outliers among the covariate. As usual, this is accomplished by setting the argument xout=TRUE. But there are serious concerns about the other assumptions associated with this method as previously noted.

Example

To illustrate how to read the output, data from the Well Elderly 2 study (mentioned at the beginning of this section) are used where the goal is to compare a control group to an experimental group based on MAPA scores using the CAR as a covariate. (The data are stored on the author's web page in the files weA1_control.txt, weB3_exp.txt.) Assuming that the data for the control group are stored in the R variable A1 and the data for the experimental group are stored in B3, the R command

```
CLASSanc(A1$cort1-A1$cort2,A1$MAPAGLOB,B3$cort1-B3$cort2,

B3$MAPAGLOB,xout=T)
```

performs the analysis. (The variables cort1 and cort2 are cortisol measures upon awakening and 30–60 minutes after awakening, and the R variable MAPAGLOB is the MAPA score.) The output looks like this:

$slope.test

	Df	Sum Sq	Mean Sq	F value	Pr($>F$)
as.factor(g)	1	41	41.36	1.171	0.2801
x	1	20	20.37	0.577	0.4482
as.factor(g):x	1	192	192.45	5.450	0.0203 *
Residuals	76	9746	35.31		

Signif. codes:	*** 0.001	** 0.01	* 0.05	0.1

$ancova

	Df	Sum Sq	Mean Sq	F value	Pr($>F$)
as.factor(g)	1	41	41.36	1.153	0.284
x	1	20	20.37	0.568	0.452
Residuals	277	9,939	35.88		

The first six lines deal with testing the hypothesis that the regression lines are parallel. The last column headed by Pr($>F$) reports p-values. What is important here is the fifth line beginning with as.factor(g):x. At the end of this line, we see 0.0203 *, which is the p-value based on the test statistic (the value 5.450) in the column headed by F value. The * indicates that the hypothesis of equal slopes is rejected at the $\alpha = 0.05$ level. However, as previously stressed, failing to reject the hypothesis of equal slopes is not compelling evidence that the regression lines are reasonably parallel. The only goal is to illustrate an approach that is sometimes used. For illustrative purposes, imagine that the assumption of parallel regression lines is accepted. What is important now is the second line after $ancova, which begins with as.factor(g). At the end of this line is the p-value, again in the column headed by Pr($> F$). The p-value is 0.284, so the hypothesis of equal intercepts would not be rejected at the 0.05 level. That is, when taking the CAR into account, no decision is made about whether typical MAPA scores are greater for the group that received intervention.

9.12.3 Heteroscedastic Methods for Comparing the Slopes and Intercepts

Still using least squares regression, this section notes that both types of heteroscedasticity can be accommodated when comparing the regression parameters of independent groups. First, consider the goal of testing the hypothesis that the regression lines are identical. That is, the goal is to test

$$H_0 : \beta_{01} = \beta_{02} \text{ and } \beta_{11} = \beta_{12}.$$

For within group heteroscedasticity, the HC4 estimator (mentioned in Chapter 8) can be used. For between group heteroscedasticity, the approach used here is based on a variation of general results derived by Johansen (1980, 1982). The method can be used when there are two or more independent variables (covariates), but the somewhat involved calculations are not described. (For more details, see Wilcox and Clark, 2015.) Instead, an R function is supplied, which is described in the next section. There is also a function for comparing the individual slopes and the intercepts. That is, the goal is to determine which parameters, if any, differ by testing two hypotheses, namely $H_0 : \beta_{01} = \beta_{02}$ (the hypothesis that the intercepts are equal), as well as $H_0 : \beta_{11} = \beta_{12}$ (the hypothesis that the slopes are equal).

9.12.4 R Functions olsJ2 and ols2ci

The R function

```
olsJ2(x1,y1, x2, y2, xout=FALSE, outfun=outpro,
    plotit=TRUE,xlab='X',ylab='Y', ISO=FALSE)
```

tests the hypothesis that two independent groups have identical regression lines when using least squares regression. The function can handle more than one covariate, in which case the arguments x1 and x2 are assumed to be matrices as described in Chapters 1 and 8. If the argument plotit=TRUE, and there is one covariate only, the function plots the regression lines. If the goal is to test the hypothesis that all of the slopes are equal, ignoring the intercept, this can be accomplished by setting the argument ISO = TRUE. (ISO stands for include slopes only.) So, if there is one covariate only, the goal is to test the hypothesis that the regression lines are parallel.

When there is more than one covariate, another goal is to determine which slopes differ. If olsJ2 rejects, this indicates that one or more of the slopes differ, but it does not indicate which ones. To determine which slopes differ, the R function

```
ols2ci(x1,y1,x2, y2, xout=FALSE, outfun=out,ISO=FALSE,
       plotit=TRUE, xlab='X', ylab='Y')
```

can be used. Although olsJ2 does not indicate which slopes differ when there is more than one covariate, it might have more power than ols2ci.

Notice that if there is only one covariate, both olsJ2 and ols2ci can be used to compare the slopes. These functions can give slightly different results. The reason is that olsJ2 is based on a test statistic that stems from Johansen (1980), while ols2ci uses a variation of Welch's test statistic described in Section 9.1.5.

Example

Consider again the Well Elderly 2 study, only now focus on the CAR and a measure of depressive symptoms. Recall that Figure 8.8 in Section 8.9.1 suggests that after intervention, the regression line for predicting the typical level of depressive symptoms, given the value for the CAR, is not straight. In particular, the nature of the association appears to depend on whether cortisol increases after awakening (CAR is negative) or whether it decreases (CAR is positive). More precisely, the nature of the association seems to change at or near where the CAR is equal to -0.05. As a check on the possibility that the regression line is not straight, the data are split into two groups based on whether the CAR is less than -0.05 and then the slopes and intercepts are compared. If the regression line is straight using all of the data, then it should be the case that the slopes and intercepts, when splitting the data as just described, are identical. (The data used in this example are stored in the file A3B3C.txt on the author's web page and differs from the data used to illustrate the classic ANCOVA method.) Here is one way of doing the analysis using R, assuming that the data are stored in the R variable A3B3C:

```
dif=A3B3C$cort1-A3B3C$cort2
left=which(dif<0-.05)
right=which(dif>=0-0.05)
olsJ2(dif[left],A3B3C$CESD[left],dif[right],A3B3C$CESD[right],
xout=TRUE)
```

The first command stores the CAR data in the R variable dif for convenience. (The R variable A3B3C$cort1 contains cortisol measures upon awakening and A3B3C$cort2 contains cortisol measures taken 30–60 minutes later. Measures of depressive symptoms are stored in the R variable A3B3C$CESD.) The next command identifies the individuals for whom CAR is less than -0.05, and the third command identifies the individuals for whom CAR is greater than or equal -0.05. The argument xout=TRUE indicates that all participants, for whom the CAR value is flagged as an outlier, are eliminated from the analysis. The slopes are estimated to be -9.444

and 32.415. The *p*-value returned by the last command is 0.003, indicating that there is fairly strong evidence that the slope is larger when the CAR is greater than or equal to -0.05 compared to when the CAR is less than -0.05. Setting the argument plotit=TRUE, the function olsJ2 returns a plot of the regression lines, indicating that they cross somewhere close to where the CAR is zero. That is, the nature of the association, after intervention, appears to depend on whether cortisol increases or decreases shortly after awakening. The R function ols2ci also rejects the hypothesis that the slopes differ. When comparing the intercepts, the *p*.value is 0.956.

9.12.5 Dealing with Outliers among the Dependent Variable

As demonstrated in Chapter 8, outliers among the dependent variable can have a substantial impact on the least squares estimator: Strong associations among the bulk of the data can be missed and the nature of the association can be poorly modeled. There are R functions for comparing robust regression lines that are aimed at dealing with this concern, which are described in the next section. Both functions use a bootstrap method. (For computational details, see Wilcox and Clark, 2015; Wilcox, 2012a.)

9.12.6 R Functions reg2ci, ancGpar, and reg2plot

When there is one covariate, the R function

```
reg2plot(x1,y1,x2,y2,regfun=tsreg, xlab='X',

    ylab='Y', xout=FALSE, outfun=out)
```

creates a scatterplot of the data with a solid line indicating the regression line for the first group and a dashed line indicating the regression line for the second group. By default, the Theil–Sen estimator is used. To plot the least squares regression lines, set the argument regfun=ols. Figure 9.8 shows the plot created by the R command

```
reg2plot(A1$cort1-A1$cort2,A1$MAPAGLOB,B3$cort1-B3$cort2,

B3$MAPAGLOB,xout=T,regfun=ols,xlab='CAR',ylab='MAPA').
```

The R function

```
ancGpar(x1,y1,x2,y2,regfun=tsreg,nboot=100,

SEED=TRUE,xout=FALSE, outfun=outpro,plotit=TRUE,

    xlab='X', ylab='Y', ISO=FALSE)
```

tests the global hypothesis that two regression lines are identical. It is a robust analog of the R function olsJ2. More than one covariate is allowed. Consistent with Chapter 8, the Theil–Sen estimator is used by default, but other robust regression estimators can be used via the argument regfun. Again, setting the argument ISO=TRUE, the global hypothesis of identical slopes is tested, ignoring the intercept.

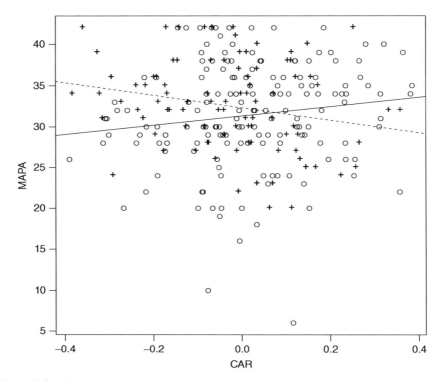

Figure 9.8   The solid line is the regression lined for the first group (the control group) for predicting MAPA scores based on CAR. The dashed line is the regression line for the second group (the group that received intervention)

The R function

```
reg2ci(x,y,x1,y1,regfun=tsreg, nboot=599, alpha=0.05,
    plotit=TRUE, xout=FALSE, outfun=outpro, xlab='X',
                        ylab= 'Y')
```

compares the individual slopes as well as the intercepts. It is a robust analog of the R function `ols2ci`.

Example

For the data in Figure 9.8, the R command

```
ancGpar(A1$cort1-A1$cort2,A1$MAPAGLOB, B3$cort1-B3$cort2,
B3$MAPAGLOB, xout=T)
```

returns a p-value equal to 0.020. So, testing at the $\alpha = 0.05$ level, reject the hypothesis that the regression lines are identical. For the R command

```
reg2ci(A1$cort1-A1$cort2,A1$MAPAGLOB, B3$cort1-B3$cort2,
B3$MAPAGLOB, xout=T)
```

a portion of the output looks like this:

```
Parameter   ci.lower   ci.upper      p.value Group 1 Group 2
        0 $-$2.986918  1.324114   0.47579299 31.945133 32.389970
        1  4.057608 22.6768410 0.01168614  5.050505 $-$9.029294
```

This indicates that for the hypothesis of equal intercepts, the p-value is 0.476, the 0.95 confidence interval for the difference between the intercepts is $(-2.987, 1.324)$, the estimate of the intercept for the first group is 31.945, and the estimate for the second group is 32.390. The p-value for the hypothesis of equal slopes is 0.012.

9.12.7 A Closer Look at Comparing Nonparallel Regression Lines

Look again at Figure 9.8 and note that when the CAR is close to zero, the typical MAPA score for the control group is estimated to be very similar to the typical score for the experimental group. When the CAR is negative, it is estimated that typical MAPA scores for the control group are less than the MAPA scores for the intervention group. But can we be reasonably certain that this is the case when the CAR is equal to -0.1? If, for example, least squares regression is used, can the hypothesis

$$H_0 : E(Y_1|\text{CAR} = -0.1) = E(Y_2|\text{CAR} = -0.1)$$

be rejected, where Y_1 and Y_2 are MAPA scores for the control and experimental groups, respectively? If not, is this hypothesis rejected when the CAR is equal to -0.2? It appears that when the CAR is positive, now the typical MAPA score is higher among the participants in the control group. But is this a reasonable conclusion when the CAR is 0.1? If not, is this a reasonable conclusion when the CAR is 0.2? The R function ancJN in Section 9.12.8 is designed to help address these questions. (For methods that deal with curved regression lines, see Wilcox, 2012b.)

9.12.8 R Function ancJN

The R function

```
ancJN(x1,y1,x2,y2, pts=NULL, regfun=tsreg,alpha=0.05,

    plotit=TRUE, xout=FALSE, outfun=out,xlab='X',

                    ylab= 'Y')
```

compares regression lines for specified values associated with the covariate. The covariate values can be specified via the argument pts. By default, pts = NULL, meaning that the function picks the points that will be used. The argument regfun indicates the regression estimator that will be used, which defaults to the Theil–Sen estimator. To use the least squares regression line, set regfun=ols. If the argument plotit=TRUE, a scatterplot of the data is produced that includes both regression lines. As usual, setting the argument xout=TRUE will eliminate outliers among the independent variables using the method specified by the argument outfun, which defaults to the MAD-median rule when there is one covariate.

Example

This is a continuation of the example in Section 9.12.6, still assuming that the data for the control group are stored in the R variable A1 and the data for the experimental group are stored in B3. Based on Figure 9.8, imagine that the goal is to compare the regression lines at the following CAR values: −0.4, −0.3, −0.2, −0.1, 0, 0.1, 0.2, and 0.3. Here are the R commands that accomplish this goal:

```
pts=seq(-0.4,0.3,0.1)

ancJN(A1$cort1-A1$cort2,A1$MAPAGLOB,B3$cort1-B3$cort2,

B3$MAPAGLOB,xout=T,regfun=ols,pts=pts)
```

The first command creates a sequence of values starting at −0.4 and extending to 0.3 in increments of 0.1. The output from the second command looks like this:

```
   X      Est1      Est2        DIF        TEST         se   ci.low
-0.4 29.06505 35.37430 -6.3092522 -3.7452696 1.6845923 -10.908
-0.3 29.63058 34.61334 -4.9827540 -3.7132998 1.3418669  -8.646
-0.2 30.19612 33.85237 -3.6562558 -3.5148909 1.0402189  -6.496
-0.1 30.76165 33.09141 -2.3297576 -2.8206938 0.8259520  -4.584
 0.0 31.32719 32.33045 -1.0032593 -1.2940911 0.7752618  -3.119
 0.1 31.89272 31.56948  0.3232389  0.3529857 0.9157280  -2.176
 0.2 32.45826 30.80852  1.6497371  1.3968902 1.1810070  -1.574
 0.3 33.02379 30.04756  2.9762353  1.9755316 1.5065491  -1.136
 ci.hi       p.value
-1.710 0.0001802001
-1.319 0.0002045743
-0.816 0.0004399347
-0.074 0.0047919916
 1.113 0.1956339522
 2.823 0.7240991788
 4.873 0.1624466046
 7.089 0.0482078572
```

The column headed by X indicates the values of the covariate (the CAR values here) where the regression lines are compared. The next two columns indicate the estimated typical value of the dependent variable based on the regression line. So, given that CAR is equal to −0.4, the regression line for the first group estimates that the typical MAPA score is 29.065 and for the second group, the regression line estimates that the typical MAPA score is 35.37. The next column reports the difference between these two estimates followed by the test statistic and the corresponding standard error, which is indicated by the column headed by se. The next two columns indicate the lower and upper ends, respectively, of a confidence interval for the difference. (These are not 0.95 confidence intervals. Rather, they are designed so that with probability 0.95, all of the confidence intervals contain the true difference with probability 0.95. Chapter 12 elaborates on what this means.) The final column headed by p.value contains the p-values. Note that for the first four rows, where the CAR values range from -0.4 to -0.1, the p-values are close to zero and the confidence intervals do not contain zero. From the point of view of Tukey's three-decision rule, decide that for CAR less than or equal to -0.1, typical MAPA scores for the control group are less than the typical values for the group that received intervention.

Notice that for the last row, where CAR is 0.3, the confidence interval contains zero. The regression lines in Figure 9.8 suggest that as the CAR increases, at some point the typical MAPA scores for the control group will be greater than the typical values for the group that received intervention. But the confidence intervals suggest that this might not be the case over the range of CAR values that were observed. Or, from the point of view of Tukey's three-decision rule, no decision about this issue should be made. Also, extrapolation should be avoided, as stressed in Chapter 8. The regression lines in Figure 9.8 might suggest that as CAR becomes increasingly positive (cortisol decreases shortly after awakening), at some point, no intervention is more effective in terms of increasing a measure of meaningful activities. But the data only extend out to CAR=0.4. There are no data providing information about typical MAPA scores when CAR is greater than 0.4.

9.13 SUMMARY

- The most common strategy for comparing two independent groups is to use means via Student's T or Welch's method. A positive feature of these methods is that when they reject, it is reasonable to conclude that the distributions differ in some manner. That is, when comparing identical distributions, they provide good control over the probability of a Type I error. When comparing symmetric, light-tailed distributions (outliers are rare), Welch's method performs reasonably well. But there are general conditions where methods based on means result in inaccurate confidence intervals and poor power relative to other methods that might be used. The ability of these methods to provide accurate confidence intervals is a complicated function of the sample sizes, skewness, heteroscedasticity, and the likelihood of encountering outliers.

- Despite the impact of outliers on the mean, situations are encountered where the mean can be argued to be a better measure of location than the median, as explained in Chapter 2. To deal with nonnormality when computing a confidence interval for the difference between the population means, a bootstrap-t method appears to be the most reliable approach with the understanding that even this method might yield inaccurate confidence intervals. Even when dealing with discrete data where there are no outliers and only a few possible values can occur, some alternative method might detect a difference that is missed when using means. The first example in Section 9.11.1 illustrates this point.

- The Wilcoxon–Mann–Whitney test is sometimes described as a method for comparing medians, but in general this is not the case. Rather, it is based on an estimate of the probability that a randomly sampled observation from the first group is less than a randomly sampled observation from the second group. But to get an accurate confidence interval for this probability, something other than the Wilcoxon–Mann–Whitney test should be used, such as Cliff's method in Section 9.6.3. Although Cliff's method is not designed to compare the medians of two independent groups, it does deal with the median of the difference between two randomly sampled participants, as explained in Section 9.6.3.

- Measuring effect size is a nontrivial issue. Cohen's d is popular, but it is based on a relatively simplistic model of reality: normality and homoscedasticity. In some situations, it might suffice. But to assume this is the case is difficult to justify. Several measures of effect size might be needed to get an accurate and deep understanding of how groups compare.

- A recommendation is to plot the data. Plots can be invaluable in terms of understanding how groups compare, as illustrated in Section 9.8. Error bars are popular, but they can be rather uninformative compared to other plots that might be used. Take advantage of boxplots as well as plots of the distributions. When dealing with discrete or categorical data, consider the plot described in Section 9.11.1.

- Sometimes, it is differences between the tails of the distributions that are important and useful. The methods in Section 9.9 can be used to deal with this issue. For discrete or categorical data, consider the methods in Section 9.11.

- Many improved methods for comparing binomial distributions have been derived. Currently, the methods in Section 9.10 appear to perform relatively well.

- The best-known method for comparing the regression lines corresponding to two independent groups is the classic ANCOVA method described in Section 9.12.1. But it has long been known that it can be unsatisfactory when standard assumptions are violated. The more modern techniques in Section 9.12 are designed to deal with the shortcomings of the classic method.

- This chapter has described several ways groups might be compared, which raises a seemingly natural question: Which method is best? But there is a better and more important question: How many methods does it take to understand how groups compare? In some situations, certain techniques might be eliminated based on substantive grounds. But often, strict adherence to a single approach is too myopic. Several methods can be required to get a useful understanding of how groups compare.

9.14 EXERCISES

1. Suppose that the sample means and variances are $\overline{X}_1 = 15$, $\overline{X}_2 = 12$, $s_1^2 = 8$, $s_2^2 = 24$ with sample sizes $n_1 = 20$ and $n_2 = 10$. Verify that $s_p^2 = 13.14$, $T = 2.14$, and that Student's T test rejects the hypothesis of equal means with $\alpha = 0.05$.

2. For two independent groups of subjects $\overline{X}_1 = 45$, $\overline{X}_2 = 36$, $s_1^2 = 4$, $s_2^2 = 16$ with sample sizes $n_1 = 20$ and $n_2 = 30$. Assume that the population variances of the two groups are equal and verify that the estimate of this common variance is 11.25.

3. Still assuming equal variances, test the hypothesis of equal means using Student's T test and the data in the last exercise. Use $\alpha = 0.05$.

4. Repeat the last problem, only use Welch's test for comparing means.

5. Comparing the results for the last two problems, what do they suggest regarding the power of Welch's test compared to Student's T test when the sample variances differ sufficiently.

6. For two independent groups $\overline{X}_1 = 86$, $\overline{X}_2 = 80$, $s_1^2 = s_2^2 = 25$, with sample sizes $n_1 = n_2 = 20$. Assume that the population variances of the two groups are equal and verify that Student's T rejects with $\alpha = 0.01$.

7. Repeat the last exercise using Welch's method.

8. Comparing the results of the last two problems, what do they suggest about using Student's T versus Welch's method when the sample variances are approximately equal?

9. For $\overline{X}_1 = 10$, $\overline{X}_2 = 5$, $s_1^2 = 21$, $s_2^2 = 29$, $n_1 = n_2 = 16$, compute a 0.95 confidence interval for the difference between the means using Welch's method and state whether a decision can be made about which group has the larger population mean.

10. Repeat the last problem, only use Student's T instead.

11. Two methods for training accountants are to be compared. Students are randomly assigned to one of the two methods. At the end of the course, each student is asked to prepare a tax return for the same individual. The amounts of the refund reported by the students are

$$\text{Method 1}: \quad 132, 204, 603, 50, 125, 90, 185, 134$$

$$\text{Method 2}: \quad 92, -42, 121, 63, 182, 101, 294, 36$$

Using Welch's test, would you conclude that the methods differ in terms of the average return? Use $\alpha = 0.05$.

12. Responses to stress are governed by the hypothalamus. Imagine you have two randomly sampled groups of individuals between the age of 60 and 65. The first shows signs of heart disease and the other does not. You want to determine whether the groups differ in terms of some measure associated with the hypothalamus. For the first group of subjects with no heart disease, the measures are

$$11.1, 12.2, 15.5, 17.6, 13.0, 7.5, 9.1, 6.6, 9.5, 18.0, 12.6.$$

For the other group with heart disease, the measures are

$$18.2, 14.1, 13.8, 12.1, 34.1, 12.0, 14.1, 14.5, 12.6, 12.5, 19.8, 13.4,$$
$$16.8, 14.1, 12.9$$

Determine whether the groups differ based on Welch's test. Use $\alpha = 0.05$.

13. The 0.95 confidence interval for the difference between the means, using Student's T, is (2.2, 20.5). What are the practical concerns with this confidence interval?

14. For the first of two binomial distributions, there are 15 successes among 24 observations. For the second, there are 23 successes among 42 observations. Test $H_0: p_1 = p_2$ with a Type I error probability of 0.05 using the Storer–Kim method followed by Beal's method. That is, use the R functions twobinom and twobicipv. Note the difference between the p-values and comment on what this suggests in terms of power.

15. A film producer wants to know which of two versions of a particular scene is more likely to be viewed as disturbing. A group of 98 individuals views the first version and 20 say that it is disturbing. Another group sees the second version and 30 of 70 people say that it is disturbing. Use the R function twobinom to test the hypothesis that the two probabilities are equal using $\alpha = 0.05$. Compare the results to those returned by the R function twobicipv.

16. It is found that among 121 individuals who take a training program on investing in commodities, 20 make money during the next year and the rest do not. With another training program, 15 of 80 make money. Test the hypothesis that the probability of making money is the same for both training programs using Equation (9.20) and a Type I error probability of 0.05. Verify that the p-value is 0.69 using the R function twobinom and that the p-value using Beal's method is 0.999

17. In a study dealing with violence between factions in the Middle East, one goal was to compare measures of depression for two groups of young males. In the first group, no family member was wounded or killed by someone belonging to the opposite faction, and the measures were

$$22, 23, 12, 11, 30, 22, 7, 42, 24, 33, 28, 19, 4, 34, 15, 26, 50, 27, 20,$$
$$30, 14, 42.$$

The second group consisted of young males who had a family member killed or wounded. The observed measures were

$$17, 22, 16, 16, 14, 29, 20, 20, 19, 14, 10, 8, 26, 9, 14, 17, 21, 16, 14,$$
$$11, 14, 11, 29, 13, 4, 16, 16, 7, 21.$$

Test the hypothesis of equal means with Student's T test and $\alpha = 0.05$, and compute a 0.95 confidence interval. Use the R function t.test to verify that Welch's test yields a p-value equal to 0.0047.

18. For the data in the last problem, the difference between the medians is -7.5 and the corresponding McKean–Schrader estimate of the standard error is $\sqrt{S_1^2 + S_2^2} = 3.93$. Verify that you do not reject the hypothesis of equal medians with $\alpha = 0.05$. Use the R function msmed to verify that the p-value is 0.057.

19. Using the data in Exercise 17, use a percentile bootstrap method to compare the medians. Note that the p-value is 0.01. This is in contrast to the result in Exercise 18, where the hypothesis of equal medians is not rejected at the 0.05 level. Comment on why the two methods give different results.

20. Repeat the analysis of the sexual attitude data, the second example in Section 9.10.2, only now use the R functions twobinom and twobicipv. Verify that the p-values are now 0.004 and 0.008, respectively.

21. Does the consumption of alcohol limit our attention span? An article in the July 10, 2006 *Los Angeles Times* described a study conducted at the University of Washington where 23 people were given enough alcohol to reach a blood alcohol level of 0.04% (half the legal limit in many states). A second group of 23 people drank no alcohol. The researchers then showed members of both groups a 25-second video clip in which two teams passed a ball back and forth and asked them to count the number of times one team passed the ball. During the clip, a person in a gorilla suit walks through the crowd, thumps its chest, and walks off. Researchers found that 11 of the 23 participants in the control group saw the gorilla, compared to 10 in the alcohol group. Verify that you do not reject the hypothesis that the two groups have the same probability of seeing the gorilla using the Storer–Kim method with $\alpha = 0.05$.

22. Despite any problems it might have, summarize how you would justify using Student's T test to compare two independent groups.

23. Summarize any practical concerns about Student's T test and comment on how they might be addressed.

24. Summarize the relative merits of comparing groups with medians.

25. For each of two independent groups, 1,000 bootstrap samples are generated and it is found that there are 10 instances where the bootstrap sample trimmed mean for the first group is less than the bootstrap sample trimmed mean for the second. There are two instances where the bootstrap sample trimmed means are equal. Determine a p-value when testing the hypothesis of equal population trimmed means.

26. Repeat the analysis of Salk's data in Section 9.1.6 using the R function t.test, only use Welch's method instead. (Salk's data are stored on the author's web page as described in Section 1.5.) Verify that the p-value is now 0.0009 compared to 0.0026 using Student's T.

27. For the self-awareness data in Table 9.1, use R to apply Yuen's method with 20% trimming. (The data are stored in the file dana_dat.txt and can be downloaded from the author's web page as described in Section 1.5.)

28. Duplicate the results for the shoulder pain data in Section 9.11.1.

29. The example in Section 9.12.8 illustrates the R function `ancJN` using a measure of meaningful activities labeled MAPAGLOB. Another measure of meaningful activities was used as well, which is labeled MAPAFREQ. (The data are stored on the author's web page in the files weA1_control.txt, weB3_exp.txt.) Repeat the example in Section 9.12.8, only use MAPAFREQ rather than MAPAGLOB. What do the results suggest regarding how the control group compares to the intervention group?

30. The last exercise is based on the least squares regression estimator. Perform the analysis again using the Theil–Sen estimator instead. How do the results compare to those based on the least squares regression estimator?

10

COMPARING MORE THAN TWO INDEPENDENT GROUPS

Chapter 9 described methods for comparing two independent groups, but often comparing more than two groups is of interest. For example, a researcher might have four methods for treating schizophrenia, in which case there is the issue of whether the choice of method makes a difference. As another example, several drugs might be used to control high blood pressure. Do the drugs differ in terms of side effects?

When comparing more than two groups, there is a collection of techniques aimed at two distinct goals. The first is to test some global hypothesis that the groups are, in some sense, identical. For instance, the hypothesis might be that all of the groups have the same mean or median. The other goal is to determine which groups differ. The first goal is the subject of this chapter. The second goal is addressed with methods in Chapter 12.

10.1 THE ANOVA F TEST

Imagine that the goal is to compare J independent groups having population means $\mu_1, \ldots, \mu_J$. A common strategy is to begin by testing

$$H_0 : \mu_1 = \cdots = \mu_J, \tag{10.1}$$

the hypothesis that all J groups have equal means. As in Chapter 9, independent groups means that the observations in any two groups are independent. In the schizophrenia example, this requirement would be met if we randomly sample participants who will undergo one of the treatments, and then these participants are randomly assigned to one and only one treatment. If, for instance, all four treatment

Understanding and Applying Basic Statistical Methods Using R, First Edition. Rand R. Wilcox.
© 2017 John Wiley & Sons, Inc. Published 2017 by John Wiley & Sons, Inc.
www.wiley.com/go/Wilcox/Statistical_Methods_R

methods were applied to the same participants, independence would no longer be a reasonable assumption and the methods covered here would be inappropriate.

This section describes the classic, best-known, and most commonly used method for testing Equation (10.1), which assumes

- Random sampling
- Normality
- Homoscedasticity, meaning that all J groups have the same (population) variance.

Letting $\sigma_1^2, \dots, \sigma_J^2$ denote the population variances, this last assumption means that

$$\sigma_1^2 = \sigma_2^2 = \cdots = \sigma_J^2. \tag{10.2}$$

For convenience, this assumed common variance is denoted by σ_p^2. *Heteroscedasticity* refers to a situation where not all the variances are equal.

The basic strategy behind the method for testing Equation (10.1), which was derived by Sir Ronald Fisher, can be described as follows. First, imagine that the null hypothesis of equal means is true. Then, the sample means corresponding to the J groups are all attempting to estimate the same quantity, yet their individual values will vary. A rough characterization of the classic method is that it attempts to determine whether the variation among the sample means is sufficiently large to reject the hypothesis of equal population means. The more variation among the sample means, the stronger the evidence that the null hypothesis should be rejected.

Let $\overline{X}_1, \dots, \overline{X}_J$ be the sample means, and momentarily, consider the case where all groups have the same sample size, which is denoted by n. We begin by computing the average of the sample means,

$$\overline{X}_G = \frac{1}{J} \sum \overline{X}_j,$$

which is called the *grand mean*. Next, we measure the variation among these means in much the same way the sample variance, s^2, measures the variation among n observations. The variation among the sample means is given by

$$V = \frac{1}{J-1} \sum (\overline{X}_j - \overline{X}_G)^2.$$

In words, V is computed by subtracting the grand mean from each of the individual means, squaring the results, adding these squared differences, and then dividing by $J - 1$, the number of groups minus 1. It can be shown that *when the null hypothesis of equal means is true*, V estimates σ_p^2/n, the assumed common variance divided by the sample size. Multiplying V by the sample size, n, yields what is called the *mean squares between groups*. More succinctly, the mean squares between groups is

$$\text{MSBG} = \frac{n}{J-1} \sum (\overline{X}_j - \overline{X}_G)^2,$$

which estimates the assumed common variance σ_p^2 *when the null hypothesis is true.* However, when the null hypothesis is false, MSBG does not estimate σ_p^2, it estimates σ_p^2 plus a quantity that reflects how much the population means differ. That is, the more unequal the population means happen to be, the larger will be MSBG, on average.

To say this in a more precise way, let

$$\overline{\mu} = \frac{1}{J} \sum \mu_j$$

be the average of the population means, and let

$$\sigma_\mu^2 = \frac{\sum (\mu_j - \overline{\mu})^2}{J - 1},$$

which represents the variation among the population means. In general, MSBG estimates

$$\sigma_p^2 + n\sigma_\mu^2.$$

This says that the value of MSBG is affected by three quantities: the variation within each group, represented by σ_p^2, the variation among the population means, which is reflected by σ_μ^2, and the sample size n. When the hypothesis of equal means is true, there is no variation among the population means, meaning that $\sigma_\mu^2 = 0$. That is, MSBG is estimating σ_p^2.

Next, let $s_1^2, \ldots, s_J^2$ represent the sample variances corresponding to the J groups. By assumption, all of these sample variances estimate the common (population) variance σ_p^2. As was done in Chapter 9, we simply average the sample variances to get a single estimate of σ_p^2, still assuming equal sample sizes. This average is called the *mean squares within groups* and is given by

$$\mathrm{MSWG} = \frac{1}{J} \sum s_j^2.$$

A key result is that when the hypothesis of equal means is true, both MSBG and MSWG are attempting to estimate the same quantity, namely the assumed common variance. When the null hypothesis is false, MSWG continues to estimate the assumed common variance, but now MSBG is estimating something larger, meaning that on average, MSBG will tend to be larger than MSWG.

Based on the results just summarized, the hypothesis of equal means is rejected if MSBG is sufficiently larger than MSWG. A convenient way of measuring the extent to which they differ is with

$$F = \frac{\mathrm{MSBG}}{\mathrm{MSWG}}. \tag{10.3}$$

Note that if each group has n observations, the total number of observations in all J groups is $N = nJ$. The distribution of F, when the null hypothesis is true, is called an *F distribution* with degrees of freedom

$$\nu_1 = J - 1,$$

and

$$v_2 = N - J.$$

That is, the F distribution depends on two quantities: the number of groups being compared, J, and the total number of observations in all of the groups, N.

Decision Rule: The hypothesis of equal means is rejected if $F \geq f$, where f is the $1 - \alpha$ quantile of an F distribution with $v_1 = J - 1$ and $v_2 = N - J$ degrees of freedom. (This is the same F distribution introduced in Chapter 8.) Tables B.5–B.8 in Appendix B report critical values, f, for $\alpha = 0.1, 0.05, 0.025$, and 0.01 and various degrees of freedom. For example, with $\alpha = 0.05$, $v_1 = 6$, $v_2 = 8$, Table B.6 indicates that the 0.95 quantile is $f = 3.58$. That is, there is a 0.05 probability of getting a value for F that exceeds 3.58 when in fact the population means are equal. For $\alpha = 0.01$, Table B.8 says that the 0.99 quantile is 6.32. This means that if you reject when $F \geq 6.32$, the probability of a Type I error will be 0.01, assuming normality and that the groups have equal variances.

The method just described for comparing means is called an *analysis of variance* or *ANOVA F* test. Although the goal is to compare means, it goes by the name analysis of variance because the method is based on the variation of the sample means relative to the variation within each group.

Presumably, most readers will apply the ANOVA F test using R or some other software package. But in case it helps, here are the computational details that include situations where the sample sizes are not equal.

The notation X_{ij} refers to the ith observation in the jth group, $i = 1, \ldots, n_j$; $j = 1, \ldots, J$. (There are n_j observations randomly sampled from the jth group.) To compute the test statistic F, first compute

$$A = \sum_{j=1}^{J} \sum_{i=1}^{n_j} X_{ij}^2$$

(in words, square each value, add the results, and call it A),

$$B = \sum_{j=1}^{J} \sum_{i=1}^{n_j} X_{ij}$$

(sum all the observations and call it B),

$$C = \sum_{j=1}^{J} \frac{1}{n_j} \left(\sum_{i=1}^{n_j} X_{ij} \right)^2$$

(sum the observations for each group, square the result, divide by the sample size, add the results corresponding to each group). Next, compute

$$N = \sum n_j,$$

$$\text{SST} = A - \frac{B^2}{N},$$

$$SSBG = C - \frac{B^2}{N}$$

(SSBG stands for sum of squares between groups),

$$SSWG = SST - SSBG = A - C$$

(SSWG stands for sum of squares within groups),

$$v_1 = J - 1,$$
$$v_2 = N - J,$$
$$MSBG = \frac{SSBG}{v_1}$$

(where MSBG stands for mean squares between groups) and

$$MSWG = \frac{SSWG}{v_2}$$

(where MWBG stands for mean squares within groups). The test statistic is

$$F = \frac{MSBG}{MSWG}.$$

Decision Rule: Reject the hypothesis of equal means if $F \geq f$, the $1 - \alpha$ quantile of an F distribution with $v_1 = J - 1$ and $v_2 = N - J$ degrees of freedom.

Example

Imagine a study aimed at comparing four groups with 10 observations in each group. That is, $J = 4$ and $n = 10$, so the total sample size is $N = 40$. Consequently, the degrees of freedom are $v_1 = 3$ and $v_2 = 36$. Figure 10.1 shows the distribution of F when the hypothesis of equal means is true. As indicated, the 0.95 quantile is $f = 2.87$, meaning that the hypothesis of equal means is rejected if $F \geq 2.87$.

Example

The computations are illustrated with the following data.

Group 1: 7, 9, 8, 12, 8, 7, 4, 10, 9, 6
Group 2: 10, 13, 9, 11, 5, 9, 8, 10, 8, 7
Group 3: 12, 11, 15, 7, 14, 10, 12, 12, 13, 14

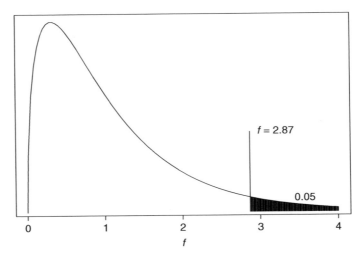

Figure 10.1 The F distribution when comparing four groups with 10 observations in each group and the hypothesis of equal means is true. That is, $J = 4, n = 10$, so $v_1 = 4 - 1 = 3$ and $v_2 = 4(10) - 4 = 36$. If the Type I error is to be $\alpha = 0.05$, reject if $F \geq 2.87$

We see that

$$A = 7^2 + 9^2 + \cdots + 14^2 = 3,026,$$

$$B = 7 + 9 + \cdots + 14 = 290,$$

$$C = \frac{(7 + 9 + \cdots + 6)^2}{10} + \frac{(10 + 13 + \cdots + 7)^2}{10}$$

$$+ \frac{(13 + 11 + \cdots + 14)^2}{10} = 2,890,$$

$$N = 10 + 10 + 10 = 30,$$

$$\text{SST} = 3,026 - 290^2/30 = 222.67,$$

$$\text{SSBG} = 2,890 - 290^2/30 = 86.67,$$

$$\text{SSWG} = 3,026 - 2,890 = 136,$$

$$\text{MSBG} = 86.67/(3 - 1) = 43.335,$$

$$\text{MSWG} = 136/(30 - 3) = 5.03,$$

so

$$F = \frac{43.335}{5.03} = 8.615.$$

The degrees of freedom are $v_1 = 3 - 1 = 2$ and $v_2 = 30 - 3 = 27$. With $\alpha = 0.01$, Table B.8 in Appendix B indicates that the critical value is $f = 5.49$. Because $8.165 \geq 5.49$, reject the hypothesis of equal means.

10.1.1   R Functions anova, anova1, aov, split, and fac2list

The built-in R function

$$aov(x \sim g),$$

used in conjunction with the R function summary or the R function anova, performs the ANOVA *F* test. Similarly to that in Chapter 9, $x \sim g$ is an R formula indicating that the data to be analyzed, often called the values of the *dependent variable*, are stored in the R variable x, and the corresponding *levels* or group identifications are contained in g. When using this function, make sure that g is a factor variable. If it is not a factor variable, the function can give highly erroneous results.

Example

A data set dealing with plasma retinol can be downloaded from Carnegie Mellon University at

http://lib.stat.cmu.edu/datasets/Plasma_Retinol.

The data are also stored on the author's web page in the file plasma_dat.txt. Here are the first 15 lines of this latter file, which provide information about the stored variables:

```
Variable Names in order from left to right:
1      AGE: Age (years)
2      SEX: Sex (1=Male, 2=Female).
3      SMOKSTAT: Smoking status (1=Never, 2=Former, 3=Current Smoker)
4      QUETELET: Quetelet (weight/(height^2))
5      VITUSE: Vitamin Use (1=Yes, fairly often, 2=Yes, not often, 3=No)
6      CALORIES: Number of calories consumed per day.
7      FAT: Grams of fat consumed per day.
8      FIBER: Grams of fiber consumed per day.
9      ALCOHOL: Number of alcoholic drinks consumed per week.
10     CHOLESTEROL: Cholesterol consumed (mg per day).
11     BETADIET: Dietary beta-carotene consumed (mcg per day).
12     RETDIET: Dietary retinol consumed (mcg per day)
13     BETAPLASMA: Plasma beta-carotene (ng/ml)
14     RETPLASMA: Plasma Retinol (ng/ml)
```

So when reading the data into R, include the skip command. Reading the data into the R variable plasma, for example, the command would be

```
plasma=read.table('plasma_dat.txt',skip=15)
```

or as explained in Section 1.3.1 the command

```
plasma=read.table(file.choose(),skip=15)
```

can be used. Once this is done, column 3 indicates the smoking status of the participants: 1=Never, 2=Former, 3=Current Smoker. Column 10 contains information on the amount of cholesterol consumed by the participant. Then, the R command

```
summary(aov(plasma[,10]~plasma[,3]))
```

attempts to perform the ANOVA F test, *but the results returned are incorrect*. The reason is that plasma[,3] is not a factor variable. Even the degrees of freedom are wrong: it reports $v_1 = 1$, but the correct value is 2. The command

```
summary(aov(plasma[,10]~as.factor(plasma[,3])))
```

performs the analysis in the correct manner. The output resembles this:

```
                        Df   Sum Sq Mean Sq F value Pr(>F)
as.factor(plasma[, 3])   2    77258   38629   2.235  0.109
```

The test statistic F is 2.235, and the p-value is 0.109.

An alternative R function is included in the file of R functions written for this book that might help avoid any problems when using aov and when the R variable g is not a factor variable. The R function is

```
anova1(x),
```

where the argument x is a matrix (or data frame) with columns corresponding to groups, or it can have list mode.

The function anova1 does not accept a formula, in contrast to the R function aov. But it is common to have data stored in a file with some R variable indicating the group to which a participant belongs. For illustrative purposes, assume this information is stored in the R variable g. Then, anova1 can be used by first using the R function

```
fac2list(x,g),
```

which was introduced in Section 9.2.3. This function sorts the data into groups based on the values in the second argument g and stores the results in an R variable having list mode that can be used with the R function anova1. The R function

```
split(x,g)
```

accomplishes the same goal.

Example

The last example is repeated using the R function anova1. The R commands are

```
z=fac2list(plasma[,10],plasma[,3])
anova1(z).
```

The first command says to take the data in column 10 of plasma and sort it into groups based on the corresponding values in column 3 of plasma. The first two lines of the output, based on the second command, resemble this:

```
$F.test
[1] 2.23471

$p.value
[1] 0.1087336
```

and are in agreement with the last example. Notice that there was no need to ensure that the R variable `plasma[,3]` is a factor variable.

A point worth stressing is that the R functions `aov` and `anova1` assume homoscedasticity—they have no option for handling unequal variances. This is a practical concern because violating the homoscedasticity assumption becomes an increasingly more serious problem as the number of groups increases. Sections 10.4.1 and 10.5.4 introduce R functions that are designed to handle unequal variances when comparing trimmed means that can be used to compare means as a special case.

10.1.2 When Does the ANOVA *F* Test Perform Well?

Similarly to the two-sample Student's *T* test in Chapter 9, if the *J* groups under study do not differ in any manner, meaning that all *J* groups have the same distribution, the ANOVA *F* test performs well in the sense that the actual Type I error probability will not exceed the specified level by very much. For example, if the goal is to have the Type I error probability equal to 0.05, the actual Type I error probability will, in general, be less than or equal to 0.05 when sampling from distributions that are nonnormal but otherwise identical. In particular, not only do the groups have equal means, they do not differ in terms of their variances or the amount of skewness. In practical terms, given the goal of controlling the probability of a Type I error, the ANOVA *F* test provides a satisfactory test of the hypothesis that *J* groups have identical distributions, meaning that if it rejects, it is reasonable to conclude that two or more groups differ in some manner.

But if the goal is to develop a test that is sensitive to means, without being sensitive to other ways the groups might differ, the ANOVA *F* test can be highly unsatisfactory. Indeed, the ANOVA *F* test suffers from problems similar to those described in Chapter 9 when using Student's *T* test. In fact, as the number of groups increases, practical problems are exacerbated. For example, in Chapter 9, it was noted that under normality, if the sample sizes are equal but the population variances differ, comparing two groups with Student's *T* controls the probability of a Type I error fairly well except possibly for very small sample sizes. But when comparing four groups with the ANOVA *F* test, this is no longer true.

Example

Suppose four groups are to be compared with equal sample sizes of 50 for each group. If all four groups have a normal distribution with a mean of 0, the first group has a standard deviation of 4, and the rest have a standard deviation of 1, the actual Type I error probability is approximately 0.088 when testing at the $\alpha = 0.05$ level. Nonnormality only makes matters worse. Although the seriousness of a Type I error depends on the situation, it has been suggested that if the goal is to have the Type I error probability equal to 0.05, at a minimum the actual Type I error probability should not exceed 0.075 (Bradley, 1978). To the extent this seems reasonable, the ANOVA F test is unsatisfactory for the situation at hand.

Perhaps, a more serious issue has to do with the ability of the ANOVA F test to detect true differences. There are situations where it performs well, such as when its underlying assumptions are true. But for a variety of reasons, it can have poor power relative to other methods that might be used. The basic reasons are the same as those illustrated in Chapter 9 when using Student's T. In fairness, situations are encountered where it makes little difference which method is used, but situations are encountered where the ANOVA F test does not come close to rejecting in contrast to more modern methods. Roughly, the more groups being compared, the more likely it is that relatively poor power will result when using the ANOVA F test due to differences in skewness, unequal variances, and outliers.

Example

Consider the following values for four groups.

Group 1: -0.89, 1.22, 1.03, 2.02, 1.41, 1.69, -1.48, 1.96, 0.44, 0.41, 1.71, 3.04, -0.63, 1.77, 2.50.

Group 2: 2.75, 0.26, 0.75, -1.52, 1.15, 1.00, 0.78, -0.01, 0.92, -0.68, 0.91, -0.41, 0.44, 0.43, 1.34.

Group 3: 0.12, -0.45, 0.37, -1.75, 1.31, 0.23, -0.53, 0.73, 0.54, -1.08, -0.65, -1.89, -0.53, 0.20, 0.09.

Group 4: 1.49, 0.10, 2.21, 0.90, -0.17, -0.84, 1.18, -0.64, -1.32, -0.89, 0.27, -0.93, 0.56, -0.27, -0.27.

These values were generated from normal distributions where the first group has a population mean of 1, and the other three have population means equal to 0. It can be seen that the ANOVA F test rejects with a Type I error probability set equal to $\alpha = 0.01$. (The p-value is 0.008.) That is, the F test makes a correct decision about whether the groups differ. But suppose one of the values in the fourth group happens to be an outlier. In particular, what if by chance the first observation in this group were 6 rather than 1.49. Now, the ANOVA F test no longer rejects with the Type I error probability set to $\alpha = 0.05$. Yet, had we compared the first three groups, ignoring the fourth, we would again reject with $\alpha = 0.01$. This illustrates that a single outlier in any group has the potential of masking true differences among the other groups, even if the other groups have normal distributions.

Example

Consider a situation where four normal distributions are to be compared, each has variance 1, the first group has mean 1, and the rest have means equal to 0. With a sample size of 15 from all four groups and the Type I error probability set at 0.05, the power of the F test is, approximately, 0.71. Now consider the same situation, only the fourth group has the mixed normal distribution shown in Figure 4.5, which is a bell-shaped, symmetric distribution with heavy tails (outliers are common). The population mean is again 0, but now the power of the F test is only 0.38. This illustrates that if the normality assumption is violated in even one group, true differences among the remaining groups can be missed as a result, even if they have normal distributions with a common variance.

Currently, the ANOVA F test is the most commonly used method when comparing multiple groups, so it is important to be aware of the method and have some sense of its relative merits. An argument for using the ANOVA F might be that there are conditions where it has relatively high power, possibly because it can be sensitive to differences among the groups that other methods tend to miss such as differences in variances or differences in the amount of skewness associated with the distributions being compared. Nevertheless, it is unrealistic to assume that the ANOVA F will have relatively high power—in many situations, some alternative method is much more likely to detect true differences.

One suggestion for trying to salvage the F test is to first test the hypothesis of equal variances, and if this hypothesis is not rejected, assume equal variances and use F. Chapter 9 pointed out that this strategy is known to fail when comparing two groups with Student's T. This strategy is again unsatisfactory when comparing more than two groups with the ANOVA F test, even when dealing with normal distributions (Markowski and Markowski, 1990; Moser et al., 1989; Wilcox et al., 1986; Zimmerman, 2004). The basic problem is that tests for equal variances do not have enough power to detect situations where violating the assumption of equal variances causes practical problems. Presumably, this is no longer true if the sample sizes are sufficiently large, but it is unclear just how large the sample sizes must be, particularly when dealing with nonnormal distributions.

10.2 DEALING WITH UNEQUAL VARIANCES: WELCH'S TEST

Many methods have been proposed for testing the equality of J means without assuming equal variances (e.g., Chen and Chen, 1998; Mehrotra, 1997; James, 1951; Krutchkoff, 1988; Alexander and McGovern, 1994; Fisher, 1935, 1941; Cochran and Cox, 1950; Wald, 1955; Asiribo and Gurland, 1989; Lee and Ahn, 2003; Scariano and Davenport, 1986; Matuszewski and Sotres, 1986; Pagurova, 1968; Weerahandi, 1995.) All of the methods just cited, plus many others, have been found to have serious practical problems (e.g., Keselman et al., 2000; Keselman and Wilcox, 1999). If the goal is to use a method that is sensitive to means, without being sensitive to other ways the groups might differ, the method described here is not completely satisfactory, but it performs reasonably well under normality and heteroscedasticity and it forms the basis of a technique that deals with nonnormality. The method is due to Welch (1951) and can be performed via the R function mentioned in Section 10.4.2 (cf. Fan and Hancock, 2012). Here are the computational details in case they are useful.

Denote the sample sizes by $n_1, \ldots, n_J$, the sample means by $\overline{X}_1, \ldots, \overline{X}_J$, and the sample variances by $s_1^2, \ldots, s_J^2$. Let

$$w_1 = \frac{n_1}{s_1^2}, w_2 = \frac{n_2}{s_2^2}, \ldots, w_J = \frac{n_J}{s_J^2}.$$

Next, compute

$$U = \sum w_j$$

$$\tilde{X} = \frac{1}{U} \sum w_j \overline{X}_j$$

$$A = \frac{1}{J-1} \sum w_j (\overline{X}_j - \tilde{X})^2$$

$$B = \frac{2(J-2)}{J^2 - 1} \sum \frac{(1 - \frac{w_j}{U})^2}{n_j - 1}$$

$$F_w = \frac{A}{1+B}.$$

When the null hypothesis is true, F_w has, approximately, an F distribution with

$$v_1 = J - 1$$

and

$$v_2 = \left[\frac{3}{J^2 - 1} \sum \frac{(1 - w_j/U)^2}{n_j - 1} \right]^{-1}$$

degrees of freedom.

Decision Rule: Reject the hypothesis of equal means if $F_w \geq f$, where f is the $1 - \alpha$ quantile of the F distribution with v_1 and v_2 degrees of freedom.

Example

Consider again the data used in the example where all four groups have normal distributions with a common variance. That is, the assumptions underlying the ANOVA F test are true. It can be seen that $F_w = 3.87$, the degrees of freedom are $v_1 = 3$ and $v_2 = 30.9$ and with $\alpha = 0.01$, the critical value is approximately 4.486. So, unlike the ANOVA F test, the hypothesis of equal means is not rejected. However, with $\alpha = 0.02$, now Welch's test rejects. The p-value for Welch's test is 0.018 compared to 0.008 when using the ANOVA F test. If the assumptions of the ANOVA F test are true, it will have better power than Welch's test, but generally the improvement is not that striking. However, when there is heteroscedasticity, Welch's test can detect a true difference among the means in situations where the ANOVA F does not, even when sampling from normal distributions.

Example

The following data illustrate that the ANOVA F and Welch's test can yield substantially different p-values, which can alter the decision about whether to reject the hypothesis of equal means.

Group 1: 53, 2, 34, 6, 7, 89, 9, 12
Group 2: 7, 34, 5, 12, 32, 36, 21, 22
Group 3: 5, 3, 7, 6, 5, 8, 4, 3

The ANOVA F test yields $F = 2.7$ with a critical value of 3.24 when the Type I error is taken to be $\alpha = 0.05$, so fail to reject. (The p-value is 0.09.) In contrast, Welch's test yields $F_w = 8$ with a critical value of 4.2, so now the hypothesis of equal means is rejected. (The p-value is 0.009.)

10.3   COMPARING GROUPS BASED ON MEDIANS

Many methods for comparing the medians of multiple groups have been derived. More formally, the goal is to test

$$H_0 : \theta_1 = \cdots = \theta_J, \qquad (10.4)$$

where $\theta_1, \ldots, \theta_J$ are the population medians. Relatively simple techniques have been proposed, but they can be rather unsatisfactory. Currently, there are two methods that seem to perform reasonably well, one of which can handle tied values. The first method uses the McKean–Schrader estimate of the standard errors in conjunction with a generalization of Welch's test. A method that performs well even when there are tied values uses a generalization of the percentile bootstrap in conjunction with an alternative estimate of the population median derived by Harrell and Davis (1982). See Wilcox (2015a) for computational details.

10.3.1   R Functions med1way and Qanova

The R function

```
med1way(x,alpha=0.05)
```

tests the hypothesis of equal medians using the McKean–Schrader estimate of the standard errors. The argument x can be a matrix or data frame with columns corresponding to groups, or it can have list mode. The function returns a test statistic, a critical value based on the Type I error probability indicated by the argument `alpha`, and a p-value. The null hypothesis is rejected if the test statistic is greater than or equal to the critical value. If there are tied values, this function should not be used.
      The R function

```
Qanova(x,q=0.5,nboot=600,MC=FALSE)
```

tests the hypothesis of equal medians using a generalization of the percentile bootstrap method. If there are tied values, this function should be used rather than med1way. Control over the Type I error probability is fairly good when every group has a sample size of 20 or more and there are no tied values. If tied values are common, sample sizes of 30 or more might be needed. Quantiles other than the median can be compared via the argument q. When comparing the quartiles and there are many tied values, the sample sizes should be at least 50. (For smaller sample sizes, use the R functions medpb and Qmcp described in Section 12.6.1.) The argument nboot indicates how many bootstrap samples are used. If a multicore processor is available, setting the argument MC=TRUE might reduce the execution time considerably. The function returns a p-value, an estimate of the population medians (or the estimate of the quantiles) and the sample sizes. (This function uses the Harrell–Davis estimator, which is better than the sample median when dealing with tied values.)

Example

Consider again the plasma retinol data used in the last example in Section 10.1.1. Comparing medians using the R commands

```
z=fac2list(plasma[,10],plasma[,3])
med1way(z),
```

the p-value is 0.25. But the function prints a warning message that there are tied values. Using, instead,

```
z=fac2list(plasma[,10],plasma[,3])
Qanova(z),
```

the p-value is 0.14, the point being that using a method that deals with tied values can make a practical difference. Section 9.9 noted that in some situations, differences in the tails of distributions occur that have practical importance. Moreover, significant differences among the upper and lower quantiles can be encountered even when no significant differences are found when comparing medians or a 20% trimmed mean. The situation at hand again illustrates that this can happen. Comparing the 0.75 quantiles with the R function Qanova by setting the argument q=0.75, the p-value is 0.017.

10.4   COMPARING TRIMMED MEANS

Welch's method is readily extended to trimmed means. A bootstrap-t method can be used as well. (For computational details, see, for example, Wilcox, 2012a, b.) These two methods can be applied with the R functions described in the next section.

10.4.1   R Functions t1way and t1waybt

The R function

$$\texttt{t1way(x,tr=0.2)}$$

tests the hypothesis of equal trimmed means using a generalization of Welch's test. To compare means, set the argument `tr=0`. The R function

$$\texttt{t1waybt(x,tr=0.2,nboot=599)}$$

uses a bootstrap-t method to test the hypothesis of equal trimmed means. The argument `nboot` indicates the number of bootstrap samples that will be used. The default value appears to control the Type I error probability reasonably well when comparing 20% trimmed means, but published papers (summarized in Wilcox, 2012b) indicate that a larger choice for `nboot` might result in more power.

Example

Consider again the plasma retinol example in Sections 10.1.1 and 10.3.1. The R commands

```
z=fac2list(plasma[,10],plasma[,3])
t1way(z,tr=0)
```

test the hypothesis that the means of the three groups are equal. The p-value is 0.134. The p-value based on the ANOVA F test is 0.109. Using a 20% trimmed mean, the p-value is 0.054, again illustrating that the choice of method can matter. (Boxplots indicate that all three groups have skewed distributions with outliers in the upper tails.) The p-value using the R function `t1waybt` is 0.068 using a 20% trimmed mean and the default number of bootstrap samples. With `nboot=999`, the p-value is 0.054.

10.5   TWO-WAY ANOVA

An important and commonly used generalization of the ANOVA F test has to do with what are called two-way designs. *One-way designs* refer to studies where multiple levels of a single factor are of interest. For example, a farmer might want to determine how different amounts of fertilizer affect the growth of her crops. If five amounts of fertilizer are under consideration, this reflects a one-way design because a single variable, amount of fertilizer, is being manipulated. There are five *levels* for this factor, which correspond to the five amounts of fertilizer that are under consideration. In the examples dealing with plasma retinol, described earlier in this chapter, there are three levels corresponding to three types of cigarette smokers.

A two-way design is similar to a one-way design, only two factors are of interest rather than just one. Consider, for example, a study aimed at understanding behavior when individuals diet in order to lose weight. In a study described by Atkinson et al. (1985) on a diet to lose weight and those who were not. So far, this is a one-way design with two levels. But the researchers wanted to understand the effects of a second factor: forced eating. Some participants were forced to consume two milk shakes, others had one milk shake, and a third group consumed no milk shakes at all. So now, we have a two-way design, where the second factor has three levels that reflect how many milk shakes were consumed. After consuming the milk shakes, the participants sampled several flavors of ice cream and were encouraged to eat as much as they wanted. The outcome measure of interest is the amount of ice cream consumed. It was found that the more milk shakes consumed by individuals not on a diet, the less ice cream they would consume later. In contrast, the dieters who had two milk shakes ate more ice cream than those who had drank one milk shake or none.

Here, the basic concepts of a two-way design are illustrated with a study where the goal is to understand the effect of diet on weight gains in rats. Specifically, four diets are considered which differ in the following: (1) amounts of protein (high and low) and (2) the source of the protein (beef and cereal). So, this is a two-way design with two levels for each factor. The results for these four groups are reported in Table 10.1 and are taken from Snedecor and Cochran (1967). Different rats were used in the four groups, so the groups are independent. The first column gives the weight gains of rats fed a low-protein diet with beef as the source of protein. The next column gives the weight gains for rats on a high-protein diet again with beef as the source of protein, and the next two columns report results when cereal is substituted for beef.

It is convenient to depict the population means as shown in Table 10.2. Table 10.2 indicates, for example, that μ_1 is the population mean associated with rats receiving a low-protein diet from beef. That is, μ_1 is the average weight gain if all of the millions of rats we might study are fed this diet. Similarly, μ_4 is the population mean for rats receiving a low-protein diet from cereal.

TABLE 10.1　Weight Gains (in Grams) for Rats on One of Four Diets

Beef Low	Beef High	Cereal Low	Cereal High
90	73	107	98
76	102	95	75
90	118	97	56
64	104	80	111
86	81	98	95
51	107	74	88
72	100	74	82
90	87	67	77
95	117	89	86
78	111	58	92

$\overline{X}_1 = 79.2, \overline{X}_2 = 100, \overline{X}_3 = 83.9, \overline{X}_4 = 85.9.$

TABLE 10.2   Depiction of the Population Means for Four Diets

		Source	
		Beef	Cereal
Amount	High	μ_1	μ_2
	Low	μ_3	μ_4

Rather than just compare the means of the four groups, often it is desired to compare the levels of each factor, ignoring the other. For example, how do the rats receiving a high-protein diet compare to those receiving a low-protein diet when the source of the protein is ignored? To illustrate how this might be done, imagine that the values of the population means are as follows:

		Source	
		Beef	Cereal
Amount	High	$\mu_1 = 45$	$\mu_2 = 60$
	Low	$\mu_3 = 80$	$\mu_4 = 90$

For rats on a high-protein diet, the population mean is 45 when consuming beef in contrast to 60 when consuming cereal. If the goal is to characterize the typical weight gain for a high-protein diet ignoring source, a natural strategy is to average the two population means, yielding $(45 + 60)/2 = 52.5$. That is, the typical rat on a protein diet gains 52.5 g.

For the more general situation depicted by Table 10.2, the typical weight gain on a high-protein diet would be $(\mu_1 + \mu_2)/2$, the average of the means over source of protein. Similarly, the typical weight gain for a rat on a low-protein diet would be $(\mu_3 + \mu_4)/2$, which in the example is $(80 + 90)/2 = 85$ g. Of course, the same can be done when dealing with the source of protein, ignoring the amount of protein. The typical weight gain for a rat eating beef, ignoring the amount of protein, is $(45 + 80)/2 = 62.5$, and for cereal, it is $(60 + 90)/2 = 75$.

What is needed is some way of testing the hypothesis that weight gain is different for a high-protein diet compared to a low-protein diet, ignoring the source of protein. One way of doing this is to test

$$H_0 : \frac{\mu_1 + \mu_2}{2} = \frac{\mu_3 + \mu_4}{2},$$

the hypothesis that the average of the populations means when the source of protein is beef is equal to the average for cereal. If this hypothesis is rejected, then there is said to be a *main effect* for the amount of protein. More generally, a main effect for the first factor (amount) is said to exist if

$$\frac{\mu_1 + \mu_2}{2} \neq \frac{\mu_3 + \mu_4}{2}.$$

Similarly, the goal might be to compare source of protein, ignoring the amount. One approach is to test

$$H_0 : \frac{\mu_1 + \mu_3}{2} = \frac{\mu_2 + \mu_4}{2},$$

the hypothesis that the average of the means in the column for beef is equal to the average for the column headed by cereal. If this hypothesis is rejected, there is said to be a **main effect** for the source of protein. More generally, a main effect for the second factor is said to exist if

$$\frac{\mu_1 + \mu_3}{2} \neq \frac{\mu_2 + \mu_4}{2}.$$

10.5.1 Interactions

There is one other important feature of a two-way design. Consider again the situation where the goal is to compare high- and low-protein diets in conjunction with two protein sources. Suppose the *population* means associated with the four groups have the values indicated in the previous section. Look at the first row (high amount of protein) and notice that the weight gain for a beef diet is 45 g compared to a weight gain of 60 g for cereal. As is evident, there is an increase of 15 g. Now, look at a low-protein diet. Switching from beef to cereal results in an increase of 10 g on average. That is, in general, switching from beef to cereal results in an increase for the average amount of weight gained, but the increase differs depending on whether we look at high or low protein. This is an example of what is called an *interaction*.

More formally, an *interaction* is said to exist if

$$\mu_1 - \mu_2 \neq \mu_3 - \mu_4.$$

In words, an interaction exists if for the first level of factor A the difference between the means is not equal to the difference between the means associated with the second level of factor A. *No interaction* means that these differences are equal. In symbols, no interaction means that

$$\mu_1 - \mu_2 = \mu_3 - \mu_4.$$

The basic ideas just described have been extended to more complex situations where the first factor has J levels and the second has K levels. Consider, for example, a study of survival times of animals given one of three poisons. This is the first factor, which has $J = 3$ levels. Further imagine that four methods aimed at treating the animals are of interest. This is the second factor, which has $K = 4$ levels. This type of design is called a J-by-K design. In the example, we have a 3-by-4 design.

TABLE 10.3 Commonly Used Notation for the Means in a J-by-K ANOVA

	Factor B			
	μ_{11}	μ_{12}	$\cdots$	μ_{1K}
	μ_{21}	μ_{22}	$\cdots$	μ_{2K}
Factor A	$\vdots$	$\vdots$	$\vdots$	$\vdots$
	μ_{J1}	μ_{J2}	$\cdots$	μ_{JK}

To describe a common approach to analyzing *J*-by-*K* designs, imagine that the population means are labeled as shown in Table 10.3. So, for example, μ_{11} is the mean of the group associated with the first level of the first and second factors. The mean corresponding to the third level of factor A and the fourth level of factor B is denoted by μ_{34}. The following example provides some indication of how the groups are often compared.

Example

Consider again the 3-by-4 design where the first factor corresponds to three types of poison and the second factor reflects four types of treatments. Using the notation in Table 10.3, μ_{11} is the mean survival time when an animal is exposed to the first poison and is given the first treatment. Similarly, μ_{12} is the mean survival time when an animal is exposed to the first poison and is given the second treatment. The *marginal mean* survival time when exposed to the first poison is just the average of the means among the four treatments. That is, the marginal mean is

$$\bar{\mu}_{1.} = \frac{\mu_{11} + \mu_{12} + \mu_{13} + \mu_{14}}{4}.$$

In a similar manner, the marginal means for the second and third poisons are

$$\bar{\mu}_{2.} = \frac{\mu_{21} + \mu_{22} + \mu_{23} + \mu_{24}}{4}$$

and

$$\bar{\mu}_{3.} = \frac{\mu_{31} + \mu_{32} + \mu_{33} + \mu_{34}}{4}.$$

A common way of comparing the levels of factor A, ignoring factor B, is to test the hypothesis that the marginal means are equal. In symbols, test

$$H_0 : \bar{\mu}_{1.} = \bar{\mu}_{2.} = \bar{\mu}_{3.}.$$

When this hypothesis is rejected, it is said that there is a main effect for factor A. In the example, this means that typical survival times, ignoring treatment, differ.

As is probably evident, comparing levels of factor B, ignoring factor A, can be handled in a similar manner. Now, for each level of factor B, the strategy is to consider the average of the population means over the levels of factor A. Then, the goal is to test the hypothesis that the resulting marginal means are equal.

Example

Consider again the previous example, only now the goal is to compare treatments, ignoring the type of poison. For each type of treatment, the average survival times over the type of poison are

$$\overline{\mu}_{.1} = \frac{\mu_{11} + \mu_{21} + \mu_{31}}{3}$$

$$\overline{\mu}_{.2} = \frac{\mu_{12} + \mu_{22} + \mu_{32}}{3}$$

$$\overline{\mu}_{.3} = \frac{\mu_{13} + \mu_{23} + \mu_{33}}{3}$$

and

$$\overline{\mu}_{.4} = \frac{\mu_{14} + \mu_{24} + \mu_{34}}{3}.$$

Then, a natural way of comparing treatments, ignoring the type of poison, is to test

$$H_0 : \overline{\mu}_{0.1} = \overline{\mu}_{0.2} = \overline{\mu}_{0.3} = \overline{\mu}_{0.4}.$$

Finally, there is the issue of interactions for the more general case of a J-by-K ANOVA design. An interaction is said to exist if there is an interaction for any two levels of factor A and any two levels of factor B.

Example

Continuing the previous two examples, consider the first and third levels of factor A. That is, focus on survival times when dealing with the first and third types of poison. Simultaneously, consider the second and fourth types of treatments. So, we are considering four means:

$$\mu_{12} \quad \mu_{14}$$

$$\mu_{32} \quad \mu_{34}$$

Extending the earlier description of an interaction in an obvious way, if $\mu_{12} - \mu_{14} = \mu_{32} - \mu_{34}$, there is no interaction among these four means. If instead $\mu_{12} - \mu_{14} \neq \mu_{32} - \mu_{34}$, there is an interaction. More generally, no interaction is said to exist if for any two levels of factor A, say j and j', and any two levels of factor B, say k and k',

$$\mu_{jk} - \mu_{jk'} = \mu_{j'k} - \mu_{j'k'}.$$

Example

Imagine that unknown to us, the population means are as follows:

		Factor B			
		Level 1	Level 2	Level 3	Level 4
	Level 1	40	40	50	60
Factor A	Level 2	20	20	50	80
	Level 3	20	30	10	40

Look at level 1 of factor A and note that the means increase by 0 as we move from level 1 of factor B to level 2. Now look at level 2 of factor A. Again, the increase is 0 between levels 1 and 2 of factor B. So for these four groups, there is no interaction. However, look again at level 1 of factor A, only now focus on levels 1 and 3 of factor B: the means increase by 10 as we move from level 1 to level 3 of factor B. In contrast, for level 2 of factor A, there is an increase of 30, which means that there is an interaction.

The focus has been on understanding what is meant by no main effects and no interactions in a two-way ANOVA design. But nothing has been said about how to test the hypotheses that there are no main effects and no interactions. Suffice it to say that these hypotheses can be tested using what are called ANOVA F tests, which assume both normality and homoscedasticity. For brevity, the tedious computational details are not provided. But an R function for performing these tests is described and illustrated in the next section. (For a detailed description of classic methods based on normality and homoscedasticity, including a wide range of experimental designs beyond what is covered here, see Kirk, 2013.)

10.5.2   R Functions anova and aov

The built-in R function anova can be used when the goal is to test the hypothesis of no main effects or no interaction in a two-way design assuming normality and homoscedasticity.

Example

Consider again the plasma retinol data and imagine that the goal is to compare groups based on two factors: sex (stored in column 2 of the R variable plasma) and smoking status (stored in column 3) in terms of the amount of cholesterol consumed (stored in column 10). When using the R function aov, connecting factors by * means that R will test the hypothesis of no main effects as well as no interactions. For convenience, assume that the data are stored in the R variable y. Then, the following command can be used:

```
anova(aov(y[,10] ~ as.factor(y[,2]) * as.factor(y[,3])))
```

Note that this R command was written to ensure that both y[,2] and y[,3] are treated as factor variables. The output resembles this:

```
Analysis of Variance Table

Response: y[, 10]    Df  Sum Sq Mean Sq F value     Pr(>F)
as.factor(y[, 2])     1  355619  355619 21.9853 4.128e-06
as.factor(y[, 3])     2   45637   22819  1.4107    0.2455
as.factor(y[, 2]):as.factor(y[, 3])
                      2   71014   35507  2.1951    0.1131
Residuals           309 4998170   16175
```

The line beginning with as.factor(y[, 2]) reports the results for the first factor. The p-value, which is in the column headed by $\Pr(> F)$, is 4.128e-06 =4.128 $\times 10^{-6}$. The line beginning with as.factor(y[, 3]) reports the results for the second factor, which has a p-value of 0.2455. So, in particular, no differences are found among the three levels of smoking status when testing at the 0.05 level. The line starting with as.factor(y[, 2]):as.factor(y[, 3]) reports the results when testing the hypothesis of no interaction; the p-value is 0.1131.

As previously noted, the * in this last R command indicates that an interaction term in the model will be used. If the * is replaced with a +, in which case the R command is now

anova(aov(y[,10] ~ as.factor(y[,2]) + as.factor(y[,3]))),

this indicates that an *additive model* will be used. That is, the hypotheses of no main effects will be performed assuming that there is no interaction. It is sometimes recommended that if the hypothesis of no interaction is not rejected, main effects should be tested assuming that the model is additive. However, results reported by Fabian (1991) do not support this strategy. The problem is that power might not be sufficiently high to justify accepting the hypothesis of no interaction.

10.5.3 Violating Assumptions

The two-way ANOVA F test assumes normality and equal variances. As was the case for the one-way design, violating these assumptions can result in the test being sensitive to features other than differences among the means. Problems do not always arise, but it is unrealistic to assume that this issue can be ignored. As before, the ANOVA F test can provide an indication that groups differ, but it might not adequately isolate the nature of the difference. As usual, power can be relatively low compared to more modern methods. There are methods aimed at allowing unequal variances, which include extensions of Welch's test based on trimmed means. Comparing trimmed means can result in better control over the Type I error probability when the goal is to be sensitive to differences in measures of location without being sensitive to other differences such as heteroscedasticity and differences in skewness. Increased power is another possibility when using trimmed means. The computational details are not provided, but R functions for comparing trimmed means are described in the next section.

10.5.4   R Functions t2way and t2waybt

The R function

$$t2way(J,K,x,tr=0.2)$$

tests the hypothesis of no main effects and no interaction using trimmed means. Homoscedasticity is not assumed. The arguments J and K indicate how many levels are associated with the first and second factors, respectively. To compare means, set the argument tr=0. The data are assumed to be stored such that the first K groups are the groups associated with the first level of first factor and the K levels of the second factor. The next K groups are the groups associated with the second level of the first factor and the K levels of the second factor, and so on. If, for example, the data are stored in the R variable x having list mode, and a 2-by-4 design is being used, the data are assumed to be arranged follows:

	Factor B			
Factor	x[[1]]	x[[2]]	x[[3]]	x[[4]]
A	x[[5]]	x[[6]]	x[[7]]	x[[8]]

where factor A is the first factor and factor B is the second factor. For instance, x[[5]] contains the data for the second level of factor A and the first level of factor B. If the data are stored in a matrix, the first K columns are assumed to be the data for the first level of factor A, the next K columns are assumed to be data for the second level of factor A, and so on.

The R function

$$t2waybt(J,K,x,tr=0.2,nboot=599)$$

uses a bootstrap-t method to test the hypothesis of equal trimmed means with data arranged in x as just described in connection with t2way.

The R functions in this section do not accept a formula. But the R function fac2list, illustrated in Section 10.4.1, can again be used to sort the data into groups.

Example

Consider again the plasma retinol example in Sections 10.1.1 and 10.3.1, only now a two-way design is used where the first factor is gender, stored in column 2 of plasma, and the second factor is smoking status, which is stored in column 3. Testing the hypotheses that there are no main effects and no interaction, using means, can be accomplished with the following R commands:

```
z=fac2list(plasma[,10],plasma[,2:3])
t2way(2,3,z,tr=0).
```

The first command sorts the data in column 10 (amount of cholesterol consumed) into groups based on gender and smoking status and stores the results in z with the groups ordered as expected by the R function t2way. The output from the second command resembles this:

```
$Qa
[1]  19.76396

$A.$p$.value
[1]  0.001

$Qb
[1]  5.51092

$B.$p$.value
[1]  0.092

$Qab
[1]  3.643692

$AB.$p$.value
[1]  0.195
```

So, the test statistic for factor A is Qa=19.76396 and the corresponding p-value is 0.001, indicating that there is a significant difference between males and females, ignoring smoking status. When testing at the 0.05 level, no significant difference is found based on smoking status, ignoring gender; the p-value is 0.092. For the hypothesis of no interaction, the p-value is 0.195.

10.6   RANK-BASED METHODS

As mentioned in the previous chapters, a possible appeal of rank-based methods is that they are insensitive to outliers, which might translate into more power compared to a method based on means. Perhaps, the most important thing to keep in mind is that they are sensitive to different features of the data compared to methods based on measures of location such as the mean, 20% trimmed mean, and median.

10.6.1   The Kruskal–Wallis Test

The best-known rank-based method for comparing multiple groups is the Kruskal–Wallis test. The goal is to test the hypothesis that J independent groups have identical distributions. A crude description of the method is that it is designed to be sensitive to differences among the ranks corresponding to the groups being compared.

For J independent groups with sample sizes $n_1, \ldots, n_J$, the method begins by pooling all $N = \sum n_j$ observations and assigning ranks. In symbols, if X_{ij} is the ith observation in the jth group, let R_{ij} be its rank among the pooled data. When there are tied values, use midranks as described in Section 9.6.1. Next, sum the ranks for each group. In symbols, compute

$$R_j = \sum_{i=1}^{n_j} R_{ij},$$

$(j = 1, \ldots, J)$. Letting

$$S^2 = \frac{1}{N-1} \left(\sum_{j=1}^{J} \sum_{i=1}^{n_j} R_{ij}^2 - \frac{N(N+1)^2}{4} \right),$$

the test statistic is

$$T = \frac{1}{S^2} \left(-\frac{N(N+1)^2}{4} + \sum \frac{R_j^2}{n_j} \right).$$

If there are no tied values, S^2 simplifies to

$$S^2 = \frac{N(N+1)}{12},$$

and T becomes

$$T = -3(N+1) + \frac{12}{N(N+1)} \sum \frac{R_j^2}{n_j}.$$

Decision Rule: The hypothesis of identical distributions is rejected if $T \geq c$, where c is some appropriate critical value. For small sample sizes, exact critical values are available from Iman et al. (1975). For large sample sizes, the critical value is approximately equal to the $1 - \alpha$ quantile of a chi-squared distribution with $J - 1$ degrees of freedom, which can be read from Table B.3 in Appendix B.

Regarding Table B.3 in Appendix B, notice the terms in the top row. The subscripts denote the quantiles. For example, under $\chi_{0.10}^2$ and in the first row where $v = 1$, you will see the entry 0.01579. This means that for a chi-squared distribution with 1 degree of freedom, the probability of getting a value less than or equal to 0.01579 is 0.1. Similarly, under $\chi_{0.975}^2$ and in the row corresponding to $v = 10$ is the entry 20.48. That is, the probability of getting a value less than or equal to 20.48, when sampling from a chi-squared distribution with 10 degree of freedom, is 0.975. So, for the situation at hand, if the goal is to have a Type I error probability $\alpha = 0.025$ when comparing $J = 11$ groups, the critical value would be $c = 20.48$.

Example

Table 10.4 shows data for three groups and the corresponding ranks. For example, after pooling all $N = 10$ values, $X_{11} = 40$ has a rank of $R_{11} = 1$, the value 56 has a rank of 6, and so forth. The sum of the ranks corresponding to each group are $R_1 = 1 + 6 + 2 = 9$, $R_2 = 3 + 7 + 8 = 18$, and $R_3 = 9 + 10 + 5 + 4 = 28$. The number of groups is $J = 3$, so the degrees of freedom are $v = 2$, and from Table B.3

TABLE 10.4   Hypothetical Data Illustrating the Kruskal–Wallis Test

\ Group 1		Group 2		Group 3	
X_{i1}	R_{i1}	X_{i2}	R_{i2}	X_{i3}	R_{i3}
40	1	45	3	61	9
56	6	58	7	65	10
42	2	60	8	55	5
				47	4

in Appendix B, the critical value is approximately $c = 5.99$ with $\alpha = 0.05$. Because there are no tied values among the N observations,

$$T = -3(10 + 1) + \frac{12}{10 \times 11} \left(\frac{9^2}{3} + \frac{18^2}{3} + \frac{28^2}{4} \right) = 3.109.$$

Because $3.109 < 5.99$, fail to reject. That is, no difference among the distributions is detected.

10.6.2   Method BDM

The Kruskal–Wallis test performs relatively well when the null hypothesis of identical distributions is true, but concerns arise when the null hypothesis is false, particularly in terms of power. An improvement on the Kruskal–Wallis test, which allows tied values as well as differences in dispersion, was derived by Brunner et al. (1997) and will be called method BDM. Again, the goal is to test the hypothesis that all J groups have identical distributions. The basic idea is that if J independent groups have identical distributions and ranks are assigned to the pooled data as was done in the Kruskal–Wallis test, then the average of the ranks corresponding to the J groups should be approximately equal. (This greatly oversimplifies the technical issues.) Method BDM is not a satisfactory test of the hypothesis of equal medians as illustrated in Section 10.7.

To apply method BDM, compute the ranks of the pooled data as was done by the Kruskal–Wallis test. Again let $N = \sum n_j$ be the total number of observations and let R_{ij} be the rank of X_{ij} after the data are pooled. Let

$$\bar{R}_j = \frac{1}{n_j} \sum_{i=1}^{n_j} R_{ij}$$

be the average of the ranks corresponding to the jth group, and let

$$Q = \frac{1}{N} \left(\bar{R}_1 - \frac{1}{2}, \ldots, \bar{R}_J - \frac{1}{2} \right).$$

The values given by Q are called the *relative effects* and reflect how the groups compare based on the average ranks. The test statistic used by method BDM is based on a function of Q that has, approximately, an F distribution. The remaining calculations are not important for present purposes, so these are not described. Readers interested in these details are referred to Brunner et al. (1997) as well as Wilcox (2012a, Section 10.8).

10.7   R FUNCTIONS kruskal.test AND bdm

The built-in R function

$$kruskal.test(x,g, \ldots)$$

performs the Kruskal–Wallis test, where x contains the data and g is a factor variable. If the data are stored in x having list mode, the R command

```
kruskal.test(x)
```

is all that is required. If the data are stored in a matrix, with columns corresponding to groups, use the command

```
kruskal.test(listm(x)).
```

If there is a factor variable, a formula can be used. That is, the function can have the form

```
kruskal.test(x ~ g).
```

The R function

$$bdm(x)$$

performs method BDM, where again the argument x can be a matrix or a data frame with J columns, or it can have a list mode.

Example

Imagine that six groups are being compared, four have a standard normal distribution and two have a normal distribution with mean zero and standard deviation 5. So, the population means and medians are equal, but the distributions have different variances. With a sample size of $n = 500$ for each group and the Type I error probability set equal to 0.05, the Kruskal–Wallis test rejects with probability 0.082 and BDM rejects with probability 0.063. So in this particular case, despite the fact that the distributions differ, both methods are relatively insensitive to the differences that exist.

Example

Imagine that four groups have distributions that are skewed with a median of zero, where the distributions have the same shape as the distribution in Figure 9.1. Also imagine that two other groups have a standard normal distribution. So, all six distributions have a median equal to zero, but they differ in other ways. With a sample size of $n = 500$ for each group and the Type I error probability set equal to 0.05, both the Kruskal–Wallis test and BDM reject with probability 0.98. That is, both methods have a high probability of detecting the difference among the distributions, but the differences have nothing to do with the medians. Moreover, if the goal is to control the probability of a Type I error given the goal of testing the hypothesis of equal medians, both methods are completely unsatisfactory: the probability of rejecting should be 0.05 because the null hypothesis is true.

Example

Consider again the plasma retinol data with the goal of comparing three groups based on smoking status. The command

kruskal.test(plasma[,10] ~ plasma[,3])

indicates that the p-value is 0.059 based on the Kruskal–Wallis test. The commands

```
z=fac2list(plasma[,10],plasma[,3])
bdm(z)
```

apply the BDM method. The resulting p-value is 0.111.

10.8 SUMMARY

- The classic ANOVA F tests in this chapter are aimed at comparing groups based on means, assuming normality and homoscedasticity. In terms of controlling the probability of a Type I error, they perform well when all groups have identical distributions. That is, not only are the means equal, the variances are equal, groups have the same amount of skewness, and so on.
- If the ANOVA F tests in this chapter reject, it is reasonable to conclude that two or more of the groups differ in some manner. But because the methods are sensitive to more than just differences among the means, there is uncertainty about how groups differ when an ANOVA F test rejects. Also, the methods in this chapter do not indicate which groups differ. (This issue is addressed in Chapter 12.)
- Generally, the more groups that are compared, the more sensitive the ANOVA F becomes to differences among the groups beyond differences among the means. That is, if the goal is to control the Type I error probability when testing the

hypothesis of equal means, the ANOVA F test becomes increasingly unsatisfactory as the number of groups increases.

- When comparing means, with the goal of being sensitive to differences among the means without being sensitive to other ways the groups might differ, heteroscedastic methods are generally better than homoscedastic methods in terms of both the Type I error probability and power.

- If the goal is to compare groups in a manner that is sensitive to measures of location (such as the median), without being sensitive to other differences that might exist, methods based on a 20% trimmed mean or median perform relatively well compared to methods based on the mean. In particular, in terms of controlling the Type I error probability, methods based on 20% trimmed means or medians perform well over a broader range of situations than methods based on means. Keep in mind, however, that for skewed distributions, comparing medians, or trimmed means is not the same as comparing means. Also, there are several perspectives that have practical value beyond using trimmed means and medians as indicated in Chapter 9. (The methods in Chapter 12 also help when dealing with more than two groups.)

- As is the case with all methods based on means, when using the methods in this chapter, power might be low relative to other methods that have been developed in recent years. But the methods designed for comparing means are routinely used, so they are important to know.

- The rank-based methods in this chapter guard against low power due to outliers. When these methods reject, it is reasonable to conclude that the distributions differ, but if the goal is to compare groups in terms of the medians, or some other measure of location, these methods are unsatisfactory. It was illustrated, for example, that when the population medians are equal, but distributions differ in other ways, rank-based methods can have a high probability of rejecting. If the goal is to control the probability of a Type I error when comparing medians, methods based on a direct estimate of the population median, which were described in Section 10.3, are better than rank-based techniques.

10.9   EXERCISES

1. Consider the following data:

Group 1	Group 2	Group 3
3	4	6
5	4	7
2	3	8
4	8	6
8	7	7
4	4	9
3	2	10
9	5	9

$$\overline{X}_1 = 4.75 \qquad \overline{X}_2 = 4.62 \qquad \overline{X}_3 = 7.75$$
$$s_1^2 = 6.214 \qquad s_2^2 = 3.982 \qquad s_3^2 = 2.214$$

Assume that the three groups have a common population variance, σ_p^2. Estimate σ_p^2.

2. For the data in the previous exercise, use R to test the hypothesis of equal means using the ANOVA F test with $\alpha = 0.05$.

3. For the data in Exercise 1, verify that Welch's test statistic is $F_w = 7.7$ with degrees of freedom $v_1 = 2$ and $v_2 = 13.4$. Then, verify that you would reject the hypothesis of equal means with $\alpha = 0.01$.

4. Using R, test the hypothesis of equal means using the ANOVA F test for the following data.

Group 1	Group 2	Group 3	Group 4
15	9	17	13
17	12	20	12
22	15	23	17

5. In the previous exercise, use the R command `apply` (described in Section 1.3.3) to compute an estimate of the assumed common variance.

6. For the data used in the last two exercises, use R to verify that the p-value based on Welch's test is 0.124.

7. For the data in Exercise 4, explain why you would get the same result using a 20% trimmed mean.

8. Why would you not recommend the strategy of testing for equal variances, and if not significant, using the ANOVA F test rather than Welch's method?

9. Five independent groups are compared with $n = 15$ observations for each group, SSBG=20 and SSWG=150. Perform the ANOVA F test with $\alpha = 0.05$.

10. Use the R function `anova1` to verify that for the following data, MSBG $= 14.4$ and MSWG $= 12.59$.

G1	G2	G3
9	16	7
10	8	6
15	13	9
	6	

11. Consider five groups ($J = 5$) with population means 3, 4, 5, 6, and 7, and a common variance $\sigma_p^2 = 2$. If the number of observations in each group is 10 ($n = 10$), indicate what is being estimated by MSBG, and based on the

information given, determine its value. That is, if the population means and common variance were known, what is the value being estimated by MSBG? How does this differ from the value estimated by MSWG?

12. For the following data, verify that ANOVA F test does not reject with $\alpha = 0.05$, but Welch's test does reject.

   Group 1: 10, 11, 12, 9, 8, 7

   Group 2: 10, 66, 15, 32, 22, 51

   Group 3: 1, 12, 42, 31, 55, 19

   What might explain the discrepancy between the two methods?

13. Using the ANOVA F test, you see that $v_1 = 5$ and $v_2 = 8$. Verify that the number of groups is $J = 4$ and the total number of observations is $N = 12$.

14. A researcher reports a p-value of 0.001 with the ANOVA F test. Describe what conclusions are reasonable based on this result.

15. Summarize the reasons you might fail to reject with the ANOVA F test.

16. Someone tests for equal variances and fails to reject. Does this justify the use of the ANOVA F test? Why?

17. A researcher reports that a test for normality was performed and that based on this test, no evidence of nonnormality was found. Why might it be unreasonable to assume normality despite this result?

18. Outline how you might construct an example where sampling is from normal distributions, Welch's test rejects, but the ANOVA F test does not.

19. Consider a 2-by-2 design with population means

		Factor B	
		Level 1	Level 2
	Level 1	$\mu_1 = 110$	$\mu_2 = 70$
Factor A			
	Level 2	$\mu_3 = 80$	$\mu_4 = 40$

State whether there is a main effect for factor A, for factor B, and whether there is an interaction.

20. Consider a 2-by-2 design with population means

		Factor B	
		Level 1	Level 2
	Level 1	$\mu_1 = 10$	$\mu_2 = 20$
Factor A			
	Level 2	$\mu_3 = 40$	$\mu_4 = 10$

State whether there is a main effect for factor A, for factor B, and an interaction.

21. For the data in the last example of Section 10.1 (used to illustrate the ANOVA F test), use the R function med1way to test the hypothesis that the population medians are equal.

22. Repeat the previous exercise with the R function Qanova. Comment on why this R function is preferable to med1way and indicate any practical concerns associated with Qanova.

23. For the data used in the last two exercises, what is the p-value using the R function t1way with 20% trimming?

24. For the data used in Exercise 21, use R to apply the Kruskal–Wallis test and method BDM with $\alpha = 0.05$ and interpret the results.

11

COMPARING DEPENDENT GROUPS

Chapters 9 and 10 focused on comparing independent groups. But often, dependent groups are compared instead. Imagine, for example, that a training program for increasing endurance is under investigation, the endurance of participants is measured before training starts, they undergo the training program for 4 weeks, and then their endurance is measured again. This is an example of what is called a *repeated measures* or *within subjects* design, simply meaning that the same individuals are repeatedly measured over time. An issue is whether there has been a change in the average endurance, but because the same participants are measured both before and after training, it is unreasonable to assume that these two measures are independent. If they are dependent, Welch's test and the two-sample Student's T test for comparing means, described in Chapter 9, are no longer valid. (They use the wrong standard error.)

As another example, consider again the study where the goal is to assess the effects of ozone on weight gain among rats. Now, however, rather than randomly sampling rats, pairs of rats from the same litter are sampled, one is assigned to the ozone-free group and the other is exposed to ozone. Because these pairs of rats are related, it is unreasonable to assume that their reactions to their environment are independent.

As a final example, consider the issue of whether men differ from women in terms of their optimism about the future of the economy. If married couples are sampled and measured, it is unreasonable to assume that a woman's response is independent of her husband's views.

Understanding and Applying Basic Statistical Methods Using R, First Edition. Rand R. Wilcox.
© 2017 John Wiley & Sons, Inc. Published 2017 by John Wiley & Sons, Inc.
www.wiley.com/go/Wilcox/Statistical_Methods_R

There are many ways two dependent groups might be compared, only a few of which are covered here. Here is a list of the more basic strategies that are described in this chapter:

1. Use some measure of location, such as the mean or median.
2. Compare measures of variation.
3. Focus on the probability that for a randomly sampled pair of observations, the first observation is less than the second observation.
4. Use a rank-based method to test the hypothesis that the distributions are identical.

11.1 THE PAIRED T TEST

There is a simple method for comparing the means of two dependent groups called the *paired T test*. The method is based on n randomly sampled pairs of observations:

$$(X_{11}, X_{12}), (X_{21}, X_{22}), \cdots, (X_{n1}, X_{n2}), \tag{11.1}$$

where each pair of observations might be dependent. These n pairs of values might represent, for example, n married couples, where $X_{11}, \cdots, X_{n1}$ denotes the responses given by the wives and $X_{12}, \cdots, X_{n2}$ are the responses given by their spouse. Next, form the *difference scores*. That is, for each pair of observations, take their difference and denote the results by

$$
\begin{aligned}
D_1 &= X_{11} - X_{12} \\
D_2 &= X_{21} - X_{22} \\
D_3 &= X_{31} - X_{32} \\
&\vdots \\
D_n &= X_{n1} - X_{n2}.
\end{aligned}
$$

Let $\overline{X}_1$ and $\overline{X}_2$ represent the sample mean for the first group (wives in the example) and the second group (husbands), respectively, and let $\overline{D}$ denote the mean of the differences. It is readily verified that

$$\overline{D} = \overline{X}_1 - \overline{X}_2.$$

Moreover, if the population means corresponding to $\overline{X}_1, \overline{X}_2$, and $\overline{D}$ are denoted by μ_1, μ_2, and μ_D, respectively, then

$$\mu_D = \mu_1 - \mu_2.$$

The goal is to test

$$H_0 : \mu_1 = \mu_2, \tag{11.2}$$

which is the same as testing

$$H_0 : \mu_D = 0. \tag{11.3}$$

Assumption: The difference scores, D, have a normal distribution.

The paired T test consists of applying the one-sample T test in Section 7.3 using the difference scores D. In the notation used here, compute

$$\bar{D} = \frac{1}{n} \sum_{i=1}^{n} D_i$$

and

$$s_D^2 = \frac{1}{n-1} \sum_{i=1}^{n} (D_i - \bar{D})^2.$$

The test statistic is

$$T_D = \frac{\bar{D}}{s_D/\sqrt{n}}.$$

Assuming that D has a normal distribution, the critical value is t, the $1 - \alpha/2$ quantile of Student's T distribution with $v = n - 1$ degrees of freedom.

Decision Rule: The hypothesis of equal means is rejected if $|T_D| \geq t$.

Confidence Interval: A $1 - \alpha$ confidence interval for $\mu_D = \mu_1 - \mu_2$, the difference between the means, is

$$\bar{D} \pm t \frac{s_D}{\sqrt{n}}.$$

As just indicated, the paired T test has $n - 1$ degrees of freedom. If the two groups are independent, Student's T test (in Section 9.1.1) has $2(n - 1)$ degrees of freedom, twice as many as the paired T test. This means that if the two variables being compared are independent, the T test in Section 9.1.1 will have more power than the paired T test. However, if Pearson's correlation for the two variables being compared is sufficiently high, the paired T test will have more power. For normal distributions, a rough guideline is that when Pearson's correlation, ρ, is greater than 0.25, the paired T test will have more power (Vonesh, 1983). The extent to which this result applies when dealing with nonnormal distributions is unclear.

Example

A company wants to know whether a particular treatment reduces the amount of bacteria in milk. To find out, counts of bacteria were made before and after the treatment is applied, resulting in the outcomes shown in Table 11.1. For instance, based on the first sample, the bacteria count before treatment is $X_{11} = 6.98$, after the treatment it is $X_{12} = 6.95$, so the reduction in the bacteria count is $D_1 = 0.03$. The goal is to determine whether, on average, the reduction differs from zero. The sample mean of the difference scores (the D_i values) is $\bar{D} = 0.258$. The sample variance of the difference scores is $s_D^2 = 0.12711$. Because the sample size is $n = 12$, $T = 2.5$ and the degrees of freedom are $v = 12 - 1 = 11$. With $\alpha = 0.05$, the critical value is $t = 2.2$, so reject. That is, there is evidence that the treatment results in a reduction in the bacteria count, on average, assuming that the difference scores have a normal distribution.

TABLE 11.1   Bacteria Counts Before and After Treatment

Sample (i)	Before Treatment (X_{i1})	After Treatment (X_{i2})	Difference $D_i = X_{i1} - X_{i2}$
1	6.98	6.95	0.03
2	7.08	6.94	0.14
3	8.34	7.17	1.17
4	5.30	5.15	0.15
5	6.26	6.28	−0.02
6	6.77	6.81	−0.04
7	7.03	6.59	0.44
8	5.56	5.34	0.22
9	5.97	5.98	−0.01
10	6.64	6.51	0.13
11	7.03	6.84	0.19
12	7.69	6.99	0.70

11.1.1   When Does the Paired T Test Perform Well?

The good news about the paired T test is that if the observations in the first group (the X_{i1} values) have the same population distribution as the observations in the second group, so in particular they have equal means, variances, and the same amount of skewness, generally Type I error probabilities substantially higher than the nominal level can be avoided. The reason is that for this special case, the difference scores (the D_i values) have a symmetric (population) distribution in which case methods based on means perform reasonably well in terms of avoiding Type I error probabilities substantially higher than the nominal level. However, when the two distributions differ in some manner, at some point this is no longer true. Again, arbitrarily small departures from normality can destroy power, even when comparing groups having symmetric distributions. If the goal is to test the hypothesis that the two variables under study have identical distributions, the paired T test is satisfactory in terms of Type I errors. But when it rejects, there is doubt as to whether this is primarily due to the difference between the means or some other way the distributions differ. With a large enough sample size, these concerns become negligible, but just how large the sample size must be is difficult to determine.

A way of reducing concerns about nonnormality is to use a bootstrap-t method, but consistent with the previous chapters, concerns remain when dealing with small-to-moderate sample sizes.

Example

Imagine that 20 pairs of observations are sampled where for time 1, the distribution is standard normal and for time 2, the distribution is skewed as shown in Figure 9.1. Further imagine that the goal is to have a Type I error probability equal to 0.05. With a sample size of $n = 20$ and a correlation $\rho = 0$, the actual probability of a Type I error is approximately 0.087. Switching to a bootstrap-t method, the Type I error probability is now 0.080.

11.1.2 R Functions t.test and trimcibt

The built-in R function

$$t.test(x)$$

can be used to perform the paired T test. If the data are stored in the R variables x and y, the command

$$t.test(x-y)$$

accomplishes this goal. Alternatively, use the command

$$t.test(x,y,paired = TRUE).$$

The bootstrap-t method can be applied with the R command

$$trimcibt(x-y,tr=0).$$

11.2 COMPARING TRIMMED MEANS AND MEDIANS

As in the previous chapters, one way of dealing with the risk of low power when comparing means is to use 20% trimmed means or medians. A possible appeal of methods for comparing 20% trimmed means is that by design, they perform about as well as the paired T test for means when the normality assumption is true. But in fairness, if a distribution is sufficiently light-tailed, comparing means might have a power advantage. If distributions are sufficiently heavy-tailed, trimmed means might provide more power. As usual, if distributions are skewed, comparing means is not the same as comparing the 20% trimmed means or the medians. Despite any concerns about the mean, there are situations where it is more appropriate than a 20% trimmed mean or median as discussed in Chapter 2. But to get relatively high power over a broad range of conditions, as well as improved control over the Type I error probability, using a 20% trimmed mean has appeal.

There is a feature of difference scores that should be noted when working with a trimmed mean or median. As noted in Section 11.1, $\overline{D} = \overline{X}_1 - \overline{X}_2$, the mean of the difference scores is equal to the difference between the means of the individual variables. However, under general conditions, this result does not generalize to a 20% trimmed mean or median. For example, if M_1, M_2, and M_D represent the sample medians of the first group, the second group, and the difference scores, respectively, then typically (but not always)

$$M_D \neq M_1 - M_2.$$

Example

As an illustration, consider the following values:

i	X_{i1}	X_{i2}	$D_i = X_{i1} - X_{i2}$
1	4	6	-2
2	7	11	-4
3	6	7	-41
4	4	9	-5
5	9	9	0

Then, $M_1 = 6$, $M_2 = 9$, and $M_D = -2$. So, we see that $M_D \neq M_1 - M_2$.

If two dependent groups have identical distributions, then the population trimmed mean of the difference scores is equal to the difference between the individual trimmed means, which is zero. In symbols, $\mu_{tD} = \mu_{t1} - \mu_{t2} = 0$. However, if the distributions differ, in general, it will be the case that $\mu_{tD} \neq \mu_{t1} - \mu_{t2}$. In practical terms, computing a confidence interval for μ_{tD} is not necessarily the same as computing a confidence interval for $\mu_{t1} - \mu_{t2}$. So, an issue is whether one should test

$$H_0 : \mu_{tD} = 0, \tag{11.4}$$

or

$$H_0 : \mu_{t1} = \mu_{t2}. \tag{11.5}$$

The latter approach is called comparing the *marginal trimmed means*. Put another way, the distributions associated with each of the dependent groups, ignoring the other group, are called *marginal distributions*. The hypothesis given by Equation (11.5) is that the trimmed means of the marginal distributions are equal. The same is true for the population medians. Let θ_1 and θ_2 be the population medians, respectively, and let θ_D be the population median of the difference scores. If the marginal distribution are identical, $\theta_D = \theta_1 - \theta_2 = 0$, but otherwise, in general, $\theta_D \neq \theta_1 - \theta_2$.

To elaborate on the difference between the two hypotheses given by Equations (11.4) and (11.5) in more concrete terms, consider a study aimed at assessing feelings of life satisfaction based on randomly sampled pairs of brothers and sisters. Testing Equation (11.4), the goal in effect is to assess how the typical brother compares to his sister. Testing Equation (11.5) instead, the goal is to compare how the typical female compares to the typical male. In terms of maximizing power, the optimal choice between these two hypotheses depends on how the groups differ, which of course is unknown.

Generally, the choice between testing Equation (11.4) rather than Equation (11.5) is more of a substantive issue than a statistical issue. For example, if an intervention study is aimed at reducing depression, one approach would be to test Equation (11.5). But it might be argued that what is more meaningful is whether the typical change in depression within each individual indicates that the intervention is effective. In this case, testing Equation (11.4) is more reasonable.

Testing Equation (11.4) using trimmed means is straightforward: Compute the difference scores as done when applying the paired T test, and then apply the methods for trimmed means in Chapters 6 and 7. As a brief reminder, the relevant R functions are as follows:

- `trimci` (non-bootstrap method for trimmed mean)
- `trimcibt` (bootstrap-t for trimmed mean)
- `trimpb` (percentile bootstrap for trimmed mean).

Assuming that the data are stored in the R variables `x` and `y`, the command `trimci(x-y)`, for example, will test the hypothesis that the difference scores have a 20% trimmed mean equal to zero.

As for testing Equation (11.5), a method is available for accomplishing this goal, but the details are not provided. Briefly, the method uses an estimate of the standard error that takes into account the correlation between the two measures. (The relevant correlation here is a Winsorized correlation.) R functions for applying the method are described in the next section.

As for the median, again methods in Chapters 6 and 7 can be applied using the difference scores. The relevant R functions are as follows:

- `sint`
- `sintv2`

When comparing the marginal medians, a percentile bootstrap method currently seems best and can be applied with the R function `dmedpb` described in the next section.

11.2.1   R Functions yuend, ydbt, and dmedpb

The R function

$$\text{yuend(x,y,tr=0.2,alpha=0.05)},$$

stored in the file Rallfun described in Section 1.4, compares the marginal trimmed means. That is, it tests H_0: $\mu_{t1} = \mu_{t2}$. The function

$$\text{ydbt(x,y,tr=0.2)}$$

compares the marginal trimmed means using a bootstrap-t method. For the special case where the goal is to compare the marginal medians, use the function

$$\text{dmedpb(x,y)}.$$

Example

This example illustrates that using difference scores can result in rejecting the null hypothesis when inferences based on the marginal trimmed means fail to to reject. In a similar manner, the marginal trimmed means can reject when a method based on the difference scores fails to reject. Consider the Well Elderly 2 study, introduced in Chapter 8, where the goal was to investigate the impact of an intervention program designed to improve the physical and emotional well-being of older adults. The measures of depressive symptoms before intervention are stored in the file CESD_before_dat.txt and the measures after intervention are stored in CESD_after_dat.txt. (Use the scan command, not the read.table command, when reading these data into R.) Using a 20% trimmed mean based on the difference scores, $p = 0.020$ using the R function trimci. The sample size is 326. Comparing the marginal trimmed means, the p-value returned by the R function yuend is 0.15. In the same study, there was interest in whether cortisol increases shortly after awakening. Prior to intervention, based on the marginal trimmed means, $p = 0.005$. But based on the difference scores, $p = 0.225$.

Example

Table 11.2 reports data, taken from Rao (1948), on the weight of cork borings from 28 trees. Of specific interest was the difference in weight for the north, east, south, and west sides of the trees. For each tree, a boring was taken from all four sides, so there is some possibility that the resulting weights are dependent. That is, methods in Chapter 8 are possibly inappropriate. Here we compare the north and east sides as well as the east and south sides. Assuming that the data for the north, east, and south sides are stored in the R variables cork1, cork2, and cork3, respectively, we first look at boxplots of the difference scores using the R command

```
boxplot(cork1-cork2,cork2-cork3).
```

TABLE 11.2   Cork Boring Weights for the North, East, South, and West Sides of Trees

N	E	S	W	N	E	S	W
72	66	76	77	60	53	66	63
56	57	64	58	41	29	36	38
32	32	35	36	30	35	34	26
39	39	31	27	42	43	31	25
37	40	31	25	33	29	27	36
32	30	34	28	63	45	74	63
54	46	60	52	47	51	52	53
91	79	100	75	56	68	47	50
79	65	70	61	81	80	68	58
78	55	67	60	46	38	37	38
39	35	34	37	32	30	30	32
60	50	67	54	35	37	48	39
39	36	39	31	50	34	37	40
43	37	39	50	48	54	57	43

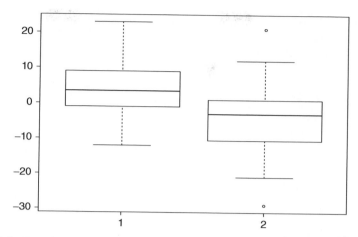

Figure 11.1 Boxplots of the difference scores based on the weight of cork borings. The left boxplot is based on the difference between north and east sides of the trees. The right boxplot is based on the east and south sides

The results are shown in Figure 11.1. Notice that the first boxplot suggests that the differences between the north and east sides have a reasonably symmetric distribution with no outliers. This might further suggest that the paired T test will give accurate probability coverage and will have relatively short confidence intervals. It is stressed, however, that the extent to which a boxplot provides a satisfactory assessment of whether accurate confidence intervals will be obtained, when working the mean, is far from clear. Using the R command `t.test(cork1-cork2)`, the 0.95 confidence interval for the population mean of the difference scores is (1.28, 7.43) and the p-value is 0.007. Using a 20% trimmed mean instead, with the command `trimci(cork1-cork2)`, the 0.95 confidence interval is (0.25, 7.41) and the p-value is 0.037. So, both methods reject at the 0.05 level, the upper ends of the confidence intervals are similar, but the lower ends differ to a fair degree despite the apparent symmetry indicated by the boxplot.

Now, consider the east and south sides. The paired T test has a p-value of 0.09. Using, instead, a 20% trimmed mean with the R command

```
trimci(cork2-cork3),
```

the p-value is 0.049. If, instead, the marginal trimmed means are compared with the R function `yuend`, the p-value is 0.12. Using, instead, medians, the p-value is 0.088.

Example

R has a built-in data set called Indometh. Each of the six participants was given an intravenous injection of indomethacin, and the goal was to understand how plasma concentrations of indomethacin change over time. In R, type Indometh and hit enter, which will return the data. The first 14 rows of data resemble this:

```
Subject time conc
      1 0.25 1.50
      1 0.50 0.94
      1 0.75 0.78
      1 1.00 0.48
      1 1.25 0.37
      1 2.00 0.19
      1 3.00 0.12
      1 4.00 0.11
      1 5.00 0.08
      1 6.00 0.07
      1 8.00 0.05
      2 0.25 2.03
      2 0.50 1.63
      2 0.75 0.71
```

The column of data headed by Subject contains the participant's code. The next column indicates the time at which blood samples were drawn (in hours). The final column indicates plasma concentrations of indomethacin (mcg/ml). There are various ways the data might be analyzed. A basic issue that can be addressed with the methods covered in this chapter is whether we can be reasonably certain that the typical plasma concentration at time 1, indicated by the value 0.25 in column 2, differs from the typical level at time 2, which corresponds to the value 0.50 in column 2.

One way to proceed is to first use the R command

```
z=fac2list(Indometh[,3],Indometh[,2]),
```

which creates an R variable z having list mode as previously described. Here, z[[1]] indicates the plasma concentrations at time 1, which is 0.25 hours, z[[2]] contains the data on concentrations at time 2 (0.50 hours), and so on. The concentrations at times 1 and 2 can be compared with the R command

```
trimci(z[[1]]-z[[2]]),
```

which tests the hypothesis that the difference scores have a population trimmed mean equal to zero. The p-value is 0.028, suggesting that the typical differences between concentrations, based on a 20% trimmed mean, have changed between times 1 and 2. In terms of Tukey's three-decision rule, decide that the typical difference is positive because the estimated difference is greater than zero. The command

```
yuend(z[[1]],z[[2]])
```

would compare the marginal 20% trimmed means. The resulting p-value is 0.013.

11.2.2 Measures of Effect Size

As discussed in Sections 7.1 and 9.7, an important issue is measuring effect size, which is a general term for measures intended to quantify the extent to which groups differ. As pointed out in Section 9.7, when comparing independent groups, different methods for measuring effect size provide different perspectives on how groups compare. Moreover, more than one measure of effect size might be needed to get a deep understanding of how groups differ. Not surprisingly, the same is true when dealing with dependent groups.

A simple approach when comparing the means of dependent groups is to use an analog Cohen's d:

$$\delta = \frac{\mu_D - 0}{\sigma_D} \qquad (11.6)$$

where μ_D and σ_D are the population mean and population standard deviation associated with the difference scores. For example, $\delta = 1.5$ indicates that the difference between the mean and zero is 1.5 standard deviations. The estimate of δ is

$$d = \frac{\overline{D}}{s_D},$$

the mean of the difference scores divided by the standard deviation of the difference scores. This might suffice in some situations, but as pointed out in Section 9.7, this approach can be misleading and generally unsatisfactory when dealing with nonnormal distributions.

Now, consider trimmed means. For difference scores, a simple variation of the method derived by Algina et al. (2005) can be used to measure effect size. For a 20% trimmed mean, the estimated effect size is

$$d_t = 0.642 \frac{\overline{D}_t}{S_{wD}},$$

where $\overline{D}_t$ is the 20% trimmed mean based on the difference scores and S_{wD} is the corresponding Winsorized standard deviation. When the difference scores have a normal distribution, d_t also estimates δ.

An approach when working with the trimmed means associated with both groups, rather than the trimmed mean of the difference scores, is to use r_e as described in Section 9.7.2. That is, use a measure that reflects the variation among the trimmed means relative to the variation within the marginal distributions. Homoscedasticity is not assumed or required. As was pointed out in Section 9.7.2, this approach has connections with a robust analog of Pearson's correlation.

One more approach is to plot the data. If dependent groups do not differ in any manner (the two dependent variables have identical distributions), then the difference scores will have a symmetric distribution about zero. The extent to which the distribution of the difference scores is skewed, or not centered around zero, provides perspective regarding how the groups differ. Boxplots, or the R function `akerd` in Section 3.2.5, can be used with difference scores. To plot the marginal distributions, use the R function `g2plot` in Section 9.8.1.

Another approach is to use the probability that for a randomly chosen pair of observations, the observation associated with group 1 is less than the corresponding observation in group 2. This can be done via the sign test, which is covered in Section 11.3.

11.2.3   R Functions D.akp.effect and effectg

The R function

```
D.akp.effect(x,y=NULL,null.value=0,tr=.2)
```

computes the measure of effect size based on difference scores, d_t, described in the previous section. As usual, the argument tr indicates the amount of trimming and defaults to 20%.

The R function

```
effectg(x,y,tr=.2)
```

computes the effect size r_e.

11.3   THE SIGN TEST

A basic approach to comparing dependent groups is the sign test. Again, we have n randomly sampled pairs of observations:

$$(X_{11},X_{12}),\cdots,(X_{n1},X_{n2}).$$

That is, X_{ij} is the ith observation from the jth group. Primarily for convenience, it is temporarily assumed that for any pair of observations, $X_{i1} \neq X_{i2}$. Let p be the probability that for a randomly sampled pair of observations, the observation from group 1 is less than the observation from group 2. In symbols,

$$p = P(X_{i1} < X_{i2}).$$

Letting $D_i = X_{i1} - X_{i2}$ ($i = 1,\cdots,n$), an estimate of p is simply the proportion of D_i values that are less than zero. More formally, let $V_i = 1$ if $D_i < 0$; otherwise, $V_i = 0$. Then, an estimate of p is

$$\hat{p} = \frac{1}{n} \sum V_i. \tag{11.7}$$

Because the number of V_i values equal to 1 has a binomial probability function, results in Section 6.7 provide a confidence interval for p. If this interval does not contain 0.5, reject

$$H_0 : p = 0.5$$

and conclude that the groups differ. If $p > 0.5$, this means that for a randomly sampled pair of observations, the first value is more likely to have the lower value, and if $p < 0.5$, the reverse is true.

Now, consider a situation where some of the D_i values are equal to zero. Given the goal of making inferences about p, one strategy is to simply ignore or discard cases where $D_i = 0$. So, if among n pairs of observations, there are N D_i values not equal to zero, an estimate of p is

$$\hat{p} = \frac{1}{N} \sum V_i. \tag{11.8}$$

11.3.1   R Function signt

The R function

```
signt(x, y = NA, alpha = 0.05,SD=FALSE)
```

tests H_0: $p = 0.5$ with the sign test as just described. If the argument y is not specified, it is assumed that either x is a matrix with two columns corresponding to two dependent groups or x has list mode. The function computes the differences $X_{i1} - X_{i2}$ ($i = 1, \cdots, n$), eliminates all differences that are equal to 0 leaving N values, determines the number of pairs for which $X_{i1} < X_{i2}$ among the N pairs that remain, and then performs the Agresti–Coull method. If SD=TRUE, the Schilling–Doi method is used instead.

Example

Various studies suggest that for the typical adult, cortisol increases within the first 30–60 minutes after awakening. The extent to which this is true has been found to be associated with various measures of stress. Does cortisol increase after awakening for the typical older adult? One way of investigating this issue is to test the hypothesis that for a randomly sampled adult, the probability of cortisol increasing is 0.5. Consider again the Well Elderly 2 study. Focusing on data collected prior to intervention, the sign test does not reject at the 0.05 level. The p-value is 0.23. That is, based on Tukey's decision rule, there is no strong empirical evidence that prior to intervention, cortisol increases shortly after awakening. For measures taken after intervention, the p-value is 0.011 indicating that cortisol is more likely to increase after awakening.

11.4   WILCOXON SIGNED RANK TEST

The sign test provides an interesting and useful perspective on how two groups differ. However, a common criticism is that its power can be low relative to other techniques that might be used. One alternative approach is the Wilcoxon signed rank test. It tests the hypothesis that the marginal distributions are identical, which is the same as testing the hypothesis that the distribution of D, the difference scores, is symmetric about zero. But it is not a satisfactory test of the hypothesis that the two groups have equal medians as illustrated at the end of this section. Moreover, when the difference scores have a skewed distribution, it can be seen that the Wilcoxon signed rank test does not test the hypothesis that the median of the difference scores is zero.

To apply it, first form difference scores as was done in conjunction with the paired T test and discard any difference scores that are equal to zero. That is, for the ith pair of observations, compute

$$D_i = X_{i1} - X_{i2},$$

$i = 1, \cdots, n$, where n indicates the number difference scores not equal to zero. Next, rank the $|D_i|$ values and let U_i denote the rank associated with $|D_i|$. (Computing ranks was described in Section 8.7.3.) So, for example, if the D_i values are 6, -2, 12, 23, -8, then $U_1 = 2$ because after taking absolute values, 6 has a rank of 2. Similarly, $U_2 = 1$ because after taking absolute values, the second value, -2, has a rank of 1. Next, set

$$R_i = U_i$$

if $D_i > 0$; otherwise,

$$R_i = -U_i.$$

Positive numbers are said to have a sign of 1, and negative numbers a sign of -1, so R_i is the value of the rank corresponding to $|D_i|$ multiplied by the sign of D_i.

When there are no tied values among the $|D_i|$ values, there is a method for determining the exact probability of committing a Type I error probability based the test statistic W, the sum of the positive R_i values. The null hypothesis of identical distributions is rejected if W is sufficiently small or sufficiently large. The R function in the next section performs the calculations.

If there are tied values among the $|D_i|$ values, or if there are no tied values and the sample size is sufficiently large, say greater than or equal to 40, the test statistic

$$W = \frac{\sum R_i}{\sqrt{\sum R_i^2}}$$

can be used. If there are no tied values, this last equation simplifies to

$$W = \frac{\sqrt{6} \sum R_i}{\sqrt{n(n+1)(2n+1)}}.$$

The null hypothesis is rejected if $|W| \geq c$, where c is the $1 - \alpha/2$ quantile of a standard normal distribution.

Rejecting with the signed rank test indicates that two dependent groups have different distributions. But a criticism is that it does not provide details about how the groups differ. For example, it does not provide a satisfactory confidence interval for the median of the difference scores. In the cork boring example, rejecting indicates that the distribution of weights differs for the north versus east side of a tree, but how might we elaborate on what this difference is? One possibility is to compute a confidence interval for the median of the difference scores using methods mentioned in

Section 11.2. Another approach is to compute a confidence interval for p, the probability that the weight from the north side is less than the weight from the east side. So, despite lower power, one might argue that the sign test provides a useful perspective on how groups compare.

Example

This example illustrates that the Wilcoxon signed rank test is not designed to test the hypothesis that two dependent groups have equal medians. Suppose 500 observations are sampled from a normal distribution and 500 observations are sampled from a distribution having the same shape as the distribution in Figure 9.1, with both distributions having a (population) median of zero. Then, the probability of rejecting at the 0.05 level exceeds 0.99. That is, the null hypothesis of equal medians is true, but with near certainty, the Wilcoxon signed rank test rejects.

11.4.1   R Function wilcox.test

The built-in R function

```
wilcox.test(x, y, paired = FALSE, exact = TRUE)
```

performs the Wilcoxon signed rank test just described by setting the argument `paired=TRUE`. (With `paired=FALSE`, the Wilcoxon–Mann–Whitney test in Section 9.6 is performed.) The argument `exact=TRUE` indicates that by default, the exact probability of a Type I error will be computed. If the sample size is large, execution time can become an issue. Evidently with a sample size of 40 or more, the approximate method for controlling the Type I error probability, where W is assumed to have a normal distribution, performs very well. That is, if $n \geq 40$, using `exact=FALSE` suffices.

11.5   COMPARING VARIANCES

A classic method for comparing the variances associated with dependent groups is the Morgan–Pitman test. As usual, we have n pairs of randomly sampled observations:

$$(X_{11}, X_{12}), \cdots, (X_{n1}, X_{n2}).$$

Set

$$U_i = X_{i1} - X_{i2}$$

and

$$V_i = X_{i1} + X_{i2},$$

$(i = 1, \cdots, n)$. That is, for the ith pair of observations, U_i is the difference and V_i is the sum. Let σ_1^2 be the variance associated with the first group, and let σ_2^2 be the variance associated with the second group. The goal is to test the hypothesis that these variances are equal. It can be shown that if

$$H_0 : \sigma_1^2 = \sigma_2^2$$

is true, then Pearson's correlation between U and V is zero. That is, the hypothesis of equal variances can be tested by testing

$$H_0 : \rho_{uv} = 0,$$

where ρ_{uv} is Pearson's correlation between U and V. Student's T test, as described in Section 8.5.2, is the classic way of testing this last hypothesis, which yields the *Morgan–Pitman test* for equal variances. But this approach assumes homoscedasticity, which in the present context means that the variance of U does not depend on the value of V. For situations where outliers tend to occur, the Morgan–Pitman test performs poorly due to heteroscedasticity (Wilcox, 2015b). To deal with heteroscedasticity, use the R function comdvar in Section 11.5.1.

11.5.1   R Function comdvar

The R function

$$\text{comdvar}(x,y)$$

compares the variances of two dependent groups. The function creates the differences and sums used by the Morgan–Pitman test and then uses the R function pcorhc4 described in Section 8.5.3. That is, the function uses a method that allows heteroscedasticity.

Example

Consider again the cork boring data for the north side and east side of a tree. Again assume that the data are stored in the R variables cork1 and cork2. The R command

$$\text{comdvar}(\text{cork1}, \text{cork2})$$

tests the hypothesis of equal variances. The p-value is 0.19. In the context of Tukey's three-decision rule, with $\alpha = 0.05$, make no decision about which side has the larger variance.

11.6   DEALING WITH MORE THAN TWO DEPENDENT GROUPS

This section summarizes methods for testing the hypothesis that two or more dependent groups have a common measure of location. As usual, first attention is focused on a classic method that is routinely used for comparing means. Then, more modern methods are described.

11.6.1   Comparing Means

The goal is to test

$$H_0 : \mu_1 = \cdots = \mu_J, \tag{11.9}$$

the hypothesis that J dependent groups have a common mean. The classic method for dealing with this goal is based on the following assumptions:

- Random sampling
- Normality
- Homoscedasticity
- Sphericity

If these assumptions are met, the resulting test statistic F has an F distribution with $v_1 = J - 1$ and $v_2 = (J - 1)(n - 1)$ degrees of freedom. That is, as was the case in Chapter 10, reject if $F \geq f$, where f is the $1 - \alpha$ of an F distribution. The computations are performed by the R functions in the next section. Readers interested in the computational details are referred to Kirk (2013) or Wilcox (2012a).

The *sphericity* assumption is met if, in addition to homoscedasticity, the correlations among all pairs of variables have a common value. To say this in a slightly more formal way, let ρ_{jk} be Pearson's correlation corresponding to groups j and k. The sphericity assumption is met if all of these correlations have a common value, ρ. The sphericity assumption is met under slightly weaker conditions than those described here (e.g., Kirk, 2013), but the details are not important for present purposes. If all of the stated assumptions are true, the Type I error probability is controlled exactly with the F test previously mentioned. There are ways of dealing with situations where the sphericity assumption is violated, which perform reasonably well when the other assumptions are true, but as is the case for all methods based on means, nonnormality can be devastating in terms of both Type I errors and power. The next section illustrates how to use a built-in R function for testing Equation (11.9) that assumes sphericity. An R function that does not assume sphericity is described in Section 11.6.4.

11.6.2   R Function aov

The classic method described in the previous section is relatively unsatisfactory given the goal of comparing means, but for completeness, it is noted that it can be applied via the built-in R function

```
aov(x ~ g),
```

which was introduced in Chapter 10. Although the goal is to test the hypothesis of equal means, a better description of this function is that it tests the hypothesis of identical distributions. As indicated, a formula convention is used, which assumes that some R variable indicates the group (or level) to which a participant belongs.

Example

Imagine that you have data stored in the R data frame mydata that resembles this:

```
    dv subject myfactor
1   1      s1       f1
2   3      s1       f2
3   4      s1       f3
4   2      s2       f1
5   2      s2       f2
6   3      s2       f3
7   2      s3       f1
8   5      s3       f2
9   6      s3       f3
10  3      s4       f1
11  4      s4       f2
12  4      s4       f3
13  3      s5       f1
14  5      s5       f2
15  6      s5       f3
```

The outcome of interest is stored in the column headed by dv (dependent variable). There are three dependent groups, which are indicated by f1, f2 and f3 in column 4. The R commands

$$\mathtt{blob = aov(dv \sim myfactor + Error(subject/myfactor),}$$

$$\mathtt{data{=}mydata)summary(blob)}$$

compute the test statistic F and the corresponding p-value. The last few lines of the output for the data at hand resemble this:

```
           Df  Sum Sq Mean Sq F value   Pr(>F)
myfactor    2 14.9333  7.4667  13.576 0.002683 **
Residuals   8  4.4000  0.5500
```

The test statistic F is equal to 13.576. The p-value is under Pr(>) and is equal to 0.002683.

11.6.3 Comparing Trimmed Means

As previously noted, when comparing two dependent groups, inferences based on difference scores are not necessarily the same as inferences based on the marginal distributions when working with trimmed means in general and the median in particular. This continues to be the case when comparing more than two groups, and again neither approach dominates the other. In terms of power, the choice of method depends on how the groups differ, which of course is unknown. Some of the examples given in this chapter illustrate that we can fail to reject when comparing the marginal trimmed means, but we reject when using difference scores, the point being that the choice of method can make a practical difference. This is not to suggest, however, that difference scores always have the highest power. The only certainty is that the reverse can happen, so both approaches are covered.

First, consider the goal of testing

$$H_0 : \mu_{t1} = \cdots = \mu_{tJ}, \qquad (11.10)$$

the hypothesis that the marginal distributions associated with J dependent groups have equal population trimmed means. Sphericity is not assumed. So, for the special case where the goal is to compare means, the method in this section appears to be a better choice for general use compared to the method in Section 11.6.1. The computations are somewhat involved and not described here. Readers interested in these details are referred to Wilcox (2012a, Section 12.2). A crude description is that the test statistic is based in part on the variation among the trimmed means. The resulting test statistic, F_t, has approximately an F distribution with degrees of freedom v_1 and v_2. If the sphericity assumption is true, the degrees of freedom are $v_1 = J - 1$ and $v_2 = (J - 1)(h - 1)$, where h is the number of observations left after trimming. For example, with 20% trimming, $h = n - 2g$ where g is $0.2n$ rounded down to the nearest integer. But to deal with situations where the sphericity assumption is not met, the degrees of freedom are adjusted based on the available data.

The method just outlined deals with the marginal trimmed means. When the goal is to compare more than two groups based on the trimmed mean of the difference scores, currently, the best strategy is to use an approach described in Section 12.8 via the R function rmmcp in Section 12.8.4.

11.6.4   R Function rmanova

The R function

```
rmanova(x,tr=0.2)
```

tests the hypothesis given by Equation (11.10). It can be used to compare means by setting the argument tr=0. As usual, the argument x can be a matrix with J columns or it can have list mode. The function automatically adjusts the degrees of freedom in a manner aimed at dealing with situations where the sphericity assumption might not be true.

11.6.5   Rank-Based Methods

This section describes two rank-based methods for comparing more than two dependent groups. The first is a classic, routinely taught technique: Friedman's test. It tests the hypothesis that all J dependent groups have identical distributions. The method begins by assigning ranks within rows. For example, imagine that for each individual, measures are taken at three different times, yielding

Time 1	Time 2	Time 3
9	7	12
1	10	4
8	2	1
⋮		

The ranks corresponding to the first row (the values 9, 7, and 12) are 2, 1, and 3. For the second row, the ranks are 1, 3, and 2, and continuing in this manner, the data become

Time 1	Time 2	Time 3
2	1	3
1	3	2
3	2	1
⋮		

Let R_{ij} be the resulting rank corresponding to X_{ij} ($i = 1, \cdots, n; j = 1, \cdots, J$), where X_{ij} is the observation in the ith row and jth column. For example, for data used here, $X_{31} = 8$ and $R_{31} = 3$. Compute

$$A = \sum_{j=1}^{J} \sum_{i=1}^{n} R_{ij}^2$$

$$R_j = \sum_{i=1}^{n} R_{ij}$$

$$B = \frac{1}{n} \sum_{j=1}^{J} R_j^2$$

$$C = \frac{1}{4} nJ(J + 1)^2.$$

If there are no ties, the equation for A simplifies to

$$A = \frac{nJ(J + 1)(2J + 1)}{6}.$$

The test statistic is

$$F = \frac{(n - 1)(B - C)}{A - B}. \tag{11.11}$$

Decision Rule: Reject if $F \geq f_{1-\alpha}$ or if $A = B$, where $f_{1-\alpha}$ is the $1 - \alpha$ quantile of an F distribution with $v_1 = J - 1$ and $v_2 = (n - 1)(J - 1)$ degrees of freedom.

Numerous rank-based methods have been proposed with the goal of improving on Friedman's test in terms of both Type I errors and power. A fundamental criticism of Friedman's test is that it assumes homoscedasticity and that the correlations among J groups have a common value. An improvement on Friedman's test that currently stands out is described by Brunner et al. (2002, Section 7.2.2), and will be called *method BPRM*. Unlike Friedman's test, ranks are assigned based on the pooled data. So, if there are no tied values, the smallest value among all Jn values gets a rank of 1, and the largest gets a rank of Jn. An R function for applying this method is described in the next section.

11.6.6 R Functions friedman.test and bprm

The built-in R function

```
friedman.test(x)
```

performs Friedman's test, where the argument x is a matrix with columns corresponding to groups. If x is a data frame, then it must be converted to a matrix. That is, use the command

```
friedman.test(as.matrix(x)).
```

This function also accepts a formula. However, no illustrations are provided because it currently seems better to use method BPRM via the the R function

```
bprm(x) .
```

The argument x is assumed to be a matrix or a data frame with J columns corresponding to groups, or it can have list mode. This function returns a p-value.

11.7 BETWEEN-BY-WITHIN DESIGNS

A between-by-within design refers to a two-way ANOVA design where the first factor involves independent groups and the second factor involves dependent groups. To illustrate one reason why such a design has practical importance, consider a study aimed at dealing with depression among young adults. Imagine that depressive symptoms are measured before treatment and again 6 months later after being treated. Further imagine that levels of depression are found to be reduced. This would seem to suggest that the experimental method has practical value, but a possible criticism is that over time, levels of depression might decrease with no intervention. A possible way of addressing this issue is to randomly assign some of the participants to a control group, measure their level of depression before the study begins and again 6 months later. The idea is to determine whether there is an interaction. That is, does the change in depressive symptoms for the experimental group differ from the change in depressive symptoms among participants who did not receive treatment?

There is a method for dealing with a between-by-within design that allows heteroscedasticity. It can be used to compare trimmed means, which includes means as a special case. The somewhat involved computational details are described in Wilcox (2012a, Section 12.6.1). Here, it is merely noted that an R function is available for performing the calculations.

11.7.1 R Functions bwtrim and bw2list

The R function

```
bwtrim(J, K, x, tr = 0.2)
```

tests hypotheses about trimmed means as described in the previous section. (The R package WRS2, mentioned in Chapter 1, contains the function `tsplit`, which performs the same calculations as `bwtrim`.) The argument J indicates the number of independent groups, K is the number of dependent groups, x is any R variable that is a matrix or has list mode, and as usual, the argument `tr` indicates the amount of trimming, which defaults to 0.2 if unspecified. If the data are stored in list mode, it is assumed that x[[1]]-x[[K]] contain the K dependent groups corresponding to the Level 1 of the first factor. For the second level among the independent groups, x[[K+1]]-x[[2K]] contain the data for the K dependent groups, and so on. If the data are stored in a matrix (or a data frame), it is assumed that the first K columns correspond to Level 1 of factor A, the next K columns correspond to Level 2 of factor A, and so on.

Example

Exercise 12 in Section 1.6 mentioned some data stored in the R variable ChickWeight, which is a matrix. There are four independent groups of chicks that received a different diet. The diet they received is indicated in column 4 (by the values 1, 2, 3, and 4). Each chick was measured at 12 different times, with times indicated in column 2. So, we have a 4-by-12 between-by-within design. Column 1 contains the weight of the chicks. To analyze the data with the R function bwtrim, the data need to be stored so that the first 12 groups correspond to the 12 times associated with diet 1, the next 12 correspond to diet 2, and so on. The R command

```
z=fac2list(ChickWeight[,1],ChickWeight[,c(4,2)])
```

accomplishes this goal. Then, the means are compared with the command

```
bwtrim(4,12,z,tr=0).
```

The p-value when comparing the four diets is 0.003. The p-value when comparing weight over time is extremely small, but of course, the result that chicks gain weight over time is not very interesting. The p-value associated with the test of no interaction is less than 0.001. That is, the increase in weight over time appears to depend on the type of diet.

In this last example, look at the last argument when using the R function fac2list, ChickWeight[,c(4,2)], and notice the use of c(4,2). This indicates that the levels of the between factor are stored in column 4 and the levels of the within factor are stored in column 2. If c(2,4) had been used, this would indicate that the levels in column 2 correspond to the between factor (the independent groups), which is incorrect.

Situations are encountered where data are stored in a matrix or a data frame with one column indicating the levels of the between factor and one or more columns containing data corresponding to different times. Imagine that, for example, three medications are being investigated regarding their effectiveness to lower cholesterol and that column 3 indicates which medication a participant received. Moreover, columns 5 and 8 contain the participants' cholesterol level at times 1 and 2, respectively. Then, the R function

```
bw2list(x, grp.col, lev.col).
```

will convert the data to list mode so that the R function bwtrim can be used. The argument grp.col indicates the column indicating the levels of the independent groups. The argument lev.col indicates the K columns where the within group data are stored. For the situation just described, if the data are stored in the R variable chol, the R command

```
z=bw2list(chol,3,c(5,8))
```

will store the data in z in the order expected by bwtrim, and the R command

```
bwtrim(3,2,z)
```

performs the analysis based on 20% trimmed means.

Example

Consider again the hangover data as described in Section 9.1.6. The first four rows of the data resemble this:

2	0	2	1
1	0	4	0
1	32	15	25
2	0	0	0

The value 1 in column 1 indicates that the participant is not the son of an alcoholic and the value 2 indicates that the participant is the son of an alcoholic. Columns 2–4 are hangover measures taken on three separate occasions. For example, the first participant is the son of an alcoholic and his hangover measures at times 1, 2, and 3 were 0, 2, and 1, respectively. Again assuming that the data are stored in the R variable hang, the R command

```
z=bw2list(hang,1,c(2:4))
```

sorts the data into groups and stores the results in the R variable z in list mode. The measures at times 1–3 are stored in z[[1]]-z[[3]] for the participants who are not the sons of alcoholics and z[[4]]-z[[6]] contain the measures for participants who are the sons of alcoholics. The R command

```
bwtrim(2,3,z)
```

tests the hypotheses of no main effects and no interaction based on 20% trimmed means.

11.8 SUMMARY

- A commonly used approach to comparing dependent groups is to test the hypothesis of equal means using the paired T test in Section 11.1 or the F test in Section 11.6.1 when dealing with more than two groups. When using the F

test, violating the sphericity assumption is a serious concern if the goal is to test the hypothesis of equal means without being sensitive to other ways the distributions might differ. Concerns can be reduced, but not eliminated, by adjusting the degrees of freedom, which is done by the R function rmanova in Section 11.5.4.

- When comparing trimmed means or medians, inferences based on difference scores are not generally the same as inferences based on the marginal distributions. Methods for both approaches are available with each providing a different perspective on how dependent groups compare.

- As in the previous chapters, methods based on means might have relatively low power compared to methods based on a trimmed mean or median. But situations are encountered where methods based on means have more power than methods based on a trimmed mean or median. In terms of controlling the Type I error probability, methods based on 20% trimmed means or medians perform well over a broader range of situations than methods based on means.

- The sign test is sometimes criticized for having relatively low power, but it provides a useful and easily interpretable perspective on how dependent groups differ, and situations are encountered where its power is relatively high.

- The rank-based methods in this chapter test the hypothesis of identical distributions. Under general conditions, they do not provide a satisfactory test of the hypothesis that groups have equal (population) medians.

11.9 EXERCISES

1. For the data in Table 11.2, perform the paired T test for means using the weights for the east and south sides of the trees. The data are stored in the file corkall_dat.txt, which can be downloaded from the author's web page as described in Section 1.5. Verify that the p-value is 0.09.

2. Repeat the previous exercise, but use 20% trimmed means instead of using the difference scores in conjunction with the R function trimci. Verify that the p-value is 0.049.

3. In Exercise 1, compare the marginal 20% trimmed means with the R function yuend and verify that now the p-value is 0.121.

4. Generally, why is it possible to get a different p-value comparing the marginal trimmed means rather than testing the hypothesis that the trimmed mean of the difference scores is zero?

5. Is it possible that the marginal trimmed means are equal but the trimmed mean based on the difference scores is not equal to zero? What does this indicate in terms of power?

6. Repeat Exercise 1, but now use a bootstrap-t method to compare the means via the R function trimcibt. Verify that the p-value is 0.091.

7. Repeat the last exercise, only now use a 20% trimmed mean. Verify that the p-value is 0.049.

8. Consider the following data for two dependent groups.

Group 1:	10	14	15	18	20	29	30	40
Group 2:	40	8	15	20	10	8	2	3

Compare the two groups with the sign test and the Wilcoxon signed rank test with $\alpha = 0.05$. Verify that according to the sign test, $\hat{p} = 0.29$, the 0.95 confidence interval for p is $(0.04, 0.71)$ and the p-value is 0.27. Also verify that the Wilcoxon signed rank test has an approximate p-value of 0.08.

9. For two dependent groups

Group 1:	86	71	77	68	91	72	77	91	70	71	88	87
Group 2:	88	77	76	64	96	72	65	90	65	80	81	72

Apply the Wilcoxon signed rank test with $\alpha = 0.05$. Verify that $W = 0.7565$ and that you fail to reject.

10. Section 11.2.1 analyzed the Indometh data, stored in R, using the R function trimci. Compare times 2 and 3 using means based on difference scores and verify that the p. value is 0.014.

11. Continuing the last exercise, plot the difference scores using the R function akerd and note that the distribution is skewed to the right, suggesting that the confidence interval for the mean might be inaccurate. Using the R function trimcibt, verify that the 0.95 confidence interval for the 20% trimmed mean of the difference scores is $(0.127, 0.543)$. Then, verify that when using the mean instead (by setting the argument tr=0), the 0.95 confidence interval is $(0.0097, 0.7969)$. Why is this second confidence so much longer than the first? Hint: Look at a boxplot of the difference scores.

12. The files CESD_before_dat.txt and CESD_after_dat.txt contain measures of depressive symptoms before and after intervention. The data can be downloaded from the author's web page as described in Section 1.5. Explain why the scan command, rather the read.table command, should be used to read the data into R. Then, use R to test the hypotheses that the difference scores have a mean, 20% trimmed mean and median equal to zero.

13. For the data used in the previous exercise, test the hypothesis that the marginal 20% trimmed means are equal.

14. For the data used in Exercises 12 and 13, perform the Wilcoxon signed rank test.

15. For the data used in Exercise 12, use the R function comdvar to compare the marginal variances.

16. The file CESDMF123_dat.txt, stored on the author's web page, contains a measure of depressive symptoms taken at three different times, which are stored in columns 2–4 and headed by CESD1, CESD2, and CESD3. Test the hypothesis that the means of these three measures are equal using

the R function `rmanova`. (The first line of the file contains labels, so use `header=TRUE` when using the R command `read.table`.)

17. For the data used in the previous exercise, test the hypothesis of identical distributions using the two rank-based methods described in Section 11.6.5: Friedman's test and method BPRM. In terms of p-values, do the methods give substantially different results?

18. Column 5 of the data file used in Exercise 16 indicates the gender of the participants (1=male and 2=female). Perform a 2-by-3 between-by-within ANOVA based on 10% trimmed means, where the first factor is gender and the second factor is the measures of depressive symptoms taken at three different times. Hint: Use the R function `bw2list`, described in Section 11.7.1, to sort the data so that the R function `rmanova` can be used.

12

MULTIPLE COMPARISONS

Chapter 10 described how to test the hypothesis that two or more independent groups have a common mean. In symbols, the goal was to test

$$H_0 : \mu_1 = \cdots = \mu_J. \tag{12.1}$$

But typically, one wants to know more about how the groups compare: which groups differ, how do they differ, and by how much?

Note that rather than test the hypothesis given by Equation (12.1), another approach is to test the hypothesis of equal means for all pairs of groups. For example, if there are four groups ($J = 4$), methods in Chapter 9 could be used to test the hypothesis that the mean of the first group is equal to the mean of the second, the mean of first group is equal to the mean of third, and so on. In symbols, the goal is to test

$$H_0 : \mu_1 = \mu_2,$$
$$H_0 : \mu_1 = \mu_3,$$
$$H_0 : \mu_1 = \mu_4,$$
$$H_0 : \mu_2 = \mu_3,$$
$$H_0 : \mu_2 = \mu_4,$$
$$H_0 : \mu_3 = \mu_4.$$

There is, however, a technical issue that needs to be taken into account. Suppose there are no differences among the groups in which case none of the six null hypotheses

Understanding and Applying Basic Statistical Methods Using R, First Edition. Rand R. Wilcox.
© 2017 John Wiley & Sons, Inc. Published 2017 by John Wiley & Sons, Inc.
www.wiley.com/go/Wilcox/Statistical_Methods_R

just listed should be rejected. To keep things simple for the moment, assume that all four groups have normal distributions with equal variances, in which case Student's T test in Chapter 9 provides exact control over the probability of a Type I error when testing any single hypothesis. Further assume that each of the six hypotheses just listed is tested with $\alpha = 0.05$. So, for *each* hypothesis, the probability of a Type I error is 0.05, but the probability of *at least one* Type I error, when performing all six tests, is approximately 0.2. That is, there is about a 20% chance of erroneously concluding that two or more groups differ when in fact none of them differ at all. With six groups, there are 15 pairs of means to be compared, and now the probability of at least one Type I error is about 0.36. In general, as the number of groups increases, the more likely we are to find a difference when none exists if we simply compare each pair of groups using $\alpha = 0.05$. An approach to this problem is to use a method that controls the probability of one or more Type I errors when performing multiple tests. A commonly used term for the probability of one or more Type I errors is the *familywise error rate* (FWE).

12.1   CLASSIC METHODS FOR INDEPENDENT GROUPS

We begin by describing classic methods for comparing the means of J independent groups that assume normality and homoscedasticity. As in Chapter 10, homoscedasticity means that the groups have equal population variances. That is,

$$\sigma_1^2 = \cdots = \sigma_J^2.$$

Concerns with these classic methods have been known for some time, but they are commonly used, so it is important to be aware of them and their relative merits.

12.1.1   Fisher's Least Significant Difference Method

One of the earliest strategies for comparing multiple groups is the so-called least significant difference (LSD) method due to Sir Ronald Fisher. Assuming normality and homoscedasticity, the method begins by testing the hypothesis given by Equation (12.1) using the ANOVA F test in Chapter 10. If the hypothesis of equal means is rejected, apply Student's T to all pairs of means. But unlike Student's T as described in Chapter 9, Fisher's LSD method takes advantage of the equal variances assumption by using the data from all J groups to estimate the assumed common variance when any two groups are compared. Under normality and homoscedasticity, this has the advantage of increasing the degrees of freedom, which in turn can mean more power.

To elaborate, suppose the ANOVA F test rejects with a Type I error probability of $\alpha = 0.05$ and let MSWG (the mean squares within groups described in Section 10.1) be the estimate of the assumed common variance. So, for equal sample sizes, MSWG is just the average of the sample variances among all J groups. Consider any two groups, say groups j and k. The goal is to test

$$H_0 : \mu_j = \mu_k, \tag{12.2}$$

TABLE 12.1   Hypothetical Data for Three Groups

G1	G2	G3
3	4	6
5	4	7
2	3	8
4	8	6
8	7	7
4	4	9
3	2	10
9	5	9

the hypothesis that the mean of the jth group is equal to the mean of the kth group. The test statistic is

$$T = \frac{\overline{X}_j - \overline{X}_k}{\sqrt{\text{MSWG}\left(\frac{1}{n_j} + \frac{1}{n_k}\right)}}.$$

(12.3)

When the assumptions of normality and homoscedasticity are met, T has a Student's T distribution with $v = N - J$ degrees of freedom, where J is the number of groups being compared and $N = \sum n_j$ is the total number of observations in all J groups.

Decision Rule: When comparing the jth group to the kth group, reject the hypothesis of equal means if

$$|T| \geq t,$$

where t is the $1 - \frac{\alpha}{2}$ quantile of Student's T distribution with $N - J$ degrees of freedom, which can be read from Table B.4 in Appendix B.

Example

The method is illustrated using the data in Table 12.1. Assume that the probability of at least one Type I error is to be 0.05. It can be seen that $\text{MSWG} = 4.14$, the sample means are $\overline{X}_1 = 4.75, \overline{X}_2 = 4.62,$ and $\overline{X}_3 = 7.75,$ and the F test rejects when the Type I error probability is $\alpha = 0.05$. So, according to Fisher's LSD method, proceed by comparing each pair of groups with Student's T test with the Type I error probability set at $\alpha = 0.05$. For the first and second groups ($j = 1$ and $k = 2$),

$$T = \frac{|4.75 - 4.62|}{\sqrt{4.14\left(\frac{1}{8} + \frac{1}{8}\right)}} = 0.128.$$

The degrees of freedom are $v = 21$, and with $\alpha = 0.05$, Table B.4 in Appendix B indicates that the critical value is $t = 2.08$. Therefore, fail to reject. That is, the F test indicates that there is a difference among the three groups, but Student's T suggests that the difference does not correspond to groups 1 and 2. Or, from the point of view of Tukey's three-decision rule, make no decision about which group has the larger mean. For groups 1 and 3,

$$T = \frac{|4.75 - 7.75|}{\sqrt{4.14(\frac{1}{8} + \frac{1}{8})}} = 2.94,$$

and because 2.94 is greater than the critical value, 2.08, reject. That is, conclude that the means for groups 1 and 3 differ and that group 3 has the larger mean. In a similar manner, conclude that the means for groups 2 and 3 differ as well because $T = 3.08$.

When the assumptions of normality and homoscedasticity are true, Fisher's method controls FWE when $J = 3$. That is, the probability of at least one Type I error will be less than or equal to α when dealing with three groups. However, when there are more than three groups ($J > 3$), this is not necessarily true (Hayter, 1986). To gain some intuition as to why, suppose four groups are to be compared, the first three have equal means, but the mean of the fourth group is so much larger than the other three that power is close to 1 when using the ANOVA F test. Consequently, with near certainty, all pairs of means will be compared with Student's T at the α level. In particular,

$$H_0 : \mu_1 = \mu_2,$$
$$H_0 : \mu_1 = \mu_3,$$
$$H_0 : \mu_2 = \mu_3,$$

will be tested each at the α level. Because all three of these hypotheses are true, the probability of at least one Type I error among these three tests will be greater than α.

12.1.2   R Function FisherLSD

The R function

```
FisherLSD(x,alpha=0.05)
```

performs Fisher's LSD method. As usual, the argument x can be a matrix or a data frame with J columns corresponding to groups or x can have list mode.

12.2   THE TUKEY–KRAMER METHOD

Tukey was the first to propose a method that controls FWE, the probability of at least one Type I error. He assumed normality and homoscedasticity (equal variances) and obtained an exact solution when all J groups have equal sample sizes. Kramer (1956) proposed a generalization that provides an approximate solution when the sample sizes are unequal, and Hayter (1984) showed that when the groups have equal population variances and sampling is from normal distributions, Kramer's method is conservative. That is, it guarantees that FWE will be less than or equal to α.

When comparing the jth group to the kth group, the Tukey–Kramer confidence interval for the difference between the means, $\mu_j - \mu_k$, is

$$(\overline{X}_j - \overline{X}_k) \pm q\sqrt{\frac{MSWG}{2}\left(\frac{1}{n_j} + \frac{1}{n_k}\right)}, \tag{12.4}$$

where n_j is the sample size of the jth group, MSWG is again the mean square within groups, which estimates the assumed common variance, and q is a constant read from Table B.9 in Appendix B, which depends on the values of α, J (the number of groups being compared), and the degrees of freedom,

$$v = N - J,$$

where again N is the total number of observations in all J groups. The critical value q can be determined with the R function

```
qtukey(p, nmeans, df),
```

where the argument p corresponds to $1 - \alpha$, the argument nmeans indicates how many groups are being compared and df indicates the degrees of freedom. For example,

```
qtukey(0.95,5,10)
```

returns 4.65, meaning that for $\alpha = 0.05$, $J = 5$ groups and 10 degrees of freedom, $q = 4.65$. When testing $H_0 : \mu_j = \mu_k$, the test statistic is

$$T = \frac{\overline{X}_j - \overline{X}_k}{\sqrt{\frac{MSWG}{2}\left(\frac{1}{n_j} + \frac{1}{n_k}\right)}}.$$

Decision Rule: Reject the hypothesis of equal means if $|T| \geq q$. Alternatively, reject if the confidence interval given by Equation (12.4) does not contain zero. Under normality, equal variances, and equal sample sizes, the probability of one or more Type I errors, when no two groups differ, is exactly α.

Example

Table 12.2 shows some hypothetical data on the ratings of three methods for treating migraine headaches. Each method is rated by a different sample of individuals. The total number of participants is $N = 23$, so the degrees of freedom are $v = N - J = 23 - 3 = 20$, the sample means are $\overline{X}_1 = 4.1$, $\overline{X}_2 = 6.125$, and $\overline{X}_3 = 7.2$, and the estimate of the assumed common variance is MSWG $= 2.13$. If the probability of at least

**TABLE 12.2   Ratings of Methods
for Treating Migraine Headaches**

Method 1	Method 2	Method 3
5	6	8
4	6	7
3	7	6
3	8	8
4	4	7
5	5	
3	8	
4	5	
8		
2		

one Type I error is to be $\alpha = 0.05$, Table B.9 in Appendix B indicates that $q = 3.58$. When comparing groups 1 and 3 ($j = 1$ and $k = 3$), the test statistic is

$$T = \frac{4.1 - 7.2}{\sqrt{\frac{2.13}{2}\left(\frac{1}{10} + \frac{1}{5}\right)}} = -5.48.$$

Because $|-5.48| \geq 3.58$, the hypothesis of equal means is rejected. The confidence interval for $\mu_1 - \mu_3$, the difference between the means corresponding to groups 1 and 3, is

$$(4.1 - 7.2) \pm 3.58\sqrt{\frac{2.13}{2}\left(\frac{1}{10} + \frac{1}{5}\right)} = (-5.12, -1.1).$$

This interval does not contain zero, so again reject the hypothesis that the population means are equal. Methods 1 and 2, as well as methods 2 and 3, can be compared in a similar manner, but the details are left as an exercise.

12.2.1   Some Important Properties of the Tukey–Kramer Method

There are some properties associated with the Tukey–Kramer method that are important to keep in mind. First, in terms of controlling the probability of at least one Type I error, the method does not assume nor does it require that we must first reject with the ANOVA F test. This is in contrast to Fisher's method, which requires that we first reject with the ANOVA F test. Second, if the Tukey–Kramer method is applied only if the ANOVA F test rejects, its properties are changed. For example, if we ignore the F test and simply apply the Tukey–Kramer method with $\alpha = 0.05$, then under normality, homoscedasticity, and when the sample sizes are equal, the probability of at least one Type I error, when none of the groups differ, is exactly 0.05. But if the Tukey–Kramer method is applied only after the F test rejects, this is no longer true, the probability of at least one Type I error will be less than 0.05 (Bernhardson, 1975). In practical terms, when it comes to controlling the probability of at least one Type I error, there is no need to first reject with the ANOVA F test to justify using the Tukey–Kramer method. If the Tukey–Kramer method is used only after the F test rejects, power can be reduced. Currently, however, a common practice is to use the Tukey–Kramer method only if the F test rejects. That is, the insight reported by Bernhardson is not yet well known.

It was previously noted that if, for example, three groups differ and have normal distributions, but there is an outlier in a fourth group, the F test can fail to reject and consequently miss the true differences among the first three groups. Notice that even if the Tukey–Kramer method is used without first requiring that the F test rejects, this problem is not necessarily corrected. The reason is that the Tukey–Kramer method is based on the sample variances of all the groups. For instance, when comparing groups 1 and 2, the sample variances from all of the groups are used to compute MSWG. The point is that if there are outliers in group 3 or 4, they can inflate the corresponding sample variances, which in turn can inflate MSWG, which can result in low power when comparing groups 1 and 2. More generally, outliers in any group can result in low power among groups where no outliers occur.

Example

Consider the following data for three groups.

G1:	268, 114, −21, 313, 128, 239, 227, 59, 379, 100
G2:	−209, −37, −10, 151, 126, −151, 41, 158, 59, 22
G3:	32, 187, −21, −54, 14, 169, −17, 304, 134, −103

It can be seen that MSWG is 15,629 and that when comparing groups 1 and 2 with the Tukey–Kramer method, $T = 4.2$. The degrees of freedom are $\nu = 27$. If the probability of at least one Type I error is to be 0.05, Table B.9 in Appendix B indicates that the critical value is $q = 3.5$, approximately. Because the absolute value of T exceeds 3.5, reject the hypothesis that groups 1 and 2 have equal means. But suppose the first two observations in the third group are increased to 400 and 500, respectively. Then, MSWG increases to 24,510 and now, when comparing groups 1 and 2, $T = 3.34$ and the hypothesis of equal means is no longer rejected even though none of the values in groups 1 and 2 were altered. A way of avoiding the problem just illustrated is to switch to one of the methods described in Section 12.4.

12.2.2   R Functions TukeyHSD and T.HSD

The Tukey–Kramer method can be applied with the R command `aov` followed by the R command `TukeyHSD`. The first command has the form

```
temp=aov(x~as.factor(g)).
```

So, the argument g must be a factor variable that is used to sort the data in x into groups based on the values in g. Then, the command

```
TukeyHSD(temp)
```

performs the Tukey–Kramer method.

If the data are stored in a matrix or data frame (with columns as groups), or list mode, the R function

```
T.HSD(x,alpha=0.05),
```

can be used.

12.3 SCHEFFÉ'S METHOD

Scheffé's method is one more classic technique that is routinely taught and used. The method can be used to compare all pairs of groups, and it is designed to control FWE (the probability of one or more Type I errors), assuming normality and that the groups have a common variance (homoscedasticity). The computational details are not provided, but a property of the method should be described. If the goal is to compare all pairs of groups, Scheffé (1959) shows that the Tukey–Kramer method is preferable because if the underlying assumptions are true, Scheffé's method will have less power compared to Tukey–Kramer. The reason is that Scheffé's method is too conservative in terms of Type I errors. That is, FWE will not be exactly 0.05, but less than 0.05 to the point that the Tukey–Kramer method will be more likely to detect true differences.

Both the Tukey–Kramer and Scheffé's method can be used for more involved comparisons. Consider a two-way ANOVA design and imagine that all pairwise comparisons among the levels of the first factor are to be performed, all pairwise comparisons among the levels of the second factor are to be performed, as well as all the tetrad differences relevant to interactions. Scheffé's method guarantees that when testing all of these hypotheses, the probability of one or more Type I errors will not exceed the specified α level, again assuming normality and homoscedasticity. As the number of hypotheses to be tested increases, at some point Scheffé's method is preferable to the Tukey–Kramer method. But similar to the Tukey–Kramer method, when the assumptions of equal variances and normality are not true, Scheffé's method can perform poorly relative to more modern techniques. Although the method is designed to compare means, a more accurate description is that it tests the hypothesis that groups have identical distributions. It might provide satisfactory confidence intervals based on means, but even under normality, if the homoscedasticity assumption is violated, this is not necessarily the case (Kaiser and Bowden, 1983).

12.3.1 R Function Scheffe

The R function

```
Scheffe(x,tr=0.2,con=0)
```

performs Scheffé's method. By default, it performs all pairwise comparisons of the means but it is not recommended for this goal. When this function is used, it prints a warning message that the R function `lincon` is probably better, which is described in Section 12.4.2. When dealing with a two-way ANOVA design, the function `Scheffe` could be used for testing all hypotheses relevant to main effects and interactions via the argument `con`. Sections 12.4.2 and 12.7.1 illustrate how the argument `con` can be used. (Also see Exercise 25.)

12.4 METHODS THAT ALLOW UNEQUAL POPULATION VARIANCES

It is known that all of the methods in the previous section can be unsatisfactory, in terms of Type I errors and providing accurate confidence intervals, when groups have unequal population variances, even when the normality assumption is true (e.g., Dunnett, 1980a; Kaiser and Bowden, 1983). As in the previous chapters, when groups do not differ in any manner, meaning that they have identical distributions, the Tukey–Kramer and Scheffé methods are satisfactory. But in terms of computing accurate confidence intervals and achieving relatively high power, they can be highly unsatisfactory under general conditions. Important advances toward more satisfactory solutions are methods that allow unequal variances. Many such methods have been proposed that are designed to control the probability of one or more Type I errors (FWE), comparisons of which were made by Dunnett (1980b), assuming normality. One of the methods that performed well in Dunnett's study is described next, which is readily generalized to the problem of comparing trimmed means.

12.4.1 Dunnett's T3 Method and an Extension of Yuen's Method for Comparing Trimmed Means

Dunnett's T3 procedure is just Welch's method described in Chapter 9, but with the critical value adjusted so that FWE is approximately equal to α when sampling from normal distributions. Let s_j^2 be the sample variance for the jth group, let n_j be the sample size, and set

$$q_j = \frac{s_j^2}{n_j}.$$

When comparing group j to group k, the degrees of freedom are

$$\hat{v}_{jk} = \frac{(q_j + q_k)^2}{\dfrac{q_j^2}{n_j - 1} + \dfrac{q_k^2}{n_k - 1}}.$$

The test statistic is

$$W = \frac{\overline{X}_j - \overline{X}_k}{\sqrt{q_j + q_k}}.$$

Decision Rule: Reject $H_0 : \mu_j = \mu_k$, the hypothesis that groups j and k have equal means, if $|W| \geq c$, where the critical value, c, is read from Table B.10 in Appendix B. A confidence interval for $\mu_j - \mu_k$, the difference between the means of groups j and k, is given by

$$(\overline{X}_j - \overline{X}_k) \pm c\sqrt{\frac{s_j^2}{n_j} + \frac{s_k^2}{n_k}}.$$

The critical value read from Table B.10 depends in part on the total number of comparisons that are to be performed. When performing all pairwise comparisons, the total number of comparisons is

$$C = \frac{J^2 - J}{2}.$$

In the illustration, there are three groups ($J = 3$), so the total number of comparisons to be performed is

$$C = \frac{3^2 - 3}{2} = 3.$$

If there are four groups *and* all pairwise comparisons are to be performed, $C = (4^2 - 4)/2 = 6$.

Example

Four methods for back pain are being investigated. For each method, 10 randomly sampled individuals are treated for 2 weeks and then they report the severity of their back pain. The results are as follows:

Method 1	Method 2	Method 3	Method 4
5	2	3	4
2	0	0	4
3	0	0	7
3	4	0	3
0	3	1	2
0	0	8	3
0	2	2	2
1	4	0	4
0	0	2	1
13	3	0	9

Tedious calculations yield the following results.

Method	Method	$|W|$	c	v
1	2	0.655	3.09	12.10
1	3	0.737	2.99	15.11
1	4	0.811	3.00	14.82
2	3	0.210	2.98	15.77
2	4	2.249	2.97	16.06
3	4	2.087	2.93	17.98

For example, when comparing methods 1 and 2, the absolute value of the test statistic is $|W| = 0.655$ and the critical value is $c = 3.09$ based on degrees of freedom $v = 12.1$, so the hypothesis of equal means is not rejected. For all other pairs of groups, again the hypothesis of equal means is not rejected.

The T3 procedure is readily extended to trimmed means. Simply apply Yuen's method as described in Section 9.3, only now the critical value is read from Table B.10, which again depends on C, the number of hypotheses to be tested. A bootstrap-t method is available as well.

12.4.2   R Functions lincon, linconbt, and conCON

The R function

```
lincon(x, con = 0, tr = 0.2, alpha = 0.05)
```

performs all pairwise comparisons using a generalization of the T3 procedure to trimmed means. To compare means, set the argument tr=0. To apply a bootstrap-t technique, use the R function

```
linconbt(x, con = 0, tr = 0.2, alpha = 0.05, nboot = 599).
```

To explain and illustrate the argument con, consider the classic problem of comparing groups to a control group. To be concrete, imagine that four experimental drugs are being considered for lowering cholesterol levels and that the goal is to compare groups taking an experimental drug to a control group that takes a placebo. So, the goal is not to compare all pairs of groups. Rather, the goal is to test

$$H_0 : \mu_1 - \mu_2 = 0,$$
$$H_0 : \mu_1 - \mu_3 = 0,$$
$$H_0 : \mu_1 - \mu_4 = 0,$$
$$H_0 : \mu_1 - \mu_5 = 0,$$

where μ_1 is the mean for the control group. An advantage of testing only these four hypotheses, rather comparing all pairs of means, is more power when controlling FWE.

Here is a way of testing these four hypotheses using R. First, create an R variable that contains the following matrix:

$$
\begin{matrix}
1 & 1 & 1 & 1 \\
-1 & 0 & 0 & 0 \\
0 & -1 & 0 & 0 \\
0 & 0 & -1 & 0 \\
0 & 0 & 0 & -1
\end{matrix}
$$

Further imagine that this matrix is stored in the R variable A, which can be done with the R function

```
conCON(J,conG=1),
```

where the argument J indicates the total number of groups and conG indicates which group is the control group. For the situation at hand, use the R command

```
A=conCON(4)$conCON.
```

Then, the R command

```
lincon(x,con=A)
```

will test four hypotheses corresponding to the four columns of A. The first column of A says to compare groups 1 and 2 ignoring groups 3–5. That is, the rows of A correspond to groups and the goal is to test $H_0: \mu_1 - \mu_2 = 0$. The second column says to compare groups 1 and 3 ignoring groups 2, 4, and 5. The third column says to compare groups 1 and 4 ignoring groups 2, 3, and 5. Finally, The fourth column says to compare groups 1 and 5 ignoring groups 2, 3, and 4.

It might help to visualize the situation in the following manner:

$$
\begin{matrix}
\mu_1 & 1 & 1 & 1 & 1 \\
\mu_2 & -1 & 0 & 0 & 0 \\
\mu_3 & 0 & -1 & 0 & 0 \\
\mu_4 & 0 & 0 & -1 & 0 \\
\mu_5 & 0 & 0 & 0 & -1
\end{matrix}
$$

Notice that if the elements in the first column are multiplied by the corresponding elements in the second column and if the results are added together, we get $\mu_1 - \mu_2$, which corresponds to the first hypothesis of interest, namely, $H_0: \mu_1 - \mu_2 = 0$. Multiplying the first column by the corresponding elements in the third column and summing the results give $\mu_1 - \mu_3$, which corresponds to the second hypothesis of interest, namely, $H_0: \mu_1 - \mu_3 = 0$. The columns of A are examples of what are called *linear contrast coefficients.* For example, the first column contains 1, −1, 0, 0, 0, which are the linear contrast coefficients associated with H_0: $\mu_1 - \mu_2 = 0$.

12.5 ANOVA VERSUS MULTIPLE COMPARISON PROCEDURES

Similar to the Tukey–Kramer method, Dunnett's T3 does not require that you first test and reject the hypothesis of equal means using the ANOVA F test or Welch's test in Section 10.2. Both the T3 and Tukey–Kramer methods are designed to control FWE when applied as previously described. As noted in Section 12.2.1, if the Tukey–Kramer method is used contingent upon rejecting the hypothesis of equal means with the ANOVA F test, its properties, in terms of the probability of a Type I error, are altered. Under normality and homoscedasticity, with equal sample sizes, FWE is controlled exactly. But if the Tukey–Kramer method is used only when the ANOVA F test rejects, the actual FWE will be smaller than intended (Bernhardson, 1975). The same is true when using Dunnett's T3. In practical terms, power will be negatively impacted.

Despite the results in Bernhardson (1975), the methods in Chapter 10 do have practical importance when performing all pairwise comparisons; they play a role in what are called step-down and step-up techniques. Variations that deal with nonnormality and unequal variances have the potential of increasing power. For details about these methods, see Wilcox (2012a, Section 13.1.5).

Another possible reason for using the methods in Chapter 10 is that they can have more power than the multiple comparison procedures covered here. That is, they might detect situations where there are true differences among the groups being compared even when something like the T3 method fails to reject for all pairs of groups.

12.6 COMPARING MEDIANS

There is a simple extension of the T3 method that can be used to compare medians rather than means when there are no tied values. For any two groups, test the hypothesis of equal medians by applying the method in Section 9.2, which is based on the sample median and the McKean–Schrader estimate of the standard errors. In symbols, let M_j and M_k be the sample medians corresponding to groups j and k and let S_j^2 and S_k^2 be the McKean–Schrader estimate of the squared standard errors. The hypothesis of equal medians is rejected when

$$\frac{|M_j - M_k|}{\sqrt{S_j^2 + S_k^2}} \geq c,$$

where the critical value c is read from Table B.10 with degrees of freedom $v = \infty$ in order to control the probability of at least one Type I error. As noted in Chapter 9, when comparing two groups, this approach appears to perform reasonably well, in terms of controlling the probability of a Type I error, provided there are no tied (duplicated) values within either group. But when there are tied values, the actual Type I error probability might be considerably larger than intended. This issue can be addressed via the percentile bootstrap in Section 9.2.2 with FWE (the probability of one or more Type I errors) controlled via Rom's method described in Section 12.8.2 or Hochberg's method in Section 12.8.3.

Example

Imagine that for five groups, all pairs of groups are to be compared using medians. Then, the total number of tests to be performed is $C = (5^2 - 5)/2 = 10$. If the FWE is to be 0.05, Table B.10 says that the critical value is $c = 2.79$. So, if for groups 1 and 2, $M_1 = 12$, $M_2 = 4$, $S_1^2 = 16$, and $S_2^2 = 22$, the test statistic is

$$\frac{12 - 4}{\sqrt{16 + 22}} = 1.3,$$

which is less than 2.79, fail to detect a difference between the population medians corresponding to groups 1 and 2. Or, in terms of Tukey's three-decision rule, make no decision about which group has the larger population median.

12.6.1   R Functions msmed, medpb, and Qmcp

The R function

```
msmed(x, con = 0, alpha = 0.05)
```

performs all pairwise comparisons of the medians using the McKean-Schrader estimate of the standard errors. It is used in the same manner as the R function lincon described in Section 12.4.2. The R function

```
medpb(x, alpha=0.05, nboot=NA, grp=NA, est=median, con=0)
```

uses a percentile bootstrap method to compare medians, which continues to perform well when there are tied values. This function defaults to comparing medians, but other measures of location can be used via the argument est. The argument con can be used as illustrated in Section 12.4.2. An additional illustration is provided in Section 12.7.1. For comparing quantiles other than the median, use the R function

```
Qmcp(x, q=0.5, con=0, SEED=TRUE, nboot=NA, alpha=0.05)
```

By default, Qmcp uses the Bonferroni method to control the probability of one more Type I errors, which is described in Section 12.8.1. With small samples sizes, the Bonferroni method is better than Hochberg's method, which is described in Section 12.8.3. With sufficiently large sample sizes, Hochberg's method can be used, but it is unknown how large the sample sizes must be.

12.7   TWO-WAY ANOVA DESIGNS

The multiple comparison procedures previously described can be generalized to a two-way ANOVA design. (Independent groups are being assumed.) But before continuing, it helps to quickly review Welch's test covered in Chapter 9, which is aimed at comparing the means of two independent groups. The goal was to test

$$H_0 : \mu_1 - \mu_2 = 0,$$

the hypothesis that the two means are equal. The strategy was to estimate the difference between the population means with the difference between the sample means: $\overline{X}_1 - \overline{X}_2$. Then, this difference was divided by an estimate of the standard error of $\overline{X}_1 - \overline{X}_2$, which is given by

$$\sqrt{\frac{s_1^2}{n_1} + \frac{s_2^2}{n_2}}.$$

This yields the test statistic

$$W = \frac{\overline{X}_1 - \overline{X}_2}{\sqrt{\frac{s_1^2}{n_1} + \frac{s_2^2}{n_2}}},$$

where s_1^2 and s_2^2 are the sample variances corresponding to the two groups being compared, and n_1 and n_2 are the sample sizes. In words, the estimate of the squared standard error of the first sample mean is given by the corresponding sample variance divided by the sample size. Similarly, the estimate of the squared standard error of the second sample mean is equal to the corresponding sample variance divided by the sample size. Finally, the estimate of the squared standard error of the difference between the means is given by the sum of the estimated squared standard errors.

To explain how Welch's test can be extended to a two-way design, it helps to begin with the simplest case: a 2-by-2 design. As explained in Chapter 10, the situation can be depicted as follows:

		Factor B
	μ_1	μ_2
Factor A		
	μ_3	μ_4

Recall from Chapter 10 that when dealing with factor A, the goal is to test

$$H_0 : \frac{\mu_1 + \mu_2}{2} = \frac{\mu_3 + \mu_4}{2}.$$

Chapter 10 described how this hypothesis can be tested, but another important approach is described here. Normality is assumed, but unlike the F test in Chapter 10, the method is designed to handle unequal variances.

It turns out to be convenient to write this last hypothesis as

$$H_0 : \mu_1 + \mu_2 - \mu_3 - \mu_4 = 0.$$

Notice the similarity between this hypothesis and the hypothesis tested by Welch's method as described in Chapter 9. Both deal with testing the hypothesis that a certain linear combination of the means is equal to zero. Welch's test is concerned with H_0: $\mu_1 - \mu_2 = 0$, the hypothesis that the difference between the means is zero.

In general, when dealing the jth group, an estimate of the squared standard error of the sample mean, $\overline{X}_j$, is given by

$$q_j = \frac{s_j^2}{n_j},$$

the sample variance divided by the sample size. With Welch's test, we get an estimate of the squared standard error of the difference between the sample means by adding the estimates of the corresponding squared standard errors. For groups 1 and 2, we use $q_1 + q_2$. More generally, for groups j and k, $\mathrm{VAR}(\overline{X}_j - \overline{X}_k)$, the squared standard error of the difference between the sample means, is estimated with $q_j + q_k$. It can be shown that for independent groups, if we add some means together and subtract out others, again the squared standard error is estimated simply by summing the corresponding estimates of the squared standard errors of the sample means. So here, when dealing with H_0 : $\mu_1 + \mu_2 - \mu_3 - \mu_4 = 0$, we estimate $\mu_1 + \mu_2 - \mu_3 - \mu_4$ with

$$\overline{X}_1 + \overline{X}_2 - \overline{X}_3 - \overline{X}_4,$$

and an estimate of the squared standard error is given by

$$q_1 + q_2 + q_3 + q_4.$$

The quantity $\mu_1 + \mu_2 - \mu_3 - \mu_4$ is an example of what is called a *linear contrast*. The resulting test statistic is

$$W = \frac{\overline{X}_1 + \overline{X}_2 - \overline{X}_3 - \overline{X}_4}{\sqrt{q_1 + q_2 + q_3 + q_4}}$$

and the degrees of freedom are based on two quantities. The first is

$$V_1 = (q_1 + q_2 + q_3 + q_4)^2,$$

the square of the sum of the estimated squared standard errors. The second is

$$V_2 = \frac{q_1^2}{n_1 - 1} + \frac{q_2^2}{n_2 - 1} + \frac{q_3^2}{n_3 - 1} + \frac{q_4^2}{n_4 - 1}.$$

The degrees of freedom are $v = V_1/V_2$.

Decision Rule: When dealing with a *single* hypothesis, the null hypothesis is rejected if $|W| \geq t$, where t is the $1 - \alpha/2$ quantile of a Student's T distribution with v degrees of freedom, which can be read from Table B.4 in Appendix B. When testing multiple hypotheses, the critical value is read from Table B.10 instead, as illustrated momentarily.

Example

As just indicated, for a 2-by-2 ANOVA design, testing the hypothesis of no main effect for Factor A corresponds to testing $H_0 : \mu_1 + \mu_2 - \mu_3 - \mu_4 = 0$. Imagine that the sample means are $\overline{X}_1 = 4$, $\overline{X}_2 = 8$, $\overline{X}_3 = 2$, and $\overline{X}_4 = 6$. An estimate of $\mu_1 + \mu_2 - \mu_3 - \mu_4$ is simply $\overline{X}_1 + \overline{X}_2 - \overline{X}_3 - \overline{X}_4 = 4$. If the sample variances are $s_1^2 = 24$, $s_2^2 = 32$, $s_3^2 = 48$, and $s_4^2 = 36$, and if the sample sizes are $n_1 = 12$, $n_2 = 8$, $n_3 = 12$, and $n_4 = 6$, then $q_1 = 24/12 = 2$, $q_2 = 32/8 = 4$, $q_3 = 4$, and $q_4 = 6$. Consequently, the estimated squared standard error of $\overline{X}_1 + \overline{X}_2 - \overline{X}_3 - \overline{X}_4$ is $q_1 + q_2 + q_3 + q_4 = 2 + 4 + 4 + 6 = 16$, so the estimated standard error is $\sqrt{16} = 4$, and an appropriate test statistic for $H_0 : \mu_1 + \mu_2 - \mu_3 - \mu_4 = 0$ is

$$W = \frac{4 + 8 - 2 - 6}{4} = 1.$$

We see that $V_1 = 16^2 = 256$,

$$V_2 = \frac{2^2}{11} + \frac{4^2}{7} + \frac{4^2}{11} + \frac{6^2}{5} = 11.3,$$

so the degrees of freedom are $v = 256/11.3 = 22.65$, in which case, if the probability of a Type I error is to be $\alpha = 0.05$, Table B.4 in Appendix B indicates that the critical value is approximately $t = 2.07$. Because $|W| < 2.07$, fail to reject the hypothesis of no main effect for factor A.

The method for dealing with factor A extends immediately to factor B. Now the goal is to test

$$H_0 : \frac{\mu_1 + \mu_3}{2} = \frac{\mu_2 + \mu_4}{2},$$

which is the same as testing

$$H_0 : \mu_1 + \mu_3 - \mu_2 - \mu_4 = 0.$$

So now, the test statistic is

$$W = \frac{\overline{X}_1 + \overline{X}_3 - \overline{X}_2 - \overline{X}_4}{\sqrt{q_1 + q_2 + q_3 + q_4}}$$

and the degrees of freedom are again V_1/V_2.

Example

The previous example is continued, only now the focus is on factor B. We have that

$$W = \frac{4 + 2 - 8 - 8}{4} = -2.5.$$

The degrees of freedom are again $v = 22.65$, the critical value is again $t = 2.07$ (still assuming that the probability of a Type I error is to be $\alpha = 0.05$), and because $|W| \geq 2.07$, reject and conclude there is a main effect for factor B.

Interactions are handled in a similar manner. The main difference is that now the goal is to test

$$H_0 : \frac{\mu_1 - \mu_3}{2} = \frac{\mu_2 - \mu_4}{2},$$

which is the same as testing

$$H_0 : \mu_1 - \mu_3 - \mu_2 + \mu_4 = 0.$$

The test statistic is

$$W = \frac{\overline{X}_1 - \overline{X}_3 - \overline{X}_2 + \overline{X}_4}{\sqrt{q_1 + q_2 + q_3 + q_4}}$$

and the degrees of freedom are again V_1/V_2.

Example

Continuing the last two examples, for the hypothesis of no interaction,

$$W = \frac{4 - 2 - 8 + 8}{4} = 0.5,$$

again the critical value (for $\alpha = 0.05$) is $t = 2.07$, and because $|W| < 2.07$, we fail to detect an interaction.

In the previous three examples, each test was performed with the probability of a Type I error set at 0.05. How might we control the probability of at least one Type I error? A simple strategy, assuming normality, is to note that a total of $C = 3$ hypotheses are to be performed, and then read a critical value from Table B.10 in Appendix B rather than Table B.4.

Example

The last three examples tested three hypotheses: (1) no main effects for factor A, (2) no main effects for factor B, and (3) no interaction. So when referring to Table B.10, the total number of hypotheses to be tested is $C = 3$. And for each of these tests, the degrees of freedom are $v = 22.65$. If we want the probability of one or more Type I errors to be 0.05, then Table B.10 indicates that the critical value is approximately $c = 2.58$. For each of the three hypotheses, the test statistic $|W|$ is less than 2.58, so none of the three hypotheses would be rejected.

12.7.1 R Function mcp2atm

As is evident, testing all of the hypotheses relevant to main effects and interactions is tedious. What is needed is an easier way of doing this with R. To illustrate how this can be done, again consider a 2-by-2 design with the means labeled as described at the beginning of this section. First, consider main effects for Factor A and recall that the null hypothesis was written as

$$H_0 : \mu_1 + \mu_2 - \mu_3 - \mu_4 = 0.$$

For Factor B, the null hypothesis is

$$H_0 : \mu_1 - \mu_2 + \mu_3 - \mu_4 = 0$$

and for the hypothesis of no interactions, it is

$$H_0 : \mu_1 - \mu_2 - \mu_3 + \mu_4 = 0.$$

Now consider

$$
\begin{array}{cccc}
\mu_1 & 1 & 1 & 1 \\
\mu_2 & 1 & -1 & -1 \\
\mu_3 & -1 & 1 & -1 \\
\mu_4 & -1 & -1 & 1
\end{array}
$$

Focus on columns 1 and 2 and notice that if the corresponding elements are multiplied and added to together, we get

$$\mu_1 + \mu_2 - \mu_3 - \mu_4,$$

which corresponds to the null hypothesis for factor A. Notice the similarity with the situation illustrated in Section 12.4.2. Focusing on columns 1 and 3, if the corresponding elements are multiplied and added to together, we get $\mu_1 - \mu_2 + \mu_3 - \mu_4$, which corresponds to the null hypothesis for factor B. Doing the same using columns 1 and 4, we get $\mu_1 - \mu_2 - \mu_3 + \mu_4$, which corresponds to the null hypothesis of no interaction. As was the case in Section 12.4.2, columns 2–4 are examples of *linear contrast coefficients*.

For a J-by-K design, the R function

```
mcp2atm(J,K,x,tr=0.2,alpha=0.05)
```

creates the relevant linear contrast coefficients and tests the hypotheses associated main effects and interactions.

Example

Here is what part of the output looks like for a 2-by-2 design:

```
$Factor.A$test
      con.num      test      crit        se        df
[1,]        1 4.198432 2.002998 0.380118 56.30864

$Factor.A$psihat
      con.num psihat  ci.lower ci.upper       p. value
[1,]        1 1.5959 0.8345238 2.357275 9.655586e-05

$conA
      [,1]
[1,]    1
[2,]    1
[3,]   -1
[4,]   -1
```

The output labeled $conA indicates the linear contrast coefficients for factor A. Note that there are four rows, which correspond to the four groups.

As in Section 12.4.2, it might help to visualize the situation as follows:

$$
\begin{array}{cc}
\mu_1 & 1 \\
\mu_2 & 1 \\
\mu_3 & -1 \\
\mu_4 & -1
\end{array}
$$

Multiplying the elements of the first column by the corresponding elements of the second column and adding the results yield $\mu_1 + \mu_2 - \mu_3 - \mu_4$. This indicates that the goal is to test H_0: $\mu_1 + \mu_2 - \mu_3 - \mu_4 = 0$. The estimate of $\mu_1 + \mu_2 - \mu_3 - \mu_4$ is under psihat and is equal to 1.5959. The value of the test statistic is 4.198 and the p-value is $9.655586e - 05 = 9.655586(10)^{-5}$. That is, levels 1 and 2 for factor A differ significantly. Results for factor B and the hypothesis of no interaction are reported in a similar manner.

Now consider a 3-by-2 design in which case the population means are depicted as follows:

		Factor B	
		μ_1	μ_2
Factor A		μ_3	μ_4
		μ_5	μ_6

Following the description of the two-way ANOVA in Chapter 10, we write the marginal means for factor A as

$$
\overline{\mu}_{1.} = \frac{\mu_1 + \mu_2}{2},
$$

$$
\overline{\mu}_{2.} = \frac{\mu_3 + \mu_4}{2},
$$

and

$$\overline{\mu}_{3.} = \frac{\mu_5 + \mu_6}{2}.$$

As was explained, no differences among the levels of factor A is taken to mean that

$$H_0 : \overline{\mu}_{1.} = \overline{\mu}_{2.} = \overline{\mu}_{3.}$$

is true. But when this hypothesis is rejected, there is no indication of which levels of factor A differ.

We begin by rewriting the null hypotheses in a more convenient form in much the same manner as was done in the 2-by-2 design. To illustrate the process, focus on testing

$$H_0 : \overline{\mu}_{1.} = \overline{\mu}_{3.}.$$

A little algebra shows that this is the same as testing

$$H_0 : \mu_1 + \mu_2 - \mu_5 - \mu_6 = 0.$$

The linear contrast coefficients are as follows:

$1, 1, 0, 0, -1, -1.$

The situation can be visualized as follows:

$$
\begin{array}{cc}
\mu_1 & 1 \\
\mu_2 & 1 \\
\mu_3 & 0 \\
\mu_4 & 0 \\
\mu_5 & -1 \\
\mu_6 & -1 \\
\end{array}
$$

Multiplying the elements of the first column by the corresponding elements of the second column yields

$$\mu_1 + \mu_2 - \mu_5 - \mu_6,$$

which corresponds to the hypothesis of interest. Main effects for factor B and interactions are handled in a similar manner.

Example

Here is a portion of the output from mcp2atm for a 3-by-2 design:

```
$Factor.A$test
     con.num       test       crit        se        df
[1,]       1  0.3854185  2.421050  0.3331979  90.59986
[2,]       2 -0.4478790  2.424420  0.3385177  85.52244
[3,]       3 -0.8409606  2.424672  0.3329949  85.16628
```

```
$Factor.A$psihat
        con.num      psihat    ci.lower   ci.upper    p. value
[1,]          1   0.1284206 -0.6782681 0.9351093 0.7008308
[2,]          2 -0.1516150 -0.9723242 0.6690942 0.6553730
[3,]          3 -0.2800356 -1.0874389 0.5273678 0.4027250

$conA
       [,1] [,2] [,3]
[1,]     1    1    0
[2,]     1    1    0
[3,]    -1    0    1
[4,]    -1    0    1
[5,]     0   -1   -1
[6,]     0   -1   -1
```

The rows of $conA correspond to the six groups having population means $\mu_1, \dots, \mu_6$. The first column of $conA indicates that $H_0: \mu_1 + \mu_2 - \mu_3 - \mu_4 = 0$ was tested; the results are reported in row 1 of $Factor.A$test and row 1 of $Factor.A$psihat. The p-value is 0.701, so the null hypothesis is not rejected. That is, no difference between levels 1 and 2 is found. Column 2 of $conA indicates that $H_0: \mu_1 + \mu_2 - \mu_5 - \mu_6 = 0$ was tested, which corresponds to comparing levels 1 and 3 of factor A. The results are reported in row 2 of $Factor.A$test and row 2 of $Factor.A$psihat. Finally, column 3 of $conA indicates that $H_0: \mu_3 + \mu_4 - \mu_5 - \mu_6 = 0$ was tested.

12.8   METHODS FOR DEPENDENT GROUPS

The methods described in the previous section take advantage of the independence among the groups when trying to control the probability of at least one Type I error. When comparing dependent groups instead, alternative methods must be used.

12.8.1   Bonferroni Method

One of the earliest methods for comparing dependent groups is based on what is known as the Bonferroni inequality. The strategy is simple: If the goal is to test C hypotheses such that FWE is equal to α, test each of the individual hypotheses at the α/C level. Put another way, the Bonferroni method rejects if the p-value is less than or equal to α/C. For the special case where all pairs of groups are to be compared,

$$C = \frac{J^2 - J}{2}.$$

In terms of ensuring that FWE does not exceed α, the only requirement is that the individual tests ensure that the Type I error probability does not exceed α/C.

Example

As a simple illustration, imagine that the means for all pairs of four groups are to be compared with FWE equal to 0.06. So, a total of $C = 6$ tests are to be performed, meaning that each test should be performed with $\alpha = 0.06/6 = 0.01$. If, for example, each group has a sample size of 11, then from Chapter 9, the critical value would be the 0.995 quantile of a Student's T distribution with degrees of freedom $v = 11 - 1 = 10$, which is read from Table B.4 in Appendix B. (A test for exact equality is being used, so the critical value would be the $1 - \alpha/2$ quantile of a Student's T distribution.) In particular, the critical value is $t_{0.995} = 3.169$. So, for example, if the paired T test is applied to groups 1 and 2 yielding $T = -2.9$, because $|-2.9|$ is less than 3.169, fail to reject. The other five tests would be performed in a similar manner.

Example

Imagine that all pairs of four dependent groups are to be compared. Then, $C = 6$ hypotheses are to be tested, and for illustrative purposes, imagine that the p-values are as follows:

Number	Test	p-Value
1	$H_0 : \mu_1 = \mu_2$	$p_1 = 0.006$
2	$H_0 : \mu_1 = \mu_3$	$p_2 = 0.025$
3	$H_0 : \mu_1 = \mu_4$	$p_3 = 0.003$
4	$H_0 : \mu_2 = \mu_3$	$p_4 = 0.540$
5	$H_0 : \mu_2 = \mu_4$	$p_5 = 0.049$
6	$H_0 : \mu_3 = \mu_4$	$p_6 = 0.014$

So, the p-value for the first hypothesis is $p_1 = 0.006$, and the p-value for the second hypothesis is $p_2 = 0.025$. If the probability of at least one Type I error is to be 0.1, the Bonferroni method says that each individual test would be rejected if its p-value is less than or equal to $0.1/6 = 0.017$. So here, hypotheses 1, 3, and 6 would be rejected.

12.8.2   Rom's Method

Several improvements on the Bonferroni method have been published, and one that stands out is a so-called sequentially rejective method derived by Rom (1990), which has been found to have good power relative to several competing techniques (e.g., Olejnik et al., 1997). To apply it, compute a p-value for each of the C tests to be performed and label them $p_1, \ldots, p_C$. Next, put the p-values in descending order and label the results $p_{[1]} \geq p_{[2]} \geq \cdots \geq p_{[C]}$. So, $p_{[1]}$ is the largest p-value, $p_{[2]}$ is the next largest, and $p_{[C]}$ is the smallest. Proceed as follows:

1. Set $k = 1$.
2. If $p_{[k]} \leq d_k$, where d_k is read from Table 12.3, stop and reject all C hypotheses; otherwise, go to step 3.

TABLE 12.3   Critical Values, d_k, for
Rom's Method

k	$\alpha = 0.05$	$\alpha = 0.01$
1	0.05000	0.01000
2	0.02500	0.00500
3	0.01690	0.00334
4	0.01270	0.00251
5	0.01020	0.00201
6	0.00851	0.00167
7	0.00730	0.00143
8	0.00639	0.00126
9	0.00568	0.00112
10	0.00511	0.00101

3. Increment k by 1. If $p_{[k]} \leq d_k$, stop and reject all hypotheses having a p-value less than or equal d_k

4. If $p_{[k]} > d_k$, repeat step 3.

5. Continue until you reject or all C hypotheses have been tested.

An advantage of Rom's method is that its power is greater than or equal to the Bonferroni approach. In fact, Rom's method always rejects as many or more hypotheses. A negative feature is that the d_k values have been computed only for $\alpha = 0.05$ and 0.01 and when the number of hypotheses is less than or equal to 10. Another limitation of Rom's method is that it assumes that the test statistics, and hence the p-values, are independent. If, for example, the goal is to test $H_0 : \mu_1 = \mu_2$ as well as $H_0 : \mu_2 = \mu_3$, the corresponding test statistics will be dependent because both contain the sample mean for the second group, $\overline{X}_2$. When this assumption is violated, simulations studies summarized in Wilcox (2012a) suggest that there are situations where Rom's method continues to perform reasonably well in terms of controlling the probability of one or more Type I errors. This appears to be the case when using robust methods that control the Type I error probability associated with each individual test.

Example

A company is considering four variations of a baked good for mass distribution. An issue is whether potential customers rate the baked goods differently, depending on which variation is used. To find out, randomly sampled individuals are asked to try a baked good produced by each method. That is, each individual consumes a baked good produced by each of the four variations. Imagine that all pairwise comparisons among the resulting four dependent groups are performed, yielding the p-values shown in Table 12.4. Further assume that you want FWE to be at most 0.05. The largest p-value is 0.62, this is greater than 0.05, so you fail to reject the corresponding hypothesis, $H_0 : \mu_2 = \mu_3$. The next largest p-value is 0.130, this is greater than $d_2 = 0.025$ (read from Table 12.3), so fail to reject $H_0 : \mu_2 = \mu_4$. The next largest is

TABLE 12.4   An Illustration of Rom's Method

Number	Test	p-Value	
1	$H_0 : \mu_1 = \mu_2$	$p_1 = 0.010$	$P_{[5]}$
2	$H_0 : \mu_1 = \mu_3$	$p_2 = 0.015$	$P_{[3]}$
3	$H_0 : \mu_1 = \mu_4$	$p_3 = 0.005$	$P_{[6]}$
4	$H_0 : \mu_2 = \mu_3$	$p_4 = 0.620$	$P_{[1]}$
5	$H_0 : \mu_2 = \mu_4$	$p_5 = 0.130$	$P_{[2]}$
6	$H_0 : \mu_3 = \mu_4$	$p_6 = 0.014$	$P_{[4]}$

0.015, this is less than $d_3 = 0.0167$, so stop and reject the corresponding hypothesis as well as those having smaller p-values. If the Bonferroni inequality had been used instead, we see that $0.05/6 = 0.00833$, so only hypothesis 3 would be rejected.

12.8.3   Hochberg's Method

A slight variation of Rom's method was derived by Hochberg (1988), which is not limited to $\alpha = 0.05$ and 0.01, and it can be used when the number of hypotheses to be tested exceeds 10. In step 2 of Rom's method, rather than read d_k from Table 12.3, set $d_k = \alpha/k$. Another appeal of Hochberg's method is that it does not assume that the test statistics and p-values are independent. (There is a weak restriction on the collection of hypotheses to be tested. But simulation studies summarized in Wilcox, 2012b, suggest that this restriction can be ignored.)

12.8.4   R Functions rmmcp, dmedpb, and sintmcp

The R function

```
rmmcp(x, con=0, tr=0.2, alpha=0.05, dif=TRUE,hoch=TRUE)
```

compares dependent groups based on trimmed means. As usual, the argument x can be a matrix or data frame with columns corresponding to groups, or it can have list mode. The function uses Hochberg's method to control the probability of one or more Type I errors. If the argument hoch=FALSE, Rom's method is applied provided $\alpha = 0.05$ or 0.01 and the number of hypotheses does not exceed 10. By default, all pairwise comparisons are performed based on difference scores in conjunction with a 20% trimmed mean. Other collections of hypotheses can be tested via the argument con as illustrated in Section 12.4.2. The argument x can be a matrix or a data frame or can have list mode. If the argument dif=FALSE, the marginal trimmed means are compared instead.

The R function

```
dmedpb(x,y=NULL,alpha=0.05,con=0,est=median,dif=TRUE)
```

compares dependent groups using a percentile bootstrap method. By default, medians are used based on difference scores, but other measures of location can be used via the argument `est`. For example, `est=mom` would compare groups based on the skipped estimator in Section 2.6. To compare the medians of the marginal distributions, set the argument `dif=FALSE`. The argument x can be a matrix or a data frame or can have list mode. If the goal is to compare two groups only and x contains the data for one of the groups (it is a vector), the data for the second group can be stored in the argument y. Again, FWE is controlled via Rom's method.

The R function

```
sintmcp(x, con=0, alpha=0.05)
```

compares groups based on the median of the difference scores using the distribution free method in Section 6.4.3 with FWE controlled via Rom's method.

12.8.5   Controlling the False Discovery Rate

Benjamini and Hochberg (1995) proposed a technique similar to Hochberg's method, assuming that C independent tests are to be performed. In step 2 of Rom's method, use

$$d_k = \frac{(C - k + 1)\alpha}{C}$$

rather than $d_k = \alpha/k$ as done by Hochberg's method. Results in Williams et al. (1999) support the use of the Benjamini–Hochberg method over Hochberg.

Example

The p-values in Table 12.4 are used to illustrate the Benjamini–Hochberg method when $\alpha = 0.05$. Because $p_{[1]} = 0.620 > 0.05$, fail to reject the fourth hypothesis. Had it been the case that $p_{[1]} \leq 0.05$, stop and reject all six hypotheses. Because a nonsignificant result was obtained, set $k = 2$, and because $C = 6$, we see that $(C - k + 1)\alpha/C = 5(0.05)/6 = 0.0417$. Because $p_{[k]} = p_{[2]} = 0.130 > 0.0417$, fail to reject the fifth hypothesis and proceed to the next step. Incrementing k to 3, $(C - k + 1)\alpha/C = 4(0.05)/6 = 0.0333$, and because $p_{[3]} = 0.015 \leq 0.0333$, reject this hypothesis and the remaining hypotheses having p-values less than or equal to 0.0333. That is, reject hypotheses 1, 2, 3, and 6, and fail to reject hypotheses 4 and 5.

A criticism of the Benjamini–Hochberg method is that situations can be constructed where some hypotheses are true, some are false, and the probability of at least one Type I error will exceed α among the hypotheses that are true (Hommel, 1988). In contrast, Hochberg's method does not suffer from this problem. In practical terms, the Benjamini–Hochberg method relaxes somewhat the control over the probability of at least one Type I error with the benefit of possibly increasing power. When performing many tests, the increase in power can be of practical importance.

Although the Benjamini–Hochberg method does not necessarily control the probability of at least one Type I error, it does have the following property. When testing C hypotheses, let Q be the proportion of hypotheses that are true and rejected. That is, Q is the proportion of Type I errors among the null hypotheses that are correct. Assume that the C test statistics are independent. If all hypotheses are false, then $Q = 0$, but otherwise Q can vary from one experiment to the next. The *false discovery rate* is the expected value of Q. That is, if a study is repeated (infinitely) many times, the false discovery rate is the average proportion of Type I errors among the hypotheses that are true. Benjamini and Hochberg (1995) show that their method ensures that the false discovery rate is less than or equal to α when performing independent tests. Results in Benjamini and Yekutieli (2001) extend this result to the case where C groups are compared to a control group as was described in Section 12.4.2. For the common situation where all pairwise comparisons are made among independent groups, in which case some of the tests are dependent, simulation results reported by Keselman et al. (1999) indicate that the Benjamini–Hochberg method continues to perform well.

12.9 SUMMARY

- Methods designed to control the probability of one or more Type I errors, which assume normality and equal variances, such as the Tukey–Kramer technique, appear to perform fairly well when all groups have identical distributions. That is, they perform well in terms of Type I errors when testing the hypothesis that groups have identical distributions. For the goal of computing accurate confidence intervals based on means, some departures from normality and unequal variances can be tolerated, but the extent to which this is true is a complicated function of the sample sizes, the type of departure from normality, the likelihood of encountering outliers, and the degree to which the variances differ.

- Among the many methods for comparing means, Dunnett's T3 performs relatively well, but there are practical reasons for considering other techniques. In particular, arguments for preferring a bootstrap-t method can be made, which can be applied with the R function `linconbt` in Section 12.4.2. Despite any advantages the T3 and bootstrap-t methods offer, not all practical problems are addressed when the goal is to compare means.

- Methods based on 20% trimmed means perform well over a relatively broad range of situations in terms of both Type I errors and power. If the results are similar to those obtained with means, this suggests that methods based on the sample means are probably satisfactory in terms of making inferences about the population means. When they differ, perhaps methods based on means remain satisfactory, but there is some uncertainty about the extent to which this is true. Also, it is prudent to keep in mind that no single method is always optimal. For example, when dealing with symmetric, light-tailed distributions, methods based on means can have more power than methods based on a 20% trimmed mean.

- Methods based on medians can be useful and effective, particularly when dealing with situations where outliers are common. An advantage of using a percentile bootstrap method is that regardless of whether tied values occur, excellent control over the probability of one or more Type I errors can be achieved, except perhaps for very small sample sizes.

- Chapter 9 pointed out that different methods for comparing groups provide a different perspective on how they differ. Moreover, the choice of method can make a practical difference in terms of how much power will be achieved. This issue remains relevant here and in fact becomes more complex. For example, comparing the medians of groups 1 and 2 might be ideal in terms of power, but when comparing groups 3 and 4, perhaps comparing means or 20% trimmed means is more effective.

12.10   EXERCISES

1. Assuming normality and homoscedasticity, what problem occurs when comparing multiple groups with Student's T test?

2. For five independent groups, the goal is to perform all pairwise comparisons of the means with FWE equal to 0.05. Assume that $n_1 = n_2 = n_3 = n_4 = n_5 = 20$, $\overline{X}_1 = 15$, $\overline{X}_2 = 10$, $s_1^2 = 4$, $s_2^2 = 9$, and $s_3^2 = s_4^2 = s_5^2 = 15$. Test $H_0 : \mu_1 = \mu_2$ using Fisher's method assuming that the ANOVA F test rejects the hypothesis that all five means are equal. Assuming normality and homoscedasticity, does Fisher's method control FWE for the situation at hand?

3. Repeat the previous problem, only use the Tukey–Kramer method.

4. For four independent groups, the goal is to perform all pairwise comparisons of the means with FWE equal to 0.05. Assume $n_1 = n_2 = n_3 = n_4 = n_5 = 10$ $\overline{X}_1 = 20$, $\overline{X}_2 = 12$, $s_1^2 = 5$, $s_2^2 = 6$, $s_3^2 = 4$, $s_4^2 = 10$, and $s_5^2 = 15$. Test $H_0 : \mu_1 = \mu_2$ using Fisher's method assuming that the ANOVA F test rejects the hypothesis that all four means are equal.

5. Repeat the previous problem, only use the Tukey–Kramer method.

6. Imagine that you compare four groups with Fisher's method and you reject the hypothesis of equal means for the first two groups. If the largest observation in the fourth group is increased, what happens to MSWG? What does this suggest about power when comparing groups one and two with Fisher's method?

7. Repeat the previous problem but with the Tukey–Kramer method.

8. For five independent groups, assume that you plan to do all pairwise comparisons of the means and you want FWE to be 0.05. Further assume that $n_1 = n_2 = n_3 = n_4 = n_5 = 20$, $\overline{X}_1 = 15$, $\overline{X}_2 = 10$, $s_1^2 = 4$, and $s_2^2 = 9$, $s_3^2 = s_4^2 = s_5^2 = 15$, test $H_0 : \mu_1 = \mu_2$ using Dunnett's T3.

9. For five independent groups, assume that you plan to do all pairwise comparisons of the means and you want FWE to be 0.05. Further assume that $n_1 = n_2 = n_3 = n_4 = n_5 = 10$ $\overline{X}_1 = 20$, $\overline{X}_2 = 12$, $s_1^2 = 5$, $s_2^2 = 6$, $s_3^2 = 4$, $s_4^2 = 10$, and $s_5^2 = 15$. Test $H_0 : \mu_1 = \mu_2$ using Dunnett's T3.

10. For four independent groups, the sample medians are $M_1 = 34$, $M_2 = 16$, $M_3 = 42$, $M_4 = 22$, and the corresponding McKean–Schrader estimates of the squared standard errors are $S_1^2 = 33$, $S_2^2 = 64$, $S_3^2 = 8$, $S_4^2 = 5$. Assuming that the goal is to test the hypothesis of equal medians for all pairs of groups

such that FWE is 0.05, determine whether you would reject when comparing groups 2 and 4.

11. In the previous problem, comment on the results if there are tied values in the first group but not the other three.

12. Imagine that two medications for treating hypertension are under investigation and that researchers want to take into account ethnic background. Here, three ethnic backgrounds are considered and labeled A, B, and C. Further imagine that the results are as follows:

		Ethnicity		
		A	B	C
		$\bar{X}_1 = 24$	$\bar{X}_2 = 36$	$\bar{X}_3 = 28$
	1	$s_1^2 = 48$	$s_2^2 = 56$	$s_3^2 = 60$
		$n_1 = 8$	$n_2 = 7$	$n_3 = 12$
Medication				
		$\bar{X}_4 = 14$	$\bar{X}_5 = 24$	$\bar{X}_6 = 20$
	2	$s_4^2 = 64$	$s_5^2 = 25$	$s_6^2 = 40$
		$n_4 = 8$	$n_5 = 5$	$n_6 = 10$

Using the method in Section 12.7, indicate the linear contrast coefficients for comparing ethnic groups A and B, ignoring type of medication. Compute the test statistic and determine whether the null hypothesis is rejected assuming that this is the only hypothesis to be tested and that the goal is to have a Type I error probability equal to 0.05.

13. In the previous exercise, imagine that the goal is to compare all pairs of groups for factor B (ethnicity) such that the probability of at least one Type I error equal to 0.05. Determine the critical value when comparing ethnic groups B and C.

14. Referring to Exercise 12, imagine that the goal is to check for interactions when dealing with ethnic groups A and B. Indicate the linear contrast coefficients. Then, test the hypothesis of no interaction for this special case assuming that no other hypotheses will be tested and that the Type I error probability is to be 0.05.

15. The p-values based on five tests are 0.049, 0.048, 0.045, 0.047, and 0.042. Based on the Bonferroni method, which would be rejected with FWE equal to 0.05?

16. Referring to the previous exercise, which hypotheses would be rejected with Rom's procedure or Hochberg's method?

17. What do the last two exercises illustrate?

18. Five tests are performed aimed at comparing the medians of dependent groups. The p-values are 0.24, 0.001, 0.005, 0.12, 0.04. Which should be rejected when using Rom's method if FWE is to be 0.05?

19. Imagine that six groups are to be compared based on their means. Indicate the null hypothesis tested by the linear contrast coefficients $1, 1, 0, 0, -1, -1$.

20. For the previous exercise, if the linear contrast coefficients are $1, -2, 0, 1, 0$, what is the null hypothesis?

21. For five groups, indicate the linear contrast coefficients for testing $H_0: 2\mu_1 - \mu_3 - \mu_5 = 0$.

22. When using R, some of the functions in this chapter allow you to specify the linear contrast coefficients via the argument con. For the previous exercise, indicate an R command that would store the linear contrast coefficients in the R variable A.

23. You have four groups and contrast coefficients stored in a matrix with two rows and four columns. Why are the linear contrast coefficients stored improperly?

24. Imagine that for four groups, the goal is to test $H_0: \mu_1 = \mu_4$ and $H_0: \mu_2 = \mu_3$. Describe an R command that creates the appropriate linear contrast coefficients.

25. For a 2-by-3 design, indicate all of the contrast coefficients relevant to interactions. Check your answer via the R command con2way(2,3), which creates the contrast coefficients for you. (They are returned in $conAB.)

13

CATEGORICAL DATA

This chapter covers some basic methods for analyzing categorical data. The simplest case is where there are only two categories, which are usually called success and failure. Assuming random sampling, such situations can be analyzed using the binomial distribution, which was introduced in Chapter 4. Contingency tables, also introduced in Chapter 4, refer to situations where there are two or more categories. The main goal here is to describe some additional methods for analyzing such data.

There are many methods for analyzing categorical data beyond those covered in this chapter (e.g., Agresti, 1990, 1996; Andersen, 1997; Lloyd, 1996; & Powers & Xie, 1999; Simonoff, 2003; Agresti, 1990; Fienberg, 1980). The focus here is on the more basic techniques that might be used.

13.1 ONE-WAY CONTINGENCY TABLES

A one-way contingency table represents a situation where each participant can be classified into one of k mutually exclusive categories. The probabilities associated with these k categories are denoted by $p_1, p_2, \ldots, p_k$. The immediate goal is to test

$$H_0 : p_1 = p_2 = \cdots = p_k = \frac{1}{k}, \tag{13.1}$$

the hypothesis that all k of these probabilities are equal. Note that for the special case $k = 2$, there are only two categories and the situation reduces to the binomial distribution. In particular, the hypothesis given by Equation (13.1) is tantamount to testing $H_0: p = 1/2$, where p is the probability of a success.

Understanding and Applying Basic Statistical Methods Using R, First Edition. Rand R. Wilcox.
© 2017 John Wiley & Sons, Inc. Published 2017 by John Wiley & Sons, Inc.
www.wiley.com/go/Wilcox/Statistical_Methods_R

Example

Consider a multiple-choice test item having five choices. One choice is correct and the other four, called distracters, are incorrect. Among students who choose the wrong answer, are choices made at random? The variable of interest is the response among students choosing one of the four distracters. Let p_1, p_2, p_3, and p_4 be the probability that, among students who failed to choose the correct answer, they picked distracter 1, 2, 3, or 4, respectively. Here, we let n represent the total number of students choosing a wrong answer. Then, if students pick a wrong response at random, it should be the case that these four probabilities are equal. In symbols, the hypothesis

$$H_0 : p_1 = p_2 = p_3 = p_4 = 1/4$$

should be true.

Let n_1 be the number of participants who belong to category 1, let n_2 be the number of participants who belong to category 2, and so on. So, the total number of participants is

$$n = \sum n_k.$$

The classic test of the hypothesis given by Equation (13.1) is based on the test statistic

$$X^2 = \frac{\sum \left(n_j - \frac{n}{k} \right)^2}{n/k}. \tag{13.2}$$

When the null hypothesis is true, and the sample size, n, is sufficiently large, X^2 will have, approximately, a chi-squared distribution with $v = k - 1$ degrees of freedom. Figure 13.1 shows chi-squared distributions with degrees of freedom $v = 2$ and $v = 4$.

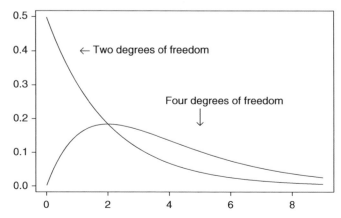

Figure 13.1   Shown are two chi-squared distributions. One has two degrees of freedom and the other has four degrees of freedom

Decision Rule: If the Type I error probability is to be α, the hypothesis of equal cell probabilities is rejected if $X^2 \geq c$, where c is the $1 - \alpha$ quantile of a chi-squared distribution with $k - 1$ degrees of freedom, which is given in Table B.3 in Appendix B. As explained in Section 10.6.1, the top row of Table B.3 in Appendix B indicates the quantile of a chi-squared distribution corresponding to the degrees of freedom indicated by the first column. For the situation at hand, the column headed by $\chi^2_{1-\alpha}$ contains the critical value c. For example, if there are 10 degrees of freedom and the desired Type I error probability is $\alpha = 0.025$, the critical value is $c = 20.48$, which can be found in the column headed by $\chi^2_{0.975}$ and the row corresponding to $v = 10$.

Example

Consider a six-sided die with each side having between one and six spots. That is, one side has a single spot, another has two spots, and so on. A gambling casino assumes that when an individual tosses the die, all six sides have the same probability of occurring. A gambler believes she can toss the die in a particular fashion so that this is not true; the belief is that some sides have a higher probability than others. To find out whether the sides have different probabilities of occurring, the gambler tosses the die 102 times and gets the following results: $n_1 = 10$, $n_2 = 15$, $n_3 = 30$, $n_4 = 25$, $n_5 = 7$, and $n_6 = 15$. That is, for 10 of the tosses 1 spot occurred, for 15 of the tosses 2 spots resulted, and so forth. To test the hypothesis that all six possibilities have the same probability, first note that the degrees of freedom are $v = k - 1 = 6 - 1 = 5$. If the Type I error probability is to be 0.05, then from Table B.3 in Appendix B, the critical value is $c = 11.0707$. Because $n = 102$, $n/k = 102/6 = 17$ and

$$X^2 = \frac{(10 - 17)^2 + \cdots + (15 - 17)^2}{17} = 22.94.$$

Because 22.94 is greater than the critical value, 11.0707, reject and conclude that the probabilities are not equal.

The method just described can be generalized to situations where the goal is to test the hypothesis that the probabilities associated with the k categories have specified values other than $1/k$. For instance, imagine that a certain medication sometimes causes a rash. For present purposes, assume that the severity of the rash is rated on a four-point scale where a 1 means no rash and a 4 means the rash is severe. Among a very large number of individuals, it is found that the proportions of individuals belonging to these four groups are $0.5, 0.3, 0.2$, and 0.1, respectively. A modification of the medication is under consideration, and one goal is to determine whether this alters the probabilities associated with the four possible outcomes. That is, the goal is to test H_0: $p_1 = 0.5$, $p_2 = 0.3$, $p_3 = 0.2$, $p_4 = 0.1$. More generally, given a set of k probabilities $p_{01}, \ldots, p_{0k}$, the goal is to test

$$H_0 : p_1 = p_{01}, \ldots, p_k = p_{0k}. \tag{13.3}$$

Among n observations, if the null hypothesis is true, the expected number of individuals falling into category 1 is np_{01}. In essence, if we focus on whether or not an individual belongs to category 1, we are dealing with a binomial random variable. That is, among the n participants, the probability of belonging to category 1 is p_{01} and the probability of not belonging to category 1 is $1 - p_{01}$. From the basic features of a binomial distribution covered in Section 4.5, the expected number of individuals falling into category 1 is np_{01}. In a similar manner, the expected number of individuals falling into category 2 is np_{02}, still assuming that the null hypothesis is true. The test statistic is

$$X^2 = \sum \frac{(n_j - np_{0j})^2}{np_{0j}}. \tag{13.4}$$

In words, the test statistic is

$$X^2 = \sum \frac{(\text{observed} - \text{expected})^2}{\text{expected}}. \tag{13.5}$$

Decision Rule: Reject the null hypothesis if $X^2 \geq c$, where c is the $1 - \alpha$ quantile of a chi-squared distribution with $k - 1$ degrees of freedom. (The distribution of X^2 when the null hypothesis is true was derived by Bienaymé, 1838.)

Example

Continuing the illustration dealing with the likelihood of getting a rash, suppose that among 88 adults taking the medication, the number of individuals corresponding to the four ratings for a rash are $n_1 = 40$, $n_2 = 30$, $n_3 = 15$, and $n_4 = 3$. This says, for example, that 40 of the 88 participants did not get a rash and 3 got the severest form. As previously noted, the goal is to test H_0: $p_1 = 0.5$, $p_2 = 0.3$, $p_3 = 0.2$, $p_4 = 0.1$. So, the expected values corresponding to the four types of rash, when the null hypothesis is true, are 44, 26.4, 17.6, and 8.8, respectively. (That is, $n = 88$, so $np_1 = 44$, $np_2 = 26.4$, $np_3 = 17.6$, and $np_4 = 8.8$.) The resulting test statistic is

$$X^2 = \frac{(40 - 44)^2}{44} + \frac{(30 - 26.4)^2}{26.4} + \frac{(15 - 17.6)^2}{17.6} + \frac{(3 - 8.8)^2}{8.8} = 5.08.$$

With $\alpha = 0.05$, the critical value is 7.8148, so the null hypothesis is not rejected.

Example

In 1988, the Department of Education conducted a survey of 17-year-old students to determine how much time they spend doing homework. Each student was classified into one of five categories: none was assigned, did not do it, spent less than 1 hour, 1–2 hours, or more than 2 hours doing homework. The percentage of students in each of these categories was found to be 20.8%, 13.4%, 27.8%, 26%, and 12%, respectively. A local school board wants to know how their students compare based on 100 randomly sampled students. That is, the goal is to test

H_0: $p_1 = 0.208$, $p_2 = 0.134$, $p_3 = 0.278$, $p_4 = 0.260$, and $p_5 = 0.120$.

TABLE 13.1   Hypothetical Data on Homework Survey

Not Assigned	Not Done	<1 Hour	1–2 Hours	>2 Hours
15	10	25	30	20

Imagine that among 100 randomly sampled students, the number of hours they study are as summarized in Table 13.1. It can be seen that $X^2 = 8.7$. If the Type I error is to be 0.05, the critical value is 9.49, so fail to reject.

13.1.1   R Function chisq.test

By default, the built-in R function

$$\texttt{chisq.test(x,p = rep(1/length(x), length(x))),}$$

performs the chi-squared test of the hypothesis given by Equation (13.1), assuming that the argument x is a vector containing count data. The hypothesis given by Equation (13.3) is tested by specifying the hypothesized values via the argument p.

Example

Imagine that participants are asked to choose their favorite brand of ice cream from among four brands and that the observed counts are 20, 30, 15, and 22. (For instance, 20 participants chose the first brand as their favorite.) Consider the goal of testing the hypothesis that all four brands have the same probability of being chosen. Here is how the analysis can be done with R:

```
oc=c(20, 30, 15, 22)
chisq.test(oc).
```

The p-value returned by this last command is 0.1468. So, if it is desired that the probability of a Type I error be less than or equal to 0.05, fail to reject the hypothesis that all four probabilities are equal to 0.25. If, instead, the goal is to test the hypothesis that the four probabilities are 0.3, 0.4, 0.1, and 0.2, now use the command

```
oc=c(20, 30, 15, 22)
chisq.test(oc,p=c(0.3, 0.4, 0.1, 0.2)).
```

The p-value returned by the last command is 0.04887.

13.1.2   Gaining Perspective: A Closer Look at the Chi-Squared Distribution

At first glance, it might appear that normality is not assumed when applying the chi-squared test just described. But this is not true. It can be shown that the test statistic, X^2, is based on a sum of squared terms, where the individual terms are approximately normal when the sample size is sufficiently large. Moreover, the formal definition of a chi-squared distribution is based on squaring independent standard normal random variables and summing them.

To illustrate the connection between a normal distribution and a chi-squared distribution, consider the special case where there are $k = 2$ categories. Now, we have the binomial probability function where p is the probability of success. Chapter 6 described how to test

$$H_0 : p = p_0$$

the hypothesis that the probability of success is equal to some specified value, p_0. Let $\hat{p}$ be the proportion of observed successes among n trials, let

$$Z = \frac{\hat{p} - p_0}{\sqrt{\hat{p}(1 - \hat{p})/n}},$$

and let c be the $1 - \alpha/2$ quantile of a standard normal distribution, which is read from Table B.1 in Appendix B. Then, reject the null hypothesis if

$$|Z| \geq c.$$

Here is the point. Note that rejecting the null hypothesis if $|Z| \geq c$ is the same as rejecting if $Z^2 \geq c^2$. It can be seen that this corresponds to assuming that Z^2 has a chi-squared distribution with one degree of freedom. In particular, the critical value c^2 corresponds to the $1 - \alpha$ quantile of a chi-squared distribution with one degree of freedom.

Example

Someone claims that for a randomly sampled stock, the probability that its value will increase after 6 months is 0.4. As a check on this claim, 20 stocks are randomly sampled and it is found that 5 gain value. So, $n = 20, p_0 = 0.4$, and the estimated probability of success is $\hat{p} = 5/20 = 0.25$. To test the claim, with a Type I error probability of 0.05, compute

$$Z = \frac{0.25 - 0.4}{\sqrt{0.25(0.75)/20}} = -1.549.$$

The critical value is $c = 1.96$, the 0.975 quantile of a standard normal distribution, which is read from Table B.1. That is, reject if $|Z| \geq 1.96$, which is the same as rejecting if $Z^2 \geq 1.96^2 = 3.8416$. The point is that 3.8416 corresponds to the 0.95 quantile of a chi-squared distribution with one degree of freedom, which can be read from Table B.3 in Appendix B.

13.2 TWO-WAY CONTINGENCY TABLES

This section describes some basic methods for analyzing a two-way contingency table.

13.2.1 McNemar's Test

Imagine a survey of 1,600 randomly sampled adults who, at two different times, are asked whether they approve of a particular political leader. At issue is whether the approval rating at time 1 differs from the approval rating at time 2. For illustrative

TABLE 13.2 Approval Rating of a Political Leader

	Time 2		
Time 1	Approve	Disapprove	Total
Approve	794	150	944
Disapprove	86	570	656
Total	880	720	1,600

purposes, suppose the results are as indicated in Table 13.2. For example, of the 1,600 respondents, 794 respond that they approve at both time 1 and time 2. The number who approve at time 1, ignoring time 2, is 944, and the number who disapprove at time 2 is 720. The estimated probability of getting an approval rating at time 1 is $944/1,600 = 0.59$.

It is convenient to write this contingency table in a more generic form as shown in Table 13.3. So, p_{11} represents the probability that a randomly sampled individual approves at both time 1 and time 2, p_{1+} is the probability of approving at time 1, ignoring time 2, and p_{+1} is the probability of approving at time 2, ignoring time 1. The frequencies associated with the possible outcomes are denoted as shown in Table 13.4. So, for example, n_{11} is the number of individuals who approve at both time 1 and time 2. The estimates of the probabilities in Table 13.3, namely p_{11}, p_{12}, p_{21}, and p_{22} are

$$\hat{p}_{11} = \frac{n_{11}}{n}, \hat{p}_{12} = \frac{n_{12}}{n}, \hat{p}_{21} = \frac{n_{21}}{n}, \hat{p}_{22} = \frac{n_{22}}{n},$$

TABLE 13.3 Probabilities Associated with a Two-Way Contingency Table

	Time 2		
Time 1	Approve	Disapprove	Total
Approve	p_{11}	p_{12}	$p_{1+} = p_{11} + p_{12}$
Disapprove	p_{21}	p_{22}	$p_{2+} = p_{21} + p_{22}$
Total	$p_{+1} = p_{11} + p_{21}$	$p_{+2} = p_{12} + p_{22}$	p_{++}

TABLE 13.4 Notation for Observed Frequencies

	Time 2		
Time 1	Approve	Disapprove	Total
Approve	n_{11}	n_{12}	$n_{1+} = n_{11} + n_{12}$
Disapprove	n_{21}	n_{22}	$n_{2+} = n_{21} + n_{22}$
Total	$n_{+1} = n_{11} + n_{21}$	$n_{+2} = n_{12} + n_{22}$	n

respectively. For example, based on the data in Table 13.2, the estimate of the probability p_{11} is $\hat{p}_{11} = n_{11}/n = 794/1,600 = 0.49625$. In words, the estimated probability of approving at both times 1 and 2 is 0.496. In a similar manner, the marginal probabilities p_{1+}, p_{+1}, p_{2+}, and p_{+2} are estimated with

$$\hat{p}_{1+} = \frac{n_{1+}}{n}, \hat{p}_{+1} = \frac{n_{+1}}{n}, \hat{p}_{2+} = \frac{n_{2+}}{n}, \hat{p}_{+2} = \frac{n_{+2}}{n},$$

respectively.

Now, consider the issue of whether the approval rating has changed from time 1 to time 2. The approval rating at time 1 is p_{1+}, at time 2 it is p_{+1}, so the change in the approval rating is

$$\delta = p_{1+} - p_{+1}. \tag{13.6}$$

This difference is estimated with

$$\begin{aligned} d &= \hat{p}_{1+} - \hat{p}_{+1} \\ &= \frac{n_{11} + n_{12}}{n} - \frac{n_{11} + n_{21}}{n} \\ &= \frac{n_{12} - n_{21}}{n}. \end{aligned}$$

In formal terms, the goal is to test

$$H_0 : \delta = 0, \tag{13.7}$$

the hypothesis that the difference between the two approval ratings is zero. The classic approach, known as McNemar's test, is based on the test statistic

$$Z = \frac{n_{12} - n_{21}}{\sqrt{n_{12} + n_{21}}}. \tag{13.8}$$

Decision Rule: If the Type I error probability is to be α, reject the hypothesis of no difference between the two probabilities if $|Z| \geq c$, where c is the $1 - \alpha/2$ quantile of a standard normal distribution read from Table B.1 in Appendix B. If the hypothesis is rejected, decide that p_{1+} is greater than p_{+1} if $\hat{p}_{1+}$ is greater than $\hat{p}_{+1}$, otherwise decide that $p_{1+} < p_{+1}$. If it is not rejected, make no decision about whether p_{1+} is less than or greater than p_{+1}.

Example

For the data in Table 13.2

$$d = \hat{p}_{1+} - \hat{p}_{+1} = 0.59 - 0.55 = 0.04$$

meaning that the change in approval rating is estimated to be 0.04. The test statistic is

$$Z = \frac{150 - 86}{\sqrt{150 + 86}} = 4.17,$$

the p-value is less than 0.001, so the data indicate that the approval rating has changed. Or, in the context of Tukey's three-decision rule, decide that the approval rating is higher at time 1.

A slight variation of McNemar's test is often recommended with the goal of improving the control over the Type I error probability. The variation is based on what is called a continuity correction, where the test statistic given by Equation (13.8) is replaced with

$$Z^2 = \frac{(|n_{12} - n_{21}| - 1)^2}{n_{12} + n_{21}}. \tag{13.9}$$

Decision Rule: Reject the null hypothesis if Z^2 is greater than or equal to the $1 - \alpha$ quantile of a chi-squared distribution with one degree of freedom. A confidence interval for δ can be computed as well. An estimate of the squared standard error of d is

$$\hat{\sigma}_d^2 = \frac{1}{n}\{\hat{p}_{1+}(1 - \hat{p}_{1+}) + \hat{p}_{+1}(1 - \hat{p}_{+1}) - 2(\hat{p}_{11}\hat{p}_{22} - \hat{p}_{12}\hat{p}_{21})\},$$

so by the central limit theorem, an approximate $1 - \alpha$ confidence interval for δ is

$$d \pm c\hat{\sigma}_d, \tag{13.10}$$

where c is the $1 - \alpha/2$ quantile of a standard normal distribution read from Table B.1 in Appendix B.

13.2.2 R Functions contab and mcnemar.test

The R function

```
contab(dat,alpha=0.05)
```

computes a $1 - \alpha$ confidence interval for δ, the difference between the marginal probabilities, where the argument dat is assumed to be a 2-by-2 matrix containing the observed frequencies. The built-in R function

```
mcnemar.test(x,y=NULL,correct=TRUE)
```

performs McNemar's test, where x is a 2-by-2 matrix or a factor object. The argument y is a factor object, which is ignored if x is a matrix. The argument correct=TRUE means that the continuity correction is used.

Example

R comes with a data set called occupationalStatus, which reports the occupational status of fathers and sons. There are eight occupational categories, but for illustrative purposes, the focus is on the first two. The data appear in R as

	Destination	
Origin	1	2
1	50	19
2	16	40

where origin refers to the father's status and destination is the son's status. An issue might be whether the probability of a category 1 among fathers differs from the corresponding probability among sons. The R command

```
contab(matrix(c(50,16,19,40),ncol=2))
```

returns

```
$delta
[1] 0.024

$CI
[1] -0.06866696  0.11666696

$p. value
[1] 0.6117234
```

Because the confidence interval contains zero, no difference in the two probabilities is detected. Or, from the point of view of Tukey's three-decision rule, make no decision about which probability is the largest. It is left as an exercise to show that the R function mcnemar.test returns a p-value equal to 0.735 with the continuity correction and 0.612 without.

13.2.3 Detecting Dependence

The next goal is to describe a classic technique for detecting dependence in a contingency table. To describe the method in concrete terms, imagine a study aimed at determining whether there is an association between personality style and blood pressure. Suppose each participant is classified as having personality type A or B and that each is labeled as having or not having high blood pressure. Some hypothetical results are shown in Table 13.5.

TABLE 13.5 Hypothetical Results on Personality and Blood Pressure

	Blood Pressure		
Personality	High	Not High	Total
A	8	67	75
B	5	20	25
Total	13	87	100

The goal is to test the hypothesis that personality type and high blood pressure are independent. The notion of independence was formally introduced in Chapter 4, but a quick review, in the context of the problem at hand, might help.

If the probability of a randomly sampled participant having a type A personality is $p_{1+} = 0.4$, and the probability of having high blood pressure is $p_{+1} = 0.2$, then based on the product rule in Chapter 4, independence implies that the probability of simultaneously having a type A personality and high blood pressure is

$$p_{11} = p_{1+} \times p_{+1} = 0.4 \times 0.2 = 0.08.$$

If, for example, $p_{11} = 0.0799999$, they are dependent although in some sense they are close to being independent. Similarly, independence implies that

$$p_{12} = p_{1+} \times p_{+2}$$
$$p_{21} = p_{2+} \times p_{+1}$$
$$p_{22} = p_{2+} \times p_{+2}.$$

In Table 13.5, $n_{11} = 8$ is the number of participants among the 100 sampled who have both a type A personality and high blood pressure. Similarly, $n_{12} = 67$, $n_{21} = 5$, and $n_{22} = 20$. The hypothesis of independence can be tested with

$$X^2 = \frac{n(n_{11}n_{22} - n_{12}n_{21})^2}{n_{1+}n_{2+}n_{+1}n_{+2}}. \tag{13.11}$$

When the null hypothesis of independence is true, X^2 has, approximately, a chi-squared distribution with one degree of freedom.

Decision Rule: Reject the hypothesis of independence if $X^2 \geq c$, where c is the $1 - \alpha$ quantile of a chi-squared distribution with one degree of freedom.

Example

For the data in Table 13.5,

$$X^2 = \frac{100[8(20) - 67(5)]^2}{75(25)(13)(87)} = 1.4.$$

With $v = 1$ degree of freedom and $\alpha = 0.05$, the critical value is 3.84, and because $1.4 < 3.84$, the hypothesis of independence is not rejected.

Generally, the chi-squared test of independence performs reasonably well in terms of Type I errors (e.g., Hosmane, 1986), but difficulties can arise, particularly when the number of observations in any of the cells is relatively small. For instance, if any n_{ij} value is less than or equal to 5, control over the Type I error probability might be unsatisfactory. There are a variety of methods for improving upon the chi-squared test, but details are not given here.

TABLE 13.6   Ratings of 100 Figure Skaters

		Rater B		
Rater A	1	2	3	Total
1	20	12	8	40
2	11	6	13	30
3	19	2	9	30
Total	50	20	30	100

The method just described is readily generalized to situations where the variables can have more than two outcomes. A common notation is to let R represent the number of possible values for the first variable and to let C represent the number of possible values for the second. Said another way, R indicates the number of rows in a contingency table and C represents the number of columns. Consider, for example, two raters who rate the same figure skaters on a three-point scale. The outcomes based on a rating of 100 skaters might look something as what is shown in Table 13.6. So here, $R = C = 3$. This table says that there were 13 instances where rater A gave a score of 2 and simultaneously rater B gave a score of 3.

In a more general context, p_{ij} represents the probability of an observation belonging to the ith row and the jth column, and n_{ij} represents the number of times, among a sample of n observations, an outcome belongs to the ith row and jth column. Moreover, for a contingency table that has R rows and C columns, independence corresponds to a situation where for the ith row and jth column,

$$p_{ij} = p_{i+}p_{+j},$$

where

$$p_{i+} = \sum_{j=1}^{C} p_{ij},$$

and

$$p_{+j} = \sum_{i=1}^{R} p_{ij}.$$

(This follows from the product rule introduced in Section 4.4.) In words, for any row, say the ith, and any column, say the jth, if we multiply the marginal probabilities, independence means that the result must be equal to the probability of being in the ith row and jth column. If for any row and column, this is not true, there is dependence.

Example

Imagine that the probabilities for the two raters considered in Table 13.6 are

Rater A	Rater B		
	1	2	3
1	0.18	0.08	0.06
2	0.14	0.05	0.19
3	0.15	0.01	0.14

Then, the probability that rater A gives a rating of 1 is $p_{1+} = 0.18 + 0.08 + 0.06 = 0.32$, the probability that rater B gives a rating of 2 is $p_{+2} = 0.08 + 0.05 + 0.01 = 0.14$, and the probability that rater B gives a rating of 3 is $p_{+3} = 0.39$. We see that $p_{1+}p_{+1} = 0.32 \times 0.47 = 0.1507$. The probability that simultaneously rater A gives a rating of 1 and rater B gives a rating of 1 is $p_{11} = 0.18$. Because $p_{11} = 0.18 \neq 0.1507$, the ratings are dependent. As usual, however, we do not know the true probabilities, so we must rely on observations to make a decision about whether there is dependence.

For the more general contingency table considered here, the hypothesis of independence can be tested with

$$X^2 = \sum_{i=1}^{R} \sum_{j=1}^{C} \frac{n\left(n_{ij} - \frac{n_{i+}n_{+j}}{n}\right)^2}{n_{i+}n_{+j}}, \tag{13.12}$$

where

$$n_{i+} = n_{i1} + \cdots + n_{iC}$$

and

$$n_{+j} = n_{1j} + \cdots + n_{Rj}.$$

In words, n_{i+} represents the total number of observations belonging to the ith row and n_{+j} is the total for column j. In Table 13.6, for example, $n_{2+} = 11 + 6 + 13 = 30$ is the number of skaters who got a rating of 2 from rater A and $n_{+1} = 20 + 11 + 19 = 50$ is the number of skaters who got a rating of 1 from rater B. When using the test statistic X^2 given by Equation (13.12), the degrees of freedom are

$$v = (R - 1)(C - 1).$$

Decision Rule: If X^2 greater than or equal to the $1 - \alpha$ quantile of a chi-squared distribution with v degrees of freedom, which is read from Table B.3 in Appendix B, reject and conclude that there is dependence.

Example

For the data in Table 13.6, it can be seen that $X^2 = 9.9$, the degrees of freedom are 4, and with $\alpha = 0.05$, the critical value is 9.49. So, the hypothesis of independence would be rejected. That is, when it comes to judging skater, there is an indication that between the ratings given by these two raters.

13.2.4   R Function chi.test.ind

Assuming that x is a matrix, the R function

$$\text{chi.test.ind}(x),$$

written for this book performs the chi-squared test of independence. Based on the help files in R, it might seem that the test of independence described here can be performed with the built-in R function chisq.test, which was described in Section 13.1.1. But the R command chisq.test(x) does not perform the test of independence just described.

Example

Consider again the data in Table 13.5. The R command

$$\text{x=matrix}(c(8,5,67,20),\text{ncol=2,byrow=T})$$

stores the data in a matrix, and the R command

$$\text{chi.test.ind}(x)$$

performs the chi-squared test of independence. The resulting p-value is 0.229.

13.2.5   Measures of Association

Simply rejecting the hypothesis of independence does not tell us how strong the association happens to be. That is, two what extent is the association important? Measuring the strength of an association between two categorical variables turns out to be a nontrivial task. This section covers some of the more basic strategies aimed at accomplishing this goal. As in the previous chapters, different methods provide different perspectives. What is required is a good understanding of what these measures tell us so that a judicious choice can be made when trying to understand data.

It helps to begin with what might seem like a reasonable approach, but which turns out to be unsatisfactory: use the p-value associated with the chi-squared test for independence. Generally, p-values are unsatisfactory when it comes to characterizing the extent to which groups differ and variables are related, and the situation at hand is no exception.

Another approach that has received serious consideration is to use some function of the test statistic for independence, X^2, given by Equation (13.12). A well-known choice is the *phi coefficient*:

$$\phi = \frac{X}{\sqrt{n}}.$$

But this measure, plus all other functions of X^2 have been found to have little value as measures of association (e.g., Fleiss, 1981; Goodman and Kruskal, 1954).

13.2.6   The Probability of Agreement

A simple yet potentially useful measure of association is the probability of agreement. In the example dealing with rating skaters, the probability of agreement refers to the probability that the two raters give the same rating to a skater. In this particular case, the probability of agreement is just $p = p_{11} + p_{22} + p_{33}$. That is, the probability of agreement is the probability that both raters give a rating of 1, or a rating of 2, or a rating of 3. For the more general case where there are R rows and R columns, the probability of agreement is

$$p = p_{11} + \cdots + p_{RR}.$$

Notice that when working with the probability of agreement, in essence, we are dealing with a binomial probability function. That is, among n observations, either there is agreement or there is not. The total number of times we get agreement is

$$n_a = n_{11} + \cdots + n_{RR},$$

and the estimate of p is just $\hat{p} = n_a/n$. Moreover, a confidence interval for the probability of agreement can be computed as described in Chapter 6. In particular, if the goal is to compute a $1 - \alpha$ confidence interval for p, let c be the $1 - \alpha/2$ quantile of a standard normal distribution, which is read from Table B.1 in Appendix B, in which case an approximate $1 - \alpha$ confidence interval for p is

$$\hat{p} \pm c\sqrt{\frac{\hat{p}(1 - \hat{p})}{n}}. \tag{13.13}$$

Equation (13.13) is the classic, routinely taught method, but as noted in Chapter 6, it is generally regarded as being rather inaccurate relative to other methods that might be used. A simple improvement is the Agresti–Coull method, which in the present context is applied as follows. Let

$$\tilde{n} = n + c^2,$$

$$\tilde{n}_a = n_a + \frac{c^2}{2},$$

and

$$\tilde{p} = \frac{\tilde{n}_a}{\tilde{n}}.$$

Then, the $1 - \alpha$ confidence interval for p is

$$\tilde{p} \pm c\sqrt{\frac{\tilde{p}(1 - \tilde{p})}{\tilde{n}}}.$$

Example

For the skating data in Table 13.6, the number of times there is agreement between the two judges is $n_a = 20 + 6 + 9 = 35$ and the total number of ratings is $n = 100$. Consequently, the estimated probability of agreement is $\hat{p} = 35/100 = 0.35$. To compute a 0.95 confidence interval for p, we see from Table B.1 in Appendix B that $c = 1.96$, so an approximate 0.95 confidence interval for p is given by

$$0.35 \pm 1.96\sqrt{0.35(0.65)/100} = (0.26, 0.44).$$

Using the Agresti–Coull method, $\tilde{n}_a = 35 + 1.96^2/2 = 36.92$, $\tilde{n} = 100 + 1.96^2 = 103.842$, $\tilde{p} = 0.3555$, and the 0.95 confidence interval is

$$0.355 \pm 1.96\sqrt{0.355(0.6445)/103.842} = (0.263, 0.448).$$

Alternatively, use the R function `acbinomci` in Section 6.7.3. The command

```
acbinomci(35,100)
```

returns the confidence interval just indicated.

13.2.7 Odds and Odds Ratio

Another approach to measuring the strength of an association is based on what is called the odds ratio. To simplify matters, attention is focused on a two-way contingency table having two rows and two columns only. Associated with each row of such contingency tables is a quantity called its *odds*. Using the notation in Table 13.3, note that for row 1, there are two probabilities associated with the two columns, namely p_{11} and p_{12}. In symbols, the odds for row 1 is

$$\Omega_1 = \frac{p_{11}}{p_{12}}. \tag{13.14}$$

Similarly, the odds for row 2 is

$$\Omega_2 = \frac{p_{21}}{p_{22}}. \tag{13.15}$$

(The symbol Ω is an upper-case Greek omega.)

Example

Consider the personality and blood pressure data shown in Table 13.5. The estimated probabilities are summarized in Table 13.7. For instance, the estimated probability

TABLE 13.7   Estimated Probabilities for Personality versus Blood Pressure

Personality	Blood Pressure		Total
	High	Not High	
A	0.08	0.67	0.75
B	0.05	0.20	0.25
Total	0.13	0.87	1.00

that, simultaneously, a randomly sampled adult has a Type A personality and high blood pressure is

$$\hat{p}_{11} = \frac{n_{11}}{n} = \frac{8}{100} = 0.08.$$

$$\hat{p}_{2|1} = \frac{0.67}{0.08 + 0.67} = 0.8933.$$

The estimate of the odds for this row is

$$\hat{\Omega}_1 = \frac{\hat{p}_{11}}{\hat{p}_{12}}$$

$$= \frac{0.08}{0.67}$$

$$= 0.12.$$

That is, given that someone has a Type A personality, the probability of having high blood pressure is estimated to be about 12% of the probability that their blood pressure is not high. Put another way, among Type A personalities, the probability of not having high blood pressure is about $1/0.12 = 8.4$ times as high as the probability that blood pressure is high. As for Type B personalities, the odds is estimated to be

$$\hat{\Omega}_2 = 0.25.$$

This says that if someone has a Type B personality, the chance of having hypertension is estimated to be about a fourth of the probability that blood pressure is not high. Notice that you can measure the relative risk of hypertension, based on personality type, by comparing the two odds just estimated. Typically, a comparison is made with their ratios. That is, use what is called the *odds ratio*, which is estimated with

$$\hat{\theta} = \frac{\hat{\Omega}_1}{\hat{\Omega}_2}$$

$$= \frac{0.12}{0.25}$$

$$= 0.48.$$

This says that among Type A personalities, the relative risk of having hypertension is about half what it is for individuals who are Type B personalities.

In terms of population probabilities, the odds ratio can be written as

$$\theta = \frac{p_{11}p_{22}}{p_{12}p_{21}},$$

and for this reason, θ is often called the *cross-product ratio*. A simpler way of writing the estimate of θ is

$$\hat{\theta} = \frac{n_{11}n_{22}}{n_{12}n_{21}}.$$

**TABLE 13.8   Mortality Rates per 100,000 Person-Years from
Lung Cancer and Coronary Artery Disease for Smokers and
Nonsmokers of Cigarettes**

	Smokers	Nonsmokers	Difference
Cancer of the lung	48.33	4.49	43.84
Coronary artery disease	294.67	169.54	125.13

Under independence, it can be shown that $\theta = 1$. If $\theta > 1$, then for participants in row 1 (Type A personality in the illustration), the odds for having high blood pressure are higher than the odds for row 2 (Type B personality). If $\theta < 1$, then the reverse is true.

All measures of association are open to the criticism that they reduce data down to a point where important features can become obscured. This criticism applies to the odds ratio, as noted by Berkson (1958) and discussed by Fleiss (1981). Table 13.8 shows the data analyzed by Berkson on mortality and smoking. It can be seen that the estimated odds ratio is

$$\hat{\theta} = \frac{10.8}{1.7} = 6.35,$$

and this might suggest that cigarette smoking has a greater effect on lung cancer than on coronary artery disease. Berkson argues that it is *only* the difference in mortality that permits a valid assessment of the effect of smoking on a cause of death. The difference for coronary artery disease is considerably larger than it is for lung cancer, as indicated in the last column of Table 13.8, indicating that smoking is more serious in terms of coronary artery disease. The problem with the odds ratio in this example is that it throws away all the information on the number of deaths due to either cause.

13.3   LOGISTIC REGRESSION

Another area of interest is a regression problem where the outcome is binary. For example, what is the probability of getting a heart attack during the next year if an individual's cholesterol level is 250? One approach to this problem is to use what is called logistic regression. For books dedicated to this topic, see, for example, Kleinbaum (1994) or Hosmer and Lemeshow (1989).

A tempting approach is to apply least squares regression as described in Chapter 8. But this is unsatisfactory, roughly because the predicted value is never equal to one of the possible outcomes, which is 1 for a success and 0 for a failure. A better approach is to use an equation designed to predict the probability of success. A commonly used strategy for dealing with this problem is the *logistic regression* function. For some independent variable X, logistic regression assumes that the probability of success is given by

$$p(X) = \frac{\exp\ (\beta_0 + \beta_1 X)}{1 + \exp\ (\beta_0 + \beta_1 X)}. \tag{13.16}$$

(The notation exp (x) refers to the exponential function, which was described in Section 4.6 in conjunction with the probability density function associated with a normal distribution.) Here, β_0 and β_1 are unknown parameters that are estimated based on the data. (Readers interested in the computational details for estimating β_0 and β_1 are referred to Hosmer and Lemeshow, 1989.) For the more general case where there are p predictors, $X_1, \ldots, X_p$, the model is

$$p(X) = \frac{\exp\ (\beta_0 + \beta_1 X + \cdots + \beta_p X_p)}{1 + \exp\ (\beta_0 + \beta_1 X + \cdots + \beta_p X_p)}. \tag{13.17}$$

Focusing on the single predictor case, if the parameter $\beta_1 > 0$, then the basic logistic regression model given by Equation (13.16) assumes that the probability of success is a monotonically increasing function of X. That is, the probability never decreases as X gets large; it stays the same or increases. If $\beta_1 < 0$, the reverse is true. Figure 13.2a shows the regression line when $\beta_1 = 1$ and $\beta_0 = 0.5$. As is evident, curvature is allowed and predicted probabilities always have a value between 0 and 1. Figure 13.2b is the regression line when $\beta_1 = -1$ and $\beta_0 = 0.5$. So now, the regression line is monotonically decreasing. (The predicted probability never increases.)

Similar to the regression methods in Chapter 8, outliers among the independent variable X can distort the results based on the logistic regression model. The R function in Section 13.3.1 can be used to check on the impact of removing outliers via the argument xout.

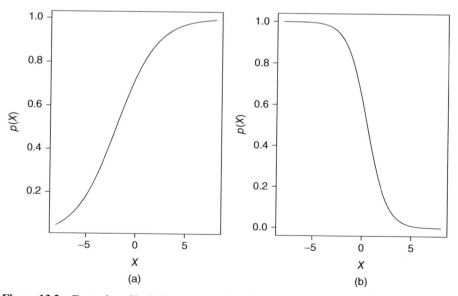

Figure 13.2   Examples of logistic regression lines based on Equation (13.16). (a) $\beta_1 = 1$ and $\beta_0 = 0.5$. Because $\beta_1 > 0$, the predicted probability is monotonically increasing. (b) $\beta_1 = -1$, and now the predicted probability is monotonically decreasing

Situations might be encountered where the true regression line is increasing over some range of X values, but decreasing otherwise. A possible way of dealing with this problem is to consider a model having the form

$$p(X) = \frac{\exp\ (\beta_0 + \beta_1 X + \beta_2 X^2)}{1 + \exp\ (\beta_0 + \beta_1 X + \beta_2 X^2)}. \tag{13.18}$$

13.3.1   R Function logreg

Leverage points (outliers among the independent variables) are a concern when using logistic regression. To help address this problem, the function

```
logreg(x,y, xout=FALSE, outfun=outpro, ...),
```

is supplied, which eliminates leverage points when the argument xout=TRUE. The argument x must be a vector or a matrix with p columns. By default, the MAD–median rule is used to detect outliers among the independent variables when there is a single predictor. (A more complex method is used if there are two or more independent variables.) The argument y must be a vector containing only one of two values: 0 or 1.

Example

Hastie and Tibshirani (1990) report data on the presence or absence of kyphosis, a postoperative spinal deformity. The independent variables are the age of the patient, in months, the number of vertebrae involved in the spinal operation, and a variable called start, which is the beginning of the range of vertebrae involved. The data can be accessed via the R command data("kyphosis", package="rpart"), in which case the data are now stored in the R variable kyphosis. It is instructive to note that in the actual data set, the presence or absence of kyphosis is indicated by "present" and "absent" in the first column of the R variable kyphosis. The command

```
flag=(kyphosis[,1]=="present")
```

converts these values to TRUE (present) and FALSE (absent) and stores the results in the R variable flag, which the R function logreg will take to be 1 and 0, respectively. Focusing on age, which is stored in column 2 of the R variable kyphosis, the R command

```
logreg(kyphosis[,2],flag)
```

returns

```
            Estimate    Std. Error    z value      Pr(>|z|)
(Intercept) -1.809351277 0.530352625 -3.411600 0.0006458269
x            0.005441758 0.004821704  1.128596 0.2590681193
```

Because the estimate of β_1 is greater than zero, the model suggests that the probability of kyphosis increases with age. However, the p-value, when testing H_0: $\beta_1 = 0$, is 0.259, so in particular, fail to reject at the 0.05 level. Removing leverage points does not alter this result. (See, however, the example in Section 13.3.5.)

13.3.2 A Confidence Interval for the Odds Ratio

The logistic regression model can be used even when the predictor X is binary. One practical advantage of this result is that it can be used to compute a confidence interval for the odds ratio, assuming that X has either the value 0 or 1. It can be shown that the odds ratio is given by

$$\Psi = e^{\beta_1},$$

where again e is approximately equal to 2.718282, the base of the natural logarithms. Letting S_{β_1} denote the estimated standard error of $\hat{\beta}_1$, the estimate of β_1, a $1 - \alpha$ confidence interval for the odds ratio is

$$\exp[\hat{\beta}_1 \pm cS_{\beta_1}], \tag{13.19}$$

where c is the $1 - \alpha/2$ quantile of a standard normal distribution.

13.3.3 R Function ODDSR.CI

The R function

```
ODDSR.CI(x, y=NULL, alpha=0.05)
```

computes a $1 - \alpha$ confidence interval for the odds ratio. If the argument y is not specified, it is assumed that the argument x is a 2-by-2 matrix that contains observed frequencies that are organized as shown in Table 13.4. Otherwise, x and y are assumed to be vectors containing 0's and 1's.

Example

For the data in Table 13.5, a confidence interval for the odds ratio can be computed with the following commands:

```
x=matrix(c(8,67,5,20),ncol=2,nrow=2)
ODDSR.CI(x)
```

13.3.4 Smoothers for Logistic Regression

Special smoothers have been proposed for the case where the outcome variable Y is binary. One such estimator is described by Hosmer and Lemeshow. Here, a slight modification of this estimator is used, where X has been standardized by replacing X with $(X - M_x)/\text{MADN}_x$, where M_x and MADN_x are the median and MADN, respectively, based on the observed X values. The estimate of $P(X)$, the probability of success given a value for the independent variable X, is

$$\hat{P}(X) = \frac{\sum w_j Y_j}{\sum w_j}, \tag{13.20}$$

where

$$w_i = I_h e^{-(X_i - X)^2}$$

and $I_h = 1$ if $|X_i - X| < h$, otherwise $I_h = 0$. (Again, e is approximately equal to 2.718282, the base of the natural logarithms.) The choice $h = 2$ appears to perform relatively well. A slight modification and generalization of this estimator can be used with $p \geq 1$ predictors, which can be applied with the R function logSM described in the next section.

13.3.5   R Functions rplot.bin and logSM

The R function

```
logSM(x, y, pyhat = FALSE, plotit = TRUE, xlab = "X", ylab =

    "Y", zlab = "Z", xout = FALSE, outfun = outpro, fr = 2)
```

computes the smoother based on Equation (13.20). It can be used with more than one predictor and appears to be a good choice for general use. When there are two predictors, the argument zlab can be used to label the z-axis. If the argument pyhat=TRUE, the function returns the predicted probability that $y = 1$ for each value in x. The argument fr corresponds to h.

An alternative approach that performs relatively well is to use an appropriate version of the running-interval smoother. This can be accomplished with the R function

```
rplot.bin(x, y, scat = TRUE, plotit = T, pyhat = F, xout = F,

    outfun = outpro, xlab = "X", ylab = "Y", zlab = "Z").
```

Again, more than one predictor is allowed.

Example

In the example in Section 13.3.1, a basic logistic regression model was used to investigate the probability of kyphosis given the age (in months) of the patient. Recall that the test of H_0: $\beta_1 = 0$ had a p-value of 0.259. That is, the basic logistic regression model fails to find an association. However, look at Figure 13.3, which shows the estimate of the regression line based on the R function logSM, and note that the line is not monotonic. That is, initially, the regression line increases with age, but at some point, it appears to decrease. This is a concern because the basic logistic regression model that was fit to the data assumes that the regression line is monotonic. That is, if the regression line increases over some range of X values, the assumption is that it

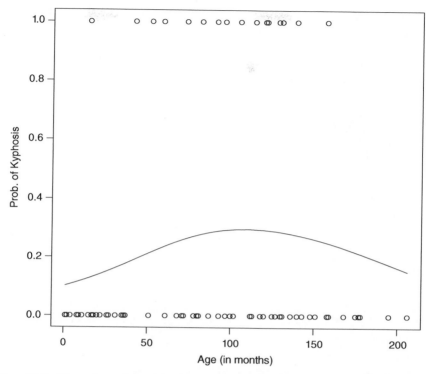

Figure 13.3 The estimated regression line suggests that the probability of kyphosis increases with age, up to a point, and then decreases, which is contrary to the assumption of the basic logistic regression model in Section 13.3

does not decrease for some other range of the predictor values. Figure 13.3 suggests considering, instead, the model given by Equation (13.18). For convenience, assume that the variable age is stored in the R variable x. This can be done with the commands

$$\texttt{xsq=cbind}\,(x, x^2)$$

```
logreg(xsq, flag)
```

where again `flag=1` indicates that kyphosis is present. The p-values for H_0: $\beta_1 = 0$ and H_0: $\beta_2 = 0$ are 0.009 and 0.013, respectively. So, in contrast to the results in Section 13.3.1, now there is an indication of an association.

13.4 SUMMARY

- The chi-squared tests in this chapter are based on a version central of the central limit theorem. That is, normal distributions play a role.
- The strength of the association in a contingency table should not be measured based on the test statistic given by Equation (13.11). In particular, the phi

coefficient should not be used. Two reasonable measures of the strength of the association are the proportion of agreement and the odds ratio.

- The basic logistic regression model assumes that the probability of some event has a monotonic association with the covariate. The smoother in Section 13.3.4 provides a partial check on the extent to which this assumption is reasonable.

13.5   EXERCISES

1. For a one-way contingency table having four categories, the frequencies corresponding to each category are as follows: 23, 14, 8, 32. Test the hypothesis that each category has the same probability. Use $\alpha = 0.05$. Check your answer using R.

2. For a one-way contingency table, the following frequencies are observed: 23, 34, 43, 53, 16. Using $\alpha = 0.01$, test the hypothesis that all five categories have the same probability. Check your answer using R.

3. A game show allows contestants to pick one of six boxes, one of which contains a large sum of money. The organizers speculate that contestants will not pick a box at random, in which case the expected amount won by contestants might be reduced by placing the money in boxes that are less likely to be chosen. To find out whether contestants choose a box at random, a study was done where potential contestants choose a box, which resulted in the following frequencies: 6, 20, 30, 35, 10, 5. Test the hypothesis that each box has the same probability of being chosen. Use $\alpha = 0.01$. Check your answer using R.

4. Imagine that 54 individuals are asked whether they agree, disagree, or have no opinion that persons with a college degree feel more satisfied with their lives. The observed frequencies are 9, 30, and 15. Test $H_0 : p_1 = p_2 = p_3$ with $\alpha = 0.05$. Check your answer using R.

5. It is speculated that the probabilities associated with four categories are 0.1, 0.3, 0.5, and 0.1. The observed frequencies are 10, 40, 50, and 5. Test this speculation using $\alpha = 0.05$. Check your answer using R.

6. It is speculated that the probabilities associated with five categories are 0.2, 0.3, 0.3, 0.1, and 0.1. The observed frequencies are 20, 50, 40, 10, and 15. Test this hypothesis using $\alpha = 0.05$. Check your answer using R.

7. Someone claims that the proportion of adults getting low, medium, and high amounts of exercise is 0.5, 0.3, and 0.2, respectively. To check this claim, you sample 100 individuals and find that 40 get a low amount of exercise, 50 get a medium amount, and 10 get a high amount. Test the claim with $\alpha = 0.05$. Check your answer using R.

8. A geneticist postulates that in the progeny of a certain dihybrid cross, the four phenotypes should be present in the ratio 9:3:3:1. So, if p_1, p_2, p_3, and p_4 are the probabilities associated with these four phenotypes, the issue is whether there is empirical evidence indicating that $H_0: p_1 = 9/16$, $p_2 = 3/16$, $p_3 = 3/16$, $p_4 = 1/16$ should be rejected. The observed frequencies corresponding to these

four phenotypes, among 800 members of the progeny generation, are 439, 168, 133, and 60. Test H_0 using $\alpha = 0.05$. Check your answer using R.

9. Does the likelihood of a particular crime vary depending on the day of the week? To find out, the number of crimes for Monday through Sunday were recorded and found to be 38, 31, 40, 39, 40, 44, and 48. Test the hypothesis that the likelihood of a crime is the same for each day of the week, using $\alpha = 0.05$.

10. For a random sample of 200 adults, each adult was classified as having a high or low income, and each was asked whether they are optimistic about the future. The results were

	Yes	No	Total
High	35	42	77
Low	80	43	123
Total	115	85	200

What is the estimated probability that a randomly sampled adult has a high income and is optimistic? Compute a 0.95 confidence interval for the true probability using the Agresti–Coull method.

11. Referring to the previous exercise, perform McNemar's test using the continuity correction with a Type I error probability of $\alpha = 0.05$.

12. In Exercise 10, would you reject the hypothesis that income and outlook are independent? Use $\alpha = 0.05$. Would you use the phi coefficient to measure the association between income and outlook? Why?

13. In Exercise 10, estimate the odds ratio and interpret the results.

14. You observe

Income (Daughter)	Income (Father)			
	High	Medium	Low	Total
High	30	50	20	100
Medium	50	70	30	150
Low	10	20	40	70
Total	90	140	90	320

Estimate the proportion of agreement and compute a 0.95 confidence interval.

15. Use the R function logSM to duplicate the plot in Figure 13.3.

APPENDIX A

SOLUTIONS TO SELECTED EXERCISES

More detailed answers for all of the exercises are located at http://dornsife.usc.edu/labs/rwilcox/books/ in the file answers_wiley.pdf.

Chapter 1

3. `sum(x)/length(x)` **4.** `sum(x[x>0])` **5.** `id=which(x==max(x))` `mean(x[-id])`, which returns 1.25. **6.** The values are -20 and -15. **7.** The average is 24.1. **9.** `sum(x)/length(x)` returns 4.8. `x-4` subtracts 4 from each value. **10.** `sum(x-mean(x))` returns 1.776357e-15, where e-15 means 10^{-15}. The exact value is zero. **11.** Two commands: `id=!is.na(m[,1])` and `m[id,]`

Chapter 2

1. (a) 22, (b) 2, (c) 20, (d) 484, (e) 27, (f) -41, (g) 2, (h) 220, (i) 12, (j) 54. **2.** (a) $\sum X_i/i$, (b) $\sum U_i^i$, (c) $(\sum Y_i)^4$. **4.** (a) $\bar{X} = -0.2$, $M = 0$, (b)$\bar{X} = 186.1667$, $M = 6.5$. **5.** $\bar{X} = 83.93$ $\bar{X}_t = 83.1$, $M = 80.5$. **6.** 338.1. **7.** (a) 30.6, (b) 120.6, (c) 1,020.6. **8.** 24.5 in all three cases. **9.** One **10.** For a 20% trimmed mean, $g + 1$, where g is $0.2n$ rounded down to the nearest integer. For the median, about half. **11.** $q_1 = -6.58$ $q_2 = 7.4$ ($j = 3$, $h = 0.41667$). **12.** $q_1 = -6$, $q_2 = 3$, ($j = 4$, $h = 0.16667$). **13.** About a fourth. **14.** Clearly, $X_{(1)}$ has a value between $X_{(1)}$ and $X_{(n)}$. If we multiply all of the values by any constant c, then in particular $X_{(1)}$ becomes $cX_{(1)}$. **16.** Range $= 18$, $s^2 = 32$, $s = 5.66$. **17.** Note that $n\bar{X} = \sum(X_i)$, So $\sum(X_i - \bar{X}) = (\sum X_i) - n\bar{X} = 0$. **18.** $s = 0.37$. **19.** $s = 11.58$. **20.** Twenty is an outlier. **21.** Both 20 and 200 are outliers. Masking. **22.** Yes. **26.** Sometimes, even with two or more outliers, the classic rule might catch all

Understanding and Applying Basic Statistical Methods Using R, First Edition. Rand R. Wilcox.
© 2017 John Wiley & Sons, Inc. Published 2017 by John Wiley & Sons, Inc.
www.wiley.com/go/Wilcox/Statistical_Methods_R

of the outliers, depending on where they are, but the boxplot rule is better at avoiding masking. **27**. $0.2 \times n = 0.2 \times 21 = 4.2$, so $g = 4$, $\overline{X}_t = 80.08$. **30**. 2. **31**. 5. The mean is least resistant and the median is the most resistant. **33**. About 20%, or more than g. **34**. $\overline{X} = 229.2$, $\overline{X}_t = 220.8$, $M = 221$, $\overline{X}_{mm} = 214.12$. **35**. 24, 24, 25, 32, 35, 36, 36, 42, 42. **37**. Smaller, because Winsorizing pulls in extreme values. $s^2 = 81$, $s_w^2 = 51.4$. **38**. Yes. **40**. $s_w^2 = 1,375.6$. **41**. $\overline{X}_t = 82$, $s_w^2 = 69.2$.

Chapter 3

1. Mean is 2.85, variance is 1.94697, sd = 1.395. **2**. Mean is 2.52, variance is 0.989, sd = 0.995. **3**. Mean is 3, variance is 1.5, sd = 1.22. **4**. Mean is 18.387, variance is 85.04, sd = 9.22. **5**. Mean is 11.1, variance is 42.3, sd = 6.5. **6**. Two values are flagged as outliers. **7**. Four values less than zero are flagged as outliers. **8**. No. **10**. The boxplot rule can declare values to be outliers that do not appear to be outliers based on a histogram. **12**. 34.6. **13**. There would be only one stem. **14**. Median = 80, quartiles = 50 and 121, IQR = 121−50 = 71, largest value not declared an outlier is 215. **15**. Values less than −56.5 or greater than 227.5 are declared outliers. **18**. When the population histogram is symmetric and outliers are rare. **19**. In some cases, 100 is sufficient but in others, a much larger sample size is needed. **20**. Generally, the boxplot is better than a histogram. **21**. Not necessarily. Situations are encountered where the sample histogram is a poor indication of the population histogram.

Chapter 4

1. No **2**. No **3**. Yes **4**. 0.5 **5**. 0. **6**. 0.5 **7**. 0.8 **8**. 0.7 **10**. Mean = 2.3, variance is 0.81, and the standard deviation is 0.9 **11**. Mean = 3.2, variance is 1.76, and the standard deviation is 1.3. **12**. $\mu - \sigma = 3.2 - 1.33 = 1.87$ and $\mu + \sigma = 3.2 + 1.33 = 4.53$. But the only possible values between 1.87 and 4.53 are 2, 3, and 4. So, the answer is $p(2) + p(3) + p(4) = 0.7$. **13**. Mean = 2, standard deviation is 0.63. **14**. Increase. **15**. Mean = 3, variance is 1.6. **16**. Smaller **17**. Larger **18**. (a) 0.3, (b) 0.03/0.3, (c) 0.09/0.3, (d) 0.108/0.18. **19**. Yes. **20**. (a) 1,253/3,398, (b) 757/1,828, (c) 757/1,253, (d) no, (e) 1,831/3,398, (f) 1−757/3,398 = 0.7777, (g) (757+496+1,071)/3,398 **21**. Yes, this can only happen if the conditional probabilities change when you are told X. **22**. Yes. **23**. Yes. **24**. (a) 0.006, (b) 0.3823, (c) 0.1673, (d) 0.367, (e) 0.7874 **25**. (a) 0.00475, (b) 0.29687, (c) 0.4845, (d) 0.688. **26**. 0.1859. **27**. 0.29848 **28**. 10.8 and 4.32 **29**. 4.4, 3.52. **30**. 0.7, 0.0105 **31**. 0.3, 0.007. **32**. (a) 0.3222, (b) 0.6778, (c) 0.302. **33**. Two heads and a tail has probability 0.44. Three heads has probability 0.343. **34**. 0.5 **35**. (a) 0.75^5, (b) 0.25^5, (c) $1 - 0.25^5 - 5(0.75)(0.25)^4$. **36**. (a) 0.5858, (b) 0.7323, (c) 0.5754, (d) 0.7265. **37**. 10, 6, 0.4, 0.0096. **38**. (a) 0.0668, (b) 0.0062, (c) 0.0062, (d) 0.683. **39**. (a) 0.691, (b) 0.894, (c) 0.799, (d) 0.928. **40**. (a) 0.31, (b) 0.885, (c) 0.018, (d) 0.221. **41**. (a) −2.33, (b) 1.93, (c) −0.174, (d) 0.3, **42**. (a) 1.43, (b) −0.01, (c) 1.7, (d) 1.28. **43**. (a) 0.133, (b) 0.71, (c) 0.133, (d) 0.733 **44**. (a) 0.588, (b) 0.63, (c) 0.71, (d) 0.95. **45**. (a) 0.383, (b) 0.683. **46**. $c = 1.96$ **47**. 1.28. **48**. 0.16. **49**. 84.45. **50**. 1−0.91. **51**. 0.87. **52**. 0.001. **53**. 0.68. **54**. 0.95. **55**. 0.115. **56**. 0.043. **57**. Yes. **58**. Small changes in the tails of a distribution can substantially alter the variance. **59**. No, could be much larger. **60**. No. **61**. Yes. **62**. Yes.

Chapter 5

1. (a) 0.885, (b) $1 - 0.885 = 0.115$, (c) 0.7705. **2.** 0.3151. **3.** 0. It is impossible to get $\hat{p} = 0.05$ when $n = 10$. **4.** Note that with $n = 25$, there are only two ways of getting $\hat{p} \leq 0.05$: when the number of successes is 0 or 1. The probability of getting 0 or 1 successes is 0.2712. **6.** 0.4. **7.** $0.4(0.6)/30 = 0.008$. **8.** (a) 0.0228, (b) 0.1587, (c) 0.9545. **9.** (a) 0.1587, (b) 0.023, (c) $0.977 - 0.023 = 0.954$. **10.** 0.023. **11.** 0.6822. **12.** 0.866. **13.** $\sqrt{160.78/9} = 4.23$. **14.** (a) 0.055, (b) 0.788, (c) 0.992 (d) $0.788 - 0.055$. **15.** (a) 0.047, (b) 0.952 (c) $1 - 0.047$, (d) $0.952 - 0.047$. **16.** Skewed, heavy-tailed distribution. **17.** Symmetric, light-tailed. **19.** No tied values. **21.** There are tied values. **22.** No. **23.** There is an outlier. $s_M = 3.60$, $s/\sqrt{n} = 17.4$. **25.** 69.4. **26.** There is an outlier. **27.** The sample mean has the smallest standard error under normality. So, if there is an ideal estimator, it must be the mean, but under nonnormality, it can perform poorly. **28.** If the distribution is heavy-tailed, meaning outliers are common, a trimmed mean or median can be more accurate on average. **29.** The standard errors can differ substantially. This was illustrated using data generated from a mixed normal distribution. See Figure 5.11. **30.** See the more detailed answers in the file mentioned at the beginning of this appendix.

Chapter 6

2. 1.28, 1.75, 2.33. **3.** $45 \pm 1.96(5/5) = (43.04, 46.96)$ **4.** $45 \pm 2.576(5/5)$. **5.** No, 0.95 CI $= (1, 141.8, 1, 158.2)$. **6.** (a) (52.55, 77.45), (b) (180.82, 189.18), (c) (10.68, 27.32). **7.** Length $= 2c\sigma/\sqrt{n}$. When n is doubled, length $= 2c\sigma/\sqrt{2n}$. Therefore, the ratio of the lengths is $1/\sqrt{2}$. That is, the length is decreased by a factor of $1/\sqrt{2}$. For $4n$, decreased by a factor of $1/2$. **8.** $\bar{X} = 19.97$. So, 0.95 CI $= (19.9602, 19.9798)$. (b) No. (c) Just because the confidence contains 20, this does not necessarily mean that $\mu = 20$. **9.** 0.99 CI $= (1.896363, 2.303637)$. **10.** 0.90 CI $= (1.62644, 1.77356)$. **11.** (a) 2.84534, (b) 2.085963, (c) 1.725. **12.** (a) (19.56179, 32.43821), (b) (122.0542, 141.9458), (c) (47, 57). **13.** (a) (16.75081, 35.24919), (b) (118.3376, 145.6624), (c) (45.28735, 58.71265). **14.** Using t.test the 0.95 confidence interval is (161.5030, 734.7075). **15.** (10.69766, 23.50234). **16.** (28.12, 39.88). **17.** (61.3, 239.2). **18.** $0.989 - 0.011 = 0.978$. **19.** 0.965. **20.** $n = 19$ and $k = 3$. 0.9993. **21.** $n = 15$, $\hat{p} = 5/15$, CI $= (0.09476973, 0.5718969)$ using Equation (6.10). Agresti-Coull method gives (0.15, 0.585). **22.** (a) 0.0064. (b) 0.0042, (c) 0.0016, (d) 0.00083. **23.** (0.0412, 0.1588). Agresti-Coull=(0.05, 0.176). **24.** (0.2618755, 0.3181245). **25.** (0.04528041, 0.07471959). **27.** (0.0000855, 0.00498) **28.** (0.1856043, 0.3143957). **29.** (0.00264542, 0.03735458). **30.** (0, 0.0183). **31.** $0.18 \pm 1.96\sqrt{0.18(0.82)/1,000}$ **33.** A large sample size might be needed. **35.** (a) $52 \pm 2.13\sqrt{12}/(0.6\sqrt{24})$. (b) $10 \pm 2.07\sqrt{30}/(0.6\sqrt{36})$. (c) $16 \pm 2.365\sqrt{9}/(0.6\sqrt{12})$. **37.** (293.6, 595.9). **38.** Under normality, the ideal estimator is the mean. So, if an ideal estimator exists, it must be the mean, but under general conditions, it performs poorly. **39.** For a 20% trimmed mean, 0.95 confidence interval is (34.8, 54.8). for the mean, it is (30.7, 58.3). **40.** There is an outlier. **41.** There are two ways of doing this. First, sort the values in t.vals: tsort=sort(t.vals). Then, use

Equation (6.13) with a=tsort[25] and b=tsort[975]. Or, let tsort=sort(abs(t.vals)) and use Equation (6.12) with t = tsort[950]. **42.** t.vals=NULL

```
for(i in 1:1000){
z=sample(x,25,replace=T)
t.vals[i]=trimci(z,tr=0,null.value=mean(x),pr=F)$test.stat
}
```

Chapter 7

1. $Z = -1.265$, Fail to reject. **2.** Fail to reject. **3.** $(74.9, 81.1)$. **4.** 0.103. **5.** 0.206. **6.** $Z = -14$, reject. **7.** Reject **8.** $(118.6, 121.4)$ **9.** Yes, because $\overline{X}$ is consistent with H_0. **10.** $Z = 10$, reject. **11.** $Z = 2.12$, reject. **16.** Might commit a Type II error. Power might be relatively low. **19.** Increase α. But Type I error probability is higher. **20.** (a) $T = 1$, fail to reject. (b) $T = 0.5$, fail to reject. (c) $T = 2.5$, reject. **21.** Power is higher when the standard deviation, s, is likely to be small. **22.** (a) $T = 0.8$, fail to reject. (b) $T = 0.4$, fail to reject. (c) $T = 2$, reject. **23.** Fail to reject because $\overline{X}$ is consistent with H_0. **24.** $T = 0.39$, fail to reject. **25.** $T = -2.61$, reject **26.** $T = 2$, fail to reject. **27.** $T = 0.75$, fail to reject. **28.** $T = -1.6$, $t = 2.26$, fail to reject. **29.** $T = 2.3$, $t_{0.99} = 2.54$, fail to reject. **30.** (a) $T = 0.6\sqrt{20}(44 - 42)/9 = 0.596$, $t = 2.2$, fail to reject. (b) $T = 0.2981$, fail to reject. **31.** Fail to reject in all three cases. **32.** $n = 10$, so the degrees of freedom are 5, $t = 2.571$, $T = -3.1$, reject. **33.** The degrees of freedom are 14, $t = 2.977$, $T = 0.129$, fail to reject. **35.** test=(mean(x)-null.value)*sqrt(length(x))/sigma. **36.** R commands: flag=which(ToothGrowth[,3]==0.5) trimci(ToothGrowth [flag,1],tr=0) returns $p = 0.018$ trimci(ToothGrowth[flag,1], tr=0.2) returns $p = 0.096$. A plot of the data indicates a skewed distribution, suggesting that a trimmed mean better reflects the typical value. **37.** The distribution is skewed. Using a median or MOM, again fail to reject.

Chapter 8

3. The least squares method minimizes the sum of the squared residuals. So, for any choice for the slope and intercept, the sum of the squared residuals will be at most 47. **4.** In Equation (8.5), $C = (n - 1)s_x^2 = 132$. So, the estimated slope is $144/288 = 0.5$. **5.** $b_1 = -0.0355$, $b_0 = 39.93$. **6.** $b_1 = 0.0039$, $b_0 = 0.485$. **8.** $b_1 = 0.0754$, $b_0 = 1.253$. **9.** $\hat{Y} = -0.0355(600) + 39.93 = 18.63$, but daily calories of 600 is greater than any value used to compute the slope and intercept. That is, extrapolation is being used. **17.** $(-2.65, -0.35)$. **18.** $(-2.948, -0.052)$. **20.** $b_1 = 3$, $b_0 = -0.5$. **21.** (a) $b_1 = 3$, $b_0 = -1$. (b) $T = -0.096$, critical value is $t = 2.43$, fail to reject. (c) $(0.602, 5.398)$. **22.** (a) $b_1 = 0.25$, $b_0 = 7$. (b) $(-0.76, 1.26)$. **23.** $(2.04, 4.14)$, indicating that the slope is greater than 2. **24.** $(2.78, 9.22)$. **25.** (a) $r = 0.8$. $T = 6.67$, reject. (b) $r = 0.5$, $T = 1.29$, fail to reject. **26.** $r = 0.5$, $T = 2.8$, $t = 1.7$, reject. This indicates dependence. **27.** (a) Yes. (b) Yes, outliers can mask a negative association. (c) Plot the data. **28.** Nothing, this does not change r. **29.** The absolute value of the slope gets larger. **30.** The residuals are larger meaning that the correlation will get smaller. **31.** The slope and intercept were chosen so as to minimize the second sum. $\overline{Y}$ is the regression line with $b_1 = 0$, so the first sum must be larger than the second. **32.** There are various ways there might be dependence that is not detected by r. **33.** Outliers, for example, can result in a large r but a poor fit. **34.** No. You need to look at the data. **35.** The confidence interval can be relatively long and is potentially inaccurate. **36.** The confidence interval can be relatively inaccurate due to using the wrong standard error.

Chapter 9

3. $T = 9.3$, reject. **4.** $W = 10.5$, reject. **5.** Welch's test might have more power. **6.** $T = 3.795$, reject. **7.** $WT = 3.795$, reject. **8.** When the sample variances are approximately equal, the choice between T and W makes little difference. **9.** $v = 31.86066$, $t = 2.037283$, CI $= (1.4, 8.6)$. **10.** CI $= (1.39, 8.61)$. **11.** No, fail to reject. **12.** $W = -1.95$, $t_{0.975} = 2.06$, fail to reject. **13.** The actual probability coverage could differ substantially from 0.95. **16.** $Z = -0.4$, CI $= (-0.13, 0.086)$. **17.** $W = 3.06$, degrees of freedom are $v = 29.54$. **19.** Difference between the means is -8.3 versus -7.5. Also, there are no outliers suggesting that the standard error of the median will be larger than the standard error of the means, which turns out to be the case. **24.** The median better reflects the typical value for skewed distributions, can have relatively high power when outliers are common. But for skewed distributions, it is possible that means have more power. The difference between the means might be larger.

Chapter 10

1. MSWG $= (6.214+3.982+2.214)/3 = 4.14$. **2.** $F = 6.05$, critical value is $f = 3.47$. **4.** $F = 4.210526$, p-value $= 0.04615848$. **5.** If the data are stored in the R variable dat, can use the R command mean(apply(dat,2,var)), which yields 25.33 **7.** With 20% trimming, no values get trimmed with this sample size. **8.** Do not know when power is high enough to detect situations where unequal variances is a practical issue. **9.** $F = $ MSBG/MSWG $= 3$, reject. **11.** MSBG estimates $2+10(2.5) = 27$. MSWG estimates 2, the common variance. Because the null hypothesis is false, MSBG estimates a larger quantity, on average. **12.** Heteroscedasticity. **14.** The distributions differ, suggesting that, in particular, the means differ. **15.** Low power due to outliers, violating the equal variance assumptions, differences in skewness, small sample sizes. **16.** No. Power of the test for equal variances might be too low. **17.** Unclear whether the test has enough power to detect a departure from normality that has practical importance. **18.** Generate data with unequal variances. **19.** There is a main effect for A and B, no interaction. **20.** There is a main effect for A and B and an interaction.

21.
```
x=list()
x[[1]]=c( 7,  9,  8, 12,  8,  7,  4, 10,  9,  6)
x[[2]]=c(10, 13,  9, 11,  5,  9,  8, 10,  8,  7)
x[[3]]=c(12, 11, 15,  7, 14, 10, 12, 12, 13, 14)
med1way(x)
```
The p-value is 0.018. **22.** The p-value is 5e$-04 = 0.0005$. **23.** 0.0022.

Chapter 11

4. The trimmed mean of the difference scores is not necessarily equal to the difference between the trimmed means of the marginal distributions. **5.** Yes, for the same reason given in Exercise 4. So, power can depend on which method is used.

Chapter 12

1. The probability of at least one Type I error can be unacceptably high. **2.** MSWG $= 11.6$, $T = |15 - 10|/\sqrt{11.6(1/20 + 1/20)} = 4.64$, $v = 100 - 5 = 95$, reject. **3.** $T = |15 - 10|/\sqrt{11.6(1/20 + 1/20)/2} = 6.565$, $q = 3.9$, reject. **4.** MSWG $= 8$, $T = |20 - 12|/\sqrt{8(1/10 + 1/10)} = 6.325$ $v = 50 - 5 = 45$, reject. **5.** $T = |20 - 12|/\sqrt{8(1/10 + 1/10)/2} = 8.94$, $q = 4.01$, reject. **6.** Increases and power decreases. **7.** Again, increases and power decreases. **8.** $W = (15 - 10)/\sqrt{4/20 + 9/20} = 6.2$, $\hat{v} = 33$, $c = 2.99$, reject. **9.** $(15 - 10)/\sqrt{.5(4/20 + 9/20)} = 8.77$, reject. **10.** $W = (20 - 12)/\sqrt{5/10 + 6/10} = 7.63$, reject **11.** Possibly invalid due to the poor estimate of the standard error. **12.** $W = (24 + 14 - 36 - 24)/\sqrt{6 + 8 + 8 + 5} = -4.23$, $v = 23$, $t_{0.975} = 2.07$. **13.** $v = 23$. Critical value equals 2.57. **14.** $W = -0.38$, $v = 23.4$, $t_{0.975} = 2.06$, fail to reject. **15.** None **16.** All of them. **17.** Both methods have as much or more power than the Bonferroni method. **19.** $H_0: \mu_1 + \mu_2 - \mu_5 - \mu_6 = 0$. **20** $H_0:$ $\mu_1 - 2\mu_2 + \mu_4 = 0$. **21.** 2, 0, −1, 0, −1. **22.** A=matrix(c(2,0,-1,0,-1)). **23.** The matrix should have four rows, which is equal to the number of groups.

Chapter 13

1. $X^2 = 17.2$, critical value $c = 7.8$. **2.** $X^2 = 26.2$, critical value $c = 13.3$. **3.** $X^2 = 46$, critical value $c = 15.1$. **4.** $X^2 = 13$, critical value $c = 5.99$. **5.** $X^2 = 5.3$, critical value $c = 7.8$. **6.** $X^2 = 5.1$, critical value $c = 9.5$. **7.** $X^2 = 20.3$, critical value $c = 5.99$. **8.** $X^2 = 6.36$, critical value $c = 7.81$. **9.** $X^2 = 4.15$, critical value $c = 12.59$.

  10. $\hat{p}_{11} = 35/200$. CI $= (0.126, 0.235)$. **12.** $X^2 = 7.4$, reject. No, phi coefficient is known to be an unsatisfactory measure of the strength of an association. **13.** $\hat{\theta} = 0.448$. Individuals with high incomes are about half as likely to be optimistic about the future. **14.** $\hat{p} = 0.4375$, 0.95 CI $= (0.385, 0.494)$.

APPENDIX B

TABLES

Understanding and Applying Basic Statistical Methods Using R, First Edition. Rand R. Wilcox.
© 2017 John Wiley & Sons, Inc. Published 2017 by John Wiley & Sons, Inc.
www.wiley.com/go/Wilcox/Statistical_Methods_R

TABLE B.1   Standard Normal Distribution

c	$P(Z \leq c)$	c	$P(Z \leq c)$	c	$P(Z \leq c)$	c	$P(Z \leq c)$
−3.00	0.0013	−2.99	0.0014	−2.98	0.0014	−2.97	0.0015
−2.96	0.0015	−2.95	0.0016	−2.94	0.0016	−2.93	0.0017
−2.92	0.0018	−2.91	0.0018	−2.90	0.0019	−2.89	0.0019
−2.88	0.0020	−2.87	0.0021	−2.86	0.0021	−2.85	0.0022
−2.84	0.0023	−2.83	0.0023	−2.82	0.0024	−2.81	0.0025
−2.80	0.0026	−2.79	0.0026	−2.78	0.0027	−2.77	0.0028
−2.76	0.0029	−2.75	0.0030	−2.74	0.0031	−2.73	0.0032
−2.72	0.0033	−2.71	0.0034	−2.70	0.0035	−2.69	0.0036
−2.68	0.0037	−2.67	0.0038	−2.66	0.0039	−2.65	0.0040
−2.64	0.0041	−2.63	0.0043	−2.62	0.0044	−2.61	0.0045
−2.60	0.0047	−2.59	0.0048	−2.58	0.0049	−2.57	0.0051
−2.56	0.0052	−2.55	0.0054	−2.54	0.0055	−2.53	0.0057
−2.52	0.0059	−2.51	0.0060	−2.50	0.0062	−2.49	0.0064
−2.48	0.0066	−2.47	0.0068	−2.46	0.0069	−2.45	0.0071
−2.44	0.0073	−2.43	0.0075	−2.42	0.0078	−2.41	0.0080
−2.40	0.0082	−2.39	0.0084	−2.38	0.0087	−2.37	0.0089
−2.36	0.0091	−2.35	0.0094	−2.34	0.0096	−2.33	0.0099
−2.32	0.0102	−2.31	0.0104	−2.30	0.0107	−2.29	0.0110
−2.28	0.0113	−2.27	0.0116	−2.26	0.0119	−2.25	0.0122
−2.24	0.0125	−2.23	0.0129	−2.22	0.0132	−2.21	0.0136
−2.20	0.0139	−2.19	0.0143	−2.18	0.0146	−2.17	0.0150
−2.16	0.0154	−2.15	0.0158	−2.14	0.0162	−2.13	0.0166
−2.12	0.0170	−2.11	0.0174	−2.10	0.0179	−2.09	0.0183
−2.08	0.0188	−2.07	0.0192	−2.06	0.0197	−2.05	0.0202
−2.04	0.0207	−2.03	0.0212	−2.02	0.0217	−2.01	0.0222
−2.00	0.0228	−1.99	0.0233	−1.98	0.0239	−1.97	0.0244
−1.96	0.0250	−1.95	0.0256	−1.94	0.0262	−1.93	0.0268
−1.92	0.0274	−1.91	0.0281	−1.90	0.0287	−1.89	0.0294
−1.88	0.0301	−1.87	0.0307	−1.86	0.0314	−1.85	0.0322
−1.84	0.0329	−1.83	0.0336	−1.82	0.0344	−1.81	0.0351
−1.80	0.0359	−1.79	0.0367	−1.78	0.0375	−1.77	0.0384
−1.76	0.0392	−1.75	0.0401	−1.74	0.0409	−1.73	0.0418
−1.72	0.0427	−1.71	0.0436	−1.70	0.0446	−1.69	0.0455
−1.68	0.0465	−1.67	0.0475	−1.66	0.0485	−1.65	0.0495
−1.64	0.0505	−1.63	0.0516	−1.62	0.0526	−1.61	0.0537
−1.60	0.0548	−1.59	0.0559	−1.58	0.0571	−1.57	0.0582
−1.56	0.0594	−1.55	0.0606	−1.54	0.0618	−1.53	0.0630
−1.52	0.0643	−1.51	0.0655	−1.50	0.0668	−1.49	0.0681
−1.48	0.0694	−1.47	0.0708	−1.46	0.0721	−1.45	0.0735
−1.44	0.0749	−1.43	0.0764	−1.42	0.0778	−1.41	0.0793
−1.40	0.0808	−1.39	0.0823	−1.38	0.0838	−1.37	0.0853
−1.36	0.0869	−1.35	0.0885	−1.34	0.0901	−1.33	0.0918
−1.32	0.0934	−1.31	0.0951	−1.30	0.0968	−1.29	0.0985
−1.28	0.1003	−1.27	0.1020	−1.26	0.1038	−1.25	0.1056
−1.24	0.1075	−1.23	0.1093	−1.22	0.1112	−1.21	0.1131
−1.20	0.1151	−1.19	0.1170	−1.18	0.1190	−1.17	0.1210
−1.16	0.1230	−1.15	0.1251	−1.14	0.1271	−1.13	0.1292

TABLE B.1 (*Continued*)

c	$P(Z \le c)$	c	$P(Z \le c)$	c	$P(Z \le c)$	c	$P(Z \le c)$
−1.12	0.1314	−1.11	0.1335	−1.10	0.1357	−1.09	0.1379
−1.08	0.1401	−1.07	0.1423	−1.06	0.1446	−1.05	0.1469
−1.04	0.1492	−1.03	0.1515	−1.02	0.1539	−1.01	0.1562
−1.00	0.1587	−0.99	0.1611	−0.98	0.1635	−0.97	0.1662
−0.96	0.1685	−0.95	0.1711	−0.94	0.1736	−0.93	0.1762
−0.92	0.1788	−0.91	0.1814	−0.90	0.1841	−0.89	0.1867
−0.88	0.1894	−0.87	0.1922	−0.86	0.1949	−0.85	0.1977
−0.84	0.2005	−0.83	0.2033	−0.82	0.2061	−0.81	0.2090
−0.80	0.2119	−0.79	0.2148	−0.78	0.2177	−0.77	0.2207
−0.76	0.2236	−0.75	0.2266	−0.74	0.2297	−0.73	0.2327
−0.72	0.2358	−0.71	0.2389	−0.70	0.2420	−0.69	0.2451
−0.68	0.2483	−0.67	0.2514	−0.66	0.2546	−0.65	0.2578
−0.64	0.2611	−0.63	0.2643	−0.62	0.2676	−0.61	0.2709
−0.60	0.2743	−0.59	0.2776	−0.58	0.2810	−0.57	0.2843
−0.56	0.2877	−0.55	0.2912	−0.54	0.2946	−0.53	0.2981
−0.52	0.3015	−0.51	0.3050	−0.50	0.3085	−0.49	0.3121
−0.48	0.3156	−0.47	0.3192	−0.46	0.3228	−0.45	0.3264
−0.44	0.3300	−0.43	0.3336	−0.42	0.3372	−0.41	0.3409
−0.40	0.3446	−0.39	0.3483	−0.38	0.3520	−0.37	0.3557
−0.36	0.3594	−0.35	0.3632	−0.34	0.3669	−0.33	0.3707
−0.32	0.3745	−0.31	0.3783	−0.30	0.3821	−0.29	0.3859
−0.28	0.3897	−0.27	0.3936	−0.26	0.3974	−0.25	0.4013
−0.24	0.4052	−0.23	0.4090	−0.22	0.4129	−0.21	0.4168
−0.20	0.4207	−0.19	0.4247	−0.18	0.4286	−0.17	0.4325
−0.16	0.4364	−0.15	0.4404	−0.14	0.4443	−0.13	0.4483
−0.12	0.4522	−0.11	0.4562	−0.10	0.4602	−0.09	0.4641
−0.08	0.4681	−0.07	0.4721	−0.06	0.4761	−0.05	0.4801
−0.04	0.4840	−0.03	0.4880	−0.02	0.4920	−0.01	0.4960
0.01	0.5040	0.02	0.5080	0.03	0.5120	0.04	0.5160
0.05	0.5199	0.06	0.5239	0.07	0.5279	0.08	0.5319
0.09	0.5359	0.10	0.5398	0.11	0.5438	0.12	0.5478
0.13	0.5517	0.14	0.5557	0.15	0.5596	0.16	0.5636
0.17	0.5675	0.18	0.5714	0.19	0.5753	0.20	0.5793
0.21	0.5832	0.22	0.5871	0.23	0.5910	0.24	0.5948
0.25	0.5987	0.26	0.6026	0.27	0.6064	0.28	0.6103
0.29	0.6141	0.30	0.6179	0.31	0.6217	0.32	0.6255
0.33	0.6293	0.34	0.6331	0.35	0.6368	0.36	0.6406
0.37	0.6443	0.38	0.6480	0.39	0.6517	0.40	0.6554
0.41	0.6591	0.42	0.6628	0.43	0.6664	0.44	0.6700
0.45	0.6736	0.46	0.6772	0.47	0.6808	0.48	0.6844
0.49	0.6879	0.50	0.6915	0.51	0.6950	0.52	0.6985
0.53	0.7019	0.54	0.7054	0.55	0.7088	0.56	0.7123
0.57	0.7157	0.58	0.7190	0.59	0.7224	0.60	0.7257
0.61	0.7291	0.62	0.7324	0.63	0.7357	0.64	0.7389
0.65	0.7422	0.66	0.7454	0.67	0.7486	0.68	0.7517
0.69	0.7549	0.70	0.7580	0.71	0.7611	0.72	0.7642
0.73	0.7673	0.74	0.7703	0.75	0.7734	0.76	0.7764

(*continued*)

TABLE B.1 (*Continued*)

c	$P(Z \le c)$	c	$P(Z \le c)$	c	$P(Z \le c)$	c	$P(Z \le c)$
0.77	0.7793	0.78	0.7823	0.79	0.7852	0.80	0.7881
0.81	0.7910	0.82	0.7939	0.83	0.7967	0.84	0.7995
0.85	0.8023	0.86	0.8051	0.87	0.8078	0.88	0.8106
0.89	0.8133	0.90	0.8159	0.91	0.8186	0.92	0.8212
0.93	0.8238	0.94	0.8264	0.95	0.8289	0.96	0.8315
0.97	0.8340	0.98	0.8365	0.99	0.8389	1.00	0.8413
1.01	0.8438	1.02	0.8461	1.03	0.8485	1.04	0.8508
1.05	0.8531	1.06	0.8554	1.07	0.8577	1.08	0.8599
1.09	0.8621	1.10	0.8643	1.11	0.8665	1.12	0.8686
1.13	0.8708	1.14	0.8729	1.15	0.8749	1.16	0.8770
1.17	0.8790	1.18	0.8810	1.19	0.8830	1.20	0.8849
1.21	0.8869	1.22	0.8888	1.23	0.8907	1.24	0.8925
1.25	0.8944	1.26	0.8962	1.27	0.8980	1.28	0.8997
1.29	0.9015	1.30	0.9032	1.31	0.9049	1.32	0.9066
1.33	0.9082	1.34	0.9099	1.35	0.9115	1.36	0.9131
1.37	0.9147	1.38	0.9162	1.39	0.9177	1.40	0.9192
1.41	0.9207	1.42	0.9222	1.43	0.9236	1.44	0.9251
1.45	0.9265	1.46	0.9279	1.47	0.9292	1.48	0.9306
1.49	0.9319	1.50	0.9332	1.51	0.9345	1.52	0.9357
1.53	0.9370	1.54	0.9382	1.55	0.9394	1.56	0.9406
1.57	0.9418	1.58	0.9429	1.59	0.9441	1.60	0.9452
1.61	0.9463	1.62	0.9474	1.63	0.9484	1.64	0.9495
1.65	0.9505	1.66	0.9515	1.67	0.9525	1.68	0.9535
1.69	0.9545	1.70	0.9554	1.71	0.9564	1.72	0.9573
1.73	0.9582	1.74	0.9591	1.75	0.9599	1.76	0.9608
1.77	0.9616	1.78	0.9625	1.79	0.9633	1.80	0.9641
1.81	0.9649	1.82	0.9656	1.83	0.9664	1.84	0.9671
1.85	0.9678	1.86	0.9686	1.87	0.9693	1.88	0.9699
1.89	0.9706	1.90	0.9713	1.91	0.9719	1.92	0.9726
1.93	0.9732	1.94	0.9738	1.95	0.9744	1.96	0.9750
1.97	0.9756	1.98	0.9761	1.99	0.9767	2.00	0.9772
2.01	0.9778	2.02	0.9783	2.03	0.9788	2.04	0.9793
2.05	0.9798	2.06	0.9803	2.07	0.9808	2.08	0.9812
2.09	0.9817	2.10	0.9821	2.11	0.9826	2.12	0.9830
2.13	0.9834	2.14	0.9838	2.15	0.9842	2.16	0.9846
2.17	0.9850	2.18	0.9854	2.19	0.9857	2.20	0.9861
2.21	0.9864	2.22	0.9868	2.23	0.9871	2.24	0.9875
2.25	0.9878	2.26	0.9881	2.27	0.9884	2.28	0.9887
2.29	0.9890	2.30	0.9893	2.31	0.9896	2.32	0.9898
2.33	0.9901	2.34	0.9904	2.35	0.9906	2.36	0.9909
2.37	0.9911	2.38	0.9913	2.39	0.9916	2.40	0.9918
2.41	0.9920	2.42	0.9922	2.43	0.9925	2.44	0.9927
2.45	0.9929	2.46	0.9931	2.47	0.9932	2.48	0.9934
2.49	0.9936	2.50	0.9938	2.51	0.9940	2.52	0.9941
2.53	0.9943	2.54	0.9945	2.55	0.9946	2.56	0.9948
2.57	0.9949	2.58	0.9951	2.59	0.9952	2.60	0.9953
2.61	0.9955	2.62	0.9956	2.63	0.9957	2.64	0.9959

TABLE B.1   (*Continued*)

c	$P(Z \le c)$	c	$P(Z \le c)$	c	$P(Z \le c)$	c	$P(Z \le c)$
2.65	0.9960	2.66	0.9961	2.67	0.9962	2.68	0.9963
2.69	0.9964	2.70	0.9965	2.71	0.9966	2.72	0.9967
2.73	0.9968	2.74	0.9969	2.75	0.9970	2.76	0.9971
2.77	0.9972	2.78	0.9973	2.79	0.9974	2.80	0.9974
2.81	0.9975	2.82	0.9976	2.83	0.9977	2.84	0.9977
2.85	0.9978	2.86	0.9979	2.87	0.9979	2.88	0.9980
2.89	0.9981	2.90	0.9981	2.91	0.9982	2.92	0.9982
2.93	0.9983	2.94	0.9984	2.95	0.9984	2.96	0.9985
2.97	0.9985	2.98	0.9986	2.99	0.9986	3.00	0.9987

TABLE B.2   Binomial Probability Function

x	0.05	0.1	0.2	0.3	0.4	*p* 0.5	0.6	0.7	0.8	0.9	0.95
n = 5											
0	0.774	0.590	0.328	0.168	0.078	0.031	0.010	0.002	0.000	0.000	0.000
1	0.977	0.919	0.737	0.528	0.337	0.188	0.087	0.031	0.007	0.000	0.000
2	0.999	0.991	0.942	0.837	0.683	0.500	0.317	0.163	0.058	0.009	0.001
3	1.000	1.000	0.993	0.969	0.913	0.813	0.663	0.472	0.263	0.081	0.023
4	1.000	1.000	1.000	0.998	0.990	0.969	0.922	0.832	0.672	0.410	0.226
n = 6											
0	0.735	0.531	0.262	0.118	0.047	0.016	0.004	0.001	0.000	0.000	0.000
1	0.967	0.886	0.655	0.420	0.233	0.109	0.041	0.011	0.002	0.000	0.000
2	0.998	0.984	0.901	0.744	0.544	0.344	0.179	0.070	0.017	0.001	0.000
3	1.000	0.999	0.983	0.930	0.821	0.656	0.456	0.256	0.099	0.016	0.002
4	1.000	1.000	0.998	0.989	0.959	0.891	0.767	0.580	0.345	0.114	0.033
5	1.000	1.000	1.000	0.999	0.996	0.984	0.953	0.882	0.738	0.469	0.265
n = 7											
0	0.698	0.478	0.210	0.082	0.028	0.008	0.002	0.000	0.000	0.000	0.000
1	0.956	0.850	0.577	0.329	0.159	0.062	0.019	0.004	0.000	0.000	0.000
2	0.996	0.974	0.852	0.647	0.420	0.227	0.096	0.029	0.005	0.000	0.000
3	1.000	0.997	0.967	0.874	0.710	0.500	0.290	0.126	0.033	0.003	0.000
4	1.000	1.000	0.995	0.971	0.904	0.773	0.580	0.353	0.148	0.026	0.004
5	1.000	1.000	1.000	0.996	0.981	0.938	0.841	0.671	0.423	0.150	0.044
6	1.000	1.000	1.000	1.000	0.998	0.992	0.972	0.918	0.790	0.522	0.302
n = 8											
0	0.663	0.430	0.168	0.058	0.017	0.004	0.001	0.000	0.000	0.000	0.000
1	0.943	0.813	0.503	0.255	0.106	0.035	0.009	0.001	0.000	0.000	0.000
2	0.994	0.962	0.797	0.552	0.315	0.145	0.050	0.011	0.001	0.000	0.000
3	1.000	0.995	0.944	0.806	0.594	0.363	0.174	0.058	0.010	0.000	0.000
4	1.000	1.000	0.990	0.942	0.826	0.637	0.406	0.194	0.056	0.005	0.000
5	1.000	1.000	0.999	0.989	0.950	0.855	0.685	0.448	0.203	0.038	0.006
6	1.000	1.000	1.000	0.999	0.991	0.965	0.894	0.745	0.497	0.187	0.057
7	1.000	1.000	1.000	1.000	0.999	0.996	0.983	0.942	0.832	0.570	0.337
n = 9											
0	0.630	0.387	0.134	0.040	0.010	0.002	0.000	0.000	0.000	0.000	0.000
1	0.929	0.775	0.436	0.196	0.071	0.020	0.004	0.000	0.000	0.000	0.000
2	0.992	0.947	0.738	0.463	0.232	0.090	0.025	0.004	0.000	0.000	0.000
3	0.999	0.992	0.914	0.730	0.483	0.254	0.099	0.025	0.003	0.000	0.000
4	1.000	0.999	0.980	0.901	0.733	0.500	0.267	0.099	0.020	0.001	0.000
5	1.000	1.000	0.997	0.975	0.901	0.746	0.517	0.270	0.086	0.008	0.001
6	1.000	1.000	1.000	0.996	0.975	0.910	0.768	0.537	0.262	0.053	0.008
7	1.000	1.000	1.000	1.000	0.996	0.980	0.929	0.804	0.564	0.225	0.071
8	1.000	1.000	1.000	1.000	1.000	0.998	0.990	0.960	0.866	0.613	0.370

TABLE B.2   (*Continued*)

x	0.05	0.1	0.2	0.3	0.4	p 0.5	0.6	0.7	0.8	0.9	0.95
n = 10											
0	0.599	0.349	0.107	0.028	0.006	0.001	0.000	0.000	0.000	0.000	0.000
1	0.914	0.736	0.376	0.149	0.046	0.011	0.002	0.000	0.000	0.000	0.000
2	0.988	0.930	0.678	0.383	0.167	0.055	0.012	0.002	0.000	0.000	0.000
3	0.999	0.987	0.879	0.650	0.382	0.172	0.055	0.011	0.001	0.000	0.000
4	1.000	0.998	0.967	0.850	0.633	0.377	0.166	0.047	0.006	0.000	0.000
5	1.000	1.000	0.994	0.953	0.834	0.623	0.367	0.150	0.033	0.002	0.000
6	1.000	1.000	0.999	0.989	0.945	0.828	0.618	0.350	0.121	0.013	0.001
7	1.000	1.000	1.000	0.998	0.988	0.945	0.833	0.617	0.322	0.070	0.012
8	1.000	1.000	1.000	1.000	0.998	0.989	0.954	0.851	0.624	0.264	0.086
9	1.000	1.000	1.000	1.000	1.000	0.999	0.994	0.972	0.893	0.651	0.401
n = 15											
0	0.463	0.206	0.035	0.005	0.000	0.000	0.000	0.000	0.000	0.000	0.000
1	0.829	0.549	0.167	0.035	0.005	0.000	0.000	0.000	0.000	0.000	0.000
2	0.964	0.816	0.398	0.127	0.027	0.004	0.000	0.000	0.000	0.000	0.000
3	0.995	0.944	0.648	0.297	0.091	0.018	0.002	0.000	0.000	0.000	0.000
4	0.999	0.987	0.836	0.515	0.217	0.059	0.009	0.001	0.000	0.000	0.000
5	1.000	0.998	0.939	0.722	0.403	0.151	0.034	0.004	0.000	0.000	0.000
6	1.000	1.000	0.982	0.869	0.610	0.304	0.095	0.015	0.001	0.000	0.000
7	1.000	1.000	0.996	0.950	0.787	0.500	0.213	0.050	0.004	0.000	0.000
8	1.000	1.000	0.999	0.985	0.905	0.696	0.390	0.131	0.018	0.000	0.000
9	1.000	1.000	1.000	0.996	0.966	0.849	0.597	0.278	0.061	0.002	0.000
10	1.000	1.000	1.000	0.999	0.991	0.941	0.783	0.485	0.164	0.013	0.001
11	1.000	1.000	1.000	1.000	0.998	0.982	0.909	0.703	0.352	0.056	0.005
12	1.000	1.000	1.000	1.000	1.000	0.996	0.973	0.873	0.602	0.184	0.036
13	1.000	1.000	1.000	1.000	1.000	1.000	0.995	0.965	0.833	0.451	0.171
14	1.000	1.000	1.000	1.000	1.000	1.000	1.000	0.995	0.965	0.794	0.537
n = 20											
0	0.358	0.122	0.012	0.001	0.000	0.000	0.000	0.000	0.000	0.000	0.000
1	0.736	0.392	0.069	0.008	0.001	0.000	0.000	0.000	0.000	0.000	0.000
2	0.925	0.677	0.206	0.035	0.004	0.000	0.000	0.000	0.000	0.000	0.000
3	0.984	0.867	0.411	0.107	0.016	0.001	0.000	0.000	0.000	0.000	0.000
4	0.997	0.957	0.630	0.238	0.051	0.006	0.000	0.000	0.000	0.000	0.000
5	1.000	0.989	0.804	0.416	0.126	0.021	0.002	0.000	0.000	0.000	0.000
6	1.000	0.998	0.913	0.608	0.250	0.058	0.006	0.000	0.000	0.000	0.000
7	1.000	1.000	0.968	0.772	0.416	0.132	0.021	0.001	0.000	0.000	0.000
8	1.000	1.000	0.990	0.887	0.596	0.252	0.057	0.005	0.000	0.000	0.000
9	1.000	1.000	0.997	0.952	0.755	0.412	0.128	0.017	0.001	0.000	0.000
10	1.000	1.000	0.999	0.983	0.872	0.588	0.245	0.048	0.003	0.000	0.000
11	1.000	1.000	1.000	0.995	0.943	0.748	0.404	0.113	0.010	0.000	0.000
12	1.000	1.000	1.000	0.999	0.979	0.868	0.584	0.228	0.032	0.000	0.000
13	1.000	1.000	1.000	1.000	0.994	0.942	0.750	0.392	0.087	0.002	0.000

(*continued*)

TABLE B.2 (*Continued*)

x	0.05	0.1	0.2	0.3	0.4	p 0.5	0.6	0.7	0.8	0.9	0.95
14	1.000	1.000	1.000	1.000	0.998	0.979	0.874	0.584	0.196	0.011	0.000
15	1.000	1.000	1.000	1.000	1.000	0.994	0.949	0.762	0.370	0.043	0.003
16	1.000	1.000	1.000	1.000	1.000	0.999	0.984	0.893	0.589	0.133	0.016
17	1.000	1.000	1.000	1.000	1.000	1.000	0.996	0.965	0.794	0.323	0.075
18	1.000	1.000	1.000	1.000	1.000	1.000	0.999	0.992	0.931	0.608	0.264
19	1.000	1.000	1.000	1.000	1.000	1.000	1.000	0.999	0.988	0.878	0.642

$n = 25$

x	0.05	0.1	0.2	0.3	0.4	0.5	0.6	0.7	0.8	0.9	0.95
0	0.277	0.072	0.004	0.000	0.000	0.000	0.000	0.000	0.000	0.000	0.000
1	0.642	0.271	0.027	0.002	0.000	0.000	0.000	0.000	0.000	0.000	0.000
2	0.873	0.537	0.098	0.009	0.000	0.000	0.000	0.000	0.000	0.000	0.000
3	0.966	0.764	0.234	0.033	0.002	0.000	0.000	0.000	0.000	0.000	0.000
4	0.993	0.902	0.421	0.090	0.009	0.000	0.000	0.000	0.000	0.000	0.000
5	0.999	0.967	0.617	0.193	0.029	0.002	0.000	0.000	0.000	0.000	0.000
6	1.000	0.991	0.780	0.341	0.074	0.007	0.000	0.000	0.000	0.000	0.000
7	1.000	0.998	0.891	0.512	0.154	0.022	0.001	0.000	0.000	0.000	0.000
8	1.000	1.000	0.953	0.677	0.274	0.054	0.004	0.000	0.000	0.000	0.000
9	1.000	1.000	0.983	0.811	0.425	0.115	0.013	0.000	0.000	0.000	0.000
10	1.000	1.000	0.994	0.902	0.586	0.212	0.034	0.002	0.000	0.000	0.000
11	1.000	1.000	0.998	0.956	0.732	0.345	0.078	0.006	0.000	0.000	0.000
12	1.000	1.000	1.000	0.983	0.846	0.500	0.154	0.017	0.000	0.000	0.000
13	1.000	1.000	1.000	0.994	0.922	0.655	0.268	0.044	0.002	0.000	0.000
14	1.000	1.000	1.000	0.998	0.966	0.788	0.414	0.098	0.006	0.000	0.000
15	1.000	1.000	1.000	1.000	0.987	0.885	0.575	0.189	0.017	0.000	0.000
16	1.000	1.000	1.000	1.000	0.996	0.946	0.726	0.323	0.047	0.000	0.000
17	1.000	1.000	1.000	1.000	0.999	0.978	0.846	0.488	0.109	0.002	0.000
18	1.000	1.000	1.000	1.000	1.000	0.993	0.926	0.659	0.220	0.009	0.000
19	1.000	1.000	1.000	1.000	1.000	0.998	0.971	0.807	0.383	0.033	0.001
20	1.000	1.000	1.000	1.000	1.000	1.000	0.991	0.910	0.579	0.098	0.007
21	1.000	1.000	1.000	1.000	1.000	1.000	0.998	0.967	0.766	0.236	0.034
22	1.000	1.000	1.000	1.000	1.000	1.000	1.000	0.991	0.902	0.463	0.127
23	1.000	1.000	1.000	1.000	1.000	1.000	1.000	0.998	0.973	0.729	0.358
24	1.000	1.000	1.000	1.000	1.000	1.000	1.000	1.000	0.996	0.928	0.723

[a]Entries indicate $P(X \leq x)$

TABLE B.3 Percentage Points of the Chi-Squared Distribution

ν	$\chi^2_{0.005}$	$\chi^2_{0.01}$	$\chi^2_{0.025}$	$\chi^2_{0.05}$	$\chi^2_{0.10}$
1	0.0000393	0.0001571	0.0009821	0.0039321	0.0157908
2	0.0100251	0.0201007	0.0506357	0.1025866	0.2107213
3	0.0717217	0.1148317	0.2157952	0.3518462	0.5843744
4	0.2069889	0.2971095	0.4844186	0.7107224	1.0636234
5	0.4117419	0.5542979	0.8312111	1.1454763	1.6103077
6	0.6757274	0.8720903	1.2373447	1.6353836	2.2041321
7	0.9892554	1.2390423	1.6898699	2.1673594	2.8331099
8	1.3444128	1.6464968	2.1797333	2.7326374	3.4895401
9	1.7349329	2.0879011	2.7003908	3.3251143	4.1681604
10	2.1558590	2.5582132	3.2469759	3.9403019	4.8651857
11	2.6032248	3.0534868	3.8157606	4.5748196	5.5777788
12	3.0738316	3.5705872	4.4037895	5.2260313	6.3037949
13	3.5650368	4.1069279	5.0087538	5.8918715	7.0415068
14	4.0746784	4.6604300	5.6287327	6.5706167	7.7895403
15	4.6009169	5.2293501	6.2621403	7.2609539	8.5467529
16	5.1422071	5.8122101	6.9076681	7.9616566	9.3122330
17	5.6972256	6.4077673	7.5641880	8.6717682	10.0851974
18	6.2648115	7.0149183	8.2307510	9.3904572	10.8649368
19	6.8439512	7.6327391	8.9065247	10.1170273	11.6509628
20	7.4338474	8.2603989	9.5907822	10.8508148	12.4426041
21	8.0336685	8.8972015	10.2829285	11.5913391	13.2396393
22	8.6427155	9.5425110	10.9823456	12.3380432	14.0414886
23	9.2604370	10.1957169	11.6885223	13.0905151	14.8479385
24	9.8862610	10.8563690	12.4011765	13.8484344	15.6587067
25	10.5196533	11.5239716	13.1197433	14.6114349	16.4734497
26	11.1602631	12.1981506	13.8439331	15.3792038	17.2919159
27	11.8076019	12.8785095	14.5734024	16.1513977	18.1138763
28	12.4613495	13.5647125	15.3078613	16.9278717	18.9392395
29	13.1211624	14.2564697	16.0470886	17.7083893	19.7678223
30	13.7867584	14.9534760	16.7907562	18.4926147	20.5992126
40	20.7065582	22.1642761	24.4330750	26.5083008	29.0503540
50	27.9775238	29.7001038	32.3561096	34.7638702	37.6881561
60	35.5294037	37.4848328	40.4817810	43.1865082	46.4583282
70	43.2462311	45.4230499	48.7503967	51.7388763	55.3331146
80	51.1447754	53.5226593	57.1465912	60.3912201	64.2818604
90	59.1706543	61.7376862	65.6405029	69.1258850	73.2949219
100	67.3031921	70.0493622	74.2162018	77.9293976	82.3618469

(continued)

TABLE B.3 (*Continued*)

v	$\chi^2_{0.900}$	$\chi^2_{0.95}$	$\chi^2_{0.975}$	$\chi^2_{0.99}$	$\chi^2_{0.995}$
1	2.7056	3.8415	5.0240	6.6353	7.8818
2	4.6052	5.9916	7.3779	9.2117	10.5987
3	6.2514	7.8148	9.3486	11.3465	12.8409
4	7.7795	9.4879	11.1435	13.2786	14.8643
5	9.2365	11.0707	12.8328	15.0870	16.7534
6	10.6448	12.5919	14.4499	16.8127	18.5490
7	12.0171	14.0676	16.0136	18.4765	20.2803
8	13.3617	15.5075	17.5355	20.0924	21.9579
9	14.6838	16.9191	19.0232	21.6686	23.5938
10	15.9874	18.3075	20.4837	23.2101	25.1898
11	17.2750	19.6754	21.9211	24.7265	26.7568
12	18.5494	21.0263	23.3370	26.2170	28.2995
13	19.8122	22.3627	24.7371	27.6882	29.8194
14	21.0646	23.6862	26.1189	29.1412	31.3193
15	22.3077	24.9970	27.4883	30.5779	32.8013
16	23.5421	26.2961	28.8453	31.9999	34.2672
17	24.7696	27.5871	30.1909	33.4087	35.7184
18	25.9903	28.8692	31.5264	34.8054	37.1564
19	27.2035	30.1434	32.8523	36.1909	38.5823
20	28.4120	31.4104	34.1696	37.5662	39.9968
21	29.6150	32.6705	35.4787	38.9323	41.4012
22	30.8133	33.9244	36.7806	40.2893	42.7958
23	32.0069	35.1725	38.0757	41.6384	44.1812
24	33.1962	36.4151	39.3639	42.9799	45.5587
25	34.3815	37.6525	40.6463	44.3142	46.9280
26	35.5631	38.8852	41.9229	45.6418	48.2899
27	36.7412	40.1134	43.1943	46.9629	49.6449
28	37.9159	41.3371	44.4608	48.2784	50.9933
29	39.0874	42.5571	45.7223	49.5879	52.3357
30	40.2561	43.7730	46.9792	50.8922	53.6721
40	51.8050	55.7586	59.3417	63.6909	66.7660
50	63.1670	67.5047	71.4201	76.1538	79.4899
60	74.3970	79.0820	83.2977	88.3794	91.9516
70	85.5211	90.5283	95.0263	100.4409	104.2434
80	96.5723	101.8770	106.6315	112.3434	116.3484
90	107.5600	113.1425	118.1392	124.1304	128.3245
100	118.4932	124.3395	129.5638	135.8203	140.1940

TABLE B.4 Percentage Points of Student's T Distribution

v	$t_{0.9}$	$t_{0.95}$	$t_{0.975}$	$t_{0.99}$	$t_{0.995}$	$t_{0.999}$
1	3.078	6.314	12.706	31.821	63.6567	318.313
2	1.886	2.920	4.303	6.965	9.925	22.327
3	1.638	2.353	3.183	4.541	5.841	10.215
4	1.533	2.132	2.776	3.747	4.604	7.173
5	1.476	2.015	2.571	3.365	4.032	5.893
6	1.440	1.943	2.447	3.143	3.707	5.208
7	1.415	1.895	2.365	2.998	3.499	4.785
8	1.397	1.856	2.306	2.897	3.355	4.501
9	1.383	1.833	2.262	2.821	3.245	4.297
10	1.372	1.812	2.228	2.764	3.169	4.144
12	1.356	1.782	2.179	2.681	3.055	3.930
15	1.341	1.753	2.131	2.603	2.947	3.733
20	1.325	1.725	2.086	2.528	2.845	3.552
24	1.318	1.711	2.064	2.492	2.797	3.467
30	1.310	1.697	2.042	2.457	2.750	3.385
40	1.303	1.684	2.021	2.423	2.704	3.307
60	1.296	1.671	2.000	2.390	2.660	3.232
120	1.289	1.658	1.980	2.358	2.617	3.160
∞	1.282	1.645	1.960	2.326	2.576	3.090

TABLE B.5   Percentage Points of the F Distribution, $\alpha = 0.10$

v_2	v_1 1	2	3	4	5	6	7	8	9
1	39.86	49.50	53.59	55.83	57.24	58.20	58.91	59.44	59.86
2	8.53	9.00	9.16	9.24	9.29	9.33	9.35	9.37	9.38
3	5.54	5.46	5.39	5.34	5.31	5.28	5.27	5.25	5.24
4	4.54	4.32	4.19	4.11	4.05	4.01	3.98	3.95	3.94
5	4.06	3.78	3.62	3.52	3.45	3.40	3.37	3.34	3.32
6	3.78	3.46	3.29	3.18	3.11	3.05	3.01	2.98	2.96
7	3.59	3.26	3.07	2.96	2.88	2.83	2.79	2.75	2.72
8	3.46	3.11	2.92	2.81	2.73	2.67	2.62	2.59	2.56
9	3.36	3.01	2.81	2.69	2.61	2.55	2.51	2.47	2.44
10	3.29	2.92	2.73	2.61	2.52	2.46	2.41	2.38	2.35
11	3.23	2.86	2.66	2.54	2.45	2.39	2.34	2.30	2.27
12	3.18	2.81	2.61	2.48	2.39	2.33	2.28	2.24	2.21
13	3.14	2.76	2.56	2.43	2.35	2.28	2.23	2.20	2.16
14	3.10	2.73	2.52	2.39	2.31	2.24	2.19	2.15	2.12
15	3.07	2.70	2.49	2.36	2.27	2.21	2.16	2.12	2.09
16	3.05	2.67	2.46	2.33	2.24	2.18	2.13	2.09	2.06
17	3.03	2.64	2.44	2.31	2.22	2.15	2.10	2.06	2.03
18	3.01	2.62	2.42	2.29	2.20	2.13	2.08	2.04	2.00
19	2.99	2.61	2.40	2.27	2.18	2.11	2.06	2.02	1.98
20	2.97	2.59	2.38	2.25	2.16	2.09	2.04	2.00	1.96
21	2.96	2.57	2.36	2.23	2.14	2.08	2.02	1.98	1.95
22	2.95	2.56	2.35	2.22	2.13	2.06	2.01	1.97	1.93
23	2.94	2.55	2.34	2.21	2.11	2.05	1.99	1.95	1.92
24	2.93	2.54	2.33	2.19	2.10	2.04	1.98	1.94	1.91
25	2.92	2.53	2.32	2.18	2.09	2.02	1.97	1.93	1.89
26	2.91	2.52	2.31	2.17	2.08	2.01	1.96	1.92	1.88
27	2.90	2.51	2.30	2.17	2.07	2.00	1.95	1.91	1.87
28	2.89	2.50	2.29	2.16	2.06	2.00	1.94	1.90	1.87
29	2.89	2.50	2.28	2.15	2.06	1.99	1.93	1.89	1.86
30	2.88	2.49	2.28	2.14	2.05	1.98	1.93	1.88	1.85
40	2.84	2.44	2.23	2.09	2.00	1.93	1.87	1.83	1.79
60	2.79	2.39	2.18	2.04	1.95	1.87	1.82	1.77	1.74
120	2.75	2.35	2.13	1.99	1.90	1.82	1.77	1.72	1.68
∞	2.71	2.30	2.08	1.94	1.85	1.77	1.72	.167	1.63

TABLE B.5 (*Continued*)

ν_2	10	12	15	20	ν_1 24	30	40	60	120	∞
1	60.19	60.70	61.22	61.74	62.00	62.26	62.53	62.79	63.06	63.33
2	9.39	9.41	9.42	9.44	9.45	9.46	9.47	9.47	9.48	9.49
3	5.23	5.22	5.20	5.19	5.18	5.17	5.16	5.15	5.14	5.13
4	3.92	3.90	3.87	3.84	3.83	3.82	3.80	3.79	3.78	3.76
5	3.30	3.27	3.24	3.21	3.19	3.17	3.16	3.14	3.12	3.10
6	2.94	2.90	2.87	2.84	2.82	2.80	2.78	2.76	2.74	2.72
7	2.70	2.67	2.63	2.59	2.58	2.56	2.54	2.51	2.49	2.47
8	2.54	2.50	2.46	2.42	2.40	2.38	2.36	2.34	2.32	2.29
9	2.42	2.38	2.34	2.30	2.28	2.25	2.23	2.21	2.18	2.16
10	2.32	2.28	2.24	2.20	2.18	2.16	2.13	2.11	2.08	2.06
11	2.25	2.21	2.17	2.12	2.10	2.08	2.05	2.03	2.00	1.97
12	2.19	2.15	2.10	2.06	2.04	2.01	1.99	1.96	1.93	1.90
13	2.14	2.10	2.05	2.01	1.98	1.96	1.93	1.90	1.88	1.85
14	2.10	2.05	2.01	1.96	1.94	1.91	1.89	1.86	1.83	1.80
15	2.06	2.02	1.97	1.92	1.90	1.87	1.85	1.82	1.79	1.76
16	2.03	1.99	1.94	1.89	1.87	1.84	1.81	1.78	1.75	1.72
17	2.00	1.96	1.91	1.86	1.84	1.81	1.78	1.75	1.72	1.69
18	1.98	1.93	1.89	1.84	1.81	1.78	1.75	1.72	1.69	1.66
19	1.96	1.91	1.86	1.81	1.79	1.76	1.73	1.70	1.67	1.63
20	1.94	1.89	1.84	1.79	1.77	1.74	1.71	1.68	1.64	1.61
21	1.92	1.87	1.83	1.78	1.75	1.72	1.69	1.66	1.62	1.59
22	1.90	1.86	1.81	1.76	1.73	1.70	1.67	1.64	1.60	1.57
23	1.89	1.84	1.80	1.74	1.72	1.69	1.66	1.62	1.59	1.55
24	1.88	1.83	1.78	1.73	1.70	1.67	1.64	1.61	1.57	1.53
25	1.87	1.82	1.77	1.72	1.69	1.66	1.63	1.59	1.56	1.52
26	1.86	1.81	1.76	1.71	1.68	1.65	1.61	1.58	1.54	1.50
27	1.85	1.80	1.75	1.70	1.67	1.64	1.60	1.57	1.53	1.49
28	1.84	1.79	1.74	1.69	1.66	1.63	1.59	1.56	1.52	1.48
29	1.83	1.78	1.73	1.68	1.65	1.62	1.58	1.55	1.51	1.47
30	1.82	1.77	1.72	1.67	1.64	1.61	1.57	1.54	1.50	1.46
40	1.76	1.71	1.66	1.61	1.57	1.54	1.51	1.47	1.42	1.38
60	1.71	1.66	1.60	1.54	1.51	1.48	1.44	1.40	1.35	1.29
120	1.65	1.60	1.55	1.48	1.45	1.41	1.37	1.32	1.26	1.19
∞	1.60	1.55	1.49	1.42	1.38	1.34	1.30	1.24	1.17	1.00

TABLE B.6   Percentage Points of the F Distribution, $\alpha = 0.05$

v_2	1	2	3	4	v_1 5	6	7	8	9
1	161.45	199.50	215.71	224.58	230.16	233.99	236.77	238.88	240.54
2	18.51	19.00	19.16	19.25	19.30	19.33	19.35	19.37	19.38
3	10.13	9.55	9.28	9.12	9.01	8.94	8.89	8.85	8.81
4	7.71	6.94	6.59	6.39	6.26	6.16	6.09	6.04	6.00
5	6.61	5.79	5.41	5.19	5.05	4.95	4.88	4.82	4.77
6	5.99	5.14	4.76	4.53	4.39	4.28	4.21	4.15	4.10
7	5.59	4.74	4.35	4.12	3.97	3.87	3.79	3.73	3.68
8	5.32	4.46	4.07	3.84	3.69	3.58	3.50	3.44	3.39
9	5.12	4.26	3.86	3.63	3.48	3.37	3.29	3.23	3.18
10	4.96	4.10	3.71	3.48	3.33	3.22	3.14	3.07	3.02
11	4.84	3.98	3.59	3.36	3.20	3.09	3.01	2.95	2.90
12	4.75	3.89	3.49	3.26	3.11	3.00	2.91	2.85	2.80
13	4.67	3.81	3.41	3.18	3.03	2.92	2.83	2.77	2.71
14	4.60	3.74	3.34	3.11	2.96	2.85	2.76	2.70	2.65
15	4.54	3.68	3.29	3.06	2.90	2.79	2.71	2.64	2.59
16	4.49	3.63	3.24	3.01	2.85	2.74	2.66	2.59	2.54
17	4.45	3.59	3.20	2.96	2.81	2.70	2.61	2.55	2.49
18	4.41	3.55	3.16	2.93	2.77	2.66	2.58	2.51	2.46
19	4.38	3.52	3.13	2.90	2.74	2.63	2.54	2.48	2.42
20	4.35	3.49	3.10	2.87	2.71	2.60	2.51	2.45	2.39
21	4.32	3.47	3.07	2.84	2.68	2.57	2.49	2.42	2.37
22	4.30	3.44	3.05	2.82	2.66	2.55	2.46	2.40	2.34
23	4.28	3.42	3.03	2.80	2.64	2.53	2.44	2.37	2.32
24	4.26	3.40	3.01	2.78	2.62	2.51	2.42	2.36	2.30
25	4.24	3.39	2.99	2.76	2.60	2.49	2.40	2.34	2.28
26	4.23	3.37	2.98	2.74	2.59	2.47	2.39	2.32	2.27
27	4.21	3.35	2.96	2.73	2.57	2.46	2.37	2.31	2.25
28	4.20	3.34	2.95	2.71	2.56	2.45	2.36	2.29	2.24
29	4.18	3.33	2.93	2.70	2.55	2.43	2.35	2.28	2.22
30	4.17	3.32	2.92	2.69	2.53	2.42	2.33	2.27	2.21
40	4.08	3.23	2.84	2.61	2.45	2.34	2.25	2.18	2.12
60	4.00	3.15	2.76	2.53	2.37	2.25	2.17	2.10	2.04
120	3.92	3.07	2.68	2.45	2.29	2.17	2.09	2.02	1.96
∞	3.84	3.00	2.60	2.37	2.21	2.10	2.01	1.94	1.88

TABLE B.6 (*Continued*)

v_2	10	12	15	20	v_1 24	30	40	60	120	∞
1	241.88	243.91	245.96	248.00	249.04	250.08	251.14	252.19	253.24	254.3
2	19.40	19.41	19.43	19.45	19.45	19.46	19.47	19.48	19.49	19.50
3	8.79	8.74	8.70	8.66	8.64	8.62	8.59	8.57	8.55	8.53
4	5.97	5.91	5.86	5.80	5.77	5.74	5.72	5.69	5.66	5.63
5	4.73	4.68	4.62	4.56	4.53	4.50	4.46	4.43	4.40	4.36
6	4.06	4.00	3.94	3.87	3.84	3.81	3.77	3.74	3.70	3.67
7	3.64	3.57	3.51	3.44	3.41	3.38	3.34	3.30	3.27	3.23
8	3.35	3.28	3.22	3.15	3.12	3.08	3.04	3.00	2.97	2.93
9	3.14	3.07	3.01	2.94	2.90	2.86	2.83	2.79	2.75	2.71
10	2.98	2.91	2.85	2.77	2.74	2.70	2.66	2.62	2.58	2.54
11	2.85	2.79	2.72	2.65	2.61	2.57	2.53	2.49	2.45	2.40
12	2.75	2.69	2.62	2.54	2.51	2.47	2.43	2.38	2.34	2.30
13	2.67	2.60	2.53	2.46	2.42	2.38	2.34	2.30	2.25	2.21
14	2.60	2.53	2.46	2.39	2.35	2.31	2.27	2.22	2.18	2.13
15	2.54	2.48	2.40	2.33	2.29	2.25	2.20	2.16	2.11	2.07
16	2.49	2.42	2.35	2.28	2.24	2.19	2.15	2.11	2.06	2.01
17	2.45	2.38	2.31	2.23	2.19	2.15	2.10	2.06	2.01	1.96
18	2.41	2.34	2.27	2.19	2.15	2.11	2.06	2.02	1.97	1.92
19	2.38	2.31	2.23	2.16	2.11	2.07	2.03	1.98	1.93	1.88
20	2.35	2.28	2.20	2.12	2.08	2.04	1.99	1.95	1.90	1.84
21	2.32	2.25	2.18	2.10	2.05	2.01	1.96	1.92	1.87	1.81
22	2.30	2.23	2.15	2.07	2.03	1.98	1.94	1.89	1.84	1.78
23	2.27	2.20	2.13	2.05	2.00	1.96	1.91	1.86	1.81	1.76
24	2.25	2.18	2.11	2.03	1.98	1.94	1.89	1.84	1.79	1.73
25	2.24	2.16	2.09	2.01	1.96	1.92	1.87	1.82	1.77	1.71
26	2.22	2.15	2.07	1.99	1.95	1.90	1.85	1.80	1.75	1.69
27	2.20	2.13	2.06	1.97	1.93	1.88	1.84	1.79	1.73	1.67
28	2.19	2.12	2.04	1.96	1.91	1.87	1.82	1.77	1.71	1.65
29	2.18	2.10	2.03	1.94	1.90	1.85	1.81	1.75	1.70	1.64
30	2.16	2.09	2.01	1.93	1.89	1.84	1.79	1.74	1.68	1.62
40	2.08	2.00	1.92	1.84	1.79	1.74	1.69	1.64	1.58	1.51
60	1.99	1.92	1.84	1.75	1.70	1.65	1.59	1.53	1.47	1.39
120	1.91	1.83	1.75	1.66	1.61	1.55	1.50	1.43	1.35	1.25
∞	1.83	1.75	1.67	1.57	1.52	1.46	1.39	1.32	1.22	1.00

TABLE B.7   Percentage Points of the F Distribution, $\alpha = 0.025$

v_2	v_1 1	2	3	4	5	6	7	8	9
1	647.79	799.50	864.16	899.59	921.85	937.11	948.22	956.66	963.28
2	38.51	39.00	39.17	39.25	39.30	39.33	39.36	39.37	39.39
3	17.44	16.04	15.44	15.10	14.88	14.74	14.63	14.54	14.47
4	12.22	10.65	9.98	9.61	9.36	9.20	9.07	8.98	8.90
5	10.01	8.43	7.76	7.39	7.15	6.98	6.85	6.76	6.68
6	8.81	7.26	6.60	6.23	5.99	5.82	5.70	5.60	5.52
7	8.07	6.54	5.89	5.52	5.29	5.12	5.00	4.90	4.82
8	7.57	6.06	5.42	5.05	4.82	4.65	4.53	4.43	4.36
9	7.21	5.71	5.08	4.72	4.48	4.32	4.20	4.10	4.03
10	6.94	5.46	4.83	4.47	4.24	4.07	3.95	3.85	3.78
11	6.72	5.26	4.63	4.28	4.04	3.88	3.76	3.66	3.59
12	6.55	5.10	4.47	4.12	3.89	3.73	3.61	3.51	3.44
13	6.41	4.97	4.35	4.00	3.77	3.60	3.48	3.39	3.31
14	6.30	4.86	4.24	3.89	3.66	3.50	3.38	3.29	3.21
15	6.20	4.77	4.15	3.80	3.58	3.41	3.29	3.20	3.12
16	6.12	4.69	4.08	3.73	3.50	3.34	3.22	3.12	3.05
17	6.04	4.62	4.01	3.66	3.44	3.28	3.16	3.06	2.98
18	5.98	4.56	3.95	3.61	3.38	3.22	3.10	3.01	2.93
19	5.92	4.51	3.90	3.56	3.33	3.17	3.05	2.96	2.88
20	5.87	4.46	3.86	3.51	3.29	3.13	3.01	2.91	2.84
21	5.83	4.42	3.82	3.48	3.25	3.09	2.97	2.87	2.80
22	5.79	4.38	3.78	3.44	3.22	3.05	2.93	2.84	2.76
23	5.75	4.35	3.75	3.41	3.18	3.02	2.90	2.81	2.73
24	5.72	4.32	3.72	3.38	3.15	2.99	2.87	2.78	2.70
25	5.69	4.29	3.69	3.35	3.13	2.97	2.85	2.75	2.68
26	5.66	4.27	3.67	3.33	3.10	2.94	2.82	2.73	2.65
27	5.63	4.24	3.65	3.31	3.08	2.92	2.80	2.71	2.63
28	5.61	4.22	3.63	3.29	3.06	2.90	2.78	2.69	2.61
29	5.59	4.20	3.61	3.27	3.04	2.88	2.76	2.67	2.59
30	5.57	4.18	3.59	3.25	3.03	2.87	2.75	2.65	2.57
40	5.42	4.05	3.46	3.13	2.90	2.74	2.62	2.53	2.45
60	5.29	3.93	3.34	3.01	2.79	2.63	2.51	2.41	2.33
120	5.15	3.80	3.23	2.89	2.67	2.52	2.39	2.30	2.22
∞	5.02	3.69	3.12	2.79	2.57	2.41	2.29	2.19	2.11

TABLE B.7 (*Continued*)

ν_2	10	12	15	20	ν_1 24	30	40	60	120	∞
1	968.62	976.71	984.89	993.04	997.20	1,001	1,006	1,010	1,014	1,018
2	39.40	39.41	39.43	39.45	39.46	39.46	39.47	39.48	39.49	39.50
3	14.42	14.33	14.26	14.17	14.13	14.08	14.04	13.99	13.95	13.90
4	8.85	8.75	8.66	8.56	8.51	8.46	8.41	8.36	8.31	8.26
5	6.62	6.53	6.43	6.33	6.28	6.23	6.17	6.12	6.07	6.02
6	5.46	5.37	5.27	5.17	5.12	5.06	5.01	4.96	4.90	4.85
7	4.76	4.67	4.57	4.47	4.41	4.36	4.31	4.25	4.20	4.14
8	4.30	4.20	4.10	4.00	3.95	3.89	3.84	3.78	3.73	3.67
9	3.96	3.87	3.77	3.67	3.61	3.56	3.51	3.45	3.39	3.33
10	3.72	3.62	3.52	3.42	3.37	3.31	3.26	3.20	3.14	3.08
11	3.53	3.43	3.33	3.23	3.17	3.12	3.06	3.00	2.94	2.88
12	3.37	3.28	3.18	3.07	3.02	2.96	2.91	2.85	2.79	2.72
13	3.25	3.15	3.05	2.95	2.89	2.84	2.78	2.72	2.66	2.60
14	3.15	3.05	2.95	2.84	2.79	2.73	2.67	2.61	2.55	2.49
15	3.06	2.96	2.86	2.76	2.70	2.64	2.59	2.52	2.46	2.40
16	2.99	2.89	2.79	2.68	2.63	2.57	2.51	2.45	2.38	2.32
17	2.92	2.82	2.72	2.62	2.56	2.50	2.44	2.38	2.32	2.25
18	2.87	2.77	2.67	2.56	2.50	2.44	2.38	2.32	2.26	2.19
19	2.82	2.72	2.62	2.51	2.45	2.39	2.33	2.27	2.20	2.13
20	2.77	2.68	2.57	2.46	2.41	2.35	2.29	2.22	2.16	2.09
21	2.73	2.64	2.53	2.42	2.37	2.31	2.25	2.18	2.11	2.04
22	2.70	2.60	2.50	2.39	2.33	2.27	2.21	2.14	2.08	2.00
23	2.67	2.57	2.47	2.36	2.30	2.24	2.18	2.11	2.04	1.97
24	2.64	2.54	2.44	2.33	2.27	2.21	2.15	2.08	2.01	1.94
25	2.61	2.51	2.41	2.30	2.24	2.18	2.12	2.05	1.98	1.91
26	2.59	2.49	2.39	2.28	2.22	2.16	2.09	2.03	1.95	1.88
27	2.57	2.47	2.36	2.25	2.19	2.13	2.07	2.00	1.93	1.85
28	2.55	2.45	2.34	2.23	2.17	2.11	2.05	1.98	1.91	1.83
29	2.53	2.43	2.32	2.21	2.15	2.09	2.03	1.96	1.89	1.81
30	2.51	2.41	2.31	2.20	2.14	2.07	2.01	1.94	1.87	1.79
40	2.39	2.29	2.18	2.07	2.01	1.94	1.88	1.80	1.72	1.64
60	2.27	2.17	2.06	1.94	1.88	1.82	1.74	1.67	1.58	1.48
120	2.16	2.05	1.95	1.82	1.76	1.69	1.61	1.53	1.43	1.31
∞	2.05	1.94	1.83	1.71	1.64	1.57	1.48	1.39	1.27	1.00

TABLE B.8   Percentage Points of the F Distribution, $\alpha = 0.01$

v_2	v_1								
	1	2	3	4	5	6	7	8	9
1	4,052	4,999	5,403	5,625	5,764	5,859	5,928	5,982	6,022
2	98.50	99.00	99.17	99.25	99.30	99.33	99.36	99.37	99.39
3	34.12	30.82	29.46	28.71	28.24	27.91	27.67	27.50	27.34
4	21.20	18.00	16.69	15.98	15.52	15.21	14.98	14.80	14.66
5	16.26	13.27	12.06	11.39	10.97	10.67	10.46	10.29	10.16
6	13.75	10.92	9.78	9.15	8.75	8.47	8.26	8.10	7.98
7	12.25	9.55	8.45	7.85	7.46	7.19	6.99	6.84	6.72
8	11.26	8.65	7.59	7.01	6.63	6.37	6.18	6.03	5.91
9	10.56	8.02	6.99	6.42	6.06	5.80	5.61	5.47	5.35
10	10.04	7.56	6.55	5.99	5.64	5.39	5.20	5.06	4.94
11	9.65	7.21	6.22	5.67	5.32	5.07	4.89	4.74	4.63
12	9.33	6.93	5.95	5.41	5.06	4.82	4.64	4.50	4.39
13	9.07	6.70	5.74	5.21	4.86	4.62	4.44	4.30	4.19
14	8.86	6.51	5.56	5.04	4.69	4.46	4.28	4.14	4.03
15	8.68	6.36	5.42	4.89	4.56	4.32	4.14	4.00	3.89
16	8.53	6.23	5.29	4.77	4.44	4.20	4.03	3.89	3.78
17	8.40	6.11	5.18	4.67	4.34	4.10	3.93	3.79	3.68
18	8.29	6.01	5.09	4.58	4.25	4.01	3.84	3.71	3.60
19	8.18	5.93	5.01	4.50	4.17	3.94	3.77	3.63	3.52
20	8.10	5.85	4.94	4.43	4.10	3.87	3.70	3.56	3.46
21	8.02	5.78	4.87	4.37	4.04	3.81	3.64	3.51	3.40
22	7.95	5.72	4.82	4.31	3.99	3.76	3.59	3.45	3.35
23	7.88	5.66	4.76	4.26	3.94	3.71	3.54	3.41	3.30
24	7.82	5.61	4.72	4.22	3.90	3.67	3.50	3.36	3.26
25	7.77	5.57	4.68	4.18	3.85	3.63	3.46	3.32	3.22
26	7.72	5.53	4.64	4.14	3.82	3.59	3.42	3.29	3.18
27	7.68	5.49	4.60	4.11	3.78	3.56	3.39	3.26	3.15
28	7.64	5.45	4.57	4.07	3.75	3.53	3.36	3.23	3.12
29	7.60	5.42	4.54	4.04	3.73	3.50	3.33	3.20	3.09
30	7.56	5.39	4.51	4.02	3.70	3.47	3.30	3.17	3.07
40	7.31	5.18	4.31	3.83	3.51	3.29	3.12	2.99	2.89
60	7.08	4.98	4.13	3.65	3.34	3.12	2.95	2.82	2.72
120	6.85	4.79	3.95	3.48	3.17	2.96	2.79	2.66	2.56
∞	6.63	4.61	3.78	3.32	3.02	2.80	2.64	2.51	2.41

TABLE B.8 (*Continued*)

v_2	10	12	15	20	v_1 24	30	40	60	120	∞
1	6,056	6,106	6,157	6,209	6,235	6,261	6,287	6,313	6,339	6,366
2	99.40	99.42	99.43	99.45	99.46	99.46	99.47	99.48	99.49	99.50
3	27.22	27.03	26.85	26.67	26.60	26.50	26.41	26.32	26.22	26.13
4	14.55	14.37	14.19	14.02	13.94	13.84	13.75	13.65	13.56	13.46
5	10.05	9.89	9.72	9.55	9.46	9.38	9.30	9.20	9.11	9.02
6	7.87	7.72	7.56	7.40	7.31	7.23	7.15	7.06	6.97	6.88
7	6.62	6.47	6.31	6.16	6.07	5.99	5.91	5.82	5.74	5.65
8	5.81	5.67	5.52	5.36	5.28	5.20	5.12	5.03	4.95	4.86
9	5.26	5.11	4.96	4.81	4.73	4.65	4.57	4.48	4.40	4.31
10	4.85	4.71	4.56	4.41	4.33	4.25	4.17	4.08	4.00	3.91
11	4.54	4.40	4.25	4.10	4.02	3.94	3.86	3.78	3.69	3.60
12	4.30	4.16	4.01	3.86	3.78	3.70	3.62	3.54	3.45	3.36
13	4.10	3.96	3.82	3.66	3.59	3.51	3.43	3.34	3.25	3.17
14	3.94	3.80	3.66	3.51	3.43	3.35	3.27	3.18	3.09	3.00
15	3.80	3.67	3.52	3.37	3.29	3.21	3.13	3.05	2.96	2.87
16	3.69	3.55	3.41	3.26	3.18	3.10	3.02	2.93	2.84	2.75
17	3.59	3.46	3.31	3.16	3.08	3.00	2.92	2.83	2.75	2.65
18	3.51	3.37	3.23	3.08	3.00	2.92	2.84	2.75	2.66	2.57
19	3.43	3.30	3.15	3.00	2.92	2.84	2.76	2.67	2.58	2.49
20	3.37	3.23	3.09	2.94	2.86	2.78	2.69	2.61	2.52	2.42
21	3.31	3.17	3.03	2.88	2.80	2.72	2.64	2.55	2.46	2.36
22	3.26	3.12	2.98	2.83	2.75	2.67	2.58	2.50	2.40	2.31
23	3.21	3.07	2.93	2.78	2.70	2.62	2.54	2.45	2.35	2.26
24	3.17	3.03	2.89	2.74	2.66	2.58	2.49	2.40	2.31	2.21
25	3.13	2.99	2.85	2.70	2.62	2.54	2.45	2.36	2.27	2.17
26	3.09	2.96	2.81	2.66	2.58	2.50	2.42	2.33	2.23	2.13
27	3.06	2.93	2.78	2.63	2.55	2.47	2.38	2.29	2.20	2.10
28	3.03	2.90	2.75	2.60	2.52	2.44	2.35	2.26	2.17	2.06
29	3.00	2.87	2.73	2.57	2.49	2.41	2.33	2.23	2.14	2.03
30	2.98	2.84	2.70	2.55	2.47	2.39	2.30	2.21	2.11	2.01
40	2.80	2.66	2.52	2.37	2.29	2.20	2.11	2.02	1.92	1.80
60	2.63	2.50	2.35	2.20	2.12	2.03	1.94	1.84	1.73	1.60
120	2.47	2.34	2.19	2.03	1.95	1.86	1.76	1.66	1.53	1.38
∞	2.32	2.18	2.04	1.88	1.79	1.70	1.59	1.47	1.32	1.00

TABLE B.9   Percentage Points of the Studentized Range Distribution

					J (Number of Groups)					
ν	2	3	4	5	6	7	8	9	10	11
$\alpha = 0.05$										
3	4.50	5.91	6.82	7.50	8.04	8.48	8.85	9.18	9.46	9.72
4	3.93	5.04	5.76	6.29	6.71	7.05	7.35	7.60	7.83	8.03
5	3.64	4.60	5.22	5.68	6.04	6.33	6.59	6.81	6.99	7.17
6	3.47	4.34	4.89	5.31	5.63	5.89	6.13	6.32	6.49	6.65
7	3.35	4.17	4.69	5.07	5.36	5.61	5.82	5.99	6.16	6.30
8	3.27	4.05	4.53	4.89	5.17	5.39	5.59	5.77	5.92	6.06
9	3.19	3.95	4.42	4.76	5.03	5.25	5.44	5.59	5.74	5.87
10	3.16	3.88	4.33	4.66	4.92	5.13	5.31	5.47	5.59	5.73
11	3.12	3.82	4.26	4.58	4.83	5.03	5.21	5.36	5.49	5.61
12	3.09	3.78	4.19	4.51	4.76	4.95	5.12	5.27	5.39	5.52
13	3.06	3.73	4.15	4.45	4.69	4.88	5.05	5.19	5.32	5.43
14	3.03	3.70	4.11	4.41	4.64	4.83	4.99	5.13	5.25	5.36
15	3.01	3.67	4.08	4.37	4.59	4.78	4.94	5.08	5.20	5.31
16	3.00	3.65	4.05	4.33	4.56	4.74	4.90	5.03	5.15	5.26
17	2.98	3.63	4.02	4.30	4.52	4.70	4.86	4.99	5.11	5.21
18	2.97	3.61	4.00	4.28	4.49	4.67	4.83	4.96	5.07	5.17
19	2.96	3.59	3.98	4.25	4.47	4.65	4.79	4.93	5.04	5.14
20	2.95	3.58	3.96	4.23	4.45	4.62	4.77	4.90	5.01	5.11
24	2.92	3.53	3.90	4.17	4.37	4.54	4.68	4.81	4.92	5.01
30	2.89	3.49	3.85	4.10	4.30	4.46	4.60	4.72	4.82	4.92
40	2.86	3.44	3.79	4.04	4.23	4.39	4.52	4.63	4.73	4.82
60	2.83	3.40	3.74	3.98	4.16	4.31	4.44	4.55	4.65	4.73
120	2.80	3.36	3.68	3.92	4.10	4.24	4.36	4.47	4.56	4.64
∞	2.77	3.31	3.63	3.86	4.03	4.17	4.29	4.39	4.47	4.55

TABLE B.9   (*Continued*)

ν	J (Number of Groups)									
	2	3	4	5	6	7	8	9	10	11
$\alpha = 0.01$										
2	14.0	19.0	22.3	24.7	26.6	28.2	29.5	30.7	31.7	32.6
3	8.26	10.6	12.2	13.3	14.2	15.0	15.6	16.2	16.7	17.8
4	6.51	8.12	9.17	9.96	10.6	11.1	11.5	11.9	12.3	12.6
5	5.71	6.98	7.81	8.43	8.92	9.33	9.67	9.98	10.24	10.48
6	5.25	6.34	7.04	7.56	7.98	8.32	8.62	8.87	9.09	9.30
7	4.95	5.92	6.55	7.01	7.38	7.68	7.94	8.17	8.37	8.55
8	4.75	5.64	6.21	6.63	6.96	7.24	7.48	7.69	7.87	8.03
9	4.59	5.43	5.96	6.35	6.66	6.92	7.14	7.33	7.49	7.65
10	4.49	5.28	5.77	6.14	6.43	6.67	6.88	7.06	7.22	7.36
11	4.39	5.15	5.63	5.98	6.25	6.48	6.68	6.85	6.99	7.13
12	4.32	5.05	5.51	5.84	6.11	6.33	6.51	6.67	6.82	6.94
13	4.26	4.97	5.41	5.73	5.99	6.19	6.38	6.53	6.67	6.79
14	4.21	4.89	5.32	5.63	5.88	6.08	6.26	6.41	6.54	6.66
15	4.17	4.84	5.25	5.56	5.80	5.99	6.16	6.31	6.44	6.55
16	4.13	4.79	5.19	5.49	5.72	5.92	6.08	6.22	6.35	6.46
17	4.10	4.74	5.14	5.43	5.66	5.85	6.01	6.15	6.27	6.38
18	4.07	4.70	5.09	5.38	5.60	5.79	5.94	6.08	6.20	6.31
19	4.05	4.67	5.05	5.33	5.55	5.73	5.89	6.02	6.14	6.25
20	4.02	4.64	5.02	5.29	5.51	5.69	5.84	5.97	6.09	6.19
24	3.96	4.55	4.91	5.17	5.37	5.54	5.69	5.81	5.92	6.02
30	3.89	4.45	4.80	5.05	5.24	5.40	5.54	5.65	5.76	5.85
40	3.82	4.37	4.69	4.93	5.10	5.26	5.39	5.49	5.60	5.69
60	3.76	4.28	4.59	4.82	4.99	5.13	5.25	5.36	5.45	5.53
120	3.70	4.20	4.50	4.71	4.87	5.01	5.12	5.21	5.30	5.37
∞	3.64	4.12	4.40	4.60	4.76	4.88	4.99	5.08	5.16	5.23

TABLE B.10   Studentized Maximum Modulus Distribution

		\multicolumn{9}{c}{C (The Number of Tests Being Performed)}								
v	α	2	3	4	5	6	7	8	9	10
2	0.05	5.57	6.34	6.89	7.31	7.65	7.93	8.17	8.83	8.57
	0.01	12.73	14.44	15.65	16.59	17.35	17.99	18.53	19.01	19.43
3	0.05	3.96	4.43	4.76	5.02	5.23	5.41	5.56	5.69	5.81
	0.01	7.13	7.91	8.48	8.92	9.28	9.58	9.84	10.06	10.27
4	0.05	3.38	3.74	4.01	4.20	4.37	4.50	4.62	4.72	4.82
	0.01	5.46	5.99	6.36	6.66	6.89	7.09	7.27	7.43	7.57
5	0.05	3.09	3.39	3.62	3.79	3.93	4.04	4.14	4.23	4.31
	0.01	4.70	5.11	5.39	5.63	5.81	5.97	6.11	6.23	6.33
6	0.05	2.92	3.19	3.39	3.54	3.66	3.77	3.86	3.94	4.01
	0.01	4.27	4.61	4.85	5.05	5.20	5.33	5.45	5.55	5.64
7	0.05	2.80	3.06	3.24	3.38	3.49	3.59	3.67	3.74	3.80
	0.01	3.99	4.29	4.51	4.68	4.81	4.93	5.03	5.12	5.19
8	0.05	2.72	2.96	3.13	3.26	3.36	3.45	3.53	3.60	3.66
	0.01	3.81	4.08	4.27	4.42	4.55	4.65	4.74	4.82	4.89
9	0.05	2.66	2.89	3.05	3.17	3.27	3.36	3.43	3.49	3.55
	0.01	3.67	3.92	4.10	4.24	4.35	4.45	4.53	4.61	4.67
10	0.05	2.61	2.83	2.98	3.10	3.19	3.28	3.35	3.41	3.47
	0.01	3.57	3.80	3.97	4.09	4.20	4.29	4.37	4.44	4.50
11	0.05	2.57	2.78	2.93	3.05	3.14	3.22	3.29	3.35	3.40
	0.01	3.48	3.71	3.87	3.99	4.09	4.17	4.25	4.31	4.37
12	0.05	2.54	2.75	2.89	3.01	3.09	3.17	3.24	3.29	3.35
	0.01	3.42	3.63	3.78	3.89	3.99	4.08	4.15	4.21	4.26
14	0.05	2.49	2.69	2.83	2.94	3.02	3.09	3.16	3.21	3.26
	0.01	3.32	3.52	3.66	3.77	3.85	3.93	3.99	4.05	4.10
16	0.05	2.46	2.65	2.78	2.89	2.97	3.04	3.09	3.15	3.19
	0.01	3.25	3.43	3.57	3.67	3.75	3.82	3.88	3.94	3.99
18	0.05	2.43	2.62	2.75	2.85	2.93	2.99	3.05	3.11	3.15
	0.01	3.19	3.37	3.49	3.59	3.68	3.74	3.80	3.85	3.89
20	0.05	2.41	2.59	2.72	2.82	2.89	2.96	3.02	3.07	3.11
	0.01	3.15	3.32	3.45	3.54	3.62	3.68	3.74	3.79	3.83
24	0.05	2.38	2.56	2.68	2.77	2.85	2.91	2.97	3.02	3.06
	0.01	3.09	3.25	3.37	3.46	3.53	3.59	3.64	3.69	3.73
30	0.05	2.35	2.52	2.64	2.73	2.80	2.87	2.92	2.96	3.01
	0.01	3.03	3.18	3.29	3.38	3.45	3.50	3.55	3.59	3.64
40	0.05	2.32	2.49	2.60	2.69	2.76	2.82	2.87	2.91	2.95
	0.01	2.97	3.12	3.22	3.30	3.37	3.42	3.47	3.51	3.55
60	0.05	2.29	2.45	2.56	2.65	2.72	2.77	2.82	2.86	2.90
	0.01	2.91	3.06	3.15	3.23	3.29	3.34	3.38	3.42	3.46
∞	0.05	2.24	2.39	2.49	2.57	2.63	2.68	2.73	2.77	2.79
	0.01	2.81	2.93	3.02	3.09	3.14	3.19	3.23	3.26	3.29

TABLE B.10 (*Continued*)

v	α	11	12	13	14	15	16	17	18	19
2	0.05	8.74	8.89	9.03	9.16	9.28	9.39	9.49	9.59	9.68
	0.01	19.81	20.15	20.46	20.75	20.99	20.99	20.99	20.99	20.99
3	0.05	5.92	6.01	6.10	6.18	6.26	6.33	6.39	6.45	6.51
	0.01	10.45	10.61	10.76	10.90	11.03	11.15	11.26	11.37	11.47
4	0.05	4.89	4.97	5.04	5.11	5.17	5.22	5.27	5.32	5.37
	0.01	7.69	7.80	7.91	8.01	8.09	8.17	8.25	8.32	8.39
5	0.05	4.38	4.45	4.51	4.56	4.61	4.66	4.70	4.74	4.78
	0.01	6.43	6.52	6.59	6.67	6.74	6.81	6.87	6.93	6.98
6	0.05	4.07	4.13	4.18	4.23	4.28	4.32	4.36	4.39	4.43
	0.01	5.72	5.79	5.86	5.93	5.99	6.04	6.09	6.14	6.18
7	0.05	3.86	3.92	3.96	4.01	4.05	4.09	4.13	4.16	4.19
	0.01	5.27	5.33	5.39	5.45	5.50	5.55	5.59	5.64	5.68
8	0.05	3.71	3.76	3.81	3.85	3.89	3.93	3.96	3.99	4.02
	0.01	4.96	5.02	5.07	5.12	5.17	5.21	5.25	5.29	5.33
9	0.05	3.60	3.65	3.69	3.73	3.77	3.80	3.84	3.87	3.89
	0.01	4.73	4.79	4.84	4.88	4.92	4.96	5.01	5.04	5.07
10	0.05	3.52	3.56	3.60	3.64	3.68	3.71	3.74	3.77	3.79
	0.01	4.56	4.61	4.66	4.69	4.74	4.78	4.81	4.84	4.88
11	0.05	3.45	3.49	3.53	3.57	3.60	3.63	3.66	3.69	3.72
	0.01	4.42	4.47	4.51	4.55	4.59	4.63	4.66	4.69	4.72
12	0.05	3.39	3.43	3.47	3.51	3.54	3.57	3.60	3.63	3.65
	0.01	4.31	4.36	4.40	4.44	4.48	4.51	4.54	4.57	4.59
14	0.05	3.30	3.34	3.38	3.41	3.45	3.48	3.50	3.53	3.55
	0.01	4.15	4.19	4.23	4.26	4.29	4.33	4.36	4.39	4.41
16	0.05	3.24	3.28	3.31	3.35	3.38	3.40	3.43	3.46	3.48
	0.01	4.03	4.07	4.11	4.14	4.17	4.19	4.23	4.25	4.28
18	0.05	3.19	3.23	3.26	3.29	3.32	3.35	3.38	3.40	3.42
	0.01	3.94	3.98	4.01	4.04	4.07	4.10	4.13	4.15	4.18
20	0.05	3.15	3.19	3.22	3.25	3.28	3.31	3.33	3.36	3.38
	0.01	3.87	3.91	3.94	3.97	3.99	4.03	4.05	4.07	4.09
24	0.05	3.09	3.13	3.16	3.19	3.22	3.25	3.27	3.29	3.31
	0.01	3.77	3.80	3.83	3.86	3.89	3.91	3.94	3.96	3.98
30	0.05	3.04	3.07	3.11	3.13	3.16	3.18	3.21	3.23	3.25
	0.01	3.67	3.70	3.73	3.76	3.78	3.81	3.83	3.85	3.87
40	0.05	2.99	3.02	3.05	3.08	3.09	3.12	3.14	3.17	3.18
	0.01	3.58	3.61	3.64	3.66	3.68	3.71	3.73	3.75	3.76
60	0.05	2.93	2.96	2.99	3.02	3.04	3.06	3.08	3.10	3.12
	0.01	3.49	3.51	3.54	3.56	3.59	3.61	3.63	3.64	3.66
∞	0.05	2.83	2.86	2.88	2.91	2.93	2.95	2.97	2.98	3.01
	0.01	3.32	3.34	3.36	3.38	3.40	3.42	3.44	3.45	3.47

(*continued*)

TABLE B.10   (*Continued*)

v	α	20	21	22	23	24	25	26	27	28
2	0.05	9.77	9.85	9.92	10.00	10.07	10.13	10.20	10.26	10.32
	0.01	22.11	22.29	22.46	22.63	22.78	22.93	23.08	23.21	23.35
3	0.05	6.57	6.62	6.67	6.71	6.76	6.80	6.84	6.88	6.92
	0.01	11.56	11.65	11.74	11.82	11.89	11.97	12.07	12.11	12.17
4	0.05	5.41	5.45	5.49	5.52	5.56	5.59	5.63	5.66	5.69
	0.01	8.45	8.51	8.57	8.63	8.68	8.73	8.78	8.83	8.87
5	0.05	4.82	4.85	4.89	4.92	4.95	4.98	5.00	5.03	5.06
	0.01	7.03	7.08	7.13	7.17	7.21	7.25	7.29	7.33	7.36
6	0.05	4.46	4.49	4.52	4.55	4.58	4.60	4.63	4.65	4.68
	0.01	6.23	6.27	6.31	6.34	6.38	6.41	6.45	6.48	6.51
7	0.05	4.22	4.25	4.28	4.31	4.33	4.35	4.38	4.39	4.42
	0.01	5.72	5.75	5.79	5.82	5.85	5.88	5.91	5.94	5.96
8	0.05	4.05	4.08	4.10	4.13	4.15	4.18	4.19	4.22	4.24
	0.01	5.36	5.39	5.43	5.45	5.48	5.51	5.54	5.56	5.59
9	0.05	3.92	3.95	3.97	3.99	4.02	4.04	4.06	4.08	4.09
	0.01	5.10	5.13	5.16	5.19	5.21	5.24	5.26	5.29	5.31
10	0.05	3.82	3.85	3.87	3.89	3.91	3.94	3.95	3.97	3.99
	0.01	4.91	4.93	4.96	4.99	5.01	5.03	5.06	5.08	5.09
11	0.05	3.74	3.77	3.79	3.81	3.83	3.85	3.87	3.89	3.91
	0.01	4.75	4.78	4.80	4.83	4.85	4.87	4.89	4.91	4.93
12	0.05	3.68	3.70	3.72	3.74	3.76	3.78	3.80	3.82	3.83
	0.01	4.62	4.65	4.67	4.69	4.72	4.74	4.76	4.78	4.79
14	0.05	3.58	3.59	3.62	3.64	3.66	3.68	3.69	3.71	3.73
	0.01	4.44	4.46	4.48	4.50	4.52	4.54	4.56	4.58	4.59
16	0.05	3.50	3.52	3.54	3.56	3.58	3.59	3.61	3.63	3.64
	0.01	4.29	4.32	4.34	4.36	4.38	4.39	4.42	4.43	4.45
18	0.05	3.44	3.46	3.48	3.50	3.52	3.54	3.55	3.57	3.58
	0.01	4.19	4.22	4.24	4.26	4.28	4.29	4.31	4.33	4.34
20	0.05	3.39	3.42	3.44	3.46	3.47	3.49	3.50	3.52	3.53
	0.01	4.12	4.14	4.16	4.17	4.19	4.21	4.22	4.24	4.25
24	0.05	3.33	3.35	3.37	3.39	3.40	3.42	3.43	3.45	3.46
	0.01	4.00	4.02	4.04	4.05	4.07	4.09	4.10	4.12	4.13
30	0.05	3.27	3.29	3.30	3.32	3.33	3.35	3.36	3.37	3.39
	0.01	3.89	3.91	3.92	3.94	3.95	3.97	3.98	4.00	4.01
40	0.05	3.20	3.22	3.24	3.25	3.27	3.28	3.29	3.31	3.32
	0.01	3.78	3.80	3.81	3.83	3.84	3.85	3.87	3.88	3.89
60	0.05	3.14	3.16	3.17	3.19	3.20	3.21	3.23	3.24	3.25
	0.01	3.68	3.69	3.71	3.72	3.73	3.75	3.76	3.77	3.78
∞	0.05	3.02	3.03	3.04	3.06	3.07	3.08	3.09	3.11	3.12
	0.01	3.48	3.49	3.50	3.52	3.53	3.54	3.55	3.56	3.57

REFERENCES

Agresti, A. (1990). *Categorical Data Analysis*. New York: John Wiley & Sons, Inc.

Agresti, A. (1996). *An Introduction to Categorical Data Analysis*. New York: John Wiley & Sons, Inc.

Agresti, A. & Coull, B. A. (1998). Approximate is better than "exact" for interval estimation of binomial proportions. *American Statistician, 52*, 119–126.

Alexander, R. A. & McGovern, D. (1994). A new and simpler approximation for ANOVA under variance heterogeneity. *Journal of Educational Statistics, 19*, 91–101.

Algina, J., Keselman, H. J. & Penfield, R. D. (2005). An alternative to Cohen's standardized mean difference effect size: a robust parameter and confidence interval in the two independent groups case. *Psychological Methods, 10*, 317–328.

Algina, J., Oshima, T. C. & Lin, W.-Y. (1994). Type I error rates for Welch's test and Jamse's second-order test under nonnormality and inequality of variance when there are two groups. *Journal of Educational and Behavioral Statistics, 19*, 275–291.

Andersen, E. B. (1997). *Introduction to the Statistical Analysis of Categorical Data*. New York: Springer-Verlag.

Asiribo, O. & Gurland, J. (1989). Some simple approximate solutions to the Behrens–Fisher problem. *Communications in Statistics—Theory and Methods, 18*, 1201–1216.

Atkinson, R. L., Atkinson, R. C., Smith, E. E. & Hilgard, E. R. (1985). *Introduction to Psychology*, 9th Edition. San Diego, CA: Harcourt, Brace, Jovanovich.

Bakker, M. & Wicherts, J. M. (2014). Outlier removal, sum scores, and the inflation of the type I error rate in T tests. *Psychological Methods, 19*, 409–427.

Barrett, J. P. (1974). The coefficient of determination—some limitations. *Annals of Statistics, 28*, 19–20.

Beal, S. L. (1987). Asymptotic confidence intervals for the difference between two binomial parameters for use with small samples. *Biometrics, 43*, 941–950.

Understanding and Applying Basic Statistical Methods Using R, First Edition. Rand R. Wilcox.
© 2017 John Wiley & Sons, Inc. Published 2017 by John Wiley & Sons, Inc.
www.wiley.com/go/Wilcox/Statistical_Methods_R

Belsley, D. A., Kuh, E. & Welsch, R. E. (1980). *Regression Diagnostics: Identifying Influential Data and Sources of Collinearity*. New York: John Wiley & Sons, Inc.

Benjamini, Y. & Hochberg, Y. (1995). Controlling the false discovery rate: a practical and powerful approach to multiple testing. *Journal of the Royal Statistical Society, B, 57*, 289–300.

Benjamini, Y. & Yekutieli, D. (2001). The control of the false discovery rate in multiple testing under dependency. *Annals of Statistics, 29*, 1165–1188.

Berger, R. L. (1996). More powerful tests from confidence interval p values. *American Statistician, 50*, 314–318.

Berkson, J. (1958). Smoking and lung cancer: some observations on two recent reports. *Journal of the American Statistical Association, 53*, 28–38.

Bernhardson, C. (1975). Type I error rates when multiple comparison procedures follow a significant F test of ANOVA. *Biometrics, 31*, 719–724.

Bienaymé, I. J. (1938). Mémoire sur la probabilité des résultats moyens des observations; demonstration directe de la règle de Laplace. *Mémoires de l'Academie de Sciences de l'Institut de France, Paris, Series Ètrangers, 5*, 513–558.

Blyth, C. R. (1986). Approximate binomial confidence limits. *Journal of the American Statistical Association, 81*, 843–855.

Box, G. E. P. (1953). Non-normality and tests on variances. *Biometrika, 40*, 318–335.

Bradley, J. V. (1978). Robustness? *British Journal of Mathematical and Statistical Psychology, 31*, 144–152.

Brown, L. D., Cai, T. T. & DasGupta, A. (2002). Confidence intervals for a binomial proportion and asymptotic expansions. *Annals of Statistics, 30*, 160–201.

Brown, M. B. & Forsythe, A. (1974). The small sample behavior of some statistics which test the equality of several means. *Technometrics, 16*, 129–132.

Browne, R. H. (2010). The t-test, p value and its relationship to the effect size and $P(X > Y)$. *American Statistician, 64*, 30–33. (Correction, 64, 195).

Brunner, E., Dette, H. & Munk, A. (1997). Box-type approximations in non-parametric factorial designs. *Journal of the American Statistical Association, 92*, 1494–1502.

Brunner, E., Domhof, S. & Langer, F. (2002). *Nonparametric Analysis of Longitudinal Data in Factorial Experiments*. New York: John Wiley & Sons, Inc.

Carroll, R. J. & Ruppert, D. (1988). *Transformation and Weighting in Regression*. New York: Chapman and Hall.

Chang, C. (2013). *R Graphics Cookbook*. Sebastopol, CA: O'Reilly Media.

Chen, S. & Chen, H. J. (1998). Single-stage analysis of variance under heteroscedasticity. *Communications in Statistics—Simulation and Computation, 27*, 641–666.

Clark, F., Jackson, J., Carlson, M., Chou, C.-P., Cherry, B. J., Jordan-Marsh, M., Knight, B. G., Mandel, D., Blanchard, J., Granger, D. A., Wilcox, R. R., Lai, M. Y., White, B., Hay, J., Lam, C., Marterella, A. & Azen, S. P. (2012). Effectiveness of a lifestyle intervention in promoting the well-being of independently living older people: results of the Well Elderly 2 Randomise Controlled Trial. *Journal of Epidemiology and Community Health, 66*, 782–790. DOI: 10.1136/jech.2009.099754.

Cleveland, W. S. (1979). Robust locally weighted regression and smoothing scatterplots. *Journal of the American Statistical Association, 74*, 829–836.

Cliff, N. (1996). *Ordinal Methods for Behavioral Data Analysis*. Mahwah, NJ: Erlbaum.

Cochran, W. G. & Cox, G. M. (1950). *Experimental Design*. New York: John Wiley & Sons, Inc.

Coe, P. R. & Tamhane, A. C. (1993). Small sample confidence intervals for the difference, ratio, and odds ratio of two success probabilities. *Communications in Statistics—Simulation and Computation, 22,* 925–938.

Coleman, J. S. (1964). *Introduction to Mathematical Sociology.* New York: Free Press.

Cook, R. D. & Weisberg, S. (1992). *Residuals and Influence in Regression.* New York: Chapman and Hall.

Cressie, N. A. C. & Whitford, H. J. (1986). How to use the two sample t-test. *Biometrical Journal, 28,* 131–148.

Cribari-Neto, F. (2004). Asymptotic inference under heteroskedasticity of unknown form. *Computational Statistics and Data Analysis, 45,* 215–233.

Cumming, G. & Maillardet, R. (2006). Confidence intervals and replication: where with the next mean fall? *Psychological Methods, 11,* 217–227.

Dana, E. (1990). Salience of the self and salience of standards: attempts to match self to standard. Unpublished Ph.D. dissertation, University of Southern California.

De Veaux, R. D. & Hand, D. J. (2005). How to lie with bad data. *Statistical Science, 20,* 231–238.

Doksum, K. A. & Sievers, G. L. (1976). Plotting with confidence: graphical comparisons of two populations. *Biometrika, 63,* 421–434.

Dunnett, C. W. (1980a). Pairwise multiple comparisons in the unequal variance case. *Journal of the American Statistical Association, 75,* 796–800.

Dunnett, C. W. (1980b). Pairwise multiple comparisons in the homogeneous variance, unequal sample size case. *Journal of the American Statistical Association, 75,* 796–800.

Emerson, J. D. & Hoaglin, D. C. (1983). Stem-and-leaf displays. In D. C. Hoaglin, F. Mosteller & J. W. Tukey (Eds.) *Understanding Robust and Exploratory Data Analysis,* pp. 7–32. New York: John Wiley & Sons, Inc.

Erceg-Hurn, D. M. and Steed, L. G. (2011). Does exposure to cigarette health warnings elicit psychological reactance in smokers? *Journal of Applied Social Psychology, 41,* 219–237. DOI: 10.1111/j.1559-1816.2010.00710.x.

Fabian, V. (1991). On the problem of interactions in the analysis of variance. *Journal of the American Statistical Association, 86,* 362–367.

Fan, W. & Hancock, G. R. (2012). Robust means modeling: an alternative for hypothesis testing of independent means under variance heterogeneity and nonnormality. *Journal of Educational and Behavioral Statistics, 37,* 137–156.

Field, A., Miles, J. & Field, Z. (2012). *Discovering Statistics Using R.* Thousand Oaks, CA: Sage Publications.

Fisher, R. A. (1935). The fiducial argument in statistical inference. *Annals of Eugenics, 6,* 391–398.

Fisher, R. A. (1941). The asymptotic approach to Behren's integral, with further tables for the d test of significance. *Annals of Eugenics, 11,* 141–172.

Fleiss, J. L. (1981). *Statisical Methods for Rates and Proportions,* 2nd Edition. New York: John Wiley & Sons, Inc.

Fung, K. Y. (1980). Small sample behaviour of some nonparametric multi-sample location tests in the presence of dispersion differences. *Statistica Neerlandica, 34,* 189–196.

Godfrey, L. G. (2006). Tests for regression models with heteroskedasticity of unknown form. *Computational Statistics and Data Analysis, 50,* 2715–2733.

Goodman, L. A. & Kruskal, W. H. (1954). Measures of association for cross- classifications. *Journal of the American Statistical Association, 49,* 732–736.

Hampel, F. R., Ronchetti, E. M., Rousseeuw, P. J. & Stahel, W. A. (1986). *Robust Statistics: The Approach Based on Influence Functions*. New York: John Wiley & Sons, Inc.

Harpole, J. K., Woods, C. M., Rodebaugh, T. L., Levinson, C. A. & Lenze, E. J. (2014). How bandwidth selection algorithms impact exploratory data analysis using kernel density estimation. *Psychological Methods*, *19*, 428–443. DOI: 10.1037/a0036850.

Harrell, F. E. & Davis, C. E. (1982). A new distribution-free quantile estimator. *Biometrika*, *69*, 635–640.

Harrison, D. and Rubinfeld, D. L. (1978). Hedonic prices and the demand for clean air. *Journal of Environmental Economics & Management*, *5*, 81–102.

Hastie, T. J. & Tibshirani, R. J. (1990). *Generalized Additive Models*. New York: Chapman and Hall.

Hayes, A. F. & Cai, L. (2007). Further evaluating the conditional decision rule for comparing two independent means. *British Journal of Mathematical and Statistical Psychology*, *60*, 217–244.

Hayter, A. (1984). A proof of the conjecture that the Tukey-Kramer multiple comparison procedure is conservative. *Annals of Statistics*, *12*, 61–75.

Hayter, A. (1986). The maximum familywise error rate of Fisher's least significant difference test. *Journal of the American Statistical Association*, *81*, 1000–1004.

Heiser, D. A. (2006). Statistical tests, tests of significance, and tests of a hypothesis (Excel). *Journal of Modern Applied Statistical Methods*, *5*, 551–566.

Hettmansperger, T. P. (1984). *Statistical Inference Based on Ranks*. New York: John Wiley & Sons, Inc.

Hettmansperger, T. P. & McKean, J. W. (1977). A robust alternative based on ranks to least squares in analyzing linear models. *Technometrics*, *19*, 275–284.

Hochberg, Y. (1988). A sharper Bonferroni procedure for multiple tests of significance. *Biometrika*, *75*, 800–802.

Hommel, G. (1988). A stagewise rejective multiple test procedure based on a modified Bonferroni test. *Biometrika*, *75*, 383–386.

Hosmane, B. S. (1986). Improved likelihood ratio tests and Pearson chi-square tests for independence in two dimensional tables. *Communications Statistics—Theory and Methods*, *15*, 1875–1888.

Hosmer, D. W. & Lemeshow, S. (1989). *Applied Logistic Regression*. New York: John Wiley & Sons, Inc.

Huber, P. J. & Ronchetti, E. (2009). *Robust Statistics*, 2nd Edition. New York: John Wiley & Sons, Inc.

Iman, R. L., Quade, D. & Alexander, D. A. (1975). Exact probability levels for the Krusakl-Wallis test. *Selected Tables in Mathematical Statistics*, *3*, 329–384.

James, G. S. (1951). The comparison of several groups of observations when the ratios of the population variances are unknown. *Biometrika*, *38*, 324–329.

Johansen, S. (1980). The Welch–James approximation of the distribution of the residual sum of squares in weighted linear regression. *Biometrika*, *67*, 85–92.

Johansen, S. (1982). Amendments and corrections: the Welch–James approximation to the distribution of the residual sum of squares in a weighted linear regression. *Biometrika*, *69*, 491.

Jones, L. V. & Tukey, J. W. (2000). A sensible formulation of the significance test. *Psychological Methods*, *5*, 411–414.

Kaiser, L. & Bowden, D. (1983). Simultaneous confidence intervals for all linear contrasts of means with heterogeneous variances. *Communications in Statistics—Theory and Methods, 12*, 73–88.

Kendall, M. G. & Stuart, A. (1973). *The Advanced Theory of Statistics*, Vol. 2. New York: Hafner.

Keselman, J. C., Cribbie, R. & Holland, B. (1999). The pairwise multiple comparison multiplicity problem: an alternative approach to familywise and comparisonwise Type I error control. *Psychological Methods, 4*, 58–69.

Keselman, H. J. & Wilcox, R. R. (1999). The "improved" Brown and Forsyth test for mean equality: some things can't be fixed. *Communications in Statistics—Simulation and Computation, 28*, 687–698.

Keselman, H. J., Wilcox, R. R., Taylor, J. & Kowalchuk, R. K. (2000). Tests for mean equality that do not require homogeneity of variances: do they really work? *Communications in Statistics—Simulation and Computation, 29*, 875–895.

Kirk, R. E. (2013). *Experimental Design: Procedures for the Behavioral Sciences*, 4th Edition. Thousand Oaks, CA: Sage.

Kleinbaum, D. G. (1994). *Logistic Regression*. New York: Springer-Verlag.

Koenker, R. & Bassett, G. (1978). Regression quantiles. *Econometrika, 46*, 33–50.

Kramer, C. (1956). Extension of multiple range test to group means with unequal number of replications. *Biometrics, 12*, 307–310.

Krutchkoff, R. G. (1988). One-way fixed effects analysis of variance when the error variances may be unequal. *Journal of Statistical Computation and Simulation, 30*, 259–271.

Kulinskaya, E., Morgenthaler, S. & Staudte, R. (2010). Variance stabilizing the difference of two binomial proportions. *American Statistician, 64*, 350–356. DOI: 10.1198/tast.2010.09096.

Lee, S. & Ahn, C. H. (2003). Modified ANOVA for unequal variances. *Communications in Statistics—Simulation and Computation, 32*, 987–1004.

Levene, H. (1960). Robust tests for equality of variances. In I. Olkin, S. Ghurye, W. Hoeffding, W. Madow & H. Mann (Eds.) *Contributions to Probability and Statistics*, pp. 278–292. Stanford, CA: Stanford University Press.

Li, G. (1985). Robust regression. In D. Hoaglin, F. Mosteller & J. Tukey (Eds.) *Exploring Data Tables, Trends, and Shapes*, pp. 281–343. New York: John Wiley & Sons, Inc.

Liu, R. G., Parelius, J. M. & Singh, K. (1999). Multivariate analysis by data depth. *Annals of Statistics, 27*, 783–840.

Lloyd, C. J. (1999). *Statistical Analysis of Categorical Data*. New York: John Wiley & Sons, Inc.

Loh, W.-Y. (1987). Does the correlation coefficient really measure the degree of clustering around a line? *Journal of Educational Statistics, 12*, 235–239.

Long, J. S. & Ervin, L. H. (2000). Using heteroscedasticity consistent standard errors in the linear regression model. *American Statistician, 54*, 217–224.

McCullough, B. D. & Wilson, B. (2005). On the accuracy of statistical procedures in Microsoft Excel. *Computational Statistics and Data Analysis, 49*, 1244–1252.

McKean, J. W. & Schrader, R. M. (1984). A comparison of methods for studentizing the sample median. *Communications in Statistics—Simulation and Computation, 13*, 751–773.

Mann, H. B., & Whitney, D. R. (1947). On a test of whether one of two random variables is stochastically larger than the other. *Annals of Mathematical Statistics, 18*, 50–60.

Markowski, C. A. & Markowski, E. P. (1990). Conditions for the effectiveness of a preliminary test of variance. *American Statistician*, *44*, 322–326.

Matuszewski, A. & Sotres, D. (1986). A simple test for the Behrens–Fisher problem. *Computational Statistics and Data Analysis*, *3*, 241–249.

Mehrotra, D. V. (1997). Improving the Brown-Forsythe solution to the generalized Behrens-fisher problem. *Communications in Statistics—Simulation and Computation*, *26*, 1139–1145.

Mélard, G. (2014). On the accuracy of statistical procedures in Microsoft Excel 2010. *Computational Statistics*, *29*, 1095–1128.

Micceri, T. (1989). The unicorn, the normal curve, and other improbable creatures. *Psychological Bulletin*, *105*, 156–166.

Miller, R. G. (1976). Least squares regression with censored data. *Biometrika*, *63*, 449–464.

Montgomery, D. C. & Peck, E. A. (1992). *Introduction to Linear Regression Analysis*. New York: John Wiley & Sons, Inc.

Moser, B. K., Stevens, G. R. & Watts, C. L. (1989). The two-sample t-test versus Satterthwaite's approximate F test. *Communications in Statistics—Theory and Methods*, *18*, 3963–3975.

Neuhäuser, M., Lösch, C. & Jöckel, K.-H. (2007). The Chen–Luo test in case of heteroscedasticity. *Computational Statistics and Data Analysis*, *51*, 5055–5060.

Newcombe, R. R. (2006). Confidence intervals for an effect size measure based on the Mann-Whitney statistics. Part 2: Asymptotic methods and evaluation. *Statistics in Medicine*, *25*, 559–573.

Ng, M. & Wilcox, R. R. (2009). Level robust methods based on the least squares regression line. *Journal of Modern and Applied Statistical Methods*, *8*, 384–395.

Ng, M. & Wilcox, R. R. (2011). A comparison of two-stage procedures for testing least-squares coefficients under heteroscedasticity. *British Journal of Mathematical and Statistical Psychology*, *64*, 244–258.

Olejnik, S., Li, J., Supattathum, S. & Huberty, C. J. (1997). Multiple testing and statistical power with modified Bonferroni procedures. *Journal of Educational and Behavioral Statistics*, *22*, 389–406.

Pagurova, V. I. (1968). On a comparison of means of two normal samples. *Theory of Probability and its Applications*, *13*, 527–534.

Pedersen, W. C., Miller, L. C., Putcha-Bhagavatula, A. D. & Yang, Y. (2002). Evolved sex differences in sexual strategies: the long and the short of it. *Psychological Science*, *13*, 157–161.

Piepho, H.-P. (1997). Tests for equality of dispersion in bivariate samples—review and empirical comparison. *Journal of Statistical Computation and Simulation*, *56*, 353–372.

Powers, D. A. & Xie, Y. (1999). *Statistical Methods for Categorical Data Analysis*. San Diego, CA: Academic Press.

Ramsey, P. H. (1980). Exact Type I error rates for robustness of Student's t test with unequal variances. *Journal of Educational Statistics*, *5*, 337–349.

Rao, C. R. (1948). Tests of significance in multivariate analysis. *Biometrika*, *35*, 58–79.

Rom, D. M. (1990). A sequentially rejective test procedure based on a modified Bonferroni inequality. *Biometrika*, *77*, 663–666.

Romano, J. P. (1990). On the behavior of randomization tests without a group invariance assumption. *Journal of the American Statistical Association*, *85*, 686–692.

Rousseeuw, P. J. & Leroy, A. M. (1987). *Robust Regression & Outlier Detection*. New York: John Wiley & Sons, Inc.

Rousseeuw, P. J. & van Zomeren, B. C. (1990). Unmasking multivariate outliers and leverage points (with discussion). *Journal of the American Statistical Association, 85*, 633–639.

Ruscio, J. & Mullen, T. (2012). Confidence intervals for the probability of superiority effect size measure and the area under a receiver operating characteristic curve. *Multivariate Behavioral Research, 47*, 201–223.

Salk, L. (1973). The role of the heartbeat in the relations between mother and infant. *Scientific American, 235*, 26–29–.

Scariano, S. M. & Davenport, J. M. (1986). A four-moment approach and other practical solutions to the Behrens-Fisher problem. *Communications in Statistics—Theory and Methods, 15*, 1467–1501.

Scheffé, H. (1959). *The Analysis of Variance*. New York: John Wiley & Sons, Inc.

Schenker, N. & Gentleman, J. F. (2001). On judging the significance of differences by examining the overlap between confidence intervals. *American Statistician, 55*, 182–186.

Schilling, M. & Doi, J. (2014). A coverage probability approach to finding an optimal binomial confidence procedure. *American Statistician, 68*, 133–145.

Sen, P. K. (1968). Estimate of the regression coefficient based on Kendall's tau. *Journal of the American Statistical Association, 63*, 1379–1389.

Silverman, B. W. (1986). *Density Estimation for Statistics and Data Analysis*. New York: Chapman and Hall.

Simonoff, J. (2003). *Analyzing Categorical Data*. New York: Springer-Verlag.

Snedecor, G. W. & Cochran, W. (1967). *Statistical Methods*, 6th Edition. Ames, IA: University Press.

Sockett, E. B., Daneman, D., Clarson, C. & Ehrich, R. M. (1987). Factors affecting and patterns of residual insulin secretion during the first year of type I (insulin dependent) diabetes mellitus in children. *Diabetes, 30*, 453–459.

Staudte, R. G. & Sheather, S. J. (1990). *Robust Estimation and Testing*. New York: John Wiley & Sons, Inc.

Stigler, S. M. (1986). *The History of Statistics: The Measurement of Uncertainty before 1900*. Cambridge, MA: Belknap Press of the Harvard University Press.

Storer, B. E. & Kim, C. (1990). Exact properties of some exact test statistics for comparing two binomial proportions. *Journal of the American Statistical Association, 85*, 146–155.

Theil, H. (1950). A rank-invariant method of linear and polynomial regression analysis. *Indagationes Mathematicae, 12*, 85–91.

Thomson, A. & Randall-Maciver, R. (1905). *Ancient Races of the Thebaid*. Oxford: Oxford University Press.

Tukey, J. W. (1977). *Exploratory Data Analysis*. Reading, MA: Addison-Wesley.

Tukey, J. W. & McLaughlin, D. H. (1963). Less vulnerable confidence and significance procedures for location based on a single sample: trimming/Winsorization 1. *Sankhya A, 25*, 331–352.

Vonesh, E. (1983). Efficiency of repeated measures designs versus completely randomized designs based on multiple comparisons. *Communications in Statistics—Theory and Methods, 12*, 289–302.

Wald, A. (1955). Testing the difference between the means of two normal populations with unknown standard deviations. In T. W. Anderson *et al* (Eds.) *Selected Papers in Statistics and Probability by Abraham Wald*. New York: McGraw-Hill.

Wechsler, D. (1958). *The Measurement and Appraisal of Adult Intelligence*, 4th Edition. Baltimore (MD): Williams & Witkins.

Weerahandi, S. (1995). ANOVA under unequal error variances. *Biometrics, 51,* 589–599.

Welch, B. L. (1938). The significance of the difference between two means when the population variances are unequal. *Biometrika, 29,* 350–362.

Welch, B. L. (1951). On the comparison of several mean values: an alternative approach. *Biometrika, 38,* 330–336.

Wickham, H. (2009). *ggplot2: Elegant Graphics for Data Analysis.* New York: Springer-Verlag.

Wilcox, R. R. (1990). Comparing the means of two independent groups. *Biometrical Journal, 32,* 771–780.

Wilcox, R. R. (2002). Comparing the variances of independent groups. *British Journal of Mathematical and Statistical Psychology, 55,* 169–176.

Wilcox, R. R. (2012a). *Modern Statistics for the Social and Behavioral Sciences: A Practical Introduction.* New York: Chapman & Hall/CRC press.

Wilcox, R. R. (2012b). *Introduction to Robust Estimation and Hypothesis Testing,* 3rd Edition. San Diego, CA: Academic Press.

Wilcox, R. R. (2013). A heteroscedastic method for comparing regression lines at specified design points when using a robust regression estimator. *Journal of Data Science, 11,* 281–291.

Wilcox, R. R. (2015a). Global comparisons of medians and other quantiles in a one-way design when there are tied values. *Communications in Statistics—Simulation and Computation.* DOI: 10.1080/03610918.2015.1071388.

Wilcox, R. R. (2015b). Comparing the variances of two dependent variables. *Journal of Statistical Distributions and Applications, 2:7.* DOI: 10.1186/s40488-015-0030-z.

Wilcox, R. R., Charlin, V. & Thompson, K. L. (1986). New Monte Carlo results on the robustness of the ANOVA F, W, and F^* statistics. *Communications in Statistics—Simulation and Computation, 15,* 933–944.

Wilcox, R. R. & Clark, F. (2013). Robust regression estimators when there are tied values. *Journal of Modern and Applied Statistical Methods, 12,* 20–34.

Wilcox, R. R. & Clark, F. (2015). Heteroscedastic global tests that the regression parameters for two or more independent groups are identical. *Communications in Statistics—Simulation and Computation, 44,* 773–786. DOI: 10.1080/03610918.2013.784986.

Wilcox, R. R., Erceg-Hurn, D., Clark, F. & Carlson, M. (2013). Comparing two independent groups via the lower and upper quantiles. *Journal of Statistical Computation and Simulation.* DOI: 10.1080/00949655.2012.754026.

Wilcox, R. R., Vigen, C., Clark, F. & Carlson, M (2013). Comparing discrete distributions when the sample space is small. *Universitas Psychologica, 12,* 1583–1595. DOI: 10.11144/Javeriana.UPSY12-5.cdds.

Wilcoxon, F. (1945). Individual comparisons by ranking methods. *Biometrics, 1,* 80–83.

Williams, V. S. L., Jones, L. V. & Tukey, J. W. (1999). Controlling error in multiple comparisons, with examples from state-to-state differences in educational achievement. *Journal of Educational and Behavioral Statistics, 24,* 42–69.

Wu, P.-C. (2002). Central limit theorem and comparing means, trimmed means one-step M-estimators and modified one-step M-estimators under non-normality. Unpublished doctoral dissertation, Department of Education, University of Southern California.

Yuen, K. K. (1974). The two sample trimmed t for unequal population variances. *Biometrika, 61,* 165–170.

Zimmerman, D. W. (2004). A note on preliminary tests of equality of variances. *British Journal of Mathematical and Statistical Psychology, 57,* 173–182.

INDEX

Understanding and Applying Basic Statistical Methods Using R, First Edition. Rand R. Wilcox.
© 2017 John Wiley & Sons, Inc. Published 2017 by John Wiley & Sons, Inc.
www.wiley.com/go/Wilcox/Statistical_Methods_R

Printed in Poland
by Amazon Fulfillment
Poland Sp. z o.o., Wrocław
01 December 2020

9746cb7a-6dcc-4246-a14c-0f835bbf0045R01